THE RISE OF MODERN EUROPE

A SURVEY OF EUROPEAN HISTORY
IN ITS POLITICAL, ECONOMIC, AND CULTURAL ASPECTS
FROM THE END OF THE MIDDLE AGES
TO THE PRESENT

FOUNDING EDITOR

WILLIAM L. LANGER

Harvard University

THE WORLD
IN THE
CRUCIBLE

1914–1919

BY
BERNADOTTE E. SCHMITT
AND
HAROLD C. VEDELER

ILLUSTRATED

1817

HARPER & ROW, PUBLISHERS, New York
Cambridge, Philadelphia, San Francisco, London
Mexico City, São Paulo, Singapore, Sydney

FIRST EDITION

Library of Congress Cataloging in Publication Data
Schmitt, Bernadotte Everly, 1886–1969.
    The world in the crucible, 1914–1919.
    (The Rise of modern Europe)
    Bibliography: P.
    Includes index.
        1. World War, 1914–1918.   2. Europe—History—1871–1918.
3. Europe—History—1918–1945.   4. World War, 1914–1918—
Influence.   5. Revolutions—Europe—History—20th century.
I. Vedeler, Harold C.   II. Title.   III. Series.
D521.S367 1984   940.3   83–48384
ISBN 0–06–015268–0

84 85 86 87 88 10 9 8 7 6 5 4 3 2 1

To the Members
of
Deck D

CONTENTS

CONTENTS

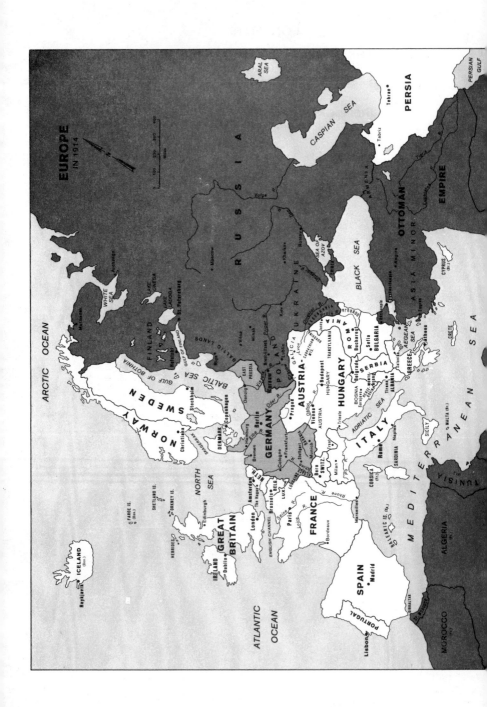

ILLUSTRATIONS

These photographs, grouped in a section, will be found following page 204.

MAPS

PREFACE

The present book covers a shorter span of time than any volume in The Rise of Modern Europe series. The question may arise whether a period so brief deserves the treatment of a separate volume. If, however, one measures a period not by years but by the stature of its events in the long historical process, the case is strong for demarking this towering time for a full book. After all, there belonged to the period the Great War, a peace of far-reaching effect, the Russian revolution, a series of revolutions in central and eastern Europe, and a transformation in the western outlook.

The Great War itself was a conflict of massive forces in four dimensions —military, political, economic, and ideological. Its scope, intensity, duration, and consequences were quite beyond the expectations of contemporaries. In the end the European empires dissolved in the furnace of war, a body of new states emerged, the map of Europe was remade essentially in its present form, and a world organization of supranational functions was created. The colonial era came to a close, and the Third World dawned in the Arab revolt and the conversion of the German colonies into mandates of the League of Nations. Monarchy as an institution of real authority received a death blow while democracy and socialism made giant advances. Two of the most creative figures of the twentieth century, Lenin and Wilson, dominated the political and ideological forces of the time. In most of Europe a radical shift occurred in the status of social classes and the distribution of power among them. In the long march of women toward equality, their position in society changed dramatically for the better. The western vision of man and his world suffered irremediable damage, and the somber, ironic cast emerging still endures.

The narrative begins with a brief discussion of the outbreak of war as a necessary introduction to the view of subsequent events. The end of the story follows the outcome of the series of revolutions, the establishment of new states and governments, and the economic and intellectual impact of the upheaval even if the strict limit of 1919 may be exceeded on occasion.

The limited time frame of the work calls for a treatment of subject differing in some respects from that of the series in general. Instead of being divided into separate chapters on economic and cultural developments, material of this nature has been integrated with other content as the account proceeds. Despite considerable attention given to military affairs, the book is not a history of the Great War but of Europe, and in certain aspects of the world, during the period of the war.

The survey is a study of war and revolution—of the remolding of Europe and much of the world. The focus of the work that gives unity to the twin themes is that the war was a revolution in itself—in military, political, and economic affairs as well as in state of mind—and the breeder of a progeny of revolutions. The war and the resultant revolutions transformed the shape and spirit of our times more profoundly than any series of events in the twentieth century to date. These revolutionary changes afford the integrating thread and the perspective of the presentation.

Among the changes was the altered relationship of Europe to the rest of the world. Hitherto Europe, identified with the western and central portions, had been the active agent transmitting its influence to every other continent. Now the running tides of influence reverse themselves. The outer world, chiefly America and Eurasian Russia, recoil on the old Europe. For the first time the Russian institutional system, power, and policy exert a major and long-lasting effect on the dominant Europe of the past. Particular consideration is directed to these phenomena through the chapter on the American entry into European affairs and the two chapters on the Russian revolution.

The chapters on the revolutions in eastern Europe are intended to pay due attention to an area sometimes neglected in a book of this scope. The area concerned is the zone of secondary countries between the Germans and the Russians. The developments of the area impinged more and more on the consciousness and policies of the Allies as the war continued. An interest in these countries is taken also from assignment in the Foreign Service to eastern Europe and from my work for six years as Director of the Office of Eastern European Affairs in the Department of State.

The fate of the continental empires and the Ottoman Empire may be treated with emphasis on the disintegration of the old formations or on the advent of the new. I have viewed the end of the Dual Empire and the Ottoman Empire from the latter standpoint. In the collapse of the Ottoman Empire the focus is on the Arab revolt and the political and territorial settlement with the new forces. In this sphere and in the disposition of the German overseas empire the view is from the origins of the Third World.

The book has long been in the making. My friend Bernadotte E. Schmitt commenced the study and for some time gathered material and prepared a draft on many topics. His numerous professional obligations and declining strength prevented him from proceeding further. At his and Dr. Langer's request I undertook to continue the project. I have endeavored to draw on Professor Schmitt's papers to the extent that his material might still be of current importance and contribute to the substance of the book within its general plan and organization. The chapters on the revolutions are entirely mine.

I regret that the volume was not finished before the death of Dr. Langer, to whom I am much indebted for his ever-ready help and his editorial review of the first nine chapters in their earlier stage. Having had the privilege of a desk on Deck D in the Library of Congress, I express deep appreciation for the resources, facilities, and personal assistance supplied by this great institution. My gratitude extends above all to the Research Facilities Section of the library but also to the Prints and Photographs Division (especially to Mr. Bernard Reilly), where I had the benefit of its special Straight Collection of wartime graphic art, and to the Map Division. The National Archives and the Archives Department of The Hoover Institution on War, Revolution and Peace were most helpful in the search for appropriate pictorial material. The Cartographic Services Laboratory of the University of Maryland has prepared the maps. To the scholars whose specialized studies have contributed to enlightenment in the field, I proffer an expression of respect and admiration for their work without which any attempt at a synthesis of this kind would be impossible.

HAROLD C. VEDELER

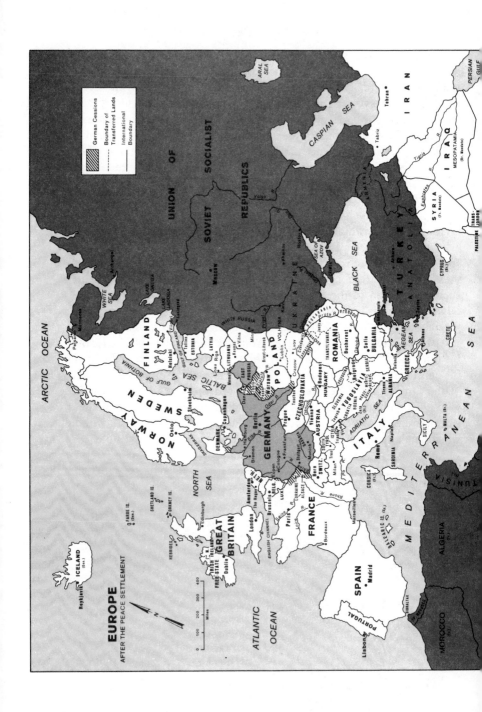

EUROPE
AFTER THE PEACE SETTLEMENT

German Cessions
Boundary of
Transferred Lands
International
Boundary

THE WORLD IN THE CRUCIBLE

1914-1919

shifts in pol power before war

alliances

"Silent war" p5 until 7/14

Chapter One

THE PLUNGE INTO WAR

1. THE INTENSIFYING DYNAMICS OF THE EUROPEAN SITUATION

NOT since the beginning of modern times had the forces of accelerating change been acting on Europe so deeply and disturbingly as in the years before the First World War. From our vantage point today we see that the most striking feature of the Europe before the war was the intensifying dynamics of the political and social situation resulting from the advance of industrial technology. The differential pace of this advance in global scope exerted profound effects in altering the international power structure of Europe and Europe's position in the world. Within the European states the progress of industrialization increasingly brought about a shift in economic and social power from the aristocracy and bourgeoisie to the masses, implying a corresponding shift in political power.

Internationally, the development shook the foundations of the classical balance of power system by differentiating the power position of members of the Pentarchy—that is, Britain, France, Prussia-Germany, Austria-Hungary, and Russia. For two and a half centuries the European political order was based on the classical balance of power, or the system of relations associated with the five great powers of the Pentarchy. Historically, the five states had been more or less equal in power, reflecting a more static society. Over the long run the members of the system shared a common interest in preventing a continental hegemony of any one state; the maintenance of the balance afforded a rough means of achieving national security conceived in terms of preserving the independence and position of the state.[1]

From 1871 to 1914 the approximate equality among the five great

1. The discussion that best clarifies the variously used term "balance of power" in application to the prewar period is in Edward V. Gulich, *Europe's Classical Balance of Power* (Ithaca, 1955), especially pp. 4–51. See also L. Claude, Jr., *Power and International Relations* (New York, 1962), 11–93, for an analysis of the meaning of the balance of power in its historical setting and for a critique of the system; Gustav A. C. Frantz, *Untersuchungen über das Gleichgewicht* (1859; Osnabrück, 1968), for a treatment of the subject as identified with the Pentarchy from the Restoration to the Crimean War and the war of Italian unity.

powers had given way to serious disparities in power owing principally to the varying advance of the technological revolution from country to country. This shift in the distribution of power had a direct relation to the origins of the war.[2] By the end of the century the German Reich was borne upward by an economic miracle to the position of Europe's chief industrial state. Germany's industrial preeminence and constant economic expansion rested on unequaled technological virtuosity, organizing powers, broad scientific and technological training provided by its institutions of higher education, and mass discipline of the workers. Indeed the Wilhelmine Reich's industrial and technological primacy afforded a better index to its general capacity to wage total war than its highly trained mass army and its second most powerful navy.

In contrast, Britain, the first industrial state in the world in 1870, saw its share of the world's manufacturing production fall from one-third in 1870 to one-seventh by 1913. Britain became the third-ranking industrial country, while France declined from second to fourth position in world production and trade. Britain's naval and imperial supremacy and France's large army gave an exaggerated impression of their strength. These manifestations of power tended to cloak symptoms of senescence, notably in regard to economic organization, industrial modernization, and capital input in industrial development.[3] The Dual Empire of Austria-Hungary still ranked as a great power but more by virtue of tradition than current realities. The once proud empire on the Danube had become a feeble conglomeration of nationalities because of internal paralysis and limited industrial capacity. Russia had towered in the east until it was left behind in the technological race. It experienced, nevertheless, two spurts of economic growth since the nineties that promised the rise of its future economic strength in the twentieth century. Italy never belonged to the Pentarchy, ranking among the great powers only by indulgence.

Thus by 1914 the Pentarchy of approximately equal powers had been transformed into a disequilibrium in which Germany was surging forward to the rank of a semisuperpower; Austria was dropping out of the circle

2. The emphasis here on the critical importance of the shift in the power structure reflects the seminal works of Ludwig Dehio, *Germany and World Politics in the Twentieth Century* (London, 1959); and F. H. Hinsley, *Power and the Pursuit of Peace* (Cambridge, England, 1967), 280–88.

3. On the change in relative economic position among Britain, France, and Germany, see David S. Landes, "Technological Change and Development in Western Europe, 1750–1914," in *Cambridge Economic History of Europe*, ed. H. J. Habakkuk and M. Poston, vol. 6 (Cambridge, England, 1965), pt. 1: 274–601.

of true great powers; Britain and France were falling back in relative power position; and Russia was spasmodically trying to overcome its weak and backward condition under an archaic state organization. Confronted with this upsetting and not fully understood phenomenon, France and Britain set about creating along with Russia the diplomatic system of the Triple Entente, directed essentially to containing Germany's assertion and growth of power. The Entente diplomacy aroused in Germany the fear of "encirclement"—of an "iron ring" being forged around the Reich. This fear of diplomatic isolation and Entente preponderance over the Triple Alliance, or Triplice, of Germany, Austria-Hungary, and Italy was fed by the growing unreliability of the Italian ally, the decline of the Dual Empire's status as a great power, and the increasing indications of Russia's military and economic capabilities in the future. It was really paradoxical that the Germans, so much in the lead in many basic ingredients of national power, should grow more and more concerned that before long the other states would join together to stop the German progress. Where it counted most, in economic and technological growth, the Germans were unstoppable by any diplomatic means.

In the endeavor to hold its own against the Entente, Germany maintained the Dual Alliance with Austria through repeated international confrontations. The question remains debatable whether the preservation of the Austrian connection virtually at any price served to support or to impede Germany's attainment of a position acceptable to both itself and its neighbors. The ultimate problem was how Europe should be organized as the old structure of interstate relations broke down under the impact of differential technological development. Upon the ability to find a solution hung the issue of peace or war.

The classical balance of power had also come under the assault of forces in the world beyond Europe. By the turn of the century there had sprung up two non-European great powers, the economic giant of the United States in the west and the rising empire of Japan in the east. The defeat of Russia by Japan in 1905, the Anglo-Japanese alliance concluded in 1902, and the gradual growth of a kind of tacit entente between Britain and the United States evidenced the impingement of these forces on power relations in Europe. The altered situation meant that in a future attempt to preserve the balance of power in Europe through war, outside powers would be drawn into the conflict—not to redress the balance, as hoped by most of the European states, but to destroy forever the Pentarchy and the old system. A new global pattern of power relations would rise, and in this configuration Europe would form a part but no longer be the political and economic center of the world.

Within the European states the ruling elites still consisted generally of the aristocracy and the upper middle classes, although the beneficiaries of privilege were being challenged by the lower bourgeoisie and the masses. Since the workers manned positions essential to the functioning of an industrial society, they controlled economic and social power as they asserted themselves in an organized manner. The masses were building the foundations of political power, if they were not yet exercising effective parliamentary functions, through popular education, universal military service, social welfare legislation, the expanding trade-union movement, development of a worker's press, extension of the franchise, and the rise of popular parties with a professional organization. Liberalism, having spent its invigorating influence, was declining everywhere while social democracy was coming forward as the movement of the future. As the liberal parties split into national or imperialist and moderate or radical groups, socialists and labor became the leading representatives of mass democracy and steadily increased their strength in parliamentary bodies. The threat of socialism hardened the determination of the privileged classes on the continent to resist radical political change and preserve their position in society. The pressure of the masses, controlled by socialist and worker organizations, for political reform consonant with their economic power was beating against the strongholds of privilege. The strains of war would sharpen this opposition of forces to the point of revolution.

From the beginning of the century to the outbreak of war, the progressive redistribution of power among the major European states had increasing effect on the shape and substance of international relations. The quickening dynamics found expression in the tensions of ever sharpening nationalism and in serious instability. A struggle for power was carried on so intensely that it assumed the nature of a silent war, referred to at that time as a "dry war" or a "latent war."[4] The silent war centered on the issue whether the old balance of power was to be preserved or whether the status quo was to be revised to conform to Germany's industrial, technical, and military primacy.

4. Professor Hans Delbrück termed the Anglo-German arms race a "dry war." Captain Widenmann, German naval attaché in London, called it a "latent war." Winston Churchill, believing that the growth of the German navy exposed Britain to dangers to its existence, demanded "a vigilance almost as tense as that of actual war." See Churchill's *The World Crisis*, 4 vols. (London, 1923–29), 1: 30.

The Wilhelmine Reich, impelled by the swelling energies and expansionist pressure of the nation, embarked on a drive for established world power. A principal means toward the goal was the construction of a powerful battle fleet to operate chiefly in the North Sea. The naval program, pressed in connection with Germany's aggressive pursuit of world trade and a career in world politics, challenged British maritime supremacy, British security in home waters, and British capacity to guarantee the balance of power on the continent. In resistance to the drive to bring about the demise of the old European system, Britain chose an unlimited naval race in preference to purchasing naval limitation at the price of withdrawal from the continent (and of German hegemony there)—a deal that Berlin offered.[5] Britain along with France and Russia moved steadily to consolidate the Triple Entente.

The silent war between the Entente and the Central Powers of Germany and Austria-Hungary continued until the July crisis of 1914.[6] The struggle was waged on the diplomatic front, but with military and naval means in close support. Thus Kurt Riezler, the close confidant of the German chancellor Bethmann Hollweg, noted, "The cannons no longer shoot but they speak in the negotiations."[7] The contestants sought the fruits of victory without resort to war itself. The protracted power struggle involved brinkmanship including the diplomacy of threat and bluff, war scares, and resort to ultimatums and mobilizations. The inevitable diplomatic confrontations risked getting out of hand and ending in a general war. That catastrophe was avoided until 1914 but not without four major crises from 1905 to 1913, bringing the threat of a European war on the horizon. The nations, gripped in this war without guns, could scarcely escape other crises, and the question casting its shadow over Europe remained whether the next one would precipitate a shooting war.[8]

5. See A.J.P. Taylor, *The Struggle for the Mastery of Europe, 1848–1918* (Oxford, 1954), 459.

6. On the general subject of the conflict, see Dehio, *Germany and World Politics*, 11–16, and his review of Ritter's *Staatkunst und Kriegshandwerk*, vol. 2, in *Historische Zeitschrift* 194 (1962): 130–38.

7. Andreas Hillgruber, "Riezlers Theorie des kalkulierten Risikos und Bethmann Hollwegs politische Konzeption in der Julikrise 1914," *Historische Zeitschrift* 202 (1966): 338.

8. Churchill refers to the exercise of brinkmanship in discussing the Agadir crisis. "It seems probable that the Germans did not mean war on this occasion. But they did mean to test the ground; and in so doing they were prepared to go to the very edge of the precipice." *The World Crisis*, 1: 46. A recent German work is direct on the point: ". . . the Reich leadership had consequently pursued a risk policy in the international crises from 1905 to 1914 hard on the brink of war." Karl-Heinz Janssen, *Der Kanzler und der General* (Göttingen, 1967), 6.

The successive crises caused each state involved to redouble exertions to sustain its position and to strengthen the camp to which it belonged. The resulting strain on the great powers was especially felt in the rapidly mounting burden of armament expenditures. The costs climbed rapidly not only because of the need to arm larger and larger masses of men but also because of the rising outlays for the constantly improving technical quality of arms and for replacement due to earlier obsolescence.

The strain revealed the increasing disparities between the major European states in their continued capacity to act as great powers. At the same time it constituted a test of national economic development and the efficient organization of the state, just as the war was to impose an even more severe trial. Austria was finding the struggle hardest to bear and was clearly falling behind in the competition. Russia's per capita expenditures for arms in 1914 were only slightly larger than Austria's, and it had to depend on French loans for defraying a major portion of these costs. France had difficulty in keeping up the pace with Germany.[9]

2. THE WORLD IN CRISIS

The assassination of Archduke Franz Ferdinand of Austria-Hungary at Sarajevo on June 28, 1914, plunged the world into a deep crisis from which it did not emerge until some five years later. The crisis proceeded through three stages: the initial diplomatic stage, ending by August 5, 1914, in the immediate declarations of war; the stage of world war, lasting until the armistice on November 11, 1918; and the concluding stage, in which the changes of the war period were institutionalized by the peace settlement and the completion of the wartime revolutions.

The diplomatic crisis of July 1914 was the logical outcome of the silent war carried on since the beginning of the century. It was similar in many ways to the preceding diplomatic crises since 1905 yet different in scope, for it joined two international conflicts. The two Moroccan crises involved European and imperialist confrontations between Germany on one side and France and Britain on the other. The crisis of 1908–1909 arising from the annexation of Bosnia by Austria-Hungary and the crisis of 1912–1913 produced by the Balkan Wars involved the Serbian problem, the composition of the Austrian multinational empire, and the opposition of Austrian

9. M. E. Howard, "The Armed Forces," in *The New Cambridge Modern History*, vol. 11, ed. F. H. Hinsley (Cambridge, England, 1962), 240–41; A.J.P. Taylor, *The Habsburg Monarchy, 1809–1918* (London, 1948), 229.

and Russian interests in the Balkans. Austria and Russia had no direct interest in the former, France and Britain no decisive interest in the latter. The July confrontation merged both conflicts in one overall European crisis, making it far graver than any of the earlier ones. It was the link between the silent war of the past years and the Great War of the next four years.[10]

The July events took the form of a diplomatic contest preliminary to the military struggle. The handling of the issues in this contest was to determine whether it would end in peace or war, what the alignment of the belligerents was to be, and where personal responsibility would rest for the shift from diplomacy to war. The First World War was not a single military conflict but three wars in one: a Balkan war over eastern European issues; a continental war over the issue of German power on the continent; and a world war in which Germany challenged Anglo-Saxon naval supremacy. The diplomatic contest finally erupted into military conflict by broadening out from a local Austro-Serbian war to a continental war of Germany and Austria against Russia and France, and then to a world war drawing in Britain and Japan.

Of six decisive acts leading to the catastrophe, the first was the Potsdam consultation of July 5–6 held by the Viennese envoy Count Alexander Hoyos, chief of cabinet and confidant of the Austrian foreign minister Count Leopold Berchtold, and the Austrian ambassador Count Laszlo Szögyeny with the kaiser and the chancellor. This resulted in a German commitment of full support for drastic action against Serbia.

The second act was the note of ultimatum delivered by Austria to the Serbian government on July 23. It was designed to be unacceptable and made a break in diplomatic relations between the two states inevitable.

Austria's declaration of war against Serbia on July 28 came as the third act, followed by the bombardment of Belgrade on July 29. The effect was to challenge Russia's interest in the Balkans and most immediately its relations to Serbia, provoking an outburst of indignation and war enthusiasm in Saint Petersburg.

The order for general mobilization in Russia on July 30 became a fourth decisive action. It provided the occasion (the decision for war was made by the German government at least twelve hours before news was re-

10. Churchill attributes the utmost importance to the compound character of the crisis. See Winston S. Churchill, *The Unknown War: The Eastern Front, 1914–1917* (London, 1941), 18.

ceived of the Russian general mobilization) for Berlin to proclaim a state of threatening war danger preliminary to German general mobilization.[11]

The fifth event was the order for German general mobilization, together with the order for French mobilization, on August 1. German mobilization closed off any last possibility of diplomacy to save the peace. Since mobilization involved carrying out a schedule of military movements, it led to the German declarations of war on Russia on August 1 and on France on August 3, as well as to the German invasion of Belgium.

The final act—the British ultimatum to Germany on August 4, with the subsequent declaration of war—proceeded directly from the invasion of Belgium. This climax to the series of actions changed the nature of the war completely, from continental to world dimensions.

With these steps the great powers passed beyond the brink. In the ensuing days the formalities in moving to a legal state of belligerence between the Entente and the Central Powers were rounded out with additional declarations of war among the participants. The war assumed global proportions on August 23, when Japan declared war on Germany.

Of the six decisive steps on the road to war, the crucial one was the blank check issued to the Austrians by William II and Bethmann Hollweg at Potsdam. All the other actions to the fatal end followed like a chain reaction.[12] Without the unlimited commitment of Berlin, Vienna would hardly have dared to take military measures on its own against Serbia at the risk of war with Russia. Prior to the completion of the Hoyos mission, the Vienna cabinet was divided on the response to make to the Sarajevo incident. Only the German pledge and Berlin's pressure for firm action removed at last the opposition of Count Stephen Tisza, the chief minister at Budapest and the strongest personality in the imperial ministry of common affairs, and produced unanimity in favor of the "daring stroke." Tisza as well as the other ministers at Vienna saw the danger of Russian intervention. But when Germany was firm, Tisza yielded, for close cooperation with Germany was the cornerstone of his policy.[13]

11. On the relationship between Russian mobilization and the German decision for war, see Imanuel Geiss, *Julikrise und Kriegsausbruch*, 2 vols. (Hannover, 1963–64), 2: 73, and his "The Outbreak of the First World War and German War Aims," *Journal of Contemporary History* 1, no. 3 (1966): 88–89.

12. J. Stengers, "July 1914: Some Reflections," *L'Annuaire d'Institute de philologie et d'histoire orientales et slaves* 17 (1963–64): 114; Geiss, *Julikrise*, 2: 722.

13. Norman Stone, "Hungary and the Crisis of July 1914," *Journal of Contemporary History* 1, no. 3 (1966): 156–68.

The Reich set in motion a "political offensive" in the July diplomacy.[14] The aims of the offensive at the risk of a European war were to help reassert the position of Austria as a great power after revelations of its weakness in recent years, thereby retaining the Dual Empire and making Austria more valuable as an ally; to force a basic revision of the Balkan situation in favor of Austria, checking the increasing influence of Russia at Belgrade and Bucharest after the Balkan Wars; and to break through the Reich's encirclement by a diplomatic success of sufficient weight to disrupt the Entente.

The Hoyos mission brought a letter to William II from Franz Joseph and a memorandum for the German government that made plain Vienna's desire to utilize Sarajevo for commencing a political offensive of broad purpose. The intention was to save the Habsburg monarchy by solving its major nationality problems and to replace the rising Russian influence in the Balkans with Austrian hegemony. It would require that Romania, whose irredentist aspirations were a threat to the integrity of the Austro-Hungarian empire second only to the Serbian nationalist goals, abandon irredentist agitation and take an unambiguous stand either for or against the Central Powers. An alliance was to be formed with a strengthened Bulgaria and a new Balkan league developed with Bulgaria, Greece, and Turkey as the nucleus under the aegis of the Triple Alliance.

The German offensive was sustained at the outset through the pressure exercised by the German ambassador at Vienna for a sharp formulation of the note to Serbia.[15] Berlin repeated demands on the Ballhausplatz for speed in declaring war on Serbia with subsequent military action. The Reich did not take any effective part in the efforts made to preserve the peace, resisting until near the end Sir Edward Grey's proposals for four-power mediation of the Austro-Serbian conflict. As late as July 28, the German chancellor neutralized, by distortions and by delay in transmission, the kaiser's "Halt-in-Belgrade" proposal for mediation. Only when British intervention threatened, did the chancellor emphatically urge Berchtold to accept a British version of this plan for mediation. By that time it was too late to prevent a general war; the military leaders were,

14. See Egmont Zechlin, "Deutschland zwischen Kabinettskrieg und Wirtschaftskrieg. Politik und Kriegführung in den ersten Monaten des Weltkrieges 1914," *Historische Zeitschrift* 199 (1964): 353–54.
15. Eberhard von Vietsch, "Der Kriegsausbruch 1914 im Lichte der neuesten Forschung," *Geschichte in Wissenschaft und Unterricht* 15 (1964): 479.

in effect, then making the decisions.

Until near the end of July, Germany insisted on localization of the conflict. The Reich rejected a settlement by the concert of Europe or in the interests of Europe as a whole. The acceptance of localization by the powers would have given Austria a license to carry out a war against Serbia alone. The Reich was in substance presenting the Entente the alternatives of a resolution of the crisis on the terms of the Central Powers or a general war. For the Entente it became a matter of resisting the success of German policy or capitulation.

On the other hand, from the standpoint of the German government, it seemed that if Austria did not react firmly to the challenge of Sarajevo, the Dual Empire would forfeit its position as a great power. If the Reich did not support Austria, it would be charged with betrayal of the ally. A blow would be struck at the alliance, and the ring of encirclement would be tightened still further. The failure to follow a vigorous course seemed to Berlin to be at the least a serious defeat for its diplomacy and at most an opportunity missed to advance the interests of Germany and its position as a continental power.

3. THE ALIGNMENT OF STATES

The diplomatic contest, ending in a general war, determined the basic alignment of powers until the entry of the United States and set the lines of the wartime struggle to win over the neutral states to the respective sides. As soon as Germany and Russia were at war with each other, it almost automatically followed that France would join in a continental conflict. France was determined to remain faithful to the alliance with Russia and to uphold the solidarity of the Entente. The ambivalent position of Britain in that system seemed, in Germany, to make British intervention uncertain. At least Bethmann Hollweg hoped for Britain's neutrality and bid for it as a cardinal point of policy in the last days of the July crisis, just as his efforts since assuming office were directed to detaching Britain from the Entente.[16]

16. The German government was divided on the possibility of Britain's neutrality. Moltke, the chief of the general staff, and Tirpitz, the state secretary of the Reich naval office, were certain of British intervention. Gerhard Ritter, *Staatskunst und Kriegshandwerk*, 4 vols. (Munich, 1959–68), 2: 271; Fritz Fischer, *Germany's Aims in the First World War* (New York, 1967), 49; A. von Tirpitz, *Politische Dokumente*, vol. 2: *Deutsche Ohnmachtspolitik im Weltkriege* (Hamburg, 1926), 180–81. Baron Ferdinand von Stumm, director of the political department of the foreign office and specialist in British affairs, believed, however, in the likelihood

On July 29 the chancellor made an offer to the British that Germany would respect the territorial integrity of France and Belgium in the event of German victory if Britain remained neutral. That he was desperate to purchase British neutrality was revealed by his proposal for a fleet agreement (discussed with the British but rejected by the kaiser) that would have conceded British naval supremacy and sacrificed the most cherished aims of William II and Admiral Alfred von Tirpitz.[17]

The failure of German diplomacy to assure British neutrality could only be reckoned a serious defeat for German policy. The defeat insured that Germany would not be free to wage a war only against France and Russia, with every prospect of victory and the achievement of uncontested supremacy on the continent. It spelled ultimate disaster for Germany inasmuch as there was no way, given the kind of military and naval preparation Germany had made, by which the Reich's power could gain effective access to the British insular fortress. Germany could find no means to subdue the center of the British Empire, which drew on worldwide resources outside Europe through command of the seas.

Britain's position toward the war critically influenced Italy's decision of August 1 for neutrality and defection from the Triplice. Italy had habitually avoided war with Britain, recognizing that it could not expose its long, unguarded coastlines and dependence on foreign food supplies to British naval power. It had of course been the Italian purpose for a generation to resist Habsburg expansion and Austrian hegemony in the Balkans. The power of the Entente and the conflict of interests with Austria in the Tyrol and the Balkans virtually predetermined Italy's decision to reject the obligations of the Triple Alliance.

Rome firmly maintained, in exchanges with Vienna and Berlin, that the *casus foederis* did not come into force because Austria had violated the terms of the treaty of alliance: Vienna had embarked on an aggressive course against Serbia and had not consulted with the Italian government in advance. Italy would therefore be guided by its own "great interests." But its attitude might change if adequate compensation could be arranged

---

of British neutrality, certainly at first. Georg Alexander von Müller, *Regierte der Kaiser?* (Göttingen, 1959), 36. The naval staff considered as late as August 3 that British neutrality was still possible. Geiss, *Julikrise,* 2: 667. The historians of today are also divided on the question. For differing views, see W. J. Mommsen, "The Debate on German War Aims," *Journal of Contemporary History* 1, no. 3 (1966): 60, and Geiss, *Julikrise,* 2: 667.

17. See A. von Tirpitz, *My Memoirs,* 2 vols. (New York, 1919), 1: 360.

in accordance with the Italian interpretation of the treaty provision on reciprocal compensation.[18]

During the following months Italy, in the stance of neutrality, continued the policy of "duality" pursued for two decades: maintaining connections with both the Triplice and the Entente while avoiding an exclusive alignment with either.[19] Italy's protracted discussions with both sides enabled it to postpone a final decision until the military situation and the results of the dual negotiations indicated whether definitive neutrality or war against Austria would best serve Italian interests. The freedom of action thus attained allowed the opportunity to make diplomatic, military, and internal preparations for any eventuality.

The negotiations with the Allies, as the Entente powers were known during the war, produced a bargain by which, for joining the Entente, Italy was promised to receive, at the peace, the South Tyrol and the Adriatic islands and littoral, assuring Italy of primacy in the Adriatic area. The deal was consummated in the secret treaty of London, signed on April 26, 1915. On May 23 the Italian government, having overcome the neutralist opposition in parliament and with the country in an internal crisis, declared war on Austria-Hungary.[20]

Before the outbreak of hostilities, the two coalitions began a diplomatic struggle to gain the intervention or at least the neutrality of Romania, Bulgaria, and Turkey. The problem facing each coalition was how to form a Balkan bloc, assuring it the most dependable support and access to the maximum military resources of the Balkans in view of the antagonisms among these states and the pro- and antirevisionist attitudes toward the treaty of Bucharest ending the Balkan Wars. Irredentist emotions directed toward Hungary compounded the difficulties for the Central Powers. Taking these factors into account, Austria chose Bulgaria as the key pin of a projected Balkan combination, and Germany chose Romania.

German diplomacy targeted on Romania had to contend with a switch from anti-Russian to anti-Austrian sentiments since the second Balkan War. The shift was associated with the prevalence of a nationalist mania that seized the public with the vision of a Greater Romania to be achieved

18. W. W. Gottlieb, *Studies in Secret Diplomacy during the First World War* (London, 1957), 169–73.

19. William A. Renzi, "Italy's Neutrality and Entrance into the Great War: A Reexamination," *American Historical Review* 73 (1968): 1415–18.

20. See below, pp. 92–95.

through the incorporation of the Romanian minority in the Dual Empire. Irredentism was further aroused by the repressive Magyarization of this minority. Adding to the threat to Austria-Hungary and to the difficulties of realizing the German objective was an active Russian and French diplomacy in Bucharest which held out to Romania the lure of acquiring Transylvania. Austria's bid for an alliance with Bulgaria also worked to alienate Romania as well as to cause friction with Germany. These influences swung Romania away from the Triplice toward a cordial relationship with Russia.

The July crisis and the beginning of the war stimulated the anti-Austrian tendencies in Romania to a new pitch of irredentist agitation and violent public attacks on the Habsburg empire. King Carol I, a Hohenzollern, vainly pleaded in the crown council of August 3, 1914, for Romania to join the Central Powers in a war against Russia. The council, moved by the public feelings against Austria and influenced decisively by the neutrality policy of Italy, took a strong stand for maintaining neutrality. Romania continued to watch alertly on the sidelines until the end of August 1916, when, after skillful negotiations with the Entente, the country joined the Allies on its own terms.[21]

Since the Balkan Wars, Bulgaria had been moving from a russophile orientation to the Austrian orbit. The shift came about primarily from the Bulgarian desire to overthrow the treaty of Bucharest and from Austrian steps to woo revanchist Bulgaria as an anti-Serbian partner in the Balkans. Both King Ferdinand, a ruler of German origin, and his government, headed by Vasil Radoslavov, favored the Central Powers. Vienna could have entered into an alliance with Sofia before Sarajevo but was held back by Berlin's preference for strengthening the alliance with Romania. Upon the outbreak of war the increasingly cordial relationship between Austria and Bulgaria, however, did not keep the wily and cautious Bulgarian king, in the face of Russian threats, from declaring neutrality and from halting negotiations with the Central Powers just short of signing a draft treaty of alliance. While drawing back from involvement in the conflict, Bulgaria made diplomatic preparations for a possible struggle with Serbia by concluding an alliance with Turkey in August 1914. After the Central Powers swept through western Russia in 1915, the attraction of their success

21. Glenn Torrey, "Irredentist Diplomacy: The Central Powers and Romania, August–November 1914," *Südost-Forschungen* 25 (1966): 285–90.

proved too strong for Bulgaria to resist, and it joined Germany and Austria in October 1915.[22]

The policy of the Ottoman Empire in 1914 and during the war was conditioned by these circumstances: the bankruptcy of the moldering multinational empire of Turks, Arabs, Kurds, Greeks, Armenians, and miscellaneous lesser groups, consisting for the most part of an oppressed and illiterate peasantry; the conflict between the Arab national movement and Turkish domination; the dependence on foreign powers through a regime of capitulations and concessions; and the diplomatic isolation of the weak, decrepit state. The Young Turks in the Committee of Union and Progress had endeavored fervently to modernize the empire and emancipate it from these circumstances. They had encouraged German investment in the Bagdad railway, utilities, mining, and agriculture as a way to resist British and French pressures. They had recently brought in a German military mission under General Otto Liman von Sanders, appointed inspector general of the Turkish army, to reorganize the armed forces.[23]

The Porte, or Ottoman government, had made unsuccessful overtures to both the Entente and the Central Powers with the view to an alliance. Whether oriented toward Germany or the Entente, the Turkish leaders detected in the July crisis an opportunity to end Ottoman isolation. The pro-Entente minister of the navy, Djemal Pasha, sounded out Paris; and to Berlin dashed Enver Pasha, a bold, colorful young officer of Napoleonic ambitions who had made himself minister of war and chief of the general staff not many months before. After neither Paris nor Berlin reacted affirmatively, Enver urgently requested of the German ambassador, Hans von Wangenheim, on July 22 admission to the Triple Alliance and German support of a Turkish-Bulgarian combination. The Reich, unable to postpone any longer a choice in its Balkan and Turkish policy, quickly negotiated with the Turks a secret treaty, signed at Constantinople on August 2, 1914. The two parties pledged that in the event of Russian

22. See James M. Potts, "The Loss of Bulgaria," in Alexander Dallin et al., *Russian Diplomacy and Eastern Europe* (New York, 1963), 194–205; C. Jay Smith, *The Russian Struggle for Power, 1914–1917* (New York, 1956), 30–33; Z.A.B. Zeman, *A Diplomatic History of the First World War* (London, 1971), 72–75.

23. See Ahmed Emin, *Turkey in the World War* (New Haven, 1930), 79–95; M. Larcher, *La guerre turque dans la guerre mondiale* (Paris, 1926), 11–27; Howard M. Sachar, *The Emergence of the Middle East, 1914–1924* (New York, 1969), 10–14; Ulrich Trumpener, *Germany and the Ottoman Empire* (Princeton, 1968), 6–14; Peter Mansfield, *The Ottoman Empire and Its Successors* (London, 1973), 14–33.

intervention in the Austro-Serbian conflict, Turkey would participate in the war and Germany would support territorial gains for Turkey in the Balkans at the expense of Russia. In addition, Germany agreed to back the abolition of capitulations.[24]

Austria quickly followed with similar discussions at Constantinople, which ended in an exchange of notes on August 5 committing the two parties to the engagements of the German treaty. The Turks ordered mobilization on August 3, but the next day sober second thoughts prompted a declaration of neutrality.[25]

For the Turks the treaties offered the hope of long-range security against the inroads of Russian imperialism and of a share in the spoils of victory over Russia. For Germany and Austria the pact provided the means of breaking the vital Entente link between Russia and western Europe via the Black Sea, influencing the Balkan states in favor of the Central Powers, and gaining access to Turkish raw materials. But the Turks postponed for three months the final decision on war, while they maintained an armed and uneasy neutrality combined with military preparations. During the time, opportunistic and fruitless approaches to the Entente were succeeded by increasing German and Austrian pressures for cooperation in the war, ending in Turkey's involvement as a belligerent by November 1.

The official Greek attitude was plagued by divided sympathies. King Constantine, the husband of the kaiser's sister and an ardent admirer of the German army, leaned toward the Central Powers; the premier Eleutherios Venizelos, a vehement nationalist dedicated to the creation of a Greater Greece, took the side of the Entente. These differences were paralleled by the conflicting royalism of the king and the democratic constitutionalism of Venizelos, which divided the nation into two groups —the royalists and the Venizelists. In the narrower Balkan frame they shared the common determination to prevent the Bulgarians from utilizing the war situation to overturn the Bucharest settlement. Unable to agree among themselves so far as the great powers were concerned, the Greeks resisted the pressures of Berlin designed to win them to the Central Powers and proclaimed neutrality. The Entente encouraged the

24. Gerard E. Silberstein, *The Troubled Alliance* (Lexington, Ky., 1970), 10–13; Larcher, *La guerre turque,* 34–38; Ahmed Enim, *Turkey in the World War,* 66–68. The full text of the treaty is given in Larcher.
25. Silberstein, *Troubled Alliance,* 13–16.

Greeks to persist in their neutrality, when in mid-August 1914 Venizelos approached Britain and France about joining them. The proposal was unwelcome to the Allies, since they feared that Greece's entry would drive Turkey into the camp of the enemy. Russia objected in the suspicion of Greek designs on Constantinople. By June 1917 the Allies nevertheless forced Greece into the war in order to further Allied operations in the Balkans.

In accordance with the ancient Anglo-Portuguese alliance, the Portuguese government informed London at once of its intention to cooperate. The parliament proclaimed the solidarity of Portugal with Britain. The latter did not find that Portugal could make any military contribution and considered that, on the contrary, the protection of its commerce and colonies would constitute a liability for the Allies. The British therefore encouraged Portugal to maintain neutrality. Its entrance into the war was postponed until Germany and Austria formally declared war on Portugal in March 1916.

The other states of Europe—the Scandinavias, Holland, Switzerland, and Spain—assumed neutrality at once. These states, small in size except for Spain, had no national aspirations to satisfy by means of war. The small states adjoining Germany by land or having close water and trade connections with that formidable power, could be seriously hurt by military participation. They utilized every resource and suffered many hardships and indignities to preserve their neutrality, and succeeded in doing so throughout the war.

The two great powers outside Europe, Japan and the United States, followed contrasting courses. The struggle that absorbed the European powers presented Japan with a unique opportunity to build up its power position in East Asia and the Pacific. Because of the Anglo-Japanese alliance of 1902, renewed in 1911, consultations commenced at once between the two allies upon the coming of the war. Britain, somewhat reluctantly, asked for Japanese help against Germany, and Japan, not loath, immediately agreed. On August 15, 1914, the Japanese presented a note "advising" the German government to withdraw all warships from Chinese and Japanese waters and to hand over to Japan the leased territory of Kiaochow before September 15, "with a view to the eventual restoration of the same to China." When the German government returned no answer to the ultimatum, Japan declared war on August 23.

The United States pronounced its neutrality and maintained it until

April 1917. The case is strong for concluding that it would have continued the status of neutrality had it not been for the unrestricted U-boat campaign. The significant shifts of states from neutrality to cobelligerent status occurred over the period from November 1914 to April 1917. Each of these shifts materially affected the balance of forces between the two coalitions, bringing advantages to one and losses in relative strength to the other. The changes exerting the decisive influence on the equilibrium were the participation of the United States and the dropout of Russia in 1917. Not until then was the definitive alignment of warring powers determined. The changes in alignment in the process proved of more consequence in affecting the outcome of the war than many of the battles.

4. THE NEVER-ENDING QUESTION

Ever since the Great War the western mind has been disturbed by the question whether the cataclysm could have been avoided. An answer to that question cannot be simple in view of the many factors that contributed to the complex set of events bringing about the great upheaval. The personal factor was evident in the Potsdam decision of William II and Bethmann Hollweg that set off the inexorable chain of diplomatic interactions in July 1914;[26] in the forward program of Berchtold that prompted vigorous Austrian action against Serbia, rejection of the Serbian reply to the ultimatum, and refusal of any attempt at mediation of the powers;[27] and in the cooperation of the Russian foreign minister Sergei Sazonov with the generals in obtaining the tsar's signature to the order for general mobilization. Sazonov's move followed from an energetic policy program adopted in February 1914 aiming at the consolidation of the Entente and the strengthening of Russian influence in the Balkans.[28]

The institutional factor made itself felt in the unstable situation existing

26. On the influences affecting the decision of William II and Bethmann Hollweg, see Michael Balfour, *The Kaiser and His Times* (London, 1964), 339–41; Egmont Zechlin, "Bethmann Hollweg, Kriegsrisiko und SPD 1914," *Der Monat* 18 (1966): 19–21; Hillgruber, "Riezlers Theorie des kalkulierten Risikos und Bethmann Hollwegs politische Konzeption in der Julikrise 1914," 347–48; Fritz Stern, "Bethmann Hollweg and the War: The Limits of Responsibility," in *The Responsibility of Power*, eds. L. Krieger and F. Stern (New York, 1967), 263–66; Karl Dietrich Erdmann, "Zur Beurteilung Bethmann Hollwegs," *Geschichte in Wissenschaft und Unterricht* 15 (1964): 536–37; Fritz Fischer, "Weltpolitik, Weltmachtstreben und deutsche Kriegsziele," *Historische Zeitschrift* 199 (1964): 341–42.

27. Hugo Hantsch, *Leopold Graf Berchtold*, 2 vols. (Graz, 1963), 2: 559–62, 647.

28. I. V. Bestuzushev, "Russian Foreign Policy February–June 1914," *Journal of Contemporary History* 1, no. 3 (1966): 93–112.

when nearly two-thirds of the European population—in Germany, Austria, and Russia—were governed under archaic political systems by obsolete ruling elites. That constitutional anachronism allowed only a few men—sometimes one or two, as in the case of the Potsdam decision—to determine foreign policy, control the armed forces, and decide for peace or war without benefit of a well-ordered deliberative process.[29] The antiquated constitutional structure failed as an organization for coordinating plans and policies of the army, navy, ministry of war, foreign office, and economic offices. These institutional rigidities combined with many feudal and authoritarian features of the regime prevented the Habsburg monarchy from solving its internal problems and encouraged the constituent nationalities to look outside the empire for the satisfaction of their aspirations. Since the crumbling empire proved incapable of enlightened self-regeneration, its fate became an international issue and a threat to peace.[30]

--The competitive expansion of million-man armies and dreadnought navies contributed to both internal and international tensions. The phenomenal growth of military establishments opened the way to enlarging the influence of the military in the affairs of government. Military and naval services acted like autonomous authorities in central and eastern Europe; the general staff was able to impose on the civilian leadership the primacy of "military necessity" over political purpose. In July 1914 the inflexibility of military planning without contingent alternatives figured prominently in moving from the diplomatic contest to war. Each general staff felt under the compulsion of immediate action to execute prepared plans so as to prevent the other side from gaining the advantage of prior military movement.[31]

-- Disturbed domestic conditions were favorable to the genesis of both war and revolution. A constitutional breakdown threatened in Germany as control of the Reichstag appeared soon to pass from the conservatives

29. In Germany responsible authority was confined to a small oligarchy of a score of officials, assisting the Kaiser and chancellor. John C. Rohl, *Germany without Bismarck* (Berkeley, 1967), 267.

30. The tsar expressed the opinion to the British ambassador in April 1913 that the disintegration of the Austrian empire was only a question of time, with the prospect of succession states being formed. The ambassador observed that "such a recasting of the map of Europe could hardly be effected without a general war." Sir George Buchanan, *My Mission to Russia*, 2 vols. (Boston, 1923), 2: 182.

31. A dominant theme of Ritter's monumental work *Staatskunst und Kriegshandwerk* is the major influence exerted by the military-technical factors in the sweep to war.

to representatives of the masses in the Social Democratic and Center parties. The feeble government of the superannuated Franz Joseph, himself a relic of the past days of Habsburg glory, and the resistance of the German and Magyar ruling groups produced an impasse over reform in the Dual Empire. Many authoritarian administrative controls in Austria, generated by the increasing internal conflict, and Hungary's tough policy of Magyarization, applied by an autocratic centralized administration, only made the crisis perpetual. The internal tensions, focusing on the threat of the Southern Slav movement to the empire, gave impetus to an uncertain and adventurous foreign policy. A sense of enervating deadlock and the loss of morale from a state in degeneration caused a feeling of fatalistic hopelessness in the empire's political centers. The ruling elites had a sense that their position in society was besieged and the survival of the empire imperiled. War was their answer to each of these dangers, their only decisive step intended to solve the nationality problem.[32]

No state was so near revolution in 1914 as Russia. The changes incident to a new spurt of industrialization, the delinquencies of an inept reactionary regime, and the acute discontent among the urban workers and the peasants revived the revolutionary movement. A strong swing of domestic opinion against the Central Powers in 1914 and the new wave of revolutionary feeling convinced Nicholas II and Sazonov that the failure to act in Serbia's behalf would precipitate a revolution and endanger the tsarist regime.[33]

⊷ In the central and eastern empires a tendency prevailed to identify between the privileged classes and the forces of militarism and extreme nationalism on the one hand and between the forces of reform, antimilitarism, and internationalism on the other. The ruling elites pressed for a vigorous foreign policy, including war if necessary, as a way to appease the dissatisfied elements at home. For them an active foreign policy was a prophylaxis against reform and revolution that would safeguard their position. This same attitude carried through the war to the uncompromising war aims they espoused. They were moved to war for the same reasons

32. See Solomon Wank, "Foreign Policy and the Nationality Problem in Austria-Hungary, 1867–1914," *Austrian History Yearbook* 3, pt. 3 (1967): 49–51; Robert A. Kann, *The Habsburg Monarchy* (New York, 1957), 96–97.

33. Stengers, "July 1914," 117–44; Jonathan French Scott, *Five Weeks: The Surge of Public Opinion on the Eve of the Great War* (New York, 1927), 177–78. On the importance of domestic conditions as a whole in bringing about the war, see Arno J. Mayer, "Domestic Causes of the First World War," in *Responsibility of Power*, 286–300.

that kept them from a compromise peace.

— The temper of the age, dominated by the explosive combination of integral nationalism and the cult of power, created a disposition to war. The cult of power expressed itself, among other ways, in the militarism, navalism, and imperialism of the era. War was viewed, by the statesmen and generals of the time, as a legitimate instrument of policy and as a normal part of the European political system. War was not to be sought, but war might be necessary to secure the independence and position of the state as a great power, the achievement of which was regarded by major governments as more important than keeping the peace. A fatalistic belief developed among many military and political leaders, no less than among publicists, that a European war was inevitable sooner or later. Some of these men, including Bethmann Hollweg, deduced the corollary that the most favorable time for waging a war should not be passed by— a conception dangerously close to the idea of preventive war. The repeated international crises and alerts were wearing down the threshold for tolerating international tension. The situation was producing a widespread feeling that, to paraphrase the Austrian quip, it might be better to end the crises than to have crisis without end.

Far beneath the surface of the actions of statesmen and governments, seismic political and social forces were rumbling in 1914, giving premonitory warnings of a vast eruption. The crust of European institutions was not adjusted to the deep political and social realities inherent in the shifts of power relations between states and between classes caused by the accelerating change incident to advancing industrialization and the technological revolution. Europe faced the critical question whether the institutional structure could be accommodated, without war or revolution, to the disruptive shifts in position from state to state, from continent to continent, from class to class, and from one ethnic group to another. The rigidities and contradictions within the old empires and the backward-looking standpoint of their ruling oligarchies raised doubts whether this was possible.

The efforts to cope with this pervasive disequilibrium involved three dominant issues: the position of Germany in the future Europe and in the world order; the organization of the multinational eastern zone of Europe, embracing Austria-Hungary and the German and Russian borderlands; and the effect of the conflict between the two social orders—of privilege and the masses—on the internal institutional systems of the European countries. The German statesmen seemed to have an instinctive sense that the old system of the Pentarchy was an anachronism that had to be replaced by some new state system. The only alternative Germany could offer was the hegemony of the Reich on the continent. The rest of Europe rejected this solution for fitting the superior power of Germany into the European order. The Entente became a coalition, and the war an Allied means for its prevention.[34]

‒ Regarding the second issue, the outbreak of the war was linked with the absence of a stable order in the multinational eastern zone conforming more to the claims of nationality. In one sense the war was a contest for control and leadership of the political reorganization of the eastern zone.[35] In practice there seemed to be no way to refashion the organization of the area along national lines without destroying the old continental empires. The focal point of the problem was the incapacity of the Dual Empire to generate a revival from within by which it might have introduced substantial democratic reform and resolved the national conflicts through a confederation of nations. Such a solution might have enabled Vienna to become the center of a stable community of nations, thereby taking over the leadership of the forces of nationality instead of being their antagonist. Vienna could then have enjoyed the friendship of the Slavs and rid itself of dependence on Germany. The failure to take the lead in reshaping the political order in the eastern zone put the political reconstruction of the area into other hands. The dying empire had outlived its historical usefulness.

In the social conflict the traditional order, which, although modified, was still essentially feudal and monarchical in much of Europe, stood opposed to the order of industrialized or mass society. The forces of resistance sought to preserve the traditional order, and the forces of democratic reform to introduce a new order adapted to the demands of an industrial society. The shape of the institutional structure within the European states was to depend on the outcome of this struggle, which in 1914 was moving toward a climax in the three empires of central and eastern Europe.

A conclusion that the war could have been avoided implies a conception of the crisis and the international system of 1914 along these lines: the

34. See René Albrecht-Carrié, "Europe and the German Problem," *Orbis* 10 (1967): 1031–45; Charles A. Fisher, "The Changing Dimensions of Europe," *Journal of Contemporary History* 1, no. 3 (1966): 3–20.

35. See Hans Kohn, "Was the Collapse Inevitable?", *Austrian History Yearbook* 3, pt. 3 (1967): 260.

world crisis was in essence a matter of diplomatic issue; the outbreak of
the war was due to the personal inadequacies and defective acts of the
individual actors handling the crisis; the war represented an aberration
rather than an inherent aspect of the international system of that time.

The underlying argument assumes that if there had been other, more
qualified personalities at the posts of decision, the system would have
functioned normally, without resort to war. As it was, the statesmen slid
into war for lack of ability to direct events. Lloyd George gave this
interpretation his imprimatur as early as 1920: ". . . no one at the head
of affairs quite meant war at that stage. It was something into which they
glided, or rather staggered and stumbled, perhaps through folly, and a
discussion, I have no doubt, would have averted it."[36] And later: "Had
there been a Bismarck in Germany, a Palmerston or a Disraeli in Britain,
a Roosevelt in America, or a Clemenceau in authority in Paris, the catastrophe might, and I believe would have been averted; . . ."[37]

The interpretation distributes responsibility among all the actors and
tends to neglect or play down the nonpersonal factors giving rise to the
war. It suggests some note of judging the policy-makers and the system
of 1914 by the standards of a subsequent age. At that time peace was not
the highest end in the conduct of international affairs, and war was a part
of the classical balance of power system, the final means of guaranteeing
the position and security of the state. War was the natural issue of the
brinkmanship of the preceding silent war. Germany pursued a diplomacy
risking war to achieve a set of policy goals implying a radical revision of
the international order: a political position corresponding to its economic
supremacy; destruction of the ring of encirclement; the status of a world
power competitive with that of the giants, the United States of the present
and Russia of the future. The Entente endeavored to prevent this and
preserve the old balance of power. The encrusted interests, rigidities, and
stalemates scarcely left any means but war and revolution to adapt international and internal relations to the multiform changes in the distribution
of power.

The system and the age were as responsible as the actors for the July
crisis and its ending in war. We can hardly imagine that any of the statesmen in office during the decade before 1914 would have acted in a

36. Scott, *Five Weeks*, 11.
37. David Lloyd George, *War Memoirs*, 6 vols. (London, 1933–36), 1: 57.

substantially different manner from those of the July crisis if they had been in power at the time. The men actually at the helm of affairs, given the preceding decade of events and all the other conditions and forces of the time, would have been almost inescapably the prisoners of those factors in discharging the practical responsibilities of office. When confronted with this question, Churchill could only conclude: "The more I reflect upon this situation, the more convinced I am that we took the only practical course that was open to us or to any British Cabinet; . . ."[38]

We come to this view. The crisis of 1914 was the fifth in a series since 1905. Each produced tensions, bitterness, and resentment, which mounted with the progress of the series. A war might have come earlier if the combination of elements in the crisis had been somewhat different, or it might have been postponed until the next crisis if certain aspects of the situation had been different in 1914. At that time the mixture of elements was just right for the explosion. Although we cannot say that war was inevitable in July 1914, we can say that, given the conditions that existed—the ambitions and goals of the great powers, their shifting strength, the institutional and domestic factors, the temper of the times, and especially the deeper forces favorable to a political upheaval—the conclusion can hardly be avoided that a great conflict was bound to break out sooner or later. We can see today in our quiet chairs, more than a half century later, better alternatives than the decisions of 1914, ones that might have prevented war. That the statesmen and generals of July after years of silent war and in the crater of the volcanic forces of the age should have taken the necessary steps to avert war is probably demanding more of humankind than we have any warrant to expect.

38. *World Crisis,* 1: 218.

Chapter Two

FORCES AND PLANS IN TOTAL WAR

1. THE WORLD UPHEAVAL

THE conflict of nations from 1914 to 1918 was not some "dull rumor of some other war."[1] The struggle ushered in a new scope of war, the first total war in the experience of mankind. Its duration, intensity, and scale exceeded anything previously known or generally expected. The day of mass warfare had arrived: million-man armies grappled with one another on the European battlefields, and in the end the number of soldiers killed amounted to more than ten million. Although the fighting was concentrated in Europe, every major state became engaged, and the conflict extended to all the seas. In one way or another the first total war involved the whole world since it had become interdependent under the forces of industrialization and global commerce.

The total war made participants of the entire nation—farm, factory, and front combining in the national effort.[2] In the description of the American Industrial Mobilization Plan of 1933, based on the experience of the Great War: "War is no longer simply a battle between armed forces in the field, it is a struggle in which each side strives to bring to bear against the enemy the coordinated power of every individual and every material resource at its command. The conflict extends from the soldier in the most forward lines to the humblest citizen in the remotest hamlet in the rear."[3] Among the major belligerents the national resources and energies, including the minds of men, were mobilized in the desperate endeavor to overcome the opponent in what seemed to be a struggle for life or death. The grim test of survival depended not only on military prowess at the front but also on

1. From "Exposure" by Wilfred Owen, the best of the war poets. See below, pp. 478–479.
2. There is no intention to imply that the workers at home and the soldiers at the front underwent comparable experiences but only to suggest that the conduct of total war depended on the activities of each.
3. Quoted in U. S., Congress, Senate, Special Committee to Investigate the Munition Industry, *Report on War Department Bills S. 1716–S. 1722 Relating to Industrial Mobilization in Wartime.* S. Rept. 944, 74th Cong., 1st sess., 1935, pt. 4, 7.

the productive organization of the whole economy and the capacity of the state itself to function effectively in new spheres of activity during severe crisis.

The vastly expanded military operations introduced a revolution in warfare as industrialization and modern technology were broadly extended to this field. Tremendous volumes of capital and labor were poured into the production of weapons for the mass armies. Human ingenuity was exerted to devise new instruments of war that might prove decisive in swinging the pendulum of advantage from the defensive to the offensive. The soldiers in the terrible ordeal of the trenches were the first to endure the fire and steel of twentieth-century industrialization on the battlefield. It is not surprising, and was in fact inevitable, that, in the environment of rapidly spreading industrialization and the expanding powers of the state, war became mechanized, impersonal, and highly organized. The range of war, moreover, was broadened to new dimensions in the political and economic sectors. These total aspects of war in modern society were carried so far that war, contrary to the Clausewitz doctrine, seemingly ceased to be the servant of policy and became instead its master.[4]

The war ended with the military defeat of the Central Powers, but it did not finish the competitive struggle among the major European states nor seriously weaken the strength of Germany and the ambitions of its nationalist forces. Since a stable, enduring settlement failed, the interwar period turned out to be only a protracted truce, and William II's vision of a second Punic war in his century was more prophetic than he knew. In the sequel of the Second World War the Nazis tried to reverse the results of the first. So far as Europe was concerned, what began with the assassination at Sarajevo ended with the unconditional surrender of Germany on May 7, 1945.[5] These wars as much as anything else have given this century of turmoil and violence its distinctive stamp.

But the far-ramifying events from 1914 to 1919 comprehended a great deal more than an international war of unprecedented proportions. Their deep influence on subsequent history had struck André Gide before the

4. Gerhard Ritter describes the altered relationship with the formulation that war became the supreme end in itself. *Das deutsche Problem* (Munich, 1962), 177–78.

5. This period impresses a number of historians as a thirty years' war of the twentieth century. For example, Gordon Wright, in this series, *The Ordeal of Total War, 1939–1945* (New York, 1968), p. xiii.

end of 1914. In a poem of that time he saw the war rising "from the very depths of humanity" as a war, "not like other wars," but one in which the "future is striving to be born. A vast future, tearing its feet as it wriggles to be free."[6]

In the process Europe was torn apart by what was, from the standpoint of the European community, a tragic civil war. It consumed much of the manpower and accumulated capital of the European states and weakened their position in relation to the rising power centers outside western and central Europe. The war dealt an irreparable blow to European civilization, from which it has never recovered.

The war thus quickened the shift in power relations already under way, bringing about the fall of Europe from its pinnacle in world affairs. Europe ceased to be the pivot of world history, and thereafter the influence of Europe visibly declined in the world at large. At the same time the power of outside states, notably the United States and Japan, expanded rapidly. That the master powers of Europe could weaken themselves by the folly of internecine war encouraged the colonial peoples to press the struggle against their domination.

Inside Europe the war eventually broadened into a revolutionary flood. In the words of De Gaulle, "The Great War is a revolution."[7] The convulsion occurred just as socialists like August Bebel, Jean Jaurès, and Lenin had foreseen it would in case of a general war. The existing class conflict between the masses and the aristocratic and bourgeois forces of resistance was submerged during the early part of the war. With more burdensome privations and dimming hopes in Russia, Germany, and Austria, the feeling against the direction of the state and against the ruling elites mounted from the end of 1916 on. The struggle to achieve political reform intensified until finally revolution had swept away three empires, and of these, two states altogether, leaving quite different successors.

This crisis of change proved to be the death crisis of the old order in Europe. The old political system with the classical balance of power and the predominantly liberal capitalist economy had been destroyed. The Russian revolution launched a worldwide political movement, riving Europe by the deep chasm of ideological differences. A series of nationalist revolutions created a zone of secondary states in eastern Europe whose

6. *The Journals of André Gide*, 2 vols. (New York, 1948), 2: 96.
7. Charles de Gaulle, *La France et son armée* (Paris, 1938), 235.

stability was uncertain. The war speeded the transfer of power to the masses, corresponding to their mighty efforts in the mass warfare. Institutions and methods of government were altered to formalize this change. The immense production of the war factories necessitated a broad extension of state powers and accustomed people to a larger sphere of state activity. A considerable part of these powers of the state under war socialism remained, and new similar ones were soon added after the war. An impetus was given to the maturing of the modern state and its complex administrative machinery. The conditions of war accelerated the movement to "mass collectivized life" through a more rapid industrialization and urbanization.

To contemporaries the upheaval became known as the Great War, and this it remained until the Second World War. Winston Churchill wrote already in October 1914: "This is no ordinary war. . . . It effaces the old landmarks and frontiers of our civilization."[8] Lord (Maurice) Hankey, who merited recognition as the secretary-general of the British direction of the war, affirmed to Lloyd George some years after the event: "The War was probably the most important episode in our national history and will dominate our destiny for generations to come."[9] The distinguished French historian Elie Halévy compared it with the Thirty Years' War and the wars of the French Revolution and Napoleon in forming one of the three great revolutionary crises in modern history.[10]

From the perspective of nearly seven decades, the shaping influence of this complex of events on our century still looms large. The world came through the crucible of change from 1914 to 1919 refashioned. More than anything else, the war separated the world of the nineteenth century from that of the twentieth. The wide range of its impact is still very much a part of our life.

The war did not of course create something entirely new nor mark a sharp break with the past. The war accelerated the process of transformation and enhanced tendencies already operating at its outbreak; it served as an agent and catalyst of changes long under way.[11] These deep secular changes, which intensified and broadened in the catastrophe of war, form

8. Churchill to Prince Louis Battenberg, *World Crisis*, 1: 435.
9. *The Supreme Command*, 2 vols. (London, 1961), 1: 5.
10. *The World Crisis of 1914–1918* (Oxford, 1930), 7.
11. See Pierre Renouvin and Jean-Baptiste Duroselle, *Introduction to the History of International Relations* (New York, 1967), 372.

our major theme. Military operations have an undeniable importance but for our purpose primarily from the standpoint of their relation to strategy, policy, the methods of war, and the organizational and other demands imposed by military operations on society and institutions.

2. THE BALANCE OF FORCES

The military establishments had been preparing for a European war ever since the last conflict of the continental powers, in 1870–71. They were organizing and equipping million-man forces while laying successive war plans. They never anticipated, however, the kind of total conflict described above except in the number of men initially engaged. Their model was not an imagined war of the future but rather an enlarged version of the Franco-German War.

The war now beginning was a war of masses—masses of men and masses of materiel. The mighty hosts marching to battle under the August sun numbered more than six million men. These were conscript forces, except those of the British, which were recruited by voluntary enlistment. In sheer number of troops fielded at the onset of hostilities, the Entente coalition, or the Allies, marshaled an impressive superiority over the Central Powers, with 199 to 137 infantry divisions and 50 to 22 cavalry divisions. They also had a combined population of more than double that of the Central Powers (279 to 120 million).[12]

The Russians provided more than half the total number of divisions available to the Allies. In spite of its size the Russian "Steam Roller" was a lumbering military machine, weighed down with many military weaknesses owing in great part to the obstacles to reform that the traditionalists had raised. The proportion of cavalry to infantry was excessive, the officer class of uneven quality and split between two factions, the staff work inefficient. The supreme command, thrown together only when the war began, possessed no actual directing authority over the operational groups into which the army was divided—the one in the northwest and the other in the southwest. The army was handicapped by a shortage of noncommissioned officers, along with ranks having a high rate of illiteracy. Russia's

12. Comparative figures for military strength vary from source to source. Ours are taken for the most part from the British official military historian, Sir James E. Edmonds, *A Short History of World War I* (London, 1961), 9–10. See also Walther Hubatsch, *Germany and the Central Powers in the World War 1914–1918* (Lawrence, Kansas, 1963), 22–23; and Anton Wagner, *Der Erste Weltkrieg* (Vienna, 1968), 16–17.

preparations in the supply and modernization of equipment were the poorest of any of the major belligerents. The field army lacked heavy artillery, yet resources had been squandered on heavy guns for antiquated fortresses (better razed than maintained). The dearth of maps and communications facilities hampered the effective movement of the Russian forces in battle; inadequate railways and poor roads deprived them of strategic mobility. Russia was obliged to compensate for the insurmountable inferiority in arms with the blood and fortitude of its soldiers.[13]

Of most serious import in the long run, this backward nation did not possess the industrial capacity and technological resources to wage total war for an extended period. Nor was the organization of the state sufficiently responsive and adaptable to the needs of war and even of survival. The incompetence and confusion in government were paralleled on the military side. General N. N. Yanushkevich, appointed chief of the general staff in 1914, was more of a clerk and courtier than a professional soldier.

France assembled 62 infantry divisions and 10 cavalry. France was obliged to call up each year more than 80 percent of potential recruits in order to maintain this large army. The capacity to expand the French army was consequently limited in contrast to the German army, which recruited annually only a little more than half the men liable for military service. The troops were of good quality on the whole and exceptionally skillful in the utilization of terrain. The reserves and most of the other troops were not as well trained as the German, and the lower and noncommissioned officers not as competent as their German counterparts. The field artillery, thanks to the famous 75-mm gun and outstanding training in gunnery, attained a high degree of excellence. The "75's" were considered to have no equal in mobility, accuracy, speed of fire, and range for their size. The deadliness of this weapon in French hands was to serve conspicuously in sustaining the esprit of the French army during the long retreat of 1914 and the battle of the Marne.[14]

The French officers' corps was scarred by the factions and antagonisms generated by the long conflict between bourgeois and laic elements on the

13. Howard, "The Armed Forces," 213; Alfred Knox, *With the Russian Army, 1914–1917,* 2 vols. (London, 1921), I, pp. xvii–xxxi; Nicholas N. Golovine, *The Russian Army in the World War* (New Haven, 1931), 49; Norman Stone, *The Eastern Front, 1914–1917* (New York, 1975), 27–32, 49–53.

14. On the value of the "75's" to the French in 1914, see Sir Edward Spears, *Liaison, 1914* (New York, 1968), 433.

one side and aristocratic and clerical on the other. Profound differences over tactics and strategy separated the school making a mystique of the offensive spirit from those upholding the defensive power of modern weapons. The first was inspired by Colonel Ferdinand Foch, who had been professor of military history at the École Supérieure de Guerre, and Colonel Loyzeau de Grandmaison, head of the operations section of the general staff. The debates between these schools focused on the issue of a general offensive at once, as opposed to a counterattack after the German plan of operations had become evident; and the issue of disposing the French forces in extended line or massing them in depth.

With some exceptions the prewar period for the French was as sterile in the introduction of new weapons as in the development of military doctrine. The Lebel rifle of 1893 was obsolete and had to be replaced in 1915. Supremely confident that the 75-mm field gun would serve all purposes of artillery, the French army let Germany eclipse it in the development of various types of heavy artillery, in the introduction of the light field howitzer, and in the use of high explosives. The French were to pay a high price for the lack of field howitzers. France, however, had been more innovative in aviation than any other European power. The separate air force of 123 planes surpassed other air services in numerical size and in technical efficiency. Thus the French could achieve an initial advantage in reconnaissance.[15]

The British had the smallest army—11 infantry divisions and 3 cavalry —of any great power. The largest part consisted of the British Expeditionary Force (BEF) of 160,000 men, an elite group of professional soldiers, better in quality than all the others. Although superior staff officers were scarce, its infantry produced the steadiest, most rapid, and most experienced rifle fire of any army. The soldiers were equipped with the Lee-Enfield rifle, ranking at the top in adaptation to the ordinary purposes of mass combat. Lighter than other rifles, it had a smooth and easy bolt action as well as outstanding durability in the wear and tear of combat use. With this weapon, the highly trained infantry was the only military force capable of utilizing the modern rapid-firing rifle to its fullest potential. In addition to this force, the British could draw on their overseas garrisons and a Territorial Army of volunteers at home. Moreover, they had estab-

15. Correlli Barnett, *The Swordbearers* (London, 1963), 246–47; De Gaulle, *La France et son armée,* 232–33.

lished the Royal Flying Corps and the Royal Naval Air Service.[16]

Britain was unprepared, however, for mass warfare on land. Like the French, the British had neglected the development of heavy artillery and the production of high-explosive shells, which were to be far more effective than shrapnel in the positional warfare of the Western Front. No trench mortars and no reliable hand grenades were available. The War Office had no stores of rifles, guns, and ammunition for the training and supply of new recruits. Only a few small factories and a limited number of machines existed for the production of materiel. The issue of munitions supply would become critical immediately.[17]

The immediate power of Britain was gathered in its command of the seas. This capability made possible a tightening economic pressure on Germany and opened to the Allied coalition the economic resources of the world. The main strength of the British fleet resided in 21 dreadnoughts, 27 predreadnought battleships, and 7 battle cruisers. To counter this force, the German High Seas Fleet would have to rely on 13 dreadnoughts, 16 predreadnoughts, and 5 battle cruisers. The margin of British superiority was to increase steadily throughout the war. Both Britain and Germany had made a beginning with submarines, but neither state had much understanding of the potentialities of the weapon or had done anything to prepare for antisubmarine warfare.[18] The direction of British naval affairs, being concentrated in the Admiralty, was more unified than the German, which was divided between the naval staff, the secretary of the naval office, and the naval cabinet of the kaiser. The British Grand Fleet, having carried out a test mobilization, was assembled in the North Sea ready for action.

The British advantages in strength, speed, heavy armament, direction, and readiness of the royal navy could not conceal certain weaknesses. The British had never created a naval staff to coordinate naval strategy and tactics, design of vessels, equipment, and training. The German fleet surpassed the British in training—especially in the execution of maneuvers, excellence of gunnery, construction of thicker and more extensive

16. Edmonds, *Short History of World War I*, 11. On the characteristics of the Lee-Enfield rifle, see C.H.B. Pridham, *Superiority of Fire* (London, 1945), 15-18.

17. Lloyd George, *War Memoirs*, 1: 126-30.

18. The figures for battleships are from Arthur J. Marder, *From the Dreadnought to Scapa Flow*, 5 vols. (London, 1961-70), 2: 4-5. For submarines, see O. Groos and Walter Gladisch, *Der Krieg in der Nordsee*, 6 vols. (Berlin, 1922-37), 1: 45; Churchill, *World Crisis*, 2: 278.

armor and the building of nearly unsinkable vessels, practices of command, and efficiency of communications. The German cruisers were faster and far ahead of the British in mine-laying; the destroyers were better equipped for torpedo warfare; the submarines for overseas use had longer range. The Germans had developed a superior Diesel engine for use in U-boats and had fitted their submarines with powerful wireless transmitters and more reliable and heavier torpedoes of stronger explosive force. In naval gunnery, the British could not be certain about the security of their explosive Lyddite, and they had not yet produced armor-piercing shells for long-range fire. The German shells were of more explosive effect and greater penetrability.[19]

The Belgian and Serbian armies were small, poorly trained, and poorly equipped for modern war.

Germany mustered an army of 87 infantry divisions and 11 cavalry of thoroughly trained troops. The noncommissioned officers formed a superb body of subordinate leaders; the reserves were so well prepared they could be inserted into the front line with the regular divisions without much loss in effectiveness. The infantry was better than the French in rifle fire, and the heavy artillery was clearly in a class by itself, with a whole range of advanced weapons. Their caliber, destructiveness, and mobility were to surprise the Allies. The field artillery had been strengthened by the adaptation of howitzers and mortars to field use.

Among other German advantages was tactical teaching that was flexible and better adapted to the firepower of current weapons. The Germans were adept in the elaborate business of mobilization, which required extraordinary precision of timing and movement. The army was more ready than others for combat, and the Reich had not only larger stocks of weapons and equipment than any other combatant but also more initial capacity in armament factories. The interior position of the Central Powers afforded Germany an advantage in mobility.[20]

Despite all these attainments, the magnificent German army had weaknesses in the directing center. The inadequacies of command were due in

19. Viscount Jellicoe, *The Grand Fleet, 1914–1916* (New York, 1919), 305–15; Tirpitz, *My Memoirs*, 1: 167–77; Groos and Gladisch, *Der Krieg in der Nordsee*, 1: 47–48; Sir William Jameson, *The Most Formidable Thing* (London, 1965), 99–101.

20. Barnett, *Swordbearers*, 41, 246; Alfred Vagts, *A History of Militarism* (New York, 1937), 211; J.F.C. Fuller, *A Military History of the Western World*, 3 vols. (New York, 1954–56), 3: 187; B. H. Liddell Hart, *The Revolution in Warfare* (New Haven, 1947), 7.

part to personal factors in a number of commanding generals. Moreover, the command was habituated to overreliance on intricate operational planning, not just for the opening battle, but for an entire campaign. Operations of this kind presented a nearly insuperable problem in coordinating direction from the center, which in turn depended on an effective system of communications and on productive reconnaissance. The German army was deficient in both, and its initial ill success in reconnaissance can be attributed to slowness in the development of military aviation, as compared with the French and the British. The expenditures for secret intelligence by the general staff had been relatively limited, and the intelligence service was small.[21]

The Germans had forged ahead of the other powers in the utilization of airships. The progress was due to the series of dirigibles built since Count Ferdinand von Zeppelin had sent his first ship into the air in 1900. In 1914, 11 dirigibles were available for military and naval use.

The Dual Empire fielded a force of 50 infantry divisions and 11 cavalry. Though modeled on the German army and led predominantly by ethnic German officers, these troops did not measure up to the German standard in equipment, training, and size relative to population. In 1914 the empire could not produce a single reserve division; just less than a third of the infantry was fully trained; and only one in five of those liable were ever called for military service. The supply of arms was limited, and uniforms were scarce. Some of the artillery, particularly the field howitzer, was outdated, but Austria had developed the first motorized heavy mortar (305 mm). This remarkable weapon was to be used by the Germans with telling effect in smashing through the Belgian and French forts.[22]

The army as a whole was deficient in cohesiveness because of the constitutional structure of the empire and the multinational composition of the forces. The differences in nationality and language increased the problems in communication and command. The official language of command was German, but the army was so organized that soldiers could communicate in their own language with the officers above them in the company. Most of the troops were seemingly loyal to the empire at the outset, although nationalist agitation under the leadership of the Czechs

21. Hubatsch, *Germany and the Central Powers in the World War*, 24.

22. Austria, Bundesministerium für Landesverteidigung, *Österreich-Ungarns letzter Krieg, 1914–1918*, 8 vols. (Vienna, 1930–38), 1: 28–32; Oskar Regele, "Die Donaumonarchie als Machtfaktor 1914," *Der Donauraum* 9 (1964): 146; Wagner, *Der Erste Weltkrieg*, 27.

was not absent within the ranks. The loyal officer corps had a good technical training but was indoctrinated with the precept of "attack at any price." The soldiers of the highest technical proficiency were the elite mountain troops and the engineers, who were provided with first-rate equipment.[23]

The generals everywhere were backward in exploiting the products of mechanized industry for warfare. While the motorized vehicle and the airplane had been introduced to military use, their immense possibilities were scarcely appreciated. The recent invention of wireless telegraphy was employed on land and sea, and technical telegraph, wireless signal, and bicycle units had been organized in the armies. Typical in many respects was the reliance on the bayonet, an utterly outmoded, suicidal weapon for assaulting a defensive line, and on the cavalry, rendered useless on the Western Front by modern weapons and motorized transport. Symbolic of the prevailing military conservatism were the French and Belgian foot soldiers, arrayed in uniforms of blue coats and red trousers as they marched valorously into battle.

There is no doubt as to which side came out of the diplomatic round of the world crisis in the stronger position. The Reich had gambled, just as German strategy was to do in the war, and failed. It failed first in localizing the Austro-Serbian conflict and then in keeping the continental war from becoming a world war. Germany had badly miscalculated not only the risks of a general war but also, because of British entry, the strength of the possible coalition of enemies in relation to its own power. After August 5, 1914, the balance of forces was irretrievably disposed against the Central Powers. Because of British entry Germany and Austria lost the war (that is, a war of victory) before the fighting ever began.

3. STRATEGIC PLANS

The initial military operations were based on plans that involved more study than those of any other campaign or undertaking of the war. All the plans, formulated for a war of the past rather than a war of the future, envisaged a quick fight of two or three months with complete victory after a decisive battle. The planners, believing that the society and economy could not withstand the ravages of prolonged war, made no preparations for extended combat and failed to foresee the need of arms and munitions on a vast scale. They devised plans for a war of movement, estimating

23. Österreich-Ungarns letzter Krieg, 1: 34–35, 39–44.

quite wrongly the defensive power of current weapons. They could not anticipate the effect of those weapons in producing a war of position, in spite of the prophecies of siege warfare in the field made by some military writers and officers below the top echelons, such as Lieutenant Colonel Emile Mayer in France and J.F.C. Fuller in Britain.

The most elaborate of the plans was the German one, devised by Count Alfred von Schlieffen, the austere, taciturn chief of the general staff from 1891 to 1906, and modified by his successor, General Helmuth von Moltke. Schlieffen, the complete military technician and aloof Prussian general, started from the assumption that a strategy of Blitzkrieg must be adopted. The question where to direct the Blitzkrieg was Germany's central strategic problem, which had preoccupied the general staff ever since the seventies; namely, the question was whether to follow an eastern or a western strategy in a two-front war. Schlieffen opted for the latter, with a plan designed for a quick battle of annihilation against France in the first stage. It was to be followed in a second stage by a campaign against Russia, after a large part of the forces had been transferred from the western to the eastern theater.[24]

In the west, the great bulk of the German troops would first execute a grandiose maneuver, the immediate object of which was to effect an entry into fortress France, where the terrain was level and the frontier least fortified. The mass of the German armies would bypass the strong barrier fortresses form Belfort to Verdun by striking through Belgium, west of the Meuse river, into northern France. The main strength was to be concentrated in five armies on the right wing, which in advancing would pivot on Metz-Thionville (Diedenhofen) in a massive wheeling move-

24. The most objective and searching study of the Schlieffen plan, and from the broadest standpoint, has been made by Gerhard Ritter, *Der Schlieffenplan—Kritik eines Mythos* (Munich, 1956). The work, which is based on Schlieffen's papers, contains the text of the plan. See also by the same author: "Le plan Schlieffen de l'état-major allemand de 1914: considérations sur sa critique militaire et politique," *Revue d'histoire moderne et contemporaine* 7 (1960): 215–32; *Staatskunst*, 2: 240–81; "Der Anteil der Militärs an der Kriegskatastrophe von 1914," *Historische Zeitschrift* 193 (1961): 72–91. Supporting the annihilation strategy of Schlieffen, of interest is Wolfgang Foerster, "Einige Bemerkungen zu Gerhard Ritters Buch 'Der Schlieffenplan,' " *Wehrwissenschaftliche Rundschau* 7 (1957): 37–44. The same author's *Graf Schlieffen und der Weltkrieg* (Berlin, 1925) is one of the better works making a military seer out of Schlieffen. Friedrich von Boetticher, *Schlieffen* (Berlin, 1957), is a more recent work favorable to Schlieffen and critical of Moltke's modifications of the Schlieffen plan. A more balanced view is presented by Walter Görlitz, *Der deutsche Generalstab*, 2d ed. (Frankfurt, 1953), 95–123.

ment extending outward as far as Lille. A much weaker left wing of two armies would undertake a diversionary defensive along the eastern frontier of France; it was to pin down as large a French force as possible, even retreating in order to draw the enemy after it.

The strong right wing was expected to push the French to the Verdun-Aisne-Oise line and, on the extreme right, to move south and west of Paris. As the city was invested, the grand envelopment would proceed to roll up the French armies against the defensive left wing of the Germans, the Lorraine fortresses, and the Swiss frontier. Since the brunt of the audacious undertaking would fall heavily on the right wing, Schlieffen worried until his death, in 1913, that it would be insufficiently reinforced to support the tremendous outflanking attempt. He proposed that in order to strengthen the right wing more, two army corps be transferred to it from the left wing in Lorraine as soon as the French had committed their forces. In addition, he called for the formation of eight new army corps of reserves to be sent behind the right wing to relieve it of investing bypassed forts and securing lines of communication.

After Schlieffen, the reflective and skeptical Moltke had some doubts about the feasibility of the plan he had inherited.[25] He modified it by eliminating the crossing of the Maastrict, or Limburg "appendix," of Holland. Moltke believed that this crossing might be likely to bring Britain into a continental war and that Germany needed Holland "as a windpipe for our access overseas."[26] Instead, a German force would seize Liège by surprise on the third day of mobilization. The purpose was to assure control of the railways through this center just west of the German border and the passage of the German armies through the Brussels-Namur defile. Another important change strengthened the left wing, when more divisions became available with the increase in the size of the army.

The revision altered the relative strength of the two wings from Schlieffen's ratio of roughly seven to one, but did not decrease the total mass on the right. The change was intended to protect the German left wing against a French breakthrough, threatened by the French army's expansion and offensive intentions of recent years. It was also to insure against a weakness in this sector that might encourage diversion of French troops to the north, thereby endangering the success of the wheeling

25. Ritter, "Der Anteil der Militärs an der Kriegskatastrophe," 80.
26. Ritter, *Staatskunst,* 2: 271.

movement. As a further measure to pin down French forces, Moltke contemplated an offensive from Lorraine.

The powerful offensive in the west imposed two requirements in the east: Austria was to bear the main burden of battle with the Russians and provide the main cover of the German rear until victory in the west would allow the large-scale transfer of troops to the eastern front; and Germany must maintain sufficient strength in the east to protect Berlin against a Russian advance and to encourage the Austrians to active combat. For this purpose one army was to be assigned to East Prussia.

German naval strategy, like the military plan, aimed at a great decisive battle, which was to take place with the British Grand Fleet in the North Sea. It was generally recognized by the high naval officers, except Tirpitz, that this encounter was out of the question until the British fleet had been cut down by sallies of surface vessels, by mines, and by submarines to a size offering the High Seas Fleet some chance of success. Meanwhile a defensive strategy would be pursued.

The Austrian plan was prepared by the chief of the general staff, Conrad von Hötzendorf, a general of active mind with a penchant for political projects beyond his official competence. The plan presupposed the full-fledged and early cooperation of the German forces in a massive move to pinch off the salient of Russian Poland by a combined attack of the Austrians from Galicia and the Germans from East Prussia. In response to Conrad's repeated importunities concerning the German contribution, Moltke finally pledged a diversionary offensive from East Prussia beyond the Narew River; he suggested a period of six weeks for victory in the west before the transfer of troops to the east to take part in the combined offensive in Poland. The extent and promptness of Austrian action against Russia would also hinge on Balkan events—the course of the offensive against Serbia and the decisions of Romania and Bulgaria for neutrality or for participation in the war.

The Austrian plan took account of alternative contingencies of war on two fronts, against Russia and Serbia (the "R" case), and of war against Serbia and Montenegro alone (the "B" case). The whole army would be divided into three masses: the main force of three armies and an army group to be concentrated in Galicia for possible operations against Russia; the "minimal group Balkans," a weaker force to consist of two armies for fighting Serbia and Montenegro; and a third force of a single army to be shifted to either front as events might determine. In the "R" case the third force would be sent to Galicia, and in the "B" case it would augment the strength of the "minimal group Balkans," along with reinforcements from the Galician armies. Before Russia became involved in the war, most of the third force was actually in transport to the Balkan theater to participate in the drive against Serbia. When Austria mobilized against Russia, this army had to be transferred to Galicia, but only after some delay and confusion.[27]

French strategic planning, evolving in a series of successive plans, had been committed since Plan VIII to the offensive, with the object of an early decisive battle near the frontiers. The famous Plan XVII, inspired by the mystic cult of the *offensive à outrance,* had the spiritual paternity of Henri Bergson and Foch, in emphasizing in its assumptions the importance of morale factors and the valor of the French soldier. It represented the actual work of Grandmaison and his associates of the general staff.[28]

The plan laid down the deployment of five armies: two were to advance toward the Saar and Lorraine preparatory to attacking in the latter area; two were to move forward opposite Metz and the Ardennes, so as to take the offensive against the Germans whichever way they came; a fifth was to be kept as a central reserve, which could be used against German forces if they marched through Belgium. The French plan was not a preconceived prescription of operations for a whole campaign; it allowed the commander-in-chief the initiative of decision after the opening battle.

The central flaw in the French strategy was to launch a general offensive for which the army had no superiority in numbers over the Germans. French intelligence badly miscalculated German frontline strength, because of the conclusion that the Germans would not join in combat their reserve formations with the regular divisions immediately. Nor did the French prepare ground defenses and dispose forces to anticipate the power and wide extension of the Schlieffen flanking movement. Through the treachery of a German officer, French intelligence had obtained information about the Schlieffen plan, but the French military had discounted it as being only the sketch for a war game. General Augustin Edouard Michel, the presumptive commander-in-chief until displaced by General Joseph Césaire Joffre, had urged in 1911 a revision of French strategy, positing Belgium as the main ground of battle. Joffre and the general staff

27. *Österreich-Ungarns letzter Krieg,* 1: 4–15; Wagner, *Der Erste Weltkrieg,* 32–37; Helmut Otto, Karl Schmiedel, and Helmut Schnitter, *Der Erste Weltkrieg* (Berlin, 1968), 40–42; Stone, *Eastern Front,* 73.
28. Theodore Ropp, *War in the Modern World* (Durham, N.C., 1959), 211.

minimized the possibility of the German main thrust coming through Belgium. Michel had similarly anticipated the use by the Germans of reserve divisions at once in the front line and had contended for a reorganization of the army by combining reserves with active troops at the regimental level.[29]

British strategy in the prewar years was altered by two decisions that ran counter to British tradition. Hitherto strategy had been predominantly maritime, in utilizing superior naval power to maintain a close blockade of enemy states, combined with economic constriction; to meet any challenge to control of the seas by decisive naval battle; and to send improvised land forces to a vital point of assistance to a continental coalition. This strategy was not too far removed from the navy's conception advanced by Sir John Fisher (who had been First Sea Lord) that the army "should be regarded as a projectile to be fired by the navy."[30] A new orientation in war planning emerged with the organization of a professional army to be used as the BEF on the continent and with the military conversations conducted with the French. These developments meant an involvement in continental affairs not previously known, a move of Britain into Europe that was to be extended with its participation in the present continental war by means of a mass army.

A major step in the change, putting into eclipse the conceptions of the old navy, came with the virtual pledge in the military conversations with the French to send the British army to France in the event of war with Germany and to concentrate the BEF around Maubeuge. These arrangements of the general staff, which were upheld and carried out in August 1914, marked the beginning of the conversion of the British army and its subsequent reinforcements into the left wing of an immense combined force committed to continental warfare on the Western Front for the duration. The effect would make "inevitable that the main strength of the Empire would be deployed in France" throughout the war. The general staff had sacrificed to the French tie Britain's freedom of strategic decision.[31]

29. Maurice Paléologue, *Un grand tournant de la politique mondiale, 1904–1906* (Paris, 1934), 63–64; Jules Isaac, "L'utilisation des réserves dans l'armée allemande en 1914," *Revue d'histoire de la guerre mondiale* 2 (1924): 317–37.

30. Paul Guinn, *British Strategy and Politics* (Oxford, 1965), 19.

31. John Terraine, *The Western Front, 1914–1918* (London, 1964), 57; Trumbull Higgins, *Winston Churchill and the Dardanelles* (New York, 1963), 35, 69.

The other significant decision was planning for a distant blockade, instead of a close one. The danger of torpedo warfare and mines to surface vessels accounted for this shift. In case of war with Germany, the distant blockade would shut off the exits from the North Sea by stationing the Grand Fleet at Scapa Flow and blocking the Straits of Dover with a lesser naval force and minefields.

Russian planning became the object of conflicting interests between the "northerners" and the "southerners," or the professional-technical strategists and the national traditionalists. The Russians were bound in the military convention with France and urged by the French general staff in the prewar Franco-Russian military conversations to conduct a strong offensive against Germany. Instead of concentrating the main Russian forces against East Prussia for an effective strike against the chief opponent, Germany, as the northerners desired, the revised Plan No. 19 was a faulty compromise, by which the Russian armies would be divided on the Prussian and Austrian fronts without sufficient strength on either for the projected purpose. The main force of four armies would be deployed against the Austrian assault for a large-scale counteroffensive in Galicia from the east and from Russian Poland in the north. Two armies were to invade East Prussia, one from the Niemen River and the other from the Narew. Each attack was to envelop and destroy the opposing forces so that the six armies might join in a general offensive thereafter against Austria and Germany. Two remaining armies were centered at Saint Petersburg and Odessa for safeguarding the flanks. The planning ended by laying out two sets of operations, with a separate army group command and front for each, which were not compatible in strategic aim or amenable to the unified direction of war.[32]

32. Stone, *Eastern Front*, 33–35, 53; Otto, Schmiedel, and Schnitter, *Der Erste Weltkrieg*, 45–46; Edmonds, *Short History of World War I*, 20.

Chapter Three

THE WAR OF PLANS

1. THE DEFEAT OF BLITZKRIEG

IT took the the general staffs of the continent forty years to evolve the operational plans in effect in 1914; it took forty days to demonstrate the unreality and bankruptcy of the planning. The period from the beginning of hostilities to the end of the battle of the Marne constitutes a distinct phase of the conflict, in which each side failed in its attempt at winning the war in a few weeks by a decisive stroke of massive scale. Military action began immediately after the mobilization and deployment of recruits, which was carried out with marvelous precision in Germany, with less efficiency in France, and with some confusion in Austria and Russia.

Even during mobilization, a German force entered Luxembourg on August 2, and the Germans crossed the border into Belgium two days later. With the aid of General Erich Ludendorff the troops captured the city of Liège after it had successfully opposed a night attack. The surrounding forts had to be reduced by heavy siege artillery, including the Austrian howitzers, the first of many surprises produced by the war. The possession of this railway center enabled the German armies to proceed with the great turning movement through Belgium.

The advancing armies met resistance but soon occupied the larger part of the country. The main Belgian forces withdrew successfully behind the fortifications of Antwerp, where they posed a threat to the German flank. At the same time, August 20, the Germans entered Brussels and a few days later captured Namur, following destruction of its forts by heavy bombardment. The garrison along with a division of troops in the field reached the French lines. The civilian population continued a resistance to the invader. On August 23 the Germans set up a system of military government in the occupied parts of Belgium known as the *gouvernement générale,* under which the country was administered during the rest of the war.[1]

---

1. See Emile Joseph Galet, *S. M. le roi Albert, commandant en chef, devant l'invasion allemande* (Paris, 1931), and as a critique A. Klobukowski, "La résistance belge à l'invasion allemande," *Revue d'histoire de la guerre mondiale* 10 (1932): 233–50; reply by Galet and rejoinder by Klobukowski, ibid., 11 (1933): 44–54.

The seven German armies moved forward according to the Schlieffen plan. The Sixth and Seventh formed the left wing in Alsace-Lorraine; the other five wheeled through Belgium and France on Metz as a fulcrum. The total force numbered about 1,500,000, approximately the same strength as that of the five French armies taking up position. Yet the German armies on the extreme right wing (the First, Second, and Third) had a superiority of more then a hundred battalions and a thousand guns over the enemy opposite them. After moving through Belgium rapidly, the German wheel reached the Belgian-French frontier by August 20.

The five French armies meanwhile undertook to execute Plan XVII. It was modified at the outset, when the commander-in-chief, Joffre, extended the French line by moving the Fifth Army farther to the northwest and installing the Fourth Army, previously intended as a central reserve, between the Fifth and the Third. The First and Second Armies launched an offensive in Lorraine against the German Sixth Army, commanded by Crown Prince Rupprecht of Bavaria. Following the Schlieffen prescriptions, Rupprecht's army fell back at first, but its command soon persuaded Moltke to abandon evasive action, and with the Seventh it attacked. The French were defeated at Morhange-Sarrebourg with heavy losses in both men and guns. The two French armies retreated across the border and established a defensive position in the strongly fortified area around Nancy. The outcome afforded the first practical demonstration that the official doctrines of Grandmaison and the assumptions underlying Plan XVII were unfounded. The French generals were conducting warfare in an unreal world of their own fancy.[2]

German success against the Lorraine offensive brought about a thoroughgoing change in the Schlieffen strategy. Moltke had already transferred six and one-half corps of reserve troops, held under the plan for support of the right-wing wheel, to the Lorraine front for the counterattack. Exaggerating the importance of the bloody victory at Morhange-

---

2. Of most use for the Marne campaign have been these informative, full-length works: Sewell Tyng, *The Campaign of the Marne, 1914* (New York, 1935); Germany, Reichsarchiv, *Der Weltkrieg 1914 bis 1918: Die militärischen Operationen zu Lande,* 14 vols. (Berlin, 1925–44), vols. 3 and 4, which are basic for an intensive study of the campaign in the west through the battle of the Marne; Henri Isselin, *The Battle of the Marne* (London, 1965); H. von Kuhl, *The Marne Campaign, 1914* (Fort Leavenworth, Kansas, 1936); Spears, *Liaison, 1914.* In addition, see Gotthard Jaesche, "Zum Problem der Marne-Schlacht von 1914," *Historische Zeitschrift* 190 (1960): 311–48, and Wilhelm Groener, *Lebenserinnerungen* (Göttingen, 1957), 150–77.

Sarrebourg, the high command (or OHL)[3] now glimpsed the prospect of breaking through the gap between the fortified centers of Epinal and Toul. Moltke, urged on by the command of the Sixth Army and some of his own staff, ordered an offensive by the Sixth and Seventh Armies against the natural and fortified defenses of the French in the Epinal-Toul-Nancy sector. The left wing rushed into a costly futile struggle of fortress warfare, lasting from August 25 to September 8, while the right wing was deep in the most critical stage of its advance and the battle of the Marne was under way. The left wing thus occupied was not called on to supply the reinforcements either to the crucial right wing or to the army in East Prussia. At the same time its attack could not prevent the French from withdrawing from the defenses on this front the equivalent of four corps to strengthen the resistance to the main German advance in the northwest.[4]

Joffre, still pursuing Plan XVII, ordered an offensive by the Third and Fourth Armies north of Metz into the Ardennes. After a series of confused, fierce engagements on August 22–23, the French attack collapsed, and the two armies withdrew. The two fruitless offensives in Lorraine and the Ardennes completed the wrecking of Plan XVII and indeed the French strategy of Blitzkrieg. The French now had to concentrate on saving themselves from the "paroxysm of danger."[5] They abandoned the initiative to the Germans, as they conducted a general retreat preparatory to a counteroffensive. The Germans unwittingly cooperated with the French through their own mistakes in the turning maneuver.

One of these critical mistakes occurred when General Alexander von Kluck, heading the First Army, was diverted, from the original direction to the southwest, to the protection of the flank of General Karl von Bülow's Second Army. The latter was fighting the French Fifth Army, which was under General Charles Lanrezac. The diversion kept Kluck from getting outside both the French line and the British army so as to envelop the Allied wing. It caused instead, a head-on collision with the British army, transported to the concentration area near Maubeuge without interference from the Germans and even without their knowledge.

3. OHL is the abbreviation for the German Oberste Heeresleitung. The equivalent for Austria-Hungary was the AOK, or Armeeoberkommando; for the French GQG, or Grand Quartier Général; for the British GHQ, or General Headquarters; and for the Russians Stavka.

4. Tyng, *Campaign of the Marne*, 61–74; Jaesche, "Zum Problem der Marne-Schlacht," 321–24; *Der Weltkrieg*, 4: 508–11.

5. De Gaulle, *La France et son armée*, 238.

This small BEF of four infantry and one cavalry division under Field Marshal Sir John French, an old cavalry officer, came into position at Mons to the left of the French line in time to encounter Kluck's advancing force. In their first battle (August 23) the British soldiers fired so rapidly with their rifles that the Germans credited them with twenty machine guns per battalion instead of the actual two. The British, however, learned how destructive the German howitzers could be. Though the German attack was halted, the British were obliged to retire when Lanrezac's Fifth Army fell back on their right.

Lanrezac had advanced to Charleroi, where he engaged in heavy fighting for three days (August 21–23) against a great part of the first three German armies of the right wing. The threat to his flank and rear from the Second and Third Armies, combined with the French defeat in the Ardennes, forced him to withdraw. The Germans missed two opportunities here to inflict serious defeats on the French; they failed to outflank Lanrezac's army or to cut off his line of retreat after he began to withdraw.

By August 24 the initial period of the campaign, often called the Battle of Frontiers, was completed. Although the Allies were in retreat or on the defensive everywhere, every Allied army had averted destruction. The Germans had muffed opportunities for a strategic envelopment and had greatly overestimated the significance of their victories over the long line from Switzerland to the Scheldt.

In the next period, from August 25 to the beginning of the Marne battle, the Germans at first met with success all along the front. Kluck's First Army posed a grave threat to the left wing and the center of the Allied forces. The Allies nevertheless skillfully conducted a strategic retreat, a gigantic turn on Verdun as a pivot. The imperturbable Joffre had come to realize finally how far the German wheeling maneuver reached. He now pursued the objective of throwing back the German armies after the Allies had gathered strength along a shorter line and the Germans had run into mounting problems of command and communications. For the purpose, Joffre began building up a new army, the Sixth under General Michel Joseph Maunoury, around Amiens. Its immediate mission was to keep Kluck's army from moving between the BEF and the coast around the Allied flank and to protect Paris.

The German armies attacked in depth, and the great wheel closed toward Paris in spite of heavy casualties. The BEF and the French Fifth Army succeeded in maintaining contact in the general retreat, although at one point Sir John French considered withdrawing the BEF from the line to a position behind the Seine for rest and reorganization. Only a hurried visit to Paris by Lord Kitchener, the British secretary for war, deflected French from this disastrous intention that would have been so fatal to Allied unity.

The string of German victories opened before Moltke the bright vista of a triumph of annihilation to be achieved, not through the consummation of the Schlieffen wheeling movement, but by a double envelopment —a "giant Cannae" converging from both ends of the German line. On August 27 he ordered a general pursuit of the Allied forces by all seven German armies. In place of the march by the right wing of three armies south and west of Paris, as prescribed in the Schlieffen plan, only Kluck's First Army was to move in this direction.[6]

The situation of the German armies was actually far less favorable than it appeared. The Germans had outrun their supplies, which were now brought up by trucks after the Belgians sabotaged their own railways. The soldiers of the right wing, in consequence of the many long marches and the unceasing combat, were an exhausted mass, their boots nearly worn off their tortured feet, their wills reinforced by brutal disciplinary measures. The system of communications was breaking down because of inadequate equipment, sabotage, and the speed of the advancing troops. Military intelligence was deficient, and the faults of command were showing. The cohesion of the right wing was beginning "to ravel to pieces."[7] Its strength was weakened not only by the mounting losses but also by diversion of two corps to East Prussia to help the German Eighth Army, one corps to invest Antwerp, forces to garrison Brussels, and more than a corps to reduce Maubeuge. These diversions cut down the first three armies of the right wing from sixteen to eleven corps. The French had the advantage of operating on close interior lines from the base of Paris, from which the radial lines of a superb network of railways reached to the front.

At the end of August the Germans departed further from the Schlieffen strategy when Lanrezac's Fifth Army skillfully attacked Bülow's forces at Guise (August 29–30). The attack could not be pressed home because the British fell back. It allowed time, nonetheless,

6. For the full text of the general directive, see Tyng, *Campaign of the Marne,* Appendix VIII, 374; for a discussion of the order, Jaesche, "Zum Problem der Marne-Schlacht," 326–27.

7. Görlitz, *Der deutsche Generalstab,* 128.

for the Fifth Army and the BEF to escape the clutch of the moving wheel. They continued their retreat until they could take part in the battle of the Marne. Guise also bought time for assembling Maunoury's Sixth Army on the German flank.

The attack caused Bülow to ask for help from Kluck, and in lending assistance Kluck had his intention strengthened to cut inward in the attempt to outflank Lanrezac's troops and strike at the rear of the French armies. The decision, taken without Moltke's approval (though he subsequently concurred) and contrary to the Schlieffen plan and the still operative general directive of August 27, shifted the First Army's line of march from west to the southeast of Paris. Maunoury's Sixth Army was left outside as a threat to the flank of the German right wing. The whole right side of five armies was forced to contract to a narrower arc to prevent gaps from rending the line. The grand strategy of Schlieffen's outflanking maneuver was well on the way to abandonment, yet it was operational necessity all along the right wing, even more than Kluck's initiative, that compelled the compression.[8]

A wave of optimism nevertheless swept over the German high command and court, with the overwhelming defeat of the Russians at Tannenberg, followed by the fall of Soissons on September 1 and by the transfer of the French government to Bordeaux on the next day. Then a turn suddenly came when the British escaped Kluck's chase and the French Fifth Army ended the possibility of its envelopment by crossing the Marne to the south. Moltke, forced by his contracting right wing and the strength of fortress Paris, ordered a narrowing of the whole loop intended to snare the Allied armies; henceforth the mass of the French forces was to be driven southeast from Paris. In the movement the First Army was ordered to fall in behind the Second Army to guard the flank rather than to serve as the cutting edge of the advance.

Kluck disregarded the order, believing his army was in a better position than the Second to gain an impressive victory by pursuit of the French. He drove after them for the next three days, across the Marne east of Paris. His push raised for the German armies the threat of destruction by envelopment of their own right flank. Moltke, seized with pessimism and nervous exhaustion at this point, feebly issued orders on September 4

8. On the importance of Guise in preparing the way for the battle of the Marne, see Terraine, *Western Front*, 126–31.

commanding both the First and Second Armies to heel right as a flank guard facing the eastern front of Paris; the other five armies were to join in driving the French forces into a still smaller sack, the focal point of which would be Verdun. The abrupt change in operations, putting the First and Second Armies on an offensive defense, surrendered the initiative to the Allies and scrapped the remnants of the Schlieffen strategy after a march of more than five hundred kilometers.

The stage was set for the battle of the Marne. The strategic opportunity for which the cool, tenacious, and resolute Joffre had prepared was at hand after the phase of the long strategic retreat. Joffre had strengthened his left wing with forces from the right until he had achieved a numerical superiority in the Marne area. The newly created Sixth Army of Maunoury was in position northwest of Paris on the flank of the German First Army. By dividing the overlarge Fourth Army, Joffre formed another new army, the Ninth under Foch, to bolster the center of the Allied line. He did not hesitate to remove some fifty generals who revealed incompetence or insufficient energy in combat. Among the latter was Lanrezac, who was replaced by Louis Franchet d'Espéry as commander of the Fifth Army. Earlier Lanrezac had shown a better and quicker grasp than Joffre of the strategic situation arising from the extended German wheel. Joffre was forced, however, to recognize that, although brilliant in military analysis, Lanrezac was too prone to professorial argument and criticism to command forcibly in action.[9] Unlike Moltke, Joffre had consulted personally with each of his army commanders, informing himself of the current situation and state of readiness of each army.

Both Joffre and General Joseph Galliéni, who as military governor of Paris had been preparing its defenses against a possible attack, perceived the new strategic situation produced by Kluck's reckless thrust to the southeast. The move had been detected by French and British aviation and by French cavalry scouts. Both Joffre and Galliéni were eager to exploit the opportunity offered by Kluck's exposed position. But Joffre had a larger objective in mind—that of beginning with an attack here a general action, a counteroffensive that would push back the entire wing of the five wheeling armies. Their invasion had created a large salient extending from Verdun to Compiègne, and Joffre's orders of September 5 for the counterstroke directed drives to be made on each flank of the

9. W. A. Stewart, "Lanrezac, Joffre, and Plan XVII," *Military Affairs* 32 (1969): 181–90.

salient, while the Allied center held strongly.[10]

The execution of these orders of Moltke and Joffre produced the battle of the Marne (September 6–10). It consisted of a series of complicated engagements in which two key developments stand out: the initiative shifted from the German to the Allied side, with a corresponding shift in morale and in the element of surprise; a gap of some thirty kilometers opened up between the German First and Second Armies as they carried out the heeling movement to the right and at the same time fought the Allied line.

The breach appeared when Kluck transferred two corps from his left wing next to Bülow's Second Army to his main force on the Ourcq River in trying to outflank Maunoury's Sixth Army. The BEF, now reinforced to an army of six divisions, advanced into this gap for the next three days against the light protective screen, chiefly cavalry, of the Germans. Though having a numerical superiority of about ten to one, the British edged forward overcautiously in the face of deceptive German maneuvers. They approached the Marne River by September 8, crossing it the next day thirty hours before any French infantry.[11]

The Allied exploitation of the gap threatened the rear of the First Army and the flank of the Second Army. The perilous situation provoked a crisis in the German high command in Luxembourg. Moltke had issued no orders to the army commanders since the beginning of the battle and had not consulted with them. Isolated and poorly informed about the position and movement of the German armies, he was overcome with doubts and suspense. After a conference in OHL he sent Lieutenant Colonel Richard Hentsch, a highly respected and intelligent senior officer of the general staff, on a trip by car to consult with the command of each of the five

10. The texts of the major orders and directives of the German and French high commands during this campaign are given in translation in Tyng, *Campaign of the Marne*, Appendices, 362–94. A controversy has long been carried on concerning the primary responsibility, whether of Galliéni or of Joffre, for the decision to order the counteroffensive. The prevailing view attributes the basic responsibility and the final victory to Joffre, although recognizing that Galliéni by telephone prodded the slow-minded Joffre to an early conclusion of his thinking and gave him wise support. Isselin, *Battle of the Marne*, 103–12, 121–25, 277–78, judiciously assesses the competing claims along this line. Spears, *Liaison, 1914*, 335–36, similarly gives the chief credit to Joffre. B. H. Liddell Hart joined the campaign in support of Galliéni; see his *The British Way in Warfare* (London, 1932), 64–71.

11. Spears, *Liaison, 1914*, 434; C. Vidal, "L'armée britannique à la bataille de la Marne," *Revue d'histoire de la guerre mondiale* 14 (1936): 345–69; General de Cugnac, "L'armée anglaise à la Marne," ibid. 15 (1937): 97–108.

armies on the right. The headquarters of the Second Army concluded with Hentsch that, if the enemy got across the Marne, both the Second and the First Armies should withdraw in such a direction as to close the breach between them. When the British were about to cross, Bülow consequently ordered the Second Army to retreat in order to escape outflanking.[12]

On that same day Hentsch visited the command of the First Army and found Kluck's force isolated; the gap between his army and Bülow's had widened to fifty kilometers, and the left wing of the French Fifth Army had joined the British in moving through the opening. Kluck's worsening position and Bülow's decision to withdraw induced Hentsch, invoking the powers accorded him orally by Moltke, to order the retreat of the First Army. Kluck's command finally yielded in spite of the desire to continue the attack against Maunoury's Sixth Army and advance on Paris. The wisdom of this action and the basis for it were thereafter closely scrutinized and long debated by the Germans. Though Hentsch carried out his mission as "Fate's messenger" with no formal mandate from Moltke, a later military inquiry and other investigations concluded that he did not exceed his authority.

The issue of the Marne battle was decided by the afternoon of September 9. The First and Second Armies were in retreat; the advance of the Third Army against Foch's Ninth Army was halted; Paris and Maunoury's Sixth Army were saved. The Sixth Army was reinforced by troops from the armies of the right wing, part of which were sent out from Paris in taxicabs. From this event arose a legend exaggerating its importance out of all proportion. The retreat of the First and Second Armies forced Moltke, now sunk in despair, to order a general withdrawal of the Third, Fourth, and Fifth Armies. By the night of September 11 all the German forces fell back all the way to Switzerland—a mass of gray figures thwarted of victory, exhausted in body, and depressed in spirit.

The "miracle of the Marne" ended as a strategic victory for the Allies without local tactical defeats for the Germans. The German armies were outmaneuvered by the Allies so that they were compelled to withdraw to escape imminent disaster. The supremely calm and confident Joffre had

12. For a thorough tracing of the Hentsch mission hour by hour and discussion of the question of his responsibility, see *Der Weltkrieg*, 4: 526–33. This and other accounts representing the German military establishment hold that the decision snatched defeat from the moment of victory. See also Groener, *Lebenserinnerungen*, 172; Kuhl, *Marne Campaign*, 18–19, 261–70.

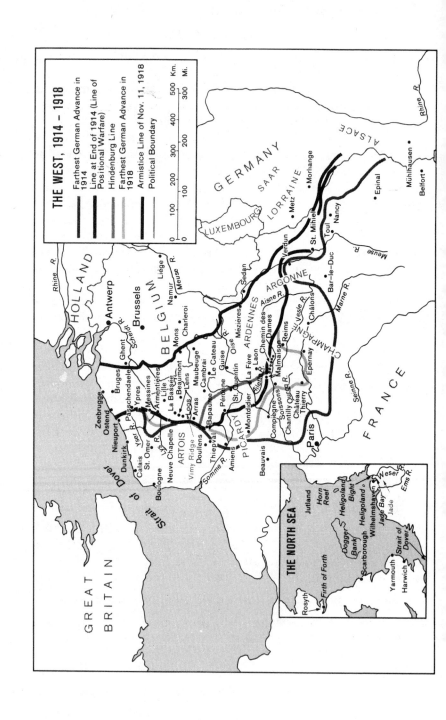

THE WEST, 1914 – 1918

|||| Farthest German Advance in 1914
|||| Line at End of 1914 (Line of Positional Warfare)
|||| Hindenburg Line
|||| Farthest German Advance in 1918
|||| Armistice Line of Nov. 11, 1918
|||| Political Boundary

Km.
0   100 200 300 400 500
Mi.
0   100 200 300

GREAT BRITAIN

HOLLAND

Rhine R.

Antwerp
Brussels
Scheldt R.
Ghent
Bruges
Ostend
Zeebrugge
Nieuport
Dunkirk
Calais
Boulogne

Strait of Dover

BELGIUM
Liège
Namur
Meuse R.
Charleroi
Mons
Maubeuge
Beaumont
Cambrai
Le Cateau
Guise
Péronne
St. Quentin
La Fère
Laon
Oise R.
Bapaume

Passchendaele
Ypres
Messines
Armentières
Lille
La Bassée
LOOS
Lens
Arras
Neuve Chapelle
St. Omer
Yser R.
Lys R.

ARTOIS
Vimy Ridge
Thiepval
Doullens
Somme R.
Amiens
PICARDY
Montdidier
Compiègne
Chantilly
Beauvais
Paris

Sedan
Mézières
ARDENNES
Chemin des Dames
Aisne R.
Malmaison
Soissons
Château Thierry
Crépy
Épernay

GERMANY
SAAR
LUXEMBOURG
LORRAINE
Metz
Morhange
Verdun
Argonne
Aisne R.
Vesle R.
Reims
Châlons
CHAMPAGNE
Marne R.
St. Mihiel
Toul
Nancy
Bar-le-Duc
Meuse R.
Seine R.

FRANCE

ALSACE
Rhine R.
Mühlhausen
Belfort
Épinal

THE NORTH SEA

Firth of Forth
Rosyth
Dogger Bank
Scarborough
Jutland
Horn Reef
Heligoland
Heligoland Bight
Wilhelmshaven
Jade Bay
Jade
Weser R.
Ems R.
Yarmouth
Harwich
Strait of Dover

accomplished a rare feat of leadership, in sustaining a long strategic retreat and then seizing the favorable moment for a general counteroffensive— one of the most difficult achievements for a military command. The French generals contrasted with the German in effective coordination of effort and in staff teamwork. The advance of the British army into the gap insured the immediate utilization of the opportunity presented the Allies.

No other battle of the war was so pregnant in consequences. It pointed to the fatal fallacy of Blitzkrieg in a time of modern defensive weapons, passing a severe verdict on the accumulation of German military mistakes since Schlieffen. The German defeat disturbed the confidence of the army in the military command, and some of the more perceptive military and civil leaders soon realized that Germany was condemned to a hopeless struggle. The victory of the Allies saved the greater part of France with its manpower and economic resources for the Entente coalition and pre- vented the catastrophe of division such as existed in the Second World War between Free and Vichy France. The outcome collapsed the myth of German invincibility that had prevailed since 1871, brought the Allies the first intimations that the Central Powers could not win the war, and deeply impressed Italy favorably toward the Entente. By insuring that the war would last a long time, the Marne created an opportunity for command of the seas to exert its slow, strangling effect. The campaign of the Marne represented par excellence the war of movement with great masses of men rapidly advancing and falling back as many sanguinary battles were waged. Its conclusion presaged a new shape of war on the Western Front—a radically different kind from the war of movement.

2. THE AFTERMATH OF MARNE

The Allies, coming out of the Marne, pursued the retreating Germans to the Aisne river. Yet the pursuit was so faltering and the German staff work in retreat so successful that the immediate fruits of victory eluded the Allies; they could not destroy German formations. The Germans entrenched themselves on the line of the Aisne, and in a bitter encounter here the Allied armies were unable to dislodge them.

After the Marne battle, the Germans resolved the crisis in command. On September 14 the kaiser replaced in effect (but not in name) the overstrained and sick Moltke, reduced to a state of despondent collapse, with General Erich von Falkenhayn, the Prussian minister of war. The general taking over from the "fallen favorite of the kaiser" was a self-contained Prussian nobleman fifty-three years old, who was imposing in appearance and had a quick mind and a readiness to assume responsibility.[13]

The defeat of Blitzkrieg at the Marne and the establishment of a front of fixed trenches along the Aisne altogether altered the strategic premises on which the war had begun. A strategy of sudden annihilation was excluded in a war between foes not too disparate in strength. Neither the new commander of the German armies nor his opponent Joffre grasped at first the significance of the change in spite of the terrible casualties suffered by both sides. Falkenhayn, moreover, no longer had the power of assault delivered by the thoroughly trained troops driving forward in the great August wheel. The exhausted soldiers needed rest and refitting, trained reserves hardly existed, and the unanticipated consumption of munitions caused a critical scarcity of supply.

These conditions and the entrenched line of the Allies along the Aisne to Noyon did not deter Falkenhayn from adhering to Schlieffen principles by resuming the offensive against the French in the effort to achieve a decisive victory. He commenced an attack aimed to envelop the Allied flank with a reconstituted Sixth Army moved to the end of the lengthening line in the north. In support of the action he conducted separate attacks from Noyon to the area around Verdun as a diversionary effort, since the Germans lacked the strength for a general offensive along this line. Some of these separate engagements produced local success, such as the creation of the St. Mihiel salient south of Verdun, but at a fearful cost in men.[14]

The Allies quite naturally tried to realize the corresponding objective of extending their line beyond and around the northern end of the German defenses. Each opponent sought to best the other by moving forces to the north from other parts of the line or by throwing in new troops in a race at mutual outflanking. In the course of the struggle, the front was pushed northward from Noyon, through Picardy, Artois, and Flanders to the Channel near Nieuport. Bitter fighting raged along this line in October and November.

During the race the British army was gradually shifted to Flanders to

13. Janssen, *Der Kanzler und der General,* 21; Görlitz, *Der deutsche Generalstab,* 16–17, 131–32.

14. Peter Graf Kielmansegg, *Deutschland und der Erste Weltkrieg* (Frankfurt, 1968), 62–64.

help check the German thrust and to be nearer its base of supply. It was reinforced by troops from home and from overseas garrisons, as well as by an Indian corps. The Belgian field army eventually took a position at the end of the line between the British and the coast after Antwerp fell. Churchill at Admiralty had hurriedly sent out three brigades of marines to help the Belgians at Antwerp, but the defenses could not resist beyond October 10 the pounding by the big Austrian and German howitzers. That they held out until then may have been instrumental in saving Dunkirk and Calais for the Allies.

The French brought a strong army into position between the BEF and Noyon, and Foch was given command of French troops operating in the northern area. Foch was established as the deputy to Joffre, with the task of coordinating the disposition of Allied forces north of Noyon. In this mission he developed cordial relations with the British.

Events were now rushing toward the climactic encounter of Ypres. The Germans strengthened their position by occupying—in addition to Antwerp—Lille, Ghent, Bruges, and the port of Ostend and Zeebrugge. They concentrated two new armies in Flanders, one of which (the Fourth) consisted largely of student volunteers and men liable for military service but not previously recruited. Falkenhayn would throw the many poorly trained youths and over-age reserve officers of this army along with other troops into a last great effort to break through and roll up the Allied line, before the establishment of a fixed front from Noyon to the sea ended the war of movement. If successful, he hoped also to obtain the Channel ports and drive the British into the sea.

The battle of Ypres, or Flanders, began on October 20 with a German attack and continued until November 22 along a front of one hundred kilometers. In the initial phase, the Belgians mustered the sea to fight for them by opening the sluices at Nieuport. The flood let loose forced the Germans to break off the fighting. Farther south, the British held their own with deadly fire by rifle and field gun. The next part, around Messines Ridge, was more confused; here the British line broke for a time against the furious assaults of the half-trained German youth of the Fourth Army, burning with patriotism and the zeal for sacrifice. They were slaughtered in a massacre of the intellectuals from the younger generation *(Der Kindermord von Ypern)*. The last phase had the limited objective of capturing at least Ypres itself, in order to avoid the impression of defeat and to make the line of the Germans more defensible. They opened a hole momentarily in the British defenses and almost succeeded in taking the city. They were too near collapse to exploit the break, however, and it was soon closed by counterattack.

After the Flanders battle the fighting abated, for a "balance of exhaustion" had been reached.[15] Falkenhayn concluded that "a further thoroughgoing success was no longer to be obtained" in Flanders[16] and, responding to calls from the eastern front for reinforcements, transferred eight divisions to Poland. The problem of waging a two-front war had become apparent to the Germans in all its inescapable and stark reality. In the next four years the German high command would have to grapple many times with the perplexities of deciding between an eastern and a western strategy, between the priorities and the proponents of each.

The failure of Falkenhayn's costly offensive caused another crisis in the OHL. Ypres so shook Falkenhayn's confidence that he remained a changed man thereafter, with a suddenly instilled tendency to caution and a deep-rooted pessimism about Germany's chances of winning the war. Falkenhayn was formally appointed Moltke's successor on November 3, but his position was weakened by criticism at the general headquarters and at the eastern command for the futile bloodbath in Flanders.

In striving for a decision, Falkenhayn used up the available reserves of the army; he overestimated its offensive strength and underestimated the defensive capabilities of the Allies—a recurrent mistake of the Germans throughout the war. The army lost faith in its power of attack and again faith in a command that would commit to a large-scale offensive forces in such poor condition to seek a major objective. Falkenhayn's critics of the eastern command claimed that he should have transferred the troops sacrificed in the western offensive to the east for a knockout blow against Russia. Doubtless the most serious mistake of command was the strained attempt to force a decision with the instrument at hand after the rigors of the Marne. The conclusion of a recent German writer seems fair enough: "Falkenhayn had sought the impossible. The task was too great for him and for the German army."[17]

The French command had learned as little as the German from the opening battles about the capabilities of firepower in modern war. Foch

15. Ibid., 69.

16. Erich von Falkenhayn, *The German General Staff and Its Decisions, 1914–1916* (New York, 1920), 35.

17. Janssen, *Der Kanzler und der General,* 26–32.

was prevented from launching a hopeless major offensive toward Courtrai-Lille only by the necessity of defense against Falkenhayn's assault. In December Joffre and Foch undertook a decisive breakthrough first in Artois north of Arras and then in Champagne, but without success and at the price of costly casualties.

For all practical purposes the battle of Ypres ended open war in the west until the offensives of 1918 and introduced the war of stalemate along a fixed front. The mud and blood of Ypres were prophetic of what was to come in the battles of the Western Front. The monsters of opposing armies writhed in desperate contention at an inordinate cost of casualties (the British 50,000 and the Germans 100,000 in this one contest) without substantial result in changing the front. By the end of Ypres the British professional army originally sent to the continent was practically wiped out. Flanders was left a shambles and Ypres a ruin. The consumption of ammunition was inconceivable. At the conclusion of the Marne, half of the accumulated supply of the French army was used up.[18] Similarly, the dearth of munitions, especially for the artillery, seriously handicapped the fall offensive of the Germans, weakening the élan of the infantry. It was already clear that total war must be a war of machines and supply, as well as of human masses.

The "race to the sea" and the Flanders fighting completed the formation of the Western Front. The entrenched lines of the two sides extended for 466 miles form Nieuport south to Noyon, then east to the north of Soissons and Reims, across the Argonne forest to the north of Verdun, and then, after curving around the St. Mihiel salient, southeast to the Swiss frontier. On the Allied side the French held all of this line except a sector of 21 miles taken over by the British (later extended to 50) and a sector of 15 by the Belgians. Except for small areas involved in the battles of 1915 and a sector evacuated by the Germans in 1917, the line changed very little from November 1914 to March 1918, when the stalemate was broken.

3. THE CLASH OF CONTINENTAL EMPIRES

The defeat of Blitzkrieg in the west disarranged the plans of the German and Austrian empires for war in the east, and the quick offensive planned to achieve a victory of annihilation was hardly more fortunate for the

18. *Mémoires du Maréchal Joffre,* 2 vols. (Paris, 1932), 2: 25.

Russian empire than for France. The problem of coordinating operations among members of each contending coalition came peculiarly into play in the east. Here the Central Powers were waging two wars at the same time, a two-front continental war and a Balkan conflict, which increased the difficulties of determining strategic objectives and the allocation of military resources. The eastern theater, where the frontier between Russia and its neighbors extended more than a thousand miles, was on a greater territorial scale but with far fewer facilities in railways and good roads for transport.

Immediately after mobilization and deployment, two Russian armies moved into East Prussia, the First, or Niemen, Army under General Paul Edler von Rennenkampf from the east, and the Second, or Narew, Army under General Alexander V. Samsonov from the south. Their objective was to envelop the German Eighth Army in East Prussia. The forces were not properly concentrated, and the various services, especially those of communication and supply for the Second Army, were not sufficiently organized.

The Eighth Army, under General Max von Prittwitz, moved forward to meet the advancing Russians. Rennenkampf's army, after crossing the border, defeated the main part of the Eighth Army at Gumbinnen. Prittwitz, whose alarm was increased by the movement of Samsonov's army from the south, reported to Moltke his intention to retire behind the Vistula and requested reinforcements. The operations division of the general staff, displeased with Prittwitz's loss of nerve, urged Moltke to replace him with General Paul von Hindenburg, who was recalled from retirement at sixty-seven years of age. He received Ludendorff as chief of staff, and the two were to form a working partnership for the duration of the war.[19]

The Russians acted on the belief that they had inflicted a major defeat on the Germans. Samsonov rushed ahead into East Prussia with an exhausted and hungry array spread over some sixty miles. Rennenkampf at the same time failed to exploit his success, advancing only haltingly without giving any assistance to Samsonov. Near Tannenberg the German forces, assembled through forced marches and rail movement, threw a net around the center of Samsonov's army and won a spectacular victory in a classic Cannae of double envelopment (August 23–31). The surrounded

19. Görlitz, *Der deutsche Generalstab,* 134.

Russians, a hundred thousand in number, were killed or taken prisoner, while the remnant of the army was forced to retreat. The victim of the German maneuver, General Samsonov, shot himself on the battlefield.[20] By this time the Germans were reinforced with the two corps that Moltke had diverted from the west during the Marne campaign. With the added strength, Hindenburg moved on Rennenkampf's army, which had fallen back to a defensive position, and attempted to outflank the Russians. Rennenkampf eluded the envelopment, but the German victory in the battle of the Masurian lakes (September 8–9) resulted in driving his army out of East Prussia. The pursuing Germans did not succeed in crossing the Niemen.

Tannenberg aroused enormous enthusiasm in Germany and from the very beginning became a subject of propaganda and myth, extending to political ramifications. Hindenburg and Ludendorff got the credit for the dazzling stroke, which really belonged to Hoffmann and the subordinate field commanders, and gained such prestige that the general staff had to listen to the inseparable pair. The deadlock in the west was seized on by them and their growing company of proponents to support the thesis that the war could be won in the east by properly diverting military strength to that theater. The political charisma that both Hindenburg and Ludendorff were to acquire went back to Tannenberg.[21]

The success of the Germans is largely explained by their technical and organizational superiority over the Russians and by the latter's faults of command, disorganized supply, and disordered communications. The Russian undertaking had not observed the axiomatic requirement of modern war that a large-scale offensive must be launched only after the most careful planning. Since their intelligence functions were almost nonexistent, the Russians developed no useful intelligence about the enemy's intentions, distribution of forces, or movements; the Germans, on the other hand, intercepted Russian radio messages sent in the clear or in easily decipherable code, revealing the schedule of movement of the

20. Max Hoffmann, *War Diaries and Other Papers*, 2 vols. (London, 1929), 1: 20, 37–42 and 2: 22–43; Knox, *With the Russian Army*, 1: 66–94; and the entire account of the Russian advance and defeat in Stone, *Eastern Front*, 54–67. The debacle of the Second Army is the grand theme of Alexandr Solzhenitsyn's novel *August 1914*, which vividly portrays the confusion and incompetence of command characterizing the offensive in East Prussia.

21. Hoffmann dispelled many of the myths about Tannenberg in "The Truth About Tannenberg," in *War Diaries*, 2: 239–334. See also Stone's treatment referred to in note 20 above.

Russian armies, the objectives of individual corps, the strength of forces. The two Russian commanders, mistrusting each other, acted on their own without cooperation; the laggard advance of Rennenkampf after Gumbinnen was accounted by a British observer on the ground to have been a main factor in Samsonov's crushing defeat.[22] Coordination was missing among corps commanders of Samsonov's army and between them and himself. The army group command having formal authority over the two Russian armies failed to provide direction or assistance to either. The Russians could not bring their numerical superiority to bear against the opposing German army, while the Germans concentrated superiority of forces against Samsonov's separate army. The Russians had committed one blunder after another; good fortune favored good planning with the Germans. Despite the brilliant success of the Germans, the victory had no strategic significance; it saved East Prussia but its effect on Russia at the time was not marked.[23]

As the allies Germany and Austria had had their differences in the conduct of foreign policy during the prewar years, so their difficulties in waging coalition warfare emerged at once. Austria initially deployed nearly half its forces for the expedition against Serbia, though Berlin urged Vienna to concentrate Austrian strength to meet the main Russian array. The persistence in the initial offensive against Serbia and the delay in shifting forces of the swing army and transport from Serbia to Galicia weakened the Austrian campaign against the Russians. The large concentration against Serbia delayed the deployment of the armies originally planned for movement to Galicia, and the difficulties were increased by inefficient staff work and by the strategic irresolution between defensive and offensive operations there.[24]

The Austrian fortunes in Serbia were soon blighted when the two invading armies were ejected by a Serbian counterattack before the end of August. The Austrian armies began a new invasion in September and a third in November, the latter reaching its high point with the capture of Belgrade. The savage fighting continued until the stubborn Serbs drove the exhausted Austrian troops in the December cold back across the

22. Knox, *With the Russian Army*, 1: 90.
23. Hoffmann, *War Diaries*, 2: 265–68, 332–34; Otto, Schmiedel, and Schnitter, *Der Erste Weltkrieg*, 62; Görlitz, *Der deutsche Generalstab*, 135–36; Kielmansegg, *Deutschland und der Erste Weltkrieg*, 53.
24. Ritter, *Staatskunst*, 2: 327–38; Stone, *Eastern Front*, 71–81.

Danube. The Serbs returned to Belgrade and other evacuated areas in triumph, having captured large quantities of much needed munitions and medical supplies. The Austrians returned home after suffering more than 200,000 casualties and a humiliating blow to their prestige. Thousands of Slav troops had surrendered. The Serbian victory over the Austrian Goliath encouraged the forces in the Balkan states favorable to the Allies and stimulated the nationalist movements within the Dual Empire.[25]

During this time the Russian "Steam Roller" was turning early Austrian success into catastrophic reverses in the Galician campaign. Following the Russian plans of long standing, four Russian armies under General Nicholas Ivanov, two from the north and two from the east, made a concentric push toward Lvov (Lemberg), the capital city of Galicia, and the great fortress of Przemyśl. The Austrians opposed the Russians with a numerically inferior force of four smaller armies, including the force shifted from the Serbian front, under the nominal command of Archduke Friedrich and the operational direction of Conrad, the chief of the general staff. Conrad, pressed by the Germans for prompt action, finally chose to oppose the advancing Russians by bold offensive operations. After two of his armies moved northward into southern Poland, the Austrians defeated the Russian host in the initial battle (Kraśnik) and advanced before Lublin. The two sides were fighting blindly, without adequate aviation and without effective intelligence services. So far the Russians had outdone the Austrians in blundering; they had hurt themselves by quarreling among commanders and by repeated shifting of command appointments.

On the north the Russians were reinforced by an additional army from Warsaw, and the mass action moved to the east, where the Austrians were engaged in severe fighting. They were compelled to withdraw to the Lvov line and then to yield Lvov. From there they had to carry out a general retreat from one river line to another until they reached the Dunajec on October 3. The Austrian armies escaped annihilation only through their interception of Russian radio messages revealing the position of key Russian forces. The Russians did not advance farther at the time but invested the fortress of Przemyśl, left behind in the Austrian retreat.[26]

This short but deadly campaign cost Austria irretrievable losses of 350,-000–400,000 casualties, between a third and a half of the troops involved,

25. Arthur J. May, *The Passing of the Hapsburg Monarchy, 1914–1918*, 2 vols. (Philadelphia, 1966), 1: 100–02.
26. For the whole campaign, see Stone, *Eastern Front*, 80–91.

and the granary and oil fields of Galicia. Many of the numerous prisoners were Slavs deserting to the Russians. The cadres of thoroughly trained officers and noncommissioned personnel were devastated; the empire could never again put officer complements of comparable quality into the field. Army morale received a profound shock, to which the critical shortages caused by the mammoth consumption and losses of military supplies contributed. The disastrous campaign enhanced the tendencies toward disintegration within the army and within the multinational empire itself. The burden of fighting fell thereafter increasingly on the German and Magyar troops in the army. The campaign caused further conflicts and recriminations between the Central Powers concerning the conduct of coalition war.

The Austrians were embittered by the failure of the Germans to effect a big transfer of troops from the west to the eastern front after the lapse of six weeks, the time Moltke had suggested for subduing the French army. Conrad, whose suspicions of German intentions were confirmed, questioned among his associates what "our secret foes the Germans are doing."[27]

The Austrian leaders were henceforth never disposed to trust the German direction of war. Because of the debilitating losses and accelerated disintegration within the army, Austria needed from this time on the increasing support of German units in the field if it was to remain a useful ally. The growing dependence augmented the difficulties of cooperation between the two. The German officers, for their part, saw in the Galician campaign clear proof of their little faith in Austrian military capabilities.[28]

With their shattered armies safe behind the Dunajec, the Austrians, both the general staff and the Ballhausplatz, appealed to Falkenhayn for immediate help, warning that they might be forced to conclude a separate peace. OHL was moved not only by this appeal but also by the threat of Russian advances from Polish territory into the valuable industrial and mining sections of Silesia and by the danger of further Austrian defeats adversely influencing Balkan opinion. In response, a newly formed Ninth Army under Hindenburg and Ludendorff drove forward from Upper Silesia against the Russians in southwest Poland until the gates of Warsaw were reached. Benefiting from this diversion, the Austrian armies behind

27. May, *Passing of the Hapsburg Monarchy,* 1: 98.
28. Kielmansegg, *Deutschland und der Erste Weltkrieg,* 55–59.

the Dunajec moved forward in Galicia and into Poland in continuous line with the Germans. They proceeded to the San river and relieved Przemyśl before their resumed offensive died down.

The Russian supreme command (Stavka) meanwhile shifted the main Russian attack from Galicia to Silesia and Poznán, aiming at a decisive thrust into Germany from Poland. The old story of intercepted radio messages of the Russians was repeated. Hindenburg's command, learning of the danger it was about to encounter, was also assisted by the confusion on the Russian side and contradictory orders of Stavka. The Germans broke off the fighting and began a retreat toward Silesia. In withdrawing, they systematically destroyed the railways and roads. This held up the Russian advance sufficiently for Hindenburg to mount a strike from Thorn at the comparatively weak right flank of the Russians.

The German counteroffensive, beginning on November 11, led to heavy fighting in cold weather at Lowicz and Lódz. Hindenburg was not able, however, to destroy the opposing armies and roll up the Russian front in a successful envelopment. The Ninth Army had to settle for safeguarding Silesia and establishing a line near the Silesian border. Hoffmann was convinced that OHL lost a major opportunity in this action by not breaking off at Ypres and transferring troops in sufficient numbers for delivering a blow that would entrap huge Russian forces in the bend of the Vistula.[29]

The central Russian offensive was covered at the same time by attacks along the flanks. In Galicia the Russians drove the Austrians back in bitter encounters, investing Przemyśl again, and in the south reaching the crest of the Carpathians and taking the Dukla pass. On the northern flank they struck forcefully in East Prussia and pushed the weakened Eighth Army back to the Masurian lakes.

Notwithstanding the serious weaknesses of the Russian military machine, the Russian armies had made a noteworthy contribution to the Allied coalition. They had twice threatened to occupy East Prussia, endangered the resources and heavy industry of Upper Silesia, successfully resisted the capture of Warsaw, and wrested most of Galicia from the Dual Empire with destructive effect on the Austrian army. The Russian achievement, combined with the collapse of the Blitzkrieg strategy in the west, brought home to the political and military leaders of the Central Powers

29. Hoffmann, *War Diaries*, 2: 61–63, 72–82; Knox, *With the Russian Army*, 1: 213–14.

of a two-front war over a prolonged period. Reflecting the
es over coordination of command and conduct of the war in the
the creation of the famous eastern command (Oberkommando
Ost). It came into being when Hindenburg was appointed on November
1 commander-in-chief of all German combat forces in the east. A further
step was thus taken in the rise of a virtually separate German military
center in the east.

Controversy intensified over strategic emphasis and division of military
strength between east and west. The eastern command, Conrad, and
various internal lobbies in Germany clamored for more troops in the east.
Falkenhayn did not yield to Conrad's demand for thirty divisions, but the
transfer of eight divisions to the east at the end of November made some
concession to the "easterners." Such questions were to become burning
issues during the next period of the war, when the two sides were confronted with a strategic quandary after the failure of Blitzkrieg.

4. FAILURE OF THE PLANS

The universal failure of the long-developed plans of the general staffs
on the continent was due generally to the firepower of modern weapons
and the inadequacies of the generals. The devastating fire of the magazine
rifle, machine gun, rapid-firing artillery, and heavy guns modernized the
defense, eliminating the cavalry as an arm of offense in total war. The
plans, all of which reflected the current military doctrines of *offense à
outrance* and the superiority of élan and will, were out of harmony with
the weapons of the time and betrayed a glaring failure to adjust strategic
conception to available military technology.

This blindness marked the military leaders as a group with a professional deficiency that must be attributed in part to their class background
and in part to their training in the war academies and general staffs. They
came for the most part from the aristocracy, or at least the aristocratic
tradition, and their training concentrated on operational, staff, and historical aspects. Both exerted a narrow class and professional influence, tend-
ing to close them off from the main social, economic, and technological
currents of the time. They could reach professional maturity without
perceiving that industrialization and mass military organization were
changing the whole nature of war.

Every national military establishment, moreover, was at fault in not
selecting from the officer corps those most fitted for the highest places.

One is struck by the number of generals who were over age for their duties (Moltke and the other German commanders in the key positions ranged from sixty-six to sixty-eight years old), weakened by bad health, lacking in energy and will, or deficient in confidence and capacity for decision. Too many commanders, such as Schlieffen himself, Sir John French, Samsonov, and Rennenkampf, were cavalry officers of the old school.

The central question is why the Schlieffen plan failed. The German high command committed without doubt its full share of mistakes. Moltke did not keep a tight, unified command over his army leaders. This was all too evident in his remaining far behind the front at general headquarters in Luxembourg without attempting any personal consultation with his army commanders until after the Marne battle. The system of communication with them otherwise broke down through delay or obstruction in the transmission of messages by telegram, telephone, or radio. German intelligence, on the disposition and strength of enemy forces, was not as good as that of the French. Under these limitations Moltke could not keep reliably informed of battle developments and reach accurate conclusions on the current situation. He thus made an excessively sanguine estimate that the French army was about to collapse when he authorized the Lorraine offensive with the aim of a double envelopment of the Allied armies.

Moltke lost operational control of his right wing, and no means existed outside himself for coordinating the actions of its separate commanders. These commanders all committed tactical blunders, with the result that the Germans missed at least three clear opportunities to win victories of encirclement. Kluck of the First Army failed to destroy the disorganized British army in retreat, and he changed his direction of march to the southeast from that of the plan, partly owing to Bülow of the Second Army, so that Maunoury was able to concentrate the Sixth Army outside the German flank. Both Kluck and Bülow could not coordinate effectively with each other in operational ideas and movements; they both had a responsibility for the gap that opened up between their armies for the Allies to exploit.[30]

In combat, Moltke's various diversions from the right wing, together with battle losses, helped the Allies gain a numerical superiority in the

30. On the mistakes of the German command, see *Der Weltkrieg*, 2: 510–41; Barnett, *Swordbearers*, 52–54.

Marne area. Moltke has been attacked above all for the offensive in Lorraine, which kept him from stripping his left wing to strengthen the moving wheel of the right. The Lorraine operation has been considered a basic alteration of the Schlieffen principles, condemning the Germans to involvement in two crucial battles that worked against each other to prevent concentration of force at a single point.[31]

At the most critical moment the high command experienced a crackup in leadership. The exhaustion and uncertainty during the campaign left Moltke a shattered man by the time of the Marne battle. Having lost both nerve and hope, he was incapable of independent decision and leaned on the unsure advice of a disorganized general staff. In a state of depression, he sent Hentsch on an anomalous mission.

The numerous mistakes in command should not obscure the fatal fallacies of the Schlieffen plan itself, most of which Ritter has set forth in a comprehensive case against the Schlieffen strategic ideas.[32] The plan was formulated entirely from the standpoint of technical military objectives, without regard for diplomatic and political considerations. In a war that began in the east to support Austria, the plan required Germany to take aggressive actions through a declaration of war against Russia, the invasion of Belgium, and an attack on France. No scheme could have been better devised to consolidate the Entente into an Allied coalition, convert a continental war into a world war, disrupt the alliance system of the Central Powers, and influence the opinion of neutrals unfavorably toward Germany and Austria. It constituted a case of pure militarism—of the surrender to "military necessity," or to the dominance of the military over the political leadership.

The plan was certain to weaken the coalition with Austria by exposing Austria to the main assault, with little relief from Germany, of the massed Russian armies at their best in training and equipment of any time in the war. The conflict in the east was to be essentially Austria's war until Germany had dispatched France in the west. Austria was embittered by the terrible losses that resulted and vulnerable to defection thereafter through a separate peace. The severe defeats accelerated the disintegration of the empire by revealing its weaknesses and increasing the disaffection of the subject nationalities.

31. Kielmansegg, *Deutschland und der Erste Weltkrieg,* 47.
32. *Schlieffen Plan.*

The plan was flawed just as much by its illusory foundations for military success. The daring formulation did not correspond with the actual state of German arming. Moltke's transfer of two corps to East Prussia has been greatly overplayed as a cause of the collapse of the plan. Even if these troops had been retained in the right wing and reinforcements shifted there from the left wing, Germany never had the combat strength for all requirements as the losses mounted with the progress of the campaign. Schlieffen's planning had projected a number of formations that never came into being, and a weakness from the beginning was the absence of a general operational reserve, since reserve units were mixed with the regular troops at the front for immediate use. Additional corps might have been formed before the war, had not the Prussian minister of war rejected the requests of the general staff on the grounds that the officers required would have to be drawn from unsuitable class elements.[33] The Wilhelmine class structure and constitutional system helped to defeat the Schlieffen plan.

For the purpose contemplated, the army was not sufficiently supplied with ammunition, machine guns, heavy artillery, and equipment for the technical services. The immense expenditures for the German navy had robbed the army of substantial materiel requirements for war in the west. In 1914 the Reich did not possess the military capabilities to make a success of the Schlieffen strategy, just as Germany had pursued before the outbreak of war a diplomacy beyond its national resources to support. Germany, indeed, was attempting the impossible against the preponderant power of the Entente.[34]

The Schlieffen plan might have been executed according to schedule under certain conditions that existed a century before, or in 1870, or in 1940, when the offensive was mobile and relatively stronger. In 1914 these conditions did not exist, and the formulation was unreal, amounting to a work of fiction produced from "the intellectual wasteland of outworn tradition."[35] It was the offspring of a professional romanticism attempting to apply Hannibal to the present without taking cognizance of either current military realities or the broader technological possibilities of industrialization applicable to warfare. This military conservatism and pro-

33. Vagts, *History of Militarism,* 207, 219.
34. See Hubatsch, *Germany and the Central Powers in the World War,* 27.
35. Leo Frhr. Geyer von Schweppenburg, "Der Kriegsausbruch 1914 und der deutsche Generalstab," *Wehrwissenschaftliche Rundschau* 13 (1963): 151.

fessional narrowness, which avoided any working familiarity with the technological aspects of contemporary civilization, was responsible for the striking incongruity between Germany's industrial and technological primacy and the backwardness of the general staff's strategic ideas.[36]

Nor did the judgments of the incredible demands made on the German soldiers by the plan point to any high degree of professional competence. The general staff did not foresee the difficulty of supplying adequately the rapidly moving right wing after the retreating Belgians destroyed railways and bridges. The military consequently failed to prepare for the need to rebuild them immediately. Without the necessary railways or motorized transport, the soldiers became exhausted from the forced marches, limited food supply, and incessant fighting. It was not anticipated how the French would exploit available technical advantages, in shifting troops, by the use of the interior lines of their fine network of railways, supplemented with numerous secured roads and motor vehicles. The outcome at the Marne ultimately turned on the race between the legs of the German soldiers and the locomotives of the French.[37]

The plan confronted the right wing of the invading armies with a dilemma beyond resolution. If the right wing extended its line to the southwest around Paris, it would be so weakened that danger would arise of penetration by the Allies. If the tip of the right wing moved inside Paris to the east, this center of Allied strength remained outside to threaten the German flank. As it was, the German line became attenuated to the point of developing a critical breach, which could be repaired only by a general withdrawal. The Schlieffen plan was asking more of the German army than was justified by a reasonable calculation of the factors of chance. It implied a tremendous gamble that all the contingencies of war would favor the Germans and none the Allies, if there was to be any hope of success. It presupposed the infallibility of the German command in its execution and incompetence on the part of the enemy in resistance.

The Schlieffen plan was linked with three deceptive ideas that were to prejudice Germany's fortunes in the war. In the first place, the plan encouraged the notion that an infallible formula existed for winning a war of the masses in a quick, easy, and inexpensive way. There was nothing

36. On the backwardness of the Schlieffen planning in relation to technological factors, see especially Karl Justrow, *Feldherr und Kriegstechnik* (Oldenburg, 1933).

37. Joffre said after the Marne, "Formerly, battles were won with the legs, now they are won with locomotives." Quoted in ibid., 292.

novel in the general conception of destroying an opponent's army by envelopment of the flank. The audacity and grandiose proportions of the Schlieffen version, however, gave it the plausibility to forego serious consideration of more prudent alternatives.[38]

Second, the plan, having the goal of a quick victory of annihilation, augured the unconditional surrender of the enemy and a victor's dictated peace. The Schlieffen strategy helped to make this the political and military objective of the German leadership from the beginning. Since the strategic significance of the Marne defeat was not revealed to the German people, it was difficult for a public opinion to develop, or be developed, in support of a compromise peace and an early end of the war.

Third, the plan was a product of the autonomy of the general staff in the determination of strategy, and it worked to consolidate that principle in the German government. The plan was prepared and later modified without the cooperation of the political leadership; an opinion was never requested of the chancellor whether it was acceptable from the standpoint of its political implications. Nor were diplomacy and naval strategy coordinated with military planning. "Military necessity" was invoked as the justification not only of strategic objectives but also of the independence of the general staff's formulations.

Many historians and military writers since 1918 have sanctified the Schlieffen plan and focused criticism on its execution. Nonetheless, our conclusion today must be that the Schlieffen strategy failed because of inherent defects as well as faulty command. It attempted far too much—to provide the formula, not just for winning a battle, but for winning a war. Since the general staff could not anticipate the nature of the war, how could it be expected that the staff chief could draft the strategic prescription for ultimate victory?

Even if the plan had been carried out successfully, there is scarcely reason to believe that the result would have ended the war with Germany the victor. The plan offered no strategic solution for the problem of a long war, and neither the assurance of French surrender after a Schlieffen victory nor the prospect of a quick and final peace in the event of French capitulation. As in 1940, Britain would have remained an implacable and

38. On feasible alternatives, see Ritter, *Schlieffen Plan*, 36–37; Ritter, "Der Anteil der Militärs an der Kriegskatastrophe," 73–74; Justrow, *Feldherr und Kriegstechnik*, 260–79; Churchill, *World Crisis*, 1: 281–82.

undefeated enemy to continue the war while America stood in the offing.[39]

When "the massive hopes of August were flown"[40] at the end of the Marne campaign, Germany had lost the war a second time (after losing it first in the July diplomatic contest). But more than the hopes of August fell at the Marne. Along with the Schlieffen strategy, the old Prussian military tradition and the aristocratic class structure went down to defeat. But out of the wreckage Germany saved the gains of Belgium and northern France, which allowed it the choice of going on the defensive in the west and resuming the offensive there at the Reich's own time. France's principal source of iron ore in the Briey basin and its chief coal mines near Lens were left in possession of the Germans, making much more difficult the French problem of producing munitions, and easing Germany's correspondingly. For the Allies the German position imposed the compulsion to recover the lost territory and so restricted their strategic flexibility.

Whatever the partial gains of any belligerent, the offensive plans for a quick victory had collapsed everywhere before the revolution in warfare. The firepower of up-to-date weapons had won over plans, and in the process had exacted an appalling price. The casualty rate on both sides during the Marne campaign was higher than at Verdun or during the last four months of the war, each side losing a half million men. By the end of 1914 French and German casualties exceeded 800,000 each. Among all the combatants, the flower of the officer class and the best trained soldiers, especially the noncommissioned personnel, were cut down, and enormous quantities of war materiel were consumed and lost. The French, Austrian, and Russian armies never fully recovered from this original hammering, and Britain faced the task of rebuilding completely the army on the continent.[41]

At the end of the initial campaigns, the generals and the statesmen, riding on the wave of the past, were surprised by a war that was entirely

39. See Janssen, *Der Kanzler und der General,* 19; Eberhard Kaulbach, "Schlieffen; zur Frage der Bedeutung und Wirkung seiner Arbeit," *Wehrwissenschaftliche Rundschau* 13 (1963): 148.

40. Tirpitz, *My Memoirs,* 2: 22.

41. Otto, Schmiedel, and Schnitter, *Der Erste Weltkrieg,* 74; C. A. Macartney, *The Habsburg Empire, 1790–1918* (London, 1968), 817; Rudolph Kiszling, *Österreich-Ungarns Anteil am Ersten Weltkrieg* (Graz, 1958), 15–16, 24; Ropp, *War in the Modern World,* 224; A.J.P. Taylor, *A History of the First World War* (New York, 1966), 18; Vagts, *History of Militarism,* 351.

different from their expectations.[42] It was a war of vast, new dimensions, manifesting a prodigious appetite for men and machines. The transition was made fully in the west from a war of movement to a war of position, or siege warfare in the field, as the capabilities of current weapons were better understood and as the soldiers of both sides surrendered to sheer exhaustion. The change confirmed the downfall of the original strategies and demonstrated the need for new tactics of breakthrough. The demand was urgent to restore the stricken armies with men and equipment; for this it was essential to proceed with the creation of a new economic organization of the state and with the total mobilization of the people for war. The failure of the longstanding war plans confronted the generals with a strategic dilemma as to what should take their place under the conditions of total war.

42. Before 1914, mistaken ideas were generally held about the nature of the next war, despite a profound and prophetic study of future war made at the turn of the century by a Polish banker, Jan Bloch, who had become a self-developed arms expert. An abbreviated English version of the study appeared under the title, *The Future of War in Its Economic and Political Relations* (Boston, 1903). The original, in Russian, was translated in full into French: *La guerre*, 6 vols. (Paris, 1898–1900).

Chapter Four

STRATEGY IN THE BALANCE

1. THE STRATEGIC DILEMMA

THE keynote of the initial phase of the war was a rapid change from a nineteenth-century war of maneuver to a war of the twentieth century, dominated by the feature of stalemate. The stalemate prevailed in three spheres: on the Western Front, with its distinctive static characteristics; in the North Sea, where neither great war fleet dared confront the other in battle to the finish except in its own sanctuary; and in the technology of warfare, in which the defense had counterbalanced the offense in a unique way. The failure of the professional plans for the conduct of the war ushered in a new set of conditions, investing the war with a peculiar quality of siege. The siege character gave rise to a baffling strategic dilemma for both sides. Kitchener voiced the frustration of all the traditionally minded generals: "I don't know what is to be done—this isn't war."[1]

The central fact of the new situation was the structure and location of the Western Front. The triplex entrenchments on both sides, protected by barbed wire, machine guns, and modern artillery, had the strategic effect of creating two barrier fortresses in close opposition to each other, from the Alps to the Channel. The German attempt in the Flanders offensive and Joffre's winter attacks in Artois and Champagne demonstrated to more discerning minds the virtual impenetrability of the barrier to frontal assault with immediately prospective forces and existing equipment. Its location and extent excluded the possibility of turning either flank by land. Thus the dominant strategic problem that preoccupied each coalition henceforth was how to get at and overcome the main strength of the other established behind this barrier.

The situation of the Central Powers took on the nature of a besieged stronghold. They were cut off from the outside world not only by the Western Front but also by a great circle barrier at sea in the form of the Allied blockade. If they were to assert power against Britain, the effective

1. J.F.C. Fuller, *The Conduct of War, 1789–1961* (New Brunswick, N.J., 1961), 160.

center of the coalition, they would have to penetrate or reach beyond both barriers. If Allied strategy was to attain maximum force, the investment of the German bloc had to be closed in the area of the Balkans and the Straits.

The war of siege stimulated a search for strategic alternatives, in the endeavor to break through the barriers. Churchill summed up the problem neatly in a war memorandum: "We must, therefore, either find another theater or another method."[2] One line of approach sought the development of new weapons that would either open up a hole in the enemy front by a mass disablement of the defenders or restore mobility and protection to the offense. In answer to these needs, the use of gas was introduced and the tank developed. At sea, the Germans turned the submarine, whose use for this purpose had not been anticipated, into a commerce-raider, and threw a blockade of their own around Britain.

The conclusion of a general or a separate peace was a second alternative. It did not require clairvoyance, but it did vision, to perceive that Germany could not win the war, while Britain could not lose it. Whether the Allies could win without the intervention of America hung over the conflict as the uncertain issue. The true logic of the prolonged stalemate and the wisest course would have been to recognize the necessity of a compromise peace before attrition bled Europe white. During 1915 little opinion on either side, however, favored peace on the basis substantially of the status quo ante. Politicians and the people would have generally looked upon a compromise settlement as a defeat and demanded an end to the war that would justify the sacrifices of the nation.

The murderous and futile battle of Ypres led to a reexamination of German policy. Falkenhayn renounced the objective of total victory over the entire enemy coalition and urged the negotiation of a separate peace of minimal war aims with France or Russia. If a separate peace could be concluded with one or the other, the Germans would have realized their long-pursued aim of breaking up the encircling Entente. The Reich would have achieved by diplomacy what the Schlieffen plan failed to achieve by military operations, the conversion of the two-front war into a war of a single front. Falkenhayn saw that if the attempt did not succeed, the prospect was for a general peace after a long process of exhaustion.[3]

2. "War Memorandum: Mechanical Power in the Offensive," *World Crisis,* 3: 563.
3. Ritter, *Staatskunst,* 3: 60, 63; Paul R. Sweet, "Leaders and Policies: Germany in the Winter of 1914–1915," *Journal of Central European Affairs* 16 (1956): 231–33; Janssen, *Der Kanzler und der General,* 48–50.

Among civilians, Bethmann Hollweg acknowledged the desirability of a separate peace with Russia but was skeptical of success in negotiating it. In the absence of a separate peace he foresaw the risk either of an unfavorable turn of the war for Germany or of its ending in "general mutual exhaustion without express military defeat of either side." Whatever his public pronouncements by way of yielding to poltical pressures or encouraging the people, his conclusions, from an objective and sober estimate of the war situation, could be only reconciled with a compromise peace.[4]

A third alternative consisted of an eastern strategy put forward for dealing with the deadlock, in opposition to the prevailing western strategy. A decision between these two possibilities aroused bitter differences on both sides and strained the unity of war direction. The "westerners" insisted on the concentration of military forces and arms on the Western Front against the main enemy without distracting sideshows or sizable diversions elsewhere that might weaken or even endanger the central position of the coalition. The "easterners" believed that eastern Europe presented opportunities among the weaker combatants, which, if exploited properly, could shorten the war and avoid the mass slaughter of the unending frontal offensives against the siege lines of the west.

The conflict over strategy rose to an intense pitch among the British. The British military leaders tended to line up as westerners, in support of the position of military conservatism. The two most forceful and active members of the cabinet and War Council, Churchill and Lloyd George, fervently advocated an eastern strategy. At the turn of the year 1914–15 they pressed vigorously for an urgent offensive of a united Balkan front with the western powers against Turkey (Churchill) or against Austria and Turkey (Lloyd George). To a large extent, though not entirely, these differences took the form of a dispute between politicians and generals and became merged with a wider conflict between the two over the conduct of the war.[5] The opinion of the French was similarly split, although the differences were less divisive than in Britain.[6]

4. Zechlin, "Deutschland zwischen Kabinettskrieg und Wirtschaftskrieg," 441–42; Sweet, "Leaders and Policies," 234.

5. See Churchill, *World Crisis,* 2: 84–90, 173–74; Lloyd George, *War Memoirs,* 1: 364–80; Fuller, *Conduct of War,* 161–62.

6. An excellent brief account of the conflict in Britain is given in the introduction of Robert Blake, ed., *The Private Papers of Douglas Haig, 1914–1919* (London, 1952), 31–32. See also Victor Bonham-Carter, *Soldier True* (London, 1963), pp. xv–xx. To the soldiers the

The forces determining the choice of the Allies between the two conceptions were weighted in favor of the western alternative. Of paramount
influence was the extent of the national territory of France occupied by
the enemy. The French public and politicians were almost solidly behind
the most direct and active effort to win it back. They supported the
doctrinal orthodoxy of the French high command, determined to take the
offensive against the enemy at the strongest point. The British command
and general staff deferred to Joffre's plans for offensives in the west as if
he had command authority over the British army. This subordinate relationship followed in natural consequence of the prewar conversations
between the British and French military staffs, the immediate transfer of
the BEF to France in 1914, its takeover of the northern portion of the
continuous Allied line, and the major French share in the defense of that
line in 1915.

A factor that could not be taken lightly in the strategic decision of the
Allies was their command of the seas. The easterners relied on this element of British strategic tradition to make possible a more flexible and
broader policy for the conduct of the war than beating away at the siege
barrier in the west. They were confident that it offered a way to bring
Allied power to bear against the most vulnerable members of the enemy
coalition and, in combination with land forces, a means to take Constantinople and the Straits in the first half of 1915, when the Turks were still
weak at that point. The forces of opposition were too strong for the Allies
to have adopted in a systematic and timely fashion so imaginative a strategy.[7]

The Allies instead were drawn into a course of wearing the enemy
down. The proclaimed objective was to blast the ever-expected breakthrough in the Western Front, if only sufficient quantities of men and
munitions could be concentrated at the point of attack. The Allied commanders rationalized the failure with the objective of attrition.

Among the Central Powers, the division between the western and
eastern strategy evolved more as a conflict between military commands

attempt of the civilians to find "a way around" the great western barrier in departure from
the views of military orthodoxy seemed a rank intrusion of the amateurs into the field of the
professional experts. This indictment by the professional military is developed in Gerald
Ellison, *The Perils of Amateur Strategy* (London, 1926).

7. This eastern strategy is cogently presented as against a negative view of offensives in
the west by C.R.M.F. Cruttwell, *The Role of British Strategy in the Great War* (Cambridge,
England, 1936), 33–44; and Guinn, *British Strategy and Politics*, 48–118.

than between civilians and military over the aim, location, and timing of offensive action. The debate at bottom concerned the question how best to wage the grim two-front war. Falkenhayn was a westerner, holding like Tirpitz that Britain, the focus of Allied power and determination as well as the directing center of the gigantic machinery of blockade, must be the ultimate objective of the German war effort.[8] The elusive problem was the waging of war against a Britain beyond the direct power of the German army. Falkenhayn found one way of striking at Britain to be through France and Russia, states that he regarded as "tools of Britain" on the continent. But Germany no longer had the military capability for delivering blows that might eliminate France or Russia at an early date. Success therefore must be sought by the limited means of "hammering into them that they were in no position to pay the price of subduing us."[9]

The method required an economy in the use of military resources and a constant pursuit of the dominant purpose of the overall strategy. Falkenhayn thus ruled out an offensive in Italy, since it would not affect the main course of the war; justified the slaughter-mill at Verdun in weakening the French determination to hold out; and cautiously limited military operations in the vast spaces of Russia to the goal of sufficient success to obtain a separate peace of reasonable terms. As a more direct means of fighting the British, Falkenhayn supported the navy's proposals for an unrestricted U-boat campaign and considered the formation of a Mitteleuropa union to supply a weapon for exerting unremitting pressure along with the submarine against Britain.[10]

The chief of the general staff did not envisage any possibility of a victory of annihilation in Russia or any way of winning the war in the east. He attached particular importance to keeping Russia isolated from its allies and thought that the combination of isolation and military pressure would aggravate domestic difficulties to the point of eliminating the country as an effective belligerent. It was absolutely essential, then, to hold the Dardanelles while opening a route to Constantinople under the control of the German bloc.[11]

The emergence of Falkenhayn's strategic ideas for the war in its entirety

8. Falkenhayn shared the view of Tirpitz that London "had always been the political nerve-center of the Entente." Tirpitz, *My Memoirs,* 2: 5.
9. Falkenhayn, *German General Staff,* 331.
10. Ibid., 78–79, 245.
11. Ibid., 61, 182, 247.

drew him into conflict with the eastern command headed by Hindenburg and Ludendorff and with Conrad. This "war within a war" was many-sided, involving professional and personal rivalry as well as difference over technical matters and the authority of OHL over the eastern command. The easterners adhered with doctrinal conviction to the Schlieffen principle that Russia could be defeated through a battle of annihilation; they were no less certain that the east should have been made the central theater of the war since November 1914. The easterners assailed Falkenhayn for a no-win policy and abused him as "that criminal" for senseless attacks at Ypres and Verdun. Holding him responsible for "the war of lost opportunities," they maintained that the military means frittered away in these vain undertakings could have achieved total victory in the east if they had been used there at the right time.[12] The easterner Conrad desired a powerful offensive against Russia in the belief that the fate of the Balkans would be determined on that front.

The chancellor and the German foreign office joined the conflict on the side of the easterners. They were convinced that an imposing success against Russia was necessary for negotiating a separate peace and exerting influence in the Balkans. It must be the preliminary to a campaign aiming to eliminate Serbia from the war. These strategic issues became focal points in the campaign against Falkenhayn's direction of the war. The campaign began with Bethmann's unsuccessful attempt in December 1915 to have Falkenhayn relieved of office and continued until the general's downfall was accomplished in August 1916.

Whether OHL turned to the west or the east, no way beckoned to escape the superiority of Allied resources, the pressure of the Allied armies, and the gradually increasing constriction of the British blockade. The struggle for the disposition of the dwindling military assets intensified the friction between the opposing parties over the problems raised by the position of the German bloc as a beleaguered fortress foreclosed from any likely road to decisive victory.

2. SIEGE WARFARE IN THE WEST

After 1914 the next stage of the war on land brought the Allies almost unrelieved disappointment and failures in every theater. The Central Pow-

12. Max Hoffmann, the actual planner of operations for Hindenburg and Ludendorff, made famous the phrase "the war of lost opportunities," in the easterners' denunciation of Falkenhayn's conduct of the war.

ers won a succession of victories, yet at the close of 1915 they were as far from ending the war on their terms as ever.

The German high command in 1915 had intended a large-scale offensive in the west, with the aim of doing sufficient damage to the Allies that they would see the hopelessness of continuing the war. Falkenhayn was reluctantly diverted from this purpose by the danger that Austria might cave in under Russian pressure after its ill-fated winter campaign in the Carpathians. In April he came to a final decision for transferring the major operations and direction of the war to the east. At the same time he was resolved on a tooth-and-nail defense in the west.[13]

The plans for Allied operations in the west were determined by Joffre, with the ardent support of Foch. Joffre incarnated the national will in fixing his unchanging purpose in this sense: "The major and best part of the German army was on our soil and the salient of its battle line was only a five days' march from the heart of France. This fact dictated to us, to us French, our duty. It is this enemy it is necessary to strike and throw back. . . . All other actions must be only eccentric to this main operation."[14] So guided, Joffre planned offensives for 1915 by concentric attacks from Artois and Champagne on the huge salient between them held by the Germans. The objective of cutting off the salient continued to be the basic French strategy to the end of the war.[15]

The French insistence on this paramount purpose controlled the conduct of the war by the Allies and relegated any other operational ideas to secondary importance; subordinated British interests to the French, maritime to continental; and accounted for the tremendous sacrifice of men and materiel on the Western Front in 1915, when the overall situation was still fluid enough for a flexible strategy to have realized opportunities at the Dardanelles. Nevertheless, when all is said and done, the question remains whether any other strategic emphasis was compatible with the solidarity of the alliance.

The Germans were the best prepared and the British the worst in 1915 for the trench warfare of the Western Front. The Germans had overcome the problem of munitions scarcity by the spring of 1915. They had in-

13. Falkenhayn, *German General Staff*, 64–65, 220.
14. Joffre, *Mémoires*, 1–2.
15. B. H. Liddell Hart, *Foch* (Boston, 1932), 169. For a sympathetic discussion of the French strategy, see John Terraine, *Douglas Haig: The Educated Soldier* (London, 1963), 125–29.

creased the distribution of heavy guns, taking many from fortresses to do so, and had equipped their troops with trench mortars, efficient and suitable hand grenades, flamethrowers, periscopes, mining equipment, and demolition explosives. They were beginning to understand, sooner than the Allies, that the current conflict was a contest in the effective utilization of mechanized production and technology in the service of war as well as in the adjustment of tactical methods of defense to modern weapons.[16]

The British steadily sent to the front fresh divisions from the Territorial Force, Kitchener's New Army, and Canada. By July 1915 they had moved twenty-one divisions to France and added a third army to the two into which the BEF had been reorganized at the end of 1914. Haig was placed in command of the First Army, and blunt, brusque Sir William Robertson, who had risen from the ranks, was made chief of staff for all the British forces in France.[17] The British soldiers had to improvise trench weapons during much of 1915. The French were in better shape but also had to improvise or make do with trench weapons poorly adapted to the purpose. The French, however, progressed rapidly during 1915 in the production of munitions, guns, and other materiel. The British did not solve the critical problem of munitions supply until 1916.[18]

After the fruitless winter offensives of the French in Artois and Champagne, the French and British projected a combined assault beginning in March. But when the British took over a section of the French line, Haig's First Army attacked alone at Neuve Chapelle (March 10). The objective was to prepare the way for a subsequent advance on the industrial city of Lille. The battle set a pattern that would be repeated many times thereafter. The British made methodical preparation and conducted a short but

16. *Der Weltkrieg,* 8: 95–97; Falkenhayn, *German General Staff,* 49.
17. Sir John French desired General Sir Henry Wilson to be chief of staff. Wilson, like French an Irishman, spoke fluent French and got on well with both Joffre and Foch; he was well suited for the difficult job of explaining British and French military men to each other. Because of previous involvement in Irish politics, Wilson was distrusted by the government, which insisted on appointing Sir William Robertson. These two generals, along with Haig, played the leading roles in the British military direction of the war. Two authoritative biographies may be noted: Basil Collier, *Brasshat: A Biography of Field Marshal Sir Henry Wilson* (London, 1961); and Bonham-Carter's study of Robertson, *Soldier True,* appearing in the American edition under the title of *The Strategy of Victory, 1914–1918* (New York, 1964).
18. Edmonds, *Short History of World War I,* 81–82; Lloyd George, *War Memoirs,* 1: 485–86; Lt. Colonel Fliecx, *Les quatres batailles de France, 1914, 1918, 1940, 1944* (Paris, 1958), 46–50.

hurricane bombardment—the most intensive per yard up to that time. The blow breached the German lines in the center, though the British were unable to exploit the penetration before the Germans brought up reinforcements and counterattacked. The machinery ran down when the initial set-program was played out.[19]

The French tried and failed in April to push back the St. Mihiel salient, and the Germans shortly afterwards attempted a limited initiative in the second battle of Ypres against both British and French forces. In the west the Germans were generally on the defensive during 1915, except for this attack and related activity on a wide front cloaking their preparations for the Gorlice strike of May in the east. Though the diversionary effort was the main purpose, the Germans desired locally to eliminate the Ypres salient if they could. The battle owes its place in history to the introduction of gas warfare in the west. Chlorine gas was released from cylinders in the trenches before the infantry moved forward and opened a gap of four and a half miles. Canadian and British reserves were rushed up to fill the breach, however thinly. The Allies restored a line largely because the Germans, regarding the new weapon with deep distrust and using it on an experimental basis, were not prepared to exploit a breakthrough they never expected. The Germans continued the attack, releasing gas several times, while the British endeavored to defend every inch of ground and even recover that already lost no matter what the cost. That cost was a massacre.[20]

In the combined spring offensive (May 9–June 18) the French attacked north of Arras. Their assault, following six days of concentrated bombardment, made a break into the German lines, throwing the German rear into disarray. The French command in this fugitive moment of success could not bring up reserves with sufficient speed and strength before the Germans filled in the gap with theirs. The combat then settled down to a grinding business of attack and counterattack for the remainder of the

19. Terraine, *Douglas Haig,* 139–45; Alan Clark, *The Donkeys* (London, 1961), 48–73. On the battles and generalship of the British on the Western Front in 1915, two opposing views are offered in these two works. The title of the latter derives from the remark of General Max Hoffmann that the British were "lions led by donkeys." It presents a severe critique, while Terraine's book makes a very affirmative defense of the Western Front approach and the commanders executing that strategy.

20. *Der Weltkrieg,* 8: 38–49; Falkenhayn, *German General Staff,* 94; B. H. Liddell Hart, *The Real War, 1914–1918* (Boston, 1930), 175–85; Liddell Hart, *Foch,* 174–81; Clark, *Donkeys,* 78–101.

second battle of Artois.[21] Haig's attempt to take Aubers Ridge, still farther north beyond La Bassée canal, was an expensive replay of Neuve Chapelle.[22]

In addition to the superior firepower of the German heavy artillery and machine guns, two chief factors accounted for the success in halting the Allied spring offensive. The first was the progressive construction of an elaborate structure of field fortifications in which a front position of complex structure including wide breastworks, shelters, dugouts, and machine gun redoubts was supplemented by a second similar zone at least two kilometers in the rear. Thus began a race, which was to continue until 1918, between the daily growth, based on current experience, in the solidity of the German defensive organization and the constant expansion of the Allied offensive materiel.[23] The second ingredient in the improved defenses of the Germans came from an operational mobility attained through building a network of military railways behind the lines and extending the system of roads in the area.

The futility of the spring offensive produced both military and political consequences. Militarily, Haig concluded that "a long methodical bombardment" was necessary to demolish the enemy's strengthened defensive system. Henceforth, during the next two years, the element of surprise obtained through a short hurricane bombardment lost its importance to destruction of the enemy's position in preparing the attack. The Allied commands were certain now that victory escaped them because of the insufficiency of troops and guns; they would consequently overcome the enemy if they accumulated more men and munitions for the next attack. A strong, fresh stimulus was given to the concentration of ever more guns, shells, and divisions on the Western Front.[24]

Among the political repercussions was a storm of criticism that was blowing up against Joffre and his headquarters staff in the officer corps, in the parliament, and with the public. The vehement attacks of Georges Clemenceau and others against Joffre, the minister of war Alexandre Millerand, and the general headquarters obliged Joffre to reorganize his

21. Joffre, *Mémoires*, 76–80; Liddell Hart, *Foch*, 182–86.
22. Blake, *Private Papers of Douglas Haig*, 92–93; Terraine, *Douglas Haig*, 148–49; Clark, *Donkeys*, 115–27.
23. *Der Weltkrieg*, 8: 56, 96–98; Fliecx, *Les quatres batailles*, 45.
24. Blake, *Private Papers of Douglas Haig*, 93; Terraine, *Douglas Haig*, 148; Liddell Hart, *Foch*, 189.

command and establish a more effective liaison with the individual armies and the army group commanders. The first signs of disaffection with the war were manifested in letters sent to the French president.[25]

In Britain the political fallout commenced with a scandal over the shortage of shells, which was agitated in the press. The newspaper baron Lord Northcliffe set off a press campaign with the purpose of getting the production of munitions moving and bringing about the downfall of Kitchener. The shell scandal did not in itself produce the cabinet crisis of May, but it was instrumental in creating a ministry of munitions headed by the human dynamo Lloyd George in the new coalition government.[26]

Joffre's offensive in the fall was planned through simultaneous attacks in Champagne and Artois to achieve a strategic breakthrough in both places. The French made their main thrust between Reims and the Argonne on September 25 in the second battle of Champagne. The assault forces, using gas and smoke after a drumfire bombardment of three days, stormed through the German front line and reached the rear position. The Germans surmounted this serious break in their defenses by applying new methods of defense in depth. In the new tactics the main resistance was put up in the second position by means of artillery drawn back to that line and stubborn counterattacks. The advancing French, having taken the German front line already largely destroyed by their own artillery preparation, were exposed without cover to the German artillery fire and counterattacking infantry. This method of defense cost the Allies heavily until 1918, when they in turn applied it against the Germans.

Joffre was soon forced to halt the slaughter, and resumption of the assault (October 6–14) was stopped quickly with trifling gain. The northern prong of the French offensive in the third battle of Artois (September 25–October 13) met with much the same fortune.

The British share in the combined offensive was "the unwanted battle" of Loos, between Lens and La Bassée. Sir John French and Haig disagreed with Joffre's plan and regarded the site for the British action in the Arras strike as unfavorable. Both the cabinet and high command desired to hold to the defensive until the British army was considerably more strength-

25. Raymond Poincaré, *Au service de la France,* 11 vols. (Paris, 1926–74), 6: 239–307 passim.

26. The factors involved in the causes and results of the shell scandal are reliably weighed from an inside knowledge by Lord Beaverbrook, *Politicians and the War, 1914–1916* (Garden City, N.Y., 1928), 87–95.

ened with troops, guns, and munitions. Kitchener, stressing the need to relieve the Russians and French, had to intervene with the British commander-in-chief to overcome his reluctance to attack.[27]

In the battle of Loos, Haig's infantry rush, preceded by a long artillery bombardment, took the enemy's first position, even breaking into the second line at some points. But Haig's divisions could not exploit the initial success, and the Germans, bringing up their reserves faster than the British, reinforced their second position and counterattacked successfully. After appalling carnage the normal state of deadlock settled down again on the front except for a new fruitless attack on October 13.[28]

The unfortunate fall offensive reaped a quarter million casualties for the Allies to 150,000 for the Germans and caused changes in the direction of the war. The battle of Loos provides a classical case of the difficulties experienced in coalition cooperation and the sacrifice of one ally's interests for another's. The clamor in France for Joffre's dismissal set off an effort to lessen his influence on operations in the west. This was done by spreading his activities from the command of the forces in France to the command of all the French forces. At the same time a new chief of the general staff was appointed, General Edouard de Castelnau, who was an army group commander opposed to extravagant offensives. The headquarters staff was purged of those more prominently associated with the plans for past offensives. The political shock effect replaced the ministry of René Viviani with a cabinet headed by Aristide Briand. The new premier supplanted the minister of war, Millerand, with Galliéni.[29]

In Britain the conduct of Sir John French at Loos forced his recall. Indignation flared up over his control of reserves so that Haig could not draw on them at the critical moment of the battle, and the army lost confidence in the methods and qualifications of the commander-in-chief. Haig replaced him as head of the British armies in France. The position of Kitchener, whose standing in the cabinet was already in decline, could not withstand the twin blows of Loos and Gallipoli. His sweeping powers as chief of the War Office were drastically reduced to the control of

27. Guinn, *British Strategy and Politics,* 89–90; Blake, *Private Papers of Douglas Haig,* 101–02.
28. See Liddell Hart, *Real War,* 186–88; Clark, *Donkeys,* 147–74.
29. On casualties, see Otto, Schmiedel, and Schnitter, *Der Erste Weltkrieg,* 98; Kielmansegg, *Deutschland und der Erste Weltkrieg,* 97; David Thomson, *England in the Twentieth Century, 1914–63* (London, 1964), 33; Clark, *Donkeys,* 1, 173. On political changes in France: Poincaré, *Au service de la France,* 7: 209–11; Liddell Hart, *Foch,* 209–10.

administrative affairs. The newly appointed chief of the imperial general staff, Sir William Robertson, formerly chief of staff of the command in France, henceforth determined military policy and became the actual military adviser of the cabinet and War Committee.[30]

The Allied campaign in 1915 reflected the offensive doctrine of the prewar French general staff and the unwarranted optimism of staff officers at general headquarters, not the French generals at the front. The tenacious attachment of western high commands to the illusion of attack and the repeated performances of the same piece made 1915 the most costly year of the war for the Allies. The French casualties swelled to 1,500,000 and the British to 300,000 in France. The successive massacres of the French soldiers without apparent effect on the course of the conflict, combined with the hardships of waging total war, caused some desire for peace in the French population. Among the poilus, the losses instilled hatred and scorn for all staff officers (the *embusqués* or "slackers").[31]

Though the fighting had the static quality of siege warfare, the conduct of war forged ahead rapidly in 1915. Besides the introduction of various kinds of gas and means of delivery, as well as the German innovations in defense, conspicuous progress was made in the broader military application of the airplane and in the more effective work of the artillery.[32] The Allies developed a standardized pattern of attack. It was prepared by a drumfire bombardment of some days, planned to demolish the front line of the enemy, accompanied by the release of gas and smoke, and carried out by three dense waves of infantry, each of which had its own function to perform. The battles of 1915 demonstrated that the set piece planned in advance could be staged successfully to the point of break-in, but the problem remained unsolved how to convert a break-in into a breakthrough. The elaborate German structure of defense, depending on one or two positions back of the front line and on defense in depth, together with the operational mobility of the Germans, rendered their front impregnable unless an overwhelming mass of men and guns was accumulated or unless a new weapon was devised for exploitation of the

30. Blake, *Private Papers of Douglas Haig,* 105–18; Sir William Robertson, *Soldiers and Statesmen,* 2 vols. (London, 1926), 1: 164–71.

31. Liddell Hart, *Foch,* 172, 188–89; Richard M. Watt, *Dare Call It Treason* (New York, 1963), 90–91.

32. On advances in aviation, see Harald Penrose, *British Aviation: The Great War and Armistice, 1915–1919* (London, 1969), 15 ff.; Andrew Boyle, *Trenchard* (New York, 1962), 153–57; Quentin Reynolds, *They Fought for the Sky* (New York, 1957), 4–16.

breakthrough. The problem of the breakthrough battle yielded to solution only in 1918, when both a decisively superior mass and a new weapon of exploitation, in the form of the tank, belonged to one side.

In the big offensives of 1915 the Allies never gained their objectives, or even any ground of consequence, in following the stereotyped and costly pattern of the breakthrough attempt. In justifying the continuation of the futile slaughter-matches, the Allied high commands enunciated a strategy of attrition, or *grignotage,* that is, "killing Germans" until the German government surrendered.[33] But the Allies suffered more deaths than the Germans in every Allied offensive of 1915. There were signs already that attrition could hurt the French sooner than the Germans; at the end of 1915 the French army had lost much of its élan and fighting power.

3. THE DRIVE OF THE GERMAN BLOC IN THE EAST

The largest operational movement and change of front during the period of hotly debated strategy occurred in the east. The Russian position at the end of campaigning in 1914 became the point of departure for the operations of both Russia and the Central Powers. The Russian armies had pushed the Germans back to the Masurian lakes in East Prussia, regained most of Galicia to the Dunajec line, and advanced into the Carpathians and Bukovina. The Russians planned a resumption of the offensive both from the Carpathian line and in East Prussia.

The Central Powers also decided to undertake offensives in the Carpathians and the Masurian area. The decisions were reached after an open clash between Falkenhayn on the one hand and the eastern command, Conrad, and Bethmann Hollweg on the other over the allocation of forces to the eastern theater. The conflict centered on the disposition of four newly formed German corps, which Falkenhayn desired to use in a spring offensive in the west. The differences brought on two leadership crises, jeopardizing retention of his position before the issue was resolved.

Falkenhayn yielded in January to the plans urged by Conrad and supported by the eastern command for conducting a gigantic pincers movement through concurrent offensives on the southern and northern flanks. Falkenhayn assigned the four new corps to the eastern command and reinforced the Austrian front in the Carpathians with German divisions. Apart from the German internal pressure on him, he came to this conclusion out

33. *Grignotage* came from Joffre's expression, *je les grignote* (I will nibble them away).

of concern for the precarious Austrian situation and from the need for a striking military success to impress the neutrals in southern Europe.[34]

The eastern campaign began with winter battles on the Carpathian front and in East Prussia. In the south, Conrad, with the aid of a newly formed Southern Army composed of both German and Austrian troops, commenced a push through the central Carpathians at the end of January. His objective was to envelop the bulk of the Russian forces in Galicia and relieve the besieged fortress of Przemyśl. The deep snow and extreme cold of the Carpathian ridges exacted a terrible toll from both sides, in men exhausted, sick, and frozen to death. Conrad failed in his efforts to drive through the Carpathians and relieve Przemyśl.[35]

The Russian counteroffensive moved ahead during this time. Przemyśl fell to the Russians on March 22, with the surrender of 120,000 men. Its capture, freeing the besieging army, enabled the Russians to gain a numerical superiority in the Carpathians. Attacked by the Germans in East Prussia, the Russians abandoned intentions of a spring offensive along the northern flank. Their armies, then concentrating pressure in the southwest, advanced to a few miles from Cracow and drove the Austrians back in the Carpathians. By the beginning of April the Russian forces had slogged through the remaining mountains, despite the acute suffering from the cold, and the Hungarian plain lay before them.

The collapse of the Austrian front and a break into Hungary were averted by the use of the Southern Army and German reinforcements, as well as by the crippling shortage of Russian rifles and munitions. In the second half of April these factors, together with the strain and exhaustion caused by the arduous winter campaign, compelled the Russians to pause in their attack on the Carpathian front. Both combatants had worn out the forces engaged and paid an enormous price in casualties: 600,000–800,000 by the Austrians and more than a million by the Russians. The Carpathian disaster aroused disaffection among the subject nationalities of the Dual Empire and undermined the structure of the army.

In the north, the eastern command anticipated the projected spring offensive of the Russians in East Prussia by setting in motion a maneuver of double envelopment against both wings of the Russian Tenth Army. In the biting wind and drifting snow of February two German armies attacked and within two weeks surrounded the greater part of the Tenth

34. *Der Weltkrieg,* 8: 617–20; Stone, *Eastern Front,* 109–11.
35. On the winter war in the Carpathians, see Kiszling, *Österreich-Ungarns Anteil am Ersten Weltkrieg,* 27–28; Otto, Schmiedel, and Schnitter, *Der Erste Weltkrieg,* 78–84.

Army in a forest near Grodno. Operating against the Russians were their inept command and poor intelligence, as well as their inadequate methods of defense. The change from snow to impassable mud and floods prevented a breakthrough, and the German success was of only tactical effect. Even so the British military observer General Knox considered this to be "the worst thing since Tannenberg."[36] By April the Russians had assembled superior numbers in the area, and the fighting quieted down. The Germans, threatened in their extended flank, pulled back, with East Prussia cleared of the invader except for the Memel district. The incalculable catastrophe for the Central Powers in the Carpathians outweighed, however, Ludendorff's gains in the north; Falkenhayn's judgment that the winter offensive would be imprudent and unprofitable was vindicated.[37]

Falkenhayn and Conrad agreed in April to attempt a breakthrough in the Gorlice-Tarnopol area, east of Cracow. The immediate purpose was to relieve the hard-pressed Austrians on the Carpathian front, but both chiefs were anxious, with the Central Powers on the defensive in the west and at the Dardanelles as well, to realize the larger objective of doing irreparable damage to the Russian war machine. Conrad saw a chance thereby to gain a free hand for dealing with Italy, and Falkenhayn to make forces available for a campaign against Serbia. Falkenhayn hoped, moreover, that an operation of the scale planned by OHL would allow him a greater direction of military affairs in the east and a reduction in the autonomous power of the eastern command.

For this action OHL, making the most careful preparation and striving for complete secrecy, gathered a striking force in the area composed of two armies of seasoned troops, one predominantly of German soldiers from the Western Front and the other Austrian with a stiffening of Germans. They were placed under the command of General August von Mackensen, subject to the formal authority of the Austrians and the real direction of OHL. The eastern command assisted with several diversionary attacks but only carried on the invasion of Lithuania and Courland as a sustained drive, engaging a concentration of large Russian forces.

The assault began on May 2, with a shattering barrage of superior artillery. The ill-constructed Russian defenses, having only shallow trenches and no dugouts, were soon flattened; the Russian artillery was almost entirely silenced. Within three days the strength of the attack and the

36. *With the Russian Army*, 1: 241.
37. Hoffmann, *War Diaries*, 2: 85–97; Stone, *Eastern Front*, 116–19.

Russian weaknesses allowed a breakthrough between Gorlice and Tar-nów. The Germans and Austrians were utilizing the methods learned in combat on the Western Front, notably in the effective use of artillery in cooperation with the infantry. The defending Russian army lacked suffi-cient reserves because of rivalry between the army group commanders in the northwest and the southwest. Nor was there mobility to transfer reserves quickly to the critical point. Gorlice and Tarnów fell, and the withering storm forced the Russians to retire on a front from the Carpathi-ans to the Vistula. Everywhere they tried to impede the onslaught of the enemy by destroying railways, roads, and bridges. The German and Aus-trian armies swept onward, however, crossing the San River on May 17 and taking the fortress of Przemyśl on June 3. The capture of Lvov on June 22 separated the Russian fronts in Galicia and Poland, ending the first phase of the drive.[38]

By midyear the eastern offensive of the Central Powers had thrown back the immense Russian effort to bring about the final defeat and elimi-nation of Austria. Galicia with its oil wells was largely regained. The Lithuanian areas were invaded, and most of Courland occupied. Russia sustained huge losses in men—more than 400,000 prisoners alone, irre-placeable trained troops, and hardly less irreplaceable arms, equipment, and supplies. Austria was now free to send sufficient forces to Italy for establishing a strong defensive position along the Isonzo. Turkey was saved from a prospective attack by the Odessa army, which the Russians were obliged to rush to Galicia. Bulgaria was moved further toward the Central Powers, and Romania delayed in entering on the side of the Allies. The victories lifted the morale on the home front in Austria-Hungary and revived the sinking confidence of the Austrian troops after the bitter and useless suffering in the "ice-hell of the Carpathians." Ger-many had so strengthened its position in relation to Russia that the chan-cellor on the proposal of Falkenhayn made overtures for a separate peace, but without success.[39]

The German and Austrian commands continued the eastern drive, with

38. Falkenhayn, *German General Staff*, 89–101; Stone, *Eastern Front*, 129–43; May, *Passing of the Hapsburg Monarchy*, 1: 107–08; Kielmansegg, *Deutschland und der Erste Weltkrieg*, 82–83; Otto, Schmiedel, and Schnitter, *Der Erste Weltkrieg*, 85–87.

39. Falkenhayn, *German General Staff*, 115; Kiszling, *Österreich-Ungarns Anteil am Ersten Weltkrieg*, 34; May, *Passing of the Hapsburg Monarchy*, 1: 109; *Schicksalsjahre Österreiches, 1908–1919: Das politische Tagebuch Josef Redlichs*, ed. Fritz Fellner, 2 vols. (Graz, 1953–54), 2: 36, 47.

THE EAST, 1914–1918

Farthest Russian
Advance in 1914

Advance of the Central
Powers in 1915

Line after Brusilov's
Advance and the
Romanian Campaign

Advance of the Central
Powers before the Treaty
of Brest-Litovsk

Political Boundary

0	100	200	300	400	500	Km.
0		100		200		300	Mi.

•Vaasa

FINLAND

Viipuri •

GULF OF FINLAND

•Tallinn

ESTONIA

Lake
Peipus

RUSSIA

Gulf of
Riga

LIVONIA

•Cecis

•Riga

LATGALE

Liepaja •

COURLAND

Dvinsk •

Dvina R.

•Memel

LITHUANIANS

Niemen R.

Kovno •

Lake
Naroch

Gumbinnen •

Vilna •

•Minsk

BALTIC SEA

Masurian
Lakes

Grodno •

Vistula R.

•Tannenberg

Narew R.

•Baranovici

Thorn •

Pripet
Marshes

Pripet R.

GERMANY

POSEN

•Novogeorgievsk

Brest-Litovsk

VOLHYNIA

Lowicz •

•Warsaw

SILESIA

•Lodz

Ivanogorod

Kovel •

Kiev •

POLAND

Lublin •

Bug R.

Kielce •

•Krasnik

•Lutsk

Cholm •

San R.

CRACOW •

Tarnow •

Lvov •

Przemysl •

Tarnopol •

•Gorlice

GALICIA

Sereth R.

Dunajec R.

CARPATHIAN MTS.

Dniester R.

Danube R.

CARPATHO-
UKRAINE

•Czernowitz

BUKOVINA

BESSARABIA

Tisza R.

MOLDAVIA

•Jassy

•Odessa

AUSTRIA-HUNGARY

TRANSYLVANIA

Pruth R.

ROMANIA

BLACK
SEA

BOSNIA

WALLACHIA

•Bucharest

Danube R.

ADRIATIC
SEA

MONTENEGRO

SERBIA

BULGARIA

efforts to knock off the Polish salient. At this point a conflict arose between Falkenhayn and the eastern command over the direction of the major thrust and the part the latter's armies would play in the campaign from this time on. Falkenhayn proposed to attain the Polish objective by the coordinated attacks of three forces: Mackensen's three Austrian and German armies advancing from the Galician front in the valley of the San River northward toward Lublin and Brest-Litovsk; another army under General Max von Gallwitz moving southward across the Narew River to the east of Warsaw to form a junction with Mackensen's armies; and a third force exerting pressure west of Warsaw. Ludendorff and Hoffmann insisted that the drive now be concentrated in the extreme north, toward Kovno and Vilna, with the aim of completing a wide pincers operation with the troops before Warsaw.

Apprehensive of the danger in the west and the uncertain situation in the Balkans, Falkenhayn desired to avoid involvements in the depths of Russia, while inflicting such damage that Germany "would not have much to fear from this opponent for an appreciable time."[40] Supported by the kaiser, Falkenhayn's more limited proposals prevailed. But the well of bitterness between Falkenhayn and the Hindenburg-Ludendorff pair was deepened. The struggle over their relative authority and the control of troops for purposes of reinforcement persisted throughout the remainder of the campaign.[41]

The three-pronged drive was launched with the attack of the Gallwitz group on July 12. The whole Polish operation was supported by advances on the flanks of Hindenburg's soldiers in Courland and the Austrians in Galicia. The front commands of the Russians had realized this danger and suggested a strategic retreat to a shorter, more defensible line, freeing frontline troops for reserves, but Stavka could not face up to this bold step. The pounding by Mackensen's army group smashed a breakthrough from the south, and the massed artillery of Gallwitz's forces blasted a breakthrough toward the Narew. On the Narew front coordination failed between two Russian armies, and the movement of reserves was mismanaged. The effect in each case was worsened by the shortage of shells. Nevertheless, the Russian resistance, strengthened with increasing num-

40. Falkenhayn, *German General Staff*, 116.
41. On the differences over eastern strategy, see *Der Weltkrieg*, 8: 340–51; Falkenhayn, *German General Staff*, 141–45, 158–67; Janssen, *Der Kanzler und der General*, 135–37, 154–57.

bers of troops, prevented the relentless push of the German and Austrian armies from closing a loop around the forces in Poland, as Stavka finally yielded to the necessity of a general retreat on the several fronts. One city and fortress after another fell to the drive of the Central Powers: Lublin on July 30, Warsaw on August 5, Kovno on August 17, Novogeorgievsk on August 19, Brest-Litovsk on August 26, and Grodno on September 2.[42] Mackensen's and Gallwitz's armies effected a common line but could do no more than conduct a frontal pursuit of the retreating Russians, who carried out a skillful retreat. Falkenhayn claimed that if Hindenburg had made more divisions available for Gallwitz's assault group, the envelopment would likely have succeeded; the eastern command insisted that if the main attack had been made in the extreme north, toward Vilna, an annihilating defeat could have been inflicted on the Russian armies.[43]

In opposition to Ludendorff's project for a great northern attack, Falkenhayn now ended the drive of OHL on the Russian front. His armies had outrun their railway communications, creating an overwhelming supply problem, and had worn down their offensive power by the long campaign. Above all, Falkenhayn was concerned about strengthening German defenses in the west in anticipating the September offensive of the Allies and was intent on assembling forces for an attack in Serbia. He agreed, however, to the further operations of the eastern command in the north and of the Austrians in the south.

The eastern offensive of the Central Powers therefore continued only on the flanks in September. Hindenburg made a new advance toward Vilna with the eastern command's favorite objective of turning the Russian flank. The Russians, having learned from the previous German operations, now eluded the trap by means of withdrawals, shortening of the front, and the shift of troops to the most threatened sector. The Germans could do no more than occupy Vilna. The eastern command contended that the push had started too late and with insufficient strength; it charged that a second great opportunity (after that of November 1914) was missed for a final blow. In the south, Conrad attempted to recover the part of eastern Galicia still held by the Russians. After initial successes the Austrians were repulsed by Russian counterattacks, and German reinforcements were necessary to secure the front without substantial gain. The flanking

42. See Stone, *Eastern Front*, 174–83.
43. Hoffmann, *War Diaries*, 2: 121.

campaigns contributed nothing of importance to the German bloc's record of success and should never have been attempted so late in the year with the limited reserves available to the Central Powers. Falkenhayn's strategic views were again demonstrated to be sound.[44] The long eastern war of movement in 1915 ended at this point. The front, which had been straightened out, reached from near Riga to near Czernowitz; the Russians had lost most of Galicia, Poland, Lithuania, and parts of Latvia and Belorussia. Falkenhayn had largely achieved his limited aims. The Russian military machine was irrevocably weakened, even though the Russian armies had escaped annihilation and Russia was still in the war. The eastern drive brought the greatest victories for the German bloc at any time of the war. Falkenhayn had also kept the Entente in the west at bay in resisting the major offensives of the Allies. In the fall Falkenhayn's diplomatic and military policies triumphed in the Balkans. All of these gains he achieved with a minimum of military reserves.

The long season of disaster wrought profound effects in Russia. Petrograd received a shock from the imminence of danger when at the height of the enemy's advance the tsar's government took steps to remove the archives and gold reserves from the capital.[45] The court camarilla made a scapegoat, not without cause, of the commander-in-chief, Grand Duke Nicholas, for the catastrophic reverses.[46] The tsar assumed supreme command of the Russian army, leaving the capital to establish himself at Stavka on September 5. The grand duke was sent off in discredit to govern the Caucasus. The actual direction of the army fell on General Michael V. Alekseev, a conscientious, hard-working, and well-informed soldier, who became the new chief of the general staff. This step would fasten on the tsar the stigma of responsibility for future defeats and strengthen the impression that the government in Petrograd was more than ever under the control of the tsarina Alexandra and the court camarilla.

The disasters at the front laid bare the creeping breakdown of the

44. Ibid., 2: 118–25; Falkenhayn, *German General Staff*, 169–70; Janssen, *Der Kanzler und der General*, 157.

45. Buchanan, *My Mission to Russia*, 1: 237; Basil Gourko, *War and Revolution in Russia, 1914–1917* (New York, 1919), 147.

46. A. A. Noskoff, *Mit der russischen Dampfwalze* (Berlin, 1939), 98–99, 198–99, ascribes to Grand Duke Nicholas excitable and violent tendencies, a lack of method and direction as commander-in-chief, and neglect of the work of the general staff and disturbance of its functions. Stone, *Eastern Front,* considers him a figurehead at the supreme command and Stavka under his head an illusion of supreme direction. See especially p. 52.

Russian army. The soldiers of 1915 were penalized by the deplorable scarcity of rifles, guns, and shells. The cruelest need of all was in rifles; soldiers often had to go to the front without arms until comrades with rifles had fallen. The scarcity of shells, which was the most critical of any year in the war, often kept batteries silent in the face of German artillery fire and forced infantry to attack without adequate or even any artillery preparation. In the words of a Russian officer, "The munitions shortage is bleeding the Russian army to death." The army also suffered from lapses in organization and planning. This was notably apparent in the failure to build defense positions in advance to which retreating units might fall back, slackness in constructing trenches, and inefficiency in handling railways and rolling stock. The drastic reduction in the number of well-trained and experienced officers made it impossible to supply officer replacements of adequate quality for the front and staffs; the dearth of noncommissioned officers was serious; a mutual lack of faith between officers and men increasingly divided them from each other; reserves were constantly insufficient; command was too often badly at fault. Under these conditions of "cannon-fodder tactics" losses shot up to inordinately high levels, along with numerous desertions and extensive malingering. During 1915 the total number of prisoners reached over one million, and there were as many killed and wounded if not more.[47]

The striking successes of the German armies were owing largely to their immense technical superiority over those of backward Russia, their capacity for efficient organization, and their skill in maneuver with masses of men. The Russians saw these strengths daily translating into astonishing military feats. The experience imbued the Germans with a psychological ascendancy over them. The notion was borne in that the Germans were more than the ordinary breed of men, certainly more than the Austrians, and "could do anything." The whole situation facing the Russian soldier in the summer of 1915 raised the question whether it was of any use to continue the fighting.[48]

47. Knox, *With the Russian Army*, 1: 217–350 passim; Buchanan, *My Mission to Russia*, 1: 236–37; Gourko, *War and Revolution in Russia*, 129–34; *Die internationalen Beziehungen im Zeitalter des Imperialismus: Dokumente aus den Archiven der zarischen und der provisorischen Regierung,* ed. M. N. Pokrovskii for the Russian and Otto Hoetzsch for the German edition, series 2, vol. 8, pt. 1 (Berlin, 1936), 321 (hereafter cited as *Die internationalen Beziehungen*); Stone, *Eastern Front,* 165–71.

48. Knox, *With the Russian Army*, 1: 349; Falkenhayn, *German General Staff,* 33; Noskoff, *Mit der russischen Dampfwalze,* 90–92, 116; *Die internationalen Beziehungen,* 103.

Chapter Five

THE PERIPHERAL WAR

1. THE STRUGGLE FOR THE SOUTHERN FLANK

THE major operations requiring the principal expenditure of men and materiel were conducted on the Western Front and in the eastern theater. A conflict of less intensity was waged on the southern flank of the primary theaters, in Europe and the Ottoman Empire, on the northern flank in the North Sea, and on the far oceans. This was the peripheral war, although the grinding effects of the Allied blockade and the consequences of the submarine campaign were by no means peripheral in significance. The peripheral war focused on the struggle for the southern flank in Italy and the Balkans, the campaign at the Dardanelles, and the course of the fight at sea.

The two camps contended actively along the southern flank in both the diplomatic and military arenas. Here Germany and Austria, completely isolated as belligerent states at the onset of the war, saw an opportunity to fashion a more powerful coalition. On the other hand, the Allies grasped at the possibility of organizing a solid anti-German bloc from Italy to the Middle East. After the victorious drive of Germany and Austria against Russia, France attached importance to a flanking movement of the Italians and Romanians by way of diverting the Germans from concentration on the western theater.[1] The diplomatic contest ended in 1916 essentially in a draw, with Turkey and Bulgaria having joined the Central Powers and Italy and Romania the Allied side. The varied struggle on the southern flank expanded widely in 1915 with the Isonzo battles after Italy's entry, the participation of Bulgaria in the war, the campaign against Serbia, the Allied operations from the Salonika base, and the fateful venture at the Dardanelles.

Italy joined the Allies after nine months of negotiations with both coalitions. Since the Marne, Premier Antonio Salandra favored eventual intervention on the side of the Entente.[2] His ministry made it clear to the

1. See *Die internationalen Beziehungen,* 182.
2. Antonio Salandra, *Italy and the Great War* (London, 1932), 94–97, 222, 279; Renzi, "Italian Neutrality," 1423–24.

Central Powers that continued neutrality must be purchased with compensations. There was no objection when the Italians expressed interest in the Albania area around Valona, which they occupied on December 25, 1914. The Austrians resisted the suggested transfer of the Trentino, though the German ambassador at Rome, Prince Bernhard von Bülow, let the Italian foreign minister, Sidney Sonnino, understand that he would work for the cession. Vienna was incensed at Bülow's "machinations."[3]

Rome's indications that its intentions extended far beyond the Trentino warned Bülow that little or no chance existed of coming to a settlement with the Italian ministry. The ambassador then set out to overthrow Salandra's government through alliance with Giovanni Giolitti and bring this neutralist to power. Giolitti offered Italy the policy choice of *parecchio* —of obtaining "a good deal" by negotiations while avoiding the risks of Salandra's course of intervention. But Austria must pay the cost with substantial concessions to make *parecchio* worthwhile. Austria followed a temporizing policy and thereafter a hard line against both Italian demands and German pressures until March 1915. When forced by its military reverses to yield, Vienna agreed to cede the Trentino and subsequently to rectify the Isonzo frontier. The offer was insufficient.[4]

The conversations with the Entente produced a clash of rival imperialisms. Salandra's government stubbornly sought "absolute security" against a future Serbian or Yugoslav predominance in the Adriatic and against Russian power at the Straits, as well as bases for economic penetration in the Balkans. Russia resisted in the endeavor to protect the interests of a Greater Serbia or a future Yugoslav state. Britain and France supported Italy on most of the differences. Against this front Sazonov was obliged, in bitter resentment, to concede on one point after another until he had sacrificed much in defense of South Slav ethnic and security claims. Italy, however, gave up its demand for Fiume, and Sazonov was in some

3. See Alberto Monticone, *La Germania e la neutralità italiana, 1914-15* (Bologna, 1971), for the latest and most comprehensive, thoroughly researched work on the conduct of Bülow's mission in Italy. Hantsch, *Berchtold,* 2: 689-713 passim; Gottlieb, *Studies in Secret Diplomacy,* 241-42.

4. Monticone, *La Germania e la neutralità italiana,* 401-05; Gottlieb, *Studies in Secret Diplomacy,* 196-97, 367-69; Zeman, *Diplomatic History of the First World War,* 28-29, 33-35; Leo Valoni, "Italo-Austrian Negotiations 1914-1915," *Journal of Contemporary History* 1, no. 3 (1966): 126, 130-32; Leo Valoni, *The End of Austria-Hungary* (New York, 1973), 60-66; Renzi, "Italian Neutrality," 1426-27; Klaus Epstein, *Matthias Erzberger and the Dilemma of German Democracy* (Princeton, 1959), 120-30.

measure placated by the secret agreement of Britain and France to Russia's claims to Constantinople and the Straits. The result was the treaty of London of April 26, 1915.[5]

The Allies paid a high price for the adhesion of Italy to the Entente. The treaty of London promised Italy, at the peace, South Tyrol, Trieste, Gorizia, Gradisca, Istria up to Fiume, the northern third of Dalmatia, most of the islands of the eastern Adriatic, essential control of Albania with possession of Valona, possession of the Dodecanese islands, all rights in Libya, an area in Asia Minor, and compensation in Africa. The territorial terms, which were soon leaked, would have sacrificed the principles of ethnic unity and self-determination to the extent of putting more than 600,000 South Slavs and 230,000 Germans under Italian dominion. The enthusiasm of the South Slavs for the Entente cooled rapidly, and Serbia's projected invasion of Hungary was canceled. Instead, the Serbs marched into Albania, to the great annoyance of the Italians. Relations within the Entente were so impaired by the friction generated in the negotiation of the treaty that they never recovered the bloom of 1914.

Upon learning of the treaty, Bülow was more resolved to overturn the Salandra-Sonnino cabinet. His hope now was thereby to nullify Rome's decision for intervention. Bülow and Giolitti moved on parallel lines toward bringing into power a neutralist ministry headed by the latter. For this purpose the Germans stepped up their pressure on the Austrians (which they remembered as Bülow's "betrayal"), and the Austrians made a last reluctant but forthcoming proposal on May 10.[6]

The Austrian offer strengthened the hand of Giolitti and the forces of neutralism. This group had the support of a majority in the chamber and in the country, including the ranks of political Catholicism and the socialists.[7] Against these forces Salandra could bring the country to war only by

5. Gottlieb, *Studies in Secret Diplomacy*, 317–58, delineates in splendid fashion the play of rival imperialisms in the negotiations and highlights the close relation between the questions of the Adriatic, the Balkans, and Constantinople. Also Smith, *Russia's Struggle for Power*, 243–68; Michael Boro Petrovich, "The Italo-Yugoslav Boundary Question, 1914–1915," in *Russian Diplomacy and Eastern Europe*, 163–70, 178–91; *Das zaristische Russland im Weltkriege: Neue Dokumente aus den russischen Staatsarchiven über der Türkei, Bulgariens, Rumaniens und Italiens in den Weltkrieg*, trans. Alfred von Wegerer (Berlin, 1927), 263–72, 289, 292, 295–306.

6. Monticone, *La Germania e la neutralità italiana*, 482–92; Zeman, *Diplomatic History of the First World War*, 36–37; Epstein, *Erzberger*, 130–34.

7. Recent Italian studies of the subject generally agree that the majority was neutralist. See Claudio Pavone, "Italy: Trends and Politics," *Journal of Contemporary History* 2, no. 1 (1967): 62.

resort to "piazza politics" in a violent internal struggle. The cabinet resigned, attributing the government crisis to Giolitti and his followers. Salandra took the issue to the streets and public squares. The cabinet crisis set off the eruption of frenzied violence to which Gabriele D'Annunzio, Benito Mussolini, and the nationalist press added fire and fury. Nationalist gangs and mobs took over the streets in the large cities with demonstrations, intimidation, and fighting, while the police and troops looked on with benevolent restraint. The cabinet of Salandra was reinstituted and parliament convened. By incipient fascist methods the mob had overruled the parliamentary majority. On May 23 Italy declared war on Austria-Hungary but not against Germany until August 27, 1916.[8]

Italy added to the Entente an army of about 875,000 men, mostly infantry. The Italian government had never found the funds to create the modern military machine of a great power, especially in heavy guns, machine guns, and airplanes. This inadequately equipped army of little military zeal was destined to fight in the extremely difficult mountainous terrain of the border area between Austria and Italy, where the Austrians controlled the crests of the heights.

General Luigi Cadorna, the commander-in-chief, deployed half the army to the south, along the front of the Isonzo River, a distance of 60 miles, and the other half over the 350 miles of the Trentino front to the north. Cadorna conducted an active defense on this longer line and in June commenced an offensive on the Isonzo front. The action marked the inauguration of a repetitive series of bloody attacks known as the eleven battles of the Isonzo, the objective of which was to win the Carso plateau and the fortress of Gorizia on the way to Trieste and a link with the Serbs. The first four of this series were fought between June and December 1915.[9]

In each of the four battles the Italians outnumbered the enemy by a ratio of nearly two to one, yet the Austrian forces, some of the Dual Empire's best soldiers, fought with vigor and spirit that were absent in combat against the Russians. Conrad had been anxious in fact to launch an offensive of his own against the Italians as soon as Rome declared war. He argued for going over to the defensive in Galicia and diverting the troops thus released to the Italian front. The Austrian commander was dissuaded from doing so by Falkenhayn, who gave priority to a Balkan over an Italian campaign.

8. On Salandra's use of "piazza politics," see Gottlieb, *Studies in Secret Diplomacy*, 384–89.
9. C.R.M.F. Cruttwell, *A History of the Great War, 1914–1918*, 2d ed. (Oxford, 1936), 445–49.

In the ill-planned Isonzo battles of 1915 the Italians conducted frontal assaults over hazardous ground against trenches cut in stone. The casualties of 250,000 men were due in part to the inadequate provision of guns and ammunition but also to the stony terrain. The large expenditure of military resources achieved no significant territorial advances. Neither was a check exerted on the German bloc's drive in the east, nor Serbia rendered benefit in staving off collapse and occupation.[10]

For Falkenhayn and Bethmann Hollweg the elimination of Serbia as a military and political force appeared a necessary step to removing the danger on the Austrian flank and swaying the uncommitted Balkan states toward the Central Powers. They saw it also serving to sustain Austria in the status of a great power. Of more immediate importance was the pressing need, if Turkey was to be saved after the opening of the Gallipoli campaign, to clear a route to Constantinople free of Romanian control for sending military aid to the Porte.

The eastern offensive and the continued neutrality of Bulgaria had previously diverted Falkenhayn from a Serbian campaign. In July he had deliberately pressed for an alliance with Bulgaria. Negotiations, begun with a Bulgarian representative at Pless—the seat of OHL, were completed on September 6. Sofia entered into a treaty of alliance and friendship, supported by a military convention, with Germany and Austria.[11]

This diplomatic coup allowed military preparation for the invasion of Serbia. Falkenhayn planned a massive envelopment of the Serbs from three sides, with combined forces twice as large as the Serbian. Mackensen assembled a German army under Gallwitz, together with an Austrian army on the Danube and Save. The two armies were to cross the rivers from the north and strike immediately for Belgrade. Two Bulgarian armies were to invade from the east in the direction of Nish and Skoplje.

On October 7, following a fierce bombardment, the two forces moved across the rivers on pontoons and barges at five different points precisely according to the masterly logistic and technical plans prepared under Colonel Hentsch of Marne fame. Three days later, they occupied Belgrade, while the Bulgarian armies openly joined the invasion, although Bulgaria did not follow with a declaration of war until October 14. The encirclement, driving the Serbian armies toward the center of the country,

10. On the four Isonzo battles of 1915 and their relation to Falkenhayn's continued drive in the east, see the discussion in Hermann Wendt, *Der italienische Kriegsschauplatz in europäischen Konflikten* (Berlin, 1936), 268–81.
11. *Der Weltkrieg*, 8: 611–13.

began to close in from three sides. Nish fell to the Bulgarians on November 5, and Falkenhayn attained at last the long-desired goal of a protected through railway to Constantinople. The invaders, however, were encountering severe trials in rain and snow storms, mud, cold, often roadless rough terrain, and disease.

The Serbs were steadily pushed back despite their dogged bravery, yet they succeeded in keeping open a route to the sea. The intended envelopment failed of completion and turned into a concentric movement. Desperately fighting the elements and typhus as well as the invaders, the surviving Serbs beat their way through the mountains of Montenegro and Albania to ports of escape. About half the troops survived to be taken off to the Greek island of Corfu, which was seized by the French in January 1915. After refitting and training by a French mission, they were brought to Salonika in the summer of 1916 to join the Allied expeditionary force of the Balkans.[12]

The Allies made a feeble effort to aid the Serbs, beginning with an expeditionary force of one British and one French division landed at Salonika from Gallipoli, with the permission of the Greek premier, Venizelos, just as the Austrian and German armies were about to cross into Serbia. The command of the joint force was assigned to General Maurice Sarrail, an officer involved in parliamentary politics whom Joffre desired to remove from France. Sarrail's advance up the Vardar valley was checked by Bulgarian resistance, and his communications were threatened by the unfriendly Greek army in his rear. The Allied army was obliged to retreat to the Salonika base. The position of the Salonika force in relation to Greece was uncertain from the beginning because the king and royalists leaned toward Germany. In this unlikely situation a sharp issue arose between Britain and France of retaining the joint army at Salonika. The British yielded at last to the French view, and the Balkan army continued for a year at this entrenched base—not inaptly called by the Germans "the greatest Allied internment camp"—before resuming operations.

The end of the Balkan campaign also caused friction among the Central Powers. Austria and Bulgaria were eager to pursue Sarrail's force beyond the Greek border and drive the Entente out of Salonika. Falkenhayn feared that the occupation of Salonika would add Greece to the enemies of the German bloc and resolutely vetoed the project, against the vehe-

12. May, *Passing of the Hapsburg Monarchy,* 1: 110–14; Falkenhayn, *German General Staff,* 198–211. See Gerard Silberstein, "The Serbian Campaign of 1915: Its Military Implications," *International Review of History and Political Science* 3 (1966): 115–32.

ment opposition of Conrad. The Austrians, having moved into Montenegro from Serbia, conquered that tiny country. They continued into Albania in order to check further Italian penetration, which had already
proceeded to the seizure of the ports of Valona and Durazzo. Both the
Germans and Austrians prevented the Bulgarians from advancing in the
Albanian area as a quarrel threatened between Bulgaria and Austria over
the issue. The Austrians went on to subdue almost one-half of Albania, and
Falkenhayn had to restrain Conrad from even more extensive operations
there. Falkenhayn kept unswervingly to this concept of limited aims in the
conduct of war, opposing the pursuit of nationalist objectives in the Balkans that would accomplish no overall strategic purpose.

2. TURKEY IN THE PERIPHERAL WAR

By November 1914 Turkey had moved from an ambivalent neutrality
to active belligerency. The declaration of neutrality in August reflected
the split within the government between the pro-German and pro-Entente
wings. In this situation the Porte, moved by opportunist tendencies and
concern for its future security, at first, like Italy, conducted a policy of
duality. The Porte approached Russia and Britain with a view to an alliance or at least a neutrality agreement. At the same time the Turks sought
extensive military assistance from Germany and concessions from both the
Central Powers. The British and French were opposed to any territorial
commitment to Turkey for fear of estranging Greece and Bulgaria to the
extent of interfering with the formation of a pro-Entente bloc in the
Balkans. Nor would the Allies agree to a treaty guaranteeing Turkey's
territorial integrity, along with pledges to abolish capitulations and terminate economic concessions. The western Allies took Turkey too lightly in
the balance of forces or were too preoccupied with the prospective partition of Turkey at the conclusion of the war to appreciate at that time the
value of its participation on the Allied side. Or it may have been that
London and Paris considered German influence at Constantinople too
strong to overcome. The enormity of this diplomatic dereliction can be
measured by the agony and costs of the Dardanelles disaster.[13]

The ultimate decision on the issue of war came into the hands of Enver
Pasha, the most powerful figure at the Porte, who was a convert to German

13. Sachar, *Emergence of the Middle East*, 27; Harry N. Howard, *The Partition of Turkey*
(Norman, Okla., 1931), 96–102; Kurt Ziemke, *Die neue Türkei* (Stuttgart, 1930), 23–31;
Smith, *Russian Struggle for Power*, 69–75; *Das zaristische Russland im Weltkriege*, 7–37 passim.

technical attainments and military efficiency. After the collapse of German strategy at the Marne and Austrian reverses in Galicia and Serbia, the Central Powers played every available card to induce Enver and other members of the government urgently to take military action. They assured the Porte of support for the return of the Aegean Islands occupied by Greece during the Balkan Wars and promised to lend the Turks assistance in the abolition of the hated capitulations. The Turks, thus encouraged, unilaterally notified the foreign representatives on September 9 that capitulations were abrogated. In October the Germans made an advance of two million gold pounds on a large loan. They organized a systematic propaganda campaign against the Entente chiefly by means of a purchased press.[14]

The decisive single factor was undoubtedly the presence of the battle cruiser *Goeben* and its companion light cruiser *Breslau* in the waters of the Golden Horn. In violation of Turkish neutrality, the Turkish government admitted to the Straits on August 10 these German warships escaping from the Adriatic.[15] The Turkish ministers invented, in reaction to Allied protests, the expedient of a fictitious sale of the two cruisers to Turkey to replace two dreadnoughts (purchased by the Turks and nearly completed in British shipyards) that the British had commandeered at the beginning of the war. The Turks supplemented this step by closing the Straits to Allied shipping on September 26.

The Germans used their two cruisers to gain full control of the Turkish navy, in which the *Goeben* and *Breslau* were incorporated. Admiral Wilhelm Souchon, in charge of the two cruisers, became the commander-in-chief of the Turkish, or rather the Turkish-German, navy, and the previously operating British naval mission was forced to withdraw. The combined fleet was strong enough to exercise a mastery of the Black Sea. Through Souchon and Liman von Sanders the Germans dominated both armed services. With the added influence of the active Germany embassy, there was some ground for the observation of a Belgian jurist in Constantinople: "The Germans have captured Turkey."[16]

The struggle in the cabinet between the activists and the majority of

14. On the general subject of Turkey's intervention, see Ulrich Trumpener, "Turkey's Entrance into World War I: An Assessment of Responsibilities," *Journal of Modern History* 34 (1962): 369–80; Silberstein, *Troubled Alliance*, 73–98; Gottlieb, *Studies in Secret Diplomacy,* 34–62; *Das zaristische Russland im Weltkriege,* 40–60; Ziemke, *Die neue Türkei,* 31–37.

15. On the escape of the German cruisers, see below, pp. 119–20.

16. Joseph Pomiankowski, *Der Zusammenbruch des Ottomanischen Reiches* (Vienna, 1928), 74, 78; Sachar, *Emergence of the Middle East,* 6.

neutralist moderates, however, continued with no promise of resolution. The final resort to drag Turkey into the war was to send the fleet into the Black Sea against the Russians. The action was taken under the pressure of Souchon and other German representatives, but through the collaboration of the Turkish war party and on the express authorization of Enver without the cabinet's approval. Souchon conducted the fleet, headed by the *Goeben* and *Breslau,* from the Bosporus, and on October 29 the warships raided Odessa and other Russian ports on the Black Sea. The expedition destroyed Russian shipping and sank a minelayer in a brush with the Russian naval forces. The Entente powers broke diplomatic relations with Turkey immediately, and on October 31 the tsar proclaimed war. A large part of the public was opposed to the war party's coup and to the Germans.[17]

This could only be a suicidal conflict for a country of such meager assets. It proved in the end to be a war of Ottoman liquidation. But before we condemn Enver and his cabinet partners for complete folly, we must answer the question whether the Turks could have followed any policy that would have avoided the overhanging fate of dissolution for the moribund empire. The Turkish activists saw no hope for security against Russia, except in alliance with the British and French or with the Germans. They believed that neutrality would provide no protection against dismemberment if the Allies won and would insure no different fate in case the Turks were defeated in alliance with the Central Powers. An alliance with Germany, when the Entente was unwilling to welcome Turkey into its coalition, offered at least a gambler's chance.[18]

During the period of neutrality, the Turks, with the assistance of the Germans, undertook both naval and military preparations for war. Souchon, with other naval officers and seamen dispatched from Germany, worked to improve the efficiency of the navy and naval installations. The Turks laid rows of mines and installed an antisubmarine net in the Narrows of the Straits. Additional minefields were planted after the Straits were closed. The Germans took command of this work and of fortified defenses at the Straits.

The amount of military assistance that Germany actually delivered to Turkey was limited before Serbia was subdued and a secure land route was

17. Silberstein, *Troubled Alliance,* 89–97; Sachar, *Emergence of the Middle East,* 21–24, 29; Pomiankowski, *Der Zusammenbruch des Ottomanischen Reiches,* 86–87.
18. See the discussion in Gottlieb, *Studies in Secret Diplomacy,* 61–62.

opened from Germany to Constantinople. Neutral Romania, situated astride the only rail route from Austria-Hungary, yielded to the pressure of the Russians and sealed the border on October 2 to all further military shipments bound for Turkey. Thereafter until the conquest of Serbia the Turks, with the Germans already in Turkey, had to shift for themselves.[19] Although the German military mission made progress in the reorganization and improvement of the army, it could be no better than the corrupt and backward state supporting it. With the incorporation of reservists the active army of 200,000 men was expanded to a force between 700,000 and 800,000 of undernourished, ragged, poorly equipped, and largely illiterate troops. The woefully thin communications of the Turkish military organization possessed no unbroken rail link from Anatolia to Syria and central Mesopotamia, since the Anatolian-Bagdad railway had not yet finished its tunnels through the mountains. Nor had it yet built but a few branch lines. Roads were no more developed, because of mountain, desert, and distance. The army depended on animal transport and seldom employed the telephone at the front; it had no wireless or airplanes during the first part of the war. In fighting the western powers, Turkey was pitting the ox against the internal combustion engine. Its forces for the defense of a far-flung and vulnerable empire had only a lacing of German technical influence.[20]

The military forces were organized in four armies, headed in fact by Enver as chief of the general staff. His German assistant, Colonel Fritz Bronsart von Schellendorf, played a major role in the technical direction of the army. German general staff officers served in the beginning as advisers and instructors among the Turkish general staff, but in the course of the war took over directly a number of positions on the general staff and command posts in the field. Liman von Sanders not only continued as head of the military mission but now assumed command of the First Army, with the charge of defending Constantinople and Gallipoli. The Second Army was deployed on the Asian shore across the Straits, and Third along the Russian border in the Transcaucasus. Forces were also distributed in Syria, Mesopotamia, the Hejas, and Yemen.

The principal mission of these armies, in the overall strategy of the

19. Ulrich Trumpener, "German Military Aid to Turkey in 1914," *Journal of Modern History* 32 (1960): 145–49.

20. Larcher, *La guerre turque,* 64–72; Sachar, *Emergence of the Middle East,* 32–35; Ahmed Emin, *Turkey in the World War,* 78–92; Otto Liman von Sanders, *Five Years in Turkey* (Annapolis, 1927), 10–12, 27–30.

Central Powers, was to deny the Entente the vital link between Russia and the west through the Straits. If possible, they were to break Britain's line of communication to India and the Pacific Dominions, support revolt among the Moslem peoples in the Entente imperial dependencies, and provide a diversion on Russia's southern flank. In pursuit of these aims the sultan-caliph proclaimed on November 14, 1914, a Holy War against the Entente enemies of Islam, as well as revolt against the Entente masters. Military operations were carried on in three areas before the Dardanelles campaign—the Persian Gulf, the Suez, and the Caucasus.

In early November 1914 the British initiated a preemptive enterprise in both military and political warfare by landing Indian troops at the estuary of the Euphrates and Tigris Rivers. The British were seeking to turn the Arabs against the Turks, or at least to friendly neutrality. Britain's immediate material interest was the protection of the oil pipeline of the Anglo-Persian Oil Company and its installations on Abadan island (on whose oil the oil-fired naval vessels depended); its larger goal was the safeguarding of the imperial lifeline to India.

The British forces, soon winning the point of junction of the rivers, pushed the Turks back with the aid of the navy and advanced to Basra. The expedition captured this seaport of Mesopotamia on November 23 and set about creating in this unlikely location a supply base and logistic center. In order to strengthen the hold on Basra, the force moved up the river on December 9 to take Qurna, where the troops built a defense system. Having secured a line a hundred and twenty miles from the sea, the British had gone far toward realizing their main original goals in "the Land of the Two Rivers." If they had stopped and held here, they would have avoided the later "Mesopotamian muddle" in which they became involved.[21]

In the second theater of operations, Egypt and the Suez Canal, Enver planned a strike at Britain's vital communications and, in connection with the expected revolt of the Senussi in Tripoli as a part of the Holy War, the recovery of Egypt for Turkish rule. The Fourth Army was organized in Syria from the local population and later stiffened with pure Turkish troops. The expedition made its way from Jerusalem by marches at night and surprised the British defenders with the arrival of ten thousand troops at the Canal in late January 1915. Exhausted from the hardships of marching through the desert rather than over the usual caravan road near the

21. A. J. Barker, *The Neglected War: Mesopotamia, 1914–1918* (London, 1967), 34–57.

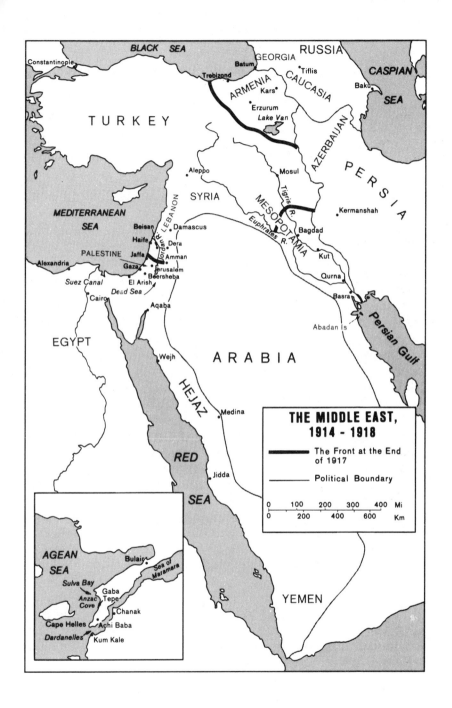

BLACK SEA

Constantinople

GEORGIA RUSSIA

Batum
Trebizond
CASPIAN SEA

ARMENIA Kars
Tiflis
Baku

CAUCASIA

TURKEY Erzurum
Lake Van

AZERBAIJAN

PERSIA

Aleppo

Mosul

SYRIA

MEDITERRANEAN SEA

Tigris R.

MESOPOTAMIA

Euphrates R.

Kermanshah

LEBANON

Beisan Damascus
Haifa Dera
PALESTINE Jaffa Amman
Gaza Jerusalem
Beersheba
El Arish
Dead Sea

Bagdad

Kut

Qurna

Basra

Alexandria

Suez Canal

Cairo Aqaba

EGYPT

Wejh

ARABIA

Abadan Is

Persian Gulf

HEJAZ

Medina

RED

Jidda

SEA

THE MIDDLE EAST,
1914 - 1918

━━━ The Front at the End
of 1917

──── Political Boundary

| 0 | 100 | 200 | 300 | 400 | Mi |
| 0 | 200 | 400 | 600 | Km |

AGEAN SEA

Bulair

Sea of Maramara

Sulva Bay

Gaba Tepe

Anzac Cove

Chanak

Cape Helles Achi Baba

Dardanelles Kum Kale

YEMEN

sea, the invaders attacked with little impetus, and the few hundred who made the crossing of the Canal by pontoons soon surrendered to the Indian infantry. The Turks were confronted with strong defenses of Indian troops, assisted by Australian and New Zealand divisions training in Egypt, and of gunboats and armored trains. Rather than assault the British defenses, the Turks began a general retreat, skillfully withdrawing the bulk of their force to Palestine without molestation.

The British received a scare from which they never recovered. Thereafter they maintained an elaborate defense system along the Canal and reinforced their troops in Egypt to excessive proportions. Other fronts, most of all that in Gallipoli, had to suffer from this Suez syndrome that was draining off the manpower and resources of the empire.[22]

In the third theater the Turks fought a campaign against the Russians in the lofty mountainous country of the Caucasus, where the gales and cold were more destructive than the enemy. This strategic area of contention afforded on the one side a gateway to the Baku oilfields and on the other a gateway to Mesopotamia. After the Turks in November halted the Russian drive from Kars toward the Turkish fortress of Erzurum, Enver was prompted by inordinate ambition personally to conduct an offensive here with the Third Army. He expected an uprising of the Tatars in the area to assist. The Turkish soldiers, having no winter clothing, shelter, or regular supplies of food, were no match for both the Russians and the winter. Enver's attempt, beginning on December 24, to turn the flank was stopped. The Russian forces under General N. N. Yudenich encircled the Third Army by a brilliant maneuver and virtually wiped it out by the latter part of January 1915. The Russians pushed the Turks back toward Lake Van as the fighting tapered off in a stalemate.[23]

These three campaigns set the stage for the Dardanelles-Gallipoli struggle. The defeat of the Turks in each suggested that, in relation to the interminable carnage and strategic paralysis of the Western Front, the time and conditions were right to strike a knockout blow at the weakest link of the Central Powers.

22. Sachar, *Emergence of the Middle East,* 39–44; C. E. Bean, *The Story of Anzac,* 2 vols. (Sydney, 1921–24), 1: 140–65; Liman von Sanders, *Five Years in Turkey,* 43–45.
23. Sachar, *Emergence of the Middle East,* 44–52; Liman von Sanders, *Five Years in Turkey,* 37–40; Edmonds, *Short History of World War I,* 106–07.

3. THE DARDANELLES DISASTER

The impulse to the Dardanelles campaign came from the appeal to the British made by Grand Duke Nicholas on January 2 for a demonstration against the Turks that might relieve the pressure on the Russians in the bitter fighting of the Caucasus. Kitchener and Churchill, the heads of war and navy, decided between them that a demonstration would be made, and Kitchener that it would be at the Dardanelles. Strategic attention had been drawn to the Straits and Constantinople from early in the war. Immediately after Turkey became an enemy, a squadron of British and French warships bombarded the outer forts of the Dardanelles. The demonstration inflicted considerable damage, without other effect than a gratuitous warning to the Turks and Germans of Entente operational interest in the area.[24]

The search for an alternative to the stalemate on the Western Front and previous strategic interest in the Dardanelles and Constantinople soon converted the demonstration promised the Russians into a serious naval undertaking intended to penetrate the Straits. Churchill's imagination soared at the prospect. Thanks to the enthusiastic eloquence and logic with which he presented the proposed project and the support given it by Kitchener, the War Council reached a provisional decision on January 13 that "the Admiralty should prepare for a naval expedition in February to bombard and take the Gallipoli Peninsula, with Constantinople as its objective." The decision was fuzzy in that a naval expedition alone could not possibly take the Gallipoli Peninsula and Constantinople; the government was committed not only to early fleet action in the Straits but also, in effect, to eventual military operations. Churchill gained the agreement of the French to participate with a naval squadron.[25]

The War Council gave definitive approval on January 28 for the Admiralty to go ahead with the attempt of the navy, unsupported by the army, to force the Straits. The government acted without cognizance of the

24. See Guinn, *British Strategy and Politics*, 53–54; Higgins, *Winston Churchill and the Dardanelles*, 57; Marder, *From the Dreadnought to Scapa Flow*, 2: 201–02; Churchill, *World Crisis*, 1: 529, 541; Sir Reginald Bacon and Francis E. McMurtie, *Modern Naval Strategy* (London, 1940), 123. Churchill defended the November bombardment, not very plausibly, in his chronicle of the war, while Jellicoe condemned it as "an unforgivable error" and Admiral Bacon as "an act of sheer lunacy."

25. See Higgins, *Winston Churchill and the Dardanelles*, 113–28; Peter Gretton, *Winston Churchill and the Royal Navy* (New York, 1969), 211–12.

misgivings of Fisher, the First Sea Lord, and other Admiralty officers. It never consulted the general staff on the feasibility of the scheme or submitted the proposal for a staff study to a combined group of naval and military experts. And the opinion was not obtained of Admiral John R. Jellicoe, the commander-in-chief of the fleet, who was opposed.[26]

A fleet headed by fourteen British and four French capital ships was concentrated before the Dardanelles under the command of Admiral Sackville H. Carden, a shore officer wanting in initiative and experience in fleet command. On the enemy side, the interval since November had been put to good advantage under the direction of Liman von Sanders, Souchon, and other Germans to extend the defenses of the Straits and Gallipoli. The defense system included minefields in front of and just inside the Narrows (some fourteen miles from the entrance to the Straits), protected by concealed minefield batteries, long guns in a series of forts, mobile howitzers, and searchlights. All of these works were guarded by outer forts at the entrance to the Dardanelles. The fleet soon discovered that the crux of the attack problem was how to sweep the minefields under the gunfire of the Turks before destroying the forts and guns—a feat possible only at close range after the minefields were swept.[27]

Twice in February the combined fleet bombarded the outer forts. The marines committed sufficient additional destruction of the outer forts and guns for Carden to attack the forts and guns inside the Straits in March. The bombardment of the inner defenses was carried out intermittently, with only parts of the fleet each time. The efforts to sweep the minefields failed entirely in the face of the destructive fire from the enemy's guns. The command was too big an assignment for Carden. Having accomplished so little and worried so much, he collapsed before attempting a new sustained attack and resigned on March 16. Carden was replaced by the second in command, Admiral John M. de Robeck, an officer of solid naval qualifications but one molded entirely according to the book.[28]

The opinion of senior officers in the Dardanelles fleet and the thought in the Admiralty and War Council were moving meanwhile toward an amphibious operation. On February 16 the War Council decided to send the 29th Division, made up of well-trained regulars from overseas garri-

26. Marder, *From the Dreadnought to Scapa Flow*, 2: 213–21; Gretton, *Winston Churchill and the Royal Navy*, 214–15.
27. Marder, *From the Dreadnought to Scapa Flow*, 2: 229–31.
28. Ibid., 233–34, 240–45; Alan Moorehead, *Gallipoli* (London, 1956), 55–61.

sons, to the Greek island of Lemnos near the Dardanelles. Under strong pressure from the French to hold the force for use on the Western Front, Kitchener retained the division in Britain until March 10. Here arises one of the many "ifs" of the Dardanelles venture. The balance of evidence supports the conclusion that if this delay of three weeks had not occurred, Gallipoli might well have been taken. It was impossible to proceed with the invasion force until the arrival of this core division at the center of concentration. If the British had set out with energy and determination on February 16 to organize a sizable land expedition for rapid attack, the only Turkish division then in Gallipoli could hardly have held out against the landing forces.[29]

When the 28th Division was released on March 10, it was joined for the combined operations with two divisions from Australia and New Zealand (the Anzacs) that had been training in Egypt, the Royal Naval Division, and a French division. Venizelos offered three more divisions for the force of some 80,000 troops, but the Russians, alarmed at the thought of Greek soldiers approaching Constantinople, denied the possibility.

Kitchener appointed General Ian Hamilton, a previous colleague of poetic, sensitive temperament and imaginative mind with a distinguished military record, to command the expedition. Both Hamilton's orders and Kitchener's parting words to him indicated that the military expedition was to play a secondary role in supporting the fleet. Action on the spot, however, was giving rise to the question whether the operation must not be primarily military, supported by the navy.[30]

The land attack was thus ordered in London as a second-class operation without adequate preparation for the functions and organization of command. Hamilton departed hastily, without a plan of operations, and did not receive the most fit and experienced generals from France whom he

29. See Churchill, *World Crisis,* 2: 187–89; Great Britain, Dardanelles Commission, *First Report* (London, 1917), 33–34; Marder, *From the Dreadnought to Scapa Flow,* 2: 235–37. Higgins, *Winston Churchill and the Dardanelles,* 148, takes an opposing view that it was not Kitchener's delay in dispatching the 29th Division, but the bad weather and the necessary reloading of the ships at Alexandria for combat that held up the landings.

30. C. F. Aspinall-Oglander, *Military Operations: Gallipoli,* 2 vols. (London, 1929–32), 1: 1; Great Britain, Dardanelles Commission, *Final Report* (London, n. d.), 10. On the choice and qualifications of Hamilton, see the admirable presentations in Henry W. Nevinson, *The Dardanelles Campaign* (London, 1918), 65–67; and Robert Rhodes James, *Gallipoli* (London, 1965), 55–58.

desired for his staff. Modern planes were not made available for reconnaissance or shrapnel-proof craft for landing.[31]

Hamilton arrived at Lemnos as the navy made the last attempt to beat down unaided the defenses of the Straits. The fleet mostly controlled the forts before and in the Narrows, but the minefield batteries and the mobile howitzers kept up such a deadly fire that the minesweepers fled without disposing of the mines. Three battleships were sunk by mines, and another put out of action, while two French battleships incurred serious damage from the gunfire. Admiral de Robeck, fearing for the safety of his remaining battleships, broke off the action. If destroyers had been used to serve as fast minesweepers and enough first-rate spotting planes to direct accurate fire against the field guns and howitzers, the outcome might have been different. Only old battleships ready for junking had been sunk, and the Admiralty and the French immediately ordered replacements for the ships destroyed or disabled.[32]

The decision was left to Admiral de Robeck whether to resume the naval attack. The commander succumbed to the conservatism of the professional navy and personal attachment to the long familiar ships he desired to spare. With the agreement of Hamilton he advised the Admiralty of his intention to await the landing of forces on Gallipoli. The Aegean fleet did not make another try, and thereafter its only part was to assist the army in a large-scale amphibious operation. There has been debate ever since whether more persistence and resolution would have carried the day. Of this Churchill was utterly convinced, and Enver and Turkish headquarters so believed.[33]

The discontinuance of the naval attacks allowed the Turks and Germans the pause of a month before the landings. The time was enough to complete the most urgent preparations for defense against the land attack of the Allies. A new army (the Fifth) was formed to take the place of the

31. Dardanelles Committee, *Final Report*, 9–10, 29; Sir Ian Hamilton, *Gallipoli Diary*, 2 vols. (London, 1920), 1: 19; John North, *Gallipoli* (1936; reprint ed., London, 1966), 65, 67; Higgins, *Winston Churchill and the Dardanelles*, 159, 161.

32. For a full account of the naval attack, see Sir Roger Keyes, *Naval Memoirs*, 2 vols. (London, 1934–35), 1: 232–48.

33. On the feasibility of passing the Straits with a further naval attempt, see the following, mostly affirmative, views in Keyes, *Naval Memoirs*, 1: 253, 276, 412, 431–57, 472 ff.; Churchill, *World Crisis*, 2: 255–59, 264–69; S. W. Roskill, *The Strategy of Sea Power* (London, 1962), 124; Liman von Sanders, *Five Years in Turkey*, 53; Nevinson, *Dardanelles Campaign*, 62; Marder, *From the Dreadnought to Scapa Flow*, 2: 248; Gretton, *Winston Churchill and the Royal Navy*, 218; Higgins, *Winston Churchill and the Dardanelles*, 163–64.

different authorities and formations previously responsible for the security of the peninsula and the Dardanelles. Liman repositioned troops and improved communications and field fortifications.[34] On the Allied side, the failure of the naval attack marked a turning point in the drift from a predominantly naval undertaking to a predominantly army show. A momentous land campaign was now set in motion on the agreement of the commanding admiral and general on the scene, with Kitchener's approval, allowing the matter to slip through the cabinet without discussion. This progressive expansion of purpose, unsupported by adequate military resources and successful diplomatic effort, typified a venture in which the involvement from the beginning was unplanned in relation to overall strategy and military means, decisions in the conduct of war were improvised from day to day, and coordinated strategic estimates were not utilized.

The original conception of the Mediterranean Expeditionary Force (MEF) had been an assemblage of troops to occupy and hold the peninsula of Gallipoli after the navy had done the primary job by getting through the Straits. The force dispatched was not large enough for a full-scale land campaign, and Kitchener did not reinforce it before the first landings. The three Greek divisions were lost through bungled diplomacy.

In preparing for the greatest amphibious operation attempted so far, Hamilton had to reload the ships from Britain for combat landings and assemble the force in Alexandria, since there were no facilities for this on Lemnos. The army was short of artillery, the artillery short of ammunition, and no one had sent out the necessities of trench warfare—periscopes, grenades, and trench mortars—or even vessels for holding water, so essential in the heat of Gallipoli. By dint of local scouring for needed items and ingenious adaptation, a miscellaneous armada was made ready to rendez-vous at Mudros Bay in Lemnos for the landings.[35]

A struggle to win control of the mountainous peninsula would become a battle of the ridges and for the commanding heights, above all for the peak Chunuk Bair dominating the Narrows. Liman disposed his six divisions in order best to protect these heights and the Asian side of the Straits near the mouth of the Dardanelles. He maintained outposts reinforced by trenches and barbed wire at the site of possible landings, while concentrat-

34. Liman von Sanders, *Five Years in Turkey*, 58–62; Aspinall-Oglander, *Gallipoli*, 1: 153.
35. Moorehead, *Gallipoli*, 109–11, 115–19, 122–27; Dardanelles Commission, *Final Report*, 16–17; North, *Gallipoli*, 76–77; James, *Gallipoli*, 77–81.

ing the bulk of the troops inland for rushing to areas of invasion. Liman held one division as a mobile reserve, under the command of an alert and energetic young officer, Lieutenant Colonel Mustapha Kemal.[36] Hamilton attacked at Cape Helles at the tip of Gallipoli and near Gaba Tebe about twelve miles to the north on the western coast. He made use of diversionary landings by the French division on the Asiatic shore and a feint near the isthmus of the peninsula. In the early morning of April 25 the men at Cape Helles, aided by a heavy naval bombardment, and the Anzacs near Gaba Tebe, without any preparatory gunfire, landed from small craft towed by tugs from the warships until the landing craft were rowed to the beaches. The Anzacs landed in some confusion at an unintended beach and moved forward in detached units that never coalesced into a coherent movement. They waged, nevertheless, a major battle for the control of the summit of Chunuk Bair. The defending Turks were retreating when Mustapha Kemal appeared with his reserve division to save the day. Kemal inspired the soldiers to fight with fanatical courage. If the Anzacs had had reserves to put in at the critical moment, or if the amazing leader Kemal had not taken charge of the Turkish defense, the Allies might have won Chunuk Bair.

During the following days the Turks made repeated frontal attacks, and the Anzacs fought fiercely to advance. The attempts of the Anzacs culminated in a big attack on May 2–3, and the Turks with reinforcements struck in suicidal waves on May 19. Neither opponent could continue the battle on that scale; the front settled down to the routine of trench warfare. The Turks retained Chunuk Bair, and the Anzacs their beachhead.[37]

At Helles three of the five landing parties of the 29th Division encountered little or no opposition. If their commands had acted with energy and initiative, there is no good reason why they should not have marched inland to join and strike the Turkish defenders in the rear before reinforcements arrived. The five beachheads linked up after wasting the immediate opportunity, while the French division from the Asiatic shore took

36. Liman von Sanders, *Five Years in Turkey*, 59–62; James, *Gallipoli*, 72 ff.; H. C. Armstrong, *Gray Wolf* (1933; reprint ed., New York, 1961), 45–46.
37. For an account of the landings and May battles by a British war correspondent, remarkable for its balance and detachment as the story of an eyewitness, see Nevinson, *Dardanelles Campaign*, 88–170. Keyes, the second-ranking officer of the fleet at Gallipoli, chronicles the events in his *Naval Memoirs*, 1: 291–330. The official presentation—one of the finest official histories to come out of the war—is the work of one of Hamilton's chief staff officers; see Aspinall-Oglander, *Gallipoli*, 1: 162–365.

up a position on the right. This advancing line tried to win the first heights of Achi Baba but could not gain the objective. Handicapped by little artillery support and inadequate equipment for this kind of warfare, they suffered severe losses against the frenzied fighting of the reinforced and entrenched Turks, who were making savage night attacks.

Two months of deadlock under a searing summer sun followed the May battles. At Helles the Allies made five intermittent, sanguinary, and largely useless frontal attacks. Otherwise the soldiers now lived a "troglodytic life" of elemental character. Disease and scarcity of ammunition plagued both the Allied troops and the Turks. The Allied soldiers felt isolated and neglected, as if caught in a trap.[38]

The feeling of neglect was deepened by the displacement of the main author of the combined enterprise. Churchill was removed from Admiralty through the May cabinet crisis, which was caused chiefly by differences between himself and the First Sea Lord Fisher, arising in great part over "this Dardanelles business" and the extent of its naval support. The War Council, the directing body for the Dardanelles campaign, did not meet after March 19 until May 14 and never had a successor until the Dardanelles Committee came into being on June 7.[39]

The new Dardanelles Committee authorized five divisions of reinforcements for Gallipoli. These effectives were dispatched with more expert landing facilities, in the form of the "beetles," armored craft with ramps. Additional balloon ships and airplanes were sent out for purposes of observation. With these reinforcements Hamilton launched a new offensive on August 6 from the Anzac beachhead and from beaches at Suvla Bay just north of Anzac cove.

At Suvla two new British divisions and at the Anzac beachhead 20,000 more troops, with supplies and guns, were secretly landed at night. At Suvla the British troops opened four beachheads with slight loss. The general move inland was delayed by the mix-up and scattering of units in landing, the issuance of unclear and conflicting orders, the absence of initiative and determined leadership, the lack of coordination between local commands, the change of objectives, the breakdown in water supply,

38. Bean, *Story of Anzac*, 2: 366–87; Hamilton, *Gallipoli Diary*, 1: 175–76, 196, 242, 368–69; Nevinson, *Dardanelles Campaign*, 171–72, 184–89; North, *Gallipoli*, 190–91; Liman von Sanders, *Five Years in Turkey*, 73–74, 79; Hans Kannengiesser, *The Campaign in Gallipoli* (London, 1928), 142–72 passim.
39. See Hamilton, *Gallipoli Diary*, 1: 240.

and the failure to establish a coherent forward movement. Sir Frederick Stopford, the general in charge of the operations, was too content with the accomplishment of landing, and the commanders under him too concerned about resting their men, to drive the troops forward at once.[40]

The tardy and confused advance toward the commanding heights frittered away golden opportunities. Liman and Colonel Hans Kannengiesser, who led Turkish soldiers against the Anzacs, were certain that a rapid British advance would have obtained the intended objective. The delay gave Liman and Kemal time to rush up two divisions from the isthmus of the peninsula. Liman placed Kemal in charge of all the forces in the Anzac-Suvla area. Kemal caught the British climbing up the heights with a headlong charge of the newly arrived Turkish troops. The broken line of the British was driven back substantially to their starting positions.[41]

As soon as the danger was past at Suvla, Kemal rushed to fortify the defenses at Chunuk Bair against the attacking New Zealanders from Anzac cove. A party of them approached the summit of Chunuk Bair the morning of August 7 and could have taken the peak, virtually undefended, if they had pushed on without delay. A group of New Zealanders, British, and Gurkhas stormed the peak on August 9 but were soon forced to retire to trenches below the crest. Kemal rallied the exhausted Turkish defenders, threw in the last regiment of reserves, and drove the attackers from their trenches in a mass charge of waves of onrushing Turks. Kemal saved the key to Gallipoli a third time since the beginning of the campaign.[42]

No part of the Gallipoli campaign so nearly achieved success as this. Thereafter military events, morale, and support in London were on the downward slope. On August 21 Hamilton's command carried out the last and largest attack at Anzac-Suvla; and, in order to repulse it, the Turks

40. On the Anzac-Suvla action as a whole, see Sir Ian Hamilton, *Final Despatch* (London, 1916); Hamilton, *Gallipoli Diary,* 2: 33–119; Dardanelles Commission, *Final Report,* 30–51; Bean, *Story of Anzac,* 2: 497–718; Aspinall-Oglander, *Gallipoli,* 2: 178–329; Nevinson, *Dardanelles Campaign,* 224–332; Keyes, *Naval Memoirs,* 1: 376–411; Kannengiesser, *Campaign in Gallipoli,* 203–27; North, *Gallipoli,* 145–239; James, *Gallipoli,* 244–309; Moorehead, *Gallipoli,* 243–97; John Hargrave, *The Suvla Bay Landing* (London, 1964); Eric Wheeler Bush, *Gallipoli* (New York, 1975), 226–84.

41. Liman von Sanders, *Five Years in Turkey,* 88; Kannengiesser, *Campaign in Gallipoli,* 219–20.

42. On the role of the New Zealanders at Chunuk Bair, see the personal narrative of a participant in Cecil Malthus, *Anzac: A Retrospect* (Christchurch, 1965); for Kemal's part, see Armstrong, *Gray Wolf,* 58, 60.

used their last reserves. Both sides had consumed too much of their strength and were too exhausted to undertake any further general assaults. A pall of lethargy, sickness, and futility descended on Hamilton's soldiers. The failure of the Anzac-Suvla action determined the fate of the Gallipoli campaign. Hamilton's high brass underwent a drastic selection out. Joffre, Haig, and Wilson persuaded Kitchener that Britain must participate in a big offensive in the west so that relief might be given the Russians on the eastern front, and support to a government and command in France dedicated to the vigorous prosecution of the war. Otherwise France might make a separate peace.[43] Time, moreover, was running out in the Balkans for any further initiative in Gallipoli. The conquest of Serbia, which was near, would permit the uninterrupted shipment of men and materiel from Germany, so strengthening Turkey as to preclude practical hope for success in a new Allied attempt. French and British divisions were diverted from Gallipoli to join the Salonika expedition at the end of September. The next month Hamilton was relieved of his command.[44]

The move to evacuate Gallipoli gathered momentum, given fresh steam by the Serbian debacle. The Conservative leader Andrew Bonar Law, "the pioneer of evacuation," and Lloyd George were moving closer together and taking a stronger line of opposition to Gallipoli, intermingled with their criticism of Kitchener. Hamilton's replacement boldly recommended withdrawal of all forces from Gallipoli.[45] Kitchener, sent out to report the Gallipoli situation, advised the evacuation of all but Helles. Finally, a severe storm and then a blizzard on Gallipoli, causing heart-rending losses in frostbite and sickness, brought the cabinet to a decision on December 7 to evacuate Anzac and Suvla.[46]

Symbolically, Churchill, the prime mover of the strategic venture, was left out of the new and smaller War Committee, which in October took the place of the Dardanelles Committee in Britain's supreme direction of war. This political casualty took to the trenches in France in command of a battalion. Kitchener returned from Gallipoli to be superseded by the new chief of the imperial general staff, General Sir William Robertson.

43. Blake, *Private Papers of Douglas Haig,* 96.
44. See Higgins, *Winston Churchill and the Dardanelles,* 211–12, 218; Guinn, *British Strategy and Politics,* 95–96.
45. Beaverbrook, *Politicians and the War,* 169–73.
46. Robertson, *Soldiers and Statesmen,* 1: 137–44; Beaverbrook, *Politicians and the War,* 179–85.

The evacuation proved the one true Allied success of the Gallipoli campaign. The step was planned in advance to the last detail and to precise schedules of movement. By complete security and ingenious ruse, the Turks were deluded into believing that the army remained in full force until the 83,000 men were secretly carried away from Anzac and Suvla to the last person during the December nights. Spurred on by Robertson, the confirmed westerner, the War Committee and the cabinet agreed to liquidate the rest of the undertaking. In the same manner the army of some 35,000 at Helles was evacuated by the night of January 8–9, just in time to escape the bad weather and a Turkish assault intended to wipe out the last of the enemy.[47] The evacuation was a shining feat of logistic efficiency, staff planning, cooperation between the services, and disciplined organization. The withdrawal without loss was the Dunkirk of the Great War—almost turning defeat into victory.

With the end of this brave, bold enterprise there has remained ever since the task of giving it a decent and just place in the gallery of history. Whatever the breadth of conception and the heroism of the men, the campaign was distinguished by some of the most brutal fighting ever known, under the worst of conditions. Of special interest in the development of the art of war, it involved the use of every variety of weapon, including the submarine and airplane, and constituted the first large-scale expedition in amphibious warfare under modern conditions.

The campaign was a poignant succession of failures. One lost opportunity followed another with momentous consequences. The debacle closed out the possibility of a grand strategic maneuver on the flank in Turkey and a means thereby of shortening the war materially. Henceforth the conflict was to be entirely a war of exhaustion and blood-drenching offensives on the Western Front, since any other possibility of opening a flank went unrealized. Dardanelles-Gallipoli thus ranks with the Marne and Jutland as a turning point in the war, not for what it accomplished strategically, but for what it failed to accomplish. If the Turkish head had been severed from the body of the empire by conquest of Constantinople, the war would have taken a different course, and Germany's allies would have been eliminated earlier. Instead of crushing the Turks early by way of Constantinople, the British had to take the long and costly route via

47. On the evacuation, see especially Nevinson, *Dardanelles Campaign*, 386–406; Bean, *Story of Anzac*, 2: 853–910; Aspinall-Oglander, *Gallipoli*, 2: 440–78; Keyes, *Naval Memoirs*, 1: 498–519; Moorehead, *Gallipoli*, 339–55.

Palestine and Mesopotamia. The failure consolidated the ascendancy of a continental over a peripheral strategy and lost the chance to liberate British strategic decision from domination by France and the westerners. The results, nevertheless, were not without benefit to the Allies. The fighting power and spirit of the Turks were sapped by the losses of some 300,000 men. The campaign contained, for the better part of a year, much of the Turkish army and war effort, drawing off Turkish forces otherwise available for the Caucasus, eliminating the Turks as a force in the Balkans, and raising a shield for the defense of Egypt and the Suez. Italy was probably brought into the war earlier than otherwise. The Allies paid a price, though not disproportionate, for these benefits in heavy casualties, amounting to just over half of the half-million soldiers committed.[48]

Victory invites celebration, and defeat, inquiry. And so with the Dardanelles disaster. The British parliament set up the Dardanelles Commission to inquire "into the origin, inception, and conduct of operations of war in the Dardanelles and Gallipoli." From that time on the strategic stroke at the Dardanelles has been the subject of the closest scrutiny and continuing controversy.

The Dardanelles Commission regarded the campaign as a mistake, setting forth its opinion "that from the outset the risks of failure attending the Expedition outweighed its chances of success."[49] The generals and others who were westerners condemned it for stealing the means of war from the west. One of the severest indictments in a serious historical work was handed down early in the Australian official history of Anzac.[50] Since this early period historical interpretation has taken, on the whole, a more favorable view, though books of a contrary vein continue to appear. The balance has been swinging toward the verdict that this was the most brilliant and imaginative strategic conception of the war, if not, as Lord Clement Attlee said, "the one strategic idea in the war."[51]

The assessment of this peripheral venture really turned on its chances of success, for there could have been no doubt of the vast consequences flowing from the Allied conquest of the Straits. Along with Enver and

48. See Aspinall-Oglander, *Gallipoli*, 2: 483, 486; Nevinson, *Dardanelles Campaign*, 406; James, *Gallipoli*, 348.
49. Dardanelles Commission, *Final Report*, 85.
50. Bean, *Story of Anzac*, particularly vol. 1, pp. 175, 201–02.
51. For example of a recent critical work, see Higgins, *Winston Churchill and the Dardanelles*. An affirmative and more representative assessment is found in the recent account by Bush, *Gallipoli*, especially p. 307.

Turkish headquarters, Liman von Sanders, officers of the German general staff in Turkey, and other foreign and naval experts stationed in Constantinople were of the opinion that the Allied fleet could have gotten through if it had made another attempt in March. Falkenhayn took it for granted "that a serious attempt at landing . . . would be bound to succeed."[52]

This peripheral strategy thus had good prospects of success if operations had been conducted properly. But operations were botched from the beginning until the end of fighting. The colossal blundering extended from the peak of authority in London to the command in Gallipoli. The Dardanelles disaster, in short, represented a conspicuous dereliction in the British war direction. The two words "drift" and "muddle" best characterize the management of the Dardanelles-Gallipoli enterprise throughout. The government drifted into a demonstration, then into a full-fledged naval assault on the Straits, into a land campaign to assist the navy, into a land campaign assisted by the navy, and finally into evacuation. The government failed to discern the eventual extent of involvement as a consequence of the initial step and set out with no comprehension of the precise strategic purpose intended in relation to the entire conduct of the war.

The resources of war consequently were thrown into the gamble in driblets, without regard to the importance of concentrating military and naval strength in combined operations before the enemy could reinforce his positions effectively. If the land forces available in August had been used in March or April, Gallipoli might have been won. The responsibility must be shared between the feeble leadership of the Asquith government, the faulty mechanism for the conduct of war, and the paralyzing lack of coordination between the various authorities concerned.

The relation was always incommensurate between the military power applied and the final objective intended. Gallipoli was treated as a second-class theater, with the expectation of achieving a victory of first-class import. The gravitational pull of the Western Front and French domination of Allied strategy kept Hamilton's forces from being adequately supplied with troops, guns, ammunition, equipment for trench warfare, planes, hospital facilities, and qualified officers. The British generals under Hamilton, selected by Kitchener on the basis of seniority, never measured up, nor did Hamilton himself, to the demands laid upon them or to the exceptionally competent command of the forceful Liman von Sanders and

52. Falkenhayn, *German General Staff*, 85.

to the inspired leadership of the fiercely energetic and bold Kemal.

Britain could have decided on either of two logical alternatives by way of assisting the Russians in this area: a diversionary demonstration, such as a purely naval bombardment involving a trifling cost, or a primary operation provided with sufficient means of war to achieve a major strategic aim. In the light of after-events the choice was clear and simple: either no Gallipoli at all or the principal front of Allied operations in Gallipoli. Unfortunately, neither course was followed.

4. THE FIGHT AT SEA

Naval policy quickly became a matter of debate both among the British and among the Germans. The British were agreed that the fleet must at once establish command of the seas and impose a distant blockade of the enemy. Beyond these objectives differences emerged concerning (1) offensive action designed to flush out the German High Seas Fleet from its havens for the decisive battle and (2) adoption of a maritime strategy employing the fleet in combined operations on the flanks of the enemy.

The First Lord of the Admiralty was the most enthusiastic advocate of a maritime, or peripheral, strategy. Churchill not only urged naval action in the Dardanelles and combined operations in Gallipoli but also the capture of the Frisian island of Borkum as a step toward a Baltic naval offensive. The proposals for utilizing supremacy at sea to circumvent the stalemate on the Western Front met resistance from Fisher, Jellicoe, and most of the senior officers of the navy. They were North Sea admirals, who were loath to see diversions of strength from the Grand Fleet, for fear of weakening it for the decisive encounter with the High Seas Fleet. They corresponded to the westerners among the generals, who would concentrate military strength on the Western Front. Their opposition to the Dardanelles project acted to limit the range of the navy's uses and worked to bring about the cabinet crisis of May 1915 and the fall of Churchill at the Admiralty. Jellicoe and other admirals also avoided an aggressive course toward the German fleet; they were concerned that fleet action in the southern part of the North Sea would enable the Germans, through the use of submarines, mines, and torpedoes, to damage the fleet to the extent of tipping the balance of naval power in this theater.

In Germany, even more uncertainty and controversy prevailed over the mission of the fleet. The war soon demonstrated, at least for the army, the poor investment made in building a political navy that, although large, was not superior or equal to the British in power. The function of the navy as the weapon of a continental military power engaged in a vast land war and at the same time in a war with the first sea power had never received serious study by the German military and naval authorities. The naval leaders expected that the British fleet would immediately lay on a close blockade and seek battle in the Helgoland Bight, where German mines and torpedoes could be used advantageously. When the British did not comply with these expectations, two lines of naval thought emerged.

Tirpitz, the foremost champion of the naval offensive, asserted that the fleet should take bold initiatives so as to inflict losses reducing the superiority of British naval power. The fleet should not wait for but seek an opportunity for full-scale battle. Constraint imposed on the High Seas Fleet "to risk nothing" against superior force would result only in "embalming the fleet." He claimed that the fleet had important technical superiorities over the British, giving the Germans a fighting chance of victory; a passive avoidance of action would damage the morale of the crews and make the navy less ready for battle; the inaction would lose the navy the support of the nation and the continued authorization of funds so that "the end of the war would be the end of the fleet."[53]

The naval staff for the most part and the chief of the kaiser's naval cabinet, Admiral Georg Alexander von Müller, recognized that the fleet was not strong enough to engage the British in the North Sea, away from German waters, with hope of success. They pursued a cautious policy of keeping the fleet "in being," while deferring a decisive action until favorable circumstances arose after the fleets were more nearly balanced in strength. The equalization would be achieved in the interim by means of minor war, or *Kleinkrieg*. This was a form of guerrilla warfare by which the Grand Fleet would be whittled down through mines, night attacks of torpedo boats, submarine warfare, and hit-and-run raids. The kaiser and the chancellor desired the preservation of the fleet substantially intact in order that it might serve as a factor in the conclusion of peace.[54]

The German naval dilemma centered on the distant blockade imposed by the British. With this means Britain could attain its primary naval

53. Tirpitz, *My Memoirs,* 2: 224, 251, 260, 344, 348; Tirpitz, *Deutsche Ohnmachtspolitik im Weltkriege,* 73–128.
54. Sir Julian S. Corbett and Sir Henry Newbolt, *Naval Operations,* 5 vols. (London, 1920–31), 1: 163; Reinhard Scheer, *Germany's High Sea Fleet in the World War* (London, 1920), 25.

objective without being vulnerable to any great extent to the weapons of the *Kleinkrieg,* which could be used to full advantage only in the German Bight and the southern part of the North Sea. A close blockade would have allowed Germany the desired conditions. On the other hand, Germany could not challenge the distant blockade without sending its fleet so far out that Britain would gain the advantage of position. Britain could maintain the blockade without a battle of the fleets; Germany could overcome it only by battle. The weight of German professional opinion concluded that Germany could not win that battle without success in the *Kleinkrieg* first, but the distant blockade precluded such success.

The German navy performed more limited but essential functions. It protected the German coasts and the bases for submarine warfare. It closed the Baltic to any Allied attack on the northern flank. Naval mastery there assured the continuous flow to Germany of Swedish iron ore and other essential Scandinavian imports. A force as large as the Tirpitz fleet, however, was not necessary for these uses, and the question arose whether some of the funds sunk in the Tirpitz dreadnoughts might not have been more wisely spent on submarines, aircraft, or additional army corps.[55]

The Grand Fleet, from its war stations in the North Sea, contained the northern passage of those waters, and the Channel Fleet guarded the Straits of Dover, blocking the other passage. British naval power otherwise was disposed principally in a Mediterranean fleet and the Asiatic squadron. Most of the German High Seas Fleet was concentrated at the mouth of the Jade River, older forces being assigned to the Baltic. In addition, the Germans had eight cruisers stationed in the Far East and West Indies; the battle cruiser *Goeben* and the light cruiser *Breslau* were in the Adriatic.

The first task of the British navy was to clear the seas of Germany's raiders—the scattered cruiser forces and five armed merchantmen. In disposing of these ships, the Germans achieved a success of large political consequences in the first naval episode of the war. The *Goeben* and *Breslau,* commanded by Souchon, eluded the chase of the more powerful British fleet in the Mediterranean and arrived at the Dardanelles unharmed on August 10. The responsibility for not seizing three different opportunities to engage the two cruisers belonged both to the faulty instructions and inadequate information provided the fleet by the Admiralty and to the lack

55. See Falkenhayn, *German General Staff,* 252; Scheer, *Germany's High Sea Fleet,* 19.

of initiative and competence of the British commander Admiral Sir Archibald Berkeley Milne. The British official history pronounces a just tribute to Souchon's action: "few naval decisions more bold and well-judged were ever taken." Through the presence of the two warships at Constantinople the Germans had the means of exerting an intense pressure on the Turks. The Porte was brought around to intervene as an ally; the Straits were closed for the duration; Russia was isolated and crippled in the prosecution of the war; and the Dardanelles campaign was initiated in an effort to overcome what Souchon had effected with his two cruisers.[56]

The Allies soon rid the far seas of the commerce-raiders. In the mission of search and destruction conducted by the Germans, the aggressive Count Maximilian von Spee, having reformed the east China squadron off Chile, won a dramatic victory of annihilation near Coronel over the British squadron off the South American station commanded by Admiral Sir Christopher Cradock.[57] Spee, now a condemned man, attempted a desperate run for home. The British intercepted his force on December 8 at the Falkland Islands with a squadron including three battle cruisers coolly detached from the Grand Fleet for the purpose. Superiority in numbers, guns, and speed were reversed, and the British made amends for the sad fate of "poor Kit Cradock" by shooting four of Spee's five cruisers into wrecks until they sank. The fifth was hunted down and sunk three months later in remote Chilean waters.[58] The other three cruisers at large, including the deadliest commerce-killer, the *Emden,* had already been destroyed before the Falklands action. Thus the battle of the Falklands ended the first phase of the naval war in accounting for the German cruisers and allowing Britain to strengthen the fleet in the North Sea theater with the squadrons from the outer oceans.

56. See above, p. 99, and Corbett and Newbolt, *Naval Operations,* 1: 56–73; Marder, *From the Dreadnought to Scapa Flow,* 2: 20–41; Geoffrey Martin Bennett, *Naval Battles of the First World War* (London, 1968), 27–48; Bacon and McMurtrie, *Modern Naval Strategy,* 99–100, 179; David Woodward, "The Escape of the *Goeben* and *Breslau,*" *History Today* 10 (1960): 232–39.

57. Corbett and Newbolt, *Naval Operations,* 1: 290–99, 315–32, 355–69; Bennett, *Naval Battles,* 69–76, 99–102; Geoffrey Martin Bennett, *Coronel and the Falklands* (New York, 1962), 22–62; Bacon and McMurtrie, *Modern Naval Strategy,* 183–85.

58. Corbett and Newbolt, *Naval Operations,* 1: 416–54; Bennett, *Coronel and the Falklands,* 109–76. Barrie Pitt, *Coronel and Falklands* (London, 1960), is a popular and dramatic narrative; the German side of the story is told by a survivor in Hans Pochhammer, *Graf Spees letzte Fahrt* (Berlin, 1918).

The first six months of the war witnessed more action in this theater than at any time before Jutland and its preliminaries in 1916. The first encounter of any significance, in the Helgoland Bight on August 28, 1914, was an operation of entrapment that set the pattern for many following actions. The British attempted to lure German destroyer patrols from the outposts of Helgoland to their destruction by two destroyer flotillas and a submarine pack, strengthened with two light cruisers and supported by a light cruiser squadron and the battle cruiser squadron of Admiral Sir David Beatty. The British attackers were saved from a German cruiser ambuscade by Beatty's battle cruisers, which rushed to the rescue in the dangerous waters of the Bight. Luck favored the British, and they sank three light cruisers and one destroyer without losing a single vessel. The Admiralty's incompetent staff work was shocking, as was the lack of coordination between the British destroyer flotillas and cruiser squadrons. The Germans, learning from this experience, took immediate steps to safeguard the Bight by laying mine barriers.[59]

The daring and resourceful British stroke confirmed British naval ascendancy and delivered a bitter blow to the untested German navy and to the kaiser. The defeat fixed the kaiser's determination not to risk further naval losses and to restrict the initiative of the fleet.

The tables, however, were shortly turned. A single German submarine caught three old armored cruisers—the "three Cressys"—without destroyer protection off the Dutch coast and sank them in quick succession, with a heavy loss of crew. The incident aroused public criticism of the Admiralty in Britain but inspired the German headquarters with enthusiasm and the kaiser with bliss.[60]

The efforts at equalization of the two navies through the *Kleinkrieg* made no headway. In frustration the commander of the High Seas Fleet, Admiral Friedrich von Ingenohl, planned a trap for catching a portion of the Grand Fleet within the grip of the whole High Seas Fleet. He dispatched Admiral Franz von Hipper's squadron of five battle cruisers as bait to raid Scarborough and sow mines along the British coast. The British utilized advance information on the German stratagem obtained by the interception and decoding of German naval messages. They set a trap to counter

59. Gretton, *Winston Churchill and the Royal Navy,* 172–74; Groos and Gladisch, *Der Krieg in der Nordsee,* 1: 210–14.
60. Marder, *From the Dreadnought to Scapa Flow,* 2: 53–59; Gretton, *Winston Churchill and the Royal Navy,* 177; Müller, *Regierte der Kaiser?,* 61.

Hipper's force with a more powerful one headed by Beatty's four battle cruisers and a squadron of six battleships from the Grand Fleet. By chance, Beatty's force and the High Seas Fleet set out to assemble off the Dogger Bank on December 16. A group of Beatty's destroyers ran into a destroyer and cruiser screen of the High Seas Fleet, and a running fight followed. Ingenohl, apprehensive that he had encountered a screen of the entire Grand Fleet, sped for home. Through mistakes Beatty missed several chances to engage Hipper's raiders. Both sides thus let slip from their grasp the rarest of opportunities to overturn, by a great victory, the distribution of naval power and radically alter the naval war.[61]

Having obtained authorization from the kaiser for the exercise of somewhat more naval initiative, Ingenohl sent out Hipper's battle cruisers on a sortie on January 24, 1915. Beatty's superior force, with the benefit of intercepted information, steamed into perfect position off Dogger Bank to meet Hipper. Though sinking one of Hipper's battle cruisers, the British "lost what should have been an unparalleled victory." (The lament of Fisher.) The fault was due to the mistakes of individuals and to the deficiencies of the inflexible system of tactical direction that discouraged the exercise of discretion and initiative in battle.[62]

The technical victory of the British and the escape of the German quarry represented to a degree a preview of Jutland. Because of their inferior gunnery the British revised the battle orders of the fleet to improve the distribution of fire. They also hurried up the work of installing the director systems of central fire control on their battle cruisers.[63]

In Germany, criticisms of the command for not sending out the main High Seas Fleet in support of Hipper led to Ingenohl's replacement by Admiral Hugo von Pohl, who had been in charge of the naval staff. After Dogger Bank and under Pohl, the Germans were still more prudent about risking the fleet. They found more likely possibilities in the U-boat and systematically applied this weapon to the war of commerce. Naval warfare during the following year until February 1916 was dominated by two

61. Marder, *From the Dreadnought to Scapa Flow*, 2: 130–34; A. Temple Patterson, ed., *The Jellicoe Papers*, 2 vols. (Shortlands, England, 1966–68), 1: 107–10; Müller, *Regierte der Kaiser?*, 75.

62. See Beatty's report to Jellicoe on the action and the latter's confidential report to Admiralty in Patterson, *Jellicoe Papers*, 1: 132–36, 145–48.

63. For accounts and discussion of the action, see Marder, *From the Dreadnought to Scapa Flow*, 2: 156–74; Groos and Gladisch, *Der Krieg in der Nordsee*, 3: 189–249; Keyes, *Naval Memoirs*, 1: 159–67.

features: the passivity of the British and German fleets and the increasing pace of the submarine and antisubmarine war. From February to September 1915 the Reich conducted a campaign of unrestricted U-boat warfare against merchant shipping in a declared zone around the British Isles.

In addition to combat duties in the North Sea sector, the British navy bore the major burden of imposing the blockade on the Central Powers. British cruisers swept the German merchant marine from the seas. The navy convoyed the army to France, the Canadian forces to Britain, and Indian troops to France. In the Mediterranean the primary responsibility for naval operations rested with France, except for the Dardanelles zone and waters off British dependencies. The French navy convoyed troops from North Africa to France and blockaded the Adriatic with a cordon of ships across the Straits of Otranto. From September 1915 on, the Germans carried on an intensive submarine campaign in the Mediterranean. The Allies, in meeting this, divided the Mediterranean into eighteen patrol zones, ten of which the French fleet patrolled and the British and Italian fleets the remainder, in a system that did not prove effective.[64]

64. Marder, *From the Dreadnought to Scapa Flow*, 2: 333–41.

Chapter Six

THE WAR OF DESPERATION

1. VERDUN

THE war in 1916, more than at any other time during the conflict, was concentrated in the struggle of stalemate on the Western Front. A victorious conclusion of the war still eluded the German bloc after a year of success in the east and generally on the southern flank. The German high command turned to the west in 1916 in an effort to convince Britain and France that it was useless to continue fighting. These two Allies, having flubbed and lost the opportunity at the Dardanelles for a true strategic alternative to the frontal assault in the west, prepared for their greatest offensive to date in France. The resulting initiatives of the two sides produced the battles of Verdun and the Somme.

These appalling contests of men against materiel typified the nature of the war of deadlock on the Western Front at its height. Elsewhere Russia, Austria, and Italy, all ill-equipped from the beginning for waging total war, were reeling from the accumulated exertions and losses. It had become a war of desperation, with no prospects of victory for either side unless unforeseen factors came into play, such as the entry of the United States. The mounting anxiety and dissatisfaction with the direction of the war brought about a change of high command both in Germany and in France and a new, more vigorous coalition government in Britain.

The Allies, endeavoring to correct the past deficiencies of coordination, held a military conference at Chantilly, the location of the French general headquarters, on December 6–8, 1915. The conference agreed on concerted early offensives of maximum effort to be launched on the principal fronts. In carrying out this agreement, Joffre and Haig planned a joint offensive on the Somme.[1]

The German strategy for 1916 was outlined by Falkenhayn in a famous memorandum submitted to the kaiser before Christmas. In this Falken-

---

1. France, Ministère de la guerre, état-major d'armée, *Les armées françaises dans la Grande Guerre,* 10 vols. (Paris, 1922–34), 4, pt. 1: 3–4, 11–15, 28–31; Robertson, *Soldiers and Statesmen,* 1: 245–46.

hayn perceived no way out for Germany until Britain was ready for peace, once France, its "best sword" on the continent, had been subdued. An unrestricted submarine campaign against British shipping, and the organization of a political and economic union on the continent formed parts of the plan for ending the war with Britain. The heart of the problem was how to eliminate France as an active military force, in view of the impenetrable barrier of the Western Front.

Falkenhayn proposed the solution of bleeding the enemy white in place (*Aufblutung auf der Stelle*) until France realized the hopelessness of continuing the war. He would limit German losses by attacking on a narrow front, with masses of materiel substituted for men to the greatest possible extent. The point of attack must be a place that would be regarded by the French nation of such military and symbolic value that the French army would fight to hold it regardless of cost. He estimated that the French were so weakened by the enormous losses of 1914–15 that they could not sustain this kind of massive assault without their morale cracking.

Falkenhayn thus rejected the Blitzkrieg battle of annihilation and the breakthrough operation in the war of position, both of which had failed a decision, for an *Aufblutung* strategy requiring presumably limited human means and taking account of psychological considerations. The method showed originality and flexibility of mind; the struggle of Verdun would test the validity of his estimate and strategic invention.[2]

The fortress system of Verdun, located in a salient astride the Meuse River, consisted of a center surrounded by two girdles of dispersed forts, beyond which extended defense positions. The system had been a pivot in the French border defenses before the war and, along with Paris at the other end, a bastion in the battle of the Marne. The high command, in the light of the destruction done the Belgian forts in 1914, had let the system deteriorate and had transferred most of its guns to active fronts.[3]

The Germans prepared to the last detail an efficient machine of assault in the Fifth Army under Crown Prince Wilhelm, masking their intensive activity by ruse and skillful concealment. They transferred divisions from

2. For the text of the memorandum, see Falkenhayn, *German General Staff*, 239–50; for a fundamental analysis of the plan and a valuable appreciation of its significance in relation to the Allied breakthrough strategy, see Hermann Ziese-Beringer, *Der einsame Feldherr: Die Wahrheit über Verdun*, 2 vols. (Berlin, 1934), 1: 26–59.

3. On the disrepair of Verdun and the reasons for it, see Wilhelm Ziegler, *Verdun*, 4th ed. (Hamburg, 1943), 51–54.

the eastern front to the west and trained storm troops especially for the attack. They placed their faith, however, in a mass accumulation of artillery and other materiel. The new Fokker monoplane gained them a momentary air supremacy. The chief of staff of the Fifth Army drafted operational plans for attacks on both banks of the Meuse, with the aim of enveloping the front forces on the right bank. But Falkenhayn limited the plan to an assault on the right bank in order to save men and materiel.[4]

The battle of Verdun lasted nearly a year and moved through four phases. In the first, the Germans struck on February 21 with nine elite divisions, following nine hours of the most intensive bombardment yet seen in the war—"an avalanche of steel and iron, of shrapnel and poisonous gas shells," as described by Pétain. Despite the storm of artillery fire and the panic created by the new German flamethrowers, the three defending divisions put up a desperate resistance. For three days of fury the Germans kept on coming and broke through the second position of the French.[5]

The resolution of the French high command saved the collapsing front. Joffre placed the defense in the hands of Pétain and rushed up reserves to form, with the troops already at Verdun, a new Second Army. During the remainder of the battle Pétain, the master of defense, continued to be the impelling force and the directing mind of the successful French resistance and the recovery of lost ground. Fresh troops and a great number of guns were brought up until an eventual army of 420,000 was assembled. An efficient motorized transport service was organized for moving men and materiel in an endless stream along the "Sacred Way" from Bar-le-Duc. The crisis was surmounted, but not without Fort Douaumont falling to the Germans.[6]

By February 27 the momentum of the German onslaught had run down, and the battle had come in effect to a standstill. Premier Briand and Joffre were agreed that the primacy of moral and political factors required resistance as if Verdun were Paris itself. From now on it was a struggle of the French army and French nation à outrance.[7]

4. Henri Philippe Pétain, *Verdun* (New York, 1930), 43; Ziese-Beringer, *Der einsame Feldherr*, 1: 146–55.

5. Pétain, *Verdun*, 58; Claude Chambard, *Mourir pour Verdun* (Paris, 1966), 15.

6. *Les armées françaises*, 4, pt. 1: 261–79, 286–88; Hermann Wendt, *Die Angriffe Falkenhayns im Maasgebiet mit Richtung auf Verdun als strategisches Problem* (Berlin, 1931), 77–86; Pétain, *Verdun*, 83–100; Ziegler, *Verdun*, 63–64. On the supply of Verdun, see especially Chambard, *Mourir pour Verdun*, 73–76.

7. On the French decision to defend Verdun, see Jean de Pierrefeu, *G.Q.G., Secteur 1*, 2 vols. (Paris, 1920), 1: 125.

The second phase commenced with Falkenhayn's attack on the left bank of the Meuse. His plan of operations had been changed because the strengthened heavy artillery of the French poured in a deadly fire on the German infantry from the left bank. The German thrust, starting on March 6, smashed over the second position of the French before grinding to a stop at key hills. On March 8 the Germans extended their assault to the right bank.

By April and May the French had brought their strength on the ground and in the air into balance with that of the Germans. The battle turned into a savage war of stalemate and attrition, focusing on the frantic struggle for the dominant hills of the left bank and the sanguinary but unsuccessful attempt of the French to recapture Fort Douaumont. The fighting in these months peculiarly marked the battle of Verdun and gave an appearance of unreality to the battered and bleeding area called "the hell" by the tortured poilus. That they could survive the inferno without a breakdown was traceable in large part to Pétain's system of replacing entire divisions with fresh ones at frequent intervals. The withdrawn divisions were reconstituted and allowed to recuperate. Four-fifths of the French army passed through the Verdun forces in this way and participated in the national effort that became a miracle of French tenacity.[8]

Verdun was now a national symbol for France and an issue of prestige for both nations. The "Meuse mill" was exacting its effects in the implacable struggle. Verdun added to the discontent of the population in Germany and Austria-Hungary; criticism of Falkenhayn was on the rise in the German bloc. A depression in morale affected some French units. In June the chamber, in secret session, attacked the high command and the conduct of the war responsible for the shocking casualties at Verdun.[9]

Joffre was determined to relieve the pressure on Verdun by accelerating the commencement of the concurrent Allied offensives agreed at Chantilly and by French participating in the Somme drive. He appealed successfully to the British and Russians to speed up the beginning of their offensives. In preparing for a share in the Somme offensive, Joffre limited Pétain to supplying replacements for Verdun only to the central group of four

8. Pétain, *Verdun*, 117–18; André Ducasse, Jacques Meyer, and Gabriel Perreux, *Vie et mort des français, 1914–1918* (Paris, 1962), 138; Jacques-Henri Lefebvre, *L'enfer de Verdun* (Paris, 1966), 30.

9. Alistair Horne, *Death of a Generation* (New York, 1970), 73–75; Chambard, *Mourir pour Verdun*, 193, 198–205.

armies, to whose command Pétain was now raised.[10]

The third phase witnessed a dramatic race between the climax of the German attacks on the Meuse and the final measures to launch the Somme offensive. During the first three weeks of June the Germans conducted preliminary attacks and captured Fort Vaux on the right bank. In the last week of the month, which was as critical as February for the French, the Germans made a desperate effort to drive through to the city of Verdun itself. With the aid of the new deadly phosgene gas, they pushed the French defense back on the right bank to the line of final resistance. Joffre answered Pétain's call for help by rushing four fresh divisions to Verdun and telling him on June 24 that the bombardment had begun in preparation for the Somme drive. The German assault slackened for want of reserves, and General Robert Nivelle, a confident aide of Pétain in command of the Second Army, struck back with counterattacks. The last crisis at Verdun ended in a week of bitter and confused fighting, much of it hand-to-hand.[11]

When Falkenhayn's attack of July 11 failed of its purpose, he stopped it and began drawing off formations for defense at the Somme. The Allies had wrested the initiative from the Germans and diverted the main theater to the Somme. The Germans had lost the battle of Verdun both in terms of the untaken city and in the failure of the *Aufblutung* strategy to prevent French participation in a large-scale offensive elsewhere.

In the last phase the French maintained an offensive posture, from the middle of July until a systematic attempt in October to recover the main fortress line and lost ground. In contrast, the differences in the German military leadership over resuming the assault were settled against further attack, with the change in high command on August 29.

The Reich's mounting accumulation of ill-fortune—the check at Verdun, the huge losses on the defensive at the Somme, the success of the Brusilov offensive in the east, the repulse of the Austrians in Italy—was experienced with rising opposition to Falkenhayn. Romania's entry against the German bloc struck as the climactic blow; Falkenhayn was recalled the next day. The kaiser appointed the Hindenburg twins to the supreme command: Hindenburg as chief of the general staff and Ludendorff as first quartermaster general. To both, Verdun was "a bleeding

10. On the significance of Joffre's limitation on Pétain, see Wendt, *Die Angriffe Falkenhayns im Maasgebiet*, 140–41.

11. Chambard, *Mourir pour Verdun*, 195–96; Ziegler, *Verdun*, 179–80.

wound, from which flowed the life blood of our forces." They halted the attack at Verdun for good.[12]

The French went over to the assault in October under the leadership of Nivelle and General Charles Mangin, a dashing, bold, even reckless, commander. Their superiority in artillery made possible a bombardment of tremendous weight, highly damaging counterbattery work, and a fully organized creeping barrage. The infantry had received extensive training on a replica of the German positions. Having achieved tactical surprise through the rolling barrage and a heavy fog, the French drove forward against the physically and mentally exhausted men of the Fifth Army. The German garrison withdrew from Fort Douaumont, and by November 2 Vaux fell without fighting. The French had regained the main fortress line.[13]

The next attack of Nivelle and Mangin, on December 15, after the same intensive preparation, regained more of the sacred ground lost to the Germans. The French captured nearly 12,000 prisoners. The battle of Verdun ended on December 18, after 302 days of the fiercest fighting.

Verdun, more a series of battles than a single action, was the longest battle in history and the greatest battle of materiel during the war for so narrow a front. No other battle of the war brought about such concentrated killing for the space involved. In this tragic bloodletting for both France and Germany, the French sacrificed more than half a million men in total casualties, while Germany's losses were almost as many.[14]

The defects in Falkenhayn's strategy were sharply revealed. He seriously underestimated the French powers of resistance and miscalculated the effects of a narrow front and the massive concentration of artillery in limiting the numbers of German infantry required. As the battle developed, the French, through constant reinforcement, reached equality with the Germans and then superiority in both arms and men.

The situation exposed the crux of the German problem: the Reich did not have sufficient military strength to take a decisive initiative against the Allies. Falkenhayn's plan offered no way to bleed France without bleeding

12. Pétain, *Verdun,* 195–97; Wendt, *Die Angriffe Falkenhayns im Maasgebiet,* 187; Erich von Ludendorff, *Ludendorff's Own Story,* 2 vols. (New York, 1920), 1: 291, 317; Marshal von Hindenburg, *Out of My Life* (London, 1920), 214.

13. *Der Weltkrieg,* 11: 166–69; Alistair Horne, *The Price of Glory* (New York, 1963), 308–14.

14. Chambard, *Mourir pour Verdun,* 316, 325; Raymond Couture and Louis Gary, *Verdun 1916: Réalités et illusions* (Pau, 1966), 36.

Germany too, and Germany could tolerate a drain of military strength even less than the Allies, in view of the balance of forces tipped against the Central Powers from the beginning. At Verdun, Falkenhayn with insufficient forces was attempting the impossible, as Moltke had done before him at the Marne and as Ludendorff was to do after him in 1918.

A main weakness of the Verdun strategy lay in the ambiguity and mutual contradiction of military objectives. While Falkenhayn aimed at draining France of its blood to the point of surrender, the tangible objective of capturing Verdun was the only one that had any meaning for the German troops and for the world. The uncertainty about the controlling purpose of the attack undermined the unity of effort and vigor of direction.[15]

The severe casualties at Verdun and the Somme nevertheless caused a sagging in the French army's spirit and created an acute problem of replacement. France's "last army" was capable of only one last major effort before going over to the defensive until 1918. The mood in France was never to have another Verdun and to end the war as quickly as possible. The conditions existed for attempting a final breakthrough offensive, and in December Joffre was displaced by Nivelle as the leader to conduct it. To Falkenhayn's Verdun strategy belonged a share of the responsibility for the 1917 offensive and for the exhaustion and moral collapse of the French army that followed.[16]

Verdun lowered the quality of the German soldier and intensified the difficulty of finding reserves. Forty-seven infantry divisions went through the Meuse mill and, because the Germans had no system of rotational relief on a divisional basis like the French (until the Somme), they came out completely exhausted and never again so ready in spirit to fight. The futile slaughter and the confused aims shook confidence in a German institutional order sending men into such a pitiless and irrational contest against the machines of death. Verdun stimulated the evolution of mind that eventually inspired the upheaval of November 1918.[17]

15. See Ritter, *Staatskunst*, 3: 221; Ziegler, *Verdun*, 66–69; Wendt, *Die Angriffe Falkenhayns im Maasgebiet*, 200–16.

16. See Ziese-Beringer, *Der einsame Feldherr*, 2: 56–175.

17. See Wendt, *Die Angriffe Falkenhayns im Maasgebiet*, 197; Ernst Kabisch, *Verdun, Wende des Weltkrieges*, 5th ed. (Berlin, 1935), 212.

2. THE SOMME

The "big push" at the Somme had its origins in the program of concurrent Allied offensive agreed at Chantilly in December 1915. Haig favored Flanders as the place for the British blow and desired more time for building up a greater concentration of guns and munitions and for better training of the inexperienced troops of Kitchener's New Armies and Territorial formations recently sent to France. As so often, however, he subordinated his own and British interests to the French, in this case in deciding on both the site and date of the offensive.[18]

The attack was to take place on a front of twenty-five miles traversing both the Somme River and the Ancre, its tributary to the north. Ever since the Marne, the Germans had been free to construct in this quiet sector the strongest defenses of any along the Western Front. The first position of trenches extended along the crest of the main ridge of the area, and the second, along another ridge, was backed by a third set of lines not yet completed. The system of integrated works was fortified with concealed strongholds in the villages and woods, strengthened by subterranean dugouts, and studded with skillfully sited machine-gun emplacements and redoubts. From its heights the Germans could look down on the British troops storming the slopes against this formidable array of the defensive art.

The intervention of Verdun in the planning for the Somme offensive shifted the main responsibility and the initiative from French to British hands. This was the first time in the war that Allied action in the west would be primarily British, and it signaled a significant step in the gradual alteration in roles between the two allies. The officially defined objectives against the bristling German defense system were: to relieve the pressure on Verdun; to wear down the strength of the enemy forces; and to prevent further transfers of German troops from the Western Front to other theaters. Beyond these declared goals, Haig's vision was set on a breakthrough allowing the German front to the north to be rolled up.[19]

The elaborate preparations involved logistics of enormous proportions in providing for the requirements of some half-million men and 100,000

18. See Blake, *Private Papers of Douglas Haig*, 121, 125, 129, 149; A. H. Farrar-Hockley, *The Somme* (London, 1964), 35, 54–56, 69–76.

19. Robertson, *Soldiers and Statesmen*, 1: 271; J. H. Boraston, ed., *Sir Douglas Haig's Despatches* (London, 1919), 20, 365–68; Blake, *Private Papers of Douglas Haig*, 157–58, Terraine, *Douglas Haig*, 200.

horses. Men of Kitchener's New Armies and the Territorial organization comprised the bulk of the fourteen attacking divisions. Both officers and men were insufficiently trained in Britain and improperly trained additionally in France. Their instruction had neglected the new methods and weapons of trench warfare, and the French and German practice of dashing forward irregularly in small groups from cover to cover. The Royal Flying Corps, however, controlled the air, thanks to Nieuport and De Haviland planes, technically more advanced than the Fokker, and to superior numbers.[20]

The principal thrust was to be made at the right of the British front by a new British army, the Fourth, set up in early March under Sir Henry Rawlinson. The French would support Rawlinson on the right with an attack of General Emile Fayolle's Sixth Army both north and south of the Somme. In resistance to the coming strike stood the German Second Army of six divisions commanded by Fritz von Below, one of the Reich's abler generals.

The British preparations closed with seven days of pounding by the guns before the final crescendo. All the thunder failed the expectations that this heavy concentration of artillery would batter down the enemy's defenses so that the infantry might come in virtually to occupy. The effectiveness of the bombardment was reduced by the inadequate training of some of the battery crews and worst of all by the defective quality of much of the ammunition.[21]

On July 1 Britain's volunteers, the flower of Kitchener's New Armies, rose from the trenches, and successive straight lines in close ranks moved forward at a slow, steady pace as if on parade. The German soldiers rushed up from the surviving dugouts to man machine-gun posts and establish a line of defense after the British barrage lifted. German shells and machine guns mowed down the advancing waves in rows. Survivors were likely to run into the death traps of barbed wire that remained intact. The more successful got through the first trenches to fight at close quarters, or even beyond to flounder about without direction in disorganized groups. Detailed arrangements planned in advance did not insure tactical control or maintain communications.

20. Edmonds, *Short History of World War I,* 179; John Harris, *The Somme* (London, 1966), 59; Brian Gardner, *The Big Push* (London, 1961), 39–40.

21. Harris, *Somme,* 69–71, 79; Farrar-Hockley, *Somme,* 95, 102; Terraine, *Douglas Haig,* 202; Gardner, *Big Push,* 63–64; Blake, *Private Papers of Douglas Haig,* 151.

In the center the Ulster division, disobeying orders, demonstrated what flexible, adaptive tactics could do in breaking the strongest German lines. The men advanced up to three miles but had to return for lack of direction, reserves, and support on the flanks. Farther south the British gained some ground, with the effective assistance of French batteries. The French achieved their territorial objectives and more in a brilliant action. The success owed much to tactical skill, experienced soldiers, elasticity of field control, and a thorough and accurate artillery preparation by an artillery having a superiority over the German greater than the British, particularly in heavy guns, including some of the new 400-mm pieces. The French seized the German first position and might have penetrated the second but for danger of exposure on their flank.[22]

The "big push" of July 1 ended as the costliest single day of battle in the war or any other war. For the British it was a cataclysmic defeat of high hopes, at the cost of 60,000 casualties, including 20,000 killed. The British had not appreciated the capacity of fortified lines to survive heavy bombardment and had not acquired proper methods of advancing infantry against enemy positions. Serious tactical faults were committed: the sacrifice of surprise, rigidity of schedule without allowing scope for the initiative of officers and troops, and the unimaginative effort to maintain momentum of advance at all costs by sending forward wave after wave of attackers.[23]

The Somme continued 141 days and, like Verdun, was not a single battle but a series of battles linked with intervening smaller actions. In the first period, two weeks of bitter fighting occurred on the British sector and the short French one north of the Somme. The Germans brought up reinforcements and more artillery, more aircraft, more machine guns. General Fritz von Below, faithfully following Falkenhayn's directive to hold every foot of ground, conducted an aggressive resistance with local counterattacks. The British carried on daily assaults against separate strong points, in which the blunders of the first day were often repeated.

The period ended with the attack of July 14, engineered by Rawlinson. The feat on a narrow front solved the problem of taking the second position of the enemy. The success was achieved by surprise, resulting

22. Farrar-Hockley, *Somme,* 156–57; Gardner, *Big Push,* 94–96; Cyril Falls, *The Great War* (New York, 1959), 250.
23. Harris, *Somme,* 82; Bonham Carter, *Soldier True,* 175. On tactical blunders, see the outstanding discussion in Terraine, *Douglas Haig,* 202–05.

from a short hurricane bombardment, the approach of the attacking troops near the German lines in the night, and the innovation of the creeping barrage.

The central period of the Somme offensive, covering the next two months, was taken up with the struggle for the dominant ridge. The advances were small from trench to trench and from one ruined village to another. The fighting for these points turned into a bloody slugging match, as the Germans reacted with stubborn counterattacks, and the operations shaped more and more into a ferocious war of attrition. The full horrors of the Somme were now brought home to the soldiers. The constant "stunts" and "shows," the battering-ram tactics, the interminable shelling, and the early exhaustion made life a hell of torments for the soldier of the Somme. Surrounded by butchery for the sake of obtaining a few yards of ground, he soon developed a cynicism about the staff officers in the rear and the purpose of the war. Survival and escape from this wasteland of ruin and misery became the one object of his life.[24]

The dimensions of the battle grew larger. The French put in their Tenth Army to the right of Fayolle's and lengthened their line south of the Somme. The Germans, sending up reinforcements, reconstituted their Somme organization into a First Army under Below and a Second Army under the dependable General von Gallwitz. They finally formed a group of three armies, commanded by Crown Prince Rupprecht of Bavaria.

After Hindenburg and Ludendorff replaced Falkenhayn in the supreme command, the German side introduced significant operational departures. They ordered the construction of a new shorter line in the rear (the Siegfried, or Hindenburg, line), extending from southeast of Arras via St. Quentin to the Laon area. Unlike Falkenhayn, the new command would withdraw to the shorter line at the right time for the sake of saving eight to ten divisions. Hindenburg and Ludendorff prepared to change the tactical emphasis through yielding ground, if necessary, so as to conserve men and through forming a more elastic defense, with fewer men in the first line.[25]

The final period commenced with another major strike, in the attack of

24. See Harris, *Somme*, 100–10; Gardner, *Big Push*, 117–22. Both of these works are written more closely from the standpoint of the men in action than most accounts. The grisly reality of the Somme for the frontline soldier is portrayed simply and movingly by a participant, in A. D. Gristwood, *The Somme* (London, 1928).

25. *Ludendorff's Own Story*, 1: 290, 313–25.

September 15. This last period was notable from a technical standpoint in three respects: the assault of September 15 established the creeping barrage as a standard part of offensive procedure; the most revolutionary weapon of land warfare was introduced, in the tank; another rapid stride was made in the progress of military aviation. The Germans brought out their new Albatross fighter, firing two guns through the propeller, with which they began to cut into the British control of the air.

Haig was anxious that the new tanks be used in "the crowning effort" of the year to achieve a decisive breakthrough to Bapaume. The British made a break in the enemy's defenses but could not widen it quickly enough before the Germans recovered and laid down a heavy fire at that point. The opportunity was lost, and the attack could not garner its objective, although the British advanced farther during the several days of fighting than in any other Somme operation. The eigtheen slow, cumbersome tanks that actually participated in combat exerted little influence on the battle. While senior officers generally were unimpressed with their promise, Haig requested a thousand tanks of London.[26]

Haig persevered thereafter, as the weather permitted, in maintaining a steady pressure on the Germans and seeking improved positions on the flanks. On September 25 the Allies attacked on a wide front and captured the Thiepval salient, or spur, on the northern flank. The Canadian corps distinguished itself in the action. When the rains of October fell, a new enemy appeared—the Somme mud. The fighting became sporadic; men, horses, and the conduct of war literally bogged down in the oozing mire. Yet, whenever the weather relented a little, Haig's men took up the fight again, often against determined counterattacks of the Germans. The gains were small, the costs large, the Somme cynicism greater.

Beginning on November 15, Haig struck once more with an attack astride the Ancre. The worst of conditions—cold, rain, and mud—soon prevailed, and a blizzard put an end to the campaign on November 18. The British won the strongly fortified anchor point on the right side of the German front, the Beaumont village and spur, and command of the Ancre valley—"a particularly heavy blow" for Ludendorff.[27]

The "blood bath" of the Somme was the supreme agony of the war, and

26. Blake, *Private Papers of Douglas Haig*, 162, 167; Terraine, *Douglas Haig*, 226–28, especially on Haig's appreciation of the tank's possibilities, in contrast to the attitude of GHQ and other commanders.

27. *Ludendorff's Own Story*, 1: 343.

this battle, along with Verdun, set the character of the war of desperation. The prolonged slaughter match inflicted losses of over 600,000 on the Allies, two-thirds of them British, and of possibly 650,000 or 680,000 on the Germans. The total losses, running to a million and a quarter men, wiped out a large part of a generation and much of the best of that generation.[28]

From this carnage the Allies gained ground thirty miles long and six to seven miles deep. It had no strategic value, and the stalemate was not broken. Haig increasingly justified the offensive for its relief value and most of all for its attritional effect and pressure on Germany toward its "complete overthrow." The main assistance to other Allies was to the French, in saving Verdun in June and July, and supporting the successful offensive there in the fall. The question nevertheless persists whether this aid would have been necessary if the French had used for the defense of Verdun the men and munitions they assembled for participation in the Somme.

The Somme did not keep Falkenhayn from sending five divisions from the west to the east, to meet the danger posed by the Brusilov offensive. Nor did it later prevent OHL from diverting troops from the Western Front for the conquest of Romania. No doubt exists that the Somme caused serious attrition of the German military strength. Both Hindenburg and Ludendorff were anxious about the state of the army in the west, the latter admitting that "we were completely exhausted on the Western Front."[29]

The defenders of Haig can rightly claim that the Somme helped to bring nearer the defeat of the Central Powers. The possibility of more "Somme fighting" was a nightmare to both Hindenburg and Ludendorff. The morale of the German soldiers was declining in August; the men were losing faith in German leadership and the handling of affairs both at the front and at home; in the last months of the battle German deserters were appearing. The Somme was the burial site of the old German army, with its superb qualities of steadfastness and fighting spirit.[30]

The mood of the German nation reflected these manifestations in a depression of spirit traceable to the excessive casualties, the tightening

28. For very good discussions of the disputed question of casualty figures, see Terraine, *Douglas Haig*, 235–36; Farrar-Hockley, *Somme*, 251–53; Gardner, *Big Push*, 235–36.
29. *Ludendorff's Own Story*, 1: 345.
30. Ibid., 364–65; Müller, *Regierte der Kaiser?*, 210; Gardner, *Big Push*, 149.

effects of the blockade, and the poor harvest in 1916. The war weariness of the people and the growing belief among moderate and leftist leaders that Germany was caught in a hopeless situation influenced the floating of its peace proposal in December. The Somme was the breeding ground of peace and revolution.[31]

The strategy of wearing down, however, worked both ways. This battle of attrition par excellence killed the finest of British volunteers, and Kitchener's New Army was entombed along with the idealism of its members in the blood-soaked soil of the Somme. Its "army of ghosts" made peace converts of the more sensitive, such as Siegfried Sassoon and Robert Graves.[32]

The attrition strategy of the Somme seemed abhorrent to many in Britain as a gruesome exercise in butchery without helping much to end the war. One reaction in political circles was represented by the peace memorandum of Lord Lansdowne. The opposite reaction was striving all the more for the knockout blow, and to this end the more efficient organization of the war direction. The latter current of opinion won out. A cabinet crisis in December swept away the weak Asquith regime for a dynamic coalition cabinet under Lloyd George, who was committed to Germany's surrender.

Lloyd George had no quarrel with Haig on winning the war, rather on the way to win it. He rejected the attrition strategy and roundly criticized the generals for the method of the Somme. But Lloyd George could not propose any other course capable of winning military and political support. Ideally, it would have almost certainly been more productive and less expensive for the western Allies to have waited until 1917 for an offensive. By that time they would have been much better supplied with munitions, artillery, planes, and tanks, while the British would have had an opportunity to give their volunteer troops more and better training.

In the actual situation, however, Haig can hardly be blamed for conducting a big offensive in 1916, since the Dardanelles failure and the outcome of Jutland removed any practical alternative. The French, not yet having suffered the prohibitive losses of prolonged attritional warfare, were not convinced that the defensive was an acceptable course, especially when they were under severe attack at Verdun. The Russians repeatedly

31. On the mood of the German people, see Müller, *Regierte der Kaiser?*, 21.
32. See Siegfried Sassoon, *Memoirs of An Infantry Officer* (London, 1930), and Robert Graves, *Good-Bye to All That* (London, 1929); also below, pp. 478–80.

clamored for more action in the west. If the coalition was to be preserved, there was no choice for the British. The defensive would only have struck Britain's allies as "phony" warfare and aroused suspicions of British intentions. The offensive was demanded, moreover, by longstanding bonds of professional cooperation and military burden sharing between the British and the French; the Somme was the fruition of the Anglo-French military talks of the prewar period.

The continued criticism of Haig for the huge losses in men nevertheless has valid ground in the tactical faults committed by the British command. It can never be forgotten how on July 1 the masses of the New Army were sent to the charge in parade-ground formation; they had neither the tactical guidance based on the experience of the French and Germans nor the leeway in orders for the initiative of officers and men to seek their objective by means of common-sense methods of survival. Rawlinson had a probably better plan, of limited steps and certainly less costly ones, for the strike of July 1. The long series of lesser attacks inflicted sacrificial casualties as well as an exhausting strain. The conclusion is hard to resist that Haig was seeking a breakthrough, or applying pressure on the enemy, or simply "killing Germans," regardless of the cost. It was a stubborn and unimaginative method of conducting the war.[33]

3. JUTLAND

Surface warfare at sea climaxed in the most intense drama of the war, the battle of Jutland, or Skagerrak, as the Germans called it. It was the first time that two national armadas, based on modern industrial technology, joined battle, and the only time in the brief age of dreadnoughts before the aircraft carrier dominated naval warfare. The encounter occurred after the Germans sent their fleet under a new command on longer and more frequent runs into the North Sea. In January 1916 Reinhard Scheer replaced Admiral von Pohl, near death by cancer, at the head of the High Seas Fleet. Before the war Scheer had risen from a middle-class background to become chief of staff in the fleet and win the reputation of a

33. Consider in this context Hindenburg's statement: "If our western adversaries failed to obtain any decisive results in the battles from 1915 to 1917 it must mainly be ascribed to a certain unimaginativeness in their generalship." *Out of My Life*, 216. Works on Haig or the Somme tend to indict or justify Haig. Illustrative of the former are Gardner, *Big Push*, and Harris, *Somme*, and of the latter Terraine, *Douglas Haig*. Terraine's book by a military expert presents an exceptionally able defense of Haig.

tactician. With the kaiser's authorization he now gave a bolder note to the activities of the fleet. At the same time a current was gathering in the Admiralty in favor of a "more active policy."[34] The pace of naval operations accelerated when each side made several attempts during the spring to entrap the other. On May 30, 1916, Scheer laid a new ambush for partial elements of the Grand Fleet, with a sweep off the coast of Norway. Hipper led his scouting force of five battle cruisers and light craft out of the Jade roads to the north, and Scheer's battle squadrons followed a little later. The Admiralty was forewarned of some German operation by way of Horn Reef through intelligence obtained in deciphering Scheer's radio messages. Jellicoe's battle fleet and Beatty's force of six battle cruisers, light craft, and attached squadron of four battleships under Admiral H. Evan-Thomas steamed out of their bases at Scapa Flow, Cromarty, and Rosyth to hunt the hunter off the Skagerrak. The Grand Fleet and the High Seas Fleet moved toward each other.[35]

On the eve of Jutland the British had an overwhelming superiority, estimated at two to one, in naval craft as a whole.[36] The two fleets about to meet were setting off against each other two different conceptions of naval construction, fleet organization, and tactics. The British skimped on durability for the sake of greater speed and gun power in building ships; the Germans aimed to commission unsinkable vessels. The British fleet, commanded by a former gunnery expert, revolved around the big gun on a fast-moving carrier; the function of lighter craft was to locate the targets for the big guns and protect their platforms, that is, the battleships against the torpedoes and mines of the enemy. The German fleet, headed by an admiral whose career had been molded by specialization in torpedo weaponry, favored a coordinated strike of all naval arms; destroyers thus had the primary offensive function of a massed torpedo attack. Jellicoe, an intellectual of mathematical mind and exceptional organizing ability,

34. Marder, *From the Dreadnought to Scapa Flow,* 2: 421–22; A. Temple Patterson, *Jellicoe: A Biography* (London, 1969), 99–102.
35. Our account of Jutland draws particularly from: Marder, *From the Dreadnought to Scapa Flow,* vol. 3; Geoffrey Martin Bennett, *The Battle of Jutland* (London, 1964); Patterson, *Jellicoe Papers;* Patterson, *Jellicoe;* Jellicoe, *Grand Fleet;* Scheer, *Germany's High Sea Fleet;* Holloway H. Frost, *The Battle of Jutland* (1936; reprint, Annapolis, 1964); Donald Macintyre, *Jutland* (London, 1957); Stuart Legg, *Jutland* (London, 1966); Langhorne Gibson and J.E.T. Harper, *The Riddle of Jutland* (New York, 1934).
36. Frost, *Battle of Jutland,* 102–03.

carefully calculated and avoided risks; Scheer, a cool, simple fighter, was willing to take a chance.[37]

Jellicoe's only idea of a battle between the two fleets was a "long-range, heavy-gun duel on parallel lines in broad daylight." This tactical rigidity became more fixed through the practice of centralized command, supported by a long tradition of implicit obedience to the commanding admiral and of waiting for orders before acting. The exercise of initiative and independent decision was smothered. The command of the High Seas Fleet paid more regard to the principle of decentralization, and senior officers enjoyed more scope for initiative.[38]

The British expected the grand encounter of the fleets to be played out as a set-piece battle. They programmed it from the beginning to end by the book, as prescribed in the elaborate orders of the Grand Fleet and supplemented by the signals of Jellicoe just before and during the action. The British tactics presupposed that the Germans would fight according to the British preconception. That Scheer would not choose self-destruction in a shoot-out line to line with a much stronger fleet was the obvious weakness in the British plan of battle.

The fight was set off with an action between battle cruisers, precipitated by Beatty's destroyers coming into contact with Hipper's destroyer screen in the early afternoon of May 31, just as Beatty reached his rendezvous west of Jutland. On contact with Beatty's battle cruisers, Hipper swung around from the northwest to the southeast to lure the British force within shot of the German battle fleet. The two carried on a running fight to the south, in which two of Beatty's six battle cruisers were sunk, apparently from the explosion of the magazine ignited by cordite flash from a penetrated turret, and his own flagship was substantially damaged. Beatty continued toward Scheer's trap until Commodore W.E.E. Goodenough's light cruiser squadron, a part of Beatty's force, sighted Scheer's line of battleships.[39]

The run to the south ended as Beatty turned north to escape destruc-

37. On the differences between Jellicoe and Scheer as fleet commanders, see Frost, *Battle of Jutland*, 108, 343; Legg, *Jutland*, 99, 141; Macintyre, *Jutland*, 30–34, 78.

38. On tactics and the practice of command, see Marder, *From the Dreadnought to Scapa Flow*, 3: 3–35; Patterson, *Jellicoe*, 103–06.

39. Until this battle the British were not aware of a specific defect in the construction of capital ships that the Germans had already discovered and corrected from their experience in the Dogger Bank action of January 24, 1915, namely, the vulnerability of the magazines to flash from hits inside the gun turrets.

tion. Hipper and Scheer joined and pursued the British battle cruiser force. Running to the north, Beatty succeeded in drawing the German fleet within range of Jellicoe's battleships, but his cruisers, except for Goodenough's exemplary job of scouting, failed to maintain contact with Scheer's fleet and report to Jellicoe on the enemy's course, speed, and formation. Beatty's battle cruisers and the battleships of Evan-Thomas, having better visibility than the Germans, registered a punishing fire on Hipper's battle cruisers and Scheer's lead battleships. A few minutes before six, Beatty's force came into visual contact with the Grand Fleet.[40]

In this first phase Beatty committed tactical faults, principally by not concentrating his battle cruisers, with the attached Fifth Battle Squadron of Evan-Thomas, before engaging Hipper. If Beatty had done this, naval experts hold that he would have destroyed Hipper's battle cruisers.[41]

The action between the main fleets turned on the manner in which Jellicoe deployed, from cruising formation of six columns of four battleships each, into a single line ahead for the tremendous gun duel. Because of the late and sometimes contradictory reporting of Beatty's scouting vessels, Jellicoe waited in rising tension but with "iron nerve" for definite information on the bearing of the approaching German battleships. He did not receive it until the enemy fleet was only seven miles away.

In view of Scheer's nearness, Jellicoe immediately decided for deployment on the port column away from the enemy. Deployment on the side toward the German battle line, Jellicoe feared, would have exposed his own battleships to a massed torpedo attack and the lead ships, in turning, to the concentrated fire of the enemy's broadsides. His decision, while taking longer for the completion of deployment, threw the British battle line directly across the head of the German fleet's advance or crossed the "T." The British had gained the most favorable and coveted position for concentrated broadside fire, from the sides of an arc on the leading German battleships. Deployment on the outer wing also obtained better visibility, by silhouetting the German ships against the skyline at sundown.

Critics, including Churchill and some admirals, have held that deployment on the farther column was an overcautious move away from the

40. For a detailed account of the battle-cruiser action, movement by movement and minute by minute, see Jellicoe, *Grand Fleet,* 316–40.

41. On the unsatisfactory aspects of the British role in the cruiser battle and the factors responsible for the deficiencies, see the excellent treatment in Marder, *From the Dreadnought to Scapa Flow,* 3: 62–79; also Bennett, *Battle of Jutland,* 94–95.

enemy; it increased the range and caused delay when it was all-important to save time for a decisive action in the remaining daylight. The greater weight of naval and historical opinion, in which the German official history shares, has, however, supported Jellicoe's decision.[42]

The fleet action began just after the British deployment got under way and continued intermittently for about two hours. The German van suddenly ran into "a sea of fire" along the entire arc, while the smoke and mist kept the Germans from making out the cloaked British battleships except for the gun flashes. Scheer coolly extricated the High Seas Fleet from this deadly peril by an intricate maneuver quite unknown to the British. From long experience, it was performed in the confusion of battle with extraordinary skill.[43]

This *Gefechtskehrtwendung* was a complete turn away from Jellicoe, or turn-around from the rear to the opposite direction, of all the ships in the battle line, covered by a destroyer attack and smoke screen. Scheer's whole fleet withdrew to the southwest. The British battleships that saw the turn-away did not report it to Jellicoe or turn themselves on their own initiative; nor did the light cruisers give him any information. When Jellicoe belatedly apprehended Scheer's movement to the rear, the British commander avoided the risk of mines and torpedoes from a retreating fleet by not giving chase. He countered with a swing of his battleships in cruising, or column, formation to the east and south, extending the fleet across the route Scheer would presumably take back to the home harbors.

During this initial clash of the fleets, lasting only ten minutes, the British heavy ships had the advantage of visibility. While being scarcely hit themselves, they hammered all but one of Hipper's battle cruisers almost out of action, and the leading German battleships hard. Earlier during the deployment, another of the great "greyhounds" of the Grand Fleet—or a battle cruiser—blew up with a magazine explosion.[44]

A half hour after Scheer vanished behind a curtain of mist, the two fleets met again, when he reversed his course in another *Gefechtskehrtwendung*. Likely intended as an escape attempt around the rear of the British fleet,

42. Bacon and McMurtrie, *Modern Naval Strategy*, 85–86; Macintyre, *Jutland*, 113–18; Marder, *From the Dreadnough to Scapa Flow*, 3: 86–94; Churchill, *World Crisis*, 3, pt. 1: 139–50; Frost, *Battle of Jutland*, 299–308. The extremely strong support of Jellicoe's action is exemplified in this judgment: "A masterly decision, it determined the outcome of the battle and the outcome of the war." Gibson and Harper, *Riddle of Jutland*, 172.

43. Scheer, *Germany's High Sea Fleet*, 152–54.

44. Jellicoe, *Grand Fleet*, 353–54.

this seeming act of suicidal folly headed the High Seas Fleet to the east actually for the center of the reformed British line.

Jellicoe, favored with a second chance, deployed his line so as to cross the "T" of the German fleet again. Scheer advanced once more into a crescent of fire. The German ships, nearly blinded from poor visibility, could shoot with little effect. At first Scheer ordered the charge of his crippled battle cruisers against the British line to cover the withdrawal of the battleships. A moment later, regaining his poise, he issued a new order that saved the battle cruisers from completing the "death ride." Under the protection of attacks by his destroyer flotillas and a barrage of smoke, he hastily executed a third turn-about to the rear, this time in some confusion. The German fleet again entered the thickening mists and disappeared to the west.

The question whether Jellicoe's response to Scheer's evasive tactics allowed the escape of the German fleet remains the central issue in the everlasting debate over Jutland. Jellicoe ordered the Grand Fleet to turn away from an expected massed torpedo attack by Scheer's flotillas. By the time Jellicoe could change course to resume action, the High Seas Fleet was gone, and in effect the battle broken off. The critics have contended that Jellicoe should have accepted the risks of torpedoes, which he exaggerated, in a turn toward the attackers; this would have allowed the pursuit of an enemy in disarray and might have brought about a decisive action and minimally the destruction of the wounded battle cruisers.[45]

The remaining daylight permitted only one more exchange between the heavy ships—the last during the battle and in fact during the war. After Jellicoe's turn-away he altered course back toward Scheer's retreating track, and the latter sought the most direct route home. A skirmish occurred as Beatty's battle-cruiser force converged on Hipper's battle cruisers, supported by the six predreadnoughts of the High Seas Fleet. Jellicoe swung the fleet to the sound of the action and was master of the situation, with his ships spread out to form a barrier ten miles long to Scheer's retreat

45. See especially the very searching examination of the case for and against Jellicoe's decision to turn away in Marder, *From the Dreadnought to Scapa Flow*, 3: 115–22; also Patterson, *Jellicoe*, 124, and Jellicoe, *Grand Fleet*, 359. Frost, *Battle of Jutland*, 370–77, gives an adverse critique of Jellicoe's tactics and the Fabian theory of naval warfare (so characterized by Frost) of taking no chances. The general criticism of the decision and its affirmed fateful significance are summarized in a single sentence by Macintyre, *Jutland*, 140: "Twenty-eight torpedoes and a fixed determination to take no chances with his battle fleet robbed Jellicoe of decisive victory."

to his bases. But the evening mist and the gathering darkness intervened to steal away the chance of "a second Trafalgar."

Jutland ended in a series of violent night actions, largely between destroyer and light cruiser forces. Jellicoe avoided a night action as "far too fluky an affair" for engaging his heavy ships. He endeavored to put the fleet in a position where it could intercept the High Seas Fleet and renew the battle at daylight. Scheer, determined to take the quickest route back by way of Horn Reef, hoped he might slip by the rear of the Grand Fleet. But he was prepared to fight his way through whatever he encountered, by way of a less dangerous alternative to a daylight meeting.

Jellicoe did not guess Scheer's intentions and left the passage via Horn Reef uncovered by surface craft. He relied on massing his destroyer flotillas at the rear to bar Scheer's escape in the night, astern of the British battle line. The resort to light craft failed its purpose when the flotillas were overrun in seven sharp actions by Scheer's fleet. It crashed the line of flotillas successfully to reach Horn Reef, and in the early forenoon of June 1 the Jade. Scheer had saved the German fleet by an audacious, resolute course at limited cost.

Jellicoe had had no inkling that Scheer's fleet had crossed the wake of the British battleships. The flotillas engaged in the night fighting had not reported, or their few messages had failed to get through to the fleet commander. At least one British battleship in the rear of the line sighted Scheer's van of dreadnoughts, and other British battleships encountered two of the wounded German battle cruisers. The British ships neither reported to Jellicoe nor opened fire on their own initiative. The Admiralty blundered grossly in not passing on to Jellicoe all of the intercepted messages on the movements and intentions of Scheer during the night. If this information had been transmitted, Jellicoe would unquestionably have headed for Horn Reef during the night and been in a position to annihilate the High Seas Fleet at daylight off Horn Reef.[46]

The British errors and omissions did much to determine the indecisive outcome of Jutland. The Germans achieved a technical success of sorts in the greater number of enemy ships destroyed, in the near unsinkability of their heavy war vessels, and in the penetrability of their shells. The British losses totaled 111,980 tons, consisting of 3 battle cruisers, 3 armored cruisers, and 8 destroyers; the German, 62,233 tons, consisting of 1

---

46. See Marder, *From the Dreadnought to Scapa Flow*, 3: 148–54; Patterson, *Jellicoe*, 129–30.

predreadnought, 1 battle cruiser, 4 light cruisers, and 5 destroyers. The Germans demonstrated the stability of their ships, given by a greater beam and more extensive subdivision into compartments; a more efficient organization for recovery from damage in battle; and, in night fighting, better training and better equipment than the British in their star shells, effective searchlights, and excellent system of recognition signals. In communications, they generally outclassed their opponent.[47]

The heavier British losses were owing chiefly to the magazine explosions in the three battle cruisers. In materiel Jutland revealed the main British defects, in vulnerable magazines and turrets and in shells of decidedly inferior power of penetration. The shooting of the two fleets on the whole has been judged about equal, though Beatty's gunnery on the run to the south was below standard.[48]

In tactical performance it is commonly agreed that Hipper was the master of them all. Scheer extricated the German fleet from catastrophe three times—twice by the adroit maneuver of the turn-away to the rear and once by his boldness in night fighting. But Scheer twice implicated the German fleet in a situation where Jellicoe's power of poised decision and tactical grasp enabled him in masterly fashion to gain an overwhelming tactical advantage over the opponent by crossing his "T." Earlier on a bright day, Jellicoe could have exploited this advantage to destroy the High Seas Fleet. Aggressiveness and risk-taking might well have sunk more German ships, but whether they offered the hope of a decisive British victory under the actual conditions of battle remains an open question.[49]

The British naval system, more than Jellicoe, accounted for the missed opportunities at Jutland—above all, the lost chance to sink the German fleet at Horn Reef. To the system belonged the meager manifestations of initiative and independent action on the part of admirals and captains at Jutland, their waiting for orders, the centralization of command, the omissions and errors in signaling, the failures in reporting, the inadequate cooperation between intelligence and operations in the Admiralty, and the blunders of Admiralty in not transmitting crucial intelligence to Jellicoe.

47. Frost, *Battle of Jutland,* 506–07; Gibson and Harper, *Riddle of Jutland,* 243–44; Macintyre, *Jutland,* 190–91.

48. Gibson and Harper, *Riddle of Jutland,* 242–43.

49. On the post-Jutland controversy over Jellicoe's handling of the fleet, see Patterson, *Jellicoe,* 230–48; also Bennett, *Battle of Jutland,* 161, and his *Naval Battles,* 259–62.

In the broader view the navy functioned as an old-fashioned system of social privilege in which officers were too narrowly recruited from class and influence. The organization lacked the invigorating effects of a general staff, staff college, and war plans. The British fleet was a mighty corporeal being without a matching brain. The outcome of the battle shocked the navy; the many lessons of Jutland served to renovate tactics, materiel, and the system of command.[50]

Jutland produced no immediate change in the strategic situation. The longer-range strategic consequence was for Germany to renounce the use of the fleet in battle in favor of unrestricted submarine warfare, and for Britain to concentrate its naval forces on a fight against the submarine peril. Jutland made the U-boat the only alternative left for German naval strategy and proved the crowning rebuttal of the Tirpitz justification of the risk navy. As the British official history appraised it, "the battle of Jutland ended one stage of naval warfare and defined the form and method of the final struggle."[51] The naval war became a trial of strength between two blockades, and the two fleets grew absorbed in measures to enforce, support, and counter these blockades. The submarine campaign was revived in September 1916, and on February 1, 1917, Germany declared unrestricted submarine warfare.

The German fleet lost its offensive mission and acted largely as the auxiliary of the U-boats—protecting their bases, guarding the approaches to Helgoland Bight, and covering the mine-laying and mine-sweeping operations in the North Sea. The inactivity of the German battleships reacted on the crews lying in port to the deterioration of their morale; their complaints over food and leave intensified; conflicts with the officers grew in number, indifference spread, and some units were already disobedient in 1916. In the fleet, the road led from Jutland to the November revolution.

Leading opinion in Britain came to realize, like Jellicoe, "that what mattered was no longer victory over the High Seas Fleet but over the submarine menace." A public outcry was raised over the Admiralty's insufficient vigor in combating the submarine peril and German destroyer attacks in the Channel. In response, the naval direction was changed: to make Jellicoe the First Sea Lord at the end of November, to raise Beatty

50. Barnett, *Swordbearers*, 184–87; Legg, *Jutland*, 141–42.
51. Corbett and Newbolt, *Naval Operations*, 4: 323.

to the command of the fleet, and to replace Lord Balfour with Sir Edmund
Carson as the First Lord of Admiralty in the Lloyd George cabinet. The
main problem faced by the new team—going back to Jutland—was ward-
ing off the submarine.[52]

Jutland reinforced Britain's supremacy at sea. Jutland nevertheless was
a strategic defeat for the Allies if viewed in the light of the momentous
consequences that would have come from annihilating the High Seas
Fleet. Its destruction would have opened up the Baltic for an easy supply
route to Russia and closer military cooperation with that ally. Sweden's
trade with Germany could have been cut off. The northern flank would
have been uncovered for amphibious operations and the submarine campaign ended quickly by elimination of the fleet's support of the U-boats
and by the freedom to demolish their bases.[53]

Jutland was of double force in extending and solidifying the war of
stalemate. The outcome had the effect of converting the maritime war into
a long stalemated struggle between two blockades. Jutland presented
the possibility of a strategic alternative to the war of attrition in France.
The failure to capitalize on the opportunity of outflanking the Western
Front to the north insured the continuance of the land stalemate and
the prolonged slaughter. For the Allies, Jutland was another Dardanelles.

4. THE RUSSIAN REVIVAL

The Russians had agreed at the conference of Chantilly in December
1915 to take part in the concerted Allied offensives of 1916. They were
not free to choose their own time for an offensive. Three times in 1916
they geared their offensive actions to the needs of the Allies by responding
to appeals for relief. The first was occasioned by the German attack at
Verdun. At the time the Russian line from Riga to Romania was organized
in three fronts, the north, the west, and the southwest, each of which was
held by an army group. On March 18 the western army group attacked
the Germans east of Vilna and repeated their efforts here until the last on
April 14. The group on the northern front made some offensive attempt
near Dvinsk and farther north along the Dvina. The Russians advanced
east of Vilna through violent assaults against thoroughly prepared German

52. Patterson, *Jellicoe*, 151.
53. See Roskill, *Strategy of Sea Power*, 120-21.

positions; they were thrown back at once or later by enemy counterattacks.[54]

This offensive has been characterized as "the last real effort of the old Russian army." It epitomized all the faults and follies of the Russian conservative military system since 1914. Although the Russians had a large numerical superiority in soldiers and guns, this was nullified by the indifference to learning from the tactical experience of the Western Front; the flagrant incompetence of command; aimless bombardment; deplorable reconnaissance; wrangling between light and heavy artillery; frequently uncooperative relations between the infantry and artillery; and confusion in the rear, supply, and transport, owing in great part to the excessive demands of an overlarge cavalry assembly. This exercise in futility, claiming a staggering toll of more than 100,000 men, clinched the case for the western and northern army groups that it was impossible to overcome the Germans. For the remainder of the war there was no further will to action on these fronts.[55]

In June the Russians altered their plans a second time, in conforming to the demands of the western Allies for a diversionary offensive. They decided in April to attack, in the middle of June, on the whole eastern front. When the Austrians struck the Italians from the Trentino in May, Cadorna and Joffre appealed for earlier action. The high command asked General A. A. Brusilov, in charge of the southwest front between the Pripet marches and the Carpathians, to attack first, on June 4. Brusilov was the only one of the commanders of the three Russian fronts who could take the field quickly with a blow already in preparation.[56]

Brusilov had gathered about him a new breed of command and staff officers who were alert students of warfare on the eastern front since 1914. This group, breaking with the musty military conservatism of the past in favor of innovations adapted to the weapons of technological warfare, presaged the emergence of a new force within the framework of the old that would be basic to the building of the future Red Army. Brusilov's solution to the problem of breakthrough was first of all to restore the factor of surprise. He took pains to make secret preparations. He endeavored to conceal from the Austrian forces opposite his armies the direction

54. A. A. Brusilov, *A Soldier's Note-Book, 1914–1918* (London, 1930), 200; Knox, *With the Russian Army*, 2: 406–11, 423; Gourko, *War and Revolution in Russia*, 167–71.

55. Stone, *Eastern Front*, 228–32.

56. Brusilov, *Soldier's Note-Book*, 222–37.

of the main thrusts toward Lutsk in Volhynia and in the area of the Dniester River. His intentions were cloaked through diversionary concentrations and attacks by each army of his group and by a short but ferocious bombardment in each case on a wider sector than in the past.

The second principle was to neutralize the enemy's use of his reserves. To the extent that Brusilov's devices succeeded in achieving surprise, the enemy would not be able to concentrate reserves at the rear of the expected sector of main attack. In order to get his own troops to the enemy's rear before the latter could bring up reserves, Brusilov adopted a systematic organization of attack, consisting of three to four waves. The first was to penetrate and occupy the first line of the enemy, the second to fill up the gaps in the first, and the third and fourth to rush ahead and take over the second and third lines opposing them. The use of his own reserves for the later waves required their hidden assembly in immense dugouts close to the front line. The front trenches were extended close to the enemy's through sapping. Additionally, his scheme of assault involved close cooperation of the artillery with the infantry, carefully targeted firing of artillery, counterbattery work dependent on aerial photography, and the training of assault troops on replicas of the Austrian trenches. With these innovational methods Brusilov's commanders succeeded brilliantly.[57]

The Russians made a breakthrough fifty kilometers wide in Volhynia in two days, capturing Lutsk on June 6. Panic seized the Austrian defenders, and the debacle spread rapidly. From Lutsk the invaders moved northward and westward to form a salient south of Kovel. In the south they broke the front at several places and drove the reeling Austrians back to the Pruth River until Czernowitz was occupied on June 17. The rout continued, and by the end of the month the Russians had raced through Bukovina to a line near the Carpathian passes. The Austrian center held at first but retreated when uncovered by the broken flanks. Brusilov's armies captured more than 200,000 prisoners by June 23.[58]

A superior tactical sense and audacity of command, along with meticulous preparation, paid off handsome rewards. Both the German and Austrian commands looked for the western army group, which had been strengthened considerably more than Brusilov's armies, to conduct the main drive against the German front. They had not reinforced the Aus-

57. Stone, *Eastern Front,* 231–39, 249.
58. Brusilov, *Soldier's Note-Book,* 249.

trian armies opposite Brusilov's, and Conrad weakened his position in Volhynia when he withdrew some of the better divisions, heavy artillery, and extensive shell to strengthen his line in the Trentino for the May offensive.[59]

On the other hand, the Russians were attacking Austrians almost entirely, for the Germans had shifted their troops largely from the Austrian portion of the eastern front to the west for the Verdun offensive. These Austrian troops varied greatly in quality. Brusilov's offensive revealed the further ethnic disintegration of the Austro-Hungarian armies. The Austrians, moreover, committed mistakes in local command and did not meet the new Russian assault tactics with suitable defenses. They concentrated too many of their troops in the first position, weakening the defenses farther to the rear, and the slowness in bringing reserves from their dugouts allowed them to be entrapped by the onrushing attack troops.[60]

The German bloc was threatened with the utter collapse of the two Austrian wings, the loss of the Galician oil wells, and the invasion of Hungary. The German command, driven to prodigious exertions, thinned out their ranks elsewhere at grave risk. It sent divisions from the German front in the east, from the west in spite of Verdun and the Somme, from the Balkans, and from local reserves to shore up the crumbling flanks of the Austrian front. Conrad was forced to halt his self-willed drive in Italy and transfer eight divisions and guns to the eastern front. The reinforcements were rushed first to the Lutsk-Kovel area. On June 16 the Germans launched a counterattack here that saved Kovel and forestalled the Russians in rolling up the remains of two routed Austrian armies.

The fate of the Russian offensive depended on two factors: the force of the Russian attacks on the western and northwest Russian fronts and the relative speed with which the two sides could bring up reinforcements. The western and northwest army groups postponed action until July, and their attacks then were minor affairs. Brusilov was outraged at this "positively criminal procedure" of the two army groups. The Germans were free to shift divisions to the south against his armies, which had to fight the Central Powers alone during June.[61]

59. The effect of Conrad's transfer of troops to the Tyrol is played down in Oskar Regele, *Feldmarschall Conrad* (Vienna, 1955), 368, and in Stone, *Eastern Front*, 244.

60. Falkenhayn, *German General Staff*, 275–87 passim; Regele, *Conrad*, 361–65; Hoffmann, *War Diaries*, 2: 137; Stone, *Eastern Front*, 249.

61. Brusilov, *Soldier's Note-Book*, 243–51; Gourko, *War and Revolution in Russia*, 176.

The futility of the attacks on the western and northwest fronts persuaded the Russian high command to divert troops to the southwest front. Two additional armies were eventually attached to Brusilov's command. This investment of reserves did not maintain the momentum of his advance. The railways behind the Russian lines were worse than those behind the German front. The British military observer General Knox pithily summarized the effect: "As so often happened in Russia, the Supreme Command ordered but the railways decided." Brusilov did not have enough reserves in the beginning to exploit the opportunity presented by his initial successes; he lost the race of transporting reinforcements thereafter; and he was deprived of the aid of strong attacks on other fronts. The Central Powers thus escaped a strategic defeat.[62]

Brusilov's advance slackened, but his armies continued to make some further headway during July and early August northeast of Kovel and in the center of the Austrian front toward Lvov. The long stretch of continuous fighting lost nearly 500,000 men and lowered the quality of the troops. With poorly trained men and superiority in shells, Brusilov reverted to the battering-ram methods of attack on a narrow front. By mid-August the Russian drive was contained in the north and center of the Austrian front without Brusilov having won the objectives of Kovel and Lvov in repeated attacks at heavy cost. But the threat was so serious that a Turkish corps was sent here to assist the defense. The front was finally stabilized when entrenched positions had been constructed and sufficient German strength thrown in.[63]

In August Brusilov's armies completed the conquest of Bukovina and moved into the Carpathians, climbing toward the crests before they were stopped. With the end of August the operations here and elsewhere on the southwest front were largely determined by Romania's entry into the war. The southwest battle line was extended four hundred miles, and action on this front was directed from now on to the support of Romania.

For a third time in the year Russia came to the aid of an ally calling for help. Apart from Russia's direct assistance in Romania, Brusilov's group attacked in September on the Volhynian-Galician front and more strongly in the Carpathian area, while one of his armies struck again in October west of Lutsk. But the exhausted and poorly trained troops, using batter-

62. Knox, *With the Russian Army*, 2: 449.
63. Ibid., 495; Stone, *Eastern Front*, 261–63.

ing-ram tactics, could maintain only diversionary action, preventing the transfer of troops opposite them to Romania. At the same time reserves were being drawn from Brusilov's and all the other Russian fronts to man the lengthened line in Romania. Brusilov's offensive had come to a close.[64]

Brusilov's brilliant series of victories was to a large extent an affair of his own and his staff. Both Hoffmann and he were convinced that the success might have been converted into a strategic decision over the Austrian army if Stavka had attacked the German front with full strength and unwavering determination.[65] In any case, Brusilov's campaign had granted immediate relief to Italy in the Tyrol, France at Verdun, and the British at the Somme. The German bloc had been compelled to withdraw twelve divisions from the Western Front, besides the eight from Italy. Romania entered the war, seeming to swing the balance still more against the German bloc. Yet it is doubtful whether Romania's late entry proved of particular military benefit to the Allies, because of the burden it imposed on Russia's dwindling military resources.

The train of reverses in the east made Falkenhayn and Conrad targets of criticism in their countries. Romania's decision to join the Entente, interpreted as a determination by Bucharest that the Central Powers would not win the war, was the last blow to the tottering position of Falkenhayn. Conrad too was to fall from grace a few months later, after the throne at Vienna had passed to Archduke Karl.

The ouster of Falkenhayn resulted from consensus at the top in Germany that the war was not being run well and a change must be made in military management. The replacement of Falkenhayn by Hindenburg and Ludendorff ended the prolonged military dualism in the German war direction and signified the complete victory of the easterners over the westerners. In the east the Bavarian prince Leopold stepped into Hindenburg's position as commander (Ober Ost), with General Hoffmann as chief of staff.

The near elimination of the Austrian military power provoked an extended crisis in the coalition relations of the Central Powers, producing a change in the coalition direction of the war. Progress was made toward a unified command, chiefly by the consolidation of German control over

64. Gourko, *War and Revolution in Russia*, 195–96.
65. Hoffmann, *War Diaries*, 2: 138. See also the judgment of Kiszling, *Österreich-Ungarns Anteil am Ersten Weltkrieg*, 51; and Falkenhayn's comments in *German General Staff*, 281.

the Austrian army. Ludendorff was elevated, in effect, to the military command of the coalition. In preserving the Austrian army as a factor in the war, further steps were taken toward its assimilation with the German.[66] The Austrian army had been brought to the verge of collapse. The casualties soared to around one million men. By the end of 1916 the military authorities were reduced to enrolling men fifty-five years old. The growing Austrian weakness made it increasingly dependent on Germany, and the dependence aggrieved Austrian opinion. The way was being prepared for the peace bid of 1917.[67]

While the Germans sustained a much lesser cost, at 350,000 casualties, the Russians paid for their victories as dearly as the Austrians for their defeats. The soldiers were exhausted from six months of steady fighting in the southwest, often in the later months over the same ground. The immense exertion without gaining a strategic victory sapped the morale of spring. By October signs of disobedience and antiwar feeling appeared in the ranks, and reports were current of antiwar propaganda spreading among the men. The despair in the army was reflected in the Russian cities, which suffered privations without now seeing a prospect of the war's end. The hopes aroused by the Russian revival were fading. Russia had made its last major military effort.[68]

5. THE SOUTHERN THEATER

The southern theater from Italy to the Middle East had no military action of strategic import at this time. It remained a theater of sideshows, where sizable military resources were invested without exploiting larger possibilities that existed. The theater was distinguished by a painful and costly want of good cooperation between coalition members. The belligerents here were secondary states that were moved to realize national aims directly with little, if any, regard for the conduct of the war as a whole. In the long run the most significant action in this area may well have been the uprising of Arabs against the rule of the Turks, heralding the revolt

66. Kiszling, Österreich-Ungarns Anteil am Ersten Weltkrieg, 46, 48; Pierre Renouvin, "Le problème du commandement unique," Revue d'histoire de la guerre mondiale 11 (1933): 349–50; Baron Artur Arz von Straussenburg, Zur Geschichte des grossen Krieges, 1914–1918 (Vienna, 1924), 127–29.

67. Kielmansegg, Deutschland und der Erste Weltkrieg, 329; May, Passing of the Hapsburg Monarchy, 1: 126.

68. Knox, With the Russian Army, 2: 488.

of the Third World that was to follow for many years.

During the winter of 1915–16 the Italians speeded up the production of guns sevenfold and introduced the *bombarda,* a big trench mortar of long range and a large destructive shell. With these arms Cadorna responded to Joffre's call for relief to Verdun, by attacking in March on both sides of Gorizia. The three days of infantry combat yielded small results, chiefly the courtesy title of the fifth battle of Isonzo for this semblance of cooperation with allies.

Before Cadorna could start an offensive under the Chantilly arrangements for concerted drives, Conrad took the initiative in the Tyrol. Conrad had requested of Falkenhayn that the Germans relieve nine Austrian divisions on the eastern front so that they would take part in the attack from the Trentino. Falkenhayn had refused on the grounds that even a success in the north would not eliminate Italy and expressed doubts whether Conrad could muster sufficient troops and guns for a favorable outcome.[69]

Conrad, paying no heed to Falkenhayn, concentrated troops and artillery in the Tyrol, including divisions of better quality and guns transferred from Galicia and Volhynia. Concealing these preparations, Conrad informed Falkenhayn of his plans the day before he attacked on May 15 in a venture of independence from the dominating German ally and a nationalist quest of vengeance against Austria's own perfidious enemy.

The Austrians penetrated Italian territory until only one ridge barred their progress to the Lombard plain. Then the momentum ran down, with their front of attack spreading out from twenty to forty miles and the Italians bringing up reinforcements. Cadorna appealed to the Russian high command for relief, and Brusilov unleashed his offensive ahead of schedule. But Conrad's drive had already come to a near halt. As the front against the Russians collapsed and the Italians counterattacked, Conrad had to retire, sacrificing a large part of the ground won.

The defeat cost the Italians nearly 300,000 casualties and overthrew the premier Salandra. For the Central Powers, however, the attempt was a sorry example of coalition warfare; it ended with no substantial territorial gains and contributed to the threat arising in the east to the whole Austrian army. Falkenhayn never relented in his conviction that the Austrian offensive was a "strategical mistake in the conduct of the war" and that even

69. Falkenhayn, *German General Staff,* 221–28.

a major blow against Italy offered no true alternative to winning the war on the main fronts.[70]

Cadorna, attracted by the less difficult terrain of the Isonzo and the nearness of the national objective of Trieste, strengthened this front for an attack by switching troops there from the Tyrol as Conrad shifted divisions to the east. With a great superiority in men and guns, Cadorna struck in August in the sixth battle of the Isonzo. The Italians won Gorizia and a surrounding bridgehead as well as a footing on the Carso, the forbidding limestone plateau to the east of the Isonzo. The victory buoyed Italian spirits and increased the Allied pressure on Romania to enter the war. A decisive breakthrough might have been possible if Cadorna had continued his drive with determination and boldness.

The opportunity could not be recaptured in the seventh, eight, and ninth battles of the Isonzo, fought in September, October, and November, respectively. Each was a short action of three days, rather overbilled as a battle, although losses mounted up on both sides.

In the Balkans the Central Powers had a weak and exposed flank, where they pursued a defensive policy determined by two clearly defined strategic goals: the maintenance of a direct line of communications with Turkey and the isolation of Russia from the western Allies. In contrast, the Allies never fixed on an agreed and sustained objective in the Balkans until the war was nearly over.

At first Sarrail's army pushed northward from the Allied base at Salonika in order to draw off pressure on Verdun. Then Sarrail was ordered to attack the Bulgarians, with a view to influencing the wavering Romanians to join the Entente. Sarrail's plans were not ready when the Allies committed themselves to an offensive of his army by the military convention with Romania of August 17. On the same day the Bulgarians, who in May had seized a foothold in Greek territory, anticipated Sarrail's repeatedly postponed action. Reinforced with two German and two Turkish divisions, the Bulgarians attacked both flanks of the Allied line. They drove back the French and the Serbs, though the advance was brought to a halt within ten days largely through fierce Serb counterattacks.

On September 12 Sarrail commenced his long delayed offensive with

70. Hoffmann had a different view of strategy in Italy. He would have mounted a large-scale attack on both fronts, in the Tyrol and on the Isonzo, at the same time rather than reject Conrad's plan. He expected such an offensive would bring about Italy's decisive defeat and presumably the outbreak of internal troubles. *War Diaries*, 2: 129.

a fully international force of five British divisions, four French, and six reformed and reequipped Serb divisions, as well as an Italian division and a Russian brigade.[71] The British, restrained by orders from home, acted only as a holding force along the Struma River front. The French and Serbs attacked west of the Vardar and drove toward the Monastir gap. The Serbs took the most difficult mountain positions and, back on Serbian soil, fought the Bulgarian occupants with the relentless fury of a tough peasant and mountain people against a hereditary enemy. The Bulgarian army, betraying defects of command, was pushed back from position to position. The army was so shaken that Ludendorff was obliged to supply a few additional German battalions. With their aid and by means of rear positions constructed by the Germans, the Bulgarians were saved from collapse.[72]

The Allied advance was checked north of Monastir, some thirty miles from the starting point, after two months of operations. In the meantime an Italian expeditionary force in southern Albania occupied Janina in northern Epirus and pushed eastward to reach Sarrail's front. The Allied "offensive," directed by an arrogant and intemperate commander, accomplished nothing of significance. The western authorities had little faith in the enterprise and gave it little support.

These operations were based, and to a considerable extent carried out, on Greek soil. Both sides played fast and loose with Greek neutrality. The Bulgarian invaders seized the port of Kavalla, where a Greek corps came into the hands of the Germans. These Greek soldiers were interned in Germany. The Allies retaliated by blockading the Greek coast and demanding the demobilization of the Greek army and a change of government. The shifty king evaded the formation of a nonparty government but complied otherwise. Later a naval demonstration forced the king to expel German agents and give the Allies control of the railways and telegraph lines.

Sarrail's constant efforts to promote the formation of a more compliant regime turned the king increasingly toward the Central Powers. Sarrail therefore supported the followers of Venizelos in setting up a "provisional

71. According to Luigi Albertini, *Venti anni di vita politica,* 2 pts., 5 vols. (Bologna, 1950–53), pt. 2, 2: 330–37, Cadorna was prepared to send a larger force to Salonika in order to strengthen the offensive against Bulgaria, but Sonnino, whose Adriatic policy made him hostile to Serbia and Greece while favorable to Bulgaria, was able to block Cadorna.
72. *Ludendorff's Own Story,* 1: 299–300, 347.

government" at Salonika. This body, of which Venizelos became the head (October 9), repudiated King Constantine and began to recruit Venizelist troops.[73]

Thoroughly disgusted with the king, the Allies moved further along the path of infringing Greek sovereignty. The French commander-in-chief in the Mediterranean seized the light ships of the Greek navy and demanded the surrender of war materiel. The king resisted, and sailors were landed to enter Athens. When they were fired on, the Allies proclaimed a blockade to force the king to yield.[74]

The treatment of the king was deeply resented by a large part of the Greek people and many of the army officers. These partisans insured that with the establishment of the Venizelist government Greece was a country divided against itself. Greece's tortuous wriggling as a neutral under the bullying of the great powers involved it in a civil war before being dragged into the world war.

Romania ended its policy of "wait and see" by declaring war on Austria-Hungary on August 27, 1916. The startling progress of Brusilov's offensive and concessions of the Allies persuaded the premier I. C. Bratianu and his colleagues that Romania's hour had come. An advance into Hungary beckoned as a victory march. Romania protected itself by a military convention with the Allied powers that not only obligated the army in Salonika to an offensive against Bulgaria but also committed Russia to continue its offensive along "the whole Austrian front," as well as to send three divisions to the Dobruja.

If the Romanians had entered the war in June or July—or even with immediate Russian assistance they had advanced rapidly across Transylvania when they declared war—it might have been possible to outflank the Austrian forces in the Carpathian area. These armies could then have been surrounded as the Romanians unlocked the Carpathians to the Russians driving forward under Brusilov. An opportunity was missed of eliminating the Austrian army, cutting the communications of Germany and Austria with the Balkans, and knocking Turkey and Bulgaria out of the war.[75]

73. Cruttwell, *History of the Great War,* 298–303.
74. Sir Basil Thompson, *The Allied Secret Service in Greece* (London, 1931), finds that the persons chiefly responsible for the Allied treatment of the Greeks were the head of the French intelligence service in Greece and the French minister of marine, Admiral M.J.L. Lacaze.
75. See Janssen, *Der Kanzler und der General,* 249; *Ludendorff's Own Story,* 1: 293, 333.

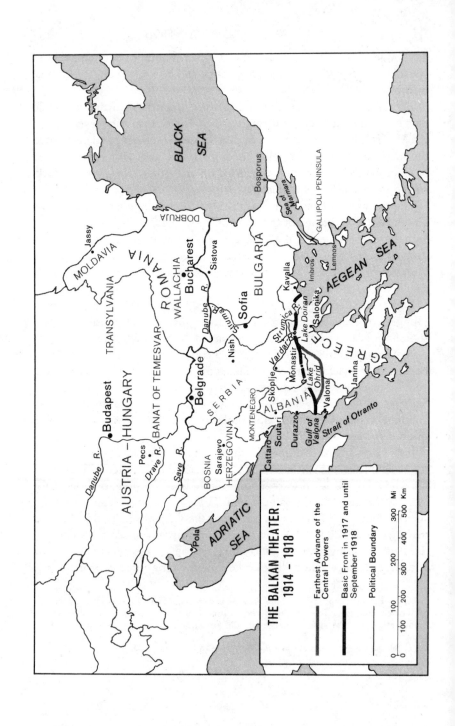

THE BALKAN THEATER,
1914 – 1918

Farthest Advance of the
Central Powers

Basic Front in 1917 and until
September 1918

Political Boundary

Mi   0   100   200   300
Km   0   100 200   300 400 500

Romania's military action was determined first of all by the nationalist aim of redeeming Transylvania with its Romanian ethnic population. For several weeks the three armies sent into Transylvania advanced "at a snail's pace" against little Austrian resistance but against difficulties of supply and derelictions of command until they occupied nearly one-third of the territory. The advance languished as troops were shifted from this front to reinforce the army deployed to the south for protecting the frontier with Bulgaria.[76]

The German bloc gripped the new enemy from both the south and the north. Mackensen, commanding a mixed army of Bulgarians, Germans, and Turks, invaded the Dobruja from Bulgaria. Although the Russians had sent three second-line divisions to aid the Romanians in the Dobruja, the mutual contempt between the two went far to thwart any hope of success. Mackensen's army swept eastward to the Black Sea and northward to the vicinity of the Delta. After these rapid moves Mackensen shifted most of his forces to the frontier south of Bucharest and stole across the Danube near Sistova. He attacked the flank of the Romanian front defending Bucharest and prepared for a dash to the capital.[77]

During this time the Romanians and Russians, operating without a coordinated plan for taking advantage of the strategic opportunity in Transylvania, allowed the Central Powers time to prepare, without hindrance, a counterstroke in the north. A new Austrian army and a new German Ninth Army under Falkenhayn deployed in Transylvania but not until four weeks after Romania's entry into the war. Falkenhayn forced two Romanian armies back to the Transylvanian Alps, while the Austrian army pushed the third Romanian army back to the Carpathians. Falkenhayn finally smashed through the defenses at one of the passes in time to beat the heavy snow. He outflanked the Romanians defending the other passes and debouched into the plains of Wallachia. The armies of Falkenhayn and Mackensen pressed forward and joined west of Bucharest. Overcoming stiff resistance, they entered the capital and the Ploesti oil fields on December 5–6.

The alarmed Russians came to the aid of the Romanians. They expanded the force in the Dobruja and lengthened Brusilov's front. Nor did they neglect to fill out gaps in the Romanian line with Russian troops. A

76. Ernst Kabisch, *Der Rumänienkrieg* (Berlin, 1938), 20–26, 33–36.
77. On the operations of Mackensen and Falkenhayn, see the account and the excellent maps in Kabisch, *Der Rumänienkrieg*.

continuous Romanian front manned by both Russian and Romanian troops was at last formed, with fixed defenses along the Sereth River against the pursuing Germans and Austrians. The victors also entrenched themselves, and a war of position followed on this front until July 1917. The Romanians had saved nearly half their army, which was reconstituted and after that improved under the training of a French military mission. A government was set up at Jassy, and the remnant kingdom in Moldavia survived under Russian shelter.[78]

Falkenhayn had conducted a brilliant campaign.[79] Yet instrumental in the Romanian debacle were also the inadequate cooperation between Russia and Romania, the inferiority in equipment and leadership of the Romanian troops, and their lack of combat experience in modern war.[80]

At the end no one could be satisfied with the belligerency of Romania. Certainly not the Romanians, who had gone the way of the Belgians and Serbs and now existed in their tiny rump state dependent on the Russians. Not the Russians, who had lost the helpful neutrality of Romania for the burdens of maintaining a new front with the reserves from other fronts and providing the Romanian troops and population with supplies. Not the Central Powers, which, though the grain, oil, and timber of Wallachia were put at their disposal, had had to commit 41 divisions to the Romanian campaign without forcing Romania out of the war and had now to assume new responsibilities of defense on an additional front of 500 kilometers.

At this time the Middle Eastern part of the southern theater formed a distinctly subsidiary area of operations. It was a peripheral wasteland where there could be no hope of an alternative to the strategy of the Western Front after the Dardanelles failure. Here operations got out of hand and sucked in large investments of Allied military means in relation to the significance of the results obtained. The area's chief strategic interest to the Allies involved the protection of the Suez Canal and the oil fields in Persia. The Russians were anxious of course to suppress the Turkish threat in the Caucasus, and both the Russians and British were obliged to put a stop to German-Turkish machinations in Persia. The German and Austrian high commands desired the war in Asiatic Turkey to divert the maximum number of Allied effectives from Europe.

78. Gourko, *War and Revolution in Russia*, 233, 236, 242.
79. See the evaluation in Kabisch, *Der Rumänienkrieg*, 183–95.
80. Brusilov, *Soldier's Note-Book*, 261–66; Gourko, *War and Revolution in Russia*, 238–40; Knox, *With the Russian Army*, 2: 503.

Outside such immediate military ends the great powers were moved by imperialist aims of current or future importance. The Germans pursued the "Egyptianization" of Turkey through their military and naval presence and through the controls extended over the use of soldiers, arms, supplies, and funds furnished the Turks.[81] The British and French supported the aspirations of Arab nationalism, not only as a means of fighting the Central Powers but also with a view to the postwar organization of these lands under their preponderant influence.

In the backward reaches of far-flung Asiatic Turkey, where communication facilities were meager, all military success depended on the ability to solve communications problems, and military operations turned into a war of communications. In communications the British had an inestimable advantage through command of the sea. By this means they could more easily reinforce and supply troops, as well as aid the Arabs in the Hejaz. They could also transport materials for building land communications. Sea mobility made possible the creation of land mobility.

The key to the possession of this advantage was the protection of the Suez Canal. The British improved its defenses in 1916 by extending a position to El Arish near the Palestine frontier, some hundred miles from the Suez. A German-Turkish expedition supported by two Austrian batteries made an unsuccessful attempt on the Canal. This ill-conceived effort of the Central Powers was their last of any consequence against the Suez.[82]

In addition to Suez-Palestine, the war in the Middle East was fought in four other theaters: the Caucasus, Persia, Mesopotamia, and the lands of the Arab revolt beginning in the Hejaz and spreading over the Arabian peninsula and Syria. In the Caucasus the Russians under Yudenich had advanced in their winter offensive of 1915 against the Third Turkish Army to Erzurum and Lake Van. They continued in 1916 with the capture of Trebizond, the important Turkish port on the Black Sea. Yudenich broke the Third Army after it attacked west of Erzurum in May and moved on Trebizond in June. The Russians pushed their front forward in a great arc from west of Trebizond through the headwaters of the Euphrates to Lake Van; they stopped after they could no longer extend their communications. A new Second Army, organized to assist the Third in Enver's

81. On the German attempt to "Egyptianize" Asiatic Turkey, see Pomiankowski, *Der Zusammenbruch des Ottomanischen Reiches*, 183–84.

82. Carl Mühlmann, *Das deutsch-türkische Waffenbündnis im Weltkriege* (Leipzig, 1940), 93–101.

grandiose plan for a flank attack against Yudenich's forces, met with defeat and went on the defensive. The theater subsided to inaction for the rest of the year.[83]

In Persia the German legation and a military mission set up in 1915 sent out agents, provided weapons, and spread money and propaganda in trying to turn local leaders and the government of the shah against the British and Russians. Outbreaks occurred against the Allies in the fall of 1915, and the gendarmerie officered by "Swedes" and adventurers revolted. The German military mission organized military formations from irregulars and the gendarme rebels. In November the Germans attempted a coup intended to bring the shah under their power.

The attempt was foiled when a column dispatched by Grand Duke Nicholas, the viceroy of the Caucasus, drove off the rebels and a contingent of Turkish troops from Mesopotamia. The Russians forced them by mid-March along the road to Bagdad to a point near the Turkish border. Three months later, the Russians crossed into Turkey, and Enver diverted a corps of the Sixth Army from Mesopotamia to defeat the Russian force. The Turkish corps invaded Persia and pushed the Russian column back to the northern part of the country. The expansive Enver entertained the Pan-Islamic project of converting Persia into a Turkish protectorate.[84]

This imperialist fantasy failed to take account of the realities of Allied power. The Russians halted the Turks in the north and established a defensive position there. The British reacted in Persia with a mission from India headed by Sir Percy Sykes, whose task was to stabilize the situation. Utilizing a force of British, Indians, and local recruits, he combated German agents and rebels, clearing one town after another. At the end of 1916 the British had gone far to restore their influence in Persia and secure this flank of the major contest in Mesopotamia.[85]

In the Mesopotamian "Paradise of the Brass Hat" (Lloyd George's term of scorn), the mismanagement and neglect caused by divided authority over the British expedition reached a peak with the surrender, forced by starvation, of Townshend's men at Kut on April 29. Even during the siege of Kut a major improvement was made through the instigation of Lloyd

83. Liman von Sanders, *Five Years in Turkey*, 129–31.

84. Barker, *Neglected War*, 171–72; Pomiankowski, *Der Zusammenbruch des Ottomanischen Reiches*, 193–94, 226.

85. Sir Arnold Talbot Wilson, *Loyalties; Mesopotamia, 1914–1917* (London, 1930), 162–75.

George. Control of the expedition was shifted from the Indian government and the secretary of state for India to the War Office, which Lloyd George headed. Under the new direction transport and medical arrangements were improved; Basra was developed as a seaport proper with adequate port facilities and port staff; and the British troops were reinforced to the extent of overwhelming preponderance over the enemy.[86] The War Cabinet cast off the curse of the British military system, the selection of commanders by seniority, and sent out General F. S. Maude as commander. Maude became a vigorous and thorough organizer of success. Other junior generals were assigned to the most responsible positions. These improvements and meticulous preparations preceded a series of attacks that culminated, with the aid of the Tigris flotilla, in the routing of the Turks at Kut on February 24, 1917. Maude chased the retreating Turks, weakened by the absence of the corps of the Sixth Army in Persia, toward Bagdad and forced the diminishing and dispirited Turkish troops to evacuate the city.[87]

The fall of Bagdad on March 11 gave notice of the weakness of the Ottoman Empire and commenced its wartime disintegration. After the British troops fanned out from Bagdad, most of Mesopotamia came into British possession. The Turkish position in Persia crumbled. Repercussions of the defeat extended throughout Islamic lands, delivering a final crushing blow to the faltering Holy War conducted since November 1914 and inviting the Arabs to join the revolt.[88]

The British, confronted with innumerable problems in restoring order and a going administration in Mesopotamia, set up a system of military government. The new administration issued an appeal for collaboration with the British "liberators," holding out vaguely the prospect of independence, self-government, and Arab union or federation. The proclamation belonged to Britain's overall policy of exploiting in political warfare the discontent and aspirations of the Arabs.

Since the Ottoman Empire's entry into the war, it was undermined by the conflict between Arab nationalism and Turkish misrule. With a view to taking advantage of this vulnerability and obtaining the assistance of the "Arab nation," Kitchener initiated contact early with the future leader of the Arab revolt, the grand sharif of Mecca, Hussein Ibn Ali. The British

---

86. Ibid., 85–200; Lloyd George, *War Memoirs*, 2: 802–31.
87. Barker, *Neglected War*, 363–76.
88. Mühlmann, *Das deutsch-türkische Waffenbündnis*, 142–43.

High Commissioner in Egypt, Sir Henry McMahon, and Hussein conducted negotiations through correspondence extending from July 1915 to February 1916. By these exchanges the British agreed to support with money and arms the independence of purely Arab areas within the Ottoman Empire except districts approximating the Syrian coast and Lebanon, where the French had a special position.[89]

With this pledge of aid Hussein was prompted to act when a Turco-German military force from Damascus departed toward Medina. Hussein was alarmed that its real purpose was his overthrow. The grand sharif set off the revolt on June 10, 1916. He and his two sons, Ali and Feisal, took the lead at once in the struggle against the Turks, and the revolt spread in the Hejaz.[90]

The fight of the Arabs became a war of national liberation in the true sense. The Arabs artfully employed a strategy of guerrilla warfare. They staged surprise attacks, made forays behind the Turkish lines as far as Syria, disrupted communications, destroyed materiel, and plundered the Turks far and wide. They took every advantage of the terrain in these swift and unnerving activities. Equipped with lighter weapons and not burdened with logistic encumbrances, they had the superior mobility for this hit-and-run warfare of the desert.[91]

These methods gained a series of military successes that attracted growing support from the Arab tribes. Hussein served as the directing center of all aspects of the revolt, and the means of handling the administrative, political, and military activities involved became the basis for the first independent Arab state. The British assisted with the use of warships, marines, and planes, and with the provision of arms, funds, supplies, and technical and political advice.

Hussein and his two sons, proceeding in this fashion, organized three armies and won control of Mecca and its seaport, Jidda. In September Haleb Pasha, who was both governor of the Hejaz and commander of its Turkish forces, surrendered, and by the end of 1916 the Turks withdrew to an entrenched position close to Medina and to the territory bordering the railway from Medina to Damascus.

From the fall of Wejh, a port far to the north of Medina, in early 1917, the Arabs maintained an unbroken initiative against the Turks. Hussein

89. Mansfield, *Ottoman Empire and Its Successors,* 37–42.
90. Suleiman Mousa, *T. E. Lawrence: An Arab View* (New York, 1966), 15 ff.
91. B. H. Liddell Hart, *Strategy* (New York, 1954), 197–99.

was proclaimed "King of the Arab Countries" by the Arabs in November 1916, and two months later was recognized by Britain and France as king of the Hejaz. He prepared for further action with the approval of the British. The spreading revolt of the Arabs was meeting with growing success. Its progress measured the failure of the Turks' Holy War.

Chapter Seven

THE WAR OF CRISIS

I. THE FRENCH CRISIS

BY 1917 the conduct of the Great War had dragged on from desperation to deep crisis. For the Allies 1917 was "the black year of the war."[1] The coalition was overtaken with four severe crises: the defection of Russia; the near collapse of France after the offensive at the Chemin des Dames; the catastrophic losses in British and neutral shipping; and the disaster of Caporetto in October. The breakup of the Entente threatened. Russia and Romania were soon to conclude separate treaties of peace, and France was an uncertainty after Chemin des Dames, and Italy after Caporetto. In this situation Britain was left like a Gibraltar to bear the brunt of the war on land and sea until France could recover and the United States could bring its force to bear. The only gleams of brightness for the Allies on these dark horizons were the conquest of the submarine menace and the entry of the United States into the war.

The strain of war mounted also for the Central Powers. Austria tottered on the verge of internal and military breakdown. The fall of Bagdad and the success of the Arab revolt gave notice of the mortal debility of Turkey. The German bloc suffered from exhaustion of troops, insufficient reserves, and shortage of manpower. The grip of larger forces tightened on the German bloc like an inescapable fate. The participation of the United States increased the balance of military and industrial strength more hopelessly than ever against the Central Powers. The Allied blockade was beginning to strangle them inexorably. A reprieve was granted by two strokes of fortune: the Russian dropout, which Ludendorff acknowledged as having saved Germany in 1917, and the aftermath of the spring offensive in France.[2]

This was in truth a bleak period for all the European belligerents. The

1. Terraine, *Douglas Haig,* 237; George Simpson Duncan, *Douglas Haig As I Knew Him* (London, 1966), 51; also the title of volume 9 for 1917, *L'année trouble,* in Poincaré, *Au service de la France.*

2. *Ludendorff's Own Story,* 2: 20, 29, 52.

sacrifices and stresses of total war were driving armies and peoples near the limits of endurance. War weariness was fracturing the unity of dedication to the prosecution of the war. People and soldiers lost faith in both the political and military direction of the war. Abetted by the events in Russia, a revolutionary change of opinion was coming to be felt among the masses. The war appeared to them to be increasingly waged less for high national purpose than for benefiting imperialist aims and salvaging the position of the ruling few.

These feelings were pronounced in Russia, Austria, Italy, and France, but the attitudes in Germany and Britain were not too far behind. The conditions produced a pressure for ending the war as quickly as possible. The pressure was manifested in two gigantic gambles, the Nivelle offensive to win a military decision at a single blow and the German campaign of unrestricted submarine warfare to reduce Britain to submission in six months. The conditions also bred peace moves and changes in government and military command—a complete revolution in Russia, the Hindenburg-Ludendorff rule in Germany, the replacement of Conrad as chief of the general staff and a new government in Vienna around the new emperor Karl, and in France the replacement of Nivelle by Pétain and the authoritarian regime of Clemenceau on the civilian side.

In Allied operational planning for 1917, the overriding strategic issue was whether the pressure on Germany was to be increased by an offensive with all available forces on the Western Front or whether the western Allies should hold to the strategic defensive until the Entente had acquired more strength through American aid and expanded tank production. The British generals and many of the French, including Joffre and Nivelle, championed the former position, while political leaders such as Lloyd George and Churchill, as well as Pétain and his sympathizers among the French generals and politicians, supported the latter. The early operational decisions for 1917 were determined by the Allied military conference held at Chantilly on November 15–16, 1916. These decisions embodied the views of Joffre and the British generals in favor of an early combined offensive, in which the British would take the larger share.[3]

After Nivelle succeeded Joffre in December 1916, the Chantilly plan was fundamentally changed. Lloyd George, who scented "the blood and

3. Blake, *Private Papers of Douglas Haig,* 180; Robertson, *Soldiers and Statesmen,* 2: 191–93. On the strategic issues of 1917, see Cruttwell, *Role of British Strategy in the Great War,* 66–73.

mud" of another Somme in the Chantilly decisions, worked to jettison the plan. True to his easterner's approach, the prime minister proposed at the Allied conference at Rome in early January a Franco-British-Italian attack on the Austrian front, directed to the capture of Vienna and the submission of Austria. When this was not welcomed by the generals, Lloyd George enthusiastically embraced Nivelle's ideas, which the French chief presented in London with self-confident plausibility.

Nivelle set out to apply the method by which he had distinguished himself at Verdun to the central bastions of the German defensive system located along the Aisne River between Soissons and Reims. In his planning, artillery preparation and a creeping barrage would cover the whole German defensive zone in that sector, that is, three or four positions of nine to twelve lines of trenches extending five to twelve miles deep. Infantry waves of several armies were to make a violent frontal assault over this distance at a single bound, without bringing up the artillery for a renewed preparation. The infantry advance was to break through the German rear in a decisive action requiring no longer than twenty-four to forty-eight hours. Reserves would immediately exploit the rupture in an open war of maneuver. The main strike and the glory of success would be shifted to the French from the British. The latter would deliver a secondary attack in a joint operation with the French in the Arras area. Despite the doubts of the British generals, the War Cabinet and Haig approved of British participation in the offensive.[4]

Nivelle's plan was in substance a dazzling formula for a quick and allegedly inexpensive victory to end the war—more a dream reflecting the desperate mood of the French nation than a consensus of professional opinion. The general, stressing the importance of determination and élan, reverted essentially to the old prewar doctrine of the *offensive à outrance* propagated by the general staff. Nivelle added a Napoleonic touch in the grandiose proportions of the strategy.

Because of heavy troop losses in 1916, the basic feature of the German bloc's military planning for 1917 was to hold to the strategic defensive on the Western Front. The Germans would seek to wear down the Allied armies by a vastly strengthened defensive system and by matching defensive tactics. The defensive consolidation included the voluntary surrender

4. Edward Louis Spears, *Prelude to Victory* (London, 1939), 42–46; Jean Galtier-Boissière, *La Grande Guerre, 1914–1918* (Paris, 1966), 377; Blake, *Private Papers of Douglas Haig,* 178, 191–94; Robertson, *Soldiers and Statesmen,* 2: 197–99.

of the salient between Arras and Soissons and withdrawal to a straight and more easily defended position, the Siegfried line (dubbed the Hindenburg line by the Allies), from south of Arras to east of Soissons. Here the Germans constructed, beginning in September 1916, a deep zone of defense, utilizing elaborate defensive devices spread through the network of trench lines. The Aisne front farther south was similarly reinforced. The high command applied a scorched-earth policy with calculated thoroughness to the area of evacuation. Most of the population was driven eastward, and the area was sown with mines and booby-traps. Beginning on March 16, the German forces withdrew to the new position in skillfully prepared and executed stages.[5]

Ludendorff's program of retirement spiked the initial British-French attack against the Arras-Soissons salient projected by Nivelle as a diversion from the main drive along the Chemin des Dames. Previous preparations of the Allies were altered and extended, as they proceeded slowly through the devastated area and then reestablished a new front. The Germans thus bought time for making more formidable their defenses on the Aisne and Arras fronts. The Allies were remiss in not attacking the Germans in the midst of withdrawal, when their vulnerability might have offered the possibility of significant success and made the Chemin des Dames unnecessary.[6]

The execution of the Nivelle plan was beset with other adverse circumstances. Friction and distrust developed between Nivelle and Haig, along with their respective headquarters staffs, over the effort of the French, assisted by the cooperation of Lloyd George, to subordinate the British command to the French. The Briand cabinet, which had appointed Nivelle, fell on March 17. The new premier, Alexandre Ribot, and the new minister of war, Paul Painlevé, had misgivings about Nivelle and his undertaking. Discussions of Painlevé with generals and political leaders, as well as a gloomy, tense meeting of the War Committee (corresponding to the British War Cabinet) with Nivelle and the army group commanders at the Compiègne headquarters (April 6), revealed that the offensive was about to be launched by a vacillating government sunk in dejection and doubt, by a commander-in-chief who had lost authority, and by group

5. Görlitz, *Der deutsche Generalstab,* 157; *Ludendorff's Own Story,* 2: 4–8; Hindenburg, *Out of My Life,* 261–62.

6. Galtier-Boissière, *La Grande Guerre,* 279; Spears, *Prelude to Victory,* 218–30; Blake, *Private Papers of Douglas Haig,* 197.

commanders who had lost faith in the operations they were about to begin. An unusually severe season put "General Winter" on the side of the Germans, delaying further the preparations and the starting date of the drive.[7]

It was too late for preparing a combined assault of the British and French forces against the entire new German line. The British alone were therefore called on to deliver the initial attack on both sides of Arras, mostly north of the area evacuated by the Germans. The attack at Arras on April 9 commenced a set-piece battle dominated by the British artillery. The weight of the bombardment, a veritable "symphony of hell," had the benefit of a perfected percussion fuse that burst the shell on contact and acted as an effective destroyer of barbed wire. The shelling was intermingled with gas ejected in drums by a new, efficient projector.[8]

The troops, at last realistically trained according to battle experience, were considerably improved over those of 1916. The British achieved tactical surprise by ruses of timing in the artillery preparation and by use of long underground galleries and tunnels by which they brought attacking troops covertly to assembly points close to the German lines.

General Sir Edmund Allenby's Third Army on both sides of Arras and the Canadian corps of the First Army on the left, opposite Vimy Ridge, attacked under the cover of a creeping barrage of crushing effect and with the aid of forty-eight tanks. They came over the defenders like "an all-engulfing maelstrom of earth, smoke, and iron," according to a German participant.[9] The Canadians captured the commanding heights of Vimy Ridge. Both their corps and the Third Army broke through the German lines in a penetration recognized by Ludendorff as producing an "extremely critical" situation, which "might have had far-reaching conse-

7. See Paul Painlevé, *Comment j'ai nommé Foch et Pétain* (Paris, 1923), 38–52; Henri Carré, *Les grandes heures du Général Pétain 1917 et la crise du moral* (Paris, 1952), 16–22; Stephen Ryan, *Pétain the Soldier* (South Brunswick, N. J., 1969), 109–13. Spears, the British liaison officer, in *Prelude to Victory,* 356–83, offers an unsurpassed account of the celebrated conference at Compiègne, for which no record was kept. Poincaré's entry on the meeting in *Au service de la France,* 9: 107–08, is too brief to be satisfactory, although revealing in conjunction with Spears's extensive version. Painlevé, *Comment j'ai nommé Foch et Pétain,* 53–54, passes over the conference too lightly, with the conclusion that it changed nothing. See also Gabriel Terrail, *Nivelle et Painlevé* (Paris, 1919), 69–77; Jere Clemens King, *Generals and Politicians* (Westport, Conn., 1971), 156–59.

8. For the battle of Arras, see Spears, *Prelude to Victory,* 308–19, 384–434; Terraine, *Douglas Haig,* 284–90; *Ludendorff's Own Story,* 2: 22–24.

9. Spears, *Prelude to Victory,* 401.

quences if the enemy had pushed further forward." Counsels of caution
ruled, however, and by frantic exertions the Germans pieced together the
broken lines with scattered units and then with orderly reinforcements.
On the right the Australian brigades of the Fifth Army broke into the
Hindenburg line on April 11 but withdrew for want of reinforcements
and artillery support.

The fighting fell off by April 12, although it continued at intervals with
small advances during the remainder of April and May. The British attack
had demonstrated how to break through the strongest German lines by
the efficient and massive use of artillery. The British were too surprised
and complacent to convert the initial success into a victory of strategic
dimensions. There was still the question whether even outstanding command and staff work would have permitted a major exploitation without
the mobility acquired by using tanks on a large scale.

Nivelle, immured in illusion, rigidly refused to the last to let unfavorable factors deter him. Adding to the handicaps was an alarming lack of
security about the oncoming offensive, the "worst kept secret of the war."
Before it commenced, the plan of operations was revealed to the Germans, who captured a prisoner bearing corps orders for the assault. Nivelle paid no heed to the doubts of many corps and divisional officers or
to the inadequacy of the artillery bombardment.

On April 16–17 Nivelle followed the British diversionary attack with
the offensive on the Aisne, or the Chemin des Dames. The assault waves
of four French armies dashed forward from Soissons to east of Reims, with
the expectation that this was the battle to end the war. They took the first
line at most points but struggled against the quagmire caused by the heavy
rains and against the deep zone of German defenses—ambushes, traps,
felled trees, concrete shelters and pillboxes, and jungles of wire entanglements. The exhausted troops fell behind their advancing barrage, exposing themselves to the deadly fire of the enemy machine gunners, who
sprang up from dugouts after the barrage passed. The tanks were used
badly with no effect; control of the air belonged to the Germans; the
inadequacy of artillery support during the battle was demoralizing. Even
shortages of artillery and small-arms ammunition developed.[10]

The advance faltered and stopped, never going beyond the first or
second line. The waves of attackers often became disorganized, and a

10. Ibid., 491 ff.; Barnett, *Swordbearers,* 206–08.

general breakdown reached from the battle zone rearward. The German counterattacks regained most of the ground won by the French. During the following days Nivelle continued the battle regardless of the commitment he gave at Compiègne to call off the offensive if the enemy's front was not ruptured within forty-eight hours. The French forced the Germans to evacuate the salient at Malmaison and cleared the Aisne valley and the road from Reims to Soissons. The offense was resumed on May 5, but under the influence of Pétain the fresh attack was staged with limited objectives. After only slight gains since May 5, the battle of Chemin des Dames, or the second battle of Aisne, came to an end on May 9.

By the ordinary standards of positional warfare, Chemin des Dames would not rank as a defeat for the French. Nivelle's record for ground and prisoners taken in proportion to losses was better than Joffre's.[11] The outcome nonetheless was a crushing defeat of French expectations and hopes. No breakthrough, no exploitation, no opening of a war of maneuver, no Napoleonic victory. By his excessive promises and pronouncements Nivelle had created the myth of a cheap, quick way to end France's misery of war. The myth now collapsed, just at the time a distinct psychological change of defeatist character had affected the French nation. The revulsion against futile combat, the inequitable distribution of war burdens, and the inability to organize more effectively on the home front were rending the patriotic *union sacrée* of enthusiastic support of the war. The long-suffering poilu, sharing the national moral reaction, was feeling "fed up" with the war, or more precisely with the way the war was being run by the command and staff officers.[12]

In this atmosphere of strain and expectation the results of the great Nivelle offensive touched off "a crisis of confidence" (Painlevé's term) within the army. The crisis forced Nivelle out of his command and a turn to a new strategy, while taking form among the front soldiers in a series of mutinies. Pétain was generally the choice of the army to save France in this hour of extreme peril. The government appointed him commander-

11. Churchill, *World Crisis,* 3, pt. 1: 281; Taylor, *History of the First World War,* 113. The French losses in this battle have been the subject of more dispute than those of any other engagement in the war because of the conflict over the advisability of the offensive. The French official figure of 96,125 for the period April 16–25 is based on the returns of Nivelle, who had an interest in keeping the estimate as low as possible. Spears, *Prelude to Victory,* 510, is confident that his total of 144,000, which was considered personally with Painlevé, is reliable to the greatest extent possible.

12. See especially Barnett, *Swordbearers,* 228–30.

in-chief of the French armies of the north and northeast, with Foch as chief of the general staff.[13]

The betrayal of promises at the Chemin des Dames after nearly three years of war and after three million casualties was at last too much for the French soldiers. The battle was conclusive in demonstrating the futility of dying when the command was incapable of victory either by the attritional attacks of Joffre or by the grand and audacious attempt of Nivelle. The poilus gave vent to their despair and bitter resentment in acts of mutiny, which continued at a crisis pitch from the latter part of April into August.[14] This "collective indiscipline," or desertions at an excessive rate, spread through a large majority of the divisions along and behind the front. The rebellious soldiers cried for peace and down with war, waved red flags, sang the Internationale, rioted, did violence against officers, attended strike meetings, resorted to drunkenness, and refused to march or to depart for the front. The "crisis of command after Chemin des Dames became a crisis of discipline" in the army.[15]

The mutinies were associated with pacifist-defeatist agitation and an outburst of strikes and workers' unrest. Yet the mutinous acts were spontaneous, without organized leadership. The poilus rebelled against taking part in further hopeless and murderous attacks. The basic factor was the loss of confidence in the command; whatever form the indiscipline took, the acts represented a protest against the manner in which the war was being conducted. The mutineers were intuitively demanding a new form of warfare, which would utilize mass artillery, tanks, and planes against the

13. Painlevé, *Comment j'ai nommé Foch et Pétain,* 78–128; Poincaré, *Au service de la France,* 9: 118–38 passim; King, *Generals and Politicians,* 164–68.

14. On the mutinies in general, see Henri Philippe Pétain, *Une crise morale de la nation française en guerre, 16 avril–23 octobre 1917* (Paris, 1966); the English translation of this work with preliminary comment drawn from his experience as British liaison officer by Sir Edward Spears in *Two Men Who Saved France* (London, 1966); Guy Pedroncini, *Les mutineries de 1917* (Paris, 1967); Watt, *Dare Call It Treason;* John Williams, *Mutiny 1917* (London, 1962); Barnett, *Swordbearers,* 208–32. Pétain's version, drafted after the war, places large responsibility for the mutinies on the "criminal pacifist propaganda" spreading from the interior of the country, its "tacit tolerance" by the public authorities, and the role of the press in criticizing military operations and publicizing the actions of the Russian revolutionaries. Pétain, nevertheless, does not neglect causes of discontent in the army, which in his opinion could have been removed before the outbreak in 1917. Pedroncini's account is the most thorough investigation of the subject, utilizing the military archives extensively. Its survey of the causes of the crisis is more balanced than Pétain's, and the study plumbs deeply the meaning of the mutinies.

15. Pedroncini, *Les mutineries,* 67–69, 280.

enemy's machine guns rather than the lives of the infantry. In comparison, defeatist propaganda was of secondary importance.[16]

In addition, the mutinies, fittingly characterized as a "professional strike," sprang from numerous concrete grievances, to which the closeted command had been insensitive. Most pervasive was the deep feeling that the staff officers—"the drinkers of blood"—treated the fighting troops impersonally, only as so much material to be thrown into the mill of mechanized war, along with guns and ammunition for the purpose of turning out decorations for the staff officers and impressive content for the communiqués. More specific complaints concerned the arbitrary and inequitable leave system, poor and insufficient food, deficient rest facilities, a severe disciplinary system, and an exasperating postal censorship. These afflictions sickened the body of the French army, and Pétain's task was to nurse the stricken being back to health.[17]

In restoring the patient, Pétain wrought the miracle of 1917 and did as great a service for the Allies as Joffre at the Marne. The saving of France from collapse avoided a Dunkirk and an entirely new shape of the war. His treatment combined a change of strategy and tactics with exceptional measures of military justice, restraint of revolutionary and pacifist agitation around troops, remedy of grievances, and reform of the army.[18]

Pétain introduced a new psychology to the French conduct of war. The altered system was called forth not only by the rebellion of the French soldiers but also by the stringency in effectives as well as by the development in mechanized arms and the massive expansion of their production. His unspectacular "strategy of patience" and "tactics of convalescence" rejected the making of attacks whatever the cost, whether the breakthrough attempt or the grandiose offensive of Napoleonic sweep. Pétain took up the strategic defensive while seeking a favorable shift in the balance of forces. A major offensive should await therefore the coming of the Americans in force and a substantial increase in French firepower and in the weight of the mechanized attack. The more powerful mechanized

16. Ibid., 179, 278, 306–12 passim; Galtier-Boissière, *La Grande Guerre*, 390.
17. Watt, *Dare Call It Treason*, 195.
18. On Pétain's means of healing in the army with the remedy of grievances and improved conditions of material existence, see his *Une crise morale* and Pedroncini, *Les mutineries*, 232–78. For the most careful analysis of the measures of military justice documented from the military archives, see also the latter, 183–231, which reveals their character of relative moderation and not ruthless repression. On the estimate of Pétain's achievement, see particularly Spears, *Two Men Who Saved France*, 62–65.

attack would be achieved through an enlarged program of producing heavy artillery, light assault tanks, and improved planes. All of these factors contributed toward a method of war designed to husband the infantry while according a preponderance to materiel and extending the mechanized means of war.

German reserves would be consumed and the offensive spirit of the French army preserved by a series of attacks with strictly limited objectives organized to the last detail and supported with maximum artillery coverage. This cool, impassive realist among many romantic militarists had long been a disciple of cannon over the bayonet. His aim was not to launch an infantry attack until massive artillery pounding obliterated the enemy's resistance, including the power of counterattack. The infantry, moving behind a creeping barrage, could then make a successful, though limited, advance at a minimum cost.[19]

Attaching such importance to the artillery, Pétain strengthened its power of attack by more flexible and effective organization of the branch and by increasing the density of guns for 1918. In his fully developed tactics, Pétain spared the infantry by the massive use of all other arms against the enemy's machine guns, field fortifications, and artillery nearest the front. He thus realized the value of aircraft as a weapon of ground fighting and gave it a place in total combat, prefiguring its future role in war. In resisting the enemy's attack, Pétain applied an active defense arranged in depth.[20]

Pétain's strategy and tactics, plus his repressive and remedial steps, restored discipline to the French army and began its revival of confidence. Pétain's work of reorganizing the French army, technically still behind the German army, created an up-to-date fighting instrument capable of sharing effectively in the Allied drive to victory in 1918. Pétain, being first of all an organizer, replaced the old ascendancy of élan and impetuous will dedicated to the quest of glory with the preeminence of intensive training, heavier firepower, flexibility and mobility through proper organization, and constant adaptation of tactics to new weapons and experience. He encouraged more initiative on the part of officers, more contact between officers and men, and more interest of the officers in the welfare of their

19. On Pétain's method of war, see Guy Pedroncini, *Pétain, général en chef, 1917–1918* (Paris, 1974), 20–21, 40–42, 109, 166, 436; Barnett, *Swordbearers,* 204, 208–09; Watt, *Dare Call It Treason,* 215–17.

20. Pedroncini, *Pétain,* 44–48, 57–62.

troops. Altogether, his measures as "doctor to the army" succeeded to a great extent in establishing a relationship of trust between Pétain and the poilu.[21]

The French command had to face the never-ceasing menace that the Germans might seize this supreme opportunity for a fatal blow. Before Pétain's cure had worked, a major offensive of the Germans could have broken through the feeble French front and captured Paris. The French authorities, by measures of tight security, successfully concealed the full proportions of the army's moral collapse. In June and July the Germans attacked on the Chemin des Dames and took back some of the ground gained in the Nivelle offensive. Pétain, however, rounded up enough dependable troops to stave off serious damage.[22]

The question was soon put to the test whether the afflicted French army was sufficiently mended and prepared under Pétain's direction to serve again as an instrument of attack. The cooperation that Pétain pledged the British in connection with the summer offensive in Flanders was limited initially to an assault by General Antoine's First Army along the Yser canal, between the Belgian army and the British forces. The attack pushed the Germans back across the canal and broke into the German third line at a small cost in casualties. Pétain had demonstrated the success of his method of obliteration by bombardment and the progress of the French army's recuperation. Similarly, this method of meticulous preparation and saturated bombardment prior to the infantry advance captured long-contested heights at Verdun on August 20, and in October reduced the fort of Malmaison. The whole front on the Chemin des Dames was improved.

2. THE PASSCHENDAELE TRAGEDY

From the time of the crisis in the French army the main responsibility for fighting the Germans fell to the British. Their operations were concentrated in the Flanders offensive widely known as the Passchendaele campaign, or the Third Ypres. The campaign from July 31 to November 10 was the dominant event of land warfare in 1917. Of all British actions on the Western Front this series has come under the severest indictment for being an obstinate venture in impassable mud that involved the wrong strategy, the wrong tactics, the wrong place, and the wrong time.

21. Williams, *Mutiny 1917*, 162. On Pétain's reorganization of the army and reforms, see Barnett, *Swordbearers*, 243–56.
22. Watt, *Dare Call It Treason*, 240–42; Williams, *Mutiny 1917*, p. ix, 164–5, 243–48.

Haig was fixed in the view that the British must conduct a large-scale western offensive in 1917, which by continued pressure would keep the Germans from recovering from past blows. He argued with unrestrained optimism before the War Cabinet that the complete concentration of British resources in a summer offensive in France might "even bring final victory this year." An offensive of this scope was the more necessary since the French had become in his sight "a broken reed" and Britain must act "to win the war by itself." Haig took up the cudgels strongly against what to his mind was "the act of a lunatic"—Lloyd George's advocacy of diverting troops and guns from France to Italy for a peripheral offensive against Austria that would end the war.[23]

The choice of Flanders for the ground of the summer offensive represented Haig's long-standing preference no less than the government's view, given fresh force by the submarine peril of 1917, of the need to drive the Germans from the Belgian coast. The Admiralty, in a state of near panic, pressed Haig with the support of half the War Cabinet to free the Belgian coast so that the German U-boat bases at Ostend and Zeebrugge could be wiped out. A strategic success at Ypres would not only clear the Belgian coast but could also rip open the German flank, holding out the possibility of rolling up the German line from the north. Of minimum tactical advantage, the troublesome Ypres salient might be removed.[24]

Flanders, however, presented disadvantages from an operational standpoint. Marshland drained by numerous ditches extended behind the coast, and at Ypres the lower ground with its heavy clay and high water table would be churned by bombardment into deep mud pitted with watery craters. The Germans were entrenched in a strongly fortified position east of Ypres, along the crest of a ridge commanding the surrounding Flanders plain. After the failure of the Nivelle offensive, they began to shift reserves to this sector in anticipation of an attack.

Out of such considerations the chief of the imperial general staff, Robertson, voiced doubts about the plan. Pétain and Foch warned that the Flanders offensive would fail. Of the War Cabinet, Lloyd George and Bonar Law, the head of the Conservative party, along with the Tory Alfred Milner, were opposed, although the prime minister could not

23. Blake, *Private Papers of Douglas Haig*, 218–19, 234–40, 245–47.
24. Ibid., 221, 227; Terraine, *Western Front*, 138–39; Guinn, *British Strategy and Politics*, 245–46; Robertson, *Soldiers and Statesmen*, 2: 243–44.

muster support for adoption of his alternative against Austria when military and naval opinion rejected it. Haig was determined nevertheless to go ahead rather than assume the defensive and wait for the Americans or accede to Lloyd George's strategy. The French in the end agreed to support "to the best of their power" an offensive in which the British would make the main attack. The vacillation and indecision of the War Cabinet continued, and Haig did not receive formal approval of his plans until six days before the beginning of the offensive.[25]

Prior to the opening of the Passchendaele campaign Haig conducted the preliminary action of winning Messines Ridge (June 7–14), a southern spur of the main ridge east of Ypres, by way of security for the British right flank. The action, carried out by "Daddy" (General Sir Hubert) Plumer and his Second Army, put into effective practice his maxims of "Trust, Training, and Thoroughness." The precepts were skillfully applied in joining long and intensive preparatory bombardment, precise counterbattery work, an overwhelming barrage 700 yards deep, and the most shattering mining operation of the war. Ludendorff found the demoralizing effect of the mine explosions "simply staggering." The British troops, including an Australian and the New Zealand division, took the ridge in an exemplary victory of siege warfare, demonstrating what could be done by thorough organization and minute planning.[26]

Haig made a critical mistake by shifting the command of the main operations from the older and methodical Plumer, who had long been in charge of this area, to the younger, more "thrusting" General Sir Hubert Gough. Plumer's Second Army was now to provide cover on the right for Gough's Fifth Army, and Antoine's First French Army, inserted between the Belgian and British forces, to protect the left.

The arrangements brought about an unfortunate change in plans and delay in preparations that made the first month of fighting coincide with heavy August rains. Gough, applying a more risky and ambitious approach to the problem, prepared essentially for a frontal attack to the north, through the lower land, on the German coastal bases, and counted on breaking through the four German positions in a big bite. The Fifth Army had to be transferred from Artois to Ypres, and Antoine's army moved

25. Blake, *Private Papers of Douglas Haig*, 219–45 passim; Terraine, *Douglas Haig*, 335–36.
26. *Haig's Despatches*, 105–09; Terraine, *Western Front*, 144; *Ludendorff's Own Story*, 2: 31. John Giles, *The Ypres Salient* (London, 1970), 140–44, pays special attention to the mining operation.

into position on the left. The six weeks of time lost gave the Germans full opportunity to strengthen their defenses in depth and to assemble reinforcements.[27]

The massive preparatory bombardment by the largest force of artillery the British had ever brought together never realized its intended purpose. It could not dominate the German artillery, and the cross fire destroyed the intricate drainage system, reducing the ground to a morass of swamps or pitting it with craters impassable to the tanks.

British historians distinguish nine different actions in the Third Ypres, falling into three phases. In the first, or Gough, phase, the initial assault by the Fifth Army (July 31–August 2) was soon halted by the vigorous counterattacks of the special German counterattack divisions and by the deadly effect of the German artillery, not silenced by the British bombardment. The onset of rain cooperated with the German defense. The French support could go no further than Antoine's action along the Yser.[28] The British had to postpone further attack for two weeks; the incessant rains of August, more than twice the average fall for the month, paralyzed the British offensive. Gough's second attack (August 16–18), in the plain west of the Ypres ridge, was a decided failure. The rest of the month, moreover, yielded Gough no success.

The August record of futility at high cost persuaded Haig to replace the tactics and leadership of Gough with those of Plumer. The second phase was a period of modest success, achieved by Plumer's characteristic method of meticulous preparations for a narrow advance of small bounds, protected by massive artillery coverage and a deep barrage. With the densest artillery concentration for any engagement during the war, Plumer attacked on higher ground east of Ypres in three steps (the battles of Menin Road Ridge, September 20–25; Polygon Wood, September 26; and Broodseinde, October 4), each according to the same pattern, and gained the crest of the Ypres ridge. Plumer's triple success spelled the triumph of a method and brought the peak of artillery's growing share in battle.[29]

The fall rains descended on the final phase of the campaign and converted the ground into "a porridge of mud." The last three battles (Poel-

27. Terraine, *Douglas Haig*, 336–40. For a critical appraisal of Gough, see Leon Wolff, *In Flanders Fields* (London, 1961), 126–27.
28. See above, p. 176.
29. Terraine, *Douglas Haig*, 356–66; Terraine, *Western Front*, 149–50.

cappelle, October 9; Passchendaele I, October 12; and Passchendaele II, October 26–November 10) were fought under agonizing conditions for infantry, gunners, and even the mules. The air force could not help the artillery; the gunners had no firm base from which to fire; and the foot soldiers, slogging forward by inches through rain and mud, bog and swamp, had trifling help from the artillery. It is this picture of frightful misery that has identified the nature and popular name of Passchendaele with the whole campaign. In these last actions there was nothing to show for the cost and suffering, except for the capture of Passchendaele village and adjoining ground on the Passchendaele ridge, which was to the credit of the Canadian corps.[30]

Haig now had no recourse but to end the dismal offensive as winter approached and five of his divisions were transferred to Italy after Caporetto. Only to a lesser degree than the Nivelle offensive was this a bitter disappointment of inflated expectations. The army in more than three months of fighting widened the Ypres salient but created in the Passchendaele salient a new and even tighter one. How high the blood toll soared remains a matter of controversy, with the casualty figures ranging from the official number of 244,897 to 400,000. The German total is even more uncertain; estimates vary from under 200,000 to 400,000. Both Lloyd George and Churchill have arraigned in the sharpest terms "this senseless campaign," in which Haig and Robertson "wore down alike the manhood and guns of the British army almost to destruction."[31]

The best that can be said for the Third Ypres from the Allied standpoint is that it helped to save the French army from imminent destruction during the moral crisis and to give Pétain a chance to accomplish the army's revival. More than half the German army in the west had to take part in the defense, "the greatest martyrdom of the war," as seen by the chief of staff of the defending army, who admitted the battle consumed German strength beyond the power to replace. The Germans nevertheless were not kept from sending divisions to Italy to encompass the Italian army in the disaster at Caporetto, from overcoming the last resistance of the Russians, and from concentrating strength for the great offensive of 1918. The

30. See E. Norman Gladden, *Ypres 1917* (London, 1967), for the personal record of a British infantryman's experiences in this nightmare.

31. Lloyd George, *War Memoirs*, 4: 2240; Churchill, *World Crisis*, 3, pt. 2: 339. Three examples of present-day works extremely critical of the Flanders offensive are: Taylor, *History of the First World War*, 124; Barnett, *Swordbearers*, 239–43; Giles, *Ypres Salient*, 217.

continuation of the offensive on the Ypres scale after August was hardly necessary for Pétain's salvation of the French army. Haig's objective thereafter, resting on a false estimate of the enemy's powers of resistance and of his own strength, accomplished no strategic purpose.[32]

The damage to the British army in the mire and mud of Ypres has also to be reckoned in the accounting. The British army, like the French and the German, had now endured too much. Its high morale was sacrificed in this hideous ordeal. So weakened by the losses and exhaustion of Ypres, the army could not prevent Cambrai from ending in a fiasco, though the mass use of tanks had effected a break-in of the German lines. The destructive effects carried over to 1918 to help collapse the British line before Ludendorff's onslaught in March.

Passchendaele had serious repercussions in Britain on the higher direction of war, exerting a divisive influence on the military and political leadership. The undertaking was associated with some divergence of view between Robertson and Haig that began to affect their cooperation. Distrust was deepened between Lloyd George on the one side and Robertson and Haig on the other. Lloyd George felt that he had been duped by the generals, whose professional competence he judged lower than before. The estrangement was mutual, and Lloyd George now worked to bring Robertson and Haig to book. By February 1918 Lloyd George had managed the fall of the chief of the general staff. Haig was too solidly entrenched in the British establishment, with the king's backing and other political support, to be accessible to Lloyd George's maneuvers. The prime minister continued putting up with the command in the field in whom he had no confidence.[33]

The question whether there was a feasible alternative to Passchendaele must start with the assumption that the saving of France required British offensive action on the Western Front. Lloyd George's strategy of an Allied blow from Italy to knock out Austria was hardly a solution. It would require a far greater effort for the Allies to deliver, particularly when the shipping situation was still critical, than for the Germans to counter. Robertson had the support of fact in repeatedly insisting to Lloyd George and the War Cabinet, "Germany could always beat us in concentrating superior force on the Italian front." These circumstances did not make it

32. *Ludendorff's Own Story,* 2: 106; Terraine, *Douglas Haig,* 372–73.
33. Bonham-Carter, *Soldier True,* 303–51; Terraine, *Western Front,* 155; Blake, *Private Papers of Douglas Haig,* 265.

credible that the Allies could shift enough divisions to this front for diverting the German danger from enfeebled France.[34]

To realize Haig's larger objectives at Ypres was to ask the impossible of the British army. Yet if Haig had kept Plumer in charge of the main action from beginning to end, Passchendaele might not have turned out quite the futile tragedy it was. More ground would undoubtedly have been gained at smaller losses. Further than this, the most likely alternative was the Pétain system of limited attacks, prodigal in the use of artillery and economic in the cost of men, while waiting for a full concentration of coalition forces, including especially the Americans. There should have been no reason why a sufficient number of these attacks, properly organized and coordinated, would not have provided an adequate shield for France's recovery. Pétain urged that this alternative of small operations with limited objectives was the proper course for both Allies. Another alternative was to have sped the production of tanks and launched a thoroughly planned Cambrai earlier in the year with the resources wasted at Ypres.[35]

The offensive at Cambrai (November 20–December 5) was notable for a revolutionary innovation in warfare—the mass action of tanks. Since its introduction on the Western Front, the tank had improved in speed, maneuverability, and specialization of purpose; and tactics had evolved in accordance with these qualities. At Cambrai, opposite the Hindenburg line south of Ypres, the command fielded nearly five hundred tanks on firm, chalk land ideal for the operations of the new weapon. The Third Army of Sir Julian Byng utilized them in a manner to achieve complete surprise. The assault began without a preparatory bombardment or even preliminary registration of targets. The tanks, advancing behind the artillery barrage, smashed down the barbed wire of the enemy, opening lanes for the infantry that followed closely. The German defenses collapsed in most places before these demoralizing monsters and the superior weight of the British. Confusion spread as a sense of helplessness seized the enemy infantrymen.

On the first day the British made an unprecedented advance, the tanks breaking through the German trench systems and the infantrymen occupying the third position with small loss of life. After this splendid success the

34. Robertson, *Soldiers and Statesmen,* 2: 241.
35. On the Cambrai alternative, see Churchill, *World Crisis,* 3, pt. 2: 347.

British were not prepared to proceed with the stage of exploitation. The operational conception had begun with the idea of a disorganizing raid, projected by the chief general staff officer of the Tank Corps, J.F.C. Fuller then lieutenant colonel, and moved on to an ambitious general assault. The planning never overcame this hybrid background and failed to take the later stage adequately into account. Because of Passchendaele and the shift of five divisions to Italy after Caporetto, the command did not possess reserves or fresh enough troops to take advantage of the breach and engage in open warfare. That the opportunity was frittered away was also due to some of the commanders, who were still too rigid in altering tactics to suit the needs and capabilities of the tanks or who lacked the independent authority to exploit local advantages that arose.[36]

The Germans rushed reinforcements to the broken lines, checked the advance, and surprised the Third Army with a successful counteroffensive on November 30. The outcome after German penetration and British withdrawal to a better line left the Germans in possession of ground in original British positions nearly as great as the gains retained by the Third Army. The Germans had not made the most of their opportunity, failing through mistakes of command to direct the main thrust where British resistance was least.

Cambrai rises as a sharp divide in the war, for here two solutions were advanced to the problem of grappling with the stalemate of the Western Front: the fleet action of tanks by the British, and the penetration tactics of special assault troops by the Germans. The British, combining the mass action of tanks with the fire of planes against enemy trenches, introduced the war of the future but were too bound down by the war of the past to reap the fruits of their ingenuity. If the British command had had vision and faith in the revolutionary innovation, Haig would have called off at an early date the slaughter at Ypres and devoted the men and materiel to adequate preparation for a Cambrai.

Ludendorff failed to learn from Cambrai that tanks were a key to victory. He did not grasp the lesson owing partly to success in destroying a number of the British tanks at Cambrai and partly to the demonstrated

36. Bryan Cooper, *The Battle of Cambrai* (New York, 1968); B. H. Liddell Hart, *The Tanks*, 2 vols. (New York, 1959), 1: 130–33; Terraine, *Douglas Haig*, 379–80; Blake, *Private Papers of Douglas Haig*, 269; Hindenburg, *Out of My Life*, 290–91. Hindenburg concludes that the British high command "seemed to have failed to concentrate the resources required to secure the execution of their plans and their exploitation in the case of success."

value of new tactics introduced two months before. The innovation replaced the long artillery preparation with a hurricane bombardment of a few hours, after which small parties of special assault troops would knife forward toward the rear and flanks as quickly as possible, leaving masses of the enemy behind them to be reduced later by subsequent waves of troops. The infiltration tactics, similar to Brusilov's, were brought out against the Russians in the capture of Riga in September, executed with devastating success at Caporetto, and used at Cambrai to steal victory from the British.

3. THE CAPORETTO DEBACLE

The decline of national morale and attrition in internal strength proceeded furthest in Austria, Italy, and Russia, each of which was racing the others toward collapse. Italy, reflecting this condition, experienced the worst military rout of the war at Caporetto. Although late in complying with the Allied decisions of Chantilly for concerted spring offensives, the Italian army attacked in the tenth battle of the Isonzo (May 12–28), winning little ground while piling up enormous casualties. The Italian command coordinated the eleventh battle of the Isonzo (August 18–September 12) with the British offensive in Flanders. Thorough preparation attended the Italians with more success in this action. They pushed the Austrians back more than five miles in the direction of Laibach.

The two battles climaxed the long train of losses and suffering inflicted by the series of Isonzo struggles. In these two "endurance contests" demanding ever larger masses of men, the casualty lists jumped to 300,000 for Italy, after it had already absorbed losses of more than three-quarters of a million since taking up arms. War weariness had taken possession of the troops, in view of the immense effort made for so small a gain in more than two years of fighting. The discontent accumulated from the professional deficiencies of command, as well as from the thoughtlessness of higher officers about the hardships of the front soldiers and the social distinction between officers and men. One of the gravest abuses was the lack of operational system, evident in the failure of infantry and artillery to cooperate and the inability to cover advancing troops with a rolling barrage. The general disillusionment of the Italian people with the war offered a fertile ground for the activities of defeatists and neutralists among socialists and church agencies, the spread of Bolshevik ideas, and the enemy's propaganda campaign. All of this added to the deteriorating spirit in the army, which was further worsened by putting into the front lines discontented workers who had been on strike.[37]

On the other hand, the last grim battle had been costly to the Austrians as well, and had convinced them that their situation was too critical to endure the expected resumption of Cadorna's offensive. The Austrians decided that it was imperative to strike first with a counteroffensive. But Austrian weakness required the participation of German strength. The previous German reluctance to divert German troops to Italy was overcome by the conclusion that this was the only means of bolstering the sinking war spirit of the Austrians and saving the empire from collapse. For the attack, the German command dispatched to Italy seven select divisions, along with air and heavy artillery, on condition that General von Below, heading the German forces, should command the entire operation.[38]

The Italian local commander sensed what was being prepared and proposed that it be broken by a preventive strike. Cadorna, however, insisted on arranging "for a stout defensive *à outrance* on the whole front."[39] At the same time the Italians deployed reserves improperly when the Austro-Germans assembled fourteen divisions against the Italian four at Caporetto.

By way of preparation, the Central Powers drenched the enemy front with propaganda pamphlets disseminating the Bolshevik stock-in-trade and the idea of Italy's subordination to British interests. The attackers, utilizing the techniques proved at Riga, began the twelfth battle of the Isonzo on October 24, with a short but overwhelming bombardment.[40] The enemy position was saturated with gas, against which the Italians had no effective protection. The infantry moved forward quickly to tear open a gap in the Italian line, and the Second Italian Army fell into panic and chaos. Terrified of the Germans and suspicious of its own officers, this army disintegrated into prisoners and stragglers. Within three days

37. Rudolf Kiszling, "Tirols und Kärntens Südgrenzen als Kampfraum im Ersten Weltkrieg," *Österreich in Geschichte und Literatur* 6 (1962): 200–01; Fuller, *Military History of the Western World*, 3: 301.
38. Kiszling, *Österreich-Ungarns Anteil am Ersten Weltkrieg*, 64–65; Kielmansegg, *Deutschland und der Erste Weltkrieg*, 371.
39. See Cadorna's letter of September 21 to Robertson and Foch; Robertson, *Soldiers and Statesmen*, 2: 252.
40. Illustrative of the formidable difficulties mastered by the Austro-Germans in preparing and launching the attack is Ernst Kabisch, *Helden in Fels und Eis* (Stuttgart, 1941), 60 ff.

Cadorna had to order a general retreat to the Tagliamento River, and within four the Italian forces had lost all the area gained since 1915. The Italians found it impossible to make a stand on the Tagliamento, the original objective of the Germans, and the rout continued to the Piave.[41] German methods and Italian feebleness had opened up a war of movement that continued until the Italians could improvise a line behind the barrier of the Piave by November 10. Ludendorff stopped the drive there, believing that a continuation would have invested military resources needed for the March offensive of 1918. In the Trentino, where the Italian troops were properly handled, the Italians firmly defeated the attempt of an army commanded by Conrad to break through to Vicenza (November 21–December 25).[42]

The disaster reduced the Italian army to a state of paralysis, and the war thereafter stagnated on this front. Cadorna blamed the debacle on the cowardice of his men, but that indeed was very little of the story. The breakdown of the losses told a great deal more: 40,000 killed and wounded, nearly 300,000 prisoners, and 350,000 deserters and stragglers. The figures make clear that the Italians were conducting a soldiers' strike, which was like that of the French earlier in the year, except that theirs was in the midst of battle rather than afterwards. The strike was against futile combat, bad leadership, and mistreatment of the rank and file.[43]

Caporetto did not put Italy out of the war, but it made of Italy a liability from then on. Along with the campaign of 1917 on the Western Front, the Russian dropout, and the elimination of Romania from the war, Caporetto contributed immeasurably to the gloom and depression in the Allied

41. Kiszling, *Österreich-Ungarns Anteil am Ersten Weltkrieg*, 65–68; May, *Passing of the Hapsburg Monarchy*, 1: 453–55. Ernest Hemingway's famous novel *A Farewell to Arms* (1929) is based on the retreat.

42. *Ludendorff's Own Story*, 2: 117.

43. On Italian losses, see Pietro Pieri, "L'Italia nella prima guerra mondiale, 1915–1918" in *Storia d'Italia*, ed. Nino Valeri, 5 vols. (Turin, 1965), 4: 866; Kiszling, "Tirols und Kärntens Südgrenzen als Kampfraum im Ersten Weltkrieg," 201. After the Italian disaster an official commission investigated the causes. Although in the nature of a whitewash, the report puts Cadorna into an unfavorable light, and V. E. Orlando, *Memorie, 1915–1919* (Milan, 1960), takes the same view. Cadorna's reply to the report is printed in his *Pagine polemiche* (Milan, 1950). Pieri, "L'Italia nella prima guerra mondiale," is similarly critical. On the other hand, Albertini, *Venti anni di vita politica*, pt. 2, 3: 143–88, defends Cadorna's conduct of the battle and lays the blame for defeat on the inadequacy of the officers, including generals, and the weakness of the government in dealing with defeatist agitation.

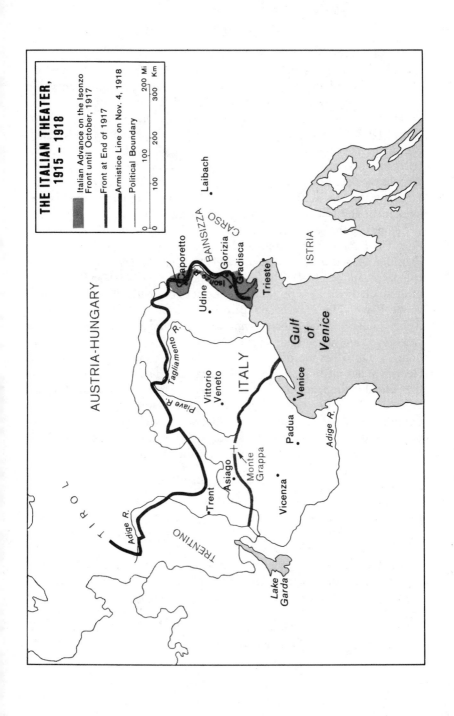

THE ITALIAN THEATER, 1915 – 1918

Italian Advance on the Isonzo Front until October, 1917

Front at End of 1917

Armistice Line on Nov. 4, 1918

Political Boundary

0   100   200 Mi
0   100   200   300 Km

AUSTRIA-HUNGARY

TIROL

Adige R.

Caporetto

Isonzo R.

BAINSIZZA

CARSO

Gorizia

Gradisca

Laibach

Udine

ISTRIA

Trieste

Tagliamento R.

Piave R.

Vittorio Veneto

ITALY

Gulf of Venice

Venice

Padua

Adige R.

Monte Grappa

Asiago

Trent

TRENTINO

Vicenza

Lake Garda

camp. Contrariwise, the decisive reverse with the other Allied setbacks lifted the Austrian spirits, propping up Austria to hold out one more year. The defeat, involving the loss of most of Venezia and the disorganization of the army, caused the formation of a new government under V. E. Orlando and prompted the replacement of Cadorna with General Armando Diaz, a younger man who had a much more perceptive understanding of the needs and psychology of Italy's soldiers. Diaz set about the reorganization of the army, and it started back on the road to recovery. The disaster excited a nationalist movement under the lead of such flamboyant extremists as D'Annunzio and Mussolini. Support of the war reawakened, and Italian morale revived quickly.

The nearly shattering blow to Italy gave an impetus to Allied cooperation. The Entente rushed help to their member in the form of six French divisions headed by Fayolle, and five British by Plumer, two of the most competent and prudent of the fighting generals of the Western Front. Four of these divisions were put into the line at once, when the Italians halted at the Piave. The French and British chiefs of general staff Foch and Robertson visited the Italian command to encourage resistance; Painlevé and Lloyd George paid similar suit to the government. Caporetto brought home to the Allies the need for better military coordination, and Lloyd George at last made progress in instituting a unified direction of the war that would at the same time provide a mechanism for controlling his own generals. The conference that met at Rapallo on November 5 to deal with the Italian crisis established the Supreme War Council. Its intended function was the determination of strategy, priorities, the distribution of forces, and other aspects of running a coalition war.

4. THE RUSSIAN DROPOUT

Neither the Allies nor the Central Powers anticipated that Russia would have dropped out of the war by the end of 1917. Indeed, a war council at Stavka in December 1916, endeavoring to comply with the decisions of the Chantilly conference of November 1916, agreed on starting a spring offensive, with the main attack to be delivered on Brusilov's southwestern front. It was doubtful, however, whether the Russian army by 1917 preserved sufficient cohesion and spirit for a sustained offensive.

Brusilov wrote later that the army had so deteriorated in quality that it had become "something like a poor kind of militia," which was "ready for revolution."[44] The mass recruits of this time, who were under inadequately trained replacements for the career officers lost in the severe casualties of 1914–15, were hardly brought under the regular military regime. The normal separation of officers and men into different castes fixed by the tsarist military code deepened. The officers lost authority with the troops, and the two mutually lost respect for each other.[45]

The political crisis produced by Nicholas II's methods of rule, the disasters at the front, and the "dark forces" in the court entourage caused a general loss of credibility for the tsarist authorities among the officers and, by reflection, in the trenches. The interminable casualties and futile attacks had taken their toll in sinking morale. The notion was taking shape in the front soldiers' consciousness that the war was an affair of the propertied and educated groups, intended to serve their interests. The army had become by and large a mass of alienated, suspicious, vengeful, and war-weary peasants possessed by the all-dominant idea that the fighting must end. Mutinies, in fact, had already occurred in 1916.[46]

The state of economic disorder made it questionable how long Russia could continue fighting. The rampant inflation had rocketed prices by four times since July 1914. A food emergency gripped the cities, and the fuel supply had become disorganized, as the transport system fell into disrepair and confusion.[47]

Before planning for the offensive could be carried further, the revolution intervened, beginning on March 12 in Petrograd. Party representatives of the Duma formed the Provisional Government, and the socialists and radicals, the Petrograd Soviet of Workers' and Soldiers' Deputies. The Russian part in the war from this time until the Bolsheviks took over power depended on the differences and power relations between these bodies and on the progress of rebellion in the army.

44. Brusilov, *Soldier's Note-Book*, 300.

45. Stone, *Eastern Front*, 166–71; Gerhard Wettig, "Die Rolle der russischen Armée im revolutionären Machtkampf 1917," *Forschungen zur osteuropäischen Geschichte* 12 (1967): 67–74.

46. Wettig, "Die Rolle der russischen Armée 1917," 76–80; Stone, *Eastern Front*, 168, 171; Allan Wildman, "The February Revolution in the Russian Army," *Soviet Studies* 22 (1970–71): 5–6; Allan Wildman, *The End of the Russian Imperial Army* (Princeton, 1980), 107–20. In relation to Brusilov's statement above, note Wildman's conclusions in *Soviet Studies* that the trench soldiers were not about to revolt in the winter of 1916–17 and that there was no general tendency in the army to mutiny.

47. See Rudolf Claus, *Die Kriegswirtschaft Russlands bis zur bolschewistischen Revolution* (Bonn, 1922).

The liberal and moderate party leaders of the Duma now in the Provisional Government believed that the new regime should continue the war in cooperation with the Allies until victory made possible the realization of Allied war aims. The Petrograd Soviet desired to end the "imperialist" war quickly, with a "democratic peace" that would further the victory of the socialist revolution. Soviet groups stood for a "democratization of the army," insuring the soldier masses full civil equality and removing the authoritarian power of command.

The acts of the Petrograd Soviet combined with the revolt of the Petrograd forces against the authority of officers and the old relationship of officers and men to undermine the organization of the army. At the same time the Soviet was winning control over the bulk of the rebellious troops. Agitators of the Soviet conducted activities among the soldiers of the capital area intended to mold them into a political following. Soviet Order No. 1 of March 15 yielded to the anarchical tendencies of the soldier masses. The order, applicable to the Petrograd area, abolished marks of subordination to officers and their power to impose punishment. Troop units were directed to elect committees of representatives to the Soviet. The committees were to control arms and their use, settle differences between officers and the troops, and along with the Soviet exercise authority over the political activities of the soldiers.[48]

The order soon acquired general force in the armed services, with the spread of its knowledge through agitators and the Soviet press. The order broke the already declining power of the officers, and, as the commanders accommodated to its effect, inaugurated a military organization structured around the committees. Discipline and the professional military direction tended to collapse in a large part of the army, except as they were licensed by the elected committees. Frequent arrests of officers took place, and sometimes lynchings, mostly in the rear; in any case, officers were deposed if they were disliked. The men spent much of their time in political discussion and in argument with officers, to the neglect of their daily duties.

Influenced by Order No. 1 and events of the revolution, the soldiers in the rear were refusing to go to the front. Numerous units were melting away or changing into bands of idlers and plundering vagrants abusing

48. On the genesis, content, promulgation, and influence of the order: John R. Boyd, "The Origins of Order No. 1," *Soviet Studies* 19 (1967–68), 359–72; Wettig, "Die Rolle der russischen Armée 1917," 149–52, 186–90; Wildman, "February Revolution in the Russian Army," 13–17; Wildman, *End of the Russian Imperial Army,* 182–96, 230–31.

both officers and the public. The progressive disorganization of the rear spread to the front. Where this happened, the men made the decisions through the committees or reacted to orders with passive or open resistance. More and more opposed to participating in offensive action, they felt that they had done their share of fighting. The formations still reliable for offensive operations were found largely among the artillery, cavalry, Cossacks, and troops most distant from the revolutionary capital.[49]

The Provisional Government bore its share of responsibility for reforms inimical to order in the army. The power of command was weakened by the abolition of the death sentence and the field court-martial. On April 29 the minister of war, bowing to the demands of the Soviet, issued a statute providing for the direct election of committees at lower levels of the military organization and indirect election of those including officers at higher levels. The committees were endowed with powers over army housekeeping, social and welfare matters, political activities incident to elections, and the use of officers' authority. The measure gave official sanction to stripping away powers of command and impetus to the formation of committees and extension of committee functions. The personnel absorbed by the committees withdrew from technical military activities an estimated 8 percent of the troops—and these the most active and intelligent of the men—at a time when the military was confronted with a manpower stringency.

The Provisional Government, under the pressure of the Soviet and with the generals divided on the question, agreed to sending to the front commissars representing jointly the government and the Soviet executive committee. These agents intervened in the decisions of the military commands as they chose to interpret their mandates from the dual Petrograd authorities. At the top the army had become a chaos of multiple authorities and at the bottom an anarchical mass of soldiery that would determine the fate of the army and of Russia.[50]

49. Wettig, "Die Rolle der russischen Armée 1917," 175–83; Golovine, *Russian Army in the World War,* 250–60. Authorities differ noticeably on the scale of desertion in the early revolutionary period. See Wettig, p. 183; Golovine, p. 260; Wildman, "February Revolution in the Russian Army," 17; Wildman, *End of the Russian Imperial Army,* 235; Marc Ferro, "The Russian Soldier in 1917: Undisciplined, Patriotic, and Revolutionary," *Slavic Review* 30 (1971), 509, 511. The last writer rejects traditional estimates on the basis of his investigation, claiming few desertions before October 1917. He apparently excludes from the category of deserters units as a whole abandoning their stations, mutineers, and revolutionaries.

50. On the Provisional Government's measures destructive of the army organization, see Wettig, "Die Rolle der russischen Armée 1917," 235–42.

In May the new minister of war, Alexander Kerensky, issued the Declaration of Soldiers' Rights. To a great extent the statement confirmed the mutual equality of officers and men in the military units and the removal of the officers' disciplinary power. For the Soviet groups it was "a great victory"; for Stavka, the last nail "driven into the coffin of the army." The military reforms as a whole democratized the army to the point of sacrificing military efficacy. The breakdown of the officers' authority allowed defeatism and antiwar feeling to come to the surface.[51]

The foreign policy program of the Soviet and the Bolsheviks was epitomized in the demand for a "general peace without annexations or indemnities on the basis of the self-determination of peoples." This was interpreted by the mass of the soldiers to confirm their ruling desire of stopping the war immediately and to justify refusal of a part in offensive action or departure for home. They were determined that the government should pursue a defensist policy along the Soviet line and gave expression to this view in individual messages.[52] The efforts of officers to induce the troops to continue fighting only made the soldiers look upon them as "the traitors" and "the internal enemy" or identify them, often unjustly, as counterrevolutionaries.[53]

The Soviet groups strengthened the appeal of their peace formula with intensive agitational activity centering in the army committees. The socialist effort for a "democratic peace" was represented as a part of the universal class struggle of the peoples against the rulers and "oppressors," who supported the continuation of the war in the pursuit of aggressive war aims. The Bolsheviks were the most active in distributing political propaganda at the front, in the form of proclamations and orders, newspapers and pamphlets, preaching antiwar and defeatist ideas.

In view of these conditions the vital question before the Allies and the Central Powers was whether Russia would remain an active belligerent. Each side hailed the coming of the revolution in the expectation that the change would strengthen its own coalition or weaken the enemy's. The western Allies, interpreting the revolution to be anti-German in character, rejoiced at being free now of the incubus of the reactionary tsarist regime. The Entente could henceforth wage political warfare as an unbreached coalition of democracies against the autocratic system. In Germany both

51. Ibid., 309–13.
52. Ferro, "Russian Soldier in 1917," 493.
53. Golovine, *Russian Army in the World War,* 267.

the civilian government and the high command saw in the revolution a means of relieving the Reich's difficult military situation.[54]

Both the western Allies and the Germans tried to influence the course of revolutionary Russia's military and internal affairs. The one worked for Russia's military revival, consolidation of a liberal political regime, and coalition solidarity with a vigorous war effort; the other for military paralysis, the increase of internal disruptive forces, and the conclusion of a separate peace with the revolutionary government. Each side became involved in the revolution as a means of conducting war against the enemy. Each facilitated, or attempted to prevent, the return of exiles who might affect the direction of events in Russia according to the interest of the coalition concerned. The Allies sent messages, representatives, delegations, and missions in the endeavor to exert maximum effect.[55]

The Germans pursued operational inactivity on the eastern front as a deliberate policy for the next several months. They coupled with this passivity an active political warfare at the front, conducted through the distribution of pacifist and defeatist publications and by fraternization with the Russian soldiers. The Russians in the front lines believed that direct contact with the German soldiers opposite them afforded a means to scotch any plan of the general staff to resume military operations. They therefore welcomed fraternization, and it soon swept the entire front with lasting effects on the Russian troops.[56]

The Provisional Government quickly assured the Allies (March 17) that Russia would fight "to the end, unswervingly and indefatigably." The government would "remain mindful of the international engagements entered into by the fallen regime and would honor Russia's word." The continuation of the war policy of the previous regime precipitated a conflict with the Petrograd Soviet over the issue of war and peace.

Russia's changing attitude toward the conduct of the war reflected the progress of this ideological and power struggle between the two bodies. The government's declaration of April 9 on war aims, forced by Soviet pressure, rejected the annexationist policy of the past and formulated

54. Robert D. Worth, *The Allies and the Russian Revolution* (Durham, N. C., 1954), 26–28.
55. Ibid., 37–44; Arno J. Mayer, *Political Origins of the New Democracy* (New Haven, 1959), 60, 88–97.
56. Wettig, "Die Rolle der russischen Armée 1917," 265–68; Ferro, "Russian Soldier in 1917," 495; *Ludendorff's Own Story*, 2: 14, 35–36.

Russia's war purpose to be the "establishment of a stable peace on the basis of the self-determination of peoples." In ambivalent fashion the statement affirmed, however, that the government was "fully observing at the same time all obligations assumed toward our allies." Fresh assurances under-cutting the main drift of this manifesto were given the Allies in a note of May 1. The note overturned the government and brought about the formation of a new, liberal-socialist cabinet. The Soviet outburst of protest to the note and the Bolshevik demonstrations in the streets obliged the new government to link publicly the Soviet formula of "a peace without annexations or indemnities" with the principle of self-determination. This pronouncement did not abandon the Allies but remained the govern-ment's public position, on which it attempted to get a "new agreement" concerning Allied war aims. The western Allies sought to keep Russia in the war without acceding to the demand.[57]

The revolutionary disturbances did not permit the resumption of mili-tary activity until four months after the March uprising. Notwithstanding the plight of the army, Stavka favored an offensive for strategic reasons.[58] The generals hoped further that an initial victory would raise the morale of the troops and check the process of disintegration. The more politically conscious soldiers suspected that Stavka desired an offensive in the inter-ests of restoring the old military system.[59]

The social circles of Petrograd were more alive to the fundamental trends than the generals. In April they were already saying to the French ambassador: "the war is dead." This perception was echoed a few days later by Poincaré in his diary: "Russia forgets the war more and more to think only of revolution."[60]

Not only did the Provisional Government approve of the offensive, but also the Soviet concurred. Now that a coalition cabinet had been formed and the enemy had not accepted the Soviet appeal for a "democratic peace," the Soviet majority could accept a continuation of the war. The war, even offensive action, became a means of exerting force in behalf of

57. See Rex A. Wade, *The Russian Search for Peace, February–October 1917* (Stanford, 1969), 12–50; Mayer, *Political Origins of the New Democracy,* 73–83.
58. See the discussion of the strategic considerations in Robert S. Feldman, "The Russian General Staff and the June 1917 Offensive," *Soviet Studies* 19 (1967–68): 531–34.
59. Golovine, *Russian Army in the World War,* 260–67; Ferro, "Russian Soldier in 1917," 494.
60. Maurice Paléologue, *La Russie des tsars pendant la Grande Guerre,* 3 vols. (Paris, 1921–22), 3: 295–96; Poincaré, *Au service de la France,* 9: 110.

"democratic peace" aims and "revolutionary democracy."[61]

In preparing the front for the offensive, the commanders combed the army for dependable divisions and selected elite shock units of reliable volunteers to head the action wherever possible. An attempt was made to condition the troops psychologically by a large-scale agitational campaign in which the officers, higher army committees, and troop commissars were joined by politicians from the Provisional Government and the Soviet, including Kerensky, the most active of all. The exhortations of the political leaders, failing to heed the dominant concern of the soldiers for a quick peace, awakened their distrust of both the government and the Soviet majority, with an increasing responsiveness to Bolshevik propaganda.[62]

On July 1 the Kerensky offensive began on the southwest front in the direction of Lvov. The most concentrated artillery preparation yet seen on the part of the Russians and the determined fighting of the shock units moved the uncertain infantry to advance wherever they met the Austrians. Within the Austrian army the forces of disintegration were also proceeding, above all among the Czech and other Slav elements. There were, however, numerous Russian units, including whole divisions, that never left the trenches. The Russians pushed through the Austrian lines but would go no farther after the enemy threw in reinforcements. It was necessary to break off action after two days, by which time a German counterattack had won back the Russian gains in large part.[63]

A few days later (July 8), an army commanded by General Lavr Kornilov quickly broke through south of the Dniester, driving the foe, mostly Austrian troops of poor quality, back to the Carpathians. The retreating Austrians were stiffened with German reinforcements, and the select units of the Russians were used up in great number. The Central Powers checked the drive and threw back the indifferent infantry mass in confusion.

The attempts to attack on the northern and western fronts were abortive affairs sabotaged by mutinous troops. On the Romanian front from the lower Sereth northwest to the Carpathians, the Russians and the reorganized Romanian army joined in an offensive (beginning July 22) that

61. Wettig, "Die Rolle der russischen Armée 1917," 315–16; Feldman, "Russian General Staff and the June 1917 Offensive," 537–38.

62. Wettig, "Die Rolle der russischen Armée 1917," 318–29.

63. On the Kerensky offensive as a whole, see ibid., 314–39; Feldman, "Russian General Staff and the June 1917 Offensive," 526–43.

overran the enemy lines for a distance of twenty kilometers. Then the Russian forces abandoned efforts to continue the advance. Mackensen counterattacked with his mixed force of Germans, Bulgarians, and Turks, beating the Russians and Romanians back.

The German bloc struck back in Galicia with a strong counterattack that rapidly broadened into a major offensive southeastward along the Lvov-Tarnopol line. The preparatory bombardment was directed by Colonel Georg Bruchmüller, the most famous artillery officer of the war. After his thorough job of demolition in seven hours, the Germans crashed through the demoralized Russian front on July 19. Panic and confusion took over; the front forces, save for the shock units, broke down into a mass flight of marauding bands of disorganized soldiery. Pressing forward along the whole southwest front of the Russians, the Germans captured Czernowitz and Bukovina within two weeks. The Russian troops, retreating from the war itself, withdrew to their own borders with only the barest resistance by the end of August.[64]

The end of fighting on the Russian front followed quickly in September with the German capture of the Riga bridgehead and neighboring islands. The Germans tried out at Riga their new tactics of penetration after Bruchmüller again conducted a short but hurricane bombardment. Once more the Russian opponent offered little resistance.[65]

The Kerensky offensive was an impossible undertaking, since it was vetoed by the bulk of the Russian soldiers. Far from reviving the morale of the troops, the offensive recoiled on the army as the final destructive blow. The action consumed the most reliable elements of the army and intensified the animosity between the officers and the mass soldiers. The discontent of the latter was aggravated to the extent often of violent reactions and even of mutinies. The measures of compulsion taken against resisting soldiers, the restoration of the death penalty, and some move to reestablish the chain of command and the authority of officers impressed the rebellious troops as an attempt to stop the revolution in the army and return to tsarism. The soldiers grew hostile toward both the Provisional Government and the Soviet. The Bolsheviks were successfully channeling the discontent into a political force destructive of the existing revolutionary regime. The Kerensky offensive thus augmented the forces of anarchy

64. See Hoffmann, *War Diaries,* 1: 185–92; *Ludendorff's Own Story,* 2: 36–41; Hindenburg, *Out of My Life,* 278–79.
65. On the use of the new German tactics at Caporetto, see above, p. 185.

and accelerated the progress of the revolution, suggesting again the indivisibility of the war and revolution in Russia.

The November coup approached, and the disintegration of the army quickened under the extremist influence of Bolshevik agents and propaganda. Stavka concluded at that time that "the army is simply a huge, weary, shabby, and ill-fed mob of angry men united by their common thirst for peace and by common disappointment." There was no longer the weapon or the will to carry on the war.[66] No force existed in the east to keep the Germans from marching to Petrograd or Moscow. But the need to assemble German divisions in the west for the spring offensive of 1918 deterred the high command from carrying the offensive farther into Russia. This urgency prompted Germany to convert the more or less de facto cessation of hostilities into a legal termination of the conflict. When the Bolsheviks in power took the initiative for an armistice, the Germans accepted the Soviet proposals. The delegations of the Central Powers and Russia concluded at Brest-Litovsk on December 15 an armistice terminating hostilities on the basis of existing positions.

In the peace parleys taken up five days later, the Russian delegation resisted German terms in prolonged debates and propagandist speeches. On February 10, 1918, Leon Trotsky gave a "pedagogical demonstration" to the world by declaring a unilateral peace and walking out of the conference. During this time the same delegations of the German bloc at Brest-Litovsk negotiated against Soviet opposition a "peace" treaty with representatives of the Ukrainian National Council (Rada), which had declared the independence of the Ukraine. This *Brotfrieden* of February 9 granted concessions, opening to the Central Powers access to food supplies and raw materials of the Ukrainian storehouse.[67]

Trotsky's misconceived ploy turned out to be an expensive experiment in new diplomacy and Bolshevik propaganda. The German high command denounced the armistice and renewed military operations. In a crazy kind of war the German divisions, satisfying the dreams of the eastward expansionists and the Ludendorff high command, sped forward (in the

---

66. Golovine, *Russian Army in the World War,* 281.
67. See the discussion of the Brest-Litovsk treaty in John W. Wheeler-Bennett, *Brest-Litovsk: The Forgotten Peace* (London, 1938), 65–228; Werner Hahlweg, *Der Diktatfrieden von Brest-Litovsk und die bolschewistische Weltrevolution* (Münster, 1960), 23–43; Winfried Baumgart, *Deutsche Ostpolitik 1918* (Vienna, 1966), 21–22.

north to Lake Peipus and the Narva) at a rate better than a mile an hour against no opposition but the winter and the almost roadless spaces of Russia.

The chastened Bolsheviks rushed to accept the terms previously offered, but the Germans delayed until they completed their advance. The Germans replied in time with Draconian proposals to be accepted within three days. The Bolshevik ruling bodies, after torturous and emotional debates, submitted to "the Tilsit peace" in order to "save the revolution." The returning Russian delegates signed the treaty of Brest-Litovsk on March 3 without negotiation. The Romanians were also eliminated from the war by an armistice on December 8 and then the separate peace of Bucharest of May 7, 1918.[68]

German and Austrian forces marched into the Ukraine to reap the advantages conferred by the treaty with the Rada. Although they encountered resistance from Bolshevik bands and Czechoslovak troops organized in Russia, they advanced to the steppes of the Don. The two vied with each other, the Germans taking Kiev and the Austrians Odessa.

The Reich's military responsibilities had not ceased in the east. Brest-Litovsk had turned over to the Germans control of the Russian borderlands, with a population of 55 million people. Dependent states were set up as the Germans came in, and the military had to remain in assuming duties of occupation, protection, and the suppression of resistance to the German practice of political and economic imperialism in the east. Lenin foresaw that the conflict would be carried on by other means: "This war will be settled in the rear, not in the trenches. . . . Germany will have to maintain larger, not fewer, forces in the east."[69]

If the Bolsheviks lost the peace of Brest-Litovsk, they ultimately won the war against Germany. Internally in Russia, the negotiations sealed the victory of the Bolsheviks. In a sense the conflict never ended; it only took on a new form of political warfare. In their Faustian traffic with the devil, the Germans provided a stage at Brest-Litovsk for Bolshevik propagandist speeches and opened Germany, through the negotiations and the peace, to an avalanche of published Bolshevik propaganda, which in the end helped to produce the German defeat and revolution. The victor's drastic peace terms boomeranged against Germany, for the Allies exploited the

68. Wheeler-Bennett, *Forgotten Peace,* 228–308; Hahlweg, *Der Diktatfrieden von Brest-Litovsk,* 43–52; Baumgart, *Deutsche Ostpolitik,* 24–27.
69. Wheeler-Bennett, *Forgotten Peace,* 288.

settlement in the most effective propaganda in demonstrating the meaning of a German victory.

There was no comfort for the Allies in Balkan affairs at this time and little for the German bloc. The Germans had forced a peace with Romania and had entry to the riches of that country. It was necessary, nevertheless, to keep military forces in Romania to support a new minority government exercising power in cooperation with the conqueror but in silent resistance from the bulk of the people. The war-weary ally Bulgaria, having occupied desired areas of Serbia, Greece, and Romania, showed little interest in carrying on the war further.

The Allies strengthened their hold on Greece by compelling the abdication of King Constantine in June and supporting the rule of the restored Venizelos government against the royalists. The Greek government under Venizelos declared war on the Central Powers on July 2, and the Greek army was expanded and trained as an Allied force. General Sarrail's army, grown to 600,000 troops, attacked in the spring and fall on the Macedonian front. The operations proved a dreary failure; it was impossible to cooperate effectively with Sarrail, and the British interest ran mainly to the Middle East rather than to the Balkans.

Chapter Eight

CRISIS AT SEA AND AMERICAN INVOLVEMENT

I. THE *HANDELSKRIEG*

THE series of Allied crises on the continent—the collapse of French morale, the defection of Russia, the submission of Romania, and the Italian "farewell to arms" at Caporetto—had a counterpart at sea in the climax of the submarine peril. The Germans launched three campaigns against merchant shipping in the years 1915–17, each the result of a critical decision taken near the beginning of the year. The sum of these decisions approximated in Bethmann Hollweg's mind the significance of the original declaration of war. No issue divided the German military and political direction of the war so deeply and fatefully as this.[1]

The extreme peril to Allied shipping and supply did not come until 1917 with the third campaign, an all-out war on commerce *(Handelskrieg, or guerre de course).* The increasing capability of the submarine fleet and the inability of the German army to end the war on the continent exerted a growing pressure for an unrestricted offensive against both Allied and neutral shipping. The destructive power of the submarines had risen markedly with the expanding size of the fleet, which by February 1917 had reached 102 U-boats available for active duty, and with the technical experience and skill acquired by the U-boat skippers since 1914.

The decision on utilizing the U-boat in economic warfare to the bitter end depended chiefly on the opposition between the increasing power of the Reich submarine constituency and the firm stand of the United States against submarine attacks endangering American lives and property. The submarine pressure groups began to form in the fall of 1914, when naval leaders were discussing the proposal for an unrestricted campaign against merchant shipping. In December Tirpitz, the secretary of state for naval affairs, in an interview with an American journalist unveiled the "miracle weapon" as a means of countering the British blockade.[2]

1. Müller, *Regierte der Kaiser?,* 146–47; Ritter, *Staatskunst,* 3: 145.
2. Arno Spindler, *Der Handelskrieg mit U-Booten,* 5 vols. (Berlin, 1932–66), 1: 27–83, 141–46; Groos and Gladisch, *Der Krieg in der Nordsee,* 3: 274; Tirpitz, *My Memoirs,* 2: 138–42.

At the beginning of 1915 the principal thrust for a submarine war on shipping came from the chief of the naval staff and the public stimulated by Tirpitz. Falkenhayn joined the submarine lobby in making unrestricted submarine war a complement to the Verdun offensive as a strategy of victory. When he pressed in 1915 for a decision on beginning an indiscriminate submarine offensive, this course had the support of the naval faction, the annexationists and conservatives, the right-wing press, the largest and most powerful economic associations of Germany, the empress and crown prince, a majority of the Reichstag members, and majorities in the state legislatures. At the end of 1916 the strength of the submarine enthusiasts was powerfully augmented by the demand of Hindenburg and Ludendorff for the unbridled use of the weapon.

The opposition arose from moderates headed by the chancellor and the chief of the foreign office, Gottlieb von Jagow, with public support confined largely to the Social Democrats.

The manner in which the submarines were to be used remained a primal issue in the determination of German strategy and the shaping of German foreign policy until the campaign of 1917. Bethmann and Jagow tenaciously held the ground, giving way only as they must, that Germany's paramount purpose in this question should be to avoid a policy choice that would bring the United States into the war. They were firmly convinced that America's entry would spell the conclusive defeat of Germany. The naval and military leaders generally or eventually took the attitude that submarines could be a successful weapon of *Handelskrieg* only if employed without restriction. For them the unrestricted use of the U-boats was essential to forcing Britain to peace terms; the matter, being a purely military question, should depend solely on military prospects regardless of the possibility of American belligerency, which they tended to see already existing to a great extent through American economic ties with the Allies. The recurrent differences materialized in a conflict between the political and military authorities, which amounted at bottom to a struggle over supremacy in the direction of the war.[3]

The submarine menace to the Allies was subject to the twists and turns of this conflict. At first Bethmann and the kaiser yielded to the pressure of the submarine proponents in the proclamation of February 4, 1915, declaring the waters around the British Isles to be a war zone barred to

3. See Karl E. Birnbaum, *Peace Moves and U-Boat Warfare* (Stockholm, 1958), 56–57; Ritter, *Staatskunst,* 3: 194–98.

all merchant ships of the enemy. If encountered, Allied ships would be sunk without assurance of saving crew and passengers, that is, without observance of the legitimate prize procedure previously followed by belligerents, or the procedure of cruiser warfare, requiring the visit and search of merchant vessels. Neutral shipping was warned about the danger of passage through the war zone.[4]

The concern of the moderates was warranted by the quick and vigorous reaction of the United States, holding the German government accountable for the loss of American life and property by submarine action. The American attitude was given more force in the sharp protests and demands of the United States in notes concerned with the sinking of the British liners *Lusitania* on May 7 and *Arabic* on August 19, 1915. The force of the American diplomatic action enabled Bethmann to prevail over the navy. From September on, submarine activities around the British Isles were limited to cruiser warfare. Since the submarines were restricted to the dangerous practice of coming to the surface and stopping the intended victim, the *Handelskrieg* in practice was suspended in British waters and shifted to the Mediterranean.[5]

In 1916 Bethmann had to make concessions to the growing power of the submarine lobby in order to ward off the whole program of U-boat warfare. A conference with the kaiser on March 4 in effect deferred unrestricted submarine warfare for an indefinite period. An order of March 13, however, authorized the U-boats to attack without warning enemy merchant ships in the war zone around Britain and armed merchant ships of the enemy outside the zone but not to make submerged attacks on enemy passenger steamers anywhere, whether armed or not. The outcome of the confrontation with the submarine champions strengthened the position of Bethmann and weakened that of Falkenhayn, particularly in relation to the failure to realize his objectives at Verdun. The chancellor succeeded in maneuvering the resignation from office of his inveterate opponent Tirpitz.[6]

The partial freeing and the partial curbing of the U-boats proved to be

4. See Spindler, *Der Handelskrieg,* 1: 87, 145.

5. See Hermann Bauer, *Reichsleitung und U-Bootseinsatz 1914 bis 1918* (Lippoldsberg, 1956), 42–43).

6. Ibid., 54–55; Birnbaum, *Peace Moves and U-Boat Warfare,* 57–64; Müller, *Regierte der Kaiser?,* 159–63; Ritter, *Staatskunst,* 3: 199–201, 204–05; Janssen, *Der Kanzler und der General,* 190–94.

no solution. The fleet command did not stress the restrictions on the U-boats in dealing with submarine commanders, and the problem of ship identification confronted the submerged U-boats. The *Sussex* crisis brought home the serious political difficulty of conducting even this form of submarine warfare. The severe American note over the torpedoing of this unarmed Channel steamer of the French on March 24 impressed circles at headquarters as "desperately near an ultimatum." The very sobering experience for both the moderates and some of the submarine advocates made it possible for Bethmann to have the war against merchant shipping around Britain retracted to the procedure of cruiser warfare. The commands of the fleet and the Flanders submarines, believing that the *Handelskrieg* conducted under such limitations was not worth the risks involved, called off the U-boats from the war on commerce in western waters. The cruiser warfare of the submarines continued only in the Mediterranean.[7]

The question of a note to inform the United States of the restrictive policy provoked a conflict between Falkenhayn and Bethmann. The general claimed that if the submarine war was not carried on, it would be necessary to abandon the effort at Verdun. He challenged the supremacy of the political side in dealing with political issues, to which belonged— the chancellor insisted—the question of averting war with the United States. The struggle between the two leaders provoked a crisis in the management of the war, both political and military. The kaiser decided against the general, and the defeat seriously undermined his position. His Verdun strategy was put more in question, his credit with the kaiser considerably lowered. The breach between the chancellor and the general had become irreparable.[8]

The response to the American note, representing the views of the moderates, overcame the *Sussex* crisis. For the next six months the submarine was employed mainly to support the operations of the fleet. But by the end of August the fleet command, whose opposition to any form of restriction was strengthened by the outcome of Jutland, had become insistent on unbridling the U-boats. The chief of the naval staff, Henning von Holtzendorff, strongly pressed by his subordinates and the fleet, again advocated the unlimited use of the submarines. Public agitation was rising

7. Müller, *Regierte der Kaiser?*, 170; Ritter, *Staatskunst*, 3: 206.
8. Janssen, *Der Kanzler und der General*, 200–01.

in behalf of employing the miracle weapon to the fullest. During the fall a definite Reichstag majority formed in favor of commencing unrestricted submarine warfare as soon as the high command considered it opportune.[9] Near the end of the year an irresistible confluence of factors determined the final stage of the Reich's submarine policy. The dualism in Germany's direction of the war ended when the center of decisive power settled in the third OHL, of Hindenburg and Ludendorff. As soon as the Romanian campaign drew to a close, they were prepared to risk the reaction of European neutrals to commencing radical submarine warfare. The losses inflicted on both the Allies and the neutrals after the U-boats resumed cruiser warfare on October 15 afforded the submarine enthusiasts arguments for uncurbing the U-boats completely. Bethmann failed to find a peace alternative that would obviate a showdown with the military and naval authorities. The final decision portended either an open breach between the political and military leadership, ravaging the unity of the country, or the submission of the civilian government to the supremacy of the general staff. The chancellor, in trying to avert either denouement, made peace efforts along a "double track" through encouraging the initiative of Wilson for American mediation and through offering a German peace bid.[10]

Just as Bethmann was attempting to gain the official approval of OHL for the peace note of December 12, Hindenburg and Ludendorff demanded that unrestricted submarine warfare should begin at the end of January. The demand initiated a series of exchanges between the military, naval, and political leaders during the next month that sharpened the differences between OHL and the chancellor. OHL aggressively asserted the primacy of the military in the settlement of the issue; the chancellor maintained in opposition that political aspects were involved—the fate of relations and immediately continuing negotiations with the United States —for which he alone had responsibility under the German system.[11]

Ludendorff and Holtzendorff were determined by early January, regardless of Bethmann, to obtain an urgent decision unleashing the submarines. A solid front of the various naval authorities and OHL, to which

9. Birnbaum, *Peace Moves and U-Boat Warfare,* 108–48 passim; Bauer, *Reichsleitung und U-Bootseinsatz,* 65–67.

10. Theobald von Bethmann Hollweg, *Betrachtungen zum Weltkrieg,* 2 vols. (Berlin, 1919–21), 2: 126 ff.; Birnbaum, *Peace Moves and U-Boat Warfare,* 135–38, 220, 267.

11. Bethmann Hollweg, *Betrachtungen,* 2: 129–31; Birnbaum, *Peace Moves and U-Boat Warfare,* 237–42, 276–82; Ritter, *Staatskunst,* 3: 368–73.

1. Enthusiasm in Berlin at the beginning of the war: Ovation before the Austrian embassy. The crowd has raised pictures of Emperor Franz Josef and Kaiser William II. *(The Hoover Institution on War, Revolution, and Peace, Stanford)*

2. Enthusiasm in London at the beginning of the war: Response at a recruiting meeting on Trafalgar Square. *(The Hoover Institution, Stanford)*

3. Maximilian Mopp, *The World War,* 1916. Oil on canvas. 21 × 17 5/8". *(Collection, The Museum of Modern Art, New York; given anonymously)*

LEADERS OF THE CENTRAL POWERS

4. Chancellor Theobald von Bethmann Hollweg. *(National Archives)*

5. General Erich von
Falkenhayn. *(National Archives)*

6. Emperor Franz Josef.
(National Archives)

7. General Paul von Hindenburg, Kaiser William II, and General Erich Ludendorff
at German general headquarters, January 1917. *(National Archives)*

LEADERS OF THE ALLIES

8. General Joseph Joffre, President Raymond Poincaré, King George V, General Ferdinand Foch, and General Sir Douglas Haig. *(The Hoover Institution, Stanford)*

9. Marshal Philippe Pétain, 1919. *(National Archives)*

10. Tsar Nicholas II and the Russian commander-in-chief Grand Duke Nicholas. *(National Archives)*

11. David Lloyd George. *(The Hoover Institution, Stanford)*

12. Georges Clemenceau. *(National Archives)*

13. Woodrow Wilson. *(The Hoover Institution, Stanford)*

14. Théophile Steinlen, *Un poilu à Pétain.* Lithograph. The frontline soldier of France became a national hero and a frequent subject of French artists and illustrators. On this page are different versions of the poilu by French artists of the time. *(Library of Congress)*

15. Fernand Léger, *Verdun: The Trench Diggers,* 1916. Watercolor, 14 1/8 × 10 3/8″. Poilus, sketched as anonymous figures in simplified, geometrical forms, suggesting a taut dynamism and the mechanized nature of the war. *(Collection, The Museum of Modern Art, New York; Frank Crowninshield Fund)*

16. Georges Scott, *L'Eclopé (The Cripple),* 1915. Reproduction of a crayon drawing in black and white. *(From album,* Le soldat français pendant la guerre. *Library of Congress)*

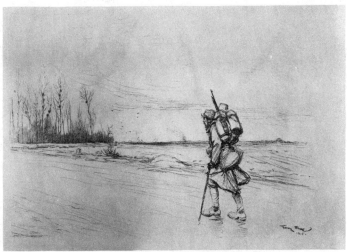

17. The British Tommy: London Scottish marching to the front in the Somme area, July 1916. *(National Archives)*

Nobbled.

"'Ow long are you up for, Bill?"
"Seven years."
"Yer lucky ——, I'm duration."

18. The character "Old Bill," a favorite of both British soldiers and civilians, often appeared in Bairnsfather's numerous drawings of the Tommies' life on the Western Front. *(From Bruce Bairnsfather,* Fragments from France, *Collections of the Library of Congress)*

19. A squad of German frontline soldiers (Corporal Adolf Hitler is marked with "x"). *(National Archives)*

20. A British Mark IV tank in action on the Western Front, November 1917. The tank above all symbolized the mechanized war. *(The Hoover Institution, Stanford)*

21. Horses bringing up the guns under cover on the Western Front. As this photograph and the one below illustrate, there was also a nonmechanized war of animal participation (horses, camels, oxen, dogs, and pigeons). Its proportions are suggested by the fact that the British alone inducted more than a million horses into military service. *(From album, La guerre, 1914–1919. Library of Congress)*

22. Bulgarian transport drawn by oxen in the Macedonian mountains. *(National Archives)*

23. Léon Broquet, A Marne 1914 scene. Reproduction of a crayon drawing in black and white. *(From album,* Carnet de route d'un territorial. *Library of Congress)*

24. Lucien Jonas, *Théatre Verdun, 2 avril, 1916 (Verdun Theater, April 2, 1916).* Reproduction of a charcoal drawing. *(From album,* Verdun mars-avril 1916. *Library of Congress)*

25. C. Léandre, *Ils ne passeront pas! (They Shall Not Pass!)* Pen and ink drawing. *(Library of Congress)*

THE HAUNTED SHIP.

Ghost of the Old Pilot. "I WONDER IF HE WOULD DROP ME *NOW!*"

[April 1st is the hundredth anniversary of Bismarck's birth.]

26. Gibing the Kaiser about Germany's predicament without Bismarck at the helm of state. (Punch, *March 31, 1915*)

27. Chancellor Bethmann Hollweg reading the German peace note of December 12, 1916 before the Reichstag. *(National Archives)*

28. The obsequies for Emperor Franz Josef on November 30, 1916, which proved to be an anticipatory service for the demise of monarchy in central and eastern Europe. *(Library of Congress)*

29. G. G., *Specimen*. Photograph of India ink drawing. A work of elaborate detail illustrative of propagandist efforts by French artists in representing the Germans at war. *(Library of Congress)*

30. Hansi (Jean Jacques Waltz), *Le Vieux Bon Dieu de Sa Majesté l'Empereur Guillaume II (The Old God of Emperor William II)*. Hand-colored woodcut. A propagandist burlesque ridiculing the German claim of "Gott mit uns." In the German heaven pictured here, Captain Saint Michael commands a band of angels on parade marching in goose step. *(Library of Congress)*

31. A propagandist caricature in water-color of the Allies: Germania raises in triumph the banner of *Einigkeit Macht Stark (Unity Brings Strength)* and the placard *Gott mit Uns* over the crying Russian bear (after the defeats of 1915), the selfish British pig, and the screeching Gallic cock. *(Library of Congress)*

32. Alfred Leete, British recruitment poster. The war posters were instruments of persuasion chiefly intended to promote recruitment, war bond drives, conservation and food production, and compassionate causes. The Kitchener poster was the most famous of all the war posters, and its design was often imitated as in the United States poster on this page. *(Imperial War Museum)*

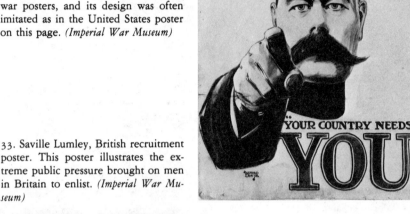

33. Saville Lumley, British recruitment poster. This poster illustrates the extreme public pressure brought on men in Britain to enlist. *(Imperial War Museum)*

34. James Montgomery Flagg, United States recruitment poster. *(National Archives)*

35. Jules Abel Faivre, *We will get them!* A widely known poster by one of the most famous poster artists of France. The four reproductions on this page are representative of the many and varied posters for war loan drives appearing in each major belligerent. *(National Archives)*

36. Georges Scott, *For the Flag! For Victory!* *(National Archives)*

37. I. Vladimirov, *Everyone must help our glorious soldiers.* *(Imperial War Museum)*

38. Luciano Mauzan, *Liberation Loan,* dedicated to the redemption of Italian-speaking lands in Austria-Hungary. *(From a photograph. The Hoover Institution, Stanford)*

39. Ludwig Holwein, *People's Fund for German War Prisoners and Civilian Internees.* Artistically, one of the best war posters by a great poster artist. *(Imperial War Museum)*

40. A. E. Foringer, United States poster. The image here was so extensively popularized and effectively used that it came to be a symbol of the Red Cross in wartime. *(Library of Congress)*

41. Every major belligerent exhorted its people to measures of food conservation and production with numerous posters like these two lower ones. *(Library of Congress)*

42. Germans are urged to plant sunflowers and poppies so as to produce oil for Germany. *(From a photograph. The Hoover Institution, Stanford)*

43. French women of Oise drawing a farm implement. A photograph widely used in Allied countries. The illustrations on this and the next two pages suggest the growing role of women in military, economic, and political affairs. *(Library of Congress)*

44. One use of the above image was in the design of this Canadian poster for the sale of Victory Bonds. *(From a photograph. The Hoover Institution, Stanford)*

45. *Everything for the war!* A Russian poster with this slogan at the top urges the subscription of war bonds. *(From a photograph. The Hoover Institution, Stanford)*

46. A group of Tommy WAACs (British Women's Army Auxiliary Corps). *(Library of Congress)*

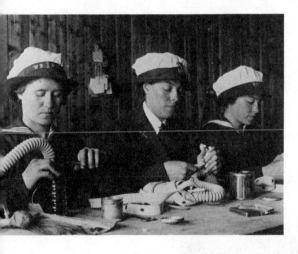

47. Members of the WRENS (British Women's Royal Naval Service) repairing respirators. *(The Hoover Institution, Stanford)*

48. Women loading incendiary bullets at the Frankfort, Ky., Arsenal in the United States. Note the dress of the women, the small flag, and the poster on the wall. *(Library of Congress)*

THE CATCH OF THE SEASON.

Conductorette (to Mr. Asquith), "COME ALONG, SIR. BETTER LATE THAN NEVER."

If You Are Good Enough for War You Are Good Enough to Vote

By MORRIS.

49. On the progress of the women's suffrage movement in Britain. (Punch, *April 4, 1917*)

50. The irrefutable logic of women's war work. (Brooklyn Magazine, *November 10, 1917*)

51. Women voting in Bavaria for the first time. *(National Archives)*

52. The worldwide inflation. (Jersey Journal, *July 18, 1915*)

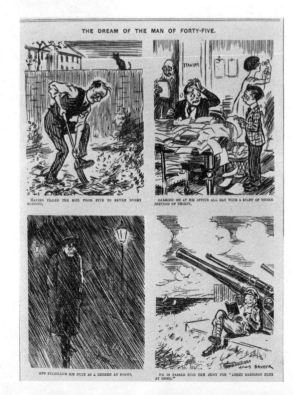

53. The life of civilians. (Punch, *July 17, 1918*)

54. André Devambez, *Le charbon (The Coal Queue).* Etching. The civilians also had to stand in queues and contend with air raids at night. *(From album,* Douze eaux-fortes. *Library of Congress)*

55. Jean Gabriel Domergue, *Nuit blanche (White night).* Lithograph. *(Library of Congress)*

56. Francisque Poulbot. Lithograph. Poulbot's war composite centers about his ever charming children but does not fail to include the poilu and refugees with the cart of all their remaining possessions. *(Library of Congress)*

57. Bessarabian village set afire by the Russians. *(German press photograph. Library of Congress)*

58. A family of Russian Poland returns to its devastated home to prepare meals on a cook stove still preserved. *(The Hoover Institution, Stanford)*

59. Serbian refugees fleeing the battle area. Note women without footwear. *(German press photograph from* Erinnerung an den Weltkrieg 1914–1918. *Library of Congress)*

60. Bruno Bielefeldt, *Die Geflüchteten (The Refugees).* Lithograph. *(From album,* Bilder aus Ostpreussens Not. *Library of Congress)*

61. Théophile Steinlen, A procession of refugees. Etching. The compassionate tendency of this versatile artist is expressed in this and the succeeding work on the same theme. *(Library of Congress)*

62. Théophile Steinlen, Refugees in flight. Drypoint. *(Library of Congress)*

63. Pierre Paulus, *Charleroi après la bataille, 1914 (Charleroi after the battle, 1914)*. Lithograph. *(Library of Congress)*

64. Louis Raemaekers, *Christendom after Twenty Centuries.* The Dutch artist Raemaekers, acclaimed as a "second Daumier," was the most celebrated cartoonist of the war period. *(From* Raemaekers' Cartoons on the European War)

65. Louis Raemaekers, *Europe 1916.* Raemaekers at his best indicted modern war and militarism for the suffering they caused humanity and the catastrophe they brought on European civilization. *(From* Raemaekers' Cartoons on the European War)

66. Hugo Krayn, *Hunger.* Lithograph. The Expressionist lithographs in *Krieg und Kunst* were antiwar in theme. (*From* Krieg und Kunst)

67. Erich Büttner, *Triumph of War.* Lithograph. (*From* Krieg und Kunst)

68. L. Moreau, *Après la victoire (After the Victory).* Wood engraving. The works of German and French artists such as those reproduced here helped to take the glory out of war. (*Library of Congress*)

69. Paul Nash, *We Are Making a New World*, 1918. Oil painting, 28 × 36″. As in this Symbolist painting, Nash conveys the "bitter truth" of the war through mutilated landscapes painted in somber tones with little or no sign of the presence of soldiers or their machines. *(Imperial War Museum)*

70. Paul Nash, *The Menin Road*, 1918. Oil painting, 84 × 168″. A monumental canvas crowning a series of some eighty works of war art by Nash. Again his passion against modern war inspired this painting of a wasteland in which man appears as a diminutive creature. *(Imperial War Museum)*

71. C. R. W. Nevinson, *The Road from Arras to Bapaume*, 1917. Oil on canvas. Painted while Nevinson was an official war artist. *(Imperial War Museum)*

72. C. R. W. Nevinson, *La Mitrailleuse (The Machine Gun)*, 1915. Oil on canvas, 24 × 20″. The machine gun group, revealing Futurist and Vorticist influences in the partially geometrical forms, sculptural effect, and dynamic tension, epitomizes the British artist's perception of the domination of the war by machines. *(The Tate Gallery, London)*

73. Otto Dix, *The War IV/3: Bombing of Lens*, 1924. Etching and drypoint, 1 1 3/4 × 9 5/8″. One of the cycle of fifty etchings called *Der Krieg (War)*, which, on the basis of drawings made during the war, documents with surgical objectivity and apocalyptic vision the horrors of the conflict. *(Collection, The Museum of Modern Art, New York; gift of Abby Aldrich Rockefeller)*

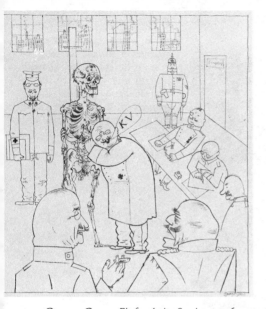

74. George Grosz, *Fit for Active Service*, 1916–17. Pen and brush and India ink, 20 × 14 3/8″. A savage and mordant satire of the German military's professed physical examination of recruits, typifying the art form of Grosz's line drawings. *(Collection, The Museum of Modern Art, New York; A. Conger Goodyear Fund)*

75. George Grosz, *Germany, a Winter's Tale*, 1917–19. Oil on canvas. A portrayal of the conditions in Germany that Grosz abhorred illustrates why he has been characterized as "the most acute satirist and social critic since Goya and Daumier." *(From a photograph. Courtesy of Peter M. Grosz. Whereabouts of the painting unknown)*

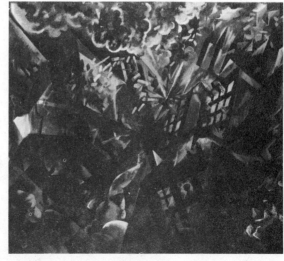

76. George Grosz, *Explosion*, 1917. Oil on composition board, 18 7/8 × 26 7/8″. A painting of the madness of modern war from Grosz's Dadaist and nihilist period. *(Collection, The Museum of Modern Art, New York; gift of Mr. and Mrs. Irving Moskovitz)*

77. Ernst Ludwig Kirchner, *Self-Portrait as Soldier*, 1915. Oil on canvas, 69.2 × 61 cm. The representation of himself, the sensitive artist, as a soldier with a hardened, expressionless face and an amputated arm symbolizes the ruinous effect of the war and military service on his artistic calling. *(Allen Memorial Museum, Oberlin College, Oberlin, Ohio)*

78. Oskar Kokoschka, *Knight Errant*, 1915. Oil on canvas, 35 3/8 × 70 7/8″. Whatever else Kokoschka's portrayal of himself as a prostrate knight errant suggests, it pictures despair associated with the war. *(The Solomon R. Guggenheim Museum)*

79. Marsden Hartley, *Portrait of a German Officer*, 1914. Oil on canvas, 68 1/4 × 41 3/8". Of the war themes of American artists represented on this page, Hartley' abstract work was painted in Germany *(The Metropolitan Museum of Art, The Alfred Stieglitz Collection, 1949)*

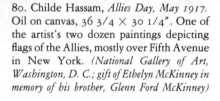

80. Childe Hassam, *Allies Day, May 1917*. Oil on canvas, 36 3/4 × 30 1/4". One of the artist's two dozen paintings depicting flags of the Allies, mostly over Fifth Avenue in New York. *(National Gallery of Art, Washington, D. C.; gift of Ethelyn McKinney in memory of his brother, Glenn Ford McKinney)*

81. J. Alden Weir, *Knitting for Soldiers*, c. 1918. Oil on canvas, 30 × 24 1/2". *(The Phillips Collection, Washington, D. C.)*

82. Larry Rivers, *History of the Russian Revolution*, 1965. Mixed media, 172 × 389". *(Hirschhorn Museum and Sculpture Garden, Smithsonian Institution)*

83. Barricade near arsenal in Petrograd raised by the first regiment to revolt in Russia, March 12, 1917. *(The Hoover Institution, Stanford)*

84. Suppressing a Bolshevik attempt to seize power in Petrograd during the July Days. *(National Archives)*

85A & 85B. Leaders of the October revolution in Russia: Lenin as chairman of the Soviet Council of Commissars (upper left) and Leon Trotsky (upper right). *(National Archives)*

86. Alexander Kerensky. *(The Hoover Institution, Stanford)*

87. German drawing pictures Entente mourning at the demise of Russia as an Ally. *(The Hoover Institution, Stanford)*

88. Proclamation of the German republic from the Reichstag building. *(National Archives)*

89. Leaders of the German revolution: Philipp Scheidemann (left) and Friedrich Ebert (right). *(National Archives)*

90. Street fighting in Berlin between Ebert forces and Spartacists. *(The Hoover Institution, Stanford)*

91. Proclamation of the Hungarian Soviet Republic in Budapest. *(National Archives)*

92. Armistice celebration in Paris. *(National Archives)*

93. The peace conference in session at the Quai d'Orsay. *(National Archives)*

94. Clemenceau, Wilson, and Lloyd George leaving the Palace of Versailles after signing the peace treaty with Germany. (*The Hoover Institution, Stanford*)

„Nur so kann Deutschland darin gebulbet werben!"

95. A German caricature of the peacemakers Lloyd George, Clemenceau, and Wilson, given wings and halos, standing with pendant swords on the prostrate body of Germany. The upper caption reads: "The foundation for the League of Nations"; and the lower: "Only in this way can Germany be tolerated." (Simplicissimus, *March 11, 1919*)

96. Berlin crowds in the Tiergarten at a rally protesting the peace terms, May 12, 1919. The slogan, "Only the 14 Points," is conspicuous. (*National Archives*)

Arthur Zimmermann, the current head of the foreign office, had gone over, had formed to require the beginning of the submarine campaign by February 1.[12]

Bethmann had no solid base of political strength for resistance. He could not command a majority in the Reichstag opposing OHL on the U-boat issue. Both the kaiser and the public, except the Social Democrats, desired not to make peace before utilizing first the wonder weapon in full force. On the basis of the improved technical capabilities of the submarine fleet and of the renewed statistical studies by the naval staff's experts, Holtzendorff was giving assurances that if the unrestricted campaign began by February, the destruction of 600,000 tons of shipping monthly would reduce Britain within five months to seeking peace.[13]

On January 8 Holtzendorff by memorandum and in private meeting with the kaiser won the monarch over to the stand of the naval staff and OHL. When the crown council began the next day at Pless, "the decision de facto" had already been reached. After a brief and perfunctory presentation of positions, the chancellor withdrew his futile opposition, and the kaiser quickly handed down a formal decision. Bethmann chose not to resign rather than force a cabinet crisis intensifying differences in the coalition and weakening the forces of cohesion at home.[14]

The step, taken without serious deliberation, was of more fateful bearing than any since Germany decided on mobilization and the invasion of Belgium. The decision was a mortal blow to any further chance of German collaboration with an American peace initiative. Indeed, it insured in a few months a break with the United States that would end in war. The outcome signified the supremacy of the military and naval power over the political in Reich policy and direction of the war. That the third OHL, as with Falkenhayn in the second, placed dependence on this method of warfare was tantamount to a confession of the technical inadequacy of the German military machine to subdue British power in a land war. The postulate that the submarine campaign would enable Germany to end the war with victory in spite of American participation added to the Schlieffen plan and the Falkenhayn strategy of 1916 another of the general staff's great and improvident gambles in the conduct of the war.

12. Birnbaum, *Peace Moves and U-Boat Warfare*, 283–314; Ritter, *Staatskunst*, 3: 375–78.
13. See Ritter, *Staatskunst*, 3: 319–23; Bauer, *Reichsleitung und U-Bootseinsatz*, 77.
14. Birnbaum, *Peace Moves and U-Boat Warfare*, 315–24; Bethmann Hollweg, *Betrachtungen*, 2: 131, 137–38; Balfour, *Kaiser and His Times*, 372.

2. THE MARITIME CRISIS

The arena of warfare at sea now shifted from the stalemate of the two vast dreadnought fleets to the implacable struggle between two systems of arms—an enormous surface array of every conceivable maritime type and submarine flotillas; between two systems of blockade; between the organizations of the two power blocs for exerting and withstanding economic pressure. Churchill was impressed at its being "in scale and stake the greatest conflict ever decided at sea." For the Germans, the High Seas Fleet became in the apt description of Admiral Scheer "the hilt of the weapon whose sharp blade was the U-boat." The Reich fleet was supporting the submarines instead of the reverse.[15]

A shipping emergency already existed before the losses of the Allies and the neutrals shot up from February 1917 on. Following the renewal of the cruiser warfare in October 1916, the Allied shipping losses flared higher in the final quarter of 1916, to an average monthly sum of 176,000 tons. Protective measures such as waiting in ports during an alarm and deviations in route were lessening the carrying capacity of available shipping. These factors, along with the earlier destruction and with the extensive diversions of commercial shipping to naval and military uses, produced a shipping stringency, which mounted to a deadly peril in 1917.

The progress of the German campaign of 1917 made the British situation somber by the end of April. Holtzendorff was attaining the norms set by the naval staff. The British losses alone exceeded 545,000 tons in April, and during that severest month of all the British, other Allied, and neutral losses reached the deadly total of 874,000 tons. And in the first six months of the German campaign the total destruction in British shipping from all causes amounted to 2,350,000 tons and in the world's shipping to more than 3,850,000. At the height of the crisis Britain's food reserves were cut down to supplies for only six weeks.[16]

It was apparent by late April that the antisubmarine war of the Allies had failed to counter the U-boat offensive. Desperation seized the First

15. See J. A. Salter, *Allied Shipping Control* (Oxford, 1921); Mancur Olson, *The Economics of the Wartime Shortages* (Durham, N. C., 1963), 75; Churchill, *World Crisis*, 4: 350; Philip K. Lundeberg, "Undersea Warfare and Allied Strategy in World War I," *Smithsonian Journal of History*, 1, no. 4 (1967): 68.

16. Great Britain, Admiralty, *Merchant Shipping (Losses)* (London, 1919), 162; C. Ernest Fayle, *Seaborne Trade*, 3 vols. (London, 1920–24), 3: 56, 91; Olson, *Wartime Shortages*, 42.

Sea Lord Jellicoe, whose black pessimism dominated his first meeting with Admiral William S. Sims after the American declaration of war. Sims attested that Jellicoe replied to his question whether there was a solution to the problem of shipping losses: "Absolutely none that we can see now." The opinion of the American ambassador Walter Hines Page supported Jellicoe: "What we are facing is the defeat of Britain." The omens of victory were on the wing toward the Germans, and the question agitating London was whether and how the navy could stop losing the war.[17]

Before the German campaign began, the British had developed a comprehensive series of measures with which to meet the submarine menace. The program extended along three lines: the protection of merchant shipping; offensive action against the U-boats; and economic measures to balance the demand for supplies and shipping with the carrying power of available tonnage. The effort was far from adequate to cope with the radical submarine attack now in progress. The main methods of protecting vessels of trade had been patrols along fixed routes and the arming of merchantmen. The latter was of material help so long as the submarine warfare kept to the surface in accordance with prize regulations, but the merchantmen were vulnerable to submerged attacks. Trade defense also utilized intelligence on U-boat cruises and patterns of action to divert ships from the danger and to keep them waiting in port until the alarm was over. On the seas, ships without escort depended on the zigzag maneuver and their speed to evade torpedoes. The mining of harbors and coasts was a further protective step.[18]

The emphasis had been on carrying the attack to the U-boat. The varied arsenal of the submarine hunters included mines, mine nets and barriers, depth charges, bombs, guns, sweeps and their improved form of paravanes, and hydrophones laid on the sea bottom. The fight against the U-boat was carried on in every medium: in the air by patrols of seaplanes, airplanes, airships, and kite balloons; under water by submarines; and on the surface by destroyers, a huge "mosquito fleet" of small craft, and the "Q-ships," steamers with concealed guns cruising the trade routes with the object of luring the U-boats into a trap.[19]

17. Patterson, *Jellicoe*, 169–71; Corbett and Newbolt, *Naval Operations*, 5: 23.
18. Marder, *From the Dreadnought to Scapa Flow*, 2: 350, 357–60; Earl Jellicoe, *The Submarine Peril* (London, 1934), p. vi; Fayle, *Seaborne Trade*, 3: 96–97.
19. Marder, *From the Dreadnought to Scapa Flow*, 2: 355–59; Jellicoe, *Submarine Peril*, 11–12, 76–80.

The British had not prepared themselves for submarine war to the finish. The foregoing technical devices and weapons had not enabled antisubmarine operations to establish a noticeable record of success. Even the spasmodic action of the Germans in 1915 and 1916 had destroyed more than three million tons of shipping. And the Germans had not been prevented from increasing impressively their average complement of U-boats engaged in operations. Some progress had been made in the adjustment of supply requirements and carriage capacity, chiefly by reduction of imports and economies in shipping, but more radical measures were necessary for the Allies to survive the crisis of 1917.[20]

Sources of encouragement appeared when the crisis was at its height. American naval cooperation began immediately after the United States declared war. Admiral Sims arranged at once for sending the first contingent of destroyers to the aid of the British. An effective means of trade defense was found in the convoy system. The technical capabilities were improved for destroying the submarines.

The disastrous shipping losses during the spring of 1917 told a sorry story about the failure of the Admiralty's methods of protecting merchant vessels. More than two years had been lost in organizing an effective system of defense. Yet the answer was at hand for Hankey, the ingenious secretary of the War Cabinet, many of the younger officers of the navy, and certain senior officers in the introduction of the convoy system.

The Admiralty under Jellicoe's professional leadership, however, resisted the strategy of convoy mainly because it had concentrated so long, in the tradition of naval activism, on fighting the U-boat rather than protecting the merchantmen. The Admiralty was thus not ready to transfer many ships from antisubmarine work to service as convoy escorts. The Admiralty also overestimated the dimensions of the escort problem.[21]

The Admiralty, supported by mercantile officers and shipowners, advanced numerous other arguments against convoy, such as the difficulty of merchant vessels keeping station and the increased size of the target presented by the convoy grouping. In refutation stood the weight of historical experience with convoys since the seventeenth century, supported more recently by the protection of troop transports by armed escorts and the success of the convoy in the French coal trade since February.

    20. Spindler, *Handelskrieg,* 4: 507, 5: 340; Roskill, *Strategy of Sea Power,* 129–30.
    21. Marder, *From the Dreadnought to Scapa Flow,* 4: 108–26, 150; Corbett and Newbolt, *Naval Operations,* 5: 5–18; Roskill, *Strategy of Sea Power,* 130–31.

Near the end of April Jellicoe and the head of the antisubmarine division in the Admiralty were converted to a trial of the convoy system. The calamitous shipping losses acted as a prime mover in jolting the Admiralty from its previous position. The promise of American naval cooperation and the discovery that the escort problem was of more manageable size than anticipated also exerted influence. Lloyd George had backed convoy since November 1916, and the intention of the prime minister, authorized by the cabinet, to investigate the existing means of antisubmarine warfare may have prompted Jellicoe somewhat sooner to a decision about to be taken.[22]

The convoy experiment was inaugurated in May with a run from Gibraltar and one from Hampton Roads. When the system was fully organized, convoys sailed from Hampton Roads, New York, Halifax, Sydney, and Gibraltar, and these were complemented with outward-bound convoys. The system was expanded to the South Atlantic with a Dakar convoy and a Sierra Leone convoy. Local convoys operated in the Mediterranean, and a convoy to and from Port Said. In addition, the convoys continued in the French coal trade and the Scandinavian trade.

The convoy system proved a phenomenal success. Shipping losses took a decided curve downward, from the monthly average of 420,000 tons during the period April–July to 196,000 for September. Nor had the experience substantiated the doubts and objections that Admiralty had raised concerning the introduction of convoy. A good deal more than a practical and effective system of trade defense, convoy became, as Admiral Sims originally suggested, the focus of the antisubmarine attack. The countermeasures of the convoy escorts were so successful that they sank 24 U-boats between August 1917 and the end of the war.[23]

Along with the decisive improvement in trade defense in 1917, the antisubmarine offensive developed more striking power. The attack was

22. Marder, *From the Dreadnought to Scapa Flow,* 4: 145, 160–64; Jellicoe, *Submarine Peril,* 108, 118, 124–31; Patterson, *Jellicoe,* 173–74; Corbett and Newbolt, *Naval Operations,* 5: 5–21. Lloyd George's account of the decision on convoys, betraying distortions and exaggerations, is related in his *War Memoirs,* 3: 1161–65. This volume of his memoirs contains the chapter entitled "The Peril of the Submarines," pp. 1120–96, which started a debate on the roles of Lloyd George and the Admiralty in coming to the convoy decision. Though Lloyd George had good reason to fault the laggard and reluctant attitude of Jellicoe and the Admiralty, this is a scornful indictment, extravagant and retributive. Jellicoe replied indirectly through the book *The Submarine Peril,* recounting the antisubmarine work of the Admiralty. See Patterson, *Jellicoe,* 249–50.

23. Corbett and Newbolt, *Naval Operations,* 128–33; Roskill, *Strategy of Sea Power,* 131.

strengthened not only by means of the convoy system but also through the depth charge and a new efficient mine (the Mark H-2 horned mine based on a German model). The arming of merchant ships in convoy with depth charges and guns converted the convoy of ships, mutually cooperating, into a kind of trap for the marauding U-boat. Thanks to the more efficient mine and its production in quantity, the mine became the most destructive weapon in the war on the U-boat. The Allies controlled the waters off the bases used by the U-boats at Ostend, Bruges, and Zeebrugge in Belgium, and Cattaro and Pola in the Adriatic. The Allied object was to sow minefields where they would "bottle up the U-boats" in those bases or entrap them as they entered or departed transit routes. The fields in the Straits of Dover and Otranto, as well as from Norway to the Orkneys, were planted as a curtain. Of these the Dover barrage was the most successful.[24]

Two other facilities contributed substantially to the better results in combating the U-boats. One was the extension of the hydrophone to ships for service at sea. The other was the improvement and expansion of British intelligence on the movements and losses of enemy submarines. The increased efficacy of the conglomerate organization fighting the submarine was indicated by the rising rate of U-boat sinkings. Even so, at the end of 1917, the Germans were able to keep up the pace of replacement with the commissioning of new submarines.[25]

The improvement in Allied antisubmarine measures and the adoption of convoy in the solution of the problem of trade defense lightened the picture for the Allies as the year of crisis came to an end. The Germans were at a loss to find means by which the convoy could be successfully countered, and their submarine strategy had not brought Britain to its knees within five months or maintained the norms promised by the naval staff. The British were making progress with economic measures planned to balance supply requirements and carriage capacity. Shipping replacements still did not cover shipping losses. Yet the British had instituted a more cohesive and efficient organization for merchant shipbuilding and embarked on a program of expanded production. In the matter of supply the British were tightening their belts further. Additional steps were being taken to extend the carrying capacity of the shipping available. Although

24. Robert M. Grant, *U-Boats Destroyed* (London, 1964), 69, 143, 159; Robert M. Grant, *U-Boat Intelligence, 1914–1918* (London, 1969), 10, 61, 80 ff.
25. Grant, *U-Boats Destroyed*, 41–43, 73; Spindler, *Handelskrieg,* 4: 507.

the submarine threat had not yet been overcome, the progress made gave assurance of survival and hope of ultimate victory at sea.[26]

3. THE ENTRY OF THE UNITED STATES INTO EUROPEAN AFFAIRS

The crises of 1917 were associated with two events that overshadowed all others in future consequences: the entry of the United States into European affairs and the Russian revolution. Conditions were ripe for America becoming a factor in the European system at this time. America had come of age as a great power, and the political structure of Europe embodied in the Pentarchy and the classical balance of power was breaking down. The creation of a new system had to extend beyond Europe, to include the strength of America as a stabilizing factor.

The war revealed that the traditional relationship of America to Europe was no longer valid. That relationship as conceived in American policy and opinion rested on the doctrine of two worlds—the old and the new, each having its separate interests. This was the essence of the isolationist temper, which desired no part of Europe in the Western Hemisphere and no political part of America in Europe. The United States had been active in driving Europe out of the Americas ever since the American revolution, and the process ended only during the Great War, through the acquisition of the Danish West Indies. The counterpart was to keep the United States out of the politics, wars, and entanglements of Europe, all of which were regarded in America's aloofness as the follies of the old world.[27]

The tradition of abstention from European politics was bred by seclusion from the competitive power system of Europe. The undisturbed apartness in which the American nation had matured to the status of the foremost great power had been possible because of British naval supremacy in the nineteenth century, common policy interests between the United States and Britain, the classical balance of power among the European Pentarchy, and the state of limited communications. The seclusion had passed away under the conditions of the twentieth century, and it was necessary to fashion a new positive relationship to Europe. Some quarters on both sides of the Atlantic had already perceived the fundamental change and its implications. Thus Sir Edward Grey consistently pursued the objective of a tacit entente between Britain and the United States;

26. See Fayle, *Seaborne Trade*, 3: 192–213.
27. See Selig Adler, *The Isolationist Impulse* (New York, 1957).

Theodore Roosevelt assumed an initiative in the holding of the Algeciras conference and in the conclusion of the Portsmouth peace treaty between Russia and Japan; and Colonel Edward M. House went on a peace mission to Europe in the summer of 1914.[28]

These were prophetic signs that the old negative relationship of the United States to Europe would no longer suffice. The war dramatically demonstrated the departure of the old physical insularity and the direct impact of European events on American citizens. The United States was forced to work out rapidly a new constructive relationship with Europe amidst the hazards and pressures of total war, above all in the cross fire of the British and German systems of maritime warfare.

It was inconceivable that the greatest power of all should remain without influence on the war and consequently without some form of involvement. The cardinal issue confronting the United States was not whether it should enter Europe at war, but how it should enter. President Wilson sensed these gravitational forces in his second inaugural address to the nation: "matters lying outside our own life as a nation over which we had no control . . . despite our wish to keep free from them, have drawn us more and more irresistibly into their own current and influence."[29] His long struggle in the period of neutrality was not to avoid entry into European affairs, not to avoid an economic or political role in Europe. It was to avoid military intervention.

Under Wilson's leadership the American government steered a very intricate course in determining the extent and forms of intervention. The nature of that course issued on the one hand from the complexity and unanticipated character of the conditions created by total war. On the other it was influenced by the division of the country between pro-German, anti-British, pro-Ally, isolationist, pacifist, and indifferent attitudes toward involvement. Time and preeminent qualities of discerning and patient leadership were required to reach a final policy of participation based on a general consensus.

The initial reaction of the government followed almost instinctively the heritage of abstention. President Wilson's proclamation of neutrality on August 19, 1914, pitched the United States on the heights of impartiality

---

28. See Edward H. Buehrig, *Woodrow Wilson and the Balance of Power* (Bloomington, Ind., 1955), 5–11; Ernest R. May, *The World War and American Isolation* (Cambridge, Mass., 1959), 8; Hajo Holborn, *The Political Collapse of Europe* (New York, 1951), 87–88.

29. Quoted in May, *World War and American Isolation*, 425.

above the conflict in Europe. From this point on, during the next five years, America made a long journey from the premise of two worlds with separate identities to the premise of a single world in which America would play the leading part. Wilson summarized the result in a speech of September 1919, defending American participation in the League of Nations. He affirmed the end of isolation "not because we chose to go into the politics of the world, but because by . . . the growth of our power we have become a determining factor in the history of mankind, and after you have become a determining factor you cannot remain isolated, whether you want to or not."[30]

The American participation in European affairs assumed four different forms: (1) the immense extension of trade and financial assistance, theoretically available to the Central Powers on the basis of American neutrality but in effect confined almost exclusively to the Allies; (2) the defense of neutral rights, which amounted to political intervention in setting the rules of maritime warfare for the twentieth century; (3) mediation to end the war and diplomatic moves to shape the peace; and (4) military intervention.

The economic role of the United States in wartime Europe expanded to large proportions prior to American military entry. Trade with the Allies swelled from approximately 825 million dollars in 1914 to over 3.214 billion in 1916. The export of war materials to the Allied countries leaped from roughly 125 million dollars in the three prewar fiscal years to 2.167 billion in fiscal 1915–17, an increase of 1,639 percent. Loans and credits extended the Allies by American bankers rose to a total of about 2.2 billion dollars.[31]

The growth of trade and financial support had come to weave a community of interest between the United States and the Allies; for the United States the relationship created prosperity; for the Allies it provided a supplementary arsenal and financial sinews of war. The shipment of munitions to the Allies aroused the indignation of the German public and

30. Quoted in Arthur S. Link, *Wilson the Diplomatist* (Baltimore, 1957), 145.
31. On the American economic ties with the Allies, see Buehrig, *Woodrow Wilson and the Balance of Power,* 88–96; Charles Callan Tansill, *America Goes to War* (Boston, 1938), especially pp. 53, 115–16; Arthur S. Link, *Woodrow Wilson and the Progressive Era* (New York, 1954), 172–73, 278–79; Daniel M. Smith, *The Great Departure* (New York, 1965), 7, 33–38; U. S., Congress, Senate, Special Committee to Investigate the Munitions Industry, *World War Financing and Industrial Expansion.* S. Rept. 944, 74th Cong., 1st sess., 1935, pt. 26, 7786.

elicited official protests from the German government, as well as a gigantic propaganda campaign and subversive activities in the United States against it. The extent of the munitions traffic seemed to the Germans to make the United States a silent partner in the Allied war effort.

The American defense of neutral rights involved the United States in a struggle with Britain and Germany to determine the rules of maritime warfare under the conditions of total war. The American government endeavored to keep the area of neutral rights as large as possible and the range of belligerent action as restricted as possible by relying on a body of international law and practice from the sailing era. Both Britain and Germany were driven by military necessity to refashion the rules of maritime warfare in a manner that would invest their own modern weapons and methods of warfare with the deadliest effect against the enemy, even though this inflicted serious injury on neutral interests. Yet scarcely any stake of either belligerent was higher than winning the toleration by the United States of the course the warring power pursued.

Through a series of orders in council and related restrictive measures, the British gradually elaborated a tight system of controls over neutral shipping for applying economic pressure against the Central Powers. Without proclaiming a legal blockade, the system of far-reaching measures largely closed off neutral trade with the German bloc, except as Britain permitted. The restrictions covered all goods, whether contraband or not, and trade directly with the Central Powers or indirectly through other neutrals with the German bloc the ultimate origin or destination.[32]

The British maritime controls were at many points incompatible with the American conception of freedom of the seas and the rights of neutrals. The all-encompassing problem of Anglo-American relations during the war was the adjustment of interest between these conflicting claims. The measures employed by the British belonged to the advantages conferred by naval supremacy, and their totality was considered essential to Britain's survival. Concessions could not therefore extend beyond matters of administration and manner of diplomatic handling. Wilson had no choice in any ultimate contention but an accommodation to the British system or a contribution to German victory.

At first the United States made a vain attempt to induce the British to accept the Declaration of London, an agreement, never ratified by Britain and the United States, that considerably enlarged and safeguarded the freedom of neutral trade. Thereafter Washington based its diplomatic case for the maximum freedom of trade on international law and practice.[33]

During 1915 the continued detention of American ships and seizures of noncontraband cargoes caused a rising tide of resentment in the United States. The new ministry of blockade in Britain tightened the system of economic warfare further in 1916. American indignation erupted when a number of American firms and individuals were blacklisted and American mail seized. Reflecting these feelings in Congress and the public, Wilson's government followed a policy of increasing resistance to the maritime controls by means of diplomatic note, House's mission to London in early 1916, and the authorization of economic sanctions.

The British maintained their maritime system in force without change. The temper of Wilson and Congress was expressed in the legislation of September 1916, granting the president discretionary authority to block imports of the Allies and deny clearance of their ships. By the end of the year 1916 the stronger American resistance united with a growing nationalism and anti-Americanism in Britain to send the relations of the two countries into a downward spiral. The bottom was never reached, owing to Wilson's rare restraint and caution in using the economic leverage authorized by Congress; to the basic acquiescence of the United States in Britain's maritime methods, while it sought adjustments and a legal record for the adjudication of future claims; to a forbearance throughout the growing differences from pressing the issues to the ultimative point where Britain's decision could mean war; and above all to the supervention of the submarine controversies and the conflicts with Germany.[34]

The Germans, compelled because of the inferiority of their fleet to rely on the revolutionary weapon of the submarine, had to cope with the peculiarly difficult problem of using it in the frame of the old rules of maritime warfare. American policy on the other hand applied the traditional code of maritime warfare in defense of neutral rights, whatever the effect might be on the efficacy of the U-boat weapon.

The German government failed by the proclamation of February 4, 1915, to obtain international acceptance of a war zone around the British

---

33. On the efforts of the United States to defend the American interpretation of maritime rights, see the story in full for 1914–15 as related in Link, *Struggle for Neutrality.*

34. See May, *World War and American Isolation,* 329–39.

Isles subject to submarine action against belligerent merchant vessels without warning where neutral ships might not enter without risk. In its strong note of February 10 the United States asserted that the "sole right" of Germany in dealing with neutral vessels on the high seas was limited to the accepted principles of visit and search. The communication supported with a warning of ultimative force the "strict accountability" required of the German government for not destroying American vessels or the lives of American citizens on the high seas.

The submarine warriors in Germany were not deterred. In April the neutral victims amounted to about one-third of the ships sunk by the U-boats. In May the *Lusitania* went down with 124 American citizens among the 1,198 lives lost. The foremost historian of the Wilson era concludes that this catastrophe "had a more jolting effect upon American opinion than any other single event of the World War." The shocking incident raised for the government and the people the dilemma of how to protect American citizens and their rights without military involvement.[35]

The response to this dilemma denounced submarine warfare as a whole and asked for its abandonment altogether. The note applied the "strict accountability" to American lives on belligerent ships and threatened "any necessary act" in upholding the rights of American citizens. Washington sent this and two additional notes in the effort to obtain Germany's disavowal of such incidents, reparation, and prevention of their recurrence. The third note, of July 21, 1915, reflected the public sentiment that the controversy should be settled without the risk of war.[36] The message departed notably from the first communication on the subject in recognizing that it was "possible and practicable" to conduct submarine operations within the bounds of the accepted practices of cruiser warfare. The note warned that acts in contravention of "a scrupulous observance of neutral rights" would be regarded "as deliberately unfriendly."

The *Arabic* and *Sussex* incidents ranked only behind the *Lusitania* in the diplomacy of the submarine controversy. The sinking of the passenger liner *Arabic* on August 19, 1915, with the loss of two American lives, tested whether the claim to immunity for American citizens on belligerent merchant vessels as an American right could be maintained without a

---

35. Link, *Struggle for Neutrality,* 372–77.
36. Ibid., 439–41.

break with Germany. By intensive and skillful negotiations Wilson and Lansing obtained the *Arabic* pledge that submarine commanders would not attack unresisting passenger liners without warning and safety of passengers and crew. Wilson had retreated from blanket opposition to the submarine war and narrowed the issue to the safety of neutral lives so far as belligerent vessels were concerned.[37]

After a lull, the German challenge to the American view of acceptable maritime warfare was renewed with the U-boat campaign of 1916. The torpedoing of the Channel steamer *Sussex* on March 24 reopened the German-American crisis over the use of U-boats. Wilson's note of April 18 reverted to the sweeping position of the first *Lusitania* note against submarine warfare in its entirety and explicitly warned of severing diplomatic relations unless Germany abandoned "its present methods of submarine warfare against passenger and freight-carrying vessels."

To this point Wilson's cautious, deliberate, even groping, diplomacy had saved the peace, but the American position had become increasingly rigid through ultimative demands and threats. This progression now arrived at the final juncture with the *Sussex* note, tantamount to a standing ultimatum in presenting Berlin the choice between curbing the U-boat or facing war with the United States. In pledging the Reich not to attack unresisting merchant vessels within and outside the war zone without warning and provision for the safety of passengers and crew, the German response of May 4 complied with the American demands by returning fully to the rules of cruiser warfare.

The *Sussex* ultimatum froze the American position in a way that would make a diplomatic rupture inescapable if Germany should resume U-boat warfare contrary to the *Sussex* pledge. Before the final storm, however, a tranquil period in German-American relations set in, following this settlement and the resolution of the unending *Lusitania* controversy in the preceding February. The German government expressed regret for the *Lusitania* incident and promised to pay reparation while avoiding an admission of illegality.[38]

The United States, the strongest great power carrying on an extensive trade with Europe, could not help but be caught in the meshes of these two innovative systems of maritime warfare. Wilson was constantly occu-

37. See May, *World War and American Isolation*, 156–67.
38. See Link, *Woodrow Wilson and the Progressive Era*, 218–19.

pied with the methods of each and ever more deeply implicated in efforts to shape the rules of each. The president felt obliged to protect American interests and thus to defend neutral rights, to sustain the national honor and dignity, to satisfy his own moral sense, and to settle on a course conducive to national unity and favorable to his own political leadership. He felt his way under uncertain conditions toward fulfilling these purposes. The course, reflecting the fluctuations of German policy and American opinion, represented a confused mixture of legal neutrality, impartiality, nonintercourse, and partisan interest that was increasingly constricted to the use of force if Germany failed to heed American demands.

The secretary of state, William Jennings Bryan, and his fraternity stood for the alternative of maintaining peace as the supreme end of policy. If this end was to be realized, logic was on the side of Bryan in the necessity for nonpartisanship and nonintercourse prohibitions.[39] But Wilson's policy diverged from Bryan's alternative, and the president's own adjuration to impartiality in thought and action rapidly gave way to a partisanship variously described as "differential neutrality" or benevolent neutrality toward the Allies.

Wilson's mediation attempts and peace actions progressively moved the United States into a deeper involvement in European affairs until it became his historical function to steer the United States in the passage from isolation to participation in European political life, to a reunion of the new and old worlds. At first he simply tried to stop the war by an immediate personal offer of good offices to the belligerents, by Bryan's mediation approaches of September 1914 to the German, British, and French ambassadors, and by Colonel House's peace mission to Europe in 1915.[40]

A further stage of mediation diplomacy was associated with House's second wartime mission to Europe, in January–February 1916, together with the preliminaries and aftermath. Wilson and House were now anxious to obtain a peace conference as a means of keeping the United States out of the war by ending the war itself. With the aim of spurring the Allies to seek a peace conference on the basis proposed in the House-Grey memorandum of February 22, 1916, Wilson publicly advanced the idea of United States participation in a postwar league of nations guaranteeing

39. On Bryan's attempt to implement the nonintercourse solution, see Link, *Struggle for Neutrality*, 62–64, 132–36, 616–25.
40. On Bryan's mediation efforts, see May, *World War and American Isolation*, 73–74; Ray Stannard Baker, *Woodrow Wilson: Life and Letters*, 8 vols. (New York, 1927–39), 5: 279–93.

the peace settlement.[41] The speech on this subject, made on May 27, 1916, before the League to Enforce Peace, bade America's "farewell to isolation."[42] The statement is recognized to be a historical landmark as significant in the relationship of the United States to Europe in the twentieth century as Monroe's message of 1823 was in the nineteenth century.[43] The revolutionary diplomacy of this stage was scarcely an impartial undertaking in mediation. It was more in the nature of cooperation with the Allies in the attempt to arrange a peace settlement with the prospect of military intervention if there was no success.

In the final period Wilson's attention was centered at first on the concert of power to be established in the guarantee of peace and then on the principles and concrete terms of the settlement. By the last months of 1916 his thoughts were turning to the terms of peace, and his identical notes of December 18 to the belligerent governments launched a peace bid calling for a statement of peace terms.[44] By 1917 Wilson had grown apprehensive that if the United States was to join with other nations in guaranteeing the peace and sharing in the new postwar order, "it must be a peace that is worth guaranteeing and preserving." He outlined the "essential terms" of such a peace in his speech of January 22, 1917, on the theme of peace without victory. He continued to discuss the issues and aims of the war in a series of memorable statements, including preeminently the war message of April 2, 1917, and his speech of January 8,

41. On House's peace venture of 1916: Charles Seymour, *The Intimate Papers of Colonel House*, 4 vols. (Boston, 1926–28), 2: 82–204 passim; Arthur S. Link, "Woodrow Wilson and Peace Moves," in *The Higher Realism of Woodrow Wilson and Other Essays* (Nashville, 1971), 100–02; Link, *Wilson the Diplomatist*, 46, 50; Charles Seymour, "The Role of Colonel House," in *Wilson's Foreign Policy in Perspective*, ed. Edward H. Buehrig (Bloomington, Ind., 1957), 19–20; Viscount Grey, *Twenty-Five Years, 1892–1916*, 2 vols. (New York, 1925), 2: 127–28.

42. William L. Langer, "From Isolation to Mediation," in *Woodrow Wilson and the World of Today*, ed. Arthur P. Dudden (Philadelphia, 1957), 38.

43. A scholar who has written some of the most interpretive works on the policy of Wilson toward Europe summarizes the historical importance of this speech thus: "Occupying a place in American history comparable to President Monroe's message to Congress of December 2, 1823, the address was a response to the circumstances of the twentieth century—as Monroe's message was a response to the circumstances of the nineteenth." Edward H. Buehrig, "Woodrow Wilson and Collective Security: The Origins," in *The Impact of World War I*, ed. Arthur S. Link (New York, 1969), 33.

44. May, *World War and American Isolation*, 366; Charles Seymour, *American Diplomacy during the World War* (Baltimore, 1934), 188; Seymour, *Intimate Papers*, 2: 403–04. The text of the American note is in Department of State circular of December 18, 1916, *Foreign Relations*, 1916, suppl., 97–99.

1918, on the Fourteen Points. The lofty tones of the epochal war message proclaimed the end of American attachment to the doctrine of the two worlds: "Neutrality is no longer feasible or desirable where the peace of the world is involved and the freedom of its peoples. . . . We have seen the last of neutrality in such circumstances."

By the standing ultimatum of the *Sussex* note Wilson's diplomacy of intervention in the rules of maritime warfare brought America to the pass where continued peace or military intervention in the war depended on German decision concerning submarine warfare or on the outcome of mediation and peace moves. The latter failed, and the Reich's unrestricted submarine campaign made it unavoidable for the United States to declare war. The American people as a whole desired peace even in 1917, but every indication suggests that they stood firmly for the defense of their national interest and honor, allowing Wilson no other choice. This conclusion represents the prevailing construction of the subject by American historians.[45] As the revisionists have done, one could presuppose a policy of nonintercourse that might have kept the United States out of the war. That course, disregarding the rights and interests of the American people, would have been entirely unacceptable to the nation.[46]

Upon entering the war, the American government and public discovered that organized military resources were not available to the extent required for supporting the new role that the United States had undertaken in European affairs. The war spirit had been slow to form, and preparedness measures had lagged in spite of the agitation conducted by the Army League, the Navy League, and the National Security League organized in December 1914. The preparedness activists, however, extended their efforts in connection with the *Lusitania* incident and the submarine controversy.

Wilson, conceding to the growing movement, battled the opposition of

45. This interpretation of American military intervention is regarded as the orthodox or neo-orthodox Wilsonian view and its representatives as the "submarine" school of scholars. Its principal recent expositors are Link and May, whose works are referred to in the foregoing footnotes. Another view emphasizes the security considerations moving Wilson and his advisers. The major recent exemplar is Buehrig, *Woodrow Wilson and the Balance of Power.* An evaluation of historiography in this field is in Daniel M. Smith, "National Interest and American Intervention, 1917: An Historical Appraisal," *Journal of American History* 52 (1965): 5–24.

46. For the revisionist case, see especially Edwin Borchard and William P. Lage, *Neutrality for the United States* (New Haven, 1937), and Tansill, *America Goes to War.* The former is more from the legal point of view, the latter from the economic.

pacifists, Progressives, and hyphenates to put through in 1916 a preparedness program of modest dimensions in relation to later necessities. The National Defense Act of June 1916 more than doubled the authorized strength of the regular army, to approximately 235,000; established a Reserve Officer Training Corps in the colleges; and furthered a project of summer training camps. Congress enacted an unprecedented schedule of naval building over three years and in the Shipping Act laid the foundations of today's merchant marine. A Council of National Defense was formed to study the means of mobilizing the resources of the nation for the purpose of defense.[47]

When the United States joined the belligerents, it had only a small military establishment of fewer than 210,000 soldiers in federal service and a second-class navy. Washington had expected that it would be called on to contribute supplies and munitions, financial assistance, and naval vessels to the Allied effort rather than a sizable army. There was surprise at the increasingly urgent calls from France and Britain for sending American soldiers to France. In response, the government acted promptly to organize a national wartime army from the small nucleus of the peacetime establishment. The National Guard was inducted into service, the National Selective Service Act was adopted, and 9,500,000 men between the ages of 21 and 31 years registered on June 5 for military duty. The United States embarked on a furious program of producing clothing and equipment for the mass army, housing it, and starting its training at home.[48]

The continuous transport of soldiers to France began in June, in time to show the American colors in Paris on July 4. General John J. Pershing had arrived with a staff to head the American Expeditionary Forces. Before the end of June he had agreed with Pétain that an independent American army would eventually take over the Lorraine sector. They also settled on St. Mihiel as the place for the first American offensive.[49]

Under pressure from Foch, projections for the size of the AEF were progressively raised from the one million men that Pershing planned to have in France by July 1, 1918. The Americans threw a bridge of soldiers across the Atlantic, until in July 1918 more than 300,000 crossed in a single month. For the first time in history American soldiers entered

47. Arthur S. Link, *Wilson*, vol. 4: *Confusions and Crises*, 1915–16 (Princeton, 1964), 327–41.
48. See John Dickinson, *The Building of An Army* (New York, 1922).
49. Edward M. Coffman, *The War to End All Wars* (New York, 1968), 4, 122–26.

Europe, and before the finish two million of them were organized in two armies.[50]

The American divisions, arriving in France with little training for modern combat, had to complete their preparation there. Only after the March offensive of the Germans could Pershing rush three divisions into line to relieve the French. At the end of May the First Division conducted an American operation by capturing Cantigny near Montdidier. The American soldiers went on to fight at Château-Thierry, Belleau Wood, Soissons, and along the Ourcq and Vesle before the major independent action in reducing the St. Mihiel salient. In that battle and the Meuse-Argonne drive the Americans made a substantial contribution to the final victory of the Allies. The most decisive military share of the Americans in the success of the coalition may well have been the moral blow to the Germans from the realization that fresh American manpower would be fed constantly and in increasing volume into the Allied drive, while they had no replacements left for their depleted ranks.[51]

The American navy could provide more immediate assistance. The first contingent of six destroyers, arriving in British waters in April 1917, grew to a force of 373 vessels operating under the command of Admiral Sims from his large headquarters staff in London. Included in these were eight battleships and 37 destroyers, as well as an array of auxiliary vessels used in the protection of convoys, patrol functions, submarine chasing, mining, and minesweeping. In the convoy operations 24 cruisers conducted transports from United States ports to the rendezvous with destroyers or other escorts near Europe.[52]

This massive effort demanded an efficient organization at home for the conduct of war, both in the directing center of military affairs and in the economic mobilization of the nation. After a stage of fumbling and stumbling during the first year, capable, hard-driving men were found to direct

50. Ibid., 127–8, 228, 357. For the solution of the transport problem in ferrying the American soldiers to France, see the recital of "the great shipping saga" by the then army chief of staff General Peyton C. March in *The Nation at War* (Garden City, N.Y., 1932), 69–103.

51. On the role of the AEF in France, see in addition to Coffman's volume already cited Frederic L. Paxson, *American Democracy and the World War*, 3 vols. (Boston and Berkeley, 1936–48), vol. 2: *America at War* (1939); Pierce G. Fredericks, *The Great Adventure* (New York, 1960); John J. Pershing, *My Experiences in the World War*, 2 vols. (New York, 1931); James G. Harbaugh, *The American Army in France* (Boston, 1936); Frederick Palmer, *John J. Pershing* (1948; reprint ed., Westport, Conn., 1970), 72–348.

52. Coffman, *War to End All Wars*, 92–101 passim.

the military and industrial mobilization programs and a structure of special wartime agencies erected to insure centralized control for gearing the economy to military requirements. On the military side, the secretary of war, Newton D. Baker, moved under the spur of Congressional inquiry and criticism from being "only half at war" to conducting his office fully at war. He reorganized the war department and installed a ruthless, determined leader of men as chief of staff, General Peyton C. March. The latter made rapid progress in bringing order to the logistic services of the general staff and war department.[53]

To the Council of National Defense and the United States Shipping Board, already existing when America declared war, was added a group of wartime executive agencies possessing extraordinary powers: the Food Administration, Fuel Administration, Railroad Administration, War Trade Board, War Industries Board, and the Committee on Public Information. The body that came to exercise the greatest scope of power and functions was the War Industries Board, operating through its committees associated with war service committees organized by industrial trade associations. Under its director, Bernard M. Baruch, acting as a czar of industry, the WIB coordinated the industrial requirements of the American military services, the civilian agencies, and the Allies. The agency determined relative priorities of the various claims as well as the best methods of meeting them.

This machinery of conducting war established a phenomenal record of national achievement. It created a massive national army from rudimentary beginnings and organized a productive system that turned out a prodigious volume of materials and supplies for the benefit of the Allies and the United States. Because America was unprepared for the war, there were nevertheless serious deficiencies that were never mastered or else overcome very late. The United States had to depend on France for 75-mm and 155-mm guns, on Britain and France almost entirely for tanks and combat planes, on British ships for transporting 49 percent of the American soldiers to Europe.[54]

With the benefit of Woodrow Wilson's clear vision and patient leadership the United States in a time of world upheaval accomplished the hazardous passage from isolation to full participation in European and

53. Daniel R. Beaver, *Newton D. Baker and the American War Effort, 1917–1919* (Lincoln, Nebr., 1966), 50–109; March, *Nation at War*, 39–56.
54. Coffman, *War to End All Wars*, 38–42, 187–206.

world affairs. However reluctantly many Americans may have accepted the object lesson, the president's policies demonstrated that isolation was no longer a feasible premise for a United States that had reached maturity in an interdependent world. Wilson dedicated himself to keeping America at peace and bringing peace to war-torn Europe. When this endeavor failed, he led the United States through the war with resolute direction and rare idealism. He set his purposes high to make this "a Peoples' War, a war for freedom and justice and self-government among all the nations of the world." At the end he had taken his country and himself to a position of preeminence in the peace making. Few men have made a deeper imprint on the history of their country or the tendencies of their age.

Chapter Nine

THE WAR OF DECISION

1. THE GERMAN DRIVES

IN 1918 the pressures and strains of total war bore down with crushing force on the Central Powers. The superior weight of Allied power, vastly augmented by the participation of the United States, moved the titanic contest to a war of decision. The immobilization of the Western Front changed to a war of movement, and on the other fronts the allies of Germany collapsed from sheer exhaustion.

The Germans at the close of 1917 were no nearer a solution of their dilemma of ending the war in spite of their conquest of Russia and Romania. The conclusion of a general peace on the basis of the status quo ante or even the status quo ante minus Alsace-Lorraine would not have the acceptance of either the German right and the military or Britain and France. The alternative of holding to the strategic defensive could be expected at best only to postpone the inevitable defeat. Rather than consider either of these possibilities, Hindenburg and Ludendorff decided for a gambler's throw of all remaining resources into an offensive in the west on the grand scale. Given the circumstances inside Germany of military supremacy and the strength of conservative and nationalist forces, this choice appears to have been unavoidable.

Before peace was made with Russia, the supreme command had begun preparations for the spring offensive in the west. Since early November the transfer of troops to the west continued at the rate of ten divisions a month on the average from Russia, Romania, and Macedonia. Specially selected assault troops were intensively trained in the offensive methods perfected at the battles of Riga and Caporetto. The new tactics of penetration had the nature of an offensive in depth, whose main elements comprised an advance combat line fed constantly with additional troops; increased firepower of the infantry advance; infiltration around strong points; the attainment of surprise by a short but intensive artillery preparation; and a rolling barrage.

The high command never had a dominant and consistent strategic purpose throughout the spring campaign. The aim, governed by tactical considerations, was to deliver a surprise blow of such preponderant weight against a weak sector as would smash through the enemy's lines and move quickly to open warfare. For this goal the Germans chose a front of about fifty miles where the French and British armies joined, the Arras-St. Quentin–La Fère sector. The Germans carried out with great secrecy and on a massive scale preparations for the attack here with three armies, one of which was the victorious army of Caporetto fame. Colonel Bruchmüller from Riga and Caporetto arranged the artillery support largely of heavy and very heavy guns. By March 20 Ludendorff had completed a masterly feat of organization and logistic arrangements.[1]

The Germans struck with a numerical superiority of twenty divisions. On the other hand, the French had come to the bottom of their reserves, and their army was still nursing its recovery of fighting spirit from the Nivelle debacle. The British army in France had been weakened by the ordeal of Passchendaele and the provision of insufficient drafts. The Lloyd George government withheld reinforcements with the purpose of discouraging Haig from another Somme or Passchendaele. Although the British were adopting the German system of defense in depth, time and insufficient labor did not permit the construction of adequate defense works.[2]

The British were the least prepared in the sector of twenty-eight miles taken over from the French in January. A new organization, the Fifth Army under Sir Hubert Gough, held the right wing, covering this extension of line. Gough's whole front was the longest and thinnest of any held by the four British armies. Haig had disposed greater strength farther north to protect the Channel ports and the key position of Arras. Lloyd George was at odds with his commander-in-chief, and he had just maneuvered the replacement of Wully Robertson, the chief of the imperial general staff, with the more compliant General Sir Henry Wilson. The resistance of Pétain and Haig had prevented the Permanent Military Representatives of the Supreme War Council from creating a coalition reserve of thirty divisions.

1. See *Ludendorff's Own Story,* 2: 219–28; Hindenburg, *Out of My Life,* 329; Liddell Hart, *Real War,* 368; Karl Tschuppik, *Ludendorff* (Boston, 1932), 173–75. The last states that "considerations of time and terrain decided everything." Foerster, *Graf Schlieffen,* 272–76, rejects this view of tactical dominance and avers that Ludendorff acted entirely in the spirit and operational manner of Schlieffen.

2. *Haig's Despatches,* 178–79; Bonham-Carter, *Soldier True,* 314–15; Edmonds, *Short History of World War I,* 377.

Ludendorff unleashed the Michael offensive on March 21, after Bruch-müller's artillery delivered a hurricane bombardment of five hours. The weight of the German avalanche both in soldiers and in guns was more than double that of the Allied resistance. With this superiority and assistance from the morning fog and their own gas and smoke, the Germans overran the first position of the British all along the front by nightfall.

Contrary to the original operational plan for the two northern armies to roll up the British forces against the coastal ports after a breakthrough, the Germans encountered during the following days unexpected resistance by General Sir Julian Byng's army at the bastion of Arras. Likewise unexpectedly, the Eighteenth Army, providing flanking protection against the French, pushed ahead rapidly in the south to Péronne and across the Somme. After some hesitation Ludendorff altered plans with a major drive on Amiens against both the French and British in exploiting the Eighteenth Army's success. By that time it was too late for breaking the reinforced line of the Allies, and Ludendorff had to acknowledge that "the enemy's resistance was beyond our strength."[3]

Gough's army, bearing the brunt of the attack, could not stem the German rush. The front was split, and a gap of twenty kilometers opened between the British and French lines as Gough's hard-pressed troops were quickly driven behind the Somme. The French sent reinforcements, but their promised counterattacks were not forthcoming. Pétain, whom Haig found "very much upset, almost unbalanced and most anxious," ordered the concentration of French troops so as to protect Paris. This move would have left the British right flank uncovered and separated the two armies of the two Allies. Dire peril arose that the Germans would cut between them to fight the Allies in two separate battles, the British for the Channel ports and the French for Paris, threatening an eventual Dunkirk.[4]

In this extremity of British need for French reserves, Haig was driven to accept, even to seek, putting the supreme control of operations in France into the hands of "General Foch or some other determined general who would fight." The conference at Doullens on March 26 therefore charged Foch "with the coordination of the Allied Armies on the Western Front." A week later at Beauvais, Foch was entrusted with "the strategic

3. Liddell Hart, *Foch,* 281–82; *Ludendorff's Own Story,* 2: 231–32; Terraine, *Douglas Haig,* 419–20.
4. Blake, *Private Papers of Douglas Haig,* 297; Ducasse, Meyer, and Perreux, *Vie et mort des français,* 369–70; Liddell Hart, *Foch,* 268–70.

direction of military operations." At last on April 14, in the shadow of catastrophic defeat, it was agreed to recognize Foch as commander-in-chief of the Allied armies in France. Foch, radiating confidence, energy, and resolution, put an end to Pétain's panic and stopped the gathering of troops for the safeguarding of Paris. Further French divisions were sent to repair the breach and maintain an unbroken front.

The Germans in the south, however, captured Montdidier and advanced to a depth of forty miles at one point. The first German offensive had achieved a breakthrough, created a large bulge in the Allied front south of the Somme, and changed the stalemate of the past into open warfare. Nevertheless, Ludendorff had not realized a strategic objective.

The German plan of campaign was ultimately directed to destroying the British forces by a knockout blow. Pursuing this aim, the Germans launched their next action in the valley of the Lys in Flanders. Forced to a lesser scale by the recent drain of reserves, the Georgette attack of April 9 was conducted along the twelve-mile front from La Bassée to Armentières. The drive overwhelmed the weakest Allied sector of the front, which was occupied by a demoralized Portuguese division long overdue for rest and scheduled for relief the night of April 9. The Portuguese collapse opened a breach that widened to thirty miles and extended ten miles in depth.

The Germans broadened the front of attack northwards beyond Ypres as the British lines yielded. The British were in critical straits because of the heavy losses of March and Foch's delayed decision to provide substantial French reserves. Thrown back on his own thin, tired forces, Haig appealed to their spirit in the ringing words: "There is no other course open to us but to fight it out. Every position must be held to the last man: there must be no retirement. With our backs to the wall, and believing in the justice of our cause, each one of us must fight on to the end."[5]

The British managed under great strain to hold out with eventual aid. Foch, on realizing his mistaken estimate of German intentions and the peril in Flanders, sent nine French divisions, and the French took over part of the British line. The Belgians extended their line some three miles, nearly to Ypres. The British themselves sent reinforcements from Britain and a division each from Italy, Palestine, and Egypt. Freshwater inunda-

5. *Haig's Despatches*, 218; Liddell Hart, *Foch*, 294 ff., 305; Edmonds, *Short History of World War I*, 306.

tions were employed in defending the region from St. Omer to Dunkirk. The onslaught was checked by these measures and by much severe fighting on the part of the British.

On April 30 Ludendorff, finding that "further attacks promised no success," called a halt to an offensive that had achieved only a tactical victory in the creation of another, though considerably smaller, salient.[6] The two German offensives broke British offensive power for three months with the staggering toll of 240,000 casualties; the cost to the French was 92,000. For the gains OHL made, it suffered losses of 348,000 and deterioration in the German fighting machine.

The German high command deferred action against the British army until a diversionary offensive could draw off the French reserves in Flanders. Ludendorff chose the Chemin des Dames ridge toward Soissons for the third assault, again for tactical reasons, because the Allies were weak in that sector. The crown prince's group of armies opened the drive with a crushing superiority in weight on May 27. Swirling forward on a front of twenty-four miles, the irresistible German flood poured in the center over the Chemin des Dames barrier, the Aisne River, and to the Vesle some twelve miles forward at the end of the first day. Ludendorff revealed his strategic opportunism—indeed a strategic aimlessness—in being lured by the surprising ease of advance into a sustained push toward Paris.

The German drive rapidly broadened and deepened to engulf Soissons and reach the Marne and Château-Thierry. The German march created a second large salient, at the apex only twenty-seven miles from Paris. The spirited fighting of two American divisions in the defense and counterattacks at Château-Thierry and Belleau Wood helped to check the assault. The indomitable confidence and galvanizing energy of Foch and the visits of Clemenceau to the front inspired resistance.

The strengthened defense of the Allies stopped the German advance by June 6. The "brilliant success" of Ludendorff "volatized" fifteen Allied divisions and threatened Paris. Still the decisive battle was as much a chimera as ever, and strength failed to continue the opportunist advance. Time and offensive power were lost for resuming the Flanders struggle.[7]

Apart from further diversion of Allied reserves from Flanders, the fourth German drive was planned for the front between Montdidier and

6. *Ludendorff's Own Story*, 2: 242.
7. Ducasse, Meyer, and Perreux, *Vie et mort des francais*, 379, 381–83.

Noyon as an extension of the Chemin des Dames offensive to improve the salient resulting from that advance and, if possible, join it with the Somme salient. The French, learning in advance of the German intention, anticipated the attack with a counterbombardment and had a defending force nearly matching the Germans in size. The ebbing German assault, which began on June 9, pushed only beyond the French second position toward Compiègne. Ludendorff saw in the enemy strength and counterattacks no prospect but further casualties and ended the offensive on June 14.

During the next month Foch and Pétain expected an attack in Champagne and concentrated reserves there to meet it. Foch and Haig, however, were not deterred from continued planning for offensive action. In this they were encouraged by two noteworthy secondary operations. One was the capture of Hamel in the Amiens area by the Australian General Sir John Monash. This model attack of July 4 was based on the most intensive and thoroughly coordinated planning and time-table precision of execution. It obtained complete surprise by using tanks and avoiding preliminary bombardment. The success afforded a demonstration project for the coming great strike of August 8.[8]

The other was a limited action in which Mangin, the thrusting hero of Verdun, employed tanks and aircraft effectively to take the high ground that dominated the German railway communications through Soissons to the Marne. The ease of advance in this action of June 28–29 suggested to Foch an operation in spoiling the German drive by anticipation.

Before the final German assault, indications had appeared that the climactic intensity of the war was imposing an intolerable strain on the German bloc. On June 15 the Austrians commenced their last offensive in Italy, a pincers operation from the Trentino and along the Piave. It was stopped mainly by French and British divisions in the mountains and by Diaz with the aid of the RAF after the Austrians had crossed the Piave. The attacking forces withdrew with casualties of 142,000. The strategic planning and disposition of forces were faulty, but of more importance, the Austrians had embarked on an enterprise too large for their shrinking resources, numerically inferior to the enemy's infantry, guns, and aircraft. Their soldiers were undernourished and their transportation facilities inadequate.

8. See Terraine, *Douglas Haig,* 449–50, for an excellent account of the operation conducted by Monash.

The train of consequences from the wreck of the offensive led straight to the collapse of the Dual Empire. The troops lost faith in the direction of the war; many believed that the undertaking "was superficial and frivolous, but particularly prepared with overhaste." The crisis in confidence, along with shortages of food, clothing, and munitions, multiplied the number of desertions and ended the offensive power of the army. The Hungarian parliament publicly blamed the high command, and a clamor arose at Budapest for freeing the Hungarian troops from the orders of Austrian generals. This fiasco and the decline of the army gave stimulus to all the ethnic and antimonarchical forces destructive of the empire. At the same time the living conditions for the people in the cities worsened drastically. The bread ration in Austria was reduced in June by half, and the limits of endurance were approaching. The specter of dissolution and revolution hung over the Habsburg dominions.[9]

In Germany disillusion and pessimism were pervasive. The brilliant but illusory victories of the four drives made the front more difficult to defend by adding the three salients and some hundred kilometers. The blood drain of nearly 700,000 casualties since March prevented the covering of losses with the semiannual levy of recruits. News of drought and poor harvest prospects in Germany and occupied territory in the east depressed spirits in general headquarters and in Berlin. On June 24 the state secretary for foreign affairs, Richard von Kühlmann, stated in a Reichstag discussion, ". . . an end to the war can hardly be expected by means of purely military decisions alone without diplomatic negotiations."[10]

At home in Germany the nutritional deprivation in the cities and the failure of the military to end the war plunged the urban masses into despair and made them increasingly responsive to the agitation of the socialists. Such influences were transmitted to the front when the soldiers on leave visited their homes or communicated with their families. The soaring number of desertions caused Ludendorff to issue an order of June 23 imposing the death penalty for the offense.

These disruptive conditions and the dwindling store of reserves raised for the high command the torturous question whether to conduct another

9. Hantsch, *Berchtold,* 2: 826; Macartney, *Habsburg Empire,* 829; Kiszling, *Österreich-Ungarns Anteil am Ersten Weltkrieg,* 81, 83.

10. Müller, *Regierte der Kaiser?,* 384–97 passim; Hans Peter Hanssen, *Diary of a Dying Empire* (Bloomington, Ind., 1955), 287–93. Because of his statement, the general staff forced the resignation of Kühlmann on July 12. He was replaced by Admiral Paul von Hintze.

costly offensive. Uncertain as he was, but believing that Germany must continue the war or submit to humiliation, Ludendorff made the gambler's choice for another drive. In an immediate attempt to ease the situation of the forces in the Marne pocket, the Germans launched on July 15 a gigantic pincers movement by two attacks, twenty kilometers apart, on each side of Reims. The two attacks by the three armies of the crown prince were to converge on Epernay and Châlons. If these were successful, the army group in Flanders of Crown Prince Rupprecht of Bavaria would join with a strike against the British. The strategy ranked in scope next to the Schlieffen plan, with which the Germans had begun military action in 1914.

Foch and Pétain had expected the next German drive to come in the Marne area and assembled strength for a planned counteroffensive beginning on July 18. The French, learning from prisoners details of the time and place of the assault, anticipated the German bombardment with a counterfire that inflicted terrible losses on the enemy infantry massed in forward position for jumping off. The attack east of Reims was met with an effective defense in depth and was stopped cold at the French main position. By noon of July 16 Ludendorff faced the reality of crushing losses and ordered the troops there to go on the defensive.

The thrust from the Marne salient west of Reims carried six German divisions across the Marne four miles. Reims seemed in danger of falling before the drive could be parried by July 17. While conferring with Rupprecht on preparations then under way for the Flanders attack, Ludendorff received news of the French counteroffensive commenced on July 18. The advance of the Germans had exposed them in a vulnerable position beyond the Marne, and the French counteroffensive suddenly raised an agonizing strategic problem. The failure east of Reims and the French counteroffensive determined Ludendorff's decision. The night of July 20–21 the German troops withdrew across the Marne. The series of great German drives ended in a crisis for the German armies and a personal crisis of nerves for the dominant figure of the general staff.[11]

2. THE COUNTEROFFENSIVE OF THE ALLIES

The series of drives without strategic result had exhausted the German war machine. Through the attrition of the German army since March, the

11. Barnett, *Swordbearers*, 335–37; *Ludendorff's Own Story*, 2: 312.

rising number of American divisions in combat, and the reinforcement of the British army in France, the balance of forces on the Western Front had now swung in favor of the Allies. The numerical superiority in Allied troops would grow until it reached 35 percent by the end of hostilities. The Allies gained superiority in aircraft as well, and an overwhelming advantage in tanks. With the second battle of the Marne, the Allies seized the initiative and kept a firm grip on it for the remainder of the war.

In the middle of the resistance to the last German assault, Foch insisted that the French proceed with the offensive scheduled for July 18 and overrode Pétain's orders to postpone it. The counteroffensive was planned to win back the whole Marne-Soissons salient by an attack of two armies on each of its two faces. General Mangin, as ardent for battle as General Patton in the next world war, led the main assault at the base of the western side. The two French armies that attacked on the western face gained complete surprise through concealing their assembly in the woods southwest of Soissons and by depending on tanks rather than on preliminary bombardment for smashing the enemy's defenses. The German lines collapsed, and the two armies moved forward quickly more than four miles, more slowly the next day against the organization of German resistance. The two armies on the eastern side, engaged at first in containing the German push south of the Marne, could not take part in the offensive against the whole salient until July 20, when without benefit of surprise they made some gains.[12]

The four French armies had reduced the size of the salient and were exercising pressure all around its perimeter. The threat of closing the loop by Mangin's penetration at the base and the determination of future strategy after the failure of the Reims-Marne drive raised the most critical questions of command for the German headquarters. The ordeal of grappling with the implications of the implacable situation—that the initiative had passed to the Allies and Germany could not win the war—threw Ludendorff into a state of nerves and a paralysis of decision. The general acknowledged the military applicability of a proposal made by Fritz von Lossberg, a general who as chief of staff of various armies had had the widest experience in defensive fighting, for assuming a strategic defensive that would be conducted by means of a progressive retirement to a succes-

12. On the role of tanks, the "Cambrai key," in the counteroffensive, see Liddell Hart, *Tanks,* 1: 15, 172–73.

sion of carefully prepared positions. Ludendorff nevertheless could not make up his mind, for political reasons, to put it into effect. After he withdrew forces from the threatened area beyond the Marne, he floundered in a quandary while the situation of the two armies in the reduced salient increased in peril. The overwrought leader proffered his resignation to Hindenburg, who refused to accept it.[13]

Hindenburg apparently forced a decision, and Ludendorff ordered a withdrawal from the pocket to the straight and shortened line of its base. By strong, if costly, resistance the Germans at least kept the mouth of the pocket open long enough for the surviving forces to escape. On August 2 the Germans abandoned Soissons and by August 5 established themselves in prepared positions behind the Aisne-Vesle line.

So ended the second battle of the Marne. As decisive as the first, it saved Paris and removed any German expectation of resuming the battle of Flanders. The momentous reversal was clearly a turning point in the great conflict, a strategic victory that justified Pétain's prudent program of producing guns, tanks, aircraft, and munitions on a gigantic scale and waiting for the Americans. The battle was no less a vindication of Foch's offensive spirit and planning but only because at last the conditions of combat fitted his conceptions through Allied superiority in strength and the supply of tanks. The unreal war had ceased to exist; the war in the minds of the Allied generals henceforth coincided with the war on the ground.[14]

For the Germans the accumulation of more than a million casualties since March was irreparable. The military direction of the war was seriously impaired by Ludendorff's disturbed condition. Victory had taken its departing flight forever. The German drives demonstrated, however, that by strengthening the attack with surprise, a tremendous battering power of artillery, heavy mobile firepower of the advancing ground forces, and tactics of penetration Ludendorff had achieved a method of breaching the enemy's lines without the necessity of tanks.[15]

The rest of the war on the Western Front concerns the manner in which the implications of the Marne battle fully materialized: how the deteriora-

13. Fritz von Lossberg, *Meine Tätigkeit im Weltkrieg 1914–1918* (Berlin, 1939), 343–50. This is the most revealing source on Ludendorff's state of mind and thinking in the July military crisis.

14. On the Foch-Pétain program, see Painlevé, *Comment j'ai nommé Foch et Pétain*, 206–11, 216–17.

15. See Görlitz, *Der deutsche Generalstab*, 163; Foerster, *Graf Schlieffen*, 272–73.

tion of the German army rapidly continued; how the offensive planning of Foch and Haig was applied on a progressively larger scale, finally encompassing the end of the war in 1918; and how the new method of Allied attack, depending on surprise and the mass use of tanks, was executed with increasing success. This progress to the end was realized in three stages: the climactic battle of Amiens, a series of limited offensives from August 12 to September 26 for the purpose of disengaging France's strategic lateral railways, and the general offensive until the armistice.

Foch approved Haig's plans for attacking east of Amiens in a limited action designed to assure the maintenance of communications and gain more room in northern France. During May, June, and July operations on the British front had been limited to a minor character, while the Germans hurled themselves against the French. This diversion allowed the British an opportunity to complete the reconstitution of their armies into an effective fighting force. For the attack on the Amiens front the Monash masterpiece of July 4 provided a model demonstration of method and the expectation of success. Foch broadened the enterprise by assigning two French armies to assist, one to participate under Haig's direction and the other to join the attack on the right.[16]

In preparation, Rawlinson and his Fourth Army went to extreme lengths to achieve what expert military opinion has judged to have been "perhaps the most complete surprise of the war." He cloaked preparations under a cover of absolute secrecy, utilizing every resource of concealment and deception. The decisive air superiority of the Allies made possible greater air support than in any engagement of the war. The British sent into battle 420 fighting tanks, along with 120 supply tanks.[17]

Rawlinson's formidable array without preliminary bombardment swept forward from battle stations on August 8 under cover of a dense ground mist and behind a creeping barrage of shattering effect. The tank fleet of monsters lumbering behind the barrage in the predawn mist produced a catastrophic shock to the badly depleted German divisions in weak defenses. In the chief strike south of the Somme, where the tanks were most successful, the Australians and Canadians cut through the panic-stricken and insubordinate enemy troops, gaining in most places their final objective six to eight miles forward by early afternoon. The attackers opened

16. Liddell Hart, *Foch*, 339–48.
17. Terraine, *Douglas Haig*, 453–54; Liddell Hart, *Tanks*, 2: 174–75; Liddell Hart, *Real War*, 432.

a gap more than eleven miles wide, and resistance of the German infantry melted away with the surrender of troops in masses.[18]

The Germans rushed up reserves and formed a new line. The attack lost momentum and coherence after the brilliant initial success. On August 9 and the following day Haig's force advanced only a few miles until they confronted the old trench lines and craters of the Somme battlefield. The attack of the two French armies lacked the vigor of the British punch but extended the battle front twenty-five miles and ended with the occupation of Montdidier. The battle of Amiens, or the third battle of the Somme, closed on August 12.

The victory of new methods and new weapons "rubbed out" sixteen German divisions. The striking disparity in losses was symptomatic of the decay in the German army. Another sign was a group of soldiers returning to the rear who greeted a division coming up to attack with cries of "strike-breakers" and "war-prolongers." Ludendorff aptly caught the battle's grave significance for the German side in the oft-quoted sentence: "August 8 was the black day of the German army in this war." The general, who received a second blow to his poise and confidence in command, at last opened his eyes to the degeneration of the German army and the superiority of Allied power. The import of the Allied supply of tanks was brought home to him. Convinced that no strategic maneuver could save Germany from defeat, he realized that "the war must be ended" and so informed the kaiser. A crown council held at Spa on August 14 agreed that an initiative for peace negotiations should be taken but after the next military success.[19]

By way of political consequences the "black day of the German army" demolished the basis of Ludendorff's authoritarian regime, which rested on military success, and opened the way for the transfer of power to a parliamentary government.[20] The defeat gave impetus to the Austrian peace movement, notably the Austrian bid in September for a separate peace.

After Amiens the Germans took to the strategic defensive in the hope of crippling the will of the Allies to continue the war and of gaining a

18. *Haig's Despatches*, 258–63. On the role of tanks and aircraft in the battle, see Fuller, *Military History of the Western World*, 3: 284–97; Liddell Hart, *Tanks*, 1: 175–84.

19. *Ludendorff's Own Story*, 2: 326, 332–35; Barnett, *Swordbearers*, 349–53.

20. Arthur Rosenberg, *The Birth of the German Republic* (1931; reprint, New York, 1962), 237–38.

tolerable peace by negotiation. It was still technically possible to carry out an orderly withdrawal to a strongly organized defensive position along the Antwerp-Meuse line and thereafter to the borders of Germany while diplomacy was at work. The German army still numbered 2,500,000, and the Germans possessed the capability of delaying the Allies by planting the routes of advance with mines and shells to be detonated by time fuses of their invention. Such was the choice the professional expert Lossberg had urged in July, and Churchill believed would have inevitably led to a peace by negotiation.[21]

The German direction of the war, however, had declined too far for adopting a systematic and coolly reasoned plan of this character. The civilian leadership was too weak and confused; the supreme command had lost its nerve and professional detachment; confidence in the military leadership had faded away; reverberations of discontent with the political system grew more ominous; the evasion of responsibility for the impending catastrophe had begun. In place of a clearly determined and faithfully executed course along this line, German strategy in the west lacked a definite overall aim during the remainder of the war. The German army retreated now here, now there, subject to the pressure of the Allies.[22]

The Allied advance resumed with expanded attacks from August 20 on. Successively, the Allied armies forced Ludendorff to retire to the Somme line, turned the Somme line in a brilliant action of the Australians, drove the Germans back to the Hindenburg line, took the outer works of the Hindenburg system, eliminated the St. Mihiel salient, and pushed the Germans largely out of the salients acquired in their drives of 1918.

The German side had suffered irreplaceable losses and the Allies lighter ones than in any earlier offensive. Ludendorff refused to concentrate the waning energies of the army on creating a strong defensive barrier along the Antwerp-Meuse line, to which the German forces could retire. Acting like Falkenhayn before him, he persisted in bitter struggle to hold every foot of ground no matter how this bit into his dwindling reserves. Unable to adjust to the reality that Germany had lost the war, he conducted an unreal war in his own mind. The intensifying conflict between what he wanted to believe and what was the actual situation made of Ludendorff by September a "completely broken man,"

21. Churchill, *World Crisis*, 4: 510–12; Kielmansegg, *Deutschland und der Erste Weltkrieg*, 657.
22. Tschuppik, *Ludendorff*, 233, 240–43; Liddell Hart, *Strategy*, 214.

who was undergoing treatment by a nerve specialist. The army as a whole had abandoned faith in the high command and in the hope of victory. The high percentage of surrenders among the German casualties revealed the spread of rot.[23]

A key to Allied success in this phase was doubtless the tank. The Germans knocked out of action many tanks by means of their artillery, but the blunder in discounting tanks without mass production either of their own tanks or of effective antitank weapons was becoming ever more apparent.

Among other instruments of victory, both the British and French now had immense quantities of munitions available for the widening battles of the counteroffensive, which consumed ammunition on a prodigious scale, even more than Passchendaele. The Allied artillery was mastering the German, and the Allies dominated the air. Their planes cooperated closely with artillery and tanks in overpowering the enemy and conducted constant attacks on German troops behind the lines and the munitions production of the Rhineland. The Allies were applying with skill the lessons learned from the Germans in the tactics of penetration.[24]

Finally, the American presence hovered over the battlefield. The British army, fully reformed and thoroughly trained and seasoned, had borne the brunt of the fighting. But the specter of defeat was raised for the Germans most of all by the flood of American troops crossing the Atlantic to France. Ludendorff conceded that "America became the deciding factor in the war."[25]

The war on the Western Front ended with the Allied general offensive of convergent action, beginning on September 26. The architects of this drive to the finish were both Foch and Haig. Under Haig's influence and with the further Allied advance, Foch had changed his campaign plan by the end of August to a general offensive, by which the ultimate victory could be won in 1918 rather than in 1919. Foch, revealed at his best in this final effort, provided a directing center and his unremitting offensive spirit; Haig, the unshakable conviction that the character of the war had changed and a decision could "be obtained in the very near future" if the pressure was maintained on the Germans at every possible point without pause. The general offensive consisted of component attacks, each con-

23. See Görlitz, *Der deutsche Generalstab*, 166–67; Müller, *Regierte der Kaiser?*, 412; Kielmansegg, *Deutschland und der Erste Weltkrieg*, 656–57.

24. Terraine, *Douglas Haig*, 461–62; Blake, *Private Papers of Douglas Haig*, 324.

25. *Ludendorff's Own Story*, 2: 276.

certed with the others, converging on the great German salient that extended from Verdun to the sea.[26]

The Allied actions to overcome the successive defense systems of the Germans began with the assault of the Americans, supported by the French, on September 26 in the Meuse-Argonne sector. The attack formed the right arm of the vast pincers closing in on the great German salient. Its immediate objective was control of the German line of communications to France and Belgium running through Sedan and Mezières. The faults of insufficient and hasty planning because of Foch's insistence on changing abruptly from the St. Mihiel operation soon retarded the advance, though a bold flanking maneuver in the first part of October induced the Germans to withdraw from the thick Argonne forest. When these problems were solved, the Americans returned successfully to the offensive in November.[27]

In the face of cabinet warnings about the possibility of an expensive failure (such as Passchendaele), Haig conducted his armies in a combined movement toward Cambrai and St. Quentin that breached the extension of the Hindenburg line to the north and then opened the line itself to British possession. This was Haig's greatest moment of the war, justifying his confidence in subduing the Germans in 1918 and insuring his reputation as a commander. With the British capture of Cambrai and the French occupation of St. Quentin, the Allies broke through to open country stretching to the center of German communications at Maubeuge. Haig reported in his despatch: "The effect of the victory upon the subsequent course of the campaign was decisive."[28] A mixed force of Belgian and French divisions conducting the Flanders offensive quickly won the strategic Ypres ridge and, after disposing of transport and supply problems, compelled the Germans to retreat from the coastal cities to their defense position along the Scheldt River.[29]

After breaking the Hindenburg line and its extension to the north, the British armies in the center had to fight their way forward slowly. The Germans kept their battle front intact, retreating from one defense position to another. Before evacuation they carried out a systematic program of destruction and transport of war materiel and looted property to Germany.

26. See Blake, *Private Papers of Douglas Haig,* 326.
27. See Liddell Hart, *Foch,* 356–62, 377–82; Liddell Hart, *Real War,* 461–68.
28. *Haig's Despatches,* 285.
29. Falls, *Great War,* 410 ff.

The French in the center, along the Aisne and Ailette Rivers, benefited from the Allied blows along the arms of the pincers. Though French action was not vigorous, the Germans retired until by early October they had lost the last of the ground taken by Ludendorff's offensives of 1918. By the end of October the Allies were biting into the Scheldt River position of the Germans and its extension southward.

The German armies were still keeping a continuous front, often with desperate fighting. The Allied advance was encountering difficulties, most of all in maintaining communications and supply over the devastated area left behind by the retreating Germans. With the aim of speeding up the German retreat, Foch and Pétain planned an offensive in Lorraine. Before it could commence, the general offensive resumed at the beginning of November with decisive results.

The shower of misfortune on the Western Front and the news of Bulgaria's collapse deepened the crisis in the German command and in the Reich political situation. The overstrained Ludendorff behaved as if "on a bed of hot coals." He and Hindenburg, "like men who have buried their dearest hopes," frantically concluded that an armistice must be obtained at once if the German army was not to risk annihilation. On September 29 a conference with the kaiser at Spa accepted their view. The kaiser approved the proposal to appeal to President Wilson for an immediate armistice and peace negotiations. The kaiser agreed as well to a "revolution from above," inaugurated by a proclamation announcing the introduction of parliamentary government. On the night of October 3–4 the new cabinet of Prince Max of Baden, formed to introduce the democratic system, dispatched the note requesting the armistice.[30]

After these critical days Ludendorff recovered his nerve and a desire for further resistance, as the German army continued to retire without the front breaking up under the Allied hammering. Wilson's October notes in reply to Germany's peace offer revealed that the Allies would enter on an armistice only on conditions making it impossible for Germany to resume combat. Ludendorff, outraged at what seemed to him a demand for unconditional surrender, now advocated in governing counsels, along with Hindenburg, the continuance of fighting supported by a national uprising. The Reichstag and the new cabinet had more realistic ideas than this suicidal gesture. The cabinet induced the kaiser to dismiss Ludendorff

30. *Ludendorff's Own Story,* 2: 374–79, 383–84; Müller, *Regierte der Kaiser?,* 424; Tschuppik, *Ludendorff,* 247–60.

on October 26. Hindenburg resigned, but the kaiser declined to accept his withdrawal. The crisis in command was resolved with the appointment of General William Groener as the first quartermaster general, in place of Ludendorff. Groener was the former chief of the army railway department and the best equipped of all the Reich military leaders in economic and technical background, and doubtless in political sense as well. For the third time the chief figure in the OHL had been found wanting, and Germany ended as it began the war, under the necessity of replacing its broken military leadership.[31]

No less decisive than the defeat of Germany on land was the final victory at sea, by the mastery of the submarine threat. The vast three-pronged exertion of the Allies in coping with the U-boat—trade defense, the antisubmarine offensive, and economic adjustment to supply and shipping shortages—achieved a repulse of the enemy at the gates comparable to that of the second Marne. Even in the fall of 1917 this immense organization of Allied, above all British, effort and resources had brought about a turn in the deadly struggle on the brink of disaster. During 1918 the crucial contest went steadily against the Germans. The convoy system was improved and extended. The Germans could neither devise tactics nor produce enough submarines to penetrate this shield. The tale of their frustration and defeat is told by the fall in British tonnage losses from 545,000 at the peak to under 200,000 per month during most of 1918, and finally to 59,000 in October just before the armistice. The decided improvement in the shipping situation was already apparent in the second quarter of the year, when the world's construction of ships exceeded losses for the first time since 1914.[32]

Corresponding to this change, the peril to the merchantman was hurled back at the U-boat itself. During the year the increasing efficacy of the Allied offense first transformed the Dover Straits into a death gauntlet for the U-boats and blocked the passage completely by August; forced the Flanders U-boat flotillas to withdraw from their bases; by mining virtually closed the German Bight to submarine transit; made the east coast of Britain nearly as dangerous as Dover; and in the Mediterranean carried the war against the U-boats to success.[33]

31. See further, below, pp. 379–80.
32. Admiralty, *Merchant Shipping (Losses)*, 162; Fayle, *Seaborne Trade*, 3: 397, 467; Corbett and Newbolt, *Naval Operations*, 5: 336–37.
33. Grant, *U-Boats Destroyed*, 93–94, 130–33; Corbett and Newbolt, *Naval Operations*, 5: 299, 337–39.

Under these conditions the efficiency and morale of the U-boat service were sharply reduced. The submarine fleet deteriorated technically from the stress of the wear and tear of continuing operations and the longer cruises through the North Sea. Throughout the year the Allies destroyed sixty-nine U-boats, and the number sunk and put out of action surpassed the number made available for service. The quality of the crews declined, and they were subjected to intolerable strain. The U-boats began to return from cruise without having discharged some or any of their torpedoes. These signs marked the clear defeat of a revolutionary weapon utilized in a grand strategy for eliminating by maritime and economic warfare the citadel and mainspring of the Allied coalition.[34]

3. THE COLLAPSE OF GERMANY'S ALLIES

The German decision to seek an armistice had been strongly influenced by the collapse of the other Central Powers. For their part they were morally ready to end the war after Germany's black day of August 8, and the ensuing defeat telegraphed a message to them that Germany's military power was sinking rapidly. The first of the Reich's allies to break down and conclude an armistice was Bulgaria on the Macedonian front.

The entry of Greece into the war in 1917 and the replacement of the controversial commander Sarrail by General Adolphe Guillaumat prepared the way for more active operations in this theater during 1918. The Venizelos government made seven divisions available for the motley army of Macedonia. Guillaumat became an eager advocate of a general offensive and set out to train the Greek divisions. Two of them won a dashing success against the salient Skradi Legen in the Bulgarian line west of the Vardar River (May 30), which tested and encouraged the Greek army.

The German drives of 1918 delayed the launching of Guillaumat's cherished project and caused his sudden recall to France. He was succeeded by Franchet d'Esperey, a hard-driving general known to the British in the Balkans as "desperate Frankie." Thanks to the repulse of the German menace and in no small part to the zealous support of Guillaumat back in France, the numerous obstacles to the general attack were cleared away. The Supreme War Council at the end of July decided on a general advance on all fronts of the war, and the offensive in Macedonia was set for the middle of September. The well-equipped Allied forces, forming

34. Grant, *U-Boats Destroyed*, 141, 145–46; Spindler, *Der Handelskrieg*, 5: 341.

an international army of twenty-six divisions, attacked from a battle line running just north of the Gulf of Valona to Monastir, then eastwards to Lake Doiran, and thence southeasternly in the valley of the Struma. The defense of the Macedonian line by the Austrian, German, and Bulgarian troops could no longer hold against a carefully organized attack. After the Allied offensive opened in France, the Germans withdrew all except three battalions. The Bulgarian troops, following six years of war, were so weary of fighting and so demoralized that they frequently deserted. Shortages of food, clothing, and munitions plagued them. Bulgaria's war casualties of 100,000 killed, 150,000 wounded, and a large number of prisoners represented an appalling sacrifice for its small population. The Bulgarian command disliked the German ally, attributing to Germany the failure to destroy the Balkan army of the Entente and the resulting burden on the Bulgarians of Macedonian defense in 1918. Germany was doubly blamed for not having supplied sufficient aid under the military convention.[35]

The war had never been popular in Bulgaria, except for its means of obtaining revenge on Serbia and regaining territory lost in the last Balkan War. When Germany paid scant regard to Bulgaria's claim in the Dobruja in making peace with Romania, the public was embittered. The government underwent a corresponding change. King Ferdinand supplanted Vasil Radoslavov, the chief proponent of the German alliance, in June 1918 with the premier Alexander Malinov, whose cabinet was favorably disposed toward the Allies.[36]

The Allied general attack commenced on September 15. French and Serb troops made the main thrust in the center west of Monastir, while British and Greek forces struck to the east around Lake Doiran. The blow in the center was brilliantly successful. The French and Serbs broke through the Bulgarian position in three days, and the Serb troops, fighting in their own country, were irresistible. Rushing on to reach the Vardar, they cut the Bulgarian armies in two and severed the communications between the Bulgarians and Germany. The advance was widened by French and Greek troops, and north of Monastir the bulk of a Bulgarian army surrendered in the field. The British and Greeks made slower prog-

---

35. See Carl Mühlmann, *Oberste Heeresleitung und Balkan im Weltkrieg* (Berlin, 1942), 209–21, on the contention between the German and Bulgarian commands over reducing the size of the German forces on the Macedonian front.
36. Pomiankowski, *Der Zusammenbruch des Ottomanisches Reiches*, 379–80.

ress to the east but, also breaking through, they entered Bulgaria and took Strumica. The Bulgarian army, fighting halfheartedly, shriveled away, and the bombing of the fading troops contributed to the rout.

The agony for Bulgaria ended with precipitate speed. The government suddenly informed President Wilson that it accepted the Fourteen Points. On September 26 Bulgarian spokesmen asked for an armistice, and Franchet d'Esperey dictated terms at once.[37] The armistice signed at Salonika on September 29 stipulated conditions essentially of unconditional surrender, including the right of Allied occupation of any strategic point desired. The Bulgarian parliament accepted the terms, but Ferdinand preferred to abdicate in favor of his son, crowned as Boris III, rather than do so.[38]

The Allies quickly took advantage of this decisive turn in Balkan affairs. Some of the Allied troops (mainly British) moved eastward and ultimately reached Constantinople. Others (French and British) advanced to the Danube to protect the reentry of Romania into the war and prepared for a march into Hungary. Still others (chiefly Serb, but some French) headed northward and recovered Macedonia and the rest of Serbia, entering Belgrade on November 1. Further west the Austrian troops were forced out of Albania, and the Italians entered Scutari on October 31.[39]

Thus in a little more than six weeks the entire Balkan peninsula was liberated. The Allies were in a position to attack Austria-Hungary from the rear. This was not necessary, for upon news of the Bulgarian armistice the Austrian and German leaders knew that the war was lost. The war had begun over a Balkan incident; it was appropriate that the beginning of its end should also take place in the Balkans.

Since the Austrian fiasco at the Piave, the degeneration of the Austrian army kept pace with the progress of dissolution and the sharpening eco-

37. For the Bulgarian effort to obtain American mediation, see Seymour, *Intimate Papers,* 4: 57–60.

38. On the negotiations and terms of the armistice, see Frederick Maurice, *The Armistices of 1918* (London, 1943), 14–15; for the text of the armistice convention, ibid., 84–85.

39. Having occupied Valona at the end of 1915, the Italians advanced to the London line of 1913 early in 1917. They moved into Epirus after the deposition of King Constantine of Greece and proclaimed an Italian protectorate over Albania. At the armistice of November 3 with Austria-Hungary, they held most of the coastal towns of Albania except Scutari, which was occupied by an inter-Allied army under a French general. On November 18 the Albanians proclaimed their independence at Tirana. See the following articles in the Revue d'histoire de la guerre mondiale: C. Vidal, "En marge de la Grande Guerre: l'Italie et l'Albanie," 16 (1938): 270–94, 337–67; J. Ancel, "L'Albanie méridionale en 1918," 17 (1939): 51–60, 170–88.

nomic crisis within the empire. The hungry, war-weary soldiers were depressed and anxious to go home, especially when revolution impended. The Austrian government was making peace bids, and almost at the stroke of twelve the emperor announced (October 16) the introduction of a federal state within the Austrian portion of the Dual Empire. The supreme command was preparing to withdraw from Venetia. Adding to the confusion was the demand of the Hungarian government that its soldiers be sent home. On October 23 companies of the non-German nationalities began to drop out of the army on their own.

The Italian commander Diaz, demanding large numbers of American troops and free munitions from Britain and France, held back from taking the offensive, regardless of these conditions in Austria and the pressure of Foch and the Supreme War Council. The continued defeat of the Germans in August and September, the collapse of Bulgaria, and the manifest disintegration within the Dual Empire convinced the Italian government that Italy must be in at the kill if it was not to risk losing the fruits of victory. Diaz organized a triple assault: on the Piave, against Monte Grappa in the north and center, and at Asiago in the mountains. The Italians aimed to break through on the Piave to Vittorio Veneto, splitting the Austrian forces on the Piave from those in the Trentino; then the latter would be rolled up in a wheeling movement to the north, while the communications of the Austrians on the river front were severed.

The Italian attack, starting on October 23, did not cross the Piave until the 27th, against the desperate resistance put up by the Austrian "array of scarecrows and skeletons." The offensive was spearheaded by five British and French divisions and materially aided by the RAF's rain of bombs and bullets. Carrying out the operational plan, the Allies broke through the courageous Austrian defense (mostly by Austro-Germans) to Vittorio and in the north to Trent and Udine.[40]

The collapse of Vienna's imperial power and the advance of the revolution of the nationalities recoiled on the armies at the front. When the Budapest parliament proclaimed a separate Hungarian state, two Hungarian divisions near Asiago refused to fight further. The mutiny spread to other Hungarian troops and to Slavic units. The fleet at Pola mutinied, and its commander, Admiral Nicholas Horthy, by Vienna's authority,

40. For a full account of the battle, see R. Moreigne, "L'effondrement militaire de l'Autriche-Hongrie," *Revue d'histoire de la guerre mondiale,* 9 (1931): 234–56, 368–91. Also Fuller, *Military History of the Western World,* 3: 308–18.

handed it over to the new government of the Serbs, Croats, and Slovenes.[41]

The emperor Karl had pursued the mirage of peace since his accession in November 1916. On August 14 the emperor, together with his foreign minister, Burián, and commander-in-chief, Arz von Straussenburg, urged on the kaiser and Ludendorff at Spa the necessity of speedy and decisive action to end the war. When their proposal was resisted by the Germans, Burián sent a separate peace note to all the belligerent governments on September 14. The approach was rebuffed by both Wilson and the Allies.[42]

The Austrians eagerly joined the Germans on October 4 in sending simultaneous notes to the Entente governments proposing an armistice and the conclusion of peace on the basis of the Fourteen Points. The Vienna cabinet of common affairs recognized that negotiation on the basis of the Fourteen Points would not be unfavorable for Austria-Hungary in many respects. Concern, however, was expressed in cabinet discussion about the application of Points IX (readjustment of the Italian boundary) and X (provision for autonomous development of the constituent nationalities).[43]

Wilson's delayed reply of October 18 declared that because of intervening events he was "no longer at liberty to accept a mere 'autonomy' of these peoples as a basis of peace." The reply produced a shock, for it indicated that the component nationalities would themselves judge what terms with the Vienna government would satisfy their national aspirations.

In the maelstrom of disintegration, the emperor appointed on October 25 a new cabinet, in which Burián was replaced by Count Julius Andrássy, son of the Andrássy who had negotiated the Austro-German alliance of 1879. He became common minister for Austro-Hungarian foreign affairs just when the common empire of the multinational provinces ceased to exist.[44] Andrássy accepted Wilson's position, appealing for an immediate armistice and a separate peace.[45]

41. Kiszling, *Österreich-Ungarns Anteil am Ersten Weltkrieg,* 92.

42. Reinhold Lorenz, *Kaiser Karl und der Untergang der Donaumonarchie* (Graz, 1959), 483–93; Victor S. Mamatey, *The United States and East Central Europe* (Princeton, 1957), 319–21.

43. Austria-Hungary, Ministerrat für gemeinsame Angelegenheiten, *Protokolle des gemeinsamen Ministerrates der österreichisch-ungarischen Monarchie* (Budapest, 1966), 688–92.

44. On October 16 the Hungarian government had pronounced a personal union only as existing between Austria and Hungary under the emperor Karl.

45. See Lewis Namier, "The Downfall of the Hapsburg Monarchy," in *Vanished Supremacies* (London, 1958), 153, 157–59; Lorenz, *Kaiser Karl,* 524–26.

Before diplomacy could bring forth a reply, the pressing appeal of the high command for urgent action carried the day with the Austrian government, and a direct approach was made to the Italians at the front for an armistice. The terms, dictated by the Supreme War Council, were passed to the Austrian armistice commission on November 1. Concurrently, a new Hungarian government, under Michael Károlyi, declared the neutrality of Hungary and ordered the Hungarian units still in the field to lay down their arms and return home. The armistice was signed on November 3 at Villa Justi near Padua. Until it became technically effective on November 4, the Italians took over 300,000 prisoners among the unresisting remnants of the broken Austrian army. This belated demonstration of military ardor and of the continued progress of Italian arms won for Italy a show of complete victory and a warrant for satisfaction at the peace settlement.[46]

The armistice terms, in Clemenceau's pungent phrase, "left the breeches of the emperor and nothing else." The usual provisions required immediate demobilization (of a nonexistent army), evacuation of occupied areas, surrender of military materiel, surrender or retirement of the fleet. The Allies gained the right to use Austro-Hungarian territory for military operations and to occupy it up to certain specified lines. Thus the Italians were able to obtain control of most, but not quite all, of the territory that they hoped to win in the peace settlement.[47]

The Romanians were even later than the Italians in garnering the prizes of victory. On November 11 Romania enacted a reprise in declaring war again on the Central Powers and advancing into Hungary. The now independent Hungary of declared neutrality no longer had an army and could offer no resistance. Károlyi asked at Belgrade for the intercession of the Allied commander Franchet d'Esperey on the ground that Hungary was friendly to the Allies. Treated sternly by the French chieftain, he was forced to conclude an armistice that permitted the Romanians to occupy Transylvania and part of the Banat of Temesvar, while allowing the Serbs and French to move up to Pecs and the Drave River. The political consequences of this armistice became evident in the final peace settlement.[48]

46. Lorenz, *Kaiser Karl*, 538–45. For the Austrian objection to the delay of twenty-four hours, see the documents in "L'armistice de Villa Justi et la cessation des hostilités austro-italiennes," *Revue d'histoire de la guerre mondiale*, 12 (1934): 61–72.
47. The protocol of the armistice is in Maurice, *Armistices of 1918*, 87–90, and Harry R. Rudin, *Armistice, 1918* (New Haven, 1944), 406–09.
48. Technically, the armistice with Hungary was a "Military Convention Regulating the Conditions Under Which the Armistice Signed Between the Allies and Austria-Hungary Is To Be Applied in Hungary." For the text, see Maurice, *Armistices of 1918*, 91–93.

After the fall of Bagdad in March 1917, the next significant strikes against the Turks were in Palestine and Syria. At the beginning of 1917 the British crossed the Palestine frontier from the defense position established at El Arish in 1916 and moved on Gaza, the gateway to Palestine, in March and April only to meet with costly repulses. London was stirred to send out from France a new commander, Sir Edmund Allenby, a forceful campaigner known as "the Bull." By way of compensating for the crises and failures in the west, Lloyd George called on Allenby to capture Jerusalem before Christmas. He received reinforcements, including two divisions from Salonika, until he possessed a decided superiority in men and arms over Falkenhayn's two opposing Turkish armies.

Allenby's offensive, launched on October 31, drove the Turks back along the entire Gaza-Beersheba line. His forces took Jaffa on November 16 and then beat down stubborn opposition in the hills around Jerusalem. When Allenby entered the city on December 11, Lloyd George had his political showpiece with two weeks to spare, even though victory yielded no great strategic benefit in the overall conduct of the war.

In 1918 the conquest of the remainder of Palestine and the move into Syria were delayed by the draft of two divisions on Allenby's manpower for reinforcing the front in France against the German onslaughts. The enemy now deployed one army entirely and another largely in Palestine under the command of Liman von Sanders, who, after having headed the defense of Constantinople, replaced Falkenhayn in March 1918. A third Turkish army was further east, in the Transjordan, fighting the Arabs and guarding the Hejaz railway. The Turkish soldiers, outnumbered five to one by the British, were half-starved men in rags and tatters, frequently sick, exhausted for lack of leave. Amply supplied only with enemy propaganda, they were short of infantry munitions, and their animals short of forage. When the decisive battle came in September, rampant desertion and lack of replacements had shrunk the strength of divisions to 1,200–1,600 rifles. Both army and people had lost the will to continue the war.[49]

Allenby's campaign of 1918 was materially assisted by the progress of the Arab revolt and the growing activity of the Arab army of Emir Feisal, the son of King Hussein. In 1917 this army, transferred to the command of Allenby, covered the right flank of the British and, after the capture of

49. Mühlmann, *Das deutsch-türkische Waffenbündnis im Weltkriege,* 214–30; Pomiankowski, *Der Zusammenbruch des Ottomanischen Reiches,* 381–83.

Wejh and Aqaba, operated against the Turks up to the Dead Sea and the Hejaz railway, which extended from Damascus to Medina. In this area the Arabs captured outposts and garrisons. The constant depredations on the Hejaz railway line, expanded northward in 1918, made a good deal more difficult the Turkish problem of supply and, along with the siege of Medina by Hussein's followers, kept the Turks from withdrawing their troops from Medina and other stations to join the armies in Palestine and the Transjordan. Feisal's men extended contact to Syria, where they agitated in favor of revolt and strengthened relations with local tribes.[50]

T. E. Lawrence, an intelligence officer attached to the British organization in Egypt, went as an adviser to assist Feisal's men in January 1917. This aficionado of Middle Eastern antiquities and things Arab spoke Arabic and took pains to dress like an Arab. His main purpose, and that of the Arab Bureau in Cairo he served, was not, however, the realization of the national independence of the Arabs but the utilization of the Arab revolt to achieve British victory in the Middle East and to bring the area under the postwar control of Britain. He soon enlarged his role in becoming the main tie between the British and the Arabs, as well as the personal emissary between Feisal and Allenby. Lawrence helped extend Arab operations to the Transjordan. The "Prince of Mecca" dramatized his Arabian activities to the point of creating his own legend.[51]

In September Allenby resumed the drive against the Turks. With the participation of Lawrence, the Arabs operating east of the Jordan conducted demolition raids on the vital railway around Dera and then captured this junction center of the line from Damascus to the Hejaz from which a branch reached to Haifa on the coast. The action, completed by September 27, severed the communications of the Turks and blocked their retreat northwards. Allenby's infantry struck west of the Jordan on September 19, pinning the Turks in a wheeling movement against the hills

50. Mousa, *T. E. Lawrence,* 66–177; Charles Edmonds (pseud.), *T. E. Lawrence (of Arabia)* (New York, 1936), 59–96 passim.
51. The figure of Lawrence and his part in the Arab revolt are a matter of sharp controversy, in a considerable literature on the subject. See the discussion in the "Bibliographical Essay" of this book. Among the contrasting versions are the early contribution to the Lawrence legend by Robert Graves, *Lawrence and the Arabs* (London, 1927); the demolition attack of the myth by Richard Aldington, *Lawrence of Arabia* (London, 1955); the critical scrutiny against the achievement of the Arabs themselves by Mousa, *T. E. Lawrence;* and the recent study of Lawrence in John E. Mack, *A Prince of Our Disorder* (Boston, 1976), treating his life predominantly from a psychiatric standpoint while casting him in the traditional role of the heroic figure in the Arab revolt.

and at the same time opening a passage along the coast for the cavalry. Through the opening, Allenby sent 15,000 desert cavalry to reach the Jordan at Beisan and seize this center of the Haifa railway. The masterly operation of the old cavalry officer Allenby was one of the very few successful cavalry actions of the war. The horse cavalry was effectively supplemented with armored cars. The RAF completely controlled the skies against the inferior German aviation. Thus British infantry, cavalry, and air cooperated with striking success in annihilating Liman's armies west of the Jordan. Thereafter Allenby's men crossed the Jordan and occupied Amman.

The British moved northwest of Jordan, and the Arabs advanced to the east. The British and Feisal's forces entered Damascus on October 1. The military breakdown and confusion—even evasion of fighting and straggling—was shocking in Liman's picture of it. The flight of the retreating Turks was racked by the demolitions of the Arabs and attacks of Bedouins; the population in towns and cities was hostile, as the people joined the Arab movement. From Damascus the British and Arabs swept on to Aleppo by October 26, at which time the Turks had sued for an armistice. Indian, Australian, New Zealand, African, and Arab troops had participated in the campaign.[52]

The British campaign in Mesopotamia had not contributed to Allenby's crushing defeat of the Turks in Palestine. After the fall of Bagdad the British concentrated on gaining control of the upper Euphrates and Tigris valleys. In the areas cleared of the Turks, the British expended much time and effort in building railroads, pacifying the country, establishing order amidst the prevailing anarchy, organizing a modern civil administration, and attempting with little result to raise and train levies of the Arabs for the British forces. From early 1918, Whitehall deliberately cut down the military investment in this political but hardly strategic theater.

The Mesopotamian command was distracted, moreover, by a sideshow within a sideshow. The fall of Russian power in the Caucasus and Persia, resulting from the Bolshevik revolution, set boiling a witches' cauldron of contention among Turks, Germans, and the British for the domination of the area and more particularly for control of Baku and its oil fields. The Turks embarked on another one of Enver Pasha's grandiose political and

52. Liman von Sanders, *Five Years in Turkey,* 268–320. As written from the British side, see the excellent brief account in Falls, *Great War,* 396–402, and his longer version in the British official history, *Military Operations: Egypt and Palestine,* vol. 2 (London, 1928).

strategic schemes in moving with military strength into and beyond the Transcaucasian Union of Georgia, Azerbaijan, and Armenia, which had been formed following the treaty of Brest-Litovsk. The British set out to build a line of communication through Persia to the Caspian, supported by the base in Mesopotamia. They were lured by the aim of driving the Turks out of the Transcaucasian Union and organizing it as a buffer state for the protection of India against an expedition of Germans and Turks. The madcap intervention of the British in the Caucasus and northern Persia was an incredible folly, planned by those far from the scene who had no appreciation of the problems involved in maintaining a line of communications and supply over a thousand miles long. London, as well, greatly exaggerated the threat to India.[53]

When Allenby destroyed the Turkish armies in Palestine, the absorption of transport and troops in the Baku enterprise kept the Mesopotamian Expeditionary Force from moving forward until October 23, and then it advanced only up the Tigris, where most of the Turkish troops had withdrawn south of Mosul. In a week of operations the British outflanked the Turkish army and brought cavalry around to its rear. The Turks were compelled to surrender on October 30, and the fall of Mosul and its oil fields on November 1 completed the delivery of Mesopotamia to the British.

The Young Turk cabinet that had taken Turkey into the war was brought down on October 13 by the catastrophe in Palestine and the advance of the victorious Allied troops on Constantinople. The Young Turks disbanded their party, and a new chapter began in the political history of Turkey. The new government rejected the unfortunate attempt of the Young Turks to solve the problem of the Ottoman Empire's survival in an alliance with Germany and reverted instead to the traditional policy of seeking the friendship and protection of the British. An approach was made to the British naval commander in the Aegean for a separate peace.

The British were ready themselves to deal separately with the Turks. Since the British had borne by far the main burden of conquering the Turks, they were determined, as the eastern question entered a new phase, that British influence should be predominant among the Allies in the

53. Mühlmann, *Das deutsch-türkische Waffenbündnis im Weltkriege,* 195, 205–12; Pomian-kowski, *Der Zusammenbruch des Ottomanischen Reiches,* 359–75; Barker, *Neglected War,* 447–53.

Middle East. Symptomatic of this intention, the British, with the cooperation of the Turkish envoys, kept the conduct of the armistice negotiations
entirely in their own hands. The exclusion of the French produced a
strong exchange of recriminations between Lloyd George and Clemenceau.[54]

The armistice signed on October 30 aboard the battleship *Agamemnon*
off the island of Lemnos stipulated these principal terms: the occupation
of Constantinople by the Allies, the opening of the Straits and Black Sea
to Allied vessels, Allied use of Turkish territory for further military operations in case of need, and the severance of relations between Turkey and
the other Central Powers. The Allies were permitted the continued occupation of the Arab lands they had conquered. The Allied armies were
welcomed by the Turkish people, who, trusting in the ideas and diplomacy
of President Wilson, believed that a new era was about to begin. Enver
Pasha, his grand designs having crumpled, fled with his chief colleagues
to foreign countries. By mid-November an Allied fleet sailed through the
Dardanelles and anchored in the Golden Horn. In the same month an
Allied force, mainly British, occupied Constantinople. The Turkish capital
remained under an international regime for four years.[55]

The extensive military operations in the Middle East had caused a
constant drain on the Allied war effort in the west and the Balkans. The
shipping necessary to sustain the troops and bases in this theater, particularly to transport the forage of the animals, made more acute the shipping
crisis of the Allies. It is generally agreed that the original objectives of
protecting Egypt and the Persian oil sources, as well as encouraging the
revolt of the Arabs, could have been satisfied by efforts of much smaller
scale and cost. The campaigns were never anything more than lesser
sideshows that became an end in themselves, largely political in character,
of providing a victory for the Allies somewhere when it could not be
gained where it counted and of achieving certain postwar aims.[56]

The political involvements originating from the wartime connection
with the Middle East were to torment Britain with endless political difficulties in future years. On November 2, 1917, the British government issued
the Balfour Declaration, by which Britain promised to facilitate "the

54. Lloyd George, *War Memoirs,* 6: 3312–15; Maurice, *Armistices of 1918,* 208–10.
55. The text of the armistice convention is in Maurice, *Armistices of 1918,* 85–87, and in
Rudin, *Armistice, 1918,* 410–11. See Ziemke, *Die neue Türkei,* 77–79.
56. See Wilson, *Loyalties,* 271, 273.

establishment in Palestine of a national home for the Jewish people." The statement expressed Britain's clear understanding "that nothing shall be done which may prejudice the civil and religious rights of the existing non-Jewish communities in Palestine." This undertaking to meet the aspirations of the Zionist movement for a Jewish state gave rise to acute antagonism between Jews and Arabs, which caused incessant turmoil in the Middle East.

The Balfour Declaration and subsequent steps in its implementation were construed by the Arabs to violate the pledges of independence and self-government given by the British. The Arabs interpreted in the same way the Sykes-Picot agreement of 1916 on a future sphere for the British in Mesopotamia and one for the French in Syria. The Arabs could only wonder to what extent the peace settlement of the Allies would follow the intent of the Sykes-Picot agreement or would adhere to the declaration issued by the British and French on November 7, 1918. The declaration stated that they desired "the establishment of national governments and administrations deriving their authority from the initiative and free choice of the indigenous populations."

4. THE END OF THE WAR

After the second battle of the Marne it was only a matter of time until Germany sued for peace. The civilians indeed had already taken initiatives toward peace in the Reichstag peace resolution of July 1917 and the peace feelers extended the British by the foreign secretary Kühlmann.[57] In the authoritarian military state of Ludendorff's supremacy no hope existed, however, of commencing serious negotiations until the supreme command decided it was time for reasonable proposals or until a revolution occurred. The progress of military defeat and steps toward an armistice thus moved along together in linkage with the political revolution.

The staff officers were by no means of the same mind concerning peace negotiations. A number of higher or extremely able staff officers believed that Germany should have moved for peace earlier in the year 1918 than after the black day of Amiens on August 8.[58] Ludendorff and Hindenburg

57. See below, pp. 465–66.
58. These officers included the crown prince, his chief of staff, General Count von der Schulenburg, the staff officer Colonel Albrecht von Thaer, and the young staff officer Captain Ludwig Beck (the future chief of the Reichswehr staff), who considered before the spring offensives that Germany should seek a compromise peace; Groener, the successor of Luden-

were far from thinking along these lines. Ludendorff, his nerves in a state of shock since July 20, was loath to take any peace step lest it react adversely on the army, the enemy, Germany's allies, the home front, and his stature as a military leader. His policy of "the strategic defensive," generated from political and personal rather than purely professional considerations, was committed "to give up no foot of ground without a stubborn fight."[59] This costly policy of wearing down the will of the enemy to continue the war stemmed from an illusion regarding the relative strength of the two sides and the possible choices before Germany.

The ominous defeat of August 8 gave the first rude jar to this world of fantasy. Ludendorff made the significance of the event sufficiently clear to the kaiser for him to conclude: "We are at the end of our strength. The war must be ended."[60] The consequent crown council at Spa on August 14 was conditioned by Ludendorff's inner conflict between some recognition of Germany's grave position and the reluctance to acknowledge to the civilian leaders the urgency of diplomatic action for ending the war. Hindenburg spoke of the necessity of shifting from the offensive to defensive operations, but the generals kept to their creed of putting only "perfectly pure wine" before the civilian leadership. Ludendorff complained about the poor spirit and discipline at home and the weakness of the government in combating defeatist and treasonable tendencies. More directly, he blamed the home authorities for not providing more recruits and for not suppressing criticism of the conduct of the war. Ludendorff had begun the shifting of blame to scapegoats for the failure of himself and the supreme command; the long process of creating the stab-in-the-back *(Dolchstoss)* legend was under way.

The conference never grappled with the nub of the problem that a lost

---

dorff, holding that a serious move for a compromise settlement should have preceded any offensive in 1918; Hoffmann, who would have had the government begin peace negotiations after the March offensive was broken off without strategic success; Colonel Max Bauer, a versatile and gifted officer who had worked with Groener in the direction of war production; Major Alfred Niemann, the liaison of OHL with the kaiser, and other staff officers, especially the younger ones, who were persuaded after the July reversal that Germany must act at once for peace. See Wolfgang Foerster, *Generaloberst Ludwig Beck: Sein Kampf gegen den Krieg* (Munich, 1953), 17; Groener, *Lebenserinnerungen,* 424–25; Hoffmann, *War Diaries,* 2: 231; Siegfried A. Kaehler, "Zur Beurteilung Ludendorffs im Sommer 1918," in *Studien zur deutschen Geschichte des 19. und 20. Jahrhunderts* (Göttingen, 1961), 247; Alfred Niemann, *Kaiser und Revolution* (Berlin, 1928), 28–32.

59. Wolfgang Foerster, *Der Feldherr Ludendorff im Unglück* (Wiesbaden, 1952), 43.
60. Niemann, *Kaiser und Revolution,* 43–45.

war had to be liquidated quickly. The dark reality was so veiled over that the conference came to a vague and inconclusive decision that a "beginning must be made for reaching an understanding with the enemy at the proper moment . . . after the next success in the west." When the Austrian leaders appeared at Spa the same day for consultation, Ludendorff put them off with illusionary assessment of the situation.[61]

During the next six weeks the dimensions of the German retreat swelled, and the process of dissolution within Austria-Hungary quickened. The sharp quarrel between the two allies over the timing and manner of floating a peace bid—between Austria's desire for an immediate appeal to all the belligerents and Germany's for the mediation of a neutral state—came to a head in Austria's separate diplomatic action of September 14. The German bloc fell into disarray as each member pursued its own separate road toward disaster and the end of the war. The diplomatic machinery of the Reich began to carry out the decision of the Spa conference, but the lumbering pace was in marked contrast to these phenomena of incipient collapse. By the end of September German diplomacy had made no tangible progress in the several attempts to commence negotiations through approaches to the Belgians, United States, and queen of the Netherlands or any serious démarche consonant with the deteriorating military situation.

Ludendorff failed in this interval to prepare either the civilian government or to articulate opinion for the hard and inevitable decisions ahead. Early in September he was telling close associates, "We no longer have any hope of winning the war." The general was deterred nevertheless from acknowledging to the chancellor and foreign secretary directly without reserve the critical state of the German army. Ludendorff let things drift in the hope that the foreign office would act on its own initiative, relieving OHL of the responsibility for urging a rescue by diplomacy. War communiqués were doctored in a misleading way, and the press censorship was constrained to withhold unpleasant war news.[62]

Ludendorff's hand was forced by the cresting of the military and political crisis during the four days of September 26–29. The confluence of convulsive events precipitated momentous decisions that introduced the

61. Pierre Renouvin, *L'armistice de Rethondes* (Paris, 1968), 37–39; Ritter, *Staatskunst*, 4: 395–97; Rudin, *Armistice, 1918*, 24–27.
62. Foerster, *Ludendorff im Unglück*, 59; Kaehler, "Zur Beurteilung Ludendorffs," 254.

democratic revolution in Germany and initiated a diplomatic course leading directly to the armistice. The news that Bulgaria was about to conclude
a separate peace deepened the impact made by the climax of the Ameri-
can-French attack on the Meuse-Argonne sector and the break by British
forces through the Hindenburg line.

The majority parties of the Reichstag, the Social Democrats, Center,
and Progressives, consummated on September 28 the formation of a solid
opposition critical of the weakness of the Hertling government and its
laggard diplomacy. A resolution of the opposition called for the formation
of a new cabinet, the introduction of a parliamentary system, an active
effort for a negotiated peace, and support of a league of nations. Similarly,
the foreign office prepared a memorandum of the same date for its head,
Admiral Paul von Hintze, who had replaced Kühlmann. The paper formulated a political and diplomatic program urging the creation of a new
government "on a broad national base" and an approach to Wilson designed to initiate peace talks on the basis of the Fourteen Points.[63]

Although subsequently denied by Ludendorff and his apologists, it is
fair to say that his anguished mind now succumbed to panic. As told in
his memoirs, he and Hindenburg quite dramatically arrived at the conclusion, each in his own office and then together in conference, that the Reich
must ask immediately for an armistice and peace negotiations.[64] A critical
conference at Spa on September 29 acted with precipitate haste on their
demand for an armistice. Ludendorff, claiming that a delay of twenty-four
or forty-eight hours would risk the loss of the army, swept the kaiser and
Hintze as well as the German nation, in a sense scarcely exaggerated,
"from the fanfare of victory to the dirge of defeat."[65] Hintze suggested,
with the approval of the conference, the "offer" of an armistice to Wilson
requesting that he call a meeting of the belligerents for peace negotiations
on the basis of the Fourteen Points.

In order to make the sudden acknowledgment of defeat more bearable
for the German people and the peace initiative more convincing to the
Allies, Hintze proposed not only a change of government in the dropping
of Chancellor Hertling but a change of political system. The conference
agreed, and Hertling resigned. The kaiser signed a decree proclaiming the
cabinet change and his acceptance of broadly representative government.

63. Ritter, *Staatskunst*, 4: 419–20.
64. *Ludendorff's Own Story*, 2: 376–77.
65. Renouvin, *L'armistice de Rethondes*, 68.

The newly designated chancellor, Prince Max of Baden, constituted a cabinet on October 3. Max had stood for a compromise peace, but his reputation for liberalism was exaggerated and he was a dynastic politician, hardly a harbinger of a new constitutional regime to countries abroad.

The new chancellor objected to requesting an armistice suddenly. He contended for delay until his government had time to announce its aims and program. In this atmosphere of sudden defeatism Hintze backed Ludendorff's frantically renewed demand, and no solid party support developed in favor of Max's position. We see in the end the ironic picture of the civilian leader, trying to hold off from an action leading eventually to capitulation, yield to the commander who, having lost his nerve, demanded an instant end to the war. This was not explained to the German public for reasons of military security, and the failure contributed to the legend of the infallible commander and the unbeaten Reich army. Hintze's ideas prevailed, and the peace policy put into effect was due primarily to him and the foreign office, though it accorded with the views and had the zealous support of the Reichstag majority.[66]

The note, approved by both the cabinet and the supreme command, was dispatched for the United States by way of Switzerland. The message commenced an exchange of notes, four on the German side (October 3, 12, 20, and 27) and four on the American side (October 8, 14, 23, and November 5), which together constitute the prearmistice agreement between the Allies and Germany. Beyond securing the end of hostilities as soon as possible, the Germans sought the foremost object, indicated in the first note, of agreement that there would be a negotiated peace on the basis of the Fourteen Points and Wilson's other announced principles. They tried to insure, through their second note, that the powers associated with the United States also accepted these principles.[67]

President Wilson was concerned to bind not only Germany but also the Allies to his program of the principles of peace. The repeated emphasis in the American notes attests that he endeavored to lay down the scarcely veiled condition for peace that the past regime of "military masters" and

66. On the authorship of the peace policy, see the discussion in Klaus Schwabe, *Deutsche Revolution und Wilson-Frieden* (Düsseldorf, 1971), 95–103.

67. The complete texts of the exchange of notes are contained in Alma Luckau, *The German Delegation at the Paris Peace Conference* (New York, 1941), 140–47. The exhaustive discussion of the prearmistice exchange in Schwabe, *Deutsche Revolution und Wilson-Frieden*, 98–226, emphasizes the factors instrumental in formulating the German notes and the German reaction to the American notes.

"monarchical autocrats" be abolished. His third note held out the prospect of imposing terms of unconditional surrender if Germany did not comply through a fundamental change in its constitution.

The German government conducted these negotiations while instituting a parliamentary system of government, dismantling the military state of OHL, and extending control over the military. The process was not accomplished without violent and disruptive encounters between Ludendorff and the civilians, when he changed his estimate of the military situation and, demanding that negotiations with the United States be broken off, called for a national uprising to make war to the bitter end. His later attempt to override the policy of the cabinet reverted to the practice of the military supremacy before the government of Prince Max. This brought his downfall and a new regime at OHL. Worst of all, the German foreign office was deprived of negotiating possibilities by Ludendorff's conduct of the war in 1918 and by his demand for an immediate armistice.

The president had to conduct dual negotiations—with both the Germans and the Allies. Since Wilson did not inform Britain and France officially at once of the first German note and consult with them about the response, the disquietude of both their governments and press was aroused about his intentions. They were concerned that Wilson, the prophet of principle, might become the arbiter of war and peace. The British, French, and Italian premiers declared jointly in a message of October 9 from Paris that the armistice conditions "cannot be fixed until after consultations with military experts." Another message of the same day appealed to the president, in view of the need not to take "decisions of supreme importance in regard to the war . . . at very short notice," to send a responsible representative of the United States government to Europe to confer with other associated governments.[68]

Compounding Wilson's difficulties was the emotional anti-Germanism generated by the war passions and propaganda. A large part of the press in the United States and the Allied countries, along with numerous members of legislative bodies, clamored for punitive terms with Germany, or unconditional surrender, or no negotiations at all until Germany had been invaded.

Under these pressures the second and succeeding notes, departing from

68. Lloyd George, *War Memoirs*, 6: 3282–83.

the moderation and civility of the first, enlarged the demands on the Germans and stated that the conditions of the armistice must be left to the judgment of the military advisers of the United States and Allied governments. The notes laid increasing stress on the necessity of instituting a system of democratic government and on accepting safeguards and guarantees that would make the resumption of hostilities by Germany impossible and the enforcement of peace terms assured.

The second note of Wilson, striking "like a bomb" in Germany, shattered the illusion that the armistice terms would permit the Germans to resume the war if the peace terms were found to be intolerable. The cabinet of Prince Max faced the agonizing decision whether to accept an agreement, tantamount to a confession of defeat, leaving the armistice and peace terms entirely to the will of the Allies and the arbitration of Wilson or to terminate negotiations with the prospect of waging a suicidal war of national resistance. Ludendorff was hopeful at this point, after regaining his composure, that the war could be continued another month, until winter interrupted the Allied attack. Max and the majority of the cabinet, backed by the estimate of Crown Prince Rupprecht of Bavaria and alive to the imminence of mass revolution, saw no chance of a better peace by continuing the war. The government therefore accepted Wilson's additional conditions.

Wilson's final note recorded the willingness of the Allies to conform the peace terms to the Fourteen Points and the other Wilsonian principles, subject to reservation on freedom of the seas and to interpretation of the principle that invaded territories must be restored. The latter was understood to mean—an augury of the reparations provisions in the future peace settlement—"that compensation will be made by Germany for all damage done to the civilian population of the Allies and their property by the aggression of Germany by land, by sea and from the air."

The Allies accepted the Wilsonian peace program except for these two reservations, by virtue of Colonel House's negotiations in Paris. He arrived there on October 26 to comply with the request of the Allied premiers. House succeeded only by posing the threat of a separate American peace if numerous objections were raised to the American program. The resolution of the issue meant that the body of the Fourteen Points was officially accepted by all parties as the governing principles for the peace settlement and that the leadership of the peace negotiations was not to be wrested from President Wilson. This was Wilson's primary purpose in the prearmistice negotiations.[69]

The prearmistice agreement represented a contractual arrangement to conclude the peace in accordance with the Wilsonian program. Wilson's notes further embodied the obligation, at least by implication, of framing a reasonable peace by negotiation on condition that the Germans instituted responsible democratic government. The Germans complied with this feature of the agreement, which undoubtedly exerted some instrumental influence in the establishment of a republic.[70] The real meaning of the Wilsonian principles, however, would depend in large part on how they were applied in the specific circumstances. There was a good deal of truth in the *Nation*'s comment that the Fourteen Points were "merely the titles of bills, which have yet to be drafted and enacted."[71]

The prearmistice agreement had an ideological character that foreshadowed the struggle between the representatives of traditional power and innovative principle at the peace conference. Wilson, conducting the war as an ideological crusade, regarded the Fourteen Points as symbolic of "the moral climax of the final war for human liberty."[72] His intervention in the political reorganization of Germany typified this standpoint. The seriousness with which Wilson intended to press the ideological approach in practical peacemaking was brought home to the European statesmen in the differences over the final prearmistice note.

The exchange of notes divided opinion along the same general lines in both Germany and the Allied countries. In Germany the Pan-Germans, the parties of the right, and a large part of the officer corps opposed the acceptance of Wilson's conditions, with demonstrations and petitions. The socialists and leftists made the strongest demands for peace, but the bulk of the Center and the Progressives supported the chancellor's efforts to end the war. Much the same alignment had formed about war aims and parliamentary reform. It would continue in the Weimar Republic over the acceptance of the new government and its policies. In the western coun-

69. For a judicious discussion of this negotiation, see Renouvin, *L'armistice de Rethondes,* 213–20; also Schwabe, *Deutsche Revolution und Wilson-Frieden,* 158, 177–82, which is critical of House.

70. William L. Langer, "Peace and the New World Order," in *Woodrow Wilson and the World of Today,* 79; John Morton Blum, *Woodrow Wilson and the Politics of Morality* (Boston, 1956), 150; Arno J. Mayer, *Politics and Diplomacy of Peacemaking* (New York, 1967), 16.

71. *Nation,* October 12, 1918, quoted in Laurence W. Martin, *Peace Without Victory* (New Haven, 1958), 189–90.

72. Blum, *Woodrow Wilson and the Politics of Morality,* 148.

tries liberals, radicals, socialists, and labor leaders applauded Wilson's initial steps in peacemaking, while many of the more conservative were critical.

The president recognized in his notes to Germany that the preparation of the armistice terms was the work of military experts and transmitted to the Allied governments the correspondence with Germany after sending the message of October 23. With the aid of papers and proposals submitted by the Military Representatives to the Supreme War Council, by the Allied commanders-in-chief, and by Admiralty, the premiers and foreign ministers, along with House, completed at Paris a text of military and naval terms. Foch's proposals for an Allied military frontier along the Rhine were adopted with amendments, in preference to Haig's simple recommendations that the occupied territories and Alsace-Lorraine be evacuated by the Germans and Metz and Strasbourg be occupied by the Allies. The terms thus agreed were approved by the SWC on November 5.[73]

Wilson's final note of that same day, incorporating the views of the Allied governments on the correspondence between the United States and Germany, informed the latter that Foch was authorized to communicate the terms of an armistice. The German armistice commission that came on November 8 to meet with Foch in the forest of Compiègne was headed by Matthias Erzberger, a leader of the Center party and a secretary of state in the expiring government of Prince Max. He had also been the prime mover of the Reichstag peace resolution. In a railway dining car at Rethondes, Foch and the other Allied representatives proffered the Allied terms, not for negotiations, but for acceptance. The German delegation was appalled by their severity. In an effort to mitigate their harshness, the Germans made counterproposals on the grounds of their necessity to prevent famine and starvation and save Germany from Bolshevism.[74]

During the November days the situation at the front and in Germany moved rapidly toward collapse. On November 1 the Allied advance was resumed all along the front, chiefly by the British driving eastward and by the Americans north from the Argonne. On November 6 the Germans

73. On the formulation of the armistice terms, see Renouvin, *L'armistice de Rethondes,* 195–208; Rudin, *Armistice, 1918,* 285–319; Blake, *Private Papers of Douglas Haig,* 330–39; Schwabe, *Deutsche Revolution und Wilson-Frieden,* 183–191.

74. On Erzberger's role in the conclusion of the prearmistice agreement and the armistice, see Epstein, *Matthias Erzberger,* 264 ff.

finally ordered a withdrawal to the line Verdun-Sedan-Namur-Antwerp. Foch's intended attack on both sides of Metz, which would have imperiled their communications with the homeland, was ready for launching when the armistice supervened. On the morning of November 11 the Americans moved up to Sedan, where Napoleon III had surrendered in 1870. The Germans had not quite reached the line to which they were ordered on November 6 to withdraw. They were nevertheless a beaten army, though not a routed army, and knew it at the time, despite the subsequently fabricated legend of "the unbeaten army in the field."[75]

At home the rebellion of the mutinous sailors at Kiel spread like a raging fire into a mass uprising of the urban population. The kaiser abdicated, a republic was proclaimed, and a socialist government formed. These unsettling events created uncertainty on both sides at Rethondes whether the German delegation possessed the full powers of the new cabinet. At last, after breathless waiting before the final meeting, Erzberger received three messages authorizing acceptance and signing of the armistice.

Acting on these messages, Erzberger made a last attempt to gain amelioration of the terms. He obtained limited concessions, mostly in extending the time of evacuation, reducing the deliveries of materiel, and narrowing the neutral zone beyond the Rhine. He failed notably to get the blockade lifted, although the Allies promised to help feed Germany.

In addition to evacuating the occupied areas and Alsace-Lorraine, the Germans were required to withdraw their armed forces from the left bank of the Rhine and the bridgeheads of Mainz and Coblenz, all of which would be occupied by the Allied armies, and from the neutral zone of ten kilometers on the right bank. War materiel, railway locomotives, rolling stock, and trucks were demanded. All submarines and the greater part of the fleet were to be surrendered. The treaties of Brest-Litovsk and Bucharest would be renounced, and the cash and securities taken from Belgium and the gold from Russia and Romania replaced. One clause ominously stipulated "reparation for damage done."[76]

75. For example, the commentary "Der Dolchstoss" by General von Kühl in Herbert Michaelis and Ernst Schraepler, eds., *Ursachen und Folgen: Vom deutschen Zusammenbruch 1918 und 1945 bis zur staatlichen Neuordnung Deutschlands in der Gegenwart,* 27 vols. (Berlin, 1959-n. d.), 2: 2.

76. Official documents on the subject are found in the English translation by the Carnegie Endowment for International Peace, *Preliminary History of the Armistice* (New York, 1924) of the Reich chancellory's work, *Vorgeschichte des Waffenstillstands* (Berlin, 1919).

The German delegation made two prophetic utterances: the Allies were repeating the errors of the conqueror already committed in the Brest-Litovsk policies; and the protest at the signing against the inhumane features of the terms ended with a cry from the depths—"A nation of seventy millions of people suffers, but it does not die."[77]

The two delegations signed the armistice at five in the morning of November 11, and six hours later it came into effect. The event, ending more than four years of agony for Europe, brought a delirium of ecstasy to the peoples of the Allied countries and feelings of relief to the German population. Now it was for the peacemakers to treat the torn world.

77. Rudin, *Armistice, 1918,* 344, 383.

Chapter Ten

THE REVOLUTION IN WARFARE

1. TECHNOLOGICAL WARFARE

APART from the political and social revolutions bred by the Great War, it introduced a revolution in warfare that might be characterized in terms of a shift from limited to unlimited, or total, war. The first total war broadened the scope of war in its qualitative aspects to make technological, political, and economic warfare the essential components of the whole process, and in its quantitative aspects amplified war to the mass scale.

The number of men called to arms was astronomical in relation to effectives participating in previous wars. During the course of the conflict Russia mobilized more than 14 million, Germany 11, France 8.5, the British Isles 6, and the remainder of the British Empire 3.5. The manpower consumed in the furnace of combat was awesome: in addition to the 10 million known dead three times that number were wounded. The million and a quarter of casualties at the Somme contrast strikingly with the numbers of killed and wounded at Sedan: some 9,000 German troops and 17,000 French in this climactic battle of the Franco-Prussian War.

The world war involved a greater number of belligerents and battles than any earlier conflict. During the Napoleonic wars 17 states participated in a series of 332 battles; in this war, 38 and 615 respectively. A war of these dimensions used up scarcely imaginable amounts of equipment and munitions. The guns of the Western Front gobbled up more ammunition in a single day of siege warfare than was fired during the whole war of 1870–71. War on the seas was in the same titanic frame: the mammoth dreadnoughts of Jellicoe's Grand Fleet weighed ten times as much as Nelson's ships and fired a projectile three times as far. Prodigious quantities of capital were necessary to feed the maw of mass war; before its finish the belligerents had spent 200 billion dollars for military purposes.[1]

The weapons and methods of war assumed a technological feature not known to past wars. Organized science was enlisted in direct technical

---

1. Hinsley, *Power and the Pursuit of Peace*, 279; Görlitz, *Der deutsche Generalstab*, 136; Barnett, *Swordbearers*, 138; Clough, *Economic History of Europe in the Twentieth Century*, 58.

support of the armed effort, signifying a turning point in the relation of science to the conduct of war. The rapid and revolutionary development of weapons technology that marks our times goes back to the First World War. New weapons of a technological and mechanized character were introduced or for the first time developed with deadly military effect, and were utilized on a massive scale. There were five of these machines that stand out and made the Great War unique to that time: the machine gun, aircraft, the tank, the submarine, and the wireless.[2]

That the mechanization of armament and the application of science and technology to the production of weapons had begun by 1914 was evident in the current arms of the magazine rifle and metal cartridges with smokeless powder and nitroglycerine explosive, the machine gun, and rapid-firing artillery, absorbing the recoil of discharge; the infancy of military aviation; the propulsion of advanced submarines by diesel engines and improved batteries; and a rudimentary wireless.

The military and naval staffs did not realize the potentialities of these modern means of war or perceive their strategic and tactical implications.[3] If the generals had properly understood the effect of the firepower of modern land weapons, they might have anticipated the stalemate of the Western Front and abandoned the prevalent doctrines of offensive warfare set forth in the writings and manuals of French and German staff officers. If the German general staff had foreseen the defensive power of current rifles, machine guns, and French 75-mm guns and fully appreciated the offensive power of their own heavy artillery of fortress-smashing calibers, they might have chosen an alternative strategy to marching through Belgium.

The revolution in warfare affected four spheres of operations: land warfare, air warfare, war at sea, and combined arms. The typical land warfare, conducted on the Western Front, has been described as the war of position, siege or fixed warfare, and stabilization. The siege warfare was murderous but not static in the sense of failure to introduce new weapons and tactics designed to break through the fixed front. The development of both, along with the experience of 1915–17, assisted the return to a war of movement in 1918.

The heavier weight of fire, from the rapid-firing arms and heavy artil-

2. Max Schwarte, *Die Technik im Weltkriege* (Berlin, 1920), 68; Sir Solly Zuckermann, *Scientists and War* (New York, 1967), 12–13.

3. See Fuller, *Military History of the Western World*, 3: 89; Fuller, *Conduct of War*, 142–43; Ropp, *Modern Warfare*, 202–03.

lery, contributed to the augmented power of the offense as well as of the defense and did not necessarily establish the superiority of the latter. The stalemate of the Western Front derived from the equilibrium of approximately matched forces, as much as from the nature of weapons and defenses; it never appeared in the east.

The characteristic feature of the war of position belonged to the intricate system of field fortications, or belts of entrenched lines.[4] Each side devoted ceaseless effort to strengthening its own system of defense and to seeking a means of breaking through the enemy's. From the lessons of Verdun and the Somme, Pétain and Ludendorff evolved the defense echeloned in depth, which endowed the defense with more punch and initiative while thinning out the defense troops so as to make them less vulnerable to hostile fire. This dynamic defense was planned to hurl the enemy back with counterattacks in depth delivered by fresh troops especially trained for the purpose.[5]

In endeavoring to achieve a breakthrough that would open the war of position into a war of movement, the Allies concentrated at first on the attempt to obtain superiority of massed artillery fire. This tactical emphasis neglected the element of surprise. The nature of the trench system and the defense in depth spurred efforts to increase the range, effective impact, and mobility of the artillery. Trench mortars were introduced in light, medium, and heavy classes. Naval and fortress guns, mounted on wheeled carriages, were drafted to add power and range to the artillery. Railway guns of heavier types were constructed, and heavy guns were moved by truck.[6]

The rolling barrage, first used at Verdun, gave more cover to the advancing infantry. In time the barrage was expanded from a curtain of fire to moving belts of fire in depth aided by smoke screens. Armies augmented the power of attack by having light mobile guns, light portable trench mortars, flame-throwers, and hand grenades. Propellants and ex-

4. On the system of defense belts, see Pascal Marie Henri Lucas, *L'évolution des idées tactiques en France et en Allemagne pendant la guerre de 1914–1918* (Paris, 1924), 38–64 passim; Watt, *Dare Call It Treason,* 75–78.

5. *Ludendorff's Own Story,* 1: 458–60; Cyril Falls, *The Nature of Modern Warfare* (London, 1941), 44–46; Lucas, *L'évolution des idées tactiques,* 203–13.

6. Terraine, *Douglas Haig,* 284, 336, 358. For a technical discussion of developments in artillery and problems of gun construction during the war, see Schwarte, *Technik im Weltkriege,* 66–81. See Aubrey Wade, *The War of the Guns* (London, 1936), for an unsurpassed memoir on the artillery war from the personal and human side.

plosives were improved, and smoke, star, and incendiary shells as well as armor-piercing and tracer bullets were installed in the armory of modern weapons.[7]

Two innovations in weaponry were designed to restore the element of surprise sacrificed in offensive warfare by the battering-ram methods of the prolonged barrage of massed artillery: gas and tanks. The maximum impact of gas and tanks derived from the demoralizing shock of the unknown. If either weapon could have been used first only after careful planning for employment on a large scale to exploit fully the shock effect, it is possible that the Germans or the British might have made a clean break through the entire defense system of the enemy.

The tank was the most revolutionary innovation in land warfare that issued from the war. The tank evolved from a slow-moving land tub to a swifter, mechanically more reliable, and more maneuverable instrument of war assuming specialized forms and functions in combat.[8] Yet the Allies never succeeded in utilizing tanks to disrupt the German rear disastrously. Haig and Foch, like the traditionalist generals and staffers, did not envisage the possibility of building a whole new set of tactics around the tanks. For the two commanders the innovation was still "an adjunct to infantry and guns," and for Kitchener "a pretty mechanical toy but of very limited military value."[9] The tank expert J.F.C. Fuller nevertheless anticipated the future role to be played by this "dominant weapon of land warfare of the twentieth century."[10] Fuller foresaw it stabbing through weak spots along a broad front of the enemy to disorganize the directing centers of the enemy's rear.

The German high command mistakenly estimated the tactical value of the tank, and the Germans never built more than a few clumsy monsters. The army devised defenses against the tank effective enough to support the high command's skepticism about the utility of the weapon. In truth the Germans had to make a choice where they put their limited supply of

7. On the advances in weaponry, see Georg Bruchmüller, *Die deutsche Artillerie in den Durchbruchschlachten des Weltkrieges,* 2d ed. (Berlin, 1922), 11–18; Lucas, *L'évolution des idées tactiques,* 173; Cyril Falls, *A Hundred Years of War* (London, 1953), 308–09.

8. On the genesis, use, and importance of the tank in the war, there are two works of unique value: J.F.C. Fuller, *Tanks in the Great War* (London, 1920), and Liddell Hart, *Tanks,* vol. 1. See also the reminiscences of Sir Ernest D. Swinton, *Eyewitness* (London, 1932).

9. On Haig's attitude toward tanks, Liddell Hart, *Tanks,* 1: 131–32; on Foch's, Terraine, *Douglas Haig,* 227; on Kitchener's, Farrar Hockley, *Somme,* 21.

10. Terraine, *Douglas Haig,* 218.

raw materials in the production of artillery, tanks, submarines, aircraft, and trucks. A huge program of tank construction would have necessitated cutbacks in building higher-powered guns and submarines. If the strategic postulate was to go for submarines, then it did not make much difference whether the high command decided for artillery and shell or for tanks. Ludendorff proved in his 1918 offensives that artillery and his new offensive tactics could breach the Allied front, but he did not have the resources to exploit the breach to strategic depth.

The tank was thus one solution for mastering stalemate—the solution by innovation in mechanized warfare. The German command invented a tactical solution to the problem of breakthrough and exploitation that restored surprise to its essential role. Surprise was to be achieved by every resource of concealment, secrecy, diversion, and hurricane bombardment of saturated coverage utilizing gas and smoke. If this was the first principle, the second was to carry out the attack by special assault troops intensively trained for the purpose. And the third was to conduct a continually sustained offense in depth by loose formations of small, heavily armed groups penetrating the weak spots as quickly as possible and bypassing points of resistance for succeeding groups to overcome.

The Allies followed similar tactics in their 1918 offensives. The mass availability of tanks made it possible for them to reduce the weight of the artillery preparation and to assist the artillery in supporting directly the forefront of the infantry attack. The firepower of the infantry was stepped up with both light and heavy machine guns, grenade rifles, grenade throwers, and light field artillery, as well as hand grenades and trench mortars. The machine gun tended to become the main infantry weapon on defense or on offense. Thus both tactics and technology offered the means of breaking the western deadlock.[11]

Another military innovation fitted into the pattern of future warfare— motor transport. Logistically, organized motor transport was introduced in supplying the defense of Verdun, and its use was extended by the Allies thereafter. The large tanks were utilized as armored troop carriers. The British employed armored cars ever since the operations at Antwerp in 1914, and eventually armored car battalions were formed.

11. On the machine gun as an infantry weapon, Pridham, *Superiority of Fire,* 75. See F.W.A. Hobart, *Pictorial History of the Machine Gun* (London, 1971), for technical specifications and description of the various models of machine guns used by the major powers. Also G. S. Hutchison, *Machine Guns, Their History and Tactical Employment* (London, 1938).

The elements of future Blitzkrieg had come into existence—the tank, motor transport, armored car formations, and the warplane. They had been employed together in a rudimentary way. It remained to combine them in operations with maximum efficacy under a new tactical doctrine, taking off from Fuller's ideas on the use of tanks and Ludendorff's tactics of penetration and offense in depth.

No arm existing in 1914 made greater strides in development than military aircraft under the stimulus of war demands. The production of armed aircraft in the thousands and of specialized types inaugurated a radically novel kind of warfare in another medium and added a new dimension to the mobility of offensive power. Changes of far-reaching import were to come about as a result in the tactics and strategy of war.[12]

At first all-purpose airplanes served the army in reconnaissance and observation. Fighter craft emerged in fitting scouting planes with machine guns. Systematic air combat appeared when mechanisms were invented in 1915 to synchronize machine-gun fire with the revolutions of the propeller, and when scout fighters were produced. In 1916 fighter planes joined action in groups of three or four, and formation flying came into practice. The team fighting of groups of planes gave rise to the tactics of aerial warfare.[13]

The rapid development of aerial photography ushered in the standard practice of planning an attack on the basis of detailed maps taken from photographs of the enemy's opposing trench system. Reconnaissance planes were equipped with wireless sets, which grew more reliable, and a wireless flight was attached to each air squadron. With these aids the air squadrons and the kite balloons became "the eyes of the artillery."[14]

Air bombing progressed from the sporadic dropping of bombs to specialized tactical and strategic bombing using bombs of varied weight and purpose as well as improved bombsights. Sustained tactical bombing from local air superiority provided a regular extension of the artillery in the preparatory bombardment and in the artillery fire during the battle. Aircraft conducted contact patrol or cooperation with the attacking infantry

12. See Edward Mead Earle, "The Influence of Air Power," in *The Impact of Air Power*, ed. Eugene M. Emmer (Princeton, 1959), 107.
13. Alexander McKee, *The Friendless Sky* (London, 1962), 23–26, 47–48; H. A. Jones, *The War in the Air*, vol. 2 (Oxford, 1928), 136–43, 156–57, 281–83; George Paul Neumann, *The German Air Force in the Great War* (London, 1921), 200–01.
14. Jones, *War in the Air*, 2: 74–129 passim, 179–80, 232–33, 251–71, 328, 331; Neumann, *German Air Force*, 41, 43, 54.

and harassed the enemy's troops at the front. In Allenby's decisive campaign against the Turks, the air destruction of combat troops in a trap anticipated the fate of the Third Reich's Seventh Army in Normandy.[15]

In the strategic bombing of England, the Germans first used the vulnerable navy Zeppelins in night raids and shifted in 1917 to daylight attacks, conducted at high cost, by two-engine heavy bombers (Gothas). They finally went to dispersed night bombing in the "first battle of Britain," in which the Gothas were joined with huge planes of the Giant class powered by four engines. The Blitz attacks sustained unacceptable losses without setting fires. Only the end of the war kept the Germans from carrying out immense fire raids with masses of a newly produced Elektron magnesium bomb. In this bomb and the Giant bomber the Germans devised the weapons and pattern of strategic warfare that would be turned in full against themselves in the next world war.[16]

The British countered the night attacks with a defense organization that included a balloon barrage, a ground complex of searchlights and guns, high-performance air fighters, and early warning arrangements. In taking up strategic air warfare, Britain perfected the Handley Page bomber, "one of the great aircraft of history," and created an autonomous and unified air force, against the bitter opposition of the RFC, Haig, and the Admiralty. An air ministry was formed, and the Royal Air Force was officially launched on April 1, 1918. The Independent Air Force of bombers delivered 550 tons of bombs on German targets, twice the tonnage Britain received in the war. An Allied Air Force was established on October 26, 1918.[17]

The air war of the future was foreshadowed by Britain's air defense organization, the IAF, and the planned Allied tactics of 1919 projecting tank-plane cooperation. The Germans, disenchanted with the power of the big bombers to inflict damage, built a postwar air force fashioned to

15. Jones, *War in the Air*, 2: 94–134 passim, 179–80, 232–33, 251–71; Neumann, *German Air Force*, 41, 43, 54.

16. On the role of the airship in the war, see especially the work of noteworthy excellence by Douglas H. Robinson, *The Zeppelin in Combat* (London, 1962). Also Ernst A. Lehmann and Howard Mingos, *The Zeppelins* (New York, 1927).

17. For the part played by airplanes, both German and British, in strategic bombing, see Raymond H. Fredette, *The First Battle of Britain, 1917–1918, and the Birth of the Royal Air Force* (London, 1966). Specifically, Penrose, *British Aviation*, 137; Fredette, *First Battle of Britain*, 197; James M. Spaight, "The Coming of Organized Air Power," in *Impact of Air Power*, 41–43; John Ehrman, *Cabinet Government and War, 1890–1940* (Cambridge, England, 1958), 101–02.

provide tactical support for the army. The British, shocked by the air invasion of their insularity, gave priority to rebuilding the RAF at first with bombers and then fighters, while neglecting the army and the creation of tactical air strength to support it. Without this belief in strategic air power, Britain might not have had in the Second World War the quality of fighter planes to beat back the Nazi foe or the heavy bombers to carry the attack to the Third Reich.[18]

The rapid advance of aviation technology during the war brought about the use of aircraft of diversified structure and the daring stride forward from wood and fabric construction to metal. The bewildering variety of engine types ranged in cylinders up to 12 and horsepower up to 450. The speed of operational planes about doubled, in attaining 120–126 miles per hour. The ceiling of the most up-to-date planes had increased to nearly 27,000 feet, and the cruising range of long-distance planes to 2,000 miles.[19]

The unproved submarine of 1914 was also destined to transform the nature of warfare. During the first six months of the war the submarine was used, like the aircraft, mainly for the purposes of reconnaissance and patrol. Offensively, both sides employed the submarine to attack the war vessels of the other. The constant menace of the submarine, or its supposed menace, imposed an inhibiting effect on the use of the battle fleets.[20] The biggest surprise afforded by the submarine in these first months was its success as a commerce-raider. The demonstration of the submarine's previously unanticipated capabilities generated the German belief of possessing a miracle weapon and proved of large influence in the Reich decision to conduct a war of commerce against Britain.[21]

The demands raised by the U-boat campaigns stimulated the evolution of the submarine as an instrument of modern warfare, and the necessities of defense against the *Handelskrieg* elicited the invention of an array of

18. Fredette, *First Battle of Britain,* 234–54.

19. Penrose, *British Aviation,* 292, 413, 436.

20. See Jellicoe's communication to the Admiralty, October 30, 1914, already revealing this concern. Patterson, *Jellicoe Papers,* 1: 75. In September 1914 the commander-in-chief of the German High Seas Fleet reported to the chief of the naval staff: "The German fleet is actually blockaded in the river mouths by the enemy's submarines during favorable weather conditions if the fleet will not expose itself to the danger of losses that will be felt." Groos and Gladisch, *Der Krieg in der Nordsee,* 2: 24.

21. Marder, *From the Dreadnought to Scapa Flow,* 2: 343; Groos and Gladisch, *Der Krieg in der Nordsee,* 2: 135–47 passim; Bernd Stegemann, *Die deutsche Marinepolitik 1916–1918* (Berlin, 1970), 23 ff.

antisubmarine devices. The Reich's capacity to produce submarines steadily expanded. The construction and equipment of the U-boats constantly
improved, not only with respect to stronger hulls and armament but also
in cruising and diving speed, increased endurance, and reliability of mechanism. Specialized types evolved for different uses, and the cruising range
of the U-boats lengthened from 2,000–2,500 to 3,600 miles.[22]

The Reich's production and improvement of submarines enabled the
Germans to destroy six million tons of Allied shipping in 1917. That the
German U-boat establishment had the power to hurt Britain and the other
Allies seriously, even when the U-boats operated according to the rules
of cruiser warfare, was apparent from the shipping losses in the campaign
beginning in October 1916. The loss of submarines in 1917 and 1918
dramatically increased over the destruction of U-boats when they hunted
according to the rules of cruiser warfare. The results clearly pointed to the
fallacious arguments of the fleet command that the conduct of the *Handelskrieg* by prize regulations was responsible for high U-boat losses.[23]

The Allied countermeasures of 1915–16 achieved but limited success.
In response to this urgent need, the depth charge was produced and a
reliable mine developed in the Mark H and Mark H-2 horned mines. The
mass production of the horned mine from 1917 on provided the means
of destroying the greatest number of U-boats, 58 altogether. With this
device the British, for the first time, could erect an effective barrier across
the Dover Straits. The turning point in the war against the U-boats arrived, however, with the full organization of the convoy system for both
the Atlantic and Mediterranean trade. The convoy system was not only a
defensive success but also allowed the Allied escort vessels to take the
offensive in strength against the U-boats operating against convoys. The
convoy supplemented, above all, with the mine won the day.[24]

The widening use of submarines and their evolving capabilities materially affected the high strategy of naval power on both sides. The primary
function of the Grand Fleet was redirected from the hunting down and
destruction of Scheer's battle force to the enforcement of the British

22. Stegemann, *Die deutsche Marinepolitik,* 26, 28, 96; Jameson, *Most Formidable Thing,*
157.
23. Stegemann, *Die deutsche Marinepolitik,* 65, 68, 72.
24. See above, pp. 240–42. Also Grant, *U-Boats Destroyed,* 74–75, 79, 93–94, 143–44;
Corbett and Newbolt, *Naval Operations,* 5: 133, 338; Jameson, *Most Formidable Thing,* 233,
246. Grant, *U-Boats Destroyed,* reports a thorough investigation of the relative efficacy of the
different methods employed in fighting the U-boats.

blockade and the support of the antisubmarine campaign. The German naval leadership similarly turned the High Seas Fleet more and more into a support for the U-boat campaign.

The submarine opened up a means of extending naval power to peripheral areas denied to surface units. British submarines attacked the extended line of Turkish communications during the Dardanelles campaign and exerted some effect in the Baltic from 1915 on. The Germans in turn helped to frustrate the Dardanelles campaign of the Allies with their U-boats. The Germans carried their submarine attack to Allied and neutral shipping off the shores of the United States, and to the Arctic supply line to Russia.[25]

This revolutionary instrument of war was not a decisive weapon, but it was the nearest thing to that weapon that came out of the war. The German mistake of gravest consequence in utilizing the U-boats was the insistence, before the Allies had developed successful antisubmarine measures, that the efficacy of the submarines depended on their unrestricted use rather than on the numbers engaged. They ignored the fact that the submarine warfare restricted to operations by prize regulations had a deadly potency. The failure to give proper weight to the value of numbers meant that they commenced the *Handelskrieg* before they were prepared to deliver the lethal blow with a mighty submarine armada and allowed the Allies an opportunity to develop antisubmarine and protective means in time to avert mortal peril. It was the story of gas and the tank over again. The Germans actually misused the weapon.[26]

In the Dardanelles campaign, the Allies inaugurated modern amphibious or combined operations of land, sea, air, and underwater forces. The marvel of Dardanelles as an amphibious and combined undertaking was the experimental use of so many new means and methods of warfare: armored landing barges equipped with landing ramps; a pontoon pier three hundred feet long, towed across the waters from the construction site on the island of Imbros to the landing place at Suvla; a converted seaplane carrier, the first ship in naval history to be used solely for this

25. Jameson, *Most Formidable Thing*, 165–69, 177–80, 199; Keyes, *Naval Memoirs*, 1: 36; Philip K. Lundeberg, "Undersea Warfare and Allied Strategy in World War I," *Smithsonian Journal of History*, 1, no. 3 (1966): 23.

26. The argument here is based mainly on Stegemann, *Die deutsche Marinepolitik*, especially pp. 66, 97, 102. Jameson, *Most Formidable Thing*, 175, holds that if Germany had conducted the campaign of 1915 with six times as many diesel-driven U-boats as were used, the Reich might have won.

function; the addition of another carrier, land planes, and two kite balloons; and the wireless. The work of the submarines came near to being
of decisive importance. This trial of naval and air support of a military
landing and of a land battle against an entrenched opponent had many
lessons to teach the generals and the admirals of the Second World War
for planning combined operations in the invasions of North Africa and
Normandy.[27]

2. POLITICAL WARFARE

This war was pushed forward to political and economic dimensions
never reached before in the history of warfare. The political warfare
focused on the struggle for the human mind and will. The political warfare
was determined by three strategic objectives. On the home front each
warring nation made extreme exertions to achieve national unity behind
the war, mobilize the civilian population for the most efficient use of
resources and the maximum output of labor, and generate an emotional
frenzy against the enemy. On the enemy front, the aim was to break down
the morale of the opponents and their will to continue the fight; the
ultimate effort centered on undermining faith in their own institutions and
fomenting revolution against the traditional state. Toward the neutral
states, the purpose was to win their cooperation and, if possible, their entry
to the coalition while limiting their support in the form of sympathy and
economic ties extended the hostile alliance.

The political side of the war was increasingly channeled in the world
ideological struggle, setting the forces of autocratic monarchy and aristocratic privilege against the forces of democracy and socialism. The war to
make the world safe for democracy was a war to make democracy trium-
phant over the old order of society.

The control and use of information afforded the principal means of
conducting political warfare. Negatively, information and communications facilities were controlled by the censorship and press policy of belligerents. Even the established democracies adopted restrictive measures,
such as the British Defense of the Realm Acts and the American Espionage
and Sedition Acts, to insure conformity of the civilian population to the
view of the war and the enemy held by the state. In executing legislation

27. Jones, *War in the Air*, 2: 8–77; Marder, *From the Dreadnought to Scapa Flow*, 2: 327–29;
Moorehead, *Gallipoli*, 239.

of this nature, governments set up a far-flung machinery of censorship to keep the mails and cables under surveillance.[28]

Through control of the news, the combatant state could convey to the world the progress of the war and the state's conduct of military operations as it would like to see the picture presented. The further purpose always operated to help fashion the solidarity of national opinion necessary for the vigorous prosecution of the war. In pursuing these ends, the British and Americans maintained a unified press policy under civilian control.[29] The French exercised a centralized control of all news relating to the war, whether military or political, through the ministry of war and its organ, the Bureau de la presse.[30]

In contrast the German government, which never created a central press office, lacked unity in the treatment of news. The general staff and the supreme command in reporting war news covered up or obscured adverse events, playing down successes of the Allies, or altogether suppressed the truth. At last the German people lost faith in their own army, and the "collapse of illusion," to use the phrase of Friedrich Meinecke, became synonymous with the collapse of the Reich.[31]

The handling of war news was intended to influence the attitude of neutrals or the enemy through the neutrals. In the ability to put forward their version of the war news, the British and French obtained a distinct advantage over the Central Powers. The British isolated Germany and Austria-Hungary by cutting the sea cables linking Germany with the outside world. The British, maintaining a cable censorship, often withheld press dispatches if not conforming to the British criteria of what the United States should learn about the war.[32]

Apart from news reports, the belligerent countries relied on an avalanche of publications, both government and private, and on public pronouncements to attain the objectives of policy on war information. Warring

28. H. C. Peterson, *Propaganda for War* (Norman, Okla., 1939), 15; James R. Mock, *Censorship 1917* (Princeton, 1941), 51–63; James R. Mock and Cedric Larson, *Words That Won the War* (Princeton, 1939), 20.

29. Peterson, *Propaganda for War*, 13; George Creel, *How We Advertised America* (New York, 1929), 83.

30. Georg Huber, *Die französische Propaganda im Weltkrieg gegen Deutschland 1914 bis 1918* (Munich, 1938), 22–23.

31. On German press control and policy, see Kurt Koszyk, *Deutsche Pressepolitik im Ersten Weltkrieg* (Düsseldorf, 1968), particularly pp. 49–50, 76–82.

32. James M. Read, *Atrocity Propaganda, 1914–1919* (New Haven, 1941), 188.

states for the first time made systematic use of mass propaganda, supported with government funds, and set up official propaganda organizations staffed with government servants to wage an intensive war of words.

The most persistent and pervasive of propaganda themes were sounded as soon as the war began. Each side attempted to pin the responsibility for the war on the other by charges of unprovoked military action, aggression, or violation of international law. The frantic diplomacy of the last days of the July 1914 crisis contained a pronounced element of political warfare; each prospective warring power was jockeying to obtain the best possible position for going to war. The war-guilt controversy did not begin in 1918 but before the first shot.

The German chancellor's most successful stroke in this propaganda skirmishing was to place the blame on Russian mobilization for German mobilization.[33] In his Reichstag speech of August 4, Bethmann Hollweg gave a summation of the propaganda case for Germany at Russia's expense. The speech presented France as the aggressor and defended Germany's entry of Belgium as a necessity that "knows no law." The statement formulated for the German nation and for the world "the psychological position for the conduct of the war."[34]

Each of the other belligerents similarly developed its propaganda case of self-defense. The French dwelt on the German guilt of declaring war and invading French and Belgian territory. The British heaped onus on the Germans for violating Belgian neutrality, making this the public basis for joining France in the war. Every warring power issued in 1914 a colored book of documents advisedly selected to point to its own innocence and to the enemy's guilt. The first of these, the German White Book, appeared under the suggestive title *How Russia and Her Ruler Betrayed Germany's Confidence and Thereby Unchained the War.*

The German thesis of Russia's war guilt won success at home but proved weak abroad. The chancellor's arguments went far to convince the Social Democrats of the necessity to defend the fatherland against the dangers of tsarism and to rally the nation behind the war.[35] The Germans, how-

33. See Geiss, "Zusammenfassung," *Julikrise,* 2: 731, and his "The Outbreak of the First World War," 88–89; also Bethmann Hollweg to Lichnowsky, August 3, 1914, Nr. 1118, *Julikrise,* 2: 664–65.

34. Zechlin, "Bethmann Hollweg, Kriegsrisiko und SPD 1914," 23.

35. German scholars generally accepted the Reich's innocence of any responsibility for the war as an article of faith. See the "Appeal of the 93" of October 4, 1914, which viewed the war in terms of "the fight for existence forced on Germany." Klaus Schwabe, *Wissenschaft*

ever, committed serious errors in conducting the initial round of the struggle for men's minds. Germany's declarations of war against Russia and France before theirs were interpreted widely by European opinion outside the Central Powers to be an aggressive action precipitating the conflict. The specious basis for declaring war against France (alleged violations of German territory from the air) only hurt Germany's credibility. The violation of Belgian neutrality was a monumental mistake in damaging Germany's psychological position, and a strategy requiring it a political blunder.

The French made the war guilt of Germany the cardinal line of their propaganda, relentlessly pursuing it throughout the war. The public opinion created by their own propaganda held the victor governments at the peace conference hostage to writing the German war-guilt thesis into the treaty of Versailles and making it a rationale for many of its punitive provisions.[36]

The accusations of brutalities and war crimes approached in political punch the central theme of the enemy's sole responsibility for the war. Both sides leveled charges of atrocities and spread atrocity reports. Accusations of war crimes were made in connection with the introduction of new weapons and strategic methods of warfare—the use of gas, unrestricted submarine war, the blockade of the British, air raids on civilians.[37] In the catalogue of propaganda on atrocities and war crimes, certain incidents received the greatest stress and scored the most effect. Ranking high on this list were the shooting of the British nurse Edith Cavell in Belgium for illegal acts, the deportation of French and Belgian civilians, the sinking of the *Lusitania,* the damage to the University of Louvain and the cathedral of Reims, and the Armenian massacres.

The furor aroused by the atrocity and war crimes propaganda recoiled on the peace conference and produced an irresistible pressure for including Part VII on "Penalties' in the treaty of Versailles. Whatever the

und Kriegsmoral (Göttingen, 1969), 22–24. The official interpretation became a doctrinal principle of the "war theology" of the Protestant and Catholic churches: "We are not responsible for the outbreak of the war; it has been forced upon us; we can witness that before God and the world." Kurt Hammer, *Deutsche Kriegstheologie (1870–1918)* (Munich, 1971), 81.

36. See F. Dickmann, "Die Kriegsschuldfrage auf der Friedenskonferenz von Paris 1917," *Historische Zeitschrift* 197 (1963): 1–101, especially p. 9.

37. See Read, *Atrocity Propaganda.* This fine product of historical scholarship is by far the best study of the subject.

peacemakers desired, they were bound by the previous propaganda campaigns.[38]

The official organizations created to conduct the propaganda activities —particularly the British ministry of information, the French Maison de la presse, and the American Committee on Public Information—formed a model for future information agencies.[39] Britain achieved the strongest and most unified direction of propaganda among the European belligerents. The machinery and volume of Russian propaganda were of little moment before the Russian revolution.[40]

The Allies acted to coordinate their informational activities in convening two gatherings in London during 1918. The one in August agreed to form an inter-Allied body with a permanent secretariat for conducting propaganda in enemy countries. A tangible and continuing practice of Allied cooperation in informational work was achieved on the Italian front, where the Inter-Allied Propaganda Commission was organized.[41]

The warring powers conveyed foreign propaganda to their own allies, to neutrals, and to enemy countries.[42] Belligerents could transmit published materials to neutrals directly by mail or, alternatively, through diplomatic channels for distribution in the neutral countries. The Germans broadcast daily to nearby neutrals from their radio installation at Nauen. Other channels to the neutrals were provided by press services, newly opened reading rooms and bureaus of information, lectures by well-

38. Ibid., p. viii and 240–85.

39. On the organization of British informational activities, see the splendid summary volume by James D. Squires, *British Propaganda at Home and in the United States from 1914 to 1917* (Cambridge, Mass., 1935), 17–40; Sir Campbell Stuart, *Secrets of Crewe House* (London, 1920), 8–36; George Bruntz, *Allied Propaganda and the Collapse of the German Empire* (Stanford, 1938), 22–28. On the French propaganda agencies, Huber, *Die französische Propaganda im Weltkrieg,* 26–69. On the American organization, Creel, *How We Advertised America,* especially pp. 3–13, 83–211, 237–81, and the later account in Mock and Larson, *Words That Won the War.*

40. The deficiency in Russian propaganda was keenly felt at the headquarters of the Russian army. *Die internationalen Beziehungen,* 373.

41. The most informative chronicle of Allied cooperation in propaganda activities is in Stuart, *Secrets of Crewe House,* 36–39, 146–99. Also Henry Wickam Steed, *Through Thirty Years, 1892–1922,* 2 vols. (Garden City, N. Y., 1924), 2: 191–96, 204–09; and below, p. 314.

42. One means of propaganda by which the Allies reached one another was through visits and tours of individuals from one country invited officially by the government of another. On the official visit of Maurice Barrès to Britain, see his *Voyage en Angleterre, l'âme française et la guerre* (Paris, 1919); on the visit of Edmund Gosse to France, *The Correspondence of André Gide and Edmund Gosse,* ed. Linette F. Brugmans (New York, 1959), 135, n. 4.

known visitors from the belligerent country, and personal correspondence.[43]

The penetration of an enemy country with propaganda often had to be indirect and covert via neutral countries.[44] Propaganda was delivered directly to occupied areas and the enemy's troops at the front as well as the population behind the front. A common practice was to drop copies of fake newspapers from the air. By 1918 the Allies had greatly advanced the technology for the direct dissemination of printed materials among the enemy. Not only did the Allies wing their words from airplanes but also sent paper missiles by mortars, hand grenades, and rockets. Balloons carried leaflets five or six hundred miles.[45]

The belligerents joined political warfare with diplomacy to influence the neutrals to enter the conflict on their side or at least to remain neutral. The Germans organized a hard-driving propaganda campaign against the British and Russians in Turkey before its entry, in which the Turkish press was brought under German influence.[46] In Bulgaria the two coalitions vied with each other in schemes for bribing the political leaders of the country and in subsidies given press organs.[47] The British, French, and Russians worked "most actively" to influence the press and the people of Italy in favor of intervention on the Allied side. The French engineered a coup by buying Mussolini to switch over from socialist pacifism to preaching nationalism and intervention in the newspaper *Popolo d'Italia*.[48]

The warring powers fixed their chief efforts on the United States. The Germans and Austrians pursued two main objectives in ranging widely over informational activities—both aboveboard and secret: to keep the United States out of the war and to block the shipment of munitions to the Allies. In this effort they resorted to espionage, intrigue, conspiracy, subversion, and sabotage. The aims of the Allies were to keep the munitions and loans flowing from America to the Entente and to woo the United States without perceptible pressure into the Allied coalition.

The Germans attempted to create diversionary trouble between the

43. Squires, *British Propaganda*, 48–63; Peterson, *Propaganda for War*, 15–32 passim.
44. Hans Thimme, *Weltkrieg ohne Waffen* (Stuttgart, 1932), 52–118; Walter Nicolai, *The German Secret Service* (London, 1924), 73, 88–99.
45. George Sylvester Viereck, *Spreading Germs of Hate* (New York, 1930), 203–07.
46. Ahmed Emin, *Turkey in the World War*, 70; Gottlieb, *Studies in Secret Diplomacy*, 59; Sachar, *Emergence of the Middle East*, 24; James, *Gallipoli*, 9.
47. *Die internalen Beziehungen*, 84–85, 235–36; Potts, "The Loss of Bulgaria," 222–26.
48. Gottlieb, *Studies in Secret Diplomacy*, 228–30.

United States and other countries. They worked to exacerbate the relations between the United States and Britain by public exploitation of the Irish rebellion and the fate of the revolutionary leader Sir Roger Casement. They conspired to embroil the United States in a war with Mexico.

The machinations of the Central Powers ran afoul of public revelations from apprehended secret records and documents that exposed the inner workings of their propaganda machinery and much of their undercover activity.[49] The Mexican adventure exploded dramatically, with the uncovering of the Zimmermann telegram of January 6, 1917. This message instructed the German minister in Mexico to propose an alliance for attacking the United States, should there be war between Germany and America.[50]

The telegram was intercepted and deciphered by the unequaled codebreakers of Room 40 at London, a group forming the center of British naval intelligence directed by that genius of intelligence work, Admiral Sir William Hall. Hall's agency tracked, with the aid of Czech-American secret agents, German and Austrian subversive activities in the United States; followed through the interception of cable traffic diplomatic action of Berlin and undercover operations of its agents; and made the biggest catch of all in the Zimmermann telegram.[51]

Its disclosure to the American government and the public revelation of the plot climaxed a long series of German intrigues inimical to the peace and security of the United States. This masterly British success in political warfare, provoking war fever in the United States, proved of major influence in bringing America into the conflict. To whatever extent German propaganda appealed to the German-American and Irish elements and certain isolationist and pacifist sectors of American society, the revelations of the undercover activities and the Zimmermann telegram were disastrous to Germany's political warfare.

In promoting revolution in the lands of the enemy or under the enemy's influence, the belligerents raised political warfare to the strategic plane and pressed its objectives on a global scale. With the support of the Turks,

49. Viereck, *Spreading Germs of Hate,* 68–74; Emanuel Victor Voska and Will Irwin, *Spy and Counterspy* (New York, 1940), 75–108.

50. On the background and transmission of this message, see Barbara W. Tuchman, *The Zimmermann Telegram* (London, 1959).

51. Sir William James, *The Code Breakers of Room 40* (New York, 1956), furnishes the fullest and best account of the work of Room 40 and Hall's handling of the Zimmermann telegram.

the Germans set out to enlist the Pan-Islamic movement in inciting revolution in Islamic countries under the sway of Britain and France. They sent agents to the subcontinent of India and entered into connections with Indian princes. The diplomatic activity and propaganda of German parties in Persia were intended not only to win it as an ally against Britain and Russia but also as a base for pressuring Afghanistan into a war against India. The Germans, British, and Russians competed in buying political support in Persia.[52]

In Africa the German political strategy of stimulating revolution reached from Egypt to central Africa in the south and to Spanish Morocco in the north. The various subversive enterprises in Africa flickered out when the British drove back the Turkish-German forces setting out to invade Egypt and revolt failed to catch fire.

Germany supported two forms of insurgency in Russia: the nationality movements in the borderlands and the forces of revolutionary socialism dedicated to the overthrow of the tsarist state. The aim of the policy of backing national revolution was the creation of states separate from Russia but dependent on Germany.[53] The Austrian policy likewise sought to weaken Russia through the liberation of the nationalities in the Russian empire bordering on Austria-Hungary. Insofar as the German promotion of the Bolshevik revolution enabled Lenin to come to power, so was it possible for the Reich to carry out the eastern policy of Germany with little hindrance from Russia and effect the mass transfer of troops to the Western Front in preparing for the offensives of 1918.

In the west the Germans could do little through political methods. They plotted the Irish uprising of 1916 with Irish revolutionaries. After bringing the Irish leader Sir Roger Casement to Germany from New York, they later landed him in Ireland from a U-boat without providing enough military support for a successful rebellion.[54] German policy promoted

52. Memoranda from Moltke to Jagow, August 2 and 5, 1914, Nrs. 1070 and 1161; Geiss, *Julikrise*, 2: 624, 697; Fritz Fischer, "Deutsche Kriegsziele, Revolutionierung und Separatfrieden im Osten 1914–1918," *Historische Zeitschrift* 188 (1959): 260–62; Fischer, *Germany's Aims in the First World War*, 121–27.
53. See above, p. 193; and Fischer, *Germany's Aims in the First World War*, 134–46.
54. Casement for his part returned to Ireland, not to lead a rebellion, but to warn against precipitating a revolt that without substantial German support would only be a bloodbath. R. R. Doerries, "Die Mission Sir Roger Casements im Deutschen Reich 1914–1916," *Historische Zeitschrift* 222 (1976): 623–24; Brian Inglis, *Roger Casement* (London, 1973), 311–13.

Flemish separatism, and the Reich attempted to penetrate the French press in the interests of sowing pacifism and defeatism.[55]

On the Entente side, the British supplemented their military operations against the Ottoman Empire with political measures to sustain the revolt of the Arabs—armed assistance, the grant of funds, and the pledge of independence from the Turks. The British gained valuable allies for delivering the death blow to the empire of the sultans and assurance that the Arab lands would remain separate entities at the peace.

The Allies turned the grand strategy of political warfare against Germany and Austria themselves. The massive propaganda offensive from the Italian front was unleashed against both the Austro-Hungarian troops and the interior of the multinational empire. The propaganda cut deeply because the Allies encouraged the subject nationalities to form national states through recognizing the national councils and armed forces they had organized. The effect combined with the growing exhaustion and hunger of the population in Austria-Hungary to set off a series of revolutions in the empire and cause its collapse. In this, Allied propaganda scored what may have been the most telling stroke of all in political warfare.

The diplomacy of the Allies and the United States and the great policy statements of Wilson laid the foundation of the propaganda attack on German autocracy and militarism. The Reich could not withstand these political assaults along with military defeat and near-starvation. The German revolution and the end of the war occurred simultaneously.

Political warfare demonstrated far more efficacy in the first total war than in the second. Political warfare had a role in bringing about the Russian and German revolutions, the breakup of the Dual Empire, the entry of the United States into the war, and the earlier ending of the conflict.[56] Its success depended only in part on methods and concentration of effort; superiority of military and economic power and attraction of ideological program were instrumental factors of much greater weight.

On a global scale the strength of Allied political warfare inhered in the idealistic and forward-looking content of its propaganda. Wilson preached, in the exalted tones of his speeches, the liberal dispensation of

55. The agent Bolo Pasha used funds of German origin for this purpose in France. Poincaré, *Au service de la France,* 10: 59–60; Wright, *Raymond Poincaré and the French Presidency,* 185–87.

56. See Holborn, *Political Collapse of Europe,* 91; Cruttwell, *Role of British Strategy in the Great War,* 86; Vagts, *History of Militarism,* 288.

democracy, freedom, self-determination, the sovereignty of small nations, permanent peace, and a new world order founded in a league of nations. The president created thereby a compelling program and made himself the supreme master of political warfare. Allied propaganda inspired with this ideology voiced the political aspirations of the age.

The Central Powers offered no political conceptions adjusted to the times with the power to compete in world appeal. Shut in by the blockade and immured in their obsolete institutional structure, the Germans suffered a "blockade of minds."[57] They could not mount a body of ideas having a universal potential like the Wilsonian principles or the Leninist ideology. While the Allies framed a political credo that won the world, the Germans could do no better than seek in Mitteleuropa essentially an arrangement for institutionalizing German supremacy on the continent. Britain and the United States went forth with the ardor of crusaders, Germany and Austria with a lack of inner conviction in their own institutional foundations and political principles.[58]

The most extreme assessment of the influence exerted by propaganda was made in Germany. The belief in the extraordinary power of propaganda was magnified after the war by the German military and conservatives. The idea that the destructive effects of Allied propaganda on the home front caused the defeat of Germany belonged to the stab-in-the-back fantasy. The political right appropriated this shallow means to restore faith in the army and the militarist state. The tendency reached its grotesque zenith in the political methods of Hitler and the Third Reich.

A postwar current of opinion elsewhere exaggerated the effect of political warfare in the past struggle. The inundation of the United States by wartime propaganda led to a reaction among historical revisionists and publicists, who attributed to it undue influence in driving America to war.[59]

57. Bethmann Hollweg, *Betrachtungen*, 2: 58.

58. On the ideological weakness of Germany and the strength of the Allies in political warfare, see Dehio, *Germany and the World War*, 94–106; and the probing of the subject to the philosophical level by Thimme, *Weltkrieg ohne Waffen*, 208–46.

59. The tendency to exaggerate the importance of propaganda in inducing the United States to go to war persisted throughout the interwar period. The isolated factor of propaganda should not be given undue weight in explaining the entry of the United States. American historians of the war period are now of the prevailing view that the great body of Americans were committed to neutrality until 1917, that is, so long as that policy best served the national interest. See Smith, *Great Departure*, 5.

The role of political warfare in the conflict is to be neither read too large nor minimized. This means of war supplied a valuable supplement to the traditional military instruments and strategies of power. Political warfare served the belligerents best when special targets of opportunity appeared on the horizon, such as the disintegrating conditions of the Austrian and Russian empires. Political warfare was the most effective when it carried an ideology of universal appeal attuned to the times. The results accomplished cost little in comparison with the war of shot and shell.[60]

During the last year of the war the Bolsheviks inaugurated a new era of political warfare, in which its objective had no relevance to the alignments of power in the war but heralded the future of ideological conflict between Communism and the free world.[61]

3. ECONOMIC WARFARE

The most familiar precedents in economic warfare, both offensive and defensive, had been set by the British blockade of the continent in the Napoleonic wars and Napoleon's counter with the Continental System. From 1914 through 1918 the dimensions of economic warfare, its techniques, its efficacy, and its more extensive involvement of neutrals expanded the practice until it became a major, if not a decisive, part of the war.[62]

In the economic war a maritime economic system was locked in a struggle à outrance with a continental system. The Allies could maintain uninterrupted contact with the overseas nations and draw on their immense resources through channels of trade and finance. The economy of the Reich, however, was less dependent on external food-supply sources, for it produced 75–80 percent of its food requirements, to Britain's 35 percent of its caloric consumption. Germany also had physically unassailable access to foods in the neighboring European neutrals. Germany was more vulnerable in the matter of raw materials.[63]

60. On the cost of British and American informational operations: Steed, *Through Thirty Years,* 2: 227, and Creel, *How We Advertised America,* 13.

61. Bolshevik methods of ideological struggle in this period are treated in Helmut Tiedemann, *Sowjetrussland und die Revolutionierung Deutschlands 1917–1919* (Berlin, 1936), 23–96.

62. On the defensive and offensive character of economic warfare, see Paul Einsig, *Economic Warfare* (London, 1940), 1–3. On the importance of economic warfare in the First World War: Salter, *Allied Shipping Control,* 1; A. C. Bell, *A History of the Blockade of Germany, Austria-Hungary, Bulgaria, and Turkey* (1937; public ed., London, 1961), 214.

63. Fayle, *Seaborne Trade,* 1: 3; Leo Grebler and Wilhelm Winkler, *The Cost of the World War to Germany and Austria-Hungary* (New Haven, 1940), 9, 12; Olson, *Wartime Shortages,* 74.

In a war waged against the Central Powers, Russia suffered the misfortune of geography. This liability fated Russia to be the victim of a double blockade, the direct one of the Central Powers and the indirect one the Allies laid around Germany and Austria. The two blockades worked to isolate Russia, disrupting its patterns of external trade.[64]

The chief weapon that each camp used to attack the economic power of the other was the blockade. In addition, each coalition of powers carried on an unceasing campaign to bend the economic activities of the neutrals to the prejudice of the enemy and the benefit of themselves.

The Allies applied the blockade against neutral trade with the enemy as well as directly against enemy trade. Britain controlled the flow of supplies through European neutrals to the enemy by trade agreements rationing the goods imported by neutrals to prewar levels. Britain utilized the leverage primarily of coal exports and provision of worldwide bunkerage, financial, and insurance facilities to secure these limitations and the use of neutral shipping in the carriage of goods between Allied ports or between Allied and neutral ports. A huge and complicated machinery evolved to enforce restrictions on enemy and neutral trade and to police the trade agreements.[65]

Germany attempted by two means to check the tendency of European neutral shipping and trade to fall under the control of the Allies. The Reich sought to intimidate neutral ships by warning that they would enter the proclaimed blockade zone around Britain at their own risk. In trade with the neutrals, Berlin exerted some counterweight to British influence through coal exports from Germany and occupied Belgium.

The neutrals of Europe were drawn into a cross fire between the blockades. Their shipping and trade were involved only in a less degree than those of the belligerents. Indeed, Norway lost about one-half of its merchant marine in the war, compared with Britain's approximately 38 percent.[66]

Each coalition fought with concentrated force to foil the other's attack by blockade. Through diplomacy, public appeal, clandestine warfare, and finally the all-out U-boat offensive, Germany combated the one-sided

---

64. Boris E. Nolde, *Russia in the Economic War* (New Haven, 1928), 22–24.

65. D. T. Jack, *Studies in Economic Warfare* (London, 1940), 108, 139–43; Fayle, *Seaborne Trade*, 2: 154–58, 401–02. On the creation and operation of the rationing system, see Bell, *History of the Blockade*, 249–400, 492–54; and on the rationing agreements, Marion C. Siney, *The Allied Blockade of Germany, 1914–1918* (Ann Arbor, 1957), 75–107.

66. Jack, *Studies in Economic Warfare*, 133–34; Olav Riste, *The Neutral Ally* (Oslo, 1965), 226.

transfusion of economic strength and transfer of arms from the United States to the Allies made possible by the latter's command of the seas. But the Germans and Austrians, being inferior in naval power, had to rely chiefly on measures of economic resistance in waging the economic war. The Allies had to complement their naval counteraction with a variety of economic adjustments to contain the peril of the shipping losses. The belligerents became engaged in a critical struggle of shortages.[67]

The relentless pressure of the blockades drove the main warring powers toward national self-sufficiency. This force and the ever-increasing need for the largest possible measure of war production compelled a reorganization of the national economy and state machinery in the form of war socialism, or *Zwangswirtschaft.* The expanded state of many agencies and tentacles directed the economic life of the nation and put into operation a planned economy for the purpose of utilizing the national resources with maximum efficiency in the prosecution of the war. The state was forced to create a mechanism for ordering priorities of allocations and distribution of scarce raw materials and manpower. In order to reduce food consumption and insure a more equitable distribution of scarce foodstuffs, the state had to institute a system of food controls—rationing, meatless days, fixed prices or ceilings, substitutions, requisitioning.

Normal patterns of production and consumption were altered drastically. Agriculture and industry had to adapt to the reduced import of primary materials or to losses from enemy occupation of national territory. (The German possession of northern France cost the French economy one-fifth of its wheat, one-half of its coal, and two-thirds of its iron production.) Many substitutions were made to compensate for shortages. The utilization of wastes was pursued intensively. The application of science and technology to industry was rapidly extended, especially in the production of ersatz articles and the creation of new industries in the chemical, metallurgical, automotive, aircraft, and communications fields. The demands of war production and the manpower shortages spurred a quickened adoption of automatic machinery, the Taylor system of efficient organization of factory work, and the methods of standardization and mass production.[68]

67. A close analyst of Britain's wartime shortages attributed the defeat of the submarine not to the convoy and the Allied naval achievements, but to certain economic adjustments to the shipping shortage. Olson, *Wartime Shortages,* 32.

68. Arthur Fontaine, *French Industry during the War* (New Haven, 1926), 16, 93–98; Maurice Crozet, *L'époque contemporaine,* 5th ed. (Paris, 1969), 17–18; D. W. Brogan, *The*

The urgent demands of factory and field for manpower were met by the employment of women, youths, child labor, older men, prisoners of war, colonial labor, and civilians from occupied areas. Women in Britain comprised 60 percent of the workers in the manufacture of shells, and in Germany 37.8 percent in typical armaments plants. Inexperienced workers caused a dilution of labor. Labor controls were instituted to insure efficient war production. In return for labor's submission to the controls and in recognition of its essential role in war production, labor gained a new influence—more scope for political activity and progress toward equal status with management in settling labor's disputes and demands.[69]

The British demonstrated extraordinary ability in defensive economic warfare. Britain's adjustments compensated for shipping losses not only by a program of building merchant ships but also by economizing of cargo space through the government control of imports, exports, food, production, and shipping. A host of new agencies sprang into being to apply many of the controls.[70] Britain was the only European belligerent that seriously tried to solve the inflationary problem by increasing its income tax and levying a war profits tax on corporations and an excess profit duty.[71]

British farming was reoriented to a more intensive agriculture. Livestock farming was extensively converted to crop production, grasslands put into crops, and vegetable production encouraged by garden "allotments." The combined reduction in food consumption and expansion in home production enabled Britain to decrease food imports by 6.7 million tons, or 63 percent, from 1913 to 1918 and save the equivalent amount of shipping tonnage. The overall management of the food supply was so efficient that at the end of the war the calories consumed per head of the population exceeded slightly the consumption at the beginning.

The crucial shortage was in shipping. Adjustments were made to use more efficiently existing British and Allied shipping. Steps were taken to clear the congestion at British ports and to expedite the handling of

---

Development of Modern France, rev. ed., 2 vols. (New York, 1966), 2: 521; Grebler and Winkler, *Cost of the World War to Germany and Austria-Hungary*, 24–54.

69. Clough, *Economic History of Europe in the Twentieth Century*, 47; Grebler and Winkler, *Cost of the World War to Germany and Austria-Hungary*, 29–31; Crouzet, *L'époque contemporaine*, 17; Kielmansegg, *Deutschland und der Erste Weltkrieg*, 191 ff.

70. On Britain's economic defense against the submarine blockade and measures to combat shortages, see Olson, *Wartime Shortages*, 23–30, 85–111.

71. Henry William Spiegel, *The Economics of Total War* (New York, 1942), 267–68; Horst Mendershausen, *The Economics of War* (New York, 1943), 223.

cargoes through port. The "Atlantic Concentration" shifted the trade from Australia and east Asia to the United States and Canada to the extent possible, so as to cut down the time of ships at sea. For the United States to provide the necessary food exports to Europe under this scheme of diversion and to feed its own armed forces, it was also obliged to undertake measures of food conservation, substitution, and expanded production.[72]

The British system of controls over shipping and supplies had parallel organizations in France and Italy. There evolved by 1918 an inter-Allied organization of control functioning through the national systems. The core part consisted of the Allied Maritime Transport Council, its Executive, and a secretariat, supplemented by the Inter-Allied Munitions Council and the Inter-Allied Food Council.[73]

In the camp of the Central Powers, Germany acted in defense against the progressive strangulation of the blockade first by organizing in August 1914 the War Raw Materials Agency. That the war economy of Germany managed so long with an insufficiency of raw materials was due to the efforts of this powerful bureau—the most successful of all the Reich's official agencies taking part in the running of the war economy.[74]

The main organs directing the German machinery for economic warfare were, however, the Prussian ministry of war and the War Office. The latter was created in November 1916 out of Ludendorff's desire to establish under the control of the high command a supreme centralized organization for managing the war economy on the model of the British ministry of munitions. This was one of a triplice of initiatives that the Hindenburg-Ludendorff team settled on, to expand the war economy of Germany and attack the all-pervasive problem of the manpower stringency.[75]

The second measure, enacted as the Auxiliary Service Law of December 5, 1916, required all males from 18 to 60 years of age not in military service to accept essential war jobs. The legislation, completed by the Reichstag, recognized the trade unions and provided for implementation and arbitration committees in which the workers would have equal representation with the employers. The rights of association and meeting were

72. Olson, *Wartime Shortages*, 87–90.
73. Salter, *Allied Shipping Control*, 88–97, 145–47, 175–85, 239.
74. Gerald D. Feldman, *Army, Industry, and Labor in Germany, 1914–1918* (Princeton, 1966), 45–52.
75. Ibid., 169–95.

confirmed for the workers. The act significantly acknowledged the political force now represented by the trade unions and the Social Democratic party. But labor turnover was not reduced nor the manpower stringency relieved.[76]

The third project was the Hindenburg program of massive war production, which set unrealistic targets of doubling the munitions output and tripling that of artillery and machine guns. This overreaching expansion was condemned to a cutback in goals and stopping of further construction of new plants, while half-finished and finished idle factories were left scattered throughout Germany. The ill-conceived effort heightened the steel scarcity and accelerated the industrial disorganization, adding to the strain that caused the great transport and coal crisis of 1916–17.[77]

The Reich contended with a growing scarcity of food from 1915 on, which was due to poor harvests and reduction in imports, as well as to withdrawal of men and horses for military use. The system of food control never approached the raw materials model or the British success in the management of the food supply. The army, self-suppliers, those in heavy work, and patrons of the black market were favored at the expense of others. The supply in surplus and deficiency areas was never equalized.[78]

The half-measures and official bungling, along with the abuses of special interests, belonged typically to the failure to achieve a unified food organization with full authority over all Reich states and groups. The rising tensions and recrimination between the rich and poor, the right and left, city and country, state and state were manifested in the increasing seriousness of strikes and food riots. The deficient administration of the food supply in truth reflected the shortcomings of the German state itself in the supreme test of total war—the incomplete unity of the Bismarckian Reich and the unreadiness to work closely together like the British in carrying out a program of food production and control.

The economic pressures of the blockade drove Germany to systematic exploitation of the occupied countries. The Reich combed out reserves of materials, machines, even whole industrial plants, especially in Belgium

76. See ibid., 535–41, for the text of the law and pp. 247–49 for an estimate of its political and social significance.

77. Ibid., 149–61, 253–73, 494–95; Grebler and Winkler, *Cost of the World War to Germany and Austria-Hungary*, 55–58.

78. Feldman, *Army, Industry, and Labor in Germany*, 104–06; Olson, *Wartime Shortages*, 139; Kielmansegg, *Deutschland und der Erste Weltkrieg*, 174–80.

and northern France for use in the German war economy. Germany drew on the iron ore of northern France, the coal of Belgium, the coal and timber of Poland, the grain and oil of Romania, and the wheat of the Ukraine.

The Reich never mastered the manpower problem or overcame the critical scarcity of coal, iron, steel, and food from the winter of 1916–17 on. The German economy was constricted until industrial output declined to 73 percent of that in 1913, agricultural production fell, the transport system was in disrepair, and food consumption sank to the level of malnutrition for many. In 1918 the ration of cereals constituted no more than 64 percent of prewar consumption, meat 18 percent, and fats 12 percent.[79]

The stringency in raw materials in the Habsburg empire and in food in Austria proper were more acute and the control machinery less effective than that in Germany. The raging inflation outstripped the inflation in Germany, as Vienna financed the war more and more by the printing press. The agricultural production in Austria fell to 41 percent of the normal yield, and in Hungary to 57 percent. In the latter part of the war deprivation was common in the cities of Austria.[80]

The economic war stimulated official and public interest among Germans and Austrians in the supranational reorganization of Central Europe. The memorandum of September 9, 1914, which government officials prepared for Bethmann Hollweg at the high noon of German victory, proposed a comprehensive economic association including Germany, Austria-Hungary, France, and Belgium to be formed after France had been eliminated from the war. The union was intended to establish the economic predominance of Germany on the continent and at the same time to create an economic and political organization, a new version of the Napoleonic Continental System, for continuing the war against Britain.[81]

Amidst the growing Mitteleuropa movement in Germany and Austria, the appearance of Friedrich Naumann's *Mitteleuropa* in October 1915 met with a sensational reception. The work envisioned Mitteleuropa issuing

79. Grebler and Winkler, *Cost of the World War to Germany and Austria-Hungary,* 27–30; Olson, *Wartime Shortages,* 81; Fayle, *Seaborne Trade,* 2: 404–05; Bell, *History of the Blockade,* 672.

80. Joseph Redlich, *Austrian War Government* (New Haven, 1929), 127; Grebler and Winkler, *Cost of the World War to Germany and Austria-Hungary,* 151; Gustav Gratz and Richard Schüller, *Der wirtschaftliche Zusammenbruch Österreich-Ungarns* (Vienna, 1930), 46; May, *Passing of the Hapsburg Monarchy,* 2: 662–68; Fayle, *Seaborne Trade,* 2: 166.

81. Zechlin, "Deutschland zwischen Kabinettskrieg und Wirtschaftskrieg," 419–47.

"from the prison of our war economy," from the common economic experience of the war. The Wilhelmstrasse in November proposed to Vienna the negotiation of an agreement for an economic community of the two empires, embracing a customs alliance and a common trade policy, along with a union of railways.[82]

In 1917 the Mitteleuropa movement lost its vigor. The public was preoccupied with internal difficulties, and interest was shifting to concern with internal reforms. The course of empire was beckoning in the east with the collapse of Russia. If the annexationists opposed the advocates of Mitteleuropa on the right, the radical socialists both in Germany and in Austria attacked on the left an arrangement that would mean the continuation of economic warfare after the peace. Swelling the opposition were the exporting, shipping, and colonial interests, which foresaw a better economic choice for Germany in the expansion of its postwar world trade.[83]

In 1916–17 the German foreign office nevertheless became more conscious of the need for continental integration. Negotiations between Berlin and Vienna on technical arrangements produced an agreement for a customs partnership that would eventually join the two empires in a free common market. Aborted by the end of the war, the enterprise remained only on paper. It was a far cry from the vision entertained by the enthusiasts for a suprastate Mitteleuropa taking its place in the world with the anticipated giant powers of the future, America, the British Empire, and Russia.[84]

82. Henry Cord Meyer, *Mitteleuropa in German Thought and Action, 1815–1945* (The Hague, 1955), 137–206 passim; Friedrich Naumann, *Mitteleuropa* (Berlin, 1915), 138–39, 263; Theodor Heuss, *Friedrich Naumann*, 3d ed. (Munich, 1968), 361–70; Gustav Gratz and Richard Schüller, *The Economic Policy of Austria-Hungary during the War in Its External Relations* (New Haven, 1928), 6–12.

83. Meyer, *Mitteleuropa*, 233–39, 250, 275–76.

84. Naumann was thinking in terms of four superpowers existing during the postwar period, among which Mitteleuropa would figure as one. *Mitteleuropa*, 165–74.

Chapter Eleven

THE FEBRUARY REVOLUTION IN RUSSIA

1. ROADS TO REVOLUTION

THE war spawned a dozen political and social revolutions, of which the Russian towered in momentous consequences for Russia itself and for the world at large. The Russian revolution, one might say, began with the revolution of 1905 and ended after the Bolsheviks came to power and consolidated their rule. Rosa Luxemburg formulated this interpretation quite simply: "the revolution of 1917 was a direct continuation of that of 1905–07."[1] Throughout these years of challenge from the opposition and response, whether concessive or repressive, from the tsarist regime, the political struggle involved a fourfold problem: the need to maintain a credible and efficacious state authority; to modernize the Russian government and economy; to integrate society; and to satisfy the aspirations of the people.

The revolution of 1905 made slight progress in solving this comprehensive problem. The tsar granted political concessions in the October Manifesto. Nicholas II then not only suppressed the further course of the revolution but backtracked. The revolution announced the coming of mass political action and produced an institutional improvisation, the soviets of workers' deputies—a form of revolutionary organization that was to be revived in the revolution of 1917. The uprising gave the socialist parties and the industrial workers training in revolution of broad scope.[2]

When the politically blind tsar turned away from the path of constitutional monarchy after the revolution, nothing was left to resist the decay of the tsardom. The government fell under the sway of mediocre favorites who were made and unmade by a camarilla around the tsarina and the debauched Grigori Rasputin. The tsarist state lost its moral authority through the corruption and obscurantist reaction of the court and the

1. Rosa Luxemburg, *The Russian Revolution* (Ann Arbor, 1961), 31, quoted by Roger Pethybridge, "The Significance of Communications in 1917," *Soviet Studies* 19 (1967): 113.
2. On the significance of the 1905 soviets, see Oskar Anweiler, *Die Rätebewegung in Russland 1905–1921* (Leiden, 1958), 79.

camarilla's intervention in government affairs.

Russia had experienced two spurts of rapid industrial growth since the 1890s, and its average annual rate of industrial growth had been higher than 5 percent since 1885. The country in 1914 nonetheless remained an economically less developed land. Its economy was primarily agrarian, and its agricultural technology was in a primitive stage. Native private capitalism and urbanization were so limited that a bourgeoisie in the western sense had scarcely emerged.[3] Russia was a great power only by import—import of capital, machinery and equipment, technology, and management.[4]

The need for integration arose from the divisions rending the Russian social body: between the state and "society," or the educated classes; and between the privileged classes and the largely uneducated masses of workers and peasants. A threat to the old order was implied by the rapidly sharpening conflict between the privileged classes and the autocracy.[5] The 1905 revolution gave notice that the chasm between the privileged classes and the masses of workers and peasants was not long to be tolerated.

During the prewar decade, the aspirations of the peoples within the empire entered the foreground of their consciousness. For the peasants and workers the desire for a better economic and social status became a motivating factor of their lives. The workers grasped for the improvement of working conditions and the guarantee of political rights. The intelligentsia and bourgeois groups wanted either fundamental reform or revolution. The policy of forced russification in the western borderlands stimulated the growth of national consciousness among the minorities. The extent to which the tsarist regime could or would go in meeting popular aspirations, both of the Russians themselves and of the minorities, was a test of survival for the tsarist state.

A number of alternatives were presented to the public during the revo-

3. On the various lines of economic advance and the manifestations of Russia's economic backwardness during the reign of Nicholas II, see *Cambridge Economic History of Europe*, vol. 6, pt. 1: 21–23, and pt. 2: 764–863; Hugh Seton-Watson, *The Russian Empire, 1801–1917* (Oxford, 1967), 517–33, 649–60. On the failure of the bourgeoisie to appear in Russia: Richard Pipes, *Russia under the Old Regime* (New York, 1974), 191–220.
4. The state of Russian backwardness in relation to the Russian revolution is treated as the focal theme in Theodore H. Von Laue, *Why Lenin? Why Stalin?*, 2d ed. (Philadelphia, 1971).
5. The subject of the acute crises caused by this conflict between the state power and educated society is developed by Leopold Haimson, "The Problem of Social Stability in Urban Russia, 1905–1917 (Part Two)," *Slavic Review* 24 (1965): 1–22.

lutionary period 1905–17 for solving Russia's fourfold internal problem. The first to receive practical effect, in partial degree, was the concept of reformist constitutional monarchy, introduced through the reforms of those two extraordinary ministers Count Sergei Witte and Petr Stolypin. Their plan was to save Russia from mass revolution by reforms, beginning with the October Manifesto, that would accord the public political freedoms and a legislative body while converting the peasantry into a prosperous rural middle class of smallholders endowed with civil rights, and the industrial workers into a group of peaceful trade unionists.

The revolution from above might well have succeeded if Stolypin had escaped assassination and retained the confidence of the tsar. Stolypin was so certain that his program offered a warranty against revolution from below that, according to Sazonov, he was accustomed to repeat: "War alone can assure the triumph of revolution in Russia. Without war, it is impossible."[6]

The other possible courses were put before the public in the ideology and programs of the political parties.[7] The principal nonsocialist party of Constitutional Democrats (Kadets) represented the enlightened gentry and professional classes. Led by the historian and publicist Paul N. Miliukov, the Kadets stood for the political westernization of Russia. They sought to establish the reign of civil and political liberties, social reform, and full-fledged constitutional democracy operating through a government responsible to, or "having the confidence of," the Duma.[8]

The Octobrist party of moderate conservatives, based on the richer gentry and big industrialists, was made up of prudent gradualists ready to accept the October Manifesto as a starting point for a constitutional re-

6. S. Sazonov, Les années fatales (Paris, 1927), 250. On the likely or possible success of the Witte-Stolypin alternative sustained in force, see the judgments of the following observers and historians: Buchanan, My Mission to Russia, 1: 161; Alexandr Kerensky, The Crucifixion of Liberty (New York, 1934), 158; Donald W. Treadgold, Lenin and His Rivals (New York, 1955), 268; Robert Conquest, V. I. Lenin (New York, 1972), 57; Adam B. Ulam, The Bolsheviks (New York, 1965), 287–88; Oliver H. Radkey, The Agrarian Foes of Bolshevism (New York, 1958), 82.

7. The role of the parties in the Duma is surveyed by Warren B. Walsh, "Political Parties in the Russian Dumas," Journal of Modern History 22 (1950): 144–50; Alfred Levin, The Second Duma (New Haven, 1940); Alfred Levin, The Third Duma, Election and Profile (Hamden, Conn., 1973); C. Jay Smith, "The Russian Third State Duma: An Analytical Profile," Russian Review 17 (1958): 201–10.

8. Thomas Riha, A Russian European: Paul Miliukov in Russian Politics (Notre Dame, 1969), 87–201; Treadgold, Lenin and His Rivals, 119–34, 192–206, 242–54; William G. Rosenberg, Liberals in the Russian Revolution (Princeton, 1974), 11–38.

gime.[9] They supported the strong government and reformist program of the Stolypin alternative. The distressing level of competence and authority to which the government sank drove the Octobrists into the opposition by 1912. The Progressives—the spokesmen of zemstvo circles, some intellectuals, and industrial and business interests of Moscow—were politically oriented between the Kadets and Octobrists.[10]

The revolutionary parties were the Socialist Revolutionaries (SRs), Mensheviks, and Bolsheviks. The agrarian socialism of the SRs stemmed from the belief that because of Russia's peculiar historical conditions— notably the communal and equalitarian tendencies of the peasantry and the artificial growth of capitalism in union with the autocratic state— Russia would follow its own distinctive road to socialism by way of socialization of the land combined with a private economy elsewhere.[11]

Each of the two factions in the Social Democratic Labor party, the Mensheviks and Bolsheviks, formed "a party within a party" of Marxist creed. In the adaptation of this ideology to Russian conditions, the two factions developed unbridgeable differences in considerable part because of Lenin's uncompromising and authoritarian disposition. A deeper difference than that between the tough and tender-minded, however, divided the two groups, namely, the traditional Russian division between "westernizers" and nativists. The Bolshevik Karl Radek flagged this distinction with the brilliant mot that "western Europe begins with the Mensheviks."[12] On the other side it is implicit in the assessment that Lenin's main intellectual achievement was to "russify" Marxism.[13]

The Mensheviks resembled the reformist Social Democratic parties of western Europe in ideological principles and party organization. They

9. It has been maintained by conservatives that the faithful observance of the October Manifesto, both by the tsar and by the Duma representatives, would alone have changed the character of the tsarist state by dividing the legitimacy of power between the people and the hereditary monarchy and its exercise between the Duma and the tsar. See V. A. Maklakov, *Préface aux interrogatoires des ministres, conseillers, généraux, hauts fonctionnaires de la cour impériale russe par la commission extraordinaire du gouvernement provisoire de 1917* (Paris, 1927), especially p. 50.

10. Riha, *Russian European*, 200–03.

11. The ideology and program of the SRs are presented in the outstanding work of scholarship by Radkey, *Agrarian Foes of Bolshevism*, 6–85.

12. Edward Hallett Carr, *The Bolshevik Revolution, 1917–1923*, 3 vols. (London, 1950–53), 1: 40.

13. John Keep, "1917: The Tyranny of Paris over Petrograd," *Soviet Studies* 20 (1968– 69): 30.

envisaged a long period of capitalist development in Russia intervening between the bourgeois-democratic and the proletarian revolutions when the conditions for the existence of a full-fledged proletarian class would be prepared by the formation of a strong trade-union movement. The Mensheviks vigorously resisted Lenin's dictatorial practices and recurrent splitting of the party.

The ideology and organization of the Bolshevik faction belonged to Lenin, the most impatient and complete revolutionary of the modern era. The ideology of this activist, rejecting socialist reformism and bread-and-butter trade unionism, was designed to accelerate Marx's timetable of history. A dictatorship of the proletariat and peasantry would complete the bouregois-democratic revolution and then proceed without pause to execute the proletarian revolution. The completion of the bourgeois revolution would ignite the socialist revolution in western Europe, and its triumph there would sustain the socialist revolution in Russia.[14]

Lenin had no confidence in the spontaneous action of the masses in initiating or putting through the revolution. A vanguard, inspiring a revolutionary consciousness in the workers, must organize the revolutionary movement and give political direction to the masses. A party capable of this role under Russian conditions must be formed as a select and secret band of professional revolutionaries unswervingly dedicated to the faith and to the leader. Lenin labeled the principle by which the party operated "democratic centralism." This was cosmetics for an authoritarian, elitist organization managed by a Russian Robespierre (the Menshevik reproach) with an unyielding intolerance of dissent.

Lenin created a formidable revolutionary machine for utilizing and directing the masses. In perceiving that the question of organization was fundamental to the success of the party and the realization of the revolution, Lenin introduced an innovation in Russian socialism and laid out the pattern for modern revolutionary movements as well as for the one-party

14. On Lenin, his thought, and the creation of the Bolshevik party: David Shub, *Lenin,* rev. ed. (Baltimore, 1966); Louis Fischer, *The Life of Lenin* (New York, 1964); Conquest, *Lenin;* Bertram D. Wolfe, *Three Who Made a Revolution* (New York, 1964); Stefan T. Possony, *Lenin: The Compulsive Revolutionary* (Chicago, 1964); Ulam, *Bolsheviks;* Treadgold, *Lenin and His Rivals;* N. D. Krupskaya, *Memories of Lenin,* 2 vols. (Moscow, 1930); Richard Pipes, "The Origins of Bolshevism: The Intellectual Evolution of Young Lenin," in *Revolutionary Russia,* ed. Richard Pipes (Cambridge, Mass., 1968), 26–52; Georg Lukács, *Lenin: A Study on the Unity of His Thought* (London, 1967); Leonard Schapiro, *The Communist Party of the Soviet Union* (New York, 1960).

state. Yet it should be said that Lenin built into this structure a place for himself as a proletarian tsar, partly owing to Russian tradition, partly in reflection of his own nature, partly because of the demands of underground warfare with the tsarist political police.[15]

2. THE STRUGGLE OVER CONSTITUTIONAL MONARCHY

The years 1907–12 were a grim period for all of the revolutionary parties. The constructive measures of the Stolypin alternative, planned to transform the tsarist autocracy into a middle-class constitutional monarchy, were joined with crushing police activity in a systematic attack on the revolutionary movement. The principal revolutionary leaders were forced to go back into exile and their parties to go underground.

A resurgent political temper made itself felt from 1912 on, to the outbreak of the war. With the assassination of Stolypin in 1911 the degeneration of the tsarist state resumed. The Bolsheviks and Mensheviks pressed political activity among the trade unions both by legal and by underground means. The Bolsheviks began publication of the legal newspaper *Pravda* and finally organized a separate party in 1912. Discontent was rife among workers and peasants. The swelling strike movement of 1912–14 culminated in the Saint Petersburg strike of July 1914, when 140,000 workers took to the street and the barricades. The strike was ended with bloody suppression by the police and Cossacks. The British ambassador recorded in his memoirs that "there had never been a time when Russian society and the Russian people had been so deeply permeated with the revolutionary spirit."[16]

The unrest of the masses merged with the outburst of nationalist indignation after the Austrian ultimatum to Serbia. Sazonov told the German ambassador during the July crisis: "Were the Russian government to tolerate this [subjection of Serbia to Austrian vassalage], there would be revolution in the country."[17]

At the outbreak of war the reaction of the masses submerged the revolutionary movement in a flood of patriotic enthusiasm. The Petersburg strike suddenly ended, and the nonrevolutionary political parties joined in a political truce with the government. The threat to the country and the

15. Alfred Meyer, *Communism*, 3d ed. (New York, 1967), 42–43; Von Laue, *Why Lenin? Why Stalin?*, 94; Ulam, *Bolsheviks*, 180.
16. Buchanan, *My Mission to Russia*, 1: 164.
17. Stengers, "July 1914," 117.

outburst of national feeling afforded the tsardom one last chance to save itself by organizing a strong and popular wartime government.

But this was beyond the capacities of the tsardom, in view of the nature of the tsar and the demands of the total war on the backward state. From the beginning the strains of the ordeal commenced to expose the inadequacy of the Russian war machine and of the tsarist state in mortal struggle with the modern giant power of Germany. By controlling the Straits and the Baltic in conjunction with the submarine campaign, the German alliance threw a blockade around Russia that gradually choked it. The economy was disrupted by the isolation, working together with the withdrawals of men from factory and farm for army service and with the disorderly evacuation of industry from areas near the front. The hordes of more than 3 million refugees overran Petersburg and Moscow. The influx imposed a mountainous burden on transportation facilities, health care, and food supply.[18] This and other wartime burdens reduced the transportation system to a shambles. Russia lost the production of the great belt of territories surrendered in the west. Under these conditions, the output of coal, iron, and steel actually dropped from 1913 to 1916.[19]

The government created a number of central wartime agencies having the status of special councils to direct the national defense and war economy. The lax and shortsighted bureaucracy, however, proved incapable of grappling with the host of new problems and effecting the required economic reorganization. Private associations came forward to man the breach the civil administrations could not fill. The previously existing zemstvos and municipalities formed in each case all-Russian unions early in the war. Along with the Red Cross they did health and welfare work. These unions, their combined union of zemstvos and municipalities, and the War Industry Committees, formed in 1915, functioned as a vast voluntary organization of national scope for procuring raw materials, distributing orders for manufactured articles, producing goods, and delivering supplies to the army. In effect, Russian society was erecting within the edifice of the autocracy the beginnings of a democratic structure of self-

18. The chaos caused by the flood of refugees is noted by a chancellery official in Michael Cherniavsky, *Prologue to Revolution* (Englewood Cliffs, N. J., 1967), 39–40. The minutes published here of the secret meetings of the council of ministers throw a revealing light on many causes of the revolution emanating from the tsarist system of government and the delinquencies of the regime.

19. See Claus, *Die Kriegswirtschaft Russlands bis zur bolschwistischen Revolution.*

government filling the more urgent and immediate needs of the people yet at the same time hollowing out the authority of both the tsar and the Duma.[20] The rotting away of the autocracy continued in wartime, and the tsardom lost legitimacy with the people. The bungling and fumbling in the conduct of the war, the government's flagrant failures of supply, and the disorganization of the home front discredited the regime thoroughly. That the tsar responded to the overwhelming tide of defeat in 1915 by taking over the supreme command at Mogilev strengthened the ascendancy of the tsarina and Rasputin.[21] The tsarina came to play the role of a virtual regent, with Rasputin acting in effect as her chief minister. The interference of the "German woman"—unpopular now also because of her German family origin—and Rasputin moved one of the family grand dukes to warn the tsar: "today it is the government which is preparing the revolution. . . ."[22] Indicative of the uninterrupted state of government crisis was the constant reshuffling of the cabinet from 1915 on.

The maneuvers of the aged chief minister, Ivan Goremykin, designed to govern without the participation of the Duma, broke the political truce between the tsar's government on the one hand and the Duma and the nonrevolutionary parties on the otehr. Numerous moderates in the Duma, both liberals and conservatives, concluded after the military disasters of 1915 that if the Duma was to participate in organizing a government that could win the war, the parties must assume the role of a political opposition. Thus prompted, many of the Kadets under the leadership of Miliukov formed, with men from other parties to their right, chiefly the Progressives and Octobrists, the Progressive Bloc in August 1915. The zemstvos and municipal councils cooperated closely. The opposition elements had already forced Goremykin's government to remove the most objectionable ministers.

20. George Katkov, *Russia 1917: The February Revolution* (New York, 1967), 6–9; Marc Ferro, *La révolution russe de 1917* (Paris, 1967), 49–50; Claus, *Die Kriegswirtschaft Russlands bis zur bolschewistischen Revolution,* 71–78. On the system of special councils installed above other government organs, see Paul P. Gronsky and Nicholas J. Astrov, *The War and the Russian Government* (New Haven, 1929), 31–42.

21. The minutes of the council of ministers disclose its soul-searching, secret debate over the tsar's decision to assume the supreme command. Cherniavsky, *Prelude to Revolution,* 137–67.

22. Robert Paul Browder and Alexander F. Kerensky, eds., *The Russian Provisional Government, 1917: Documents,* 3 vols. (Stanford, 1961), 1: 17–18. Bernard Pares, "Rasputin and the Empress: Authors of the Russian Collapse," *Foreign Affairs* 6 (1927–28): 140–54.

The Progressive Bloc controlled the Duma with a majority, and the Kadets controlled the bloc. This majority pursued the goal of forming a moderate liberal government that "enjoyed the confidence of the country," or in brief of introducing constitutional monarchy without structural change. The bloc hoped for such a government to establish a firm and active authority that would save the state from the wreckage of military disaster and the monarchy from extinction in revolution from below. Otherwise the bloc espoused a program of advancing the rights of religious and national minorities and enacting reforms in behalf of the zemstvos, cooperatives, labor unions, and various employee groups.[23]

The attempt of the bloc to obtain the adoption of its program united with the debacle at the front and the tsar's imminent assumption of the supreme command to precipitate a deep political crisis in August–September 1915. Some members of the cabinet, including Sazonov, were sympathetic with the bloc as an antirevolutionary force, and the opposition's program was not unacceptable to most of the ministers. Like the bloc leaders, they were opposed to having Goremykin remain the head of the cabinet. Their collective letter to the tsar calling attention to differences with the chief minister and imploring Nicholas not to proceed with the assumption of the supreme command brought the crisis to a head.[24]

The tsar, influenced by the tsarina, prorogued the Duma and retained Goremykin. Thereafter Nicholas gradually dismissed the leading ministers opposed to Goremykin and friendly to the Duma majority. The Progressive Bloc had offered the tsar a solution for legitimizing the monarchy on a new foundation with the support of the Duma. If the tsar had accepted faithfully this initiative in "last-chance politics," it would, in Miliukov's belief, have removed the barriers to the eventual goal of a parliamentary state and saved the monarchy and Russia from revolution.

The Progressive Bloc and the ascendancy of the Kadets in the Duma continued down until the revolution. The bloc made few if any gains in the parliamentary struggle against the government. The Kadets lacked the

23. On the formation of the Progressive Bloc and its program: Thomas Riha, "Miliukov and the Progressive Bloc in 1915: A Study in Last-Chance Politics," *Journal of Modern History* 32 (1960): 16–20; Riha, *Russian European*, 218–31; Rosenberg, *Liberals in the Russian Revolution*, 39–42.

24. The text of the collective letter to the tsar is in Cherniavsky, *Prelude to Revolution*, 166–67. On the differences between Goremykin and the other ministers, see the minutes of the ministerial meeting of August 21, 1915, in ibid., 150–65; Riha, "Miliukov and the Progressive Bloc," 21–22.

determined leadership and organizational unity to play more than a passive part. As leader of the conservative wing of the party, Miliukov counseled patient waiting until the end of the war and championed nationalist war aims. The left wing of the party, increasingly critical of Miliukov's position and tactics, urged the party to take up the leadership of the popular movement, organize the masses, develop a closer relationship with the revolutionary parties, step up the struggle against the government, and work for the creation of a new constitutional order.[25]

By the fall of 1916, the pressure of the Kadet left wing on the party leadership intensified, as it reflected the more radical mood of the public. The tsar appointed more "gravediggers of the old regime" to ministerial posts. The crisis of political authority intensified. The war weariness and the progressive impoverishment of the people were translated into a revolutionary discontent.

Conceding to this change in public attitude, Miliukov at the reopening of the Duma session on November 1 delivered a historical and widely circulated indictment of the regime. This and other attacks in the Duma disposed the tsar no more than ever to make constitutional concessions, even though Grand Duke Nicholas tried to persuade him that the only alternative would be the loss of the throne.[26]

As the revolution approached, the conservative and moderate leaders of the Progressive Bloc would not rely on action of the masses and could not obtain constitutional reform by concession from Nicholas II. At this dead end they resorted to the methods of conspiracy. The plotters assassinated Rasputin in the hope that his elimination would provide the key to removing Alexandra to a convent or to the Crimea. They were unable to proceed any further with their scheme. Plans were also hatched, but never carried out, to dethrone Nicholas II by means of a palace coup.[27]

3. THUNDER ON THE LEFT

In contrast, the socialist parties during the war took no significant part in the affairs of the Duma. Both Bolshevik (five) and Menshevik (seven) deputies joined in August 1914 in a vehement declaration denouncing the war. Their public opposition subjected both organizations to closer surveillance and increased repression. A few months later, the Bolshevik

25. Riha, *Russian European*, 244–50; Rosenberg, *Liberals in the Russian Revolution*, 42–43.
26. An adverse view of Miliukov's speech is given in Katkov, *February Revolution*, 190–95.
27. Riha, *Russian European*, 275–77; Katkov, *February Revolution*, 173–77, 193–203.

deputies, along with other Bolshevik leaders, were arrested by the police and sentenced to exile in Siberia. The Bolshevik press organ *Pravda* was closed down. The tightened police controls and harsher repression kept the socialist party organizations in disarray until the fall of 1916. The more meaningful developments in the Russian revolutionary movement were taking place outside Russia. The impact of the war internationalized the Russian revolutionary movement. This transformation was linked with a division among the Russian socialists between the social patriots, or defensists, the pacifist internationalists, and the revolutionary defeatists. The extremes of the first believed in unconditional support of the war; the last considered the defeat of Russia to be the means of bringing down the tsarist autocracy.[28]

Lenin, the most uncompromising of the defeatists, welcomed the coming of the war in presenting the long-desired but unexpected opportunity for the socialists to overturn the capitalist system. A "merciless" struggle must therefore be conducted against "patriotism" and for a socialist revolution; the present imperialist war must be turned into a European civil war. From his refuge in Switzerland the Bolshevik leader expounded this internationalism with an inflexible, defiant will and activist purpose that steadily gained converts to Bolshevism among the Russian exiles. Lenin gave himself with fierce energy and unyielding self-discipline to building up again the Bolshevik organization shattered by the war.[29]

Of the other socialist groups the Menshevik pacifist internationalists rejected Lenin's defeatist position for the view that the war should be halted as soon as possible by a peace without annexations or indemnities. The SR defensists from the schismatic Social Revolutionaries abandoned the goal of immediate socialist revolution and approached the Menshevik concept of revolution and Menshevik policy on economic and social questions. The ideological basis was thus laid for collaboration between the two groups—a collaboration that was to underlie the support extended the Provisional Government by the soviets.[30]

The SR left center, a party majority headed by Viktor Chernov, sup-

28. The divisions among the socialists are discussed in Branko Lazitch and Milorad M. Drachkovitch, *Lenin and the Comintern* (Stanford, 1972), 5–19.

29. Ulam, *Bolsheviks*, 300–02; Olga Hess Gankin and H. H. Fisher, *The Bolsheviks and the World War* (Stanford, 1940), 136–46.

30. Schapiro, *Communist Party of the Soviet Union*, 144–45; Radkey, *Agrarian Foes of Bolshevism*, 88–103.

ported defense and at the same time a peace without victory guaranteeing the right of self-determination. Chernov's position otherwise corresponded to Lenin's internationalism, to the extent of maintaining that the desired peace settlement could be achieved only by a European revolution overthrowing the existing social order. An extremist part of the internationalist wing deviated from Chernov's stand toward Lenin's until the Bolshevik coup, when it would split off to form the separate party of the Left SRs.[31]

A comparable shift favorable to Lenin was occurring among the Mensheviks. In Paris Trotsky and others associated with the paper *Nashe Slovo (Our Word)* were "seeing Lenin in a new light" and moving along the path from Menshevism to Bolshevism.[32]

In the transformation of the parochial Russian revolutionary movement, eventually channeled in Bolshevism, into a world movement and organization, it was first of all emancipated from tutelage to European Social Democracy to become a completely independent force. That the socialists of Germany and France almost uniformly supported the war shocked the Russian socialists. In disillusioned reaction Lenin castigated these western socialists for defiling the name of "Social Democrat" by their chauvinist betrayal of the workers and renunciation of the class struggle. Russian Social Democrats and true Marxists should go back to the Marxism of the Communist Manifesto and to the name of Communists. Seized with this idea in 1914, Lenin never dropped it, although he did not put it into effect in Russia until March 8, 1918.[33]

The broadening of the party name Communist from national to international significance was coupled with the formation of a new International. From 1914 on Lenin was determined to break with the social patriots of the old International and see formed a new International of true revolutionary socialists. Lenin turned his indefatigable energies to putting together a following, the nucleus of an international organization, subscribing to his views on the war.[34]

The international following began to emerge in two famous confer-

31. Radkey, *Agrarian Foes of Bolshevism*, 102–26.
32. Isaac Deutscher, *The Prophet Armed* (New York, 1965), 220–24.
33. Ulam, *Bolsheviks*, 304, 407.
34. For Lenin's September Theses on the war charging that the betrayal of socialism by the majority of the leaders in the Second International had caused its ideological and political collapse, see Gankin and Fisher, *Bolsheviks and the World War*, 140–43.

ences in Switzerland that the socialists held at Zimmerwald in September 1915 and at Kienthal in April 1916. The Zimmerwald manifesto, at bottom a pacifist internationalist statement, summoned "the working class to reorganize and begin the struggle for peace"—"for a peace without annexations or war indemnities."[35] Lenin realized no success in having the Zimmerwald meeting displace, or break away from, the International Socialist Bureau (the Second International). The conference established the International Socialist Committee, with a secretariat at Bern to promote peace and maintain relations between socialist parties in wartime. Lenin, however, united an informal group that accepted his ideas on the war and formed its own bureau. This more radical group received the name of the Zimmerwald left.[36]

In representing the peace advocates and the revolutionary internationalists among the national parties of socialists, the conference gave birth through its program and Bern committee to the Zimmerwald movement. The movement contained two strands, the formal organization at Bern and Lenin's informal body, the Zimmerwald left. Lenin was on the way to becoming the major force in extremist socialism. The rising discontent with the costs and conduct of the war won growing support for the Zimmerwald movement and new converts to the Zimmerwald left. The old Second International became increasingly moribund. These trends were clear at Kienthal, where the greater influence of the Zimmerwald left surfaced in the more radical manifesto and resolutions.

The International Socialist Committee at Bern, enthusiastic over the Russian revolution, moved its seat to Stockholm in order to be nearer the source of salvation. At Stockholm a third Zimmerwald conference convened, in September 1917. The meeting was of little or no significance, and the committee continued a steady decline as the center of interest shifted to the revolution and Bolshevik party in Russia. The organization was formally dissolved with the formation of the Comintern.[37]

The Zimmerwald left went its own way, with its own platform and draft resolutions, waging an unrelenting struggle against the social patriots. The remaining life of the Zimmerwald movement passed to the left. The group was gradually converted into the Comintern or the Third International, which was formally established at Moscow in March 1919.

35. The text of the Zimmerwald manifesto is in ibid., 32–33.
36. Lazitch and Drachkovitch, *Lenin and the Comintern*, 12–13.
37. Gankin and Fisher, *Bolsheviks and the World War*, 466–78, 631–47, 683–88.

Concurrently with the rise of the leader and the Marxist-Leninist organization for promoting the proletarian revolution throughout Europe, Lenin was formulating in 1916 its creed in a theoretical work entitled *Imperialism, the Highest Stage of Capitalism.* The treatise fixed on the theme that the present war was an imperialist conflict and that its end would not bring lasting peace unless the imperialist or bourgeois governments were overthrown through the revolutionary triumph of socialism.[38]

The socialist campaign against the war and its influence in preparing the ground for revolution in Russia were reinforced by the program of German political warfare in the east and the deepening impact of the war on the Russian state and people of the empire. The German foreign ministry and general staff collaborated in plying the Russian prisoners of war with propaganda, extending aid to members of the Russian Social Democratic party, causing agents and propaganda to be sent into Russia, arranging in April 1917 for the return through Germany of Lenin and several convoys of political exiles, and subsidizing Bolshevik propaganda in Russia.[39]

The unending crisis of the regime sped in the fall of 1916 irresistibly toward the collapse of the state. The politicians in the Duma were expressing sharper criticism, more determined opposition, more insistent demands for a more effective ministry having the confidence of the country. The army was exhausted, the soldiers mutinous and anxious about conditions at home.

The hounds of war were biting the urban masses ever more deeply, apart from the loss of fathers and sons at the front, with the rapidly rising living costs and the sharpening food crisis. A critical shortage of fuel compounded the misery. The long food lines, more frequent and more impatient, were taking on the nature of manifestations that easily turned into demonstrations and riots in the streets. In the fall of 1916 there began a series of strikes, both economic and political in character, possibly under central direction.[40]

By January 1917 the spreading strike movement and the more frequent

38. See Ulam, *Bolsheviks,* 310–12.
39. On the extent of the German subversive activities and their part in the Russian revolution: George Katkov, "German Political Intervention in Russia during World War I" and the discussion of this paper, in *Revolutionary Russia,* 63–96; Michael Futrell, *Northern Underground* (New York, 1963), 120–92; Z.A.B. Zeman, ed., *Germany and the Revolution in Russia* (New York, 1958), especially p. 65.
40. Browder and Kerensky, *Russian Provisional Government,* 1: 7; Shub, *Lenin,* 182; Ferro, *La révolution russe,* 55, 60–61.

food riots were on the point of turning into rebellion. In the midst of the unrest the Duma reconvened on February 27. Prior to its meeting, the Duma leader M. V. Rodziano pressed on the tsar the urgent need to form a responsible ministry, lest there break out uncontrollable revolution and anarchy. The Workers' Group of the Central War Industries Committee appealed for "the full democratization of the country." The group summoned the Petrograd workers to march to the Tauride Palace and present their demands to the Duma. The tsar's government arrested the leaders of the group. The tsar disregarded their demands, the warnings of Rodzianko, and the prophetic utterances in the Duma debate on the national crisis. The deputy Kerensky from the Trudovik workers' party forewarned his listeners of "the flashes of lightning that are already flaring here and there across the sky of the Russian Empire."[41]

4. THE OVERTHROW OF THE TSARIST STATE

The tsarist state was only a crumbling shell. The power of the regime had completely drained away in the loss of the tsar's legitimacy—his acceptability to all classes of the people. The tottering remains of the structure were brought down by the broadening movement from demonstrations, riots, and strikes in January and February to rebellion of the workers and mutiny of the garrison forces in Petrograd. The question before the nation of the tsar's untenability was not settled by a coup of the Duma, the palace, or the army, but by a solution from the streets that we are accustomed to call the February revolution.

The revolutionary events began on March 8 (February 23 in the Julian calendar)[42] with demonstrations in the streets of Petrograd initiated to celebrate International Women's Day but joined by striking workers locked out of the Putilov metal works and persons crying for food. During the first three days the demonstrations swelled in volume, and the strike became general. The demonstrators committed sporadic violence against the hated police, who found it beyond their resources to disperse the milling crowds. Troop detachments and Cossacks fraternized with the people. When the movement broadened, the tsar at Mogilev ordered the commandant of the Petrograd military district to suppress all disorders at once.

41. Browder and Kerensky, *Russian Provisional Government,* 1: 20.
42. The date of February 23 is according to the Julian calendar, then in effect in Russia. The dates throughout these chapters on the Russian revolution are according to the western calendar, adopted by Russia in February 1918.

In executing the tsar's order on March 11, the troops fired on crowds that refused to break up. The rioting grew more serious, and casualties occurred more widely. The soldiers were more disturbed at the shooting of civilians. Mutinous men in three companies of the Pavlovsky regiment stopped firing their guns on the people and began firing on a police detachment. The leaders were arrested, and by evening the government forces seemed about to bring the situation under control. During the day Rodzianko, in the hope of saving the monarchy, made a desperate though futile appeal to the tsar for a government of public confidence.

On the "unforgettable" day of March 12—to quote N. N. Sukhanov, the Menshevik actor in the revolution and intimate recorder of its events —"the hour of decison, for which generations had labored, had clearly arrived."[43] Two climactic things happened to transform the demonstrations and riots into a revolution overthrowing the autocratic state. Mutinous soldiers went over to the workers, and, following the tsar's decree proroguing the Duma, its leaders and representatives of the Petrograd workers and revolutionary political organizations formed new government bodies.

The soldiers from the garrison forces led by the Volinsky regiment in an irrevocable revolt mingled with the crowds and entered the demonstrations. They embarked with the workers on a round of liberating political prisoners and seizing or smashing the symbols of the old regime. In these forays soldiers and workers together captured the Peter and Paul fortress —the Russian Bastille—and occupied key districts. The government was incapable of any effective resistance. Political power passed to the revolutionary masses in a revolt so devoid of leaders that it has been called an "anonymous revolution."[44] The issue of the authority that would take the place of the imperial government was now thrust before the Duma leaders and the Petrograd workers' organizations.

The leaders of the Progressive Bloc still hoped for a safe-and-sane movement in which they might save the monarchy and restore order. They avoided defiance of the tsar in holding a Duma session and con-

43. N. N. Sukhanov, *The Russian Revolution, 1917,* ed. Joel Carmichael (London, 1955), 34. This personal record of the revolution by a socialist journalist having connections with the revolutionary leaders captures the the revolutionary surge and confusion with extraordinary immediacy.
44. William Henry Chamberlin, *The Russian Revolution, 1917–1921,* 2 vols. (1952; New York, 1965), 1: 73. The uprising, or "Great Mutiny," of the Petrograd soldiers is examined intensively, with a fresh look on the basis of fundamental research in Wildman, *End of the Russian Imperial Army,* 121–58.

stituted instead, along with two representatives of the revolutionary parties, Kerensky and the Menshevik N. S. Chkheidze, a Provisional Committee of the Duma. The headlong rush of events and the pressure of the revolutionary soldiers around and inside the Tauride Palace drove the committee to announce the intention of forming a new government.[45]

On the same day "the headquarters of the revolution" was organized in the left and opposite wing of the Tauride from where the Duma deputies gathered. Leaders of the workers and cooperatives, together with Menshevik deputies of the Duma, convoked a meeting that night of the workers' delegates, who were joined by representatives of the military units participating in the uprising. Beginning with 250 persons of uncertain credentials, the Petrograd Soviet met amidst scenes of revolutionary fervor that made Sukhanov feel himself "in the very crucible of great events, the laboratory of the revolution." The Soviet elected a presidium of three Duma deputies, headed by Chkheidze, with Kerensky one of the two deputy chairmen, and an executive committee.[46]

The revolution was giving birth to two centers of revolutionary authority while the question of the monarchy's survival in any form was still up in the air. The tsar made a single effort at the last moment to retain his throne and the dynasty by military means. The march on Petrograd never materialized because of the intervention of Rodzianko, the chairman of the Provisional Committee of the Duma, and the absence of support by the commanding generals. At Pskov, the headquarters of the northern front, Nicholas stubbornly resisted for hours the proposal to change him into a constitutional monarch. The tsar finally yielded, on learning that both Alekseev, the chief of the general staff, and the commander of the northern front backed the move.

The tsar's acceptance of responsible government came too late to keep pace with the march of revolutionary events. Influenced by the messages that Alekseev solicited of the commanding generals, most of whom favored immediate abdication, Nicholas abdicated in favor of the tsarevich and a little later extended the abdication to the son also. The deed of abdication signed March 15 transmitted the throne to Grand Duke Mi-

45. Browder and Kerensky, *Russian Provisional Government*, 1: 22–23, 43–47; Kerensky, *Crucifixion of Liberty*, 273–78; Alexandr Kerensky, *The Catastrophe* (New York, 1927), 12–28.

46. Sukhanov, *Russian Revolution*, 39–40, 57–64, 69–72; Browder and Kerensky, *Russian Provisional Government*, 1: 23, 70–76.

chael, with the enjoinder that Michael conduct affairs "in complete agreement with the representatives of the people."[47]

The fate of the monarchy was not settled until after the formation of the
Provisional Government. The new government was created by an agree-
ment between representatives of the Duma Provisonal Committee and the
Soviet executive committee to accept the cabinet proposed by the one and
the program demanded by the other. Headed by the weak, retiring liberal
Prince George Lvov, the cabinet was composed predominantly of Kadets
and Octobrists. The dominant personalities were the foreign minister
Miliukov and the radical Kerensky, the minister of Justice.

The effectiveness and stability of government—indeed the very existence of the Provisional Government—would depend on the mutual relations of the two organs of state power. The prevailing opinion in the
Soviet executive committee interpreted the uprising and the functioning
of the national liberal government just organized to be a bourgeois phase
in the revolution, lasting only until the "democratic" forces acquired the
material means and experience of administration sufficient to effect the
socialist transformation. During this phase the bourgeois government
should act, in effect, as the executive agent of the Soviet. Clothed with
revolutionary power, the Soviet set itself the task of guiding the democratic movement, more specifically exerting pressure on the Provisional
Government and monitoring its work. This ideological approach impelled
the Soviet executive committee to veto the participation of any of its
members in the cabinet. Kerensky, however, defied the committee and
entered the cabinet.[48]

The use of the term "dyarchy" in the sense of two conflicting and equal
powers conveys a misleading impression of the revolutionary authority.
Though the ultimate goals of the Soviet and the first Provisional Government were opposed to each other, the two bodies were in accord on many
immediate measures. The government's initial acts constituted a joint
program. The responsibility was joint for extending political freedoms to
persons in the armed forces, replacing the police by a militia under local
control, deciding not to disarm or withdraw from Petrograd the insurrec-

47. Katkov, *February Revolution,* 295–346, gives an extended account of the influences
inducing the tsar's abdication.

48. Sukhanov, *Russian Revolution,* 104, 119, 137–44, 187; Oskar Anweiler, "The Political
Ideology of the Leaders of the Petrograd Soviet in the Spring of 1917," in *Revolutionary
Russia,* 119.

tionary military units, and dismantling the highly centralized administrative machine in favor of a comprehensive system of self-administration for which the people were not prepared. These measures robbed the state authority of power and licensed anarchy.[49]

A duality of equal state power never existed. The Provisional Government came into being without the sanction of legitimacy, either the legitimacy of the revolution or the legitimacy of the constitution. The national organization of soviets peaking in the Petrograd Soviet possessed the legitimacy of the revolution through representing, and enjoying the support of, the revolutionary masses.

The Provisional Government had no clear constitutional links either with the Duma or with the monarchy. The Provisional Government was created by the Duma Provisional Committee, but the latter was only a private group of former members of the Duma constituted by the party leaders. The Duma itself had ceased to exist when the Duma leaders decided against the urging of Kerensky not to defy the tsar's proroguing decree and hold an official meeting of the Duma on March 12. Constitutional continuity that might have been provided through the further existence of the monarchy failed on Grand Duke Michael's renunciation of the throne.[50]

By his renunciation, the Romanov dynasty ended after a history of three centuries, and the institution of monarchy expired. Nicholas and his family were arrested on March 21, confined to Tsarskoe Selo near Petrograd, and more than a year later killed at Ekaterinburg. This train of events made the Provisional Government a de facto republic suspended in air without a supporting tie either to the tsar or to the Duma. In consequence the Provisional Government throughout its existence was engaged in a constant and fruitless quest for a credible authority.

5. THE STRUGGLE FOR CONTROL OF THE REVOLUTION

Originating in the Petrograd area and Moscow, the revolutionary flood swept from these centers throughout the land and continued rising until

49. See the perspicacious comments on the incorrectness of the term "dyarchy" by Leonard Schapiro, "The Political Thought of the First Provisional Government," in *Revolutionary Russia*, 105.

50. Both the liberal revolutionary Kerensky (*Catastrophe*, 12–13) and the monarchist historian Katkov (*February Revolution*, 410–13) point out the deficiencies of the Provisional Government in constitutional legitimacy. See also the discussion of the constitutional issue in Gronsky and Astrov, *War and the Russian Government*, 52–57.

it crested with the Bolshevik takeover and the formation of the Soviet state. The revolution, rushing onward and outward, took the form of a great outburst of debate and organizational activity after the restraints of the old regime were removed. The people, erupting in Russian spontaneity, embraced their new freedoms with a wild ardor. They were moved by an elemental urge to express their ideas and demands in meetings, public speeches, petitions, resolutions, and the suddenly expanded press. Newspapers sprang up like mushrooms; the Petrograd Soviet came out immediately with *Izvestiya,* and the Bolshevik party a few days later resumed the publication of *Pravda.* Trade unions and the revolutionary parties now plunged into activity, and soviets formed far and wide. Their model, the Petrograd Soviet, had grown to nearly 3,000 members by the second half of March. The estimated number of soviets mounted to 400 in May, 600 in August, and 900 in October.[51]

As the revolution surged on, the attitude of the masses turned more extremist, or at least more democratic. The composition of the soviets altered, by the process of recall and replacement, from a membership commonly having the moderates in the ascendant after March to bodies controlled by extremist intellectuals by summer and fall. The town councils and zemstvos were also reconstituted with more democratic elements.

From May on, the outbreak of popular spontaneity shifted toward violence and anarchy. A veritable peasant revolt broke out in the self-help seizures of estates and the expulsion or killing of landlords. Workers were moving on their own or with the aid of the local soviet and with petitions to the central political organs to improve their situation: to introduce the eight-hour day, raise their wages, install factory committees, and take over control of the factories. Subject nationalities were seizing the opportunity for autonomy or independence.[52]

Both the Provisional Government and the Petrograd Soviet adopted measures that reflected the revolutionary temper of the masses. The Provisional Government first enacted the program agreed with the Soviet and announced in the proclamation on the formation of the cabinet. Beginning with a grant of full political amnesty, the government established civil liberties, introduced jury trial, and abolished the penalties of death and

51. Von Laue, *Why Lenin? Why Stalin?,* 104, 106; Ferro, *La révolution russe,* 126–28; Anweiler, *Die Rätebewegung in Russland,* 131, 140.
52. Von Laue, *Why Lenin? Why Stalin?,* 105, 107; Ferro, *La révolution russe,* 170–203; Marc Ferro, "The Aspirations of Russian Society," in *Revolutionary Russia,* 143–57.

exile, extraordinary courts, all judicial discrimination based on class, religion, and nationality, and the centralized police system with the Okhrana secret police.

More representative government was advanced by the introduction of equal rights for women and reform of local administration and self-government, including the adoption of new electoral procedures based on universal, equal, direct, and secret voting. The government proclaimed the independence of Poland, prepared for local autonomy in Latvia and the Ukraine, and reformed the administration of Turkestan and the Caucasus.[53]

Of the economic reforms, the eight-hour day was quickly approved for plants and factories. The workers' committees, or factory committees, received recognition, and the trade unions complete freedom of activity. Arbitration boards were inaugurated to settle industrial disputes.

These democratic reforms did not save the government from destructive mistakes. The government deprived itself of any reliable means of enforcing its authority. It moved too slowly in preparing the law for the elections to the Constituent Assembly. The crucial delays concerned the failure to legalize the land settlement that the peasants were already making for themselves and conclude a war that the populace felt to be hopeless.

The relations between the Provisional Government and the Petrograd Soviet, heading the subsidiary soviet organization throughout the country, determined the future of the revolution. The relationship, in essence, was a matter of reconciliation or conflict between the bourgeois class (in Russian meaning) and the revolutionary democracy of which the Soviet was the embodiment. The choice between these two was not made until the Bolsheviks consolidated their power at the end of the civil war and liquidated the bourgeoisie as a class.

The Provisional Government and the Soviet could agree on a body of immediate reforms and pragmatic policies. The fundamental conflict concerning ultimate issues of power and ideology surfaced over control of the army and foreign policy. The Soviet assured its supremacy of power by asserting control of the army. The Provisional Government challenged the Soviet's ascendancy by asserting control of foreign policy.

53. On the political reforms, see Kerensky, *Catastrophe*, 123–25; and his *Crucifixion of Liberty*, 296–97.

The Soviet extended its political influence to the military organization by Orders No. 1 and 2. These orders established the supremacy of elected committees of soldiers and sailors in the armed services and subordinated the military branch to the Soviet in political actions. They went far to solidify the division between the officer corps and the revolutionary ranks in relation to the two state authorities. The soldiers regarded the Soviet as the state power providing leadership and support of their interests. The officers accorded their loyalty to the Provisional Government as the legitimate successor regime to which appeal might be made in behalf of the traditional military establishment.[54]

The most peremptory issue of 1917 for all parties and both state powers concerned war and peace. The Kadet foreign minister, Miliukov, committed the government to observe the alliances and secret treaties of the war period and to fight "shoulder to shoulder" with the Allies to victory. The Soviet was united in opposition to Miliukov's announced war aims. The Soviet moderates sought a general negotiated peace; the Bolsheviks appealed to the growing impatience and radicalism of the masses with the demand for an immediate and separate peace.[55]

The Soviet increased the pressure on Miliukov to change the official position toward the war when the main party leaders returned from exile in April and early May. The spectrum of political leadership in Petrograd now attained its full range. The contending forces of the revolutionary drama—the bourgeois Kadets and the Provisional Government, the Soviet, and the Bolsheviks—had rounded into position. The partnership between the Menshevik and SR bands of Siberian Zimmerwaldists formed the basis of the Menshevik-SR bloc of moderates that prevailed as the ruling force in the Soviet until the Bolshevik ascendancy in the fall.[56]

The power of the Soviet to press its policy positions on the Provisional Government was also strengthened by the evolution of that body. The Soviet's functions had rapidly expanded in scope, less by intention than by the demands made upon it for assistance by the people and by local, municipal, and state institutions. It was constantly subtracting activities from the civil administration commensurate with its real power and

54. Feldman, "The Russian General Staff and the June 1917 Offensive," 527–33. On Order No. 1, see above, pp. 190–91; on Order No. 2, Browder and Kerensky, *Russian Provisional Government*, 2: 851–52.
55. Wade, *Russian Search for Peace*, 142–48.
56. Radkey, *Agrarian Foes of Bolshevism*, 134–42, 152–55.

thereby enhancing its authority. The Soviet tended to displace the government.[57]

Soviet representations for the renunciation of Miliukov's expansionist aims therefore won the sympathy of Kerensky and in time the support of a cabinet majority. Miliukov was obliged to concede the compromise declaration of April 9 supporting a peace based on self-determination. The reluctant Miliukov, however, hedged the concession in the formulation and restricted the announcement to an appeal to the people at home. The ambiguous compromise and Miliukov's personal conduct of foreign policy gave the impression that he pursued one line at home and another abroad.[58]

The most vigorous attacks were leveled by the returning Lenin and Chernov. Lenin, having crossed Germany in the famous "sealed" train, arrived from Sweden at the Finland Station as a "bright, blinding, exotic beacon" in the revolutionary storm.[59] Lenin immediately took an uncompromising stand on three central points of internal affairs and tactics: no support for the Provisional Government; no dealings with the Soviet majority; and no unity with the Mensheviks in a single party. His program in the April Theses set out the same hard line on the question of war and peace that he had taken since 1914. From this position he opened a heavy fire on the foreign policy of Miliukov.[60]

The onslaught against "Miliukov-Dardanelski" did not divert him from continuing the double game. On May 1 he assured the Allies of pursuing the common struggle "to a decisive victory." The spontaneous storm of wrath aroused thereby provoked a government crisis. Workers and soldiers poured into the streets to demonstrate to the cries of "Down with Miliukov" and "Down with the Provisional Government." Bolshevik agents and papers mobilized protest, and banners were bearing the slogan, "All Power to the Soviet." When middle-class groups of students and officers held counterdemonstrations in support of Miliukov, a confrontation of classes occurred with bloodshed and deaths.[61]

The outcome revealed the fragility of the government's position. For

57. Sukhanov, *Russian Revolution*, 307–08, 326.
58. See above, pp. 193–94.
59. Sukhanov, *Russian Revolution*, 273–74.
60. Shub, *Lenin*, 216–23.
61. See Ferro, *La révolution russe*, 315–23; Kerensky, *Catastrophe*, 136–37; Sukhanov, *Russian Revolution*, 315–21.

two months the Soviet tried the experiment of expecting the nonsocialist government to execute the foreign policy of the revolutionary socialist democracy. And for two months the government, or at least Miliukov, attempted to ignore the demands of the Soviet and the revolutionary masses in following the expansionist war aims of the tsarist state. A majority of the ministers concluded that an end must be put to this situation of conflict and tension in which the government exercised the responsibility without the power and the Soviet commanded the credible authority (rooted in the will of the people) and the physical power (residing in the loyalty of the soldiers) without the responsibility.

The Mensheviks were compelled at last to abandon their doctrinaire opposition to taking part in the government. In response to the appeals of Prince Lvov and the demands of Kerensky, the Soviet executive committee agreed to the organization of a coalition government and negotiated with the ministers its composition and program. The British and French diplomatic representatives exerted an influence in making Kerensky the leading figure in place of Miliukov. The latter had no recourse but to resign when the Kadet party denied him collective support in opposition to the formation of a coalition.[62]

The new cabinet, completed on May 18, had more socialists than Kadets. Prince Lvov remained the chief minister, Kerensky received the ministry of war, and the Ukrainian sugar king Michael Tereshchenko, an influential member of the old government, the ministry of foreign affairs. The Soviet representatives would control the cabinet's decisions much of the time. But Kerensky would act increasingly in a nonpartisan capacity to assert the independent authority of the Provisional Government.

From the outbreak of the militant mass action in March, a struggle was waged until the conclusion of the civil war as to who was to control the revolution. The conflict over foreign policy, sharpening to a focus over the removal of Miliukov, and the issue of the formation of a coalition government represented the initial phase of the struggle. The contest at bottom was for power between the conservative middle-class forces of the revolution and the Soviet (or soviet democracy). Miliukov had proposed to settle the crisis with a conservative solution aimed to secure the supremacy of the government through the organization of a solidly nonsocialist

62. Wade, *Russian Search for Peace*, 44–48; Rosenberg, *Liberals in the Russian Revolution*, 111–16; Riha, *Russian European*, 315–16.

cabinet. His fall, together with the formation of the coalition government, defeated the scheme.

The settlement registered the victory of the Soviet and the demise of the Progressive Bloc. The experiment in coalition government was in some sense a transient exercise in class collaboration between the left liberal middle class and the moderate democratic socialists. The conservative forces of the revolution that had reluctantly attempted to grasp its leadership at the beginning had failed and now became an opposition to the government. They had no chance of acquiring political power again, except through civil war. It is doubtful in any case that the Kadets, without a power base in a developed and strong middle class and without the ability to win the support of the right or the left, could ever have succeeded in steering the revolution from the Duma system to the safe haven of a full-fledged parliamentary state.[63]

Henceforth the struggle until September would engage four political forces: the Provisional Government, the moderate revolutionary democracy headed by the Soviet majority, the revolutionary extremism encouraged and exploited by the Bolsheviks, and the counterrevolutionary right. In this confused arena the government and the Soviet were often to be aligned on policy during the period of the latter's conditional cooperation. Tension would develop later when extremist influence rose in the Soviet and the government sought to act with greater independence. Each of the two extremes, on the right and on the left, opposed the other forces. The February revolution came to an end with the rise of this complex conflict, and the prelude to October began.

63. See the discussion of the reasons for the failure of Miliukov and the Kadets in Riha, *Russian European,* 333–46; and Rosenberg, *Liberals in the Russian Revolution,* 465–73.

Chapter Twelve

THE OCTOBER REVOLUTION IN RUSSIA

I. THE RADICAL CHALLENGE

THE Provisional Government was beset from the beginning until the October revolution with a series of government crises. In truth, the Provisional Government reeled through a permanent crisis. Characteristically, the first coalition government lasted, like the predecessor, for two months, when it was brought down by a new crisis. The question before the Russian people that could not be answered until October, and not finally until the end of the civil war, was the identity of the successor regime to the fallen tsardom. The search for a viable state authority thus went on.

The coalition ministry was still but "half a government," or even less, with the ebbing of its power. The rise of radical influence kept pace with the mounting antiwar sentiment and dissatisfaction with the paralyzed state authority. The most serious challenge came from the Bolsheviks, who seized on these trends to make three attempts in June and July to overthrow the Provisional Government.

The new government had two paramount problems forced upon it: the question of war and peace and the July uprising. The coalition government adopted the foreign policy program of the Soviet, namely, a general negotiated peace to be achieved according to the formula of "a peace without annexations or indemnities, and based on the rights of nations to decide their own affairs." The two authorities, however, pursued the same policy by different routes. The government employed official diplomacy with the object of organizing an inter-Allied conference for the revision of Allied war aims. The Soviet proceeded through the nonofficial channels of international socialism in the endeavor to assemble a peace conference of socialists at Stockholm. The conference was intended to exert pressure in the belligerent countries so as to make possible the government conference on war aims.

By mid-June the foreign policy of the revolution had won no discernible success, neither through the official nor the Soviet channel. The government's diplomacy had met with rebuffs of the Allies, which closed the avenues to initiating an inter-Allied conference on war aims. The indifference of the western Allies to revolutionary Russia's interests suggested that a receptive hearing could be obtained only by a demonstration of military power.[1]

A twist of circumstance had turned the diplomacy of peace into the motive for a military offensive. The disastrous July offensive[2] renewed the wave of antiwar passion and the discontent with the Provisional Government. Many were turning away from support of the Soviet majority and falling under Bolshevik influence.

By July the days of bright promise of the revolution were over. The initial revolutionary euphoria had waned as government and Soviet could not end the war; resolve the crisis of food and fuel supply in the cities; stop the runaway inflation; relieve the conflicts between the workers and management over hours and conditions of work and over the role of factory committees; implement a new general land reform; satisfy the aspirations of the component nationalities; and restore order at home. The failure to fulfill the exaggerated hopes of the revolution frustrated the masses and caused in them a fever of restlessness.

Anarchy, invading every corner of the land, became the sovereign condition. Almost any organization was asserting an authority of its own while rejecting the remnant of state authority embodied in the Provisional Government. The number of strikes increased month by month, and direct action and appropriation of land spread widely. Acts of rebellion were occurring; the Kronstadt Soviet, for example, was conducting itself as the "Kronstadt republic." The growing radicalism reflected the deepening currents of the revolution. Political elements that could catch hold of this movement of radical democracy might ride the surge of anarchy to power.[3]

The Bolsheviks were giving evidence that they might be the chosen ones. Bolshevik agitation and propaganda, aided by money from the Germans, were winning converts in the factories and barracks.[4] The Bolsheviks took positions to appeal to the more important social groups—for "workers' control" in industry, for seizure of land by the peasants without

1. Wade, *Russian Search for Peace*, 51–87.
2. See above, pp. 195–96.
3. For conditions in Russia at this time: Ferro, *La révolution russe*, 385–443.
4. Concerning Bolshevik funds from German sources, see above, p. 337, n. 39; also Ulam, *Bolsheviks*, 349; Shub, *Lenin*, 243–48.

indemnity, for regional autonomy and the right of national minorities to secede, for an immediate end of the war to be realized only by the downfall of capitalism and the winning of power by the proletariat.

The moderate socialists saw in the soviets only instrumentalities serving the transition to a permanent democratic order; Lenin perceived their all-importance in providing a "weapon for waging war against capitalism." For him a soviet republic was the ultimate goal and the only "possible form of revolutionary government." The Bolsheviks thus attacked far and wide the Provisional Government and the system of divided authority with the slogan, "All Power to the Soviets." Bolstering their political power with physical power and preparing for the future coup, the Bolsheviks organized a party militia dubbed the Red Guard.[5]

The Bolsheviks were on their way, if not at a rapid clip until August, from being the tiny insignificant party of February to the leading party of the soviets in October. By May the soviet at the radical center of Kronstadt and the factory committees generally had come into the power of the Bolsheviks. By mid-June they commanded a majority in the workers' section of the Petrograd Soviet. They returned about 20 percent of the vote in the Petrograd elections to district councils conducted at the end of May. This was close to the total Kadet vote.[6]

In reaction to the progressive advance of the revolution, a movement began to take shape on the right. The right campaigned against the direction and effects of the revolution. The movement found supporters in the officer corps, the church, Cossacks, the rightest press, former Octobrists, and an increasing number of discontented Kadets.

With the approach of July the alignments of the civil war and the attendant somber mood were emerging. The contending alignments of the right, the moderate democratic socialists or "conciliators," and the radical left consisting of the Bolsheviks and their allies could not reach a settlement of the lost war or the revolution by means of agreement. The tendency to resolve the central issue of the revolution by violence and armed force had come uppermost. From the standpoint of demo-

5. Carr, *Bolshevik Revolution*, 1: 79–82; Shub, *Lenin*, 221–23; Anweiler, *Die Rätebewegung in Russland*, 175–76.

6. Von Laue, *Why Lenin? Why Stalin?*, 112; Chamberlin, *Russian Revolution*, 1: 155; Anweiler, *Die Rätebewegung in Russland*, 222; Sukhanov, *Russian Revolution*, 389; William G. Rosenberg, "The Russian Municipal Duma Elections of 1917: A Preliminary Computation of Returns," *Soviet Studies* 21 (1969–70): 135–40.

cratic government and established freedoms, it had become a lost revolution.

These tendencies were evident in the disturbances of June and July, in which the Bolsheviks tried to overturn the Provisional Government by violent demonstrations and in the last of the three attempts to seize political power. The demonstrations and riots associated with the third attempt took place on July 16 and 17, giving the name of the July Days to the event. The uprising had one of its main causes in the explosive unrest produced among the Petrograd regiments by Kerensky's offensive and summons for service at the front. In this, as in the two previous episodes, the militants raised the banner and cry of "All Power to the Soviets." The demonstrations were called off after the melee of shooting and looting exacted the blood price of 400 lives.[7]

The Bolshevik attempt at a coup failed. The uprising was an improvised affair, staged without planning and systematic direction. Lenin's position was damaged by a collection of documents that the minister of justice published with the intention of revealing the Bolshevik leader to be a German agent supported by German funds. The country at large was not responsive to the uprising in Petrograd. Kerensky rushed to the front, from which he ordered reliable regiments to the capital. The news of their coming damped the fires of insurgency and had much to do with the dispersal of the sailors from Kronstadt. The Cossacks remained loyal to the government and the Soviet. The "Bolsheviks had been in a hurry to pluck the unripe fruit and got poisoned."[8]

Upon the collapse of the uprising, the provisional Government took steps to neutralize the threat of the Bolsheviks. Their headquarters were occupied, and their top leaders arrested, except Lenin and Grigori Zinoviev, who fled to hideouts in Finland. The government closed down *Pravda* and resumed the practice of suppressing newspapers and preventing political meetings. Yet these halfway and halfhearted measures never went to the lengths of suppressing the Bolshevik party or bringing Lenin to trial. The moderate socialists were loath, as always, to take repressive and resolute measures against another socialist party and, vastly under-

7. An extended chronicle of the July Days is found in Chamberlin, *Russian Revolution,* 1: 166–90; Sukhanov, *Russian Revolution,* 424–82; and the study in depth by Alexander Rabinowitsch, *Prelude to Revolution: The Petrograd Bolsheviks and the July 1917 Uprising* (Bloomington, Ind., 1968).

8. Sukhanov, *Russian Revolution,* 501; Chamberlin, *Russian Revolution,* 1: 172 ff.

estimating the Bolshevik peril to democracy, saw the main danger on the right.[9]

The Bolshevik party leaders were by no means depressed by the outcome of this rehearsal for October. They detected a good chance of success for another trial when conditions were more favorable. They had learned the necessity of careful preparation and organization. Lenin concluded that new tactics symbolized by a new slogan must be devised.

The Sixth Congress of the Bolshevik party, meeting on August 9, therefore settled on a new and more forthright formula, variously phrased: "all power to the revolutionary proletariat," "dictatorship of the proletariat and the poorest peasantry," and "the complete liquidation of the dictatorship of the counterrevolutionary bourgeoisie." Lenin's actual goal remained the seizure of power by the Bolsheviks in the name of the proletariat. The Bolsheviks fixed on two means to achieve this end: the factory committees and the soviets. Whenever the Bolsheviks acquired a majority in the soviets, they would become an agency of the revolution—a means not only of preparing for the conquest of power but also for the creation of a soviet and not a parliamentary republic.[10]

2. THE SEARCH FOR POLITICAL STABILITY

Coincident with the July uprising was the beginning of a cabinet crisis lasting several weeks. Its duration disclosed the growing gravity of the internal political situation. From this time until the October revolution the conflict between the right and left sharpened acutely, and from the end of August the influence of the Bolsheviks rose rapidly. In the efforts to halt the quickening slide to chaos, a desperate search was conducted for an authority to save the country.

The cabinet crisis, beginning on July 15, lasted until August 6. Kerensky was now the man of the hour, acceptable to both the moderate socialists of the Soviet and to the conservatives, but he could not conclude the organization of the second coalition government until he received the cooperation of the central executive committee of the All-Russian Congress of Soviets and the congress of the Kadet party. The new cabinet had a socialist majority, though a less radical complexion than the previous one. The second coalition was supported for the moment, in reaction to

9. Ulam, *Bolsheviks*, 350; Shub, *Lenin*, 242–43.
10. On the role of the soviets, see Anweiler, *Die Rätebewegung in Russland*, 178–79.

the July uprising, by a wave of public sentiment favorable to the government and hostile to the Bolsheviks.

The Bolshevik party had to go underground. The support of workers and soldiers in the capital receded. The reverse, nonetheless, seems to have affected the masses in the provinces but slightly. The party continued to operate effectively, with Lenin giving directions from the hideout in Finland. The leadership was actually strengthened by the entry of Trotsky's group into the organization. At the end of July the Sixth Congress, which elected Trotsky to the central committee, represented a membership that had grown from about 80,000 in April to over 200,-000.[11]

In his memoirs Kerensky presents the picture of a national convalescence, gathering in strength between the July uprising and the Kornilov affair. The verdict of history is quite different. The impotent Provisional Government could not curb the swelling anarchy or check the disintegration in the army. The coalition failed to inspire the confidence of either the right or the Soviet moderates. Suspended decision and unrelieved instability were the benchmarks of the divided state authority.

Under these conditions the question how to create a viable government out of Kerensky's tottering regime or how to supplant it altogether became the political preoccupation of the right and left opposition. Kerensky, for his part, made frantic efforts at organizing some kind of institutional authority that would sustain his faltering government. The first venture was the All-Russian State Conference of 2,400 delegates held in Moscow from August 25 to August 28. Kerensky was unable to exert any effective leadership while the conservatives on the right constantly clashed with the representatives of the mass organizations and the left. The nonsocialists could unite on no common position, and their right wing was unresponsive to efforts of the moderate socialists to accommodate to liberal and conservative demands. The Bolsheviks boycotted the conference, staging a general strike in protest. The conference ended without accomplishing any substantial work or founding any continuing organization.[12]

The State Conference assisted the counterrevolutionary movement that

11. Georg von Rauch, *A History of Soviet Russia* (New York, 1972), 49; Chamberlin, *Russian Revolution*, 1: 185–86; Ulam, *Bolsheviks*, 489–90.

12. Rosenberg, *Liberals in the Russian Revolution*, 212–18; Alexander Rabinowitch, *The Bolsheviks Come to Power* (New York, 1976), 110–116; Chamberlin, *Russian Revolution*, 1: 200–05; Gronsky and Astrov, *War and the Russian Government*, 85–87.

reached a high point in the Kornilov affair. The right, in lionizing the Cossack general Kornilov, built him up as the strong man who could save the country. An occasion arose for coordinating relations among the various industrial, business, landowner, and military officer groups that had organized or utilized existing organizations, preeminently Stavka, to oppose the onward march of the revolution. Their purpose was to fight Bolshevism by the establishment of a military dictatorship.

The candidate for a dictator who might save the floundering country was the colorful personality and war hero Kornilov. His candidacy had gained momentum when the general returned to the front from commanding the Petrograd garrison to champion the restoration of order and discipline in the army. Having won credit in the July offensive, Kornilov was appointed by Kerensky to be commander-in-chief of the army.

The Kornilov plot was an exceedingly involved and mishandled affair. Both Kornilov and Kerensky aimed to restore the army's fighting power, strengthen the government, and safeguard it against the Bolshevik threat. That these common interests were overridden by differences ending in the insubordination of Kornilov and the publicizing of a plot can be attributed in large part to the desire of each to use the other for his own purposes and to the blundering importunities of meddlers and intermediaries.

Kornilov's program of August 16 would restore the death sentence for both civilian and military persons, as well as the authority of officers by restricting the power of commissars and soldiers' committees. Units oriented toward revolution were to be purged or disbanded. After some ambivalence and delay Kerensky agreed to the program.

The issue bringing the rupture was the handling of the reorganization of government, in which Kerensky at first concurred. The report of the matter by self-appointed intermediaries between Kornilov and Kerensky allowed each to gain the impression that the other was cooperating in the reordering of government according to his own ideas. Actually, Kornilov was moving to obtain the transfer of all military and civilian authority to the commander-in-chief and the introduction of martial law in Petrograd. Kornilov warned Kerensky to come to Stavka for his own safety.

Kerensky was shocked to realize that not only would he have a secondary place in the government reorganized by Kornilov but that his life might be in jeopardy. Kerensky thereupon abruptly dismissed Kornilov (September 9), and a release by another minister proclaimed news of a conspiracy. Kerensky ordered a halt to the movement of troops toward the capital initiated by both Kornilov and himself. The general refused to give up his command and canceled Kerensky's order to stop the transfer of troops. The front commanders supported Kornilov, but the masses and the Petrograd soviets, along with most soldiers in the capital and the Kronstadt and other Baltic sailors, organized against the Kornilov movement. Between the propaganda plied to the troops advancing toward Petrograd by the agents of the revolution and the obstructions to their progress raised by the railroad workers and telegraph operators, the troops came to a stop and disintegrated as an organized force. Kornilov, deprived of support to commence a civil war, had no alternative but to surrender to arrest at Mogilev on September 14. Kerensky assumed the position of commander-in-chief.[13]

The abortive Kornilov affair sapped the remaining strength of the Provisional Government and doomed the organization of resistance on the right to the Bolshevik seizure of power. Kerensky's blundering and treatment of Kornilov alienated the conservative forces and caused a rupture with the officer corps. The split deepened between officers and men; numerous officers were lynched or shot by the rank and file, allegedly for conspiring counterrevolution. Kerensky could no longer enlist military forces to defend his government against the Soviet and the Bolsheviks.

The episode raised an insuperable barrier between the one organized political force of national scope among the conservatives, that is, the Kadets, and the moderate socialists. The last chance was spoiled, if one existed, to organize an anti-Bolshevik alliance against Lenin's capture of power. The encouragement of Kornilov by the right wing of the Kadets branded the party with the mark of counterrevolution among the masses and destroyed their political influence. The divisive effect contributed to the splitting off of the Left SRs from the main body and their diversion to the aid of the Bolsheviks. The Mensheviks and SRs lost supporters rapidly.

On the other hand, the Kornilov debacle rehabilitated the Bolshevik party and set the stage for the Bolshevik coup. Workers and soldiers came

13. There is an enormous body of literature on the Kornilov affair. Among recent writings are James D. White, "The Kornilov Affair—A Study in Counter-Revolution," *Soviet Studies* 20 (1968–69): 187–205; Harvey Asher, "The Kornilov Affair: A Reinterpretation," *Russian Review* 29 (1970): 286–300; Rabinowitch, *Bolsheviks Come to Power*, 94–167; Rosenberg, *Liberals in the Russian Revolution*, 221–33. Kerensky published his version in *The Prelude to Bolshevism* (New York, 1919).

flocking into local party organizations. The bolshevization of the soviets spurted; in September the Petrograd and then the Moscow Soviet fell under the control of the Bolsheviks, while the soviets in other cities, though not all, soon followed. The Bolsheviks increased their strength in the elections to the unions, factory committees, and central and district councils of the cities. The Bolsheviks had suddenly become a mass party and were rapidly on the way to being the chief one. The Bolshevik-controlled soviets in a number of cities and provincial centers were seizing political power. Events were clearly moving toward the solution of the problem of state authority—the solution by "coalescence" of the soviets and the Bolshevik party as the ruling force. The solution of a soviet state, or soviet democracy, was fixing its hold on the masses, and in their eyes this was what the Bolshevik program had come to represent.[14]

The Bolsheviks profited from cooperation with the moderate socialists in the Committee for Struggle with Counterrevolution, formed to resist the Kornilov forces. This body authorized the rearming and expansion of the Red Guard. In eclipse after the July Days, the Red Guard quickly grew to become the storm troops of the October revolution. The cooperation of all socialists against counterrevolution revived feelings of socialist solidarity, minimizing the awareness of risk from the Bolsheviks.

Kerensky was forced to make concessions to the post-Kornilov mood. The Bolshevik leaders were released from prison. Of these, Trotsky was elected chairman of the Petrograd Soviet on October 6, just in time to be at the helm when the October revolution began. On the other side, Kerensky arrested officers of actual or possible Kornilov taint and some nonsocialist politicians. Although the Provisional Government had deferred for months a decision on the form of government—until the Constituent Assembly should meet—Kerensky now proclaimed a republic.

The Kornilov affair tended to identify the Provisional Government more than ever as the personal government of Kerensky. With the favor of the officers lost and with the soviets falling under Bolshevik domination, the government no longer had a basis of support. Kerensky could only resort to desperate improvisations in the attempt to keep the sinking regime afloat.

The strains produced by the Kornilov episode broke the second coali-

14. Anweiler, *Die Rätebewegung in Russland,* 222–32; Rabinowitch, *Bolsheviks Come to Power,* 167.

tion on September 14. Unable to put together a new coalition, Kerensky hit on the expedient of a Directory of five members. The central executive committee of the All-Russian Soviet gagged at this intimation of a Kerensky dictatorship and laid the problem before the Democratic Conference. The latter represented largely the propertyless elements of the preceding Moscow State Conference and various organizations of the revolutionary democracy. The conference, convened on September 27, approved the formation of a coalition but voted the exclusion of Kadets. A coalition without the Kadets was scarcely a coalition between socialists and bourgeois groups. Kerensky succeeded at last in forming the third coalition government, mainly socialist, on October 6.

The final initiative to bring together behind Kerensky's government the non-Bolshevik socialists and the nonsocialist democratic forces materialized in the Provisional Council of the Republic, or Preliminary Parliament, an assembly of 550 members drawn preponderantly from the socialist parties and groups but also from the nation's organizations. Opening scarcely more than two weeks before the Bolshevik coup, the Preliminary Parliament spent the time in interminable discussion. The talk was no more than a confabulation of ghosts having no relevancy for the perilous hour and for the increasingly radicalized masses. The Bolshevik delegation, in withdrawing on the first day, violently assailed the Preliminary Parliament and the Provisional Government. Trotsky's scorn, poured on "this government of treason" and the allegedly counterrevolutionary assembly, was a declaration of war to the death against both. Of deeper significance, the abrupt departure of the Bolsheviks presaged their coming conflict with the moderate democrats.

3. THE BOLSHEVIK CONQUEST OF POWER

That war on the Kerensky government was waged with vigor during the following weeks in the press and in agitation among the workers and soldiers. The conditions were ripe for the coup, now that the Bolsheviks had won political control of the Petrograd Soviet and other soviets.[15] Lenin, impatiently watching the political tide surge in favor of the Bolsheviks, stormed from his Finnish hideout to the party leaders in Petrograd on the urgency of starting an uprising. Here in hiding, the "compul-

15. See Dietrich Geyer, "The Bolshevik Insurrection in Petrograd," in *Revolutionary Russia,* 179.

sive revolutionary" devoted himself to planning the strategy of the Bolshevik coup and issuing instructions on technical arrangements for its execution while trying to finish the exercise in utopian anarchism called *State and Revolution.* This work spun out for Bolshevik mythology a paradise of freedom and equality "without police, without a standing army, without an officialdom," to be achieved through the progressive transition to communism beginning after the proletarian revolution.[16]

Lenin encountered extreme difficulty in converting the party leadership to the need to strike with armed force after the Bolshevik political success in the soviet and other organs. Lenin and Zinoviev came secretly out of the underground to attend the historical meeting of the divided central committee at which Lenin's motion was approved on October 23 only following discussion lasting much of the night.

In this bitter internal struggle of the party, Trotsky was a brother in spirit to Lenin in ardently desiring an immediate rising. His exertions at this point were prodigious in preparing the Bolshevik takeover from two vantage points: as chairman of the Petrograd Soviet, he ran it for the benefit of the coup and, as the dominant member of the Military Revolutionary Committee, he created the machinery for victory. The Bolsheviks turned the latter body, formed by the Soviet for the defense of Petrograd, into the chief agency of the armed uprising. Trotsky and the Military Revolutionary Committee played the part of the "general staff of the insurrection," and Lenin went back to his hiding.[17]

Trotsky's brilliant contribution to the October revolution was to insure that the transfer of state power to the Bolsheviks would be accomplished under the dual cover of Soviet legality and a defensive operation against the Germans and the counterrevolution. But the seizure of military power was assured through the preceding political victory of capturing the Petrograd and Moscow Soviets.[18] For this Lenin was primarily responsible. Together Lenin and Trotsky made the October revolution.

The October revolution moved through three acts: first, the Bolsheviks won political power by gaining a majority in the Petrograd and other soviets; second, after the political victory the transfer of military power was effected through the Military Revolutionary Committee bringing the

16. Perceptive comments on *State and Revolution* are made in Rodney Barfield, "Lenin's Utopianism: *State and Revolution,*" *Slavic Review* 30 (1971): 45–46.

17. Deutscher, *Prophet Armed,* 287–306.

18. Geyer, "The Bolshevik Insurrection in Petrograd," in *Revolutionary Russia,* 178–79.

Petrograd garrison under its control; and third, the Provisional Government was deposed, and the armed uprising and the organization of a Bolshevik government were confirmed by the Congress of Soviets.

As the Military Revolutionary Committee wrested authority over garrison units from the Provisional Government, it took over weapon depots, seized strategic communication points, and won the decisive Peter and Paul fortress. Trotsky softened up the opposition by a war of words to gain maximum support for the side of the Bolsheviks and their allies, the Left SRs, and to isolate the Kerensky government at the same time that the socialist opponents were disarmed psychologically. The conspirators entered on the third act when Kerensky on November 5 started a crackdown on the left. The minister belatedly ordered the closing down of the Bolshevik press, the arrest of the Bolshevik leaders free on bail, the prosecution of the Military Revolutionary Committee, and the posting of cadets to guard vital centers.

At this signal the machinery of the insurrection went into high gear from the center in the Smolny Institute, the headquarters of the Bolshevik party and the location of the Military Revolutionary Committee. In the evening of November 6 Lenin came out of his hiding place in the Vyborg district to take command of an insurrection well under way and already assured of immediate success owing to the exertions of Trotsky. During the night the Military Revolutionary Committee moved boldly from the cover of defending the revolution to an open effort to overthrow the Provisional Government.[19] Detachments from the Petrograd regiments and from the Red Guard seized the Tauride Palace, bridges (with the assistance of the cruiser *Aurora* in one case), and the city's power station. Kerensky spent the night in a vain attempt to muster troops capable of saving his government. The next morning he escaped from the city and tried to rally sufficient forces from the surrounding area to march on the capital. The Provisional Government fell without mass demonstrations and without resistance in a virtually bloodless uprising. On November 7 the Military Revolutionary Committee completed the physical takeover of police, government offices, the railways, remaining communication facilities, and the central positions of the economy.[20]

19. Rabinowitch, *Bolsheviks Come to Power*, 268–69, which weighs carefully the evidence concerning Lenin's responsibility for the shift.

20. The most recent and judicious tracing of the course of the revolution is in Rabinowitch, *Bolsheviks Come to Power*.

The Bolsheviks used the Second Congress of Soviets, meeting on November 7, to vest their takeover of the state with a semblance of legitimacy. The congress celebrated the passing of political power to the Bolsheviks. The socialist moderates denounced the armed uprising and withdrew from the congress. Trotsky dismissed the "pure in heart" with the taunt reverberating down the years: ". . . let them go! They are just so much refuse which will be swept into the garbage-heap of history."[21]

From Smolny the congress validated the Bolshevik conquest of power by proclamations on peace and land and by approval of the new Bolshevik cabinet. Lenin appealed from the rostrum of victory to the peoples and governments of the warring nations to begin immediately negotiations for a peace without annexations and indemnities. The decree on land abolished private property in land and placed the land of landlords, state, and church at the disposal of district agrarian committees and peasant soviets. Thus was sanctioned the peasant revolution in land appropriation.

The last action introduced the soviet system of government, lodging government authority in a body of ministers named, in departure from despised bourgeois practice, the Council (Soviet) of People's Commissars (Sovnarkom). The list of commissars in the decree recognized Lenin as chairman and included Trotsky for foreign affairs and Stalin for nationalities.

The Bolsheviks had not yet won the country. The government officials and employees of the state bank opposed the Bolshevik authority by a campaign of strikes and sabotage. The Menshevik and SR deputies from the Soviet Congress and opposition leaders of the Petrograd Soviet and the Peasant Soviet joined with the Petrograd city council to organize the Committee for the Salvation of the Country and the Revolution. This center proclaimed an uprising of the cadets involving more fighting than the Bolshevik insurrection before it was snuffed out.[22]

The efforts of the Petrograd opposition bodies were all in vain, and by the end of November these survivals of the previous regime had ceased to exist. Kerensky's rescue operation from Pskov, the headquarters of the northern front, failed completely. Kerensky escaped in dis-

21. See the dramatic reports of this momentous session by the eyewitnesses, John Reed, *Ten Days That Shook the World* (New York, 1919), 86–94, and Sukhanov, *Russian Revolution,* 631–40, 644–47.
22. S. P. Melgunov, *The Bolshevik Seizure of Power,* eds. Sergei P. and Boris S. Pushkarev (Santa Barbara, Cal., 1972), 119–44 passim.

guise to hide until he could leave Russia.

In Moscow the opposition formed a Committee of Public Safety. Cadets, officers, and armed students answered its appeal and waged a violent struggle for a week until surrendering to stronger Bolshevik forces aided by reinforcements from Petrograd.

Outside the two capital cities and the area of subject nationalities, the Bolsheviks captured power through an apparatus of revolution consisting of party committees, factory committees, trade unions, Red Guard units, soviets, and the zemstvos and municipal councils. The Bolsheviks worked to take over control of as many of these mass organs as possible, most of all the soviets, and then to utilize them in the direct seizure of power. Where the democratic opposition took coherent form, it was organized around the committees of public safety or the salvation committees created under the lead of the city councils. In some places the contention continued until it was swallowed up in the civil war.[23]

The Bolshevik revolution was a political war against three forces—the conservatives, the democratic socialists, and the borderland nationalities. Both the conservatives and the democratic socialists fell victim to illusions that paralyzed the organization of an effective opposition to the Bolshevik conquest of power. The hopes of conservatives and democratic socialists alike hinged finally on the military. The Kornilov affair had killed any inclination of the military to intervene in the civil sphere or to assume any political responsibility. Like the democrats, the generals failed to comprehend the significance of the Bolshevik coup or the means required for successful resistance.

Stavka and the front commanders were therefore no more successful than Kerensky in opposing the Bolshevik regime. The new authorities took over control of the armed forces and replaced the generals and front commanders. The Bolshevik rulers decreed the election of officers, abolition of titles, and the vestment of military authority in elected committees.

The socialist moderates by and large were so preoccupied with the threat from the right that they did not perceive the danger to democracy from the extremist left. They were reluctant to try to organize force

23. John Keep, "October in the Provinces," in *Revolutionary Russia*, 180–93; Anweiler, *Die Rätebewegung in Russland*, 245, 247–48. Such inquiries as these and Ronald Grigor Suny, *The Baku Commune, 1917–1918* (Princeton, 1972), draw attention to the great variety in the pace and pattern of the revolution in the provinces, a subject that the western study of the revolution had tended to neglect in its concentration on the two capitals.

against the conspirators because of their own democratic sensitivities and the damage to socialist solidarity. The non-Bolshevik socialists were habitually misled by the illusion that it would be possible to form an all-socialist government with the Bolsheviks. The Bolsheviks, yielding to the pressure of the railway workers' union, entered into negotiations on this question with the other socialist parties and certain trade unions. The Bolsheviks stopped these unsuccessful negotiations after two weeks. The differences generated in the discussion ruptured the ranks of the anti-Bolshevik forces. The Bolsheviks formed an alliance with the Left SRs and through the latter's good offices brought the peasants as a political force over to the Bolshevik camp. With the merger of the Peasants' Congress and the Soviet Congress the Left SRs formed a separate party, and several of them entered the Council of Commissars in December.[24]

By the beginning of 1918 the Bolsheviks had extended their authority over most of Russia and far into Siberia. Pronounced resistance, however, continued in the Ukraine and other areas of national revolt. The irreconcilable Russian opposition rallied around the Cossacks in the southeast. Kornilov, Anton Denikin, and other generals who had supported Kornilov escaped from the Mogilev area to gather at Rostov. At this anti-Bolshevik stronghold the generals began the organization of forces for civil war.

The regime consolidated power by enacting rapidly a program bearing the party stamp. The government ended the war with the peace of Brest-Litovsk and worked at a furious pace from November to February to create new organs of authority and introduce broad political and institutional changes. Beginning with the creation of the Council of People's Commissars (Sovnarkom), the Bolsheviks fashioned a new state structure, dissolved the old organs of administration, organized workers' militia units to exercise police functions, and introduced new courts. Since the frontier established by the treaty of Brest-Litovsk put in jeopardy the security of Petrograd, the government moved the capital to Moscow.

The economic and social structure was transformed through a stream of measures legalizing workers' control of industry, extending state control or nationalization to private enterprise, seizing gold in private hands, and

24. Melgunov, *Bolshevik Seizure of Power,* 184–85; Leonard Schapiro, *The Origins of the Communist Autocracy* (London, 1955), 70–80.

canceling the public debt. Confiscation, requisition, extortion, and inflation wiped out the classes of property and privilege. Russia was converted into a proletarian state through the equalization of poverty.

Social reforms granted women equality with men, established civil marriage, removed disabilities from illegitimacy, and enacted the separation of church and state. The last measure opened a campaign to neutralize the church and its social influence. The old Julian calendar was replaced by the Gregorian, involving an advance on February 14 of thirteen days in the reckoning of time. The archaic Cyrillic alphabet was simplified.

The elections for and the meeting of the Constituent Assembly sharpened the struggle between the Bolshevik regime and the democratic forces. The elections on November 25, the date finally fixed by the Kerensky government, returned an impressive majority for the democratic forces.[25] Lenin acted at once to safeguard the Bolshevik dictatorship against the democracy of the Constituent Assembly. The authorities arrested several deputies to the assembly and some of the Kadet leaders. Sovnarkom banned the Kadet party on charges of counterrevolutionary involvements. Lenin's Theses on the Constituent Assembly, contending that "a republic of soviets is a higher form of the democratic principle than the conventional bourgeois republic with its constituent assembly," spelled out clearly the final repudiation by the Bolsheviks of parliamentary democracy. They now officially attributed a proletarian character to the October revolution, which the other socialists held still to be in a democratic stage. The difference made the democratic socialists counterrevolutionaries in the eyes of the Bolsheviks, and the Constituent Assembly— a contrivance of bourgeois democracy—a counterrevolutionary threat.[26]

The implicit peril soon became a bitter reality for the democratic elements. The Constituent Assembly, allowed to meet a single day on January 8, rejected the idea of a soviet state and adopted instead a decree proclaiming Russia to be a democratic federative republic. The Bolshevik and Left SR delegates then withdrew. The authorities closed the session that night by force, and the Soviet central executive committee formally dissolved the assembly. This was the second coup of the Bolsheviks—a second resort to armed force to establish Bolshevik rule and insure the realization of the soviet constitution. The question of dual power was at last settled once and

25. See Oliver H. Radkey, *The Election to the Russian Constituent Assembly of 1917* (Cambridge, Mass., 1950).

26. Carr, *Bolshevik Revolution*, 1: 113–14; Melgunov, *Bolshevik Seizure of Power*, 190–91.

for all; the conflict between the democratic and the socialist revolutions was resolved by strangling the democratic one.[27]

The dissolution of the Constituent Assembly ended the last immediate challenge to the Bolshevik hold on power. Henceforth, if Bolshevik rule was to be overthrown, its fall would have to come through civil war. The revolution that began in 1905 came to a close at this point, although from the standpoint of the regime surviving the military challenge of the civil war the period of the revolution extended to 1921.

There is no basis in objective history for accepting the premise of Communist determinism that the October revolution was the necessary fulfillment of the February revolution. That October followed February can reasonably be attributed to the assets of the Bolsheviks and the mistakes of the democratic forces in relation to the conditions in Russia created by history and the war. The Bolshevik party emerged from the years of factional strife and conspiratorial conflict with the tsarist police a tempered instrument of revolution without a comparable rival. The Bolsheviks had on their side the two great Russian personalities of the era— Lenin and Trotsky. It must be recognized that the Bolsheviks were better politicians than their rivals: their program epitomized in the slogans "Peace, Land, and Bread" and "All Power to the Soviets" had stronger appeal to the masses than anything advanced by the other parties; and the Bolsheviks carried out an extremely active and resourceful campaign to win the political support of mass organizations in the summer and fall of 1917.[28]

The primary dereliction of the democratic parties was the inability of their instrument, the Provisional Government, to govern—to take convincing steps toward solving the critical problems of the day, peace, land, order, and the form of government. The democratic socialists and many of the nonsocialists seriously underestimated the Bolshevik threat. The democratic socialists were unwilling to face up to the real meaning of Bolshevik rule.

The fatal weakness of the opposition lay in the failure of all the main non-Bolshevik political forces—the conservatives on the right, the Kadets, and the democratic socialists—to unite in an anti-Bolshevik coalition, making concessions to mass demands and organizing a dependable mili-

27. Treadgold, *Twentieth-Century Russia*, 158–59; Chamberlin, *Russian Revolution*, 1: 368–71; Schapiro, *Origin of the Communist Autocracy*, 80–88.
28. Rabinowitch, *Bolsheviks Come to Power*, 311.

tary force. In the attempt to consolidate the right, the Kadet leadership branded itself with the stigma of counterrevolution, sacrificed party unity, and forfeited any chance of cooperation with the moderate socialists.[29] The political purity of the moderate socialists raised an obstacle to their joining with the bourgeois groups against the Bolsheviks. Always conscious of the Bolsheviks as another and brother socialist party, they were constrained by the illusion of socialist solidarity. Their doctrinal prejudices made them conscious of the need to save the revolution, but from the bourgeoisie rather than from the Bolsheviks.[30]

4. THE SHAPING OF THE SOVIET STATE

The essential configuration of the Soviet state was fixed in the first years largely by Lenin, with principal help from Trotsky. The party ideology as amended by the chief writings of Lenin was the direct formative influence in this process. The Soviet state was molded in conformity with the personality and thought of Lenin. His intolerance of dissent and exaltation of proletarian dictatorship, or the dictatorship of the vanguard, were impressed first on the party and then the state. Lenin's institutional improvisations charted the evolution of the early Soviet state. The conditions of war—at the end of an exhausting total war and during a most bitter and brutal civil war—exerted a determining effect in many ways. And pervasive in the workshop of state-making were the patterns of the past, the Russian autocratic tradition and the messianic impulse.

The emerging state presented the following features, identified with the Soviet regime ever since.

1. *A Soviet system.* The democratic socialists believed for the most part that the constitution to have been framed by the Constituent Assembly should provide for a democracy of the western type. This would displace the Petrograd Soviet, the All-Russian Congress of Soviets, and other soviets. The Bolsheviks in power rejected the idea and adopted immediately a system of soviets. The constitutional decree of November 8, enacted by the Second Congress of Soviets, provisionally approved a Soviet, or Council of People's Commissars, responsible to the Congress

---

29. See Rosenberg, *Liberals in the Russian Revolution,* 214–17.
30. On this general subject, Melgunov, *Bolshevik Seizure of Power,* 170–97. W. E. Mosse, "The February Regime: Prerequisites of Success," *Soviet Studies* 19 (1967): 100–08, discusses the factors accounting for the difference between the German and Russian socialists in defending democracy against the extreme left.

of Soviets and its central executive committee. The Soviet Congress, sovereign in name, was in actuality a soviet dominated by the Bolshevik majority. This system that overlay Bolshevik rule was supported by the way in which the masses throughout the civil war thought of the spontaneously formed soviet as their own freely elected organ of self-government, whether of factory, regiment, town, district, or village.[31]

The next step in Soviet constitutional development was the Declaration of Rights of the Toiling and Exploited People, approved by the Third Congress of Soviets on January 23. The declaration made the Soviet system Russia's permanent form of government and proclaimed: "the Russian Soviet Republic is established on the basis of a free union of free nations, as a federation of national Soviet republics." In this fashion the Bolsheviks reconciled their avowed principle of self-determination with the preservation of most of the old territorial Russian state.[32]

The constitution of the Russian Socialist Federal Soviet Republic, adopted unanimously by the Fifth Congress of Soviets on July 10, 1918, incorporated the Declaration of Rights of the Toiling and Exploited People. The soviets, the democratic creation of the people, were taken over by the Bolsheviks to form a pyramid of local soviets and district, county, provincial, and regional congresses ascending at the top to the All-Russian Soviet and its central executive committee. The constitution regularized the soviets as the source of sovereignty, electoral agencies for constituting the higher soviet organs, local government organs, and the machinery of a centralized administration. In that administration each soviet was responsible for executing the resolutions of higher soviet bodies.

The soviet structure thus erected became the hallmark of the subsequent constitutions of Russia and the Soviet Union. The soviets afforded the seeming mechanism through which proletarian class rule would be carried out. The actual apparatus of power was reared elsewhere, and the soviet edifice was relegated to the semblance of a screen for the real governing machinery in the party.[33]

2. *A socialist state.* Committed by ideology and constitution to building a socialist state, the Bolsheviks had to face up to the problem of beginning

31. See Anweiler, *Die Rätebewegung in Russland,* a study that traces the process through which the soviets from their origins in the revolution of 1905 were converted into the Soviet state of the Communists.

32. Carr, *Bolshevik Revolution,* 1: 117–23.

33. Ibid., 1: 124–35; Anweiler, *Die Rätebewegung in Russland,* 274–85.

from an economy in disintegration. The regime resorted initially there-fore to measures of state capitalism. The authorities regularized the popu-lar practice by which factory committees spontaneously took over control of individual plants and joined the committees in a centralized machinery of councils corresponding to the system of soviets.

This unsuccessful experiment yielded to the establishment of the Su-preme Economic Council by decree of December 18. Absorbing the machinery of workers' control, the Supreme Economic Council created a system of regional, provincial, and local economic councils parallel to the structure of the soviets. At the top, the All-Russian Congress of Councils of National Economy surmounted the organization. With the cooperation of the old management and technical personnel, the Supreme Economic Council gradually fashioned a centralized industrial administration founded in the wartime central agencies and practices for the control of industry.[34]

Moving on from haphazard to systematic nationalization, Sovnarkom decreed on June 28, 1918, that all the major branches of industry be nationalized. The Supreme Economic Council organized an administra-tion for each branch. This decree might be considered to have inaugurated the phase of war communism—the socialist economic system under the conditions of civil war and foreign intervention—in industry.[35] Later de-crees completed the formal nationalization of all but small concerns and put industrial enterprises under the management of the Supreme Eco-nomic Council. The conditions and exigencies of the civil war stimulated the centralization of industrial organization and the concentration of pro-duction.

The law on the socialization of land, adopted by the Congress of Soviets on February 19, 1918, ordained the collective system of agriculture to be an objective essential to socialism but provided for the land to be dis-tributed by the land sections of the soviets. The process transferred 86 percent of the confiscated land to the peasantry, 11 percent to the state, and 3 percent to agricultural collectives.[36]

34. The wartime agencies and controls are treated in S. O. Zagorsky, *State Control of Industry in Russia during the War* (New Haven, 1928).

35. There is no precise time recognized for the beginning of the civil war and war communism. David Footman, *Civil War in Russia* (New York, 1961), 22, dates the first round of the civil war from January 1918; Carr, *Bolshevik Revolution,* 2: 147, 172, dates war communism from the summer of 1918.

36. Carr, *Bolshevik Revolution,* 2: 43–48.

The harassing agrarian problem was how to extract food from the rural areas for the undernourished urban population when conditions of inflation and scarcity yielded nothing in the market place to compensate the producing peasant. The Bolsheviks used detachments of workers and poor peasants for the dual purpose of assisting the collection of food supplies and splitting the peasantry through the organization of the poorer and middle peasants against the kulaks (the richer 10 percent).[37] Agrarian policy evolving from this beginning under the impact of the civil war produced war communism in agriculture. Its basic objectives remained the forced collection of food surpluses from the more productive peasants and the promotion of the collectivist revolution in the countryside.

The pursuit of both purposes provoked peasant resistance and agrarian conflict.[38] The peasant concealed his stocks and went on strike against producing beyond family needs. The peasant's aim was not to become a "rural proletarian" on a collective farm but to maintain a small independent holding. Rather than establishing an agriculture of large units, the regime ended in 1920 with a redistribution largely equalizing the farm unit as a small holding. At the end of war communism, the Communists had solved none of the long-range problems of Russian agriculture nor found a solution through state compulsion for increasing food supplies for the towns. The situation was prepared for the adoption of a Menshevik policy of incentives and for the introduction of the New Economic Policy.[39]

The disruption of trade relations between town and country caused by the world war and the revolution quickly drove the Soviet authorities to the state control of distribution. The state organization of domestic trade, entailing state trading monopolies, replaced the normal mechanism of private trade. The trading monopolies fixed prices for commodities according to political, economic, and social ends. The fixed prices in conjunction with the conditions of scarcity necessitated a system of rationing and gave rise to a far-flung black market. In the long run, the state monopoly of trade encouraged the growth of a "moonlight" economy on the side in which individuals carried on their own private trade or craft.

37. Jan M. Meijer, "Town and Country in the Civil War," in *Revolutionary Russia*, 265–66.
38. During this period there occurred numerous peasant uprisings, the chief cause of which was the forced requisitioning of food products, but other factors also operated. Ibid., 267–71.
39. For agricultural policy as a whole, Carr, *Bolshevik Revolution*, 2: 43–55, 147–72.

Similarly, the government nationalized foreign trade and confined the conduct of foreign commerce entirely to state organs authorized for the purpose.

In the Soviet environment central economic planning took root naturally from the urge to modernize Russia as quickly as possible, pivotally through a program of heavy industry necessitating the planned coordination of its requirements with those of the whole economy, and from the need for an agency to complement the state trading system in replacing the automatic regulator of the market place for the mutual adjustment of individual economic ends. The Council of Commissars authorized on February 22, 1921, the creation of the "state general planning comission," or Gosplan. The time of NEP was not favorable for the development of its powers. Gosplan had to await a later day to emerge as an effective planning authority.[40]

3. *A one-party state.* The Soviet constitution, which never mentioned the Communist party, provided in the structure of the soviets a decorative front that concealed the actuality of the one-party state. The Communist party exercised a monopoly of political power that became fully institutionalized after the civil war. The progress toward this outcome began as soon as the Bolsheviks came to power, when the regime closed conservative papers and some liberal and socialist ones. A big stride was taken in banning the Kadet party after the elections to the Constituent Assembly.[41]

The political marriage with the Left Social Revolutionaries was short-lived. The Left SRs carried their furious opposition to the government's German policy embodied in the peace of Brest-Litovsk and to the coercion and extortion of the peasants as far as impulsive revolts in Moscow, Petrograd, and some provincial cities (July 1918). These harebrained actions were quickly suppressed. The party was denounced and subjected to a punitive reign of repression. The extinction of this opposition force went hand in hand with the effort to preserve the unity of the Bolshevik party, divided over the issue of the peace. The opposition in the party crystallized in the movement of the Left Communists, led by Nikolai Bukharin.[42]

40. Ibid., 2: 360–83.
41. James Bunyan and H. H. Fisher, eds., *The Bolshevik Revolution, 1917–1918* (Stanford, 1934), 219–22; Chamberlin, *Russian Revolution,* 1: 365, 367.
42. On Bukharin and the Left Communist movement, see Stephen F. Cohen, *Bukharin and the Bolshevik Revolution* (New York, 1973), 62–69; Robert Vincent Daniels, *The Conscience of the Revolution* (Cambridge, Mass., 1960).

The overt opposition of the Left SRs and the full involvement of the regime in the civil war precipitated a campaign of administrative harassment of the socialist parties. The sharpened weapons of terror were turned against the old ruling groups and the intelligentsia. The Communist party was the only one left free to conduct political activities, for groups differing from the Communists were considered counterrevolutionary. The socialist parties barely managed to hang on during the time of civil war. The adoption of NEP, advocated by the Mensheviks, ended even this limited sufferance. The Communists could not allow the socialist parties to score the point that the Mensheviks were right and the policies of war communism wrong. From this time on, the other parties died away, and the Communist party became identified with the state. The soviets turned into the mere instrument and public forum of the single Communist party.[43]

4. *An autocratic state.* The wellsprings of the Communist autocracy were the principles of the Soviet constitution and the ideology of Lenin. The Soviet constitution of 1918 prescribed no limitations on the powers of the state, set forth no instrument of fundamental principles controlling laws, incorporated no bill of civil rights, and provided for no separation of powers or system of checks and balances. This far departure from the conceptions of western democracy issued from the soil of tsarist absolutism and perpetuated the tsarist tradition of the autocratic state.

The Leninist formula of the dictatorship of the proletariat and the toiling peasantry implied that Bolshevik rule would wage the class war against the other classes with all the attributes of state power. Lenin's elitist theory of the vanguard, depreciating the initiative and decision of the masses and upholding the leadership of a select group of professional revolutionaries, buttressed an authoritarian role of the party, strengthened by Lenin's proclivity to tolerate no compromise. The minority support of the Bolsheviks, revealed by the returns from the elections to the Constituent Assembly, prevented them from maintaining a monopoly rule, except by crushing the opposition with force, terror, police methods, and in the end a prolonged and savage civil war. The aggrandizement of government power through the system of war communism gave a strong thrust to the rise of a bureaucratic dictatorship. The anarchy and chaos attending the

43. Schapiro, *Communist Party of the Soviet Union,* 195–96, 218–19; and his *Origin of the Communist Autocracy.*

end of the hopeless international war and the revolutionary turmoil demanded, moreover, a strict exercise of social discipline, which only a firm state authority could instill.

The instruments of the Communist autocracy belonged to both the state and the party. The principal ones of the state were the Red Army, the Cheka, the system of courts, and the devices for the control of labor. Having first relied on a militia and then on a "democratized" army (elective soldiers' organizations and elective officers), the regime decreed in January 1918 the organization of the Worker-Peasant Red Army. The progress of the Red Army from a "democratized" organization of voluntary recruitment to a professional one directed by competent officers and manned by compulsory military service was chiefly advanced by the professionalism at the heart of Trotsky's creative methods and the lessons of the eastern front in the civil war. The Red Army, hammered out in the forge of the civil war under the shaping and ruthless direction of Trotsky, grew to a force of five million men within two and a half years and laid the foundations of future Soviet military power.[44]

The use of arbitrary violence and organized terror against the individual suspected of opposition to the regime was institutionalized in the Soviet security apparatus called the Cheka. This system of centralized political police originated in the creation on December 20, 1917, of an extraordinary commission to fight counterrevolution. This agency and its successors were to evolve into the foremost organization, in effect a state within a state, for upholding the Communist autocracy and repressing the rights of individuals—the cornerstone of the system of compelling conformity and suppressing dissidence. The Cheka soon widened its functions to cover speculation, profiteering, banditry, and negligence of duty. The Cheka maintained concentration camps for political prisoners, organized its own special troops, and deeply invaded the judicial province.[45]

The Soviet system of justice derived from Decree No. 1 on the Courts, which the Council of People's Commissars laid down in December 1917. The decree abolished the entire court system of the past and founded both people's courts and revolutionary tribunals. The latter, which became

44. Deutscher, *Prophet Armed*, 405–28; John Erickson, "The Origins of the Red Army," in *Revolutionary Russia*, 224–56.
45. John Scott, *The Cheka* (typed form; St. Antony's College, Oxford, 1953); Samuel Kucherov, *The Organs of Soviet Administration of Justice* (Leiden, 1970), 55–70; Bunyan and Fisher, *Bolshevik Revolution*, 574–77, 580.

virtually an arm of the Cheka, had sweeping jurisdiction over cases of counterrevolution, sabotage, profiteering, stoppage of work, curtailment of production, and other offenses. When the judicial system was regularized in 1922, wide discretionary power in applying terror in political cases was made a fundamental principle of the criminal code. Instead of protecting the rights of the individual and the rights of property, the courts were organs for the execution of Soviet policy.[46]

The requirements of the civil war and the nationalization of industry, as well as Communist theory, contributed to the statization of labor. When the state became the employer in nationalized industry, labor was held to be a service to the state and a universal obligation. Labor came under compulsions that Bukharin and other Communist writers rationalized in the "workers' state" as "the self-organization of the masses."[47] The means of compulsion extended to workers' courts and sentences to concentration camps to insure the observance and proper performance of the labor service obligation. The trade unions, having been diverted from their traditional practices and having become identified with the state, participated in the mobilization of the labor force for obligatory service and took a leading role in implanting the new socialist discipline.[48]

The Communist party apparatus exercised dominant power in the Soviet autocracy after the Soviet system emerged in basic form. The Eighth Congress, of March 1919, gave the new name of Communist to the party and improved its rudimentary organization by creating three subordinate organs of the central committee: the Political Bureau (Politburo) to decide matters of policy; the Organizational Bureau (Orgburo) to assign personnel; and a Secretariat in charge of staff departments of the central committee. The Politburo soon came to control the central committee, to which it was formally responsible, and to govern the whole machinery of the Communist autocracy. With this Lenin, who had been at first as head of government a "dictator by persuasion," became a dictator by command and an object of veneration verging on a cult of personality.

By means of the central staff and the control established over local party organs by the central committee, the party fashioned a centralized and full-length administrative apparatus. During this process the party took the place of the soviet bodies as the organs of authority and decision, to leave

46. Kucherov, *Soviet Administration of Justice,* 3–55.
47. Cohen, *Bukharin and the Bolshevik Revolution,* 92.
48. Carr, *Bolshevik Revolution,* 2: 199–216.

the soviet congresses and committees only vestigial functions of window-dressing. The party apparatus also extended its control functions over the armed services, the Cheka organization, the judiciary, and other state agencies. The party assumed the role of guide, leader, and watchdog in relation to the public agencies. The Communist apparatus had installed itself in a position to control and supervise the entire life of the people.

The ever-growing recruitment of party officials to handle these manifold activities created a bureaucratic machine parallel to the state bureaucracy. The latter rapidly formed with the state enlarging its functions in the institutionalization of war communism. The party membership furnished officials not only for positions within the party and government but also personnel for managerial and office staff in industry, the trade unions, and cooperatives. A new ruling class (over 600,000 party members by March 1920) had come into existence to be masters of the Soviet state. The Communist autocracy was a bureaucratic state par excellence, given to the excesses of a "totalitarian bureaucracy."[49]

5. *The center of a world movement.* The Bolsheviks attributed universal bearing not only to the revolutionary experience but also to the organization making it possible and to the creed supporting the Soviet state. Lenin and his party propagated Bolshevism with messianic fervor in terms of a cosmic phenomenon and on this basis founded a world movement.

When the Communist movement emerged abroad, Lenin gave it an institutional form connecting the various parties with the Moscow center. A congress of 44 handpicked delegates, drawn mostly from Russians and former war prisoners, founded the Communist International in March 1919. The congress met in Moscow to hold a war conclave against the socialism of the west and its Second International. The second congress of the Comintern, in July 1920, was attended by representatives of a number of mass socialist or labor parties. The meeting adopted the Twenty-One Points, requiring constituent parties to be recast in the image of the Communist party of Russia and to submit to decisions of the Comintern. The executive committee was to be located in and controlled by Moscow. The congress approved statutes establishing a centralized organi-

49. On the place of the party in the Soviet state, see Schapiro, *Communist Party in the Soviet Union,* 243–70. Both Lenin and Trotsky were severe critics of the rapidly expanding bureaucracy. On January 24, 1922, Lenin wrote: "We are being sucked into a foul bureaucratic swamp." On the bureaucratic features of the Communist autocracy, Fischer, *Life of Lenin,* 578–96.

zation in which the member parties "represent in fact and in effect one unified Communist party throughout the world," directed by the executive committee.[50]

The Communist International lasted until its dissolution in 1943. Its disappointed hopes and successive defeats grew out of two illusions. One was that a revolutionary temper prevailed in Europe outside the Soviet Union, and the other that the Russian revolutionary experience and the principles of the Bolshevik party organization could be translated literally to the western milieu. The Comintern's insistence that total obeisance must be rendered to its repeated swings of policy turned the member parties into abject antinational dependencies of Moscow. Its effect proved a major factor in splitting the socialist and labor movement in Europe and in thereby weakening the defenses against the triumph of Mussolini and Hitler.[51]

50. The text of the Twenty-One Points is in Julius Braunthal, *History of the International,* 2 vols. (New York, 1967), 2: 537–42.

51. On the formation and nature of the Comintern, see the insider's account, written in 1939, by F. Borkenau, *World Communism* (Ann Arbor, 1962), 161–220; Braunthal, *History of the International,* 2: 162–229; Lazitch and Drachkovitch, *Lenin and the Comintern,* 50–569.

Chapter Thirteen

THE REVOLUTION IN GERMANY

I. THE OCTOBER REVOLUTION

THE underlying political issue in the Reich's internal affairs during the war was the possibility of the German revolution, that is, the replacement of the semiabsolutist monarchy and the authoritarian military state of Ludendorff with a parliamentary system of responsible government. The issue was covered over during the first years of the war by the political truce, which froze the domestic political situation and operated against the parties of the masses aspiring to political power. When the *Burgfrieden* broke down under the strains of the prolonged war, the question of changing Germany's political system surfaced as the fundamental point of national decision during 1917–18. The engrossment with the issue came to a head in a revolution of two phases, the quiet transformation of the Reich into a parliamentary state under a constitutional monarch and the mass movement producing a democratic republic and not a state on the Soviet model. The first engaged the government of Prince Max in October, the second the socialists in power thereafter.

Bismarck, William II, and Ludendorff belonged to the progenitors of the revolution, though the natal cause was the lost war. The state form given the Reich by Bismarck put the rule of Germany into the hands of the privileged few, headed by the monarch and chancellor, while excluding Social Democracy, the organ and the medium of the masses, from political power and responsibility. The kaiser failed to democratize the antiquated monarchy. By remaining with the high command during the war in his office of supreme war lord, he demonstrated his complete uselessness in military affairs and secluded himself from civilian functions in an empty life at general headquarters. William II thus made the monarch for many Germans a palpable superfluity and, owing in part to the propaganda of the Allies, a symbol of wrong policies and the accumulated misfortunes of the war.

Ludendorff, acting from OHL (the supreme command) as "mayor of the palace,"[1] usurped the kaiser's powers of supreme war lord to create an authoritarian military state. This rule was identified internally with the repression of civil rights and resistance to political reform and externally with the goal of a victor's peace. Being the leading factor among the Pan-Germans, annexationists, Fatherland party, and other rightists, Ludendorff did much to polarize political forces into two broad alignments and channel political contention between two centers. These were the military-conservative power and the majority bloc of Reichstag parties— the Majority Social Democrats, Progressives, and Center.[2]

The majority bloc emerged in July 1917 in support of the peace resolution. The most significant assertion of parliamentary influence appeared in the organization and policy activity of the interparty committee, comprising the leaders of the majority parties of the Reichstag.[3] The bloc dared not, however, provoke a trial of strength with Ludendorff and had no political will to force a showdown on the issue of parliamentary responsibility so long as Ludendorff's military state retained the sanction of continued military success. When military defeat proved irreversible, the barrier against the pent-up demand for political reform collapsed. Currents of action then broke free toward revolutionary change.

One action was an initiative of the interparty committee of the Reichstag concerned with the formation of a new government. By September 1918 it was clear to the majority deputies that the Social Democrats must be taken into the government, for they formed the backbone of the Reichstag coalition and their influence increased in proportion to the rise of popular unrest. The Social Democrats decided for participation in a new government if it met their basic political demands. Their demands embraced the introduction of a parliamentary state for the Reich and of universal and equal suffrage in the federal states; immediate restoration of the civil rights suppressed in wartime; elimination of Ludendorff's *Neben-*

---

1. Rosenberg, *Birth of the German Republic*, 129.
2. Communist historiography would not accept this analysis of polarization. The East German historians find rather a division between the revolutionary masses headed by the Spartacists on the one side and the right-opportunist Social Democrats, the rightist elements of the Independent Socialists, and the trade unions cooperating with the imperialist ruling classes on the other. See Leo Stern, *Der Einfluss der Grossen Sozialistischen Oktoberrevolution auf Deutschland und die deutsche Arbeiterbewegung* (Berlin, 1958); Hellmut Weber, *Ludendorff und die Monopole* (Berlin, 1966).
3. Erich Matthias and Rudolf Morsey have called attention to the importance of the interparty committee by their collection of documents, *Der interfraktionelle Ausschuss 1917–18*, 2 vols. (Düsseldorf, 1959).

regierung and removal of military institutions exerting political influence; unreserved avowal of the peace resolution and support of a league of nations; restoration and indemnification of Belgium. The bloc parties negotiated an agreed program substantially along the lines of the Social Democratic program. The resolution, approved by the interparty committee on September 28, outlined a policy for a new government that was in essence an invitation to the submissive octogenarian Hertling to withdraw from being chancellor and a move to end Ludendorff's military regime.[4]

The second action was taken by the highest officials of the foreign office to introduce a "revolution from above" in order to forestall a revolution from below. The advocacy by Hintze, the foreign secretary, of forming a new government on "the broadest national basis" meant the acceptance of the Social Democrats in the executive.[5]

The third action was that of Ludendorff, who informed both the secretary of foreign affairs and the chancellor that it was indispensable to reconstruct the government with the inclusion of men having the confidence of the Reichstag. This abrupt change marked not only the force of the impression made on Ludendorff by the irretrievable military defeat but also the attempt to pin responsibility for the lost war on the scapegoat of the more leftward politicians. Ludendorff told the department chiefs of the general staff: "They [the new men to be brought into the government] are now to eat the soup that they have cooked for us."[6]

The increasingly serious strikes and demonstrations of the industrial workers amounted to a fourth action. Their growing emphasis on political demands strengthened the power of the Social Democrats, who were the only party of the Reichstag majority having close contact with the bulk of the workers and trade unions as well as control over them.

At the end of the tense month of September, the confluence of these initiatives commenced the October revolution. Under pressure from

4. Erich Matthias and Rudolf Morsey, eds., *Die Regierung des Prinzen Max von Baden* (Düsseldorf, 1962), pp. xi–xvi. This work has rescued from neglect and underestimation the significance of the initiative recounted above. See also Prinz Max von Baden, *Erinnerungen und Dokumente,* ed. Golo Mann and Andreas Burckhardt (Stuttgart, 1968), 34, 310–16; from the Social Democratic side, Hermann Heidegger, *Die deutsche Sozialdemokratie und der nationale Staat 1870–1920* (Göttingen, 1956), 192–93; from the Centrist side, Epstein, *Matthias Erzberger,* 258–59; and Friedrich Payer, *Von Bethmann Hollweg bis Ebert* (Frankfurt, 1923), 85–86.

5. See above, p. 288; Payer, *Von Bethmann Hollweg bis Ebert,* 82.

6. Siegfried A. Kaehler, "Der Waffenstillstandsforderung der O.H.L.," in *Studien zur deutschen Geschichte des 19. und 20. Jahrhunderts,* 261, 264.

Ludendorff and Hintze, the imperial conference at Spa on September 29 made with incredible haste two of the most critical decisions taken during the reign of the kaiser: to alter the form of government through the introduction of parliamentary responsibility and to seek an immediate armistice. Opposed to any steps toward a parliamentary system, the surprised Hertling resigned at once. The kaiser's rescript of September 30 announcing the end of the Hertling government laid down the principle of parliamentary responsibility: "It is therefore my will that men having the confidence of the people take part broadly in the rights and duties of the government."[7]

The composition of the new government and the distribution of offices were negotiated with the leaders of the Reichstag majority. In the choice of a new chancellor, Prince Max of Baden, this "good and reasonable man" who had opposed the submarine war and Ludendorff's 1918 offensives, seemed the only available candidate acceptable to the court, OHL, and the majority bloc. The epochal change was completed on October 3 after Max had negotiated a program with the Reichstag leaders and the Kaiser had approved the new government. Social Democrats (Philipp Scheidemann and Gustav Bauer) were admitted to the cabinet for the first time.[8]

Although Max lacked the political experience and the physical stamina for sustained leadership,[9] the cabinet of "the last imperial and the first parliamentary chancellor" during its brief spell terminated the military regime of Ludendorff and shaped the form of responsible government adopted while all but concluding the peace negotiations. The supreme command's political powers were speedily shorn. The war cabinet rejected Ludendorff's strong stand of October 17 for breaking off negotiations with Wilson and making war "to the last man for the sake of German honor." The general was obliged to agree to a declaration of OHL that the supreme command "considered itself no power factor in political matters" and "it therefore bore no political responsibility."[10]

7. The text of the rescript is in Prinz Max, *Erinnerungen und Dokumente*, 317.
8. Payer, *Von Bethmann Hollweg bis Ebert*, 89–109; Prinz Max, *Erinnerungen und Dokumente*, 318–31, 340–42.
9. Philipp Scheidemann, *Memoiren eines Sozialdemokraten*, 2 vols. (Dresden, 1928), 2: 179, 195–96, estimates on the whole adversely Max's qualifications for being chancellor. See Matthias and Morsey, *Die Regierung des Prinzen Max*, pp. xxv–xxix, for a largely unfavorable profile of Max and Mann's Introduction to Prinz Max, *Erinnerungen und Dokumente*, 15–30, for a sensitive appreciation of the prince's worthy traits.
10. Prinz Max, *Erinnerungen und Dokumente*, 444–45.

Ludendorff nevertheless had OHL issue an order to the army declaring that Wilson's answer in his third prearmistice note (October 24) was "unacceptable for us soldiers." This challenge allowed no choice but the dismissal of Ludendorff or the resignation of Prince Max. The kaiser's dropping of Ludendorff settled the issue of military supremacy and ended the authoritarian military state. Ludendorff found a haven in Sweden to write his memoirs and nurse his bitterness. The uncontrolled internal administration of the district commanding generals was put under restraint.[11]

The institutional changes, improvised provisionally, were written into the Reich constitution by legislation of October 28 passed by the Reichstag and Bundesrat. The revised constitution specified that the chancellor and his representatives were responsible for the conduct of office to the Reichstag and Bundesrat rather than to the kaiser. Members of the Reichstag were to be entirely free to hold office in the government. The Reichstag became the dominant organ of government, the Bundesrat of federal princes now assuming the position of an upper house.

The system of parliamentary responsibility operated through the effective mechanism of the inner, or war, cabinet and the interparty committee of the Reichstag majority. Both the inner and the larger cabinet evolved from the optional meeting of the secretaries of state with the chancellor during the Hertling period. The main element in the inner cabinet consisted of the several secretaries of state without portfolio, who were the leaders of the majority parties in the Reichstag and members of the interparty committee. They acted as parliamentary secretaries linking closely the cabinet and the interparty committee of the Reichstag.[12]

The October revolution achieved a constitutional shift in political power between the classes, creating the foundational structure of the Weimar democracy and establishing the influence of the coalition of political parties that prevailed in the Weimar period. During the latter part of his government Max and the cabinet were increasingly preoccupied with the question whether this "crowned democracy" could be maintained in the face of military defeat and the prospects of a severe peace. Beginning with the Spartacists and radical left of the Independent Social Democrats, an antimonarchical sentiment was rising to invade the circles of the Major-

11. See above, p. 290.
12. Matthias and Morsey, *Die Regierung des Prinzen Max,* pp. xxxi–xxxviii.

ity Socialists, the bourgeois parties, and bourgeois intellectuals. Wilson's more explicit interventionist stance toward the German constitution seemed to make the kaiser an obstacle to the attainment of peace. The surge of hope in the first part of October when immediate peace appeared in sight gave way to frustration and unrest in the last part of the month when no result was yet at hand. On October 25 the Social Democratic press came out in support of abdication as a necessary means to peace. Particularist feelings and sentiment against the kaiser reinforced each other in the south German states. The pressures on the cabinet mounted to bring about the monarch's abdication.[13]

The October revolution had parliamentarized the monarchy in orderly fashion but had not disposed of the monarchical question. Peace had not yet come, and neither the people at home nor the nations abroad were yet convinced of the authenticity of the constitutional transformation. And the democratic revolution had not been extended to the federal states and the local governments. The remaking of the Reich did not come in time or reach far enough to forestall the revolution of the masses.

2. THE MASS REVOLUTION

The revolution in October was a revolution from above; the revolution in November was a mass movement. The mass revolution was a complex event in which three streams merged in the total revolutionary flux: a spontaneous uprising of sailors, soldiers, and workers against the war and against the Prussian system of militarism and privilege; the efforts of the Social Democrats supported by the other majority parties to extend and safeguard the democratic, parliamentary state; and the attempt of the Spartacists and the radical wing of the Independent Socialists to stage a socialist revolution with the political power lodged in the councils of workers and soldiers.[14]

The rebellion began with the mutiny of the crews on battleships at Kiel and Wilhelmshaven, when the fleet was ordered on October 28–30 to prepare for a sortie. The rank and file revolted against a "death ride"

13. Müller, *Regierte der Kaiser?*, 425; Payer, *Von Bethmann Hollweg bis Ebert*, 147; John L. Snell, "Die Republik aus Versäumnissen," *Die Welt als Geschichte* 15 (1955): 210–17; Prinz Max, *Erinnerungen und Dokumente*, 386; Hanssen, *Diary of a Dying Empire*, 336; Matthias and Morsey, *Die Regierung des Prinzen Max*, 440.
14. Interpretations along this line are discussed in relation to other views of the November revolution in Georges Castellan, "La révolution allemande de novembre 1918," *Revue d'histoire moderne et contemporaine* 16 (1969): 40–51.

intended by the admirals only to save the honor and the future of the German navy from the stigma of turning over an intact fleet to the enemy at the peace settlement. The arrest of the mutineers touched off the uprising of sailors, soldiers, and workers at Kiel on November 3. The participants formed revolutionary councils and asked not only for an amnesty for those arrested but also raised political demands, including the conclusion of an armistice and peace, assurance of more democratic relations between officers and men, abdication of William II, and extension of equal suffrage to all, both men and women. The spontaneous action that commenced only with the object of freeing the imprisoned sailors had turned into a revolutionary movement of broad political expectations.[15]

From Kiel the mutinous sailors carried the revolutionary torch through the cities of the German coast and to the soldiers and workers. The outburst swept concurrently through southern, central, and western Germany, reaching Berlin at the last on November 9. The spontaneous mass character of the revolution was demonstrated by the suddenness with which it broke out over the whole of Germany. The only groups with a determined will to revolution were the Spartacists, the "Bremen left radicals," and the revolutionary shop stewards, located chiefly in Berlin. The Spartacists had taken over the Russian model for their goal, although they saw no necessity of forming a strong centralized party of the Lenin type. The revolution was not begun or made by the socialists, yet they provided whatever direction there was.[16]

At this stage the revolution met with no appreciable opposition. Councils of workers and soldiers were formed; public buildings and offices were seized or controlled; republics were proclaimed in the individual federal states; the masses were admitted to political power through the acquisition of controlling office by the Majority and Independent Socialists. The political system was being altered corresponding to the real distribution of economic and social power between the classes. The old regime seemed to fall of its own anachronistic weight. The October revolution took place too late in adapting an obsolete system to modern conditions. The break-

15. Mann's Introduction to Prinz Max, *Erinnerungen und Dokumente*, 49–50; A. J. Ryder, *The German Revolution of 1918* (Cambridge, England, 1967), 140–42; Gilbert Badia, *Histoire de l'Allemagne contemporaine (1917–1962)*, 2 vols. (Paris, 1962), 1: 99–100.

16. Ryder, *German Revolution*, 142–49; Gilbert Badia, *Le Spartakisme* (Paris, 1967), 175–78; Eberhard Kolb, *Die Arbeiterräte in der deutschen Innenpolitik 1918–1919* (Düsseldorf, 1962), 38–85 passim.

down even threatened the dismemberment of the Reich; separatist movements came to life in Bavaria, the Rhineland, and Silesia.[17]

The organ of revolutionary authority suddenly appeared in the form of workers' and soldiers' councils. These burgeoning improvisations for taking direct action consisted, according to the circumstances, of sailors, of soldiers, of workers, of peasants, or of combinations of these groups, and in certain cases of middle-class elements. The function of the councils depended on alternative conceptions of the revolutionary goal. The socialist moderates, mainly the Social Democrats, or Majority Socialists, stood for a democratic order obtained by parliamentary means. They would leave the existing organs of administration to carry on their normal duties, while the councils exercised a regulative function during the transitional period until a national assembly framed the prescriptions for a permanent system of democracy. The Spartacists and the radical left of the Independent Socialists conceived the councils to be sovereign bodies for inaugurating and ruling the socialist society.[18]

The councils swayed between these principles and groups. They sometimes seized political power, acting in the capacity of an executive or legislative body. They sometimes exerted control over the local administrative authorities, or collaborated with the municipal council or the state organs, or contented themselves with revolutionary demonstrations. It was a haphazard patchwork of institutional departures, saved from chaos largely by the efforts of the old officials in daily administration.

Of all parts of Germany, the mass revolution struck Bavaria and Berlin with the most turbulence and the largest train of political effects. The Bavarian revolution, aided by the rising separatist sentiment, broke out under the leadership of Kurt Eisner, a Jewish editor and political writer who had joined with other dissidents in organizing the Independent Socialist party in 1917. Released from political imprisonment on October 14, 1918, he reappeared on the public scene as a prophet of revolution. The Bavarian monarchy was driven by the ground swell of unrest and political opposition to introduce constitutional reform, but it was too long delayed to avert Eisner's uprising in Munich on November 7.

17. Badia, *Le Spartakisme*, 187; Payer, *Von Bethmann Hollweg bis Ebert*, 165–66; A. Joseph Berlau, *The German Social Democratic Party, 1914–1921* (New York, 1949), 193–95; Hanssen, *Diary of a Dying Empire*, 364.

18. Kolb, *Die Arbeiterräte*, 57–59, 83–101, 285 ff.; Heidegger, *Die deutsche Sozialdemokratie*, 227–29; Badia, *Le Spartakisme*, 155–57.

A council of workers, soldiers, and peasants was formed, and in its name Eisner proclaimed the Bavarian People's Republic. Representatives from this body joined with liberals and socialists of the the old Landtag in creating a provisional state council to function until a Bavarian constitutent assembly was called. Eisner became the chief minister of a cabinet to which he was obliged to admit Majority Socialists equally with the Independent Socialists. From Munich the revolution with its councils spread elsewhere in Bavaria, weakening in progress from the capital.[19]

The Bavarian revolution never had a destination, and the Eisner regime never achieved stability or avoided confusion. The Eisner revolution nevertheless dealt the final blow to the Prussian monarchy and the Wilhelmine Reich. The revolt intensified the demand elsewhere for the abdication of the kaiser and bore the message that if the unity of Germany was to be restored, the remainder of the country must also become republics.

The political problem of the Eisner regime and the successor revolutionary governments in Bavaria overshadowing all others was how to integrate the complete parliamentary state and the system of councils. The Independent Socialists desired to augment the influence of the councils by making them a legislative organization auxiliary to the parliament; the Majority Socialists set out to minimize the councils by putting them under the state administration. The cabinet therefore remained a divided and ineffective coalition, and the array of councils a jumble of bodies with undefined authority.

The revolutionary program of the Independent Socialists soon suffered a series of defeats. In general, the old administrative officials had to be retained, and almost all the councils were brought under the control of cabinet ministers. The broad opposition to a system of councils was evident in the attitude of two new parties emerging at this time, the Bavarian People's party (Catholics and monarchists) and the German Democratic party in Bavaria (former Progressives, some liberals, representatives of the German Peasants' League). When the first state congress of workers' and soldiers' councils met on December 19, it rejected overwhelmingly the move to make the council system "the basis of the constitution of the socialistic republic." The elections of January 12 for a Bavarian constituent assembly returned a conclusive victory for the parliamentary state. This

19. Our account of the Bavarian revolution follows principally two studies: Allan Mitchell, *Revolution in Bavaria, 1918–1919* (Princeton, 1965), and Helmut Neubauer, *München und Moskau 1918–1919* (Munich, 1958).

"voting down" of the socialist revolution signified that councils could not be institutionalized in the political system except by means of force applied by a minority against the will of the majority.

The revolution in Berlin changed the German government from the parliamentary monarchy to a republic without proceeding so far as the inauguration of a socialist state. The revolutionary tide during the first week of November and Wilson's more definite intervention in Germany's internal structure raised a baffling dilemma both for Prince Max and for the Social Democrats. For Max it was how his continued efforts might overcome the kaiser's stubborn resistance to voluntary abdication and save the monarchy by avoiding the deposition of William II either from the streets or by the Allied powers. For the Social Democrats it was how to compete with the Independent Socialists for the leadership of the increasingly revolutionary masses while remaining part of a government that seemed to bring neither peace nor the removal of the discredited kaiser.

The reluctant leadership of the Social Democrats, opposed by nature to revolution but driven by the mounting pressure from below, decided that "there was nothing else to do. We were obliged to jump into the revolution if we did not want to lose the leadership of the masses."[20] On November 7 Scheidemann, acting for the Social Democrats, submitted to Max an ultimatum demanding the abdication of the kaiser and the renunciation of the throne by the crown prince, as well as larger Social Democratic influence in the cabinet. On November 8 reports of mass manifestations in the rest of Germany accumulated, and news arrived that the rulers of Bavaria, Württemberg, Brunswick, and Mecklenburg had yielded their thrones. These reports jarred the interparty committee of the Reichstag into calling for abdication of the monarch.[21]

The continued refusal of William II to surrender the throne deprived all parties of further choice and introduced on November 9 a day of momentous events in Berlin and the general headquarters at Spa, from which was born the German republic. In Berlin the workers, at last authorized by the Social Democratic executive, came out of the factories on strike. They took to the streets in a massive demonstration in which the

20. This explanation of the SPD decision was given by a party member in the Reichstag on November 9. Hanssen, *Diary of a Dying Empire*, 349.

21. Charles B. Burdick and Ralph H. Lutz, eds., *The Political Institutions of the German Revolution, 1918–1919* (New York, 1966), 32–38; Prinz Max, *Erinnerungen und Dokumente*, 581–94; Payer, *Von Bethmann Hollweg bis Ebert*, 159–61.

troops joined. That morning Max still tried to salvage the monarchy and control the revolution as his office repeatedly urged the kaiser to abdicate immediately.

At Spa, November 9 was a frenetic day of indecision over the attitude of the troops and the abdication question. Groener, now the effective chief of the general staff in place of Ludendorff, boldly advised the kaiser: "the army will march back home peacefully in good order under its leaders and commanding generals, but not under the command of Your Majesty, for it no longer supports Your Majesty." At length William II under Berlin's increased pressure renounced the imperial office but remained the king of Prussia. This decision, when telephoned to Berlin, was understood to mean the kaiser's full abdication. The kaiser's entourage failed to dispatch the promised text of an abdication statement on time. The action of workers and soldiers in Berlin widened in an irresistible movement. The Social Democratic ministers submitted their resignations by telephone from the Reichstag. Prince Max could wait no longer if he was to avert deposition of the kaiser by the revolutionary populace. Max issued a declaration announcing (1) the renunciation of the throne by the kaiser and crown prince, (2) the intention to install a regency and to propose the appointment of the Social Democratic leader Fritz Ebert as chancellor, and (3) the introduction of a bill providing for elections to a constituent assembly.[22]

Ebert accepted the proffered chancellorship and, bearing witness to a concern that continuity be maintained with the past, issued his first proclamation: "The former Reich chancellor Prince Max of Baden has transferred to me with the agreement of all the secretaries of state the conduct of business of the Reich chancellor." Outside the chancellor's office the revolution was on the march in the streets. Amidst this massive wave of movement Scheidemann, rising to the fervor of the crowd, proclaimed the German republic from a balcony of the Reichstag. By this precipitate and irrevocable act, drawing Ebert's reprimand, Scheidemann certified the fall of the monarchy.[23]

At Spa the news of the Berlin proclamations finally shattered the delu-

22. Groener, *Lebenerinnerungen*, 456–61; Niemann, *Kaiser und Revolution*, 136–40; Prinz Max, *Erinnerungen und Dokumente*, 597–99.

23. Prinz Max, *Erinnerungen und Dokumente*, 600–07; Payer, *Von Bethmann Hollweg bis Ebert*, 163–65; Ryder, *German Revolution*, 153; Waldemar Besson, *Friedrich Ebert* (Göttingen, 1963), 63.

sion of William II that he might still march home peacefully with a Prussian division as Prussian king but not as emperor. Arrangements were made for his refuge, and toward five o'clock in the morning he departed with his closest associates for Holland, first by personal train and then by automobile. There, at Doorn, the past ruler of imperial splendor was to spend the rest of his days being a country gentleman. At that moment of history the curtain fell on the reign of William II, the era of the German empire, the kingdom of Prussia, and the Hohenzollern dynasty.[24]

The Conservatives and monarchists remained unreconciled in the conviction that the army would have supported the kaiser if he had led the troops home in a fight against the revolution. They denounced Prince Max, Groener, and Scheidemann for being "the gravediggers of the Hohenzollern dynasty, the kingdom of Prussia, and the German empire." The Conservatives attempted to assemble a historical record to substantiate their case. The record and the argument became a part of the conservative mythology utilized in the attack on the Weimar Republic.[25]

Ebert, Scheidemann, and another Social Democrat joined Hugo Hasse (head of the Independent Socialists) and two of his associates in forming a provisional executive called the Council of People's Commissars. The Social Democrats, politically much stronger than the Independent Socialists, made the coalition on the basis of parity in the interests of strengthening the government through socialist unity before the masses and with the hope of controlling better the revolutionary movement. Karl Liebknecht's Spartacists refused to participate when the Social Democrats rejected the demand of the Independents for government by workers' and soldiers' councils.[26]

Concurrently, an organization of revolutionary councils was taking shape in Berlin. On November 10 an assembly of workers' and soldiers' councils of the capital set up a revolutionary authority in the Executive Committee of the Workers' and Soldiers' Councils of Great Berlin. By working closely with the trade unions and by taking a strong stand on the principles of parity and socialist unity, the Majority Socialists thwarted the

24. Groener, *Lebenserinnerungen,* 449, 462–64; Niemann, *Kaiser und Revolution,* 141–42.
25. The historical record of the Conservatives and their argument are set forth in Kuno Graf Westarp, *Das Ende der Monarchie am 9. November 1918,* ed. Werner Conze (Berlin, 1952).
26. Ryder, *German Revolution,* 153–54; Erich Matthias, Introduction to *Die Regierung der Volksbeauftragten 1918–19,* ed. Susanne Miller (Düsseldorf, 1969), pp. xx, xxvi.

attempts of the Spartacists, shop stewards, and Independents to control this executive body completely and advance their concept of the state.[27]

The masses had come into full political power through the formation of a government entirely socialist in composition. Ebert's government was legitimated by the past regime and by the revolution—both by the transfer of the chancellorship from Prince Max and by the sanction of the street and the Berlin councils. Its validation rested finally on the confidence of the general population except the radical left that it offered the only hope of maintaining order, achieving a peace, solving the problems of supply, and protecting Germany against the triumph of Bolshevism. The over-shadowing question, now that the democratic revolution had been carried out, was whether it would move on to a socialist revolution of the Soviet type. Henceforth a bitter struggle of forces would ensue over the destination of the revolution.[28]

3. THE FIGHT OVER THE COURSE OF THE REVOLUTION

The forces of the moderate socialists and the left radicals conducted the fierce, internecine fight in three arenas: in the revolutionary councils of workers and soldiers, in the governments of the republic and certain member states, and in the streets with arms. The focus of the conflict was the direction and ultimate goal of the revolution in Germany as a whole, although the struggle was intense only in some of the larger cities.

The two sides differed in accordance with the positions they had taken in the schism that had previously divided them. The Social Democrats, or Majority Socialists, true to their reformist traditions and previous coopera-tion with the bourgeois parties, were determined that the revolution should proceed along the middle way of constitutional continuity. They strove to limit the revolution to the institutionalization of an effectively functioning democracy and the preservation of the capitalist economic order in all the component states of Germany. Seeking the salvation of Germany from chaos first, they would leave socialist reforms to come in due course by means of parliamentary legislation. The left radicals aimed to destroy the old system root and branch so that they might quickly build a new rational order of socialist republics. They rallied to the cry of "All

27. Eberhard Kolb, ed., *Der Zentralrat der deutschen socialistischen Republik* (Leiden, 1968), p. xv.

28. On the legitimation of Ebert's government, see Matthias, Introduction to *Die Regierung der Volksbeauftragten*, pp. xvii–xxx.

Power to the Councils" as the only way of achieving socialism.

In this conflict the Social Democratic party had the advantages of a highly centralized national organization with an experienced and firm-handed leadership acting in league with the bulk of the trade unions. The moderate socialists additionally possessed the support of the bourgeois groups and the old officials, along with the cooperation of the army leadership. In the councils they could frequently gain control through the sheer weight of their numbers. If the ultimate test came, they could mobilize, and were prepared to use, elemental armed force.

The struggle was carried on through all arenas to a finish notably in Berlin and Munich. In Berlin Ebert stressed the transitional character of the regime of People's Commissars and minimized the councils as a passing phenomenon of the revolutionary movement.[29] The Ebert government preserved an organic link with the past system in three fields that were to influence profoundly the shaping of the Weimar Republic: the army organization, the administrative bureaucracy, and the cooperation of the majority parties.

The survival of the army cadres resulted from the mutual needs of the generals and the Social Democratic leaders. On the initiative of Groener, a compact was made with Ebert. Groener put the army at the disposal of Ebert, in return for which the latter agreed that his government would uphold the authority of the officers and discipline in the army as well as resist Bolshevism. The powers of the officers received an official confirmation of the People's Commissars. From then on Ebert maintained a "hot line" to Groener for the conduct of confidential conversations.[30]

The generals derived from the alliance the cooperation of the only possible political authority having both mass support and the determination to resist the creation of a Soviet system. They could now organize from the dissolving formations returning from the Western Front and the east volunteer units in the Free Corps and later the Reichswehr in the Weimar Republic. Through the pact the army became a power factor in the transitional government of Ebert and in the Weimar state. Ebert acquired the police force with which to suppress disorder, stamp out the Soviet republics in Bavaria and Bremen, put down the January uprising in Berlin, and throw back the Spartacist challenge. The bargain with Groener, however,

29. Besson, *Friedrich Ebert*, 65–66.
30. Groener, *Lebenserinnerungen*, 467, relates how the alliance began.

checked attempts to organize a republican guard and encouraged the rebirth of militarism and a rising current of counterrevolution.

Ebert preserved continuity from the old bureaucracy to the administrative structure of the provisional government and the Weimar Republic by keeping in office the department heads and their staffs. This insured the functioning of the administrative apparatus without a break in the interests of maintaining public order. In the long run, the solution put much of the machinery of the democratic government into the hands of its ideological enemies. Almost all the former secretaries of state remaining as heads of departments were in fact bourgeois politicians. Though they did not have formal responsibility for policy decisions, their conduct of office in practice inevitably assumed a political character. Their work with the Social Democrats in the provisional government thus represented a continued cooperation of the majority parties.[31]

The revolutionary government of the People's Commissars remained in power from November 10 until the National Assembly met at Weimar on February 6, 1919. In this theater of contest the Social Democrats steadily solidified their control of the cabinet despite the parity principle of composition. Ebert chaired the cabinet at once, and the bureaucracy and the army command considered Ebert to be the chancellor. The three commissars from the Social Democrats took a united stand in policy decisions, while the influence of the Independent Socialists was weakened by their frequent differences. In effect, the Social Democrats took over possession of the essential apparatus of administration and policy decision.[32]

The government of the People's Commissars consolidated and enlarged democratic gains by the proclamation of November 12. The act restored civil liberties, ending censorship and further restrictions of martial law; established universal, equal, and secret suffrage for both sexes in all elections; and, in addition to restoring the prewar legal rights of labor, instituted the eight-hour day and prescribed for unemployment relief. Negotiations between the Ruhr industrialists and the trade unions produced an agreement of November 15, which extended official recognition to the independent trade unions and the practice of collective bargaining.[33]

The government and the Social Democrats had to fight not only for the

31. See Matthias, Introduction to *Die Regierung der Volksbeauftragten*, pp. xxvi, lv–lvii.

32. Ibid., lxxvi–lxxxix; Kolb, *Die Arbeiterräte*, 123–25.

33. Schulthess's *Europäischer Geschichtskalender*, 59 (1918), pt. 1: 474–76, 486–88; Ryder, *German Revolution*, 166.

security of the democratic revolution but also for the survival of Germany. The People's Commissars grappled with the formidable problems of converting the German state and economy from war to peace and of formulating policies for a new era. In the west the troops had to be brought back east of the Rhine; in the east the German armies had to be withdrawn from the Russian borderlands. While demobilizing the returning soldiers, the government took initial steps to organize some kind of armed force for defending the government against putchist attempts. The People's Commissars acted decisively to keep Germany from dismemberment and protected Germany in the east against the Poles until the Versailles conference fixed the boundary with Poland. Of acute difficulty was the determination of a policy toward Bolshevik Russia, since its ambassador, Adolf Joffe, had been expelled on November 5 for subversive activities in lending agitational and financial support to the left radicals, chiefly the Spartacists.

The struggle to limit the revolution, identified with the differences over government by council or by parliament, centered in the decision whether and when to elect a constituent assembly. Ebert and his Social Democratic colleagues saw in a national assembly the only valid means of determining Germany's future system of government and the assurance of framing a democratic constitution for Germany. In the cabinet, the Social Democrats argued for fixing the elections at an early date; the Independents urged delay in the hope that the councils meanwhile could make a permanent imprint on Germany's institutional structure. Following prolonged disagreement, the cabinet at last set the date of elections on February 16.

The differences over this aspect of revolutionary policy were coupled with conflicts between the Council of People's Commissars and the Executive Committee of the Berlin councils as to where the supreme revolutionary authority resided. Although composed in equal numbers of Majority and Independent Socialists, the Executive Committee was dominated by the latter, and the views of the left extremists, who were unalterably opposed to convening a national assembly, often prevailed.

The Workers' and Soldiers' Councils of Great Berlin had created the Executive Committee as a provisional central organ of the workers' and soldiers' councils of Germany and confirmed the Council of People's Commissars without limiting the competence of each. These functional ambiguities, combined with the meddlesome interference of the Executive Committee in central and local administration, not to mention its obstructiveness and incompetence, sharpened the conflict between the two revolutionary bodies.[34]

These twin issues concerned with the holding of a constituent assembly and the determination of the fulcrum of revolutionary authority moved along toward resolution with the General Congress of the Workers' and Soldiers' Councils of Germany meeting in Berlin on December 16–20. Both its composition and work pointed to the moderate democratic expectations of the working masses. In the congress the radical Independents attacked the Council of People's Commissars and warned of the danger of counterrevolution. The Social Democratic delegates put through, with an overwhelming majority, a motion by which the assembly conferred legislative and executive power on the Council of People's Commissars. The measure created a Central Council of the Workers' and Soldiers' Councils for exercising a "parliamentary supervision" over the German and Prussian cabinets.[35]

The Independent Socialist delegates tried to obtain from the congress the power for the Central Council to pass legislation or at least to approve or reject legislation before its promulgation. In view of their failure, the Independents abstained in the election of a slate to the Central Council. Their self-denial allowed the congress to elect the members of the Central Council entirely from the Social Democratic party. The Executive Committee remained, but with jurisdiction restricted to Berlin.[36]

These changes in the central conciliar organization relieved the tension between it and the Council of People's Commissars. The members of the Central Council, composed entirely of Social Democrats, conducted business as a solid party group, working in close cooperation with the party leaders Ebert and Scheidemann among the People's Commissars.

The question of a national assembly came before the congress on a motion of the Social Democrats to advance the agreed date of February 16 to January 19 for holding the elections. Their purpose in earlier elections was to check the increasing agitation of the Spartacists and radical Independents associated with growing tendencies to putchist action.

There was widespread public support for the Social Democratic alternative of a national assembly and a parliamentary system rather than a

34. Kolb, *Der Zentralrat,* pp. xvi–xxi.
35. Ibid., pp. xxvii–xxx: Schulthess's *Europäischer Geschichtskalender,* 59 (1918), pt. 1: 573–75.
36. Kolb, *Der Zentralrat,* pp. xxxi–xxxv.

conciliar organization for the German constitutional settlement. The reactionaries, conservatives, liberals, many intellectuals, and the bourgeois press rallied behind a national assembly. The elections to the General Congress of the Workers' and Soldiers' Councils demonstrated that the Social Democrats, with their stand for a national assembly, clearly predominated in strength among the working classes and trade unions.

The isolation of the Independents and the Spartacists on the constitutional issue was revealed by the vote in the congress on the question of a national assembly. The Social Democratic motion carried overwhelmingly, while the countermotion of the radical Independents for a system of councils was defeated by 344 to 98. These two votes together constituted the decisive ballot of the revolution, signifying that it would be cut off at the point of a democratic constitution for a parliamentary state. Beyond this action the congress adopted radical demilitarization measures and an abortive resolution on the socialization of industries.[37]

The session of the congress ended in a conclusive triumph for the Social Democratic majority and an irreparable defeat for the Independents, most of all the radical left. The self-denying decision of the Independents not to participate in the Central Council prepared the way for another act of withdrawal and isolation—their resignation from the Council of People's Commissars on December 29. They were taking these steps under the increasing pressure of the left radicals.

The growing exclusion of the Independents from the central institutional arena drove them in the long run down the road of Spartacist putchism or back to reunion with the Majority Socialists. The effect solidified the differences between the disparate elements of the Independents and destroyed the last basis for the existence of a single party. The next step in this process of disintegration was the final break between the Independents and Spartacists and the formation of the separate Communist party from the Spartacist group. Its program was full socialization and government by councils, its tactics violence and nonparticipation in the parliamentary process instituted with the Weimar assembly. The struggle at this point was to sharpen into a rudimentary civil war.

37. Schulthess's *Europäischer Geschichtskalender*, 59 (1918), pt. 1: 584–86; Burdick and Lutz, *Political Institutions of the German Revolution*, 222–23.

4. THE DEFEAT OF THE RADICAL LEFT

The Majority Socialists had won in the revolutionary political bodies the contest with the left radicals over the guiding concept of the revolution. The left radicals then carried the struggle from the forum of the revolutionary political bodies to a trial of strength in the streets. This shift raised for the Majority Socialists in power the dilemma of utilizing armed force to protect the government and their own supremacy without encouraging remilitarization and counterrevolution.

The conflict of force went back to putchist disorders in Berlin on December 6. On that date a group of soldiers attempted to arrest the Executive Committee of the Berlin councils, and another band of soldiers demonstrated for Ebert as president of Germany. A Spartacist crowd, preparing to protest against the plan for a national assembly, turned its demonstration against these incidents. Troops of the government intervened, with some loss of life. These incidents, regarded widely in Berlin and in the Executive Committee to be related parts of a counterrevolutionary plot, intensified the friction between the Executive Committee and the People's Commissars and heightened the differences within the Independents between the government collaborators and the radicals. An implacable conflict was now certain between the Spartacists and the Ebert leadership.

The next resort to force occurred in the sailors' revolt of December 23–24. A dispute arose between the authorities and the People's Naval Division, a contingent of pilfering and rebellious sailors who installed themselves in the buildings of the imperial palace, over arrears of pay and their evacuation. Their arrest and detention of the Berlin commandant Otto Wels led to Ebert and two other Social Democratic members of the People's Commissars asking the minister of war to bring about Wels's release. The minister's troops shelled the palace with guns and killed some thirty people. A settlement was made with the sailors for their pay and enrollment in the republican guard. An indignant crowd, incited by Liebknecht and radical Independents, took over the offices of the socialist paper *Vorwärts* on Christmas day. The Spartacists forced the staff to publish an issue attacking Ebert's government before they vacated the building.[38]

38. Ryder, *German Revolution*, 188–91; Arthur Rosenberg, *A History of the German Republic* (London, 1936), 59–64.

Suspicious of Ebert's relationship with Groener, the Independent Socialist Commissars found in the incident an example of the "encroachments of the military leaders and the supreme command upon the revolution" and proof of the need to implement immediately the demilitarization measures adopted by the General Congress of the Workers' and Soldiers' Councils.[39] When the Central Council failed to give the assurances about demilitarization desired by the Independent Socialists, their members withdrew from the Council of People's Commissars. Gustav Noske took charge of army and naval affairs, and another Social Democrat occupied one of the other vacated posts. Henceforth the cabinet of five Social Democrats acted in the name of the government of Germany and not as the Council of People's Commissars.

The polarization within the socialists and workers peaked quickly. The Independent Socialists also withdrew from the Prussian government in which they had participated with the Majority Socialists. By January 1, 1919, the Spartacists, seceding from the Independent Socialists, had formed a separate Communist party under the leadership of Liebknecht and Rosa Luxemburg.[40] The January uprising sealed in bitterness and blood the divisions within the revolutionary movement between the democrats and left radicals.

The January uprising, known also as the Spartacist uprising, was precipitated by the dismissal of the Independent Socialist Emil Eichhorn from his office of chief of the Berlin police. The now solidly Social Democratic government of Prussia could no longer tolerate in this position a controversial figure whose security police had sided with the opposition to the government in the past rebellious actions. Independent Socialists, shop stewards, and Communists rallied to the support of Eichhorn on January 5 by organizing the largest demonstration ever held before in the center of the city. Once more the activists seized the house of *Vorwärts* and this time other newspapers as well.

The leaders of the demonstration were prompted by the activism of the participating masses and the prospect of support from the sailors, the Berlin garrison, and troops in nearby areas to attempt a seizure of power inaugurating the "second revolution." The leaders formed a revolution-

39. Burdick and Lutz, *Political Institutions of the German Revolution*, 156.
40. The only full-length biographical study of Liebknecht is by the East German Heinz Wohlgemuth, *Karl Liebknecht* (Berlin, 1973). J. P. Nettl, *Rosa Luxemburg*, 2 vols. (London, 1966) stands first in quality and importance among the writings on Luxemburg.

ary committee under three heads, representing the Independents, the Communists, and the shop stewards. The last, engaged in competitive militancy with the Communists, gave the main push to this reckless venture. The activists rushed into an inevitable showdown with the Social Democrats, against the better judgment of Rosa Luxemburg and some of the other leaders.[41]

The revolutionary committee, starting a general strike, declared the "Ebert-Scheidemann government" deposed and proclaimed that the committee had "taken over the business of government for the time being." The action was badly prepared and conducted; the expected aid from sailors and soldiers was not forthcoming; the desultory street fighting was confined to a few hundred civilians. The demonstrators occupied a number of public buildings, and for a time the government found itself in a precarious situation.

Attempts to negotiate an understanding between the government and various revolutionary groups were futile. The issue was not negotiable, for it involved a decisive struggle for power. The Spartacists were unyielding; the government, Central Council, Social Democratic party, and the supreme command were ready to use armed force as soon as it was available for overcoming the rival contender. The military force for suppressing the "second revolution" was organized by Noske, who was made commander-in-chief for Berlin. Noske took up the unwelcome task with the words: "Someone has to be the bloodhound. I will not shirk the responsibility."[42] The several thousand troops that he assembled were composed mainly of Free Corps, being formed by the generals, although volunteer regiments were recruited from socialists and trade union members. From the night of January 10–11 the forces of order began freeing the city from the Spartacist hold. The uprising was stamped out with a fierce passion. The Free Corps, taking to the assignment with a vengeance, committed numerous atrocities against the captured revolutionaries. The toll of victims included both Liebknecht and Luxemburg, who were murdered brutally.[43]

41. On the January uprising, see Ryder, *German Revolution*, 200–07; Rosenberg, *History of the German Republic*, 74–86; Badia, *Le Spartakisme*, 247–57; Nettl, *Rosa Luxemburg*, 2: 761–72; Eric Waldman, *The Spartacist Uprising of 1919 and the Crisis of the German Socialist Movement* (Milwaukee, 1958).

42. Kolb, *Der Zentralrat*, 220.

43. On the murder of Liebknecht and Luxemburg, see Nettl, *Rosa Luxemburg*, 2: 772–82; Elizabeth Hannover-Drück and Heinrich Hannover, eds., *Der Mord an Rosa Luxemburg und Karl Liebknecht: Dokumentation eines politischen Verbrechens* (Frankfurt, 1967).

The mismanaged insurrection baptized the infant Communist party with the experience of reckless and futile revolutionary action. Instead of giving warning that there should be no recurrence, it set an example that was followed. In Bremen on January 10 the minority Communists took over political power as the dictatorship of the proletariat. With the participation of the left Independents, they recast the membership of the ruling workers' and soldiers' council and armed the workers. Noske's troops then moved into Bremen and installed a government of Social Democrats. The Communists set up a dictatorship in Brunswick with similar consequences. In March the Communists attempted to utilize a general strike in Berlin for the purpose of overthrowing the government and replacing the National Assembly with councils. Rioting and street fighting broke out, and the Communists were defeated at a cost of some 1,200 lives.

The Communists eventually rode to the top of the revolutionary wave in Munich and introduced a soviet regime. This was the final stage in a series of ever more radical regimes since the November uprising. Bavaria, indeed, experienced three successive revolutions. The first, or Eisner's, revolution was doomed by the results of the elections for the Bavarian Constituent Assembly, revealing that the Independent Socialists had minimal political support.[44] Eisner was left dangling between the radical leftists on the one side and most of the Bavarian constituency on the other. Persuaded by the Social Democrats to resign, Eisner was assassinated by a counterrevolutionary on February 21 before he could submit the resignation of his cabinet to the Constituent Assembly at its first meeting.

The second revolution was distinguished by a rising confrontation between the proponents of a councils system and those of a parliamentary republic. The radicalization of the Munich councils was stimulated by the election results and the Communist penetration of the councils system. The election returns convinced the conciliar leaders of the necessity of direct action against the Bavarian assembly if the councils system was to be preserved. The radicalism in Munich found expression in the formation of the Revolutionary Central Council.

The congress of councils from all Bavaria, convening on February 25, claimed sovereign power and attempted to install a new provisional cabinet. The Social Democrats, however, rejected participation of their party

44. The Independent Socialists obtained only 2.5 percent of the vote. See the table of election returns in Franz Schade, *Kurt Eisner und die bayerische Sozialdemokratie* (Hannover, 1961), 83.

on the grounds that a legally constituted cabinet must be appointed by the Constituent Assembly. In accordance with the will of the country for parliamentary government, the Constituent Assembly met on March 17–18 and authorized a cabinet headed by the Social Democrat Johannes Hoffmann and composed almost entirely of socialists to exercise both executive and legislative power.

The Hoffmann administration ended the interim of no ministry but not the stalemate between the parliamentary and conciliar systems. The embittered radical leftists were determined to realize a republic of councils even though this was not possible against the will of the majority without the use of force. The radical forces were infused with fresh strength by the formation of the Communist International on March 3 and by the proclamation of the Hungarian Soviet Republic on March 20. The Bavarian Communists were revitalized through the work of the Russian-born Eugen Leviné, sent out by the party head in Berlin, in reorganizing the party and editing the party newspaper *Rote Fahne* with new vigor. The Hoffmann government made no noticeable progress in rescuing the foundering economy. The radicalization of the councils, particularly of the soldiers, continued.

April ushered in the third revolution, with a flight to anarchy. Crowds took to rhe streets, the unemployed and armed soldiers ranged over Munich, inflammatory protests and resolutions flared up. When Hoffmann ordered a convocation of the Constituent Assembly to deal with the tense situation, the Revolutionary Central Council declared against its convening and proclaimed a soviet republic on April 7. A Council of People's Commissars was formed of radical Independent Socialists and intellectuals of anarchist tendencies. The commissars commenced the organization of a Red Army and came out with a shower of paper proclamations and orders for inaugurating "a true socialist system" under the dictatorship of the proletariat.

The newly proclaimed republic lasted only six days. Hoffmann's rump government moved to Bamberg and retained authority in the greater part of Bavaria. Hoffmann recruited a voluntary force in northern Bavaria for restoring his government in Munich and laid a blockade around the capital. The Communists attacked the regime as nothing but a sham soviet republic in the hands of dilettantes, and it fell victim to these tactics. The Communists took over power in the midst of wild confusion and instituted the real soviet regime on April 13, with Leviné as the chief executive.

The downfall of the revolutionary government was certain from the beginning. The rest of Germany would muster whatever military force was necessary to extinguish a soviet regime in Bavaria, seceding in effect from the German union to enter into ties with Soviet Russia. Any hope of support from neighboring states expired when Romanian forces invaded Soviet Hungary and the Austrian socialists suppressed the Communist uprising in Vienna. The Red Army in Munich, though enlarged, was never welded together into a coherent, disciplined force. Hoffmann's inexorable blockade and a general strike paralyzed economic life in the capital. The support and supply of the expanded army led to measures of confiscation.

When Hoffmann attacked with a superior military force of some 35,000 men, the regime was already breaking down internally, because of the resentment caused by the unpopular measures and dissension within the leadership. The advancing army of Hoffmann's government, consisting of a people's militia, Free Corps, and a contribution of troops provided by Noske, assaulted Munich on April 30 and gained complete command of the city by May 3. The resistance was obliterated ruthlessly. The councils system was liquidated in the blood of 600 dead.

The Communists in Germany had recklessly challenged the Social Democrats in power and resorted to force when the conditions of success were absent. These experiences laid a policy track of costly and futile political adventurism that continued to be followed into the Weimar years. The Communists thereby ended any prospect for the further advance of the revolution. The German and Bavarian governments fell back on the Free Corps for insuring their survival and the unity of Germany. These units with their uncontrolled excesses thus received an official sanction.

In the struggle for power and control of the revolution, the Social Democrats won not only by the conquest of the radicals with military force but also through the elections to the National Assembly. The ballots cast on January 19, 1919, demonstrated the support of the great majority of the people for the parliamentary republic.[45] On February 6 the elected delegates convened in the Thuringian town of Weimar and elected Ebert provisional president of the republic. The new provisional government, headed by Scheidemann, was constituted from the Social Democrats,

45. For the election results, see the table in Badia, *Histoire de l'Allemagne contemporaine,* 1: 139.

Center, and Democrats (former Progressives). These three parties formed the Weimar coalition, which was to provide the Reichstag majorities for the republic. Surviving constitutions and revolutions, this grouping revived the coalition of majority parties going back through the time of Prince Max's government to the combination supporting the peace resolution of 1917.

The formation of the Weimar government, along with the military suppression of left-radical activism, brought the German revolution to a close. The revolutionary settlement produced the middle-class democratic state conceived by the leaders of the Majority Socialists, destroyed by the Nazis, and revived after 1945. Its structure was established by the advanced constitution for a parliamentary system that the National Assembly drafted and unveiled to the public at Weimar on August 11, 1919.

The revolution ended without real progress in socialization, and the demilitarization measures of the revolution were renounced in practice because Hindenburg and Groener opposed them. A new militarism took its rise from Noske's order of January 19 confirming the officers' power of command and dependence on the Free Corps for protection. Noske used the Free Corps on a large scale in suppressing political disorders. A veritable civil war was carried on during the first half of 1919 against the leftists and a considerable portion of the working class. A counterrevolution developed more and more steam as armed power shifted form the revolutionary soldiers, now demobilized, and workers to the rightist forces.

The failure of the republican government under the leadership of the Majority Socialists to achieve substantial progress in socialization and establish a conciliar system in any recognizable form alienated the left. The abortive demilitarization and the discredit cast by the Free Corps terrorism hardened that alienation. There was no surviving socialist party strong enough to provide political leadership in Germany, and the middle classes were moving toward the right. The right was increasingly inclined to self-help and putchist violence. The Weimar republic was condemned to political instability.

The Social Democrats and historians following their line have adhered to the conventional interpretation that there was no alternative to the Social Democratic course in the revolution except Bolshevism.[46] This

46. See Matthias, Introduction to *Die Regierung der Volksbeauftragten,* p. xv.

view has been challenged recently on convincing grounds. If the Ebert government, the Social Democratic leadership, and the trade unions had not taken a negative attitude toward the councils as a whole, the government might have used the democratic (contrasted with the dictatorial and soviet type) councils to democratize the civil service in the townships and provinces without endangering the organization of a parliamentary state.[47] The Ebert government, moreover, relied too easily on the old army leaders and Free Corps formations without devoting sufficient determination and energy to organizing republican security forces. That it could be done was suggested by the volunteer regiments that participated effectively against the Spartacist uprising. The Austrian socialists also formed a people's army prepared at once to put down a Communist putsch and reject the machinations of monarchist officers.

If the ideological intransigence of both the Majority and Independent Socialists had not prevented socialist unity, the government would have been strengthened with broader mass support. The right-wing Independents argued that socialist unity would have improved the chances of progress, despite the difficulties, in democratizing the civil service and of securing demilitarization, socialization, and socialist control of the National Assembly.

47. Kolb, *Die Arbeiterräte*, 360–83.

Chapter Fourteen

THE SLAVIC REVOLUTIONS IN EASTERN EUROPE

I. THE FORMATION OF NATIONAL PROGRAMS
AND ORGANIZATIONS

At the end of the war period the nationalities in the zone between the Germans and the Russians achieved national unity and independence in a series of revolutions that brought about a general territorial reorganization of eastern Europe. The central area of revolution in eastern Europe was the Austro-Hungarian empire. There three types of revolution converged: the national, the democratic, and the socialist. The democratic revolution embraced the exercise of self-determination, the establishment of republics, the introduction of parliamentary government with universal suffrage, and a shift of political power from the privileged classes to the masses. The socialist revolution made a prominent thrust in Hungary, where a short-lived soviet republic came into existence, and in Austria, where the Communist challenge was thrown back by the Social Democrats.

In Russia and Germany the revolution transformed the political system; in the Habsburg empire it destroyed the territorial state. The growing opposition of the subject nationalities turned against the government and then the state. The government at Vienna continued to demonstrate that it was incapable of constitutional reform dealing with the problem of nationalities in a reasonable fashion. The repressive methods of war government affronted the Slav nationalities more than the others, for, being suspect of political unreliability, they were subjected to harsher restrictions and punitive measures. The liberal Joseph Redlich was convinced that this wartime system of rule "contributed more than any other single factor to the political and national breakup of the monarchical machine."[1] Most of the politically articulate people in these nations were gradually converted from loyal subjects of the crown, believing that their aspirations could be satisfied within the empire, to insistent claimants of indepen-

1. Redlich, *Austrian War Government,* 79.

dence.[2] The Russian revolution and the eastern peace settlement stimulated the desire for peace, political action of the workers and socialists, urban ferment, and the movement for national independence. From this background the revolutionary movement developed in a manner distinctive of each nationality. The movement among the Slavic nationalities for the most part proceeded along two roads: at home some kind of organization carried on an opposition to the wartime policies of the government, or fought the monarchy itself, and asserted the claims of nationality; abroad a committee of political exiles conducted the movement toward national independence and unity, winning support among the Allies.

These nationality movements passed through several phases of broadening agreement among the national population on goals and methods as international recognition was progressively won. The first phase, until the end of 1916, was characterized by the formation of national programs and organizations. The Czech movement formed the fulcrum of the national revolutions in the Habsburg empire. With far-reaching vision Thomas G. Masaryk put into effect a triple design for making the Czechoslovak state: the conversion of the western countries to the Czech aims, the formation of a Czechoslovak army, giving weight to the Czechoslovak claim, and the functioning of a revolutionary organization at home.[3]

Masaryk initiated the home efforts by holding underground meetings in Prague of radical leaders from the political parties and the gymnastic society called the Sokol. The Mafia, or secret committee in which the group organized itself in March 1915, promoted the national revolution with a daring work of intelligence gathering, sabotage, encouragement of defeatism, communication with the revolutionary organization abroad, and maintaining a support base for it at home.[4] The revolutionary nationalists had to contend with division between the russophiles and the west-

2. Z.A.B. Zeman, *The Break-Up of the Habsburg Empire, 1914–1918* (London, 1961), 50–63.

3. This historical achievement is recounted in Masaryk's own story, *The Making of a State* (London, 1927). The latest biography of Masaryk is in Zbyněk Zeman, *The Masaryks* (New York, 1976).

4. For the organization and activities of the Mafia: Eduard Beneš, *My War Memoirs* (London, 1928), 37–54, 74–75; the memoirs by Jan Hajšman, *Česká Mafie* (Prague, 1932) and *Mafie v rozmachu,* 2d ed. (Prague, 1934); Milada Paulova's broad-ranging histories of the revolutionary movement, *Dějiny Maffie* (Prague, 1937) and *Tainý výbor (Maffie) a spolupráce s Jihoslovany v letech 1916–1918* (Prague, 1968).

erners. They were subjected in 1915 to an intensified police surveillance, which led to the arrest of the mainstays of the Mafia. Eduard Beneš, the foremost lieutenant of Masaryk, was obliged to escape abroad. These conditions moved most of the political parties in 1916 to join in creating the Czech Union and the National Committee. The first comprised the Czech deputies to the lower house of the Reichsrat, or the Austrian parliament. The second was organized to support the undertakings of the Czech Union and to be "the highest moral authority" in other fields of political life.[5]

In December 1914, Masaryk, the elderly professor, set out from Prague on what became a political pilgrimage of four years abroad. From a center in London, Masaryk headed the movement's activities of organization and enlightenment in the Allied countries.[6] He established a powerful unity of direction among the westerners, both exiles and immigrants, through the Czechoslovak National Council, which was founded in 1916 with its secretariat in Paris. The Paris center, directed by Beneš, waged an unceasing campaign in behalf of creating a Czechoslovak army and state.

The threat to unity came from the russophiles and Russia. The Czechs and Slovaks in that country organized a Czechoslovak contingent in the Russian army and the League of Czechoslovak Societies in Russia. The league sought the establishment of an independent national state under a Romanov king.

The partitions of Poland caused the emergence of two Polish Piedmonts —Galicia in Austria and Congress Poland, or the kingdom of Poland, in Russia. The complexity of the Polish situation gave rise to alternative programs for the attainment of Polish union and independence. (1)Roman Dmowski and his middle-class National Democratic party of Warsaw, proceeding from the base in Russian Poland, aimed to restore Poland with a federative status within the Russian empire.[7] (2)The Austrian solution, advanced in western Galicia, supported the formation of an independent state with Austrian aid.[8] (3)The program of independent Polish effort was

5. Zeman, *Break-Up of the Habsburg Empire*, 115–16; Paulova, *Tainý výbor*, 49–56.

6. On Masaryk's activities in London, see Harry Hanak, *Great Britain and Austria-Hungary during the First World War* (London, 1962), 101–28, 174–88; R. W. Seton-Watson, *Masaryk in London* (Cambridge, England, 1943); Beneš, *My War Memoirs*, 86–88.

7. Paul Roth, *Die politische Entwicklung in Kongress Polen während der deutschen Okkupation* (Leipzig, 1919), 9–10.

8. Przemysław A. Szudek, "Rebirth and Independence, 1918–1939," in *Modern Poland between East and West*, ed. Jan Ostaszewski (London, 1971), 10–11.

championed by Jozef Pilsudski, the imposing leader of the nationalist wing of the radical Polish socialist party (PPS). Pilsudski insisted that the Poles must achieve an independent and democratic republic by a struggle of their own military forces. He had trained a legion of volunteer "riflemen" in Galicia, including recruits from Russian Poland, for the future Polish army.[9]

The defeat of Russia in 1915, which returned eastern Galicia to Austria and delivered most of Russian Poland to the occupation of the Central Powers, dealt a fatal blow to the russophile orientation. In November Dmowski departed Petrograd for the west, where with other National Democrats and conservatives he undertook to mobilize support for a free Poland.

German policy toward Poland removed any chances of the Austrian solution being realized. The occupying powers divided Russian Poland into two areas of military administration, the northern one under the German government-general of Warsaw and the southern one under the Austrian government-general of Lublin. At first the Germans gave the Austrians to understand that Berlin accepted the Austrian solution by which Russian Poland would be united with Galicia in an autonomous kingdom within the Habsburg monarchy. German policy was dominated thereafter by the objectives of forming a barrier Polish state dependent on Germany and effecting a political status for the Poles that would permit the recruitment of Polish troops.

The feasibility of the Pilsudski alternative depended on the extent to which the Poles themselves could control their military forces and build political institutions within the system of the Central Powers. Obliged at the outset of war to enter his legion into the Austrian army, Pilsudski concentrated on creating through his agents a secret network of military forces in Russian Poland called the Polish Military Organization (POW).

Within occupied Poland the parties of independence formed the Central National Committee, made up chiefly of the PPS, the People's party (based in the peasantry), and the National Union of Workers. The "Independents," among which Pilsudski was the ruling power, opposed further recruitment for the legion unless it was placed under his independent command. Pilsudski resigned his command of Poles in the Austrian army,

9. Ibid., 11; Werner Conze, *Polnische Nation und deutsche Politik im Ersten Weltkrieg* (Cologne, 1958), 40–41, 52–56.

though the Austrian government accorded the legion more of a national identity with the status of the Polish auxiliary corps.[10]

Because of Ludendorff's pressure to recruit Polish troops, the German and Austrian emperors proclaimed on November 5, 1916, the intention to establish a Polish state in the form of a constitutional monarchy with its own army. Coupled with the appeal for Polish recruits, the proclamation met with an unfavorable reception. The recruits would be merged with the Polish legion to form the Polish army under German control. In the hope of winning Polish political cooperation, the two governments-general dealt with the demands of the activist political parties for the establishment of Polish political institutions by setting up an advisory State Council.[11]

By the beginning of 1917 the formation of Pilsudski's underground organization the POW and the creation of the State Council despite its limited functions afforded the Poles two forms in which the embryonic structure of a Polish government could gradually take shape under the occupation. The reborn Polish state would be ready to break out of the shell once the military power of Germany and Austria collapsed.

The national feelings of the Ukrainians in the Habsburg empire, located chiefly in eastern Galicia, Bukovina, and the Carpatho-Ukraine, had been stirred by the political and economic dominance of the Poles in Galicia and by the growing agitation and other russification activities of Russian agents. The politically conscious Ukrainians were divided between three groups: the loyalists, seeking in Galicia a status that would secure them against the dominant Poles; the ardent nationalists, envisaging the eventual creation of an independent state of all the Ukrainians to be attained through cooperation with the Habsburg monarchy; and the russophiles, identifying with the Ukrainians in the eastern or Russian Ukraine.[12]

The Ukrainian delegates to the Reichsrat founded the Ukrainian National Council to rally their countrymen of the empire in the fight against Russia. Political émigrés from the eastern Ukraine, cooperating with the local Ukrainians, organized at Lvov in Galicia the Union for the Liberation of the Ukraine, with the aim of founding a fully independent Ukrainian

10. Conze, *Polnische Nation und deutsche Politik*, 156–62; May, *Passing of the Hapsburg Monarchy*, 1: 370–71.

11. Conze, *Polnische Nation und deutsche Politik*, 216–51 passim; Roth, *Die politische Entwicklung in Kongress Polen*, 45–52.

12. Zeman, *Break-Up of the Habsburg Monarchy*, 4–13.

state. The organization (moving later to Vienna and then Berlin) attempted to promote rebellion in the eastern Ukraine and opened communications with a clandestine group in Kiev despite the Russian efforts since the beginning of the war to exterminate "Ukrainianism." The nationalists in the eastern Ukraine mostly pursued the goal of an autonomous state within Russia.[13]

The ruthless and corrupt regime of sweeping russification imposed by the Russian occupation of eastern Galicia strengthened pro-Austrian tendencies when the Austrians returned in 1915. Thereafter the immediate objective of the Ukrainian political leaders of the empire, organized since May 1915 in the General Ukrainian Council, was the establishment of an autonomous crownland of east Galicia.

The existence of three related but different ethnic groups—the Serbs, Croats, and Slovenes—with diverse historical experience and cultural traditions complicated the course of the South Slav national movement and transmitted to the future Yugoslav kingdom the problem of the multinational state that the Habsburg empire could not solve. Reflecting these divergencies, the Serbs, Croats, and Slovenes had two organizations in exile, the Serbian government and the South Slav Committee. The two were engaged in a prolonged and passionate dispute over the method of achieving independence and the structure of the future state.

The movement toward a new South Slav political organization advanced along the three tracks laid down by the South Slav Committee, the Serbian cabinet, and the political leaders inside Croatia and Slovenia. The South Slav Committee was constituted by exiles under the direction of Dr. Ante Trumbić, the principal political leader of the Dalmatian Croats. Having moved from Paris to London, the committee with the unflagging aid of the Slav historian Robert W. Seton-Watson and the journalist Wickam Steed conducted a campaign for the dissolution of the Habsburg empire and the nullification of the treaty of London (Italy's main support for claims to certain Yugoslav lands along the Adriatic).[14] The cabinet of Nikola Pašić, first in Belgrade and later in exile, pursued unrelentingly the

13. Oleh S. Fedyshyn, *Germany's Drive to the East and the Ukrainian Revolution, 1917–1918* (New Brunswick, N. J., 1971), 30–41; Dmytro Doroshenko and Oleh W. Gerus, *A Survey of Ukrainian History* (Winnipeg, 1975), 592–93; May, *Passing of the Hapsburg Monarchy*, 1: 372–73.
    14. P. D. Ostović, *The Truth about Yugoslavia* (New York, 1952), 54–61; Hanak, *Great Britain and Austria-Hungary*, 70–90.

aim of uniting from the Serbian Piedmont as a base all South Slavs and organizing the new state in the form of a centralized kingdom. The leaders of the Croat and Slovene parties moved in early 1915 to support the work of the Trumbić committee.[15]

2. THE RADICALIZATION OF THE POLITICAL MOVEMENTS

In the second phase, extending through 1917 to the spring of 1918, the political movements of the eastern zone were radicalized through the influence of the Russian revolution and the American crusade for a liberal world order. The war revealed more openly its revolutionary character, pitting democratic-socialist forces against a conservative-autocratic order in a growing ideological conflict. The cardinal tenets of autonomy, self-determination, and democracy propagated by the liberal and revolutionary side, were identified with the cause of the nationalities. The eastern borderlands became a theater and the subject nationalities an object of political warfare. The shift of opinion influenced moderate political leaders and organizations at home toward a unity of national purpose with the national organs abroad. The advance toward unity strengthened the position of the national organizations in exile and contributed to their international recognition as official bodies.

The more favorable disposition of the Allies and the United States toward the radical aspirations of the nationalities was heralded by the Allies' note of January 10, 1917, replying to Wilson's inquiry of December 18, 1916, concerning peace terms, Wilson's address of January 22 on peace without victory, and pronouncements of the revolutionary government of Russia about the nationalities. These statements committed the Allies and the United States to the reorganization of Europe on the basis of "respect for nationalities," or the principle of self-determination.

The nationality movements were encouraged to go over to the offensive in pressing more radical aims. When Emperor Karl convened the Reichs-

15. On the national programs of the South Slav Committee and the Serbian cabinet and the differences between them, see the articles by Charles Jelavich, "Nikola P. Pašić: Greater Serbia or Jugoslavia?," *Journal of Central European Affairs* 11 (1951): 133–52, and Dragovan Šepić, "The Question of Yugoslav Union in 1918," *Journal of Contemporary History* 3, no. 4 (1968): 33–38. Pašić's policy and the differences between him and the South Slav Committee have been a matter of controversy since the war. Ostović, *Truth about Yugoslavia,* presents an account favorable to the committee, and Alex N. Dragnich, *Serbia, Nikola Pašić, and Yugoslavia* (New Brunswick, N.J., 1974), 111–33, a pro-Serb defense of Pašić. Šepić strikes a balance between these two types of interpretation.

rat for the first time during the war on May 30, 1917, the Czech delegates presented a single policy statement that asked for the transformation of "the Habsburg monarchy into a federal state consisting of free and equal national states" and for "the unification of all the branches of the Czechoslovak nation in one democratic state."[16] The South Slavs and the Ukrainians announced comparable programs in a notable demonstration of cooperation among the Slavs. For the Slav nationalities the program declarations of May became charters of national revolution.[17]

In giving expression to the more radical and assertive turn of the Polish movement, the State Council made ultimative demands for the formation of a Polish cabinet and the institution of a regency. On May 28 a large meeting in Cracow of Galician political leaders and representatives from Congress Poland declared for an independent state of Great Poland with access to the sea. This resolution became the program of the national movement.[18]

Pilsudski withdrew from the State Council together with the left represented by the POW and the Pilsudski socialists. The nationalist leader mobilized both to propagandize against the German plan for a Polish army. The Germans arrested Pilsudski on July 22 and imprisoned him in Germany. Pilsudski was made a martyr and the national movement more revolutionary. Ludendorff's scheme to recruit Polish forces went down to defeat. The Polish auxiliary corps was returned to the Austrian command.

The Polish pressures accounted for the constitutional patent of the two emperors (September 12), introducing a Council of Regency of three members, who would appoint a cabinet. These organs were to have legislative, administrative, and judicial authority of limited degree. The administration of justice and the educational system were subsequently transferred to Polish officials.

Abroad, the Poles, chiefly Dmowski and the National Democrats, advanced the program of an independent Great Poland through the Polish National Committee, founded in Lausanne in 1917 and later moved to Paris. Ignace Paderewski effectively campaigned in the United States for

16. For the text of the declaration, see Hajšman, *Mafie v rozmachu*, 73.
17. Zeman, *Break-Up of the Habsburg Monarchy*, 124–27; Lorenz, *Kaiser Karl*, 350–53; Jozef Lettrich, *History of Modern Slovakia* (New York, 1955), 47. On the declaration of the South Slavs: Paulova, *Tainy výbor*, 235–46; Šepić, "The Question of Yugoslav Union," 39.
18. The account of the national movement in Congress Poland and Galicia during this phase largely follows Conze, *Polnische Nation und deutsche Politik*.

the aims of the committee while links were forged with the Polish-American organizations. The committee obtained recognition, accorded first by the French government on September 20, 1917, as an official Polish organization entitled to represent Polish interests in the Allied countries. The committee's political authority over the autonomous Polish army in France, organized since the Nivelle debacle, was recognized by the French government on March 20, 1918.[19]

The political leadership of the committee was followed by the National Democratic organizations of Congress Poland, Galicia, and Prussia. The Polish national movement thus had three rival centers of policy and direction—the committee, the Warsaw government, and the Pilsudski apparatus embodied in the POW and the PPS.

The Czechoslovak National Council attained earlier success in regularizing the status of the military forces under its control. Masaryk, upon coming to revolutionary Russia in May 1917, took firm control of the bulk of the Czechoslovak movement there. His leadership assisted the transformation of the Czechoslovak brigade into an army of 35,000–40,000 men, later known as the Czechoslovak legion. In December 1917 the Supreme War Council of the Allies recognized the Czechoslovak troops in western countries as constituting an autonomous Czechoslovak army under the French command. It was agreed that the Czechoslovak corps in Russia would become a part of this army. When Masaryk departed from Petrograd in March 1918 traveling across Siberia for the United States, the necessary arrangements that he had negotiated with the French and with the Soviet authorities seemed in order for moving the legion via Vladivostok to France.[20]

Near the end of this phase of the national movements, Lloyd George's speech to the Trades Union Congress on January 5, 1918, and Wilson's on the Fourteen Points three days later espoused "genuine self-government" or "the freest opportunity of autonomous development" for the peoples of Austria-Hungary, as well as the erection of an independent Poland. The statements combined an advocacy of self-determination for the nationalities, with the purpose of preserving the monarchy and winning Austria for a separate peace. The program of the Fourteen Points encountered vehement criticism from the political exiles and the radicals

19. Titus Komarnicki, *Rebirth of the Polish Republic* (London, 1957), 162, 172–79.
20. For Masaryk's work in Russia, see J.F.N. Bradley, *La Légion tchécoslovaque en Russie, 1914–1920* (Paris, 1965), 48–70.

at home, for they were dedicated to the establishment of completely independent states.

3. THE MARCH TOWARD NATIONAL INDEPENDENCE

In the third phase of the national movements, the Allies publicly accepted the program of the political exiles and the radicals at home, and the nationalities advanced toward independent statehood. The Entente powers shifted policy from advocacy of autonomy for the subject nationalities to promoting the dissolution of the Habsburg empire. The change occurred primarily because of the necessities of war arising from the German offensive of March 1918, and the failure of diplomacy to separate Austria from Germany demanded a new political and diplomatic course. The altered approach involved a strategy of political warfare based on the thesis that if the Dual Empire could not be detached from Germany it should be destroyed through the victory of revolutionary nationalism fostered by every means of official statement and propaganda.

The political campaign against the empire was carried out with the aid of the exile committees. The extent to which unity of purpose could be demonstrated among the exile leaders and between them and the Allies, the more effect the political offensive would have on the Austrian government and the subject nationalities. The most difficult of these problems involving unity of aim originated in (1)the conflict between the Pašić government of Serbia and the South Slav Committee of Trumbič over the liberation of the South Slavs and the organization of the future Yugoslav state and (2)the conflict between the treaty of London and the Yugoslav aspirations to the Dalmatian coast.

The Pašić and Trumbič organs surmounted their bitter differences in agreeing to the Declaration of Corfu on July 20, 1917. "The Magna Carta of Yugoslav liberty," so characterized by Masaryk, projected the establishment of a "Kingdom of the Serbs, Croats, and Slovenes" under the Serbian royal house and posited the equal status of the three ethnic branches in a "free, national, and independent state." For the South Slavs the declaration laid the foundation of Yugoslavia, though it left for future settlement, by a constituent assembly, the question of a federal or a centralized structure of the democratic and parliamentary state.[21]

21. May, *Passing of the Hapsburg Monarchy,* 2: 589–90; Ostović, *Truth about Yugoslavia,* 82–85; Jelavich, "Nikola P. Pašić: Greater Serbia or Jugoslavia?," 138–39; Dragnich, *Serbia,*

The "pact of Rome," agreed at the Congress of Oppressed Nationalities during April 8–11, 1918, demonstrated impressively the solidarity of the nationalities in the common struggle for independence and dissolution of the Habsburg monarchy. Publicly, the congress pledged cooperation between the nationalities of Austria-Hungary in the efforts to achieve their independence and amicable settlement of territorial questions between the Yugoslav nation and Italy according to "the principle of nationality and the right of self-determination." Confidential resolutions appealed to the Allied governments to declare the liberation of the nationalities to be a war aim; and to recognize autonomous national armies under the jurisdiction of the national committees as Allied cobelligerent forces.[22]

From this time the national movements marched toward victory along two routes: the Allied recognition of the exile organizations as official bodies that represented the interests of the nationalities in emerging to independent statehood; and the final radicalization of the national movements at home by which the goals of independence and republican democracy became generally acceptable. The Rome congress was a landmark in this progress. Clemenceau approved its actions; the British government endorsed the national aims proclaimed at Rome; the American government expressed "great interest" in the proceedings of the congress. An inter-Allied commission on political warfare operating on the Italian front exploited its work and spirit in the propaganda offensive conducted against the nationality contingents of the Austro-Hungarian forces.[23]

In the wake of the Rome congress the Czechoslovak National Council negotiated a convention (April 22) with Premier Vittorio Orlando, allowing the formation of a Czechoslovak army in Italy recruited from prisoners of war. The agreement put the army under the Italian command, but under the political authority of the council. Influenced by this action and by the British proponents in Italy of political warfare, the British govern-

Nikola Pašić, and Yugoslavia, 116–17. Valiani, *End of Austria-Hungary,* 194–97, reflects a negative view of the declaration in terming it "the so-called Corfu agreement."

22. Mamatey, *United States and East Central Europe,* 243–45; Valiani, *End of Austria-Hungary,* 221–40. The latter treats extensively the Italo-Yugoslav discussions leading up to the congress. For the Italian nationalist view of the Rome pact in Italo-Yugoslav relations, see Gabriele Paresce, *Italia e Jugoslavia dal 1915 al 1929* (Florence, 1935), 35–46.

23. May, *Passing of the Hapsburg Monarchy,* 2: 601–03; Mamatey, *United States and East Central Europe,* 248, 260–61. On the interest of Italian intelligence officers in exploiting "the national idea" in political warfare against the Austro-Hungarian forces, see Cesare Pettorelli Lalotta Finzi, *"I. T. O." Note di un capa del servizio informazoni d'armato (1915–1918),* 2d ed. (Milan, 1934), 179–82, 193, 212.

ment accorded the National Council the status of the "supreme organ of the Czecho-Slovak movement in the Allied countries" and recognized the army as "an organized unit operating in the Allied Cause." The Czechoslovaks now had three separate armed forces—in Russia, France, and Italy.[24]

The intended transfer to France of the two Czechoslovak divisions dispersed in southern Russia raised unending difficulties with the Soviet authorities for the Czechoslovak troops. By the latter part of May these units were spread out from the Volga to Vladivostok in an isolated world of tense uncertainty. When the Soviets moved to disarm the legion by military force, the soldiers took up the fight to gain control of the Siberian railroad and join their dispersed forces so that they all might reach Vladivostok. Needing allies, the Czechoslovak troops leagued with the White military groups and with the White regimes that sprang up in Siberia. The separate bodies of experienced soldiers moved on one center after another against poorly trained and poorly organized Bolshevik troops until they joined in control of the whole railroad and a large part of Siberia within three months.[25]

The legion's action crystallized the decision of the Allies and the United States to intervene in Siberia. The military successes made possible the replacement of Soviet authority with White rule in central Siberia. The stimulus thus given to anti-Bolshevik activity elsewhere, along with the resistance of the peasants in Russia and the intervention of the Allies, provoked an almost insurmountable crisis for the Soviet regime.[26]

Expected replacements for the disillusioned legionaries were not forthcoming from the Allies or the White Russians. Beginning in October

24. Mamatey, *United States and East Central Europe*, 247, 248; Zeman, *Diplomatic History of the First World War*, 356–57; Josef Logau, *Československé Legie v Italie, 1915–1918* (Prague, 1922).

25. The following recent works of varying emphasis offer together a survey of the legion and its anabasis: Bradley, *La Légion tchécoslovaque en Russie;* Gerburg Thunig-Nittner, *Die tschechoslowakische Legion in Russland* (Wiesbaden, 1970); George F. Kennan, *The Decision to Intervene* (Princeton, 1958). On the legion's military operations, see František V. Steidler, *Československé hnutí na Rusi* (Prague, 1922); Thunig-Nitten, *Die tschechoslowakische Legion,* 57–64.

26. The influences bringing Wilson to the decision for intervention and the grounds on which he placed it receive authoritative treatment in Kennan, *Decision to Intervene,* especially pp. 340–62, 381–404. Lloyd George judged the situation of the legion to be "the determining factor in our Siberian expedition." *War Memoirs,* 6: 3180, and John Albert White, *The Siberian Intervention* (Princeton, 1950), 236.

1918, they withdrew to the railway zone and from intervention in political affairs. They were mired down until Allied transports evacuated them from Vladivostok over the months from December 1919 to September 1920. The legion's saga of exploits and participation in the Allied intervention contributed to the recognition of the Czechoslovaks as Allies with the right to independence.

From June to October 1918 the Allies progressively extended recognition to the exile committees and commitment to the independence of the eastern nationalities. The popularization of the Czechoslovak movement by the legion's struggle in Siberia and by the active lobbying of Masaryk built up an American opinion in support of recognition. Masaryk won personal acclaim on a tour of American cities having Czech and Slovak communities and made direct representations to Secretary of State Robert Lansing and President Wilson.

Lansing and Wilson yielded to these influences and to the force of French and British example. In a statement of September 3 they based recognition on a "state of belligerency" existing between the Czechoslovaks organized in the Czechoslovak National Council and the German and Austro-Hungarian empires. Reaching beyond the stated policy of the Allies, the American declaration recognized "the Czecho-Slovak National Council as a *de facto* belligerent Government," with which the United States government was prepared to enter formally into relations.[27]

Until the prearmistice negotiations with Germany no other exile committee received comparable recognition. The Polish National Committee made progress only in regard to the status of the army. France recognized the Polish army in the west as an Allied force of cobelligerent status and on September 28 signed a convention with the committee by which its authority was established over the Polish army in France.

In the homelands the revolutionary temper spread through the Habsburg empire. The national movements took on an increasingly radical cast against the backdrop of deteriorating economic and military conditions accompanied by changing ministries and ministers. In the midst of this mounting unrest, the Croat and Slovene leaders more and more preached Yugoslav unity in the open and independence in secret. The South Slav and Czech deputies worked together in the Reichsrat, taking common positions in opposition to the government at Vienna, which seemed to be

27. Mamatey, *United States and East Central Europe,* 298–309.

losing its grip before the approaching flood of catastrophe. As Wilson's policy toward the nationalities evolved and as the ideas of the Russian revolution were grasped in relation to the faltering military fortunes of the Central Powers, the parliamentary opposition to governmental policies was transformed into a determination to break away from the empire itself.

During this period the Polish government advanced little in expanding the administrative structure on the way to building the Polish state. The Warsaw government was thwarted in the renewed endeavor to create a Polish army. The Germans forced the capitulation of Polish formations organized from soldiers of the disintegrating Russian army when they resisted demobilization. A large part of one corps escaped across the Dnieper and made its way north to Murmansk, from which the soldiers were transported to France to form the core of the Polish army in France.

The Council of Regency and its cabinets followed, since Brest-Litovsk, an activist policy of rapprochement with the Germans based on these principles: renunciation of Poznán's incorporation into the Polish territorial state; territorial compensation in the Polish ethnographic areas to the east; and the inclusion of Poland in a Mitteleuropa association beneficial to Polish security and economic interests. This collaborationist policy of a regime identified with conservative-clerical support aroused broad attack.

The Germans could not take advantage of the opportunity for a constructive settlement. It was not possible to moderate the extremist demands of Ludendorff, the Pan-Germans, and the annexationists for acquiring a large border zone from the Poles. Nor could the negotiations between Germany and Austria on a Polish settlement come to any conclusion. The negotiations became interlocked with the prolonged discussions concerning the formation of a central European union in the economic and military spheres. The Mitteleuropa parleys continued until October 11 without final issue and without benefit to the Polish negotiations.[28]

28. It had been apparent since 1916 that the formation of a Mitteleuropa and the solution of the Polish problem were inextricably linked. Paul R. Sweet, "Germany, Austria-Hungary and Mitteleuropa: August 1915–April 1916," *Festschrift für Heinrich Benedikt*, ed. Hugo Hantsch and Alexander Novotny (Vienna, 1957), 206. The interconnection between the problems of the Polish state, German and Austrian relations, and Germany's position in Europe is exemplified in the thought of Riezler, the political confidant of Bethmann Hollweg. For an advocate like Riezler the formation of a Mitteleuropa constitutional union would solve all these persistent issues in one settlement. See his *Tagebücher*, 380, 382.

4. THE TRIUMPH OF THE SLAVIC REVOLUTIONS

The fall of the eastern empires burst the barriers to the achievement of independent statehood by the nations of the eastern zone. The end of the war celebrated the victory of the national revolutions. The abortive attempts of Emperor Karl to introduce constitutional reform demonstrated once again that the only way to transform the empire was to destroy it. The work of the exile committees, the ideas and example of the Russian revolution, the Wilsonian principles, and the Allied political warfare raised the expectations and strengthened the will of the nationalities. At the end the Habsburg monarchy had neither the military power and the will to rule nor the attraction of an idea to sustain its survival. However desirable the preservation of this Danubian community was in theory, the empire was in the reality of the time a historical relic that simply collapsed.

The rising assertiveness of the nationalities broke out into conclusive revolutionary action triggered by three events of the empire's collapse: the peace note of October 4 addressed to President Wilson; the imperial manifesto of October 16; and Wilson's reply of October 18 to the Austrian note. The peace note accepted the Fourteen Points as the basis of negotiations.

The imperial manifesto announced the intention of transforming the Austrian portion of the empire into a federative union of free German, Czech, South Slav, and Ukrainian nations. The manifesto made for the complete separation of Austria and Hungary and offered no way to gain the unity in each case of the Czechoslovaks and Yugoslavs. The belated manifesto fueled the national revolutions and legitimated the revolutionary transfer of the existing administrative organization to the nationalities.[29]

Wilson's message of October 18 found autonomy for the nationalities to be no longer a sufficient basis for peace because of intervening developments. The nationalities themselves would determine "as members of the family of nations" what must be done to satisfy their claims. Wilson's refusal to negotiate with Vienna on the basis of the Fourteen Points fell like a death sentence on the monarchy but sounded the final drive to the nationalities to achieve independence and unity.

The national revolution of the Czechs and Slovaks came to a close more smoothly than any other. Abroad the Czechoslovak National Council

---

29. Lorenz, *Kaiser Karl,* 510–12; May, *Passing of the Hapsburg Monarchy,* 2: 771–72; Count Julius Andrassy, *Diplomacy and War* (London, 1921), 255; Rudolf Neck, ed., *Österreich im Jahre 1918: Berichte und Dokumente* (Munich, 1968), 66–67.

informed the Allied governments (October 14) that it had now become the Czechoslovak provisional government. The French government immediately extended recognition. Masaryk in the United States prepared a declaration of independence, and his text was released on October 18.[30]

On October 28 the National Committee occupied the administrative offices of the capital at Prague, while political demonstrations took over Wenceslas Square. The presence of the American flag at the creation celebrated the close association of the United States with the birth of the Czechoslovak republic and symbolized the western stamp of the new state. The National Committee approved the same evening the "law on the establishment of an independent Czechoslovak state." The date of October 28 thus remains to the present time the national holiday for those Czechoslovaks who are still loyal to their democratic origins and the western tradition.

The Slovak political parties formed the Slovak National Council on October 30. Its Declaration of the Slovak Nation proclaimed the separation of the Slovak people from Hungary and their becoming "a part of the Czecho-Slovak nation." The Hungarian authorities despatched troops to resist the union of the Slovaks with the Czechs. Prague had to occupy Slovakia to install the Slovak government set up first in Moravia by Dr. Vavro Šrobár.[31]

In Prague the National Committee adopted on November 13 the provisional constitution for a parliamentary republic and called for the meeting of a Revolutionary National Assembly. The next day this body of proved Czech leaders and Slovak representatives selected by the Slovak National Council elected Masaryk president of the republic and members of the new government. Masaryk returned to Prague just before Christmas to the resounding acclaim of his countrymen for being the masterly maker of their state.[32] The new-born republic was confronted with two intractable problems, the relations with the Slovaks and the dissatisfaction of the German minority of three million included within the Czech historical boundaries.

The completion of the Yugoslav national revolution was more complex. On October 5–6 the South Slav parties of both Austria and Hungary established at Zagreb the National Council of the Slovenes, Croats, and

---

30. Mamatey, *United States and East Central Europe*, 330–32.
31. Lettrich, *History of Modern Slovakia*, 49–51; for the text of the declaration, pp. 288–89.
32. Schulthess's *Europäischer Geschichtskalender*, 59 (1918), pt. 2: 107–10.

Serbs, under the presidency of the Slovene leader Dr. Anton Korošec. The National Council issued a call for the unity of the South Slavs in a democratic and independent state and assumed the functions of a governing body for the South Slavs. As the street celebrated independence along with the names of Masaryk and Wilson, the Croatian diet at Zagreb transferred its powers to the National Council on October 29. The Slovenes affirmed their independence, and the governor of Bosnia-Herzegovina soon turned over the administration of these lands to the National Council.[33]

This organ, however, failed to acquire any international legal sanction. Pašić, heading the government of the established Serbian state, constantly competed for recognition of a rival aim, the right of Serbia to represent all the South Slavs and to liberate and absorb the South Slav lands of the Habsburg realm. It proved impossible for the Trumbić South Slav Committee and the National Council to combine with the status of an Ally.

The South Slav spokesmen were no more successful with the Declaration of Geneva, negotiated with Pašić by the representatives of the Trumbić committee, the Serbian opposition, and the Zagreb National Council. In this Pašić agreed to recognition of the National Council as the government of a South Slav state to function jointly with the Serbian government until a constituent assembly devised permanent institutions for the combined state. The Serbian government in Corfu rejected the agreement.

The basis for a federal state was destroyed. The Zagreb National Council, isolated from the Yugoslav leaders abroad and confronted with the advancing Italian army, agreed to unite with Serbia without conditions. The regent Alexander then proclaimed "the union of Serbia with the lands of the state of the Slovenes, Croats, and Serbs in the kingdom of the Serbs, Croats, and Slovenes."[34]

The constituent assembly adopted a constitution for a centralized state reflecting the interests of the Serbian ruling forces. The state emerged as the most direct successor of the Habsburg empire in its legacy of unsolved multinational problems. The failure to frame a federative structure for the union taking account of the major differences in race, culture, and tradi-

33. Ostović, *Truth about Yugoslavia*, 74-76; May, *Passing of the Hapsburg Monarchy*, 2: 779-80.
34. Ostović, *Truth about Yugoslavia*, 95-98; Šepić, "The Question of Yugoslav Union," 42-43; Jelavich, "Nikola P. Pašić: Greater Serbia or Jugoslavia?," 148-49; Dragnich, *Serbia, Nikola Pašić, and Yugoslavia*, 124-25.

tion destined the kingdom to internecine turmoil during the interwar period and civil war during the Second World War.

From the Italo-Yugoslav quarrel of the war period the new kingdom acquired a provocative foreign policy problem that was to harass Italo-Yugoslav relations until the Trieste settlement after the Second World War. Following the armistice with Austria, the Italian and Serbian forces competed in a tense race to occupy the Dalmatian littoral and adjoining lands. The Italians advanced beyond the line drawn by the treaty of London and unsuccessfully attempted to prevent the union of Montenegro with the state of the Serbs, Croats, and Slovenes. The strife over the Yugoslav boundary along the Adriatic brought before the peace conference at Paris one of its most disruptive problems.

The liberation of Poland and the union of the national lands were beset by bloody struggle with other national elements and contention among three Polish groups. The first of these groups existed in the regency regime at Warsaw and its supporters primarily among the landed nobility and bureaucratic class. The second group was dominated by the middle-class National Democrats in all the Polish lands and abroad. The group controlled a military force in the Polish army in France, which Britain on October 11 and the United States on November 1 recognized "under the supreme political authority of the Polish National Committee, as autonomous, Allied, and co-belligerent." The third group consisted of the anticollaborationist leftists organized in the Polish Socialist party (PPS) and the Polish Military Organization (POW) of the national hero Pilsudski.

The revolution moved ahead rapidly during the second half of October. The ferment surfaced in big demonstrations in Warsaw and in strikes and manifestations fomented by the leftists. The moderates and leftists in Cracow seized the administrative offices in the Galician capital and formed a Polish regional government.[35]

At the beginning of November the POW mobilized openly in the Lublin government-general and wrested control from the Austrian military. When the Warsaw government attempted to install its authority in Lublin, the POW staged a coup that ended with the creation of a "provisional people's government of the Polish republic." This leftist government proclaimed the end of the Council of Regency and the introduction

35. Komarnicki, *Rebirth of the Polish Republic*, 238.

of far-reaching agrarian reforms and measures of socialization.[36]

No hope existed of coalescing the contending political forces while Pilsudski remained in a German prison. On November 10 the liberated leader returned to Warsaw in magnificent triumph. Acclaimed head of the state, he became a healing agent of magical power. Pilsudski liquidated the crumbling remains of the German military administration and arranged for the rapid removal of the occupying troops. The Lublin government and the regency submitted to his authority and dissolved themselves. A cabinet was organized mainly from the PPS, former members of the Lublin government, and the People's party. Pilsudski notified other governments that an independent and united Poland had been formed and requested the Allies to send to Poland the Polish troops that had fought with them. The unrepresentative leftist government, however, encountered strong opposition from many quarters. The western European governments denied recognition because of their close relations with Dmowski's Polish National Committee.

The untenable dualism was resolved by Pilsudski and Paderewski after the latter's return in early January 1919. Paderewski put together a ministry of specialists, which signaled a victory for the National Democrats. The Allies recognized the new government, and Dmowski dissolved the Polish National Committee. The constituent Sejm, elected by direct, equal, and secret suffrage for both men and women, opened on February 11, 1919. It confirmed both Pilsudski and Paderewski in office and set to work on preparing a constitution for the Polish republic.[37]

The regeneration of Poland still required union with the remaining Polish lands. The cession of Poznan and other areas of Prussian Poland to the republic and the determination of Poland's western boundary were effected by the treaty of Versailles. The Poles fought the Ukrainians in fierce encounters to win eastern Galicia, and the peace conference accepted the Polish claim to this area as a part of the historical province of Galicia. In the east the boundary was not fixed until a war with the Soviets produced the line established by the treaty of Riga in 1921.

The end of the war afforded the opportunity to round out the Romanian national state with the acquisition of Bessarabia, Bukovina, Transylvania, Maramures, Crişane, and the Romanian section of the Banat. The comple-

36. Ibid., 238, 247; Conze, *Polnische Nation und deutsche Politik,* 397–400.
37. Komarnicki, *Rebirth of the Polish Republic,* 247–62; Roth, *Die politische Entwicklung in Kongress Polen,* 131–39.

tion of Romanian unity was accomplished through the wartime treaty of alliance with the Entente, the actions of national councils and assemblies in the Romanian irredenta, the work of the National Council of National Unity at Paris, the dispatch of Romanian troops to Transylvania, the Banat, and Bukovina, and finally the peace settlement.[38]

38. See R. W. Seton-Watson, *A History of the Roumanians* (London, 1934), 509–11, 519–34; A. Otetea, *The History of the Romanian People* (Bucharest, 1970), 456–61; Constantin C. Giurescu, *The Making of the Romanian National Unitary State* (Bucharest, 1975), 147–53; Miron Constantinescu, Constantin Daicoviciu, and Stefan Pascu, *Histoire de la Roumanie* (Paris, 1970), 308–11.

Chapter Fifteen

THE ARRESTED REVOLUTIONS IN EASTERN EUROPE

I. THE REVOLUTION WITHOUT NATIONALISM IN AUSTRIA

THERE were three countries in eastern Europe in which the revolution experienced an arrested development or an unmistakable defeat in one or more aspects. The triumph of the national revolution among the Czechs, Slovaks, Poles, and Yugoslavs reduced the Habsburg monarchy to two residual legatees of independent statehood. German Austria and Magyar Hungary were separated from the Dual Empire as states in their own right less by their own efforts than by the revolutionary action of the Habsburg Slavs. The revolution in German Austria created a democratic republic under the leadership and strong influence of Social Democracy without a vibrant nationalism to sustain the rump state or a faith in its future.[1] In Hungary a revolutionary convulsion swung from the leftist extreme of a soviet republic to the reactionary and revisionist extreme of Admiral Horthy's regime. The movement to build an independent state completely miscarried in the western and eastern Ukraine.

When the Slav nationalities broke up the empire, the Reichsrat representatives of the German Austrians effected a "parliamentary revolution" demanded by the Social Democrats. The deputies constituted themselves on October 21, 1918, the Provisional National Assembly of German Austria. The assembly unanimously resolved to form an independent German Austrian state embracing all lands of German population within the empire. The assembly adopted a provisional constitution drafted by the esteemed socialist and future president of the second Austrian republic Karl Renner. This instrument vested sovereignty in the Provisional Assembly and the executive pow-

1. Mary MacDonald, *The Republic of Austria, 1918–1934* (London, 1946), 1, attributes the undoing of the first Austrian republic mainly to "the lack of an Austrian national consciousness strong enough to infuse any organic unity into the life" of the state. Another writer notes that the people had no "ready-made patriotism" toward the remnant German Austria. Elizabeth Barker, *Austria, 1918–1972* (Coral Gables, Fla., 1973), 10. See also Neck, Introduction to *Österreich im Jahre 1918*, 21.

ers of the emperor in a State Council, which controlled the cabinet.[2]
That the next step in the Austrian revolution was the speedy establishment of a democratic republic was due to the firm purpose of the Social Democrats and the pressure of the masses. At the end of the war the old army disintegrated into a rabble of returning soldiers animated by a revolutionary spirit. In Vienna they engaged in street demonstrations, plundered private property, organized a Red Guard, and formed soldiers' councils. The unemployed and half-starved workers also took to the streets in manifestations and formed workers' councils. Many joined the people's republican army (Volkswehr).[3]

The sentiment for a republic was rising from Vienna to the provinces. The State Council and the Provisional Assembly were driven to settle the basic constitutional question immediately after the emperor Karl renounced on November 11 any part in the state affairs of German Austria. The assembly adopted unanimously the next day a proclamation making German Austria a democratic republic. The assembly fixed the date of February 16, 1919, to elect representatives to a constituent national assembly. Universal, equal, direct, and proportional suffrage for both men and women was established. After the constituent national assembly met, a coalition government of Social Democrats and Christian Socials was formed and the State Council ended.[4]

The attempted putsch by the newly formed Red Guard and the Communists when the republic was proclaimed was an augury of the trials that the embattled state would undergo in its infancy. The struggle for economic survival and the defense of the democratic republic against Bolshevik insurrection threw down the greatest challenge but hardly more than did a settlement with separatist tendencies and the determination of Austria's permanent constitution. The economic dislocations of the war period were compounded by the severance of German Austria from the balanced economic community that constituted the prewar Danubian realm of the Habsburgs. The terms of the peace treaty with Austria were designed to punish the new state in place of the old monarchy rather than to assist the

2. Charles A. Gulick, *Austria from Habsburg to Hitler*, vol. 1 (Berkeley, 1948), 53–54; F. L. Carsten, *Revolution in Central Europe, 1918–1919* (London, 1972), 21–22; Barker, *Austria, 1918–1972*, 27–29. The text of the resolution is in Neck, *Österreich im Jahre 1918*, 76–78.

3. Otto Bauer, *Die österreichische Revolution* (1923; new ed., Vienna, 1962), 78–79, 82, 108–113.

4. Lorenz, *Kaiser Karl*, 457–58; Walter Goldinger, *Geschichte der Republik Österreich* (Munich, 1962), 18–24.

424   THE WORLD IN THE CRUCIBLE

republic in weathering the postwar economic storms. The treaty amputations, slicing off the valuable economic districts inhabited by German Austrians in the Sudetenland, Bohemia, and Moravia, left a truncated state of 6,500,000 instead of a larger, more sustainable entity of over ten million, if these areas had been included in Austria. The rump republic began its life in a grim struggle for economic viability without union with Germany, federation with the succession states, or a free economic union in eastern Europe.[5]

Like the Social Democrats in Germany, those in Austria faced the same dual problem of insuring the success of the democratic revolution against the Communist revolutionaries on the one hand and against the reactionary right of aristocracy, military officers, and bureaucracy on the other. They accomplished this feat with an alternative that showed more political skill and astuteness than the solution of their German counterparts. This was due in large measure to the character of the Volkswehr and the use made of the workers' and soldiers' councils. Admittedly, the Austrian party did not suffer the deep schism of the German Social Democrats.

The Volkswehr was a professional army recruited for pay from unemployed workers. The people's army was organized by the Social Democratic party's military expert Julius Deutsch from the ministry of defense. The nuclei were his secret groups of party members within the old army, who recruited reliable men from the former troops for the Volkswehr and influenced the selection of soldiers' councils. The Austrian Social Democrats kept to the principle of maintaining the unity of the workers' movement. Deutsch therefore admitted the Red Guard into the republican Volkswehr. Subjection to its command provided some means of control over these militants.[6]

The Social Democrats were similarly instrumental in the admission of the Communists to the workers' councils. The Communist party was a small fringe of the proletarian movement organized amidst the disorders of January 1918. The first, and scarcely prepared, Communist attempt to seize power ended in an ignominious fiasco before the parliament building.

5. On the formidable economic difficulties confronted by Austria, see Gratz and Schüller, *Der wirtschaftliche Zusammenbruch Österreich-Ungarns;* Karl R. Stadler, *The Birth of the Austrian Republic, 1918–1921* (Leiden, 1966), 163–84; David Fales Strong, *Austria (October 1918– March 1919): Transition from Empire to Republic* (New York, 1939), 180–223.
6. For the organization of the Volkswehr: Bauer, *Die österreichische Revolution,* 111–13; Carstens, *Revolution in Central Europe,* 78–107 passim.

The establishment of soviet republics in Hungary and Bavaria encour-aged a second attempt at a coup. The Hungarian regime converted its legation into a center of Bolshevik agitation and an agency for the trans-mittal of funds to the local Communist party. The struggle against Com-munist putchism was fought out with the dependable Volkswehr and on the ground of the workers' councils. Deutsch's Volkswehr and the police suppressed the outbreak of April 17, 1919, against the parliament build-ing. The Social Democrats won a subsequent trial of strength in the central workers' council of Vienna by defeating the Communist motion of non-confidence in the Social Democratic members of the government.[7]

The Communists planned their most serious effort for June 15 on the initiative of Béla Kun in Hungary. The organizers set out to lure the soldiers of the Volkswehr into a demonstration supporting the workers. A soviet republic was to be established following this disturbance.

The Social Democrats utilized the Volkswehr, the police, and the work-ers' councils to oppose the execution of these plans. By maintaining the unity of the workers in the revolutionary councils, the workers' movement was turned against the Communist aims. The Communists were left with-out a solid base of support. The Social Democratic secretary of state for internal affairs had more than a hundred leaders of the Communist party arrested on the night before the planned coup. The next day the city police, supported by the Volkswehr, resisted, with the death of seventeen persons, the attempt to take the police building where the arrested leaders were detained. When the national conference of the workers' councils met subsequently in Vienna, the majority rejected the Communist goal of a soviet republic and reserved appeals for mass action to the sole compe-tence of the workers' councils. Although the efforts to achieve a soviet regime were abortive, the revolutionary government put into effect re-forms characteristic of the socialist or social welfare state.[8]

The separatist tendencies of the provinces were stimulated by the end of the highly centralized wartime government and the disappearance of the monarchy without the rise of a national feeling. The less urban, more

7. Bauer, *Die österreichische Revolution*, 151–53; also Goldinger, *Geschichte der Republik Österreich*, 29.

8. Gulick, *Austria from Habsburg to Hitler*, 82; Bauer, *Die österreichische Revolution*, 153–55; Goldinger, *Geschichte der Republik Österreich*, 30–34. Goldinger gives more credit to the Vienna police and their chief than to the Social Democrats for the arrest of the Communists and suppression of the Communist attempt. For the workers' councils, see Carstens, *Revolu-tion in Central Europe*, 108–26.

conservative provinces, where the Christian Social party was strongest, manifested an antipathy toward the socialist government in Vienna. The struggle for food, supplies, and fuel under conditions of extreme scarcity fostered restrictive economic practices between provinces that exacerbated their relations. The main parties differed fundamentally about the structure of the republic. The Christian Socials, fearing the power of "Red Vienna," desired a federal state in which each province would have extensive rights of self-government and adequate representation in the central legislature; the Social Democrats, fearing the less democratic trends in the provinces, desired a unitary state with a unicameral legislature. Thus a bitter conflict took place between the separatist and centralist forces.[9]

The constitution of 1920 incorporated a compromise between the two tendencies that assured the Austrian state against control by a particularist minority. The constitution capped the democratic revolution in establishing a federal and parliamentary republic. Sovereignty was lodged in the National Assembly, and the upper house or Federal Council, in which representation was determined according to population, was given only a suspensive veto.[10]

The republic was a fresh creation, separate from the old Austria. This was recognized in the constitutional settlement by the name of German Austria adopted for the new state and by the declaration that German Austria regarded itself as a part (autonomous) of Germany. The peace conference, denying Austria the rights of the succession states, required the republic to renounce its name and the incorporation of the Sudetenland, German Bohemia, and German Moravia, as well as the prospect of Anschluss with Germany.

The weakest point of the residual republic was the arrested revolution by which the birth of the Austrian state took place without the exercise of self-determination and without the consciousness and conviction of a national identity. It required the painful experience of Anschluss with the Third Reich and the ordeal of the Second World War to instill a faith in Austria's own viability and a national patriotism. Yet the Social Democrats had guided the infant state through the political minefields of 1918–20 with remarkably sound judgment and political maturity. This verdict is justly deserved: "It was the historic achievement of Austrian Social De-

9. MacDonald, *Republic of Austria*, 2–22, gives a résumé of the differences between the centrifugal and centralist forces.
10. Ibid., 23–45, for the constitution of 1920.

mocracy that it prevented the emergence of a revisionist movement, which did so much damage to the Weimar system in Germany, as well as any Communist adventure which in turn might have caused a right-wing reaction as in Hungary."[11]

2. FROM REVOLUTION TO COUNTERREVOLUTION IN HUNGARY

In Hungary the revolution passed through three stages of mounting radicalism before giving way to the counterrevolution and White terror: the separation from Austria, making Hungary a completely independent state, a democratic revolt against the repressive rule of the Magyar oligarchy, and a Bolshevik movement eventuating in a Communist seizure of power.

Since the Hungarian government had acted in the Dual Empire as an independent state in all but name, the Magyar rulers had no great national goal to achieve. The catastrophic defeat at the end of the war made the separation from Austria a vital issue for the first time. The ending of the dualism was precipitated by the decision of the Austrian part of the monarchy to introduce a federal organization. A public declaration of Hungary's chief minister announced the status of a personal union with Austria (through the common monarch Karl), on which basis Hungary would independently organize its political, economic, and defense affairs.[12]

But the conditions in Hungary were ripening by October for a revolutionary outbreak. The influence of the "Red Count" Michael Károlyi was soaring with the Budapest public. His drumbeat of attacks on Budapest's last ministry of the old regime and his demand for democratic elections and the breakup of the big estates brought down the government on October 23. A surging tide of revolutionary disorders lifted Károlyi to power. Responding to the public clamor, Károlyi formed the Hungarian National Council, drawn from the reform parties. This body was already in essence an opposition government and the count already tapped by the Budapest crowds to be "the People's Premier." A large part of the public went over to the National Council, which declared its sole authority to speak for the Hungarian nation. The monarch Karl, as the king of Hungary, was forced to appoint Károlyi the chief minister on October 31. Soldiers broke into the home of Tisza and, before his family, killed that

11. Stadler, *Birth of the Austrian Republic*, 9.
12. Lorenz, *Kaiser Karl*, 509.

stern and redoubtable symbol of the old Magyar supremacy.[13]

Károlyi quickly composed a coalition government from the three parties of the National Council—his own United Party of Independence, the Social Democrats, and Oscar Jászi's Radical party of "middle-class socialists." On the formation of this revolutionary government "Budapest and the whole country had turned in a single night to a fanatical republicanism." An "extended National Council" met on November 16 to pass unanimously a resolution creating a "people's republic independent from all other countries." Károlyi was elected president of the provisional republic.[14]

On coming into power, the Károlyi democracy found itself presiding over "an avalanche of social dissolution." The new government suffered from a debilitating lack of cohesion in organization and a lack of unity in the coalition's program. Political power remained divided between the ministry, the National Council, the Budapest soldiers' council, and the military force for protecting the democratic revolution.

The democratic government was undermined by Allied policy and the failure of the nationalities program. The harsh terms of the armistice were retributive. The original line demarking areas to come under Allied occupation removed from Hungarian control about one-half of the former territory and failed to establish a line roughly according to the final boundaries set by the peace conference. The Allies consequently shifted the demarcation line several times, alarming Hungary and disturbing relations with its neighbors.[15] The minister of nationalities, Jászi, tried unsuccessfully to transform the multinational Hungary into an "eastern Switzerland" of coordinate nationalities joined with neighboring states in a Danubian federation of equal and autonomous members.[16]

It became clear that power belonged to the Social Democrats as the only effective political force with a national party apparatus. But a Social Demo

13. Michael Károlyi, Memoirs, Faith without Illusion (London, 1956), 105–19; Oscar Jászi, Revolution and Counter-Revolution in Hungary (London, 1924), 29–34; Gabor Vermes, "The October Revolution in Hungary: From Károlyi to Kun," in Hungary in Revolution, 1918–19, ed. Iván Völgyes (Lincoln, Nebr., 1971), 36–38.

14. Jászi, Revolution and Counter-Revolution in Hungary, 48–53; Károlyi, Memoirs, 142–43.

15. Alfred D. Low, The Soviet Hungarian Republic and the Paris Peace Conference, Transactions of the American Philosophical Society, n.s., vol. 53, pt. 10 (Philadelphia, 1963), 13–15.

16. Jászi, Revolution and Counter-Revolution in Hungary, 38, 57–59; Vermes, "The October Revolution in Hungary," 43–45.

cratic government would be threatened by the two political extremes hitherto excluded from the political bodies of the democratic revolution: the forces of counterrevolution, beginning to spring up from the old ruling classes, the former officers, students, and refugees from the areas occupied by the Allies; and the revolutionary socialists seeking in their discontent ways to transform the democratic state into a "pure socialist republic."

The situation was further destabilized by the arrival in Budapest on November 6 of Béla Kun and a conspiratorial band of Hungarian Bolsheviks. These men from the prisoner of war camps in Russia were "graduates of the October revolution" who brought to the capital the nucleus of a Communist organization for transplanting the Bolshevik revolution and the soviet state to Hungary.[17]

In Budapest Kun, an assiduous organizer and talented journalist, united the Hungarian party group of Russia with socialist opposition at home in founding the Communist party on Hungarian soil. The energetic recruitment program of the Communists and a saturation campaign of agitation and propaganda, conducted through the newspaper the *Red Gazette,* weakened the control by the Social Democrats over the Budapest workers' council. The pressure on the party leadership was strong enough for it to force the fall of the Károlyi government on January 8, 1919. A more leftist cabinet came into office, with increased representation from the Social Democrats.[18]

The Communists, taking measures to mobilize the masses, pushed ahead vigorously toward a second revolution. The belated defensive actions of the Social Democrats and the government, including the arrest of sixty-eight Communists headed by Béla Kun, did not forestall a political crisis. The government's position deteriorated through its indecision over land reform and elections for a constituent assembly, through the economic blockade and armistice policy of the Allies, and through the growing strength of the counterrevolutionary and Communist movements in reaction against each other. The left wing of the Social Democrats gained

17. On the transformation of Béla Kun from an organization Social Democrat to an influential Communist leader, see L. Tökés, *Béla Kun and the Hungarian Soviet Republic* (New York, 1967), 49–81. On Béla Kun's career as a revolutionary, see the same author, "Béla Kun; The Man and the Revolutionary," in *Hungary in Revolution,* 170–207.

18. Tökés, *Béla Kun and the Hungarian Soviet Republic,* 99–115; Vermes, "The October Revolution in Hungary," 51–54.

control of the executive and most of the local committees and councils of the party. A hysteria was seizing the politically conscious public.

Into this tinder bed of instability was now thrown an explosive factor —the Allied note of March 18 summoning the Hungarian government to withdraw its troops to the line of 1916 drawn by the treaty of Bucharest. Unable to accept the ultimatum and remain in power, the government resigned at once.[19] The issue was thrust squarely before the Hungarian Social Democrats: cooperation with the Communists in a Soviet-style revolution or cooperation with the bourgeois classes in defense of the democratic republic. Put on trial like the German socialists under similar conditions, the Social Democratic party failed the test.

The Hungarian Soviet Republic issued from the unity pact of March 21 between the Social Democratic executive and the imprisoned Communists. The two agreed to form the Socialist party of Hungary and take over the government. Throughout the existence of the Hungarian Soviet Republic, the Communists were engaged in an unceasing power struggle with the old Social Democrats and the trade union organization in the regime's major political bodies: the Revolutionary Governing Council and the Budapest workers' and soldiers' council. The old Social Democratic organization, coupled with the trade union bureaucracy, proved the stronger and rapidly absorbed the disunited party apparatus of the Communists.[20]

Basic to the division between the Communists and the Social Democrats were the differences over the nature of the proletarian state and methods of rule. The Social Democratic leaders rejected Communist terrorism and the typical machinery of the police state.

The first several weeks were given over to a rage of extremist experiment, covering wholesale socialization, public creation of jobs, operation

19. Low, *Soviet Hungarian Republic and the Paris Peace Conference*, 40, pins responsibility on the Entente ultimatum without reservation for bringing Béla Kun to power.

20. Tökés, *Béla Kun and the Hungarian Soviet Republic*, 134–67 passim; Iván Völgyes, "Soviet Russia and Soviet Hungary," in *Hungary in Revolution*, 165. After the fall of the Hungarian Soviet Republic Lenin and the Comintern leaders found in the Hungarian case a classical demonstration of the consummate error in joining with the Social Democrats to make a proletarian state. The lesson driven home by the Hungarian experience that only the vanguard of the Communist party could conduct a proletarian revolution was a major influence in reorganizing the Comintern in 1920 into a tight and exclusive group of Communist parties completely under Moscow's control. See David T. Cattell, "The Hungarian Revolution of 1919 and the Reorganization of the Comintern in 1920," *Journal of Central European Affairs* 11 (1951): 27–38.

of low-rent apartment houses, and a number of enlightened social and educational measures. This frenzy of reform struck the already prostrate economy with cataclysmic force and caused deep social convulsion. The government never succeeded in coping with the economic and social chaos or the bloated bureaucracy of unqualified and corrupt officials.[21]

The scope and speed of revolutionary reform soon encountered strong objection, most vehemently from the middle classes and the peasantry. The latter had special cause for grievance in the conversion of the social-ized farmlands into agricultural collectives. Among the angry opposition, there was in the making a counterrevolutionary movement, strengthened by the activity of Horthy's agents. At the same time the moderate Social Democrats were reacting against the extremism of the left Communists.[22]

The regime committed a critical mistake also in foreign affairs. An entente with Soviet Russia was expected to bring military and diplomatic aid, and alliance with other soviet states arising from the spread of the proletarian revolution to bulwark the Hungarian Soviet Republic. Kun promoted proletarian revolt in surrounding states from Hungary as a secondary center by means of agitation, propaganda, subversion, organiza-tional work, newspaper publications (a Slovak daily and a Czech weekly), and financial assistance.[23]

These roseate expectations prompted Kun to blunder in rejecting an offer of the Allies carried to Budapest by General Jan Smuts at the begin-ning of April. The Allies proposed to negotiate a new and more advanta-geous line for Hungary with Romania than that set in March and to lift the blockade. When the proposals were rejected, the Romanians on their own initiative commenced on April 16 a drive to the Tisza river in Hun-gary beyond the previous demarcation line.[24]

The Romanian march was halted only sixty miles from Budapest by the diplomatic veto of the Allies and by workers' battalions desperately orga-

21. Frank Eckelt, "The Internal Policies of the Hungarian Soviet Republic," in *Hungary in Revolution*, 61–88; Jászi, *Revolution and Counter-Revolution in Hungary*, 132–42.

22. Eckelt, "The Internal Policies of the Hungarian Soviet Republic," 82–86; Jászi, *Revolution and Counter-Revolution in Hungary*, 126–31.

23. Eva S. Balogh, "Nationality Problems of the Hungarian Soviet Republic," in *Hungary in Revolution*, 95, 112–17; Zsuzsa L. Nagy, "Problems of Foreign Policy before the Revolu-tionary Governing Council," in *Hungary in Revolution*, 123–24.

24. Alfred D. Low, "Soviet Hungary and the Paris Peace Conference," in *Hungary in Revolution*, 143–47; Nagy, "Problems of Foreign Policy before the Revolutionary Govern-ing Council," 126–27.

nized to meet the national emergency. The forces of the Czechoslovak republic also crossed the Slovak military demarcation line to attack Hungary. During the second half of May the rejuvenated and reorganized Hungarian army, however, stopped the Romanian advance and repulsed the Czechoslovak troops. The Hungarians then pressed forward into more than one-third of Slovakia and arranged for the proclamation of the Slovak Soviet Republic in the occupied area.

The Slovak Soviet Republic was already doomed by the intervention of the Allies. Their ultimatums (June 8 and 13) ordered the revolutionary government to stop hostilities against Czechoslovakia and to withdraw within the permanent frontiers assigned Hungary by the peace conference. The regime had no alternative but to acquiesce. The frontiers thus accepted were confirmed by the treaty of Trianon. The boundaries allowed Hungary to retain more than one-half of the territory won in its offensive and required Romania to vacate districts clearly Magyar east of the Tisza. On the withdrawal of the Hungarian Red Army from Slovak territory, the Slovak Soviet Republic ended after an existence of less than three weeks.[25]

The end of the Hungarian Soviet Republic was near. The final days were filled with plots and counterplots from one side of the political spectrum to the other. The moderate socialist leaders resigned from the Revolutionary Governing Council, and a new one was formed chiefly from the Communists. Amidst this carnival of conspiracies reflecting the public revulsion against the prevalent anarchy, corruption, and tyranny, there occurred the humiliating defeat of an offensive undertaken against the Romanians on the Tisza, who had not withdrawn to the frontiers assigned by the peace conference. The government could not stop the Romanian advance on Budapest or negotiate with the Allies. The failure set off the revolt against Bolshevism and the Hungarian Soviet Republic. On August 1, 1919, the Revolutionary Governing Council resigned, and the Soviet republic ended its 133 days of turbulent existence. Kun and his closest comrades boarded the "commissars' special" train for Austria, from which he was later to go into exile in Russia.

A government of right and moderate Social Democrats quickly succumbed to counterrevolution. The invading Romanians entered Budapest and occupied the city until fall. Hungary fell victim to the Horthy regime

25. Low, "Soviet Hungary and the Paris Peace Conference," 146–50.

and the White terror. The Horthy counterrevolution of convulsive nationalism and anti-Semitism turned to obliterating not only all traces of the proletarian revolution but the democratic revolution of October as well.

3. THE DEFEAT OF THE NATIONAL REVOLUTION IN THE UKRAINE

The realization of Ukrainian national aspirations was frustrated by conflict with neighboring nations and states: with the Poles over eastern Galicia, with Romania over Bessarabia and Bukovina, and with the Soviets over the separation of Kievan Ukraine from Russia. The collapse of the Habsburg monarchy stirred the political leaders of the Ukrainian lands of the Dual Empire to meet at Lvov on October 18, 1918, to create the Ukrainian National Council. This body proclaimed the founding of the Western Ukrainian Republic, consisting of the portions of the Dual Empire inhabited by Ukrainians. The council constituted itself "the people's government of the western Ukraine." Ukrainian troops hastily organized from the dissolved Austrian army took control of Lvov and other towns of eastern Galicia. These moves led to the entry of Polish troops, and on November 22 they captured Lvov. The fighting continued until the Ukrainians in Galicia were subdued. The Polish claim to all of Galicia based on its historical boundaries was established by force and Allied diplomacy.[26]

On the appeal of the local Romanians to Bucharest, Romanian troops occupied Bukovina and smothered the hopes of its Ukrainians for independence as a part of the new state of the Western Ukraine. With the separation of Slovakia from Hungary, the Ukrainians of the Carpatho-Ukraine expressed the desire in their local councils for detachment from Hungary. The most practical hope for some measure of autonomy seemed to be to go along with the Slovaks into the Czechoslovak republic, a solution that was supported by an assembly in Prešov.

The Russian revolution gave the signal for the national movement in the eastern Ukraine to take open institutional form in the prompt organization of a governing body called the Ukrainian Central Council, or Rada. Thereafter the national movement ran a stormy course through three unstable revolutionary regimes: the Rada (March 17, 1917, to April 29, 1918), the Hetmanate (to December 14, 1918), and the Directory (to

---

26. Michael Yaremko, *Galicia-Halychyna (a Part of Ukraine): From Separation to Unity* (Toronto, 1967), 209–18; John S. Reshetar, *The Ukrainian Revolution, 1917–1920* (Princeton, 1952), 229–30.

July 1920). Though dominated by the Social Democrats and Social Revolutionaries, the Rada was broadly representative of the political parties and workers' organizations, professional associations, and the soldiers. The Rada claimed an autonomy of the Ukraine within a federated and democratic Russia. Prolonged exchanges between the Rada and the Russian Provisional Government never resolved the issues over the powers of the Rada machinery and the status of the Ukraine in revolutionary Russia.[27]

The Bolshevik government of Russia opposed self-determination for the Rada by floating a rival Ukrainian Soviet Republic and invading with the Red Guard. Fighting back with its Ukrainian forces, the Rada proclaimed the independence of the Ukraine and signed a separate treaty of peace with the Central Powers at Brest-Litovsk. The Rada accepted the aid of German military forces in driving out the Bolsheviks. But once the German military was inside the Ukraine, the land became in reality an occupied country and a granary for the Central Powers.

The confusion incident to socialist land reform and the ineffectiveness of the Rada—a "pseudo-government" in the view of the Germans—brought about increasing intervention of the German military in economic and administrative affairs. This trend continued until the coup of April 29, engineered by the League of Landowners and General Paul Skoropadsky, a large landowner, in collusion with the Germans. Skoropadsky, installing himself as "Hetman of all the Ukraine," dissolved the Rada and set up a dictatorship under the control of the German occupying authorities. The Hetmanate improved the administrative organization and restored the system of private property, while advancing cultural ukrainization through the establishment of two Ukrainian universities, a Ukrainian Academy of Science, and a Ukrainian State Theater.

The Hetmanate was, however, the architect of its own ruin to a considerable extent. The regime followed a policy of repression and took on an antinational character owing to the haven that the Ukraine became for Russian Kadets, Octobrists, and anti-Bolshevik Russian officers and activities. The rising opposition was strengthened by the increasing dissidence of the peasantry. The Hetman failed to build a real Ukrainian army.

During the last months of the war German policy shifted from treating

27. For the revolution in the Ukraine: Reshetar, *Ukrainian Revolution;* Fedyshyn, *Germany's Drive to the East and the Ukrainian Revolution;* Oleh S. Pidhainy, *The Formation of the Ukrainian Republic* (Toronto, 1966); Michael Hrushevsky, *A History of Ukraine,* ed. O. J. Frederiksen (New Haven, 1941), 511–57.

the Ukrainian state as an "occupied German satellite" to encouraging more signs of independence and a national character. When the shadows of catastrophe imposed a frantic urgency, the Reich government anxiously prepared for salvaging a separate and independent Ukrainian state under German influence in the postwar period. The Central Powers promised military aid and pressed for organizing an army of 85,000.

The Hetman nevertheless forsook the popular appeal of independent statehood by proclaiming suddenly on November 14 the goal of uniting the Ukraine with Russia in a federal organization and installed an all-Russian cabinet to carry out the policy. The action set off an armed uprising previously planned by the opposition centering in the Ukrainian National Union, the sanctuary of the former Rada circles. When the Germans withdrew from Kiev, the troops of the Directory, which led the opposition, entered the capital on December 14, 1918, and the Hetman abdicated.

Assuming power as the provisional government of the revolutionary period, the Directory introduced a radical program of social reform. The Directory drained its energies in conflict with the rival Bolshevik Provisional Workers' and Peasants' Government of the Ukraine and the Ukrainian Bolshevik party, organized in Moscow as a part of the Russian Bolshevik party. The Red Army invaded the country, capturing Kiev on February 4, 1919. During the rest of its time the Directory was fated to a migratory existence and progressive decline. By December 1919 the Red Army occupied most of the country, and Simon Petlyura, principal member of the Directory at that time and its principal commander, took refuge in Warsaw. With Polish aid the Ukrainian forces resumed the struggle against the Red Army, while the Poles invaded the Ukraine and reached Kiev. When the revived Red Army carried the offensive into Poland, the remnants of the Ukrainian troops retreated with the Poles. Petlyura's government, or what remained of it, set itself up in Poland as a government in exile.

The Ukrainian national movement achieved neither unity nor independence. A primary reason was the divisive character of the movement. The people of the two Ukraines were divided by differing political jurisdictions, historical development, and cultural tradition. Their different aims and different antagonists created an obstacle to effective political and military cooperation. Inside the eastern Ukraine there was a cleavage between those who desired autonomy in a federative union with Russia and those who worked for the creation of a separate and independent state. A consensus on the form of government was lacking between the advocates of Bolshevism, of a non-Bolshevik soviet system, of a non-Communist socialist state, of a nonsocialist democratic republic, and of a Hetmanate. Of larger significance, the national movement was not strongly developed primarily on account of the almost entire absence of an ethnic bourgeoisie.

Chapter Sixteen

THE BALTIC REVOLUTIONS

1. THE ESTONIAN REVOLUTION

THE Baltic revolutions were of three strands—national, democratic, and socialist—characteristic of the time. The rise of a national movement had taken place in the Estonian, Latvian, Lithuanian, and Finnish lands during the second half of the nineteenth century, and the world war and the Russian revolution created the conditions from which the national movement could come to fruition. In the winning of independence, Finland was forced to fight a war of liberation from Soviet Russia with German assistance, and the other three nations had to go to war against both the Germans and the Soviets. In the end, the Soviet regime introduced into each of the four countries was overthrown and a democratic republic was established.

The territory of the Estonians had been incorporated in the Russian empire since the early part of the eighteenth century. The main political force in the national movement had been the antagonism generated by the political and economic dominance of the Baltic German minority in Estonian society and the oppressive russification program of the tsars.

As in Latvia, Russian participation in the war brought special repressive measures and economic suffering. These conditions moved the Estonian leaders after the outbreak of the February revolution in Russia to frame a draft law providing for home rule. The Russian Provisional Government responded with the decree of Estonian autonomy of April 12, 1917. Estonia was thereby legally constituted as a single administrative and cultural entity whose powers of self-government were to be exercised through a National Council of democratically elected representatives. Authorization was obtained to form an Estonian regiment of soldiers.[1]

The elected National Council, meeting for the first time on July 14,

---

1. Evald Uustalu, "Die Staatsgründung Estlands," *Von den baltischen Provinzen zu den baltischen Staaten,* ed. Jürgen von Hehn, Hans von Rimscha, and Hellmuth Weiss (Marburg, 1971), 275–76; Stanley W. Page, *The Formation of the Baltic States* (Cambridge, Mass., 1959), 71–72.

1917, pronounced the national objective to be the complete autonomy of a democratic Estonia within a federative Russian empire. After the Bolshevik coup in Petrograd, the Estonian Bolsheviks with the aid of the Russians instituted Bolshevik rule, which the Russian Soviets recognized as the "Estonian Soviet Republic." The National Council reacted to the Bolshevik challenge with a resolution that declared a practical separation from Russia: a democratically elected constituent assembly would determine Estonia's future form of government; until the convening of the constituent assembly the National Council would exercise supreme power in Estonia; and a Council of Elders would act for the National Council when not in session.[2]

When the German armies resumed their eastern march in February 1918, they moved into Estonia, and the Bolshevik regime ended on the withdrawal of the Bolsheviks and the Russians. The Council of Elders secretly transferred its power to the Committee for Saving Estonia. The committee published on February 23–24 a declaration of Estonian independence and formed a provisional Estonian government. Rather than accept this exercise of self-determination, the German military set up an exploitative occupation regime that allowed no political activity.[3]

The treaty of Brest-Litovsk stipulated that Estonia and Livonia would no longer be under Russian sovereignty and would be occupied by a German police force until security was insured by "proper national institutions." However objectionable the occupation regime was to the Estonian people, the German occupation immediately rid the country of Bolshevik rule and the Red terror. In the long run it insured the detachment of Estonia from Russia and made Estonia's future an international problem.

In creating "proper national institutions," the Germans convened a packed United Provinces Council, which asked for the permanent military protection of the German Reich for Estonia and Livonia and for the formation of a constitutional monarchy out of Estonia, Livonia, and Courland. The state thus created was to be joined with the Reich in a personal union through the Prussian king. This subterfuge for self-determination only strengthened the tenacious resistance of the Estonians to

2. The text of the resolution is quoted in Page, *Formation of the Baltic States*, 77.
3. Uustalu, "Die Staatsgründung Estlands," 282–83; Karl-Heinz Janssen, "Die baltische Okkupationspolitik des deutschen Reiches," in *Von den baltischen Provinzen zu den baltischen Staaten*, 240.

the occupation regime and its repressive practices.[4]

During 1918 the international recognition of an independent Estonia made progress. In response to the activities of the National Council's envoys, the British government on May 3 extended provisional recognition to the National Council as an independent de facto body. By late summer the Estonians in London were operating, in effect, a diplomatic mission under the designation of the "Estonian Provisional Legation." France granted the Estonians a corresponding status. The formation of an Estonian legion in northern Russia to assist the Allied intervention helped to gain sympathy for Estonia. The treaty of August 27, 1918, supplementary to the treaty of Brest-Litovsk, bolstered the legal separation of Estonia from Russia by requiring the renunciation of Russia's sovereignty over Estonia and Livonia.[5]

The November revolution in Germany made it possible for the Estonian provisional government to function with the approval of the German military administration but against the objection of the Baltic barons. The Council of Elders formed a coalition cabinet and returned its own powers to the assembled National Council. The provisional government negotiated with the Germans the treaty of Riga of November 18–19, arranging for the withdrawal of German forces. The treaty signified the de facto recognition of Estonia by Germany.

The existence of the emerging Estonian state was endangered by an invasion of the Estonian and Latvian Bolsheviks, supported by an offensive of the Red Army. The Estonian Bolsheviks proclaimed the establishment of the Estonian Workers' Commune, and the Soviet government immediately recognized it by the name of the Estonian Soviet Republic. The Bolshevik invaders occupied one-half of the country by December 10 and soon commenced the battle for the capital, Tallinn. The reconstituted Estonian army overcame the extreme peril with the aid of a Finnish military contingent of over 2,700, Swedish and Danish volunteers, and British warships and arms shipments. In addition, the North Army of White Russian volunteers fought with the Estonian forces. The Estonians

4. Page, *Formation of the Baltic States*, 100–06; J. Hampden Jackson, *Estonia* (London, 1941), 134–35.

5. Edgars Andersons, "Die baltische Frage und die internationale Politik der alliierten und assozierten Mächte bis zum November 1918," in *Von den baltischen Provinzen zu den baltischen Staaten*, 264–65; Malbone W. Graham, *The Diplomatic Recognition of the Border States*, pt. 2: *Estonia* (Berkeley, 1939), 244–45.

relieved Tallinn and drove the Bolsheviks back beyond the Estonian areas by February 24, 1919. The peace treaty of Tartu, concluded with the Soviets on February 2, 1920, gave juridical sanction for the independent state.[6]

Internally, the national and democratic revolution was completed by the work of the constituent assembly. Its constitution of June 15, 1920, established a democratic republic reposing sovereignty in a unicameral legislature elected on a direct, secret, and universal franchise.

2. THE LATVIAN REVOLUTION

The Latvian lands had constituted an integral part of the Russian state since they were acquired through the territorial expansion of Peter the Great and the partitions of Poland. On the eve of the war the national movement aspired to the overthrow of the supremacy of the Baltic barons in the Latvian area and to the achievement of national autonomy.

The war struck the Latvians with a murderous fury. For three years Latvian soil was an eastern battleground. The German armies drove through Courland to the Daugava (Dvina) river in 1915, captured Riga and surrounding districts in September 1916, and occupied most of the remaining Latvian territory in February 1918. The retreating Russians carried out a scorched earth policy, and the military administration of the Germans squeezed the land mercilessly for the benefit of the Reich economy.

This fate strengthened the desire for national autonomy and stimulated organizational activity in the national movement. The great dispersal of Latvian refugees in Russia occasioned the founding of the Latvian Refugee Aid Committee. The committee became a network of national purpose with branches in all parts of the empire. The émigrés established the Latvian National Committee in Switzerland to cultivate western opinion in favor of Latvian autonomy. More directly significant in promoting Latvian patriotism and the formation of an independent state, was the organization of the Latvian rifle battalions (later regiments) in the Russian army. The Rifles remaining in Latvia in 1918 formed the building blocks of the national army that fought for its liberation.

After the February revolution had broken out, the Russian Provisional

6. Page, *Formation of the Baltic States*, 127–29, 177–81; Uustalu, "Die Staatsgründung Estlands," 291–92; Graham, *Diplomatic Recognition of the Baltic States: Estonia*, 257–301; Jackson, *Estonia*, 145–46.

Government failed to address itself satisfactorily to the numerous public resolutions asking for the attainment of autonomy and unity of the Latvian provincial areas.[7] The unreceptiveness of the Provisional Government and its progressive breakdown influenced the national movement in a more radical direction toward seeking an independent Latvian state.

The power of Bolshevism grew among the councils, soviets, and assemblies that proliferated in unoccupied Latvia. The greater part of the Latvian Rifles was converted into "a spearhead of the revolution." Latvia was ahead of Petrograd in the progressive transfer of power to the Bolsheviks. When the October uprising occurred in Russia, the Latvian Bolsheviks took part on direct orders of agents from Petrograd and effectively supported the seizure of power in the Russian capital. The Bolsheviks made the executive committee of the Soviet of Workers', Landless Peasants', and Soldiers' Deputies the central organ of rule in unoccupied Latvia.[8]

Two underground organizations arose to lead the national struggle for true self-determination and independence: the Provisional National Council and the Democratic Bloc. A representative assembly, convoked at Valka on the Estonian-Latvian frontier by the Latvian Refugee Aid Committee, constituted itself the Latvian Provisional National Council (November 16–19, 1917). The Bolshevik conquest of power in Russia and the subordination of the Latvian Bolsheviks to Lenin spurred the council at its meeting of January 28–31, 1918, to resolve that Latvia should become an independent democratic republic. The council's envoys eventually took up representational activities at London and Paris.[9]

The Provisional National Council firmly opposed the designs of the German annexationists and the Baltic barons to attach the greater part of Latvia to the Reich. The peace of Brest-Litovsk partitioned Latvia between Germany and Russia, leaving Courland and Riga a protectorate of Germany, the rest of Livonia subject to German occupation, and Latgale still in the possession of Russia. The Provisional National Council denounced this "act of violence against the right of the people to self-determination"

7. The text of the most important of these resolutions is in Alfred Bilmanis, ed., *Latvian-Russian Relations: Documents* (Washington, 1944), 42.
    8. Andrew Ezergailis, *The 1917 Revolution in Latvia* (Boulder, Colo., 1974), 104–253 passim, particularly p. 251; Uldis Ģērmanis, "Die Autonomie-und Unabhängigkeitsbestrebungen der Letten," in *Von den baltischen Provinzen zu den baltischen Staaten,* 52–56.
    9. Arveds Schwabe, *The Story of Latvia* (Stockholm, 1950), 35; Arnolds Spekke, *History of Latvia* (Stockholm, 1951), 323. For the text of the November resolution, see Bilmanis, *Latvian-Russian Relations,* 42–43.

THE WORLD IN THE CRUCIBLE

as being null and void and demanded the creation of an independent and indivisible Latvian state under international guarantee.[10]

In occupied Latvia the Democratic Bloc of political parties acted as the center of resistance to the plans of the German expansionists and the Baltic barons. When they attempted in the fall of 1918 to create a united Baltic state under the hereditary rule of the kaiser, the Democratic Bloc protested strongly the formation of its organizing body, the Council of the Baltic States.[11]

The unyielding resistance of the Latvian Provisional National Council and the Democratic Bloc was joined with the German internal opposition to the Baltic annexationist schemes to thwart the kaiser and the Latvian collaborators. A Council of Regency for a united Baltic state, however, was elected by an assembly packed with Baltic barons and Latvian collaborators. The German military allowed this provisional authority to organize a Baltic Landeswehr. A project for colonizing Courland with Germans was initiated.[12]

Rather than these remnants of the German imperium, a British note on armistice day presaged the future. The note granted "provisional recognition to the Latvian National Council as a de facto independent body" and agreed to receive the Latvian envoy "as the informal diplomatic Representative of the Latvian Provisional Government."[13]

The German revolution permitted the Latvian national and democratic movement to go forward. The Provisional National Council and the Democratic Bloc came out into the open in Riga. Their long discussions resulted in the organization of the Latvian People's (or State) Council. On November 18 the council declared the founding of the "self-governing, independent, democratic republic of Latvia." The national day of free

10. Malbone W. Graham, *The Diplomatic Recognition of the Border States*, pt. 3: *Latvia* (Berkeley, 1941), 405–06; Bilmanis, *Latvian-Russian Relations*, 49–52.

11. Ģērmanis, "Die Autonomie- und Unabhängigkeitsbestrebungen der Letten," 45–46; Alfred Bilmanis, *A History of Latvia* (Princeton, 1951), 292. On the formation and party composition of the Democratic Bloc, see Bruno Kalniņš, "Die Staatsgründung Lettlands," in *Von den baltischen Provinzen zu den baltischen Staaten*, 297–302.

12. Bilmanis, *History of Latvia*, 302–04. On the German internal opposition to the imperialist projects in the Baltic area, see Arved Freiherr von Taube, "Die baltisch-deutsche Führungsschicht und die Loslösung Livlands und Estlands von Russland," in *Von den baltischen Provinzen zu den baltischen Staaten*, 146–47, 152, 186–88.

13. Andersons, "Die baltische Frage und die internationale Politik der allierten und assozierten Mächte," 272; Graham, *Diplomatic Recognition of the Border States: Latvia*, 407; Bilmanis, *Latvian-Russian Relations*, 58.

Latvians has been celebrated on that day ever since. The statement also proclaimed the formation of the Latvian provisional government, which the Germans recognized as the successor power to the occupation regime.[14]

The fledgling government was forced to fight a war of liberation for nearly two years. The Russian Red Army, entering the country on December 2, occupied over three-fourths of Latvia. The Russian Bolsheviks set up the Soviet Republic of Latvia to be the model of the Soviet state outside Russia. The transplanting of the Red terror and revolutionary tribunals gave the Latvians a foretaste of what was to come in 1940.[15]

Anti-Bolshevik forces were built up with military aid from the Germans, the British, and the Estonians. General Rüdiger von der Goltz, sent from Finland to take command of the German troops in the Baltic area, reconstituted and reinforced the Iron Division of Free Corps soldiers. This unrepentant imperialist perceived the opportunity to revive German eastern policy under the guise of an anti-Bolshevik crusade.[16] The Latvian government expanded its own armed forces and entered into military cooperation with the Estonians through a northern army organized with their assistance.

These measures paved the way for the liberation of Courland. At first, however, General von der Goltz instigated the organization of a puppet government of Balts and Latvian collaborators at Liepāja, where the Latvian government had withdrawn. The capital of Riga was taken by the Landeswehr of the Balts in an orgy of slaughtering Bolsheviks. The Latvian and Estonian forces, continuing the fight against the Bolsheviks, forced them back from northern Latvia. After the fall of Riga, the Landeswehr and the Germans turned from the war against the Bolsheviks to fighting the Latvians and the Estonians. The Balts and the Germans were irretrievably defeated at Cēsis on June 22, 1919. The Riga armistice of July 3 required the Reich Germans to be repatriated and the Landeswehr to become a unit of the Latvian army. The Latvian forces entered Riga, and the legal government returned to the capital.

14. Bilmanis, *History of Latvia,* 307–08; Schwabe, *Story of Latvia,* 37–38; Spekke, *History of Latvia,* 344–45; Kalniņš, "Die Staatsgründung Lettlands," 308–12. The text of the declaration and the statement of the political platform of the People's Council are in Bilmanis, *Latvian-Russian Relations,* 59–60.

15. Page, *Formation of the Baltic States,* 135–40.

16. Rüdiger Graf von der Goltz, *Als politischer General im Osten* (Leipzig, 1936), 85–86.

Von der Goltz tried one more gambit in attempting to keep a hold on the Baltic lands. The German commander leagued with the White Russian adventurer Colonel Paul Bermondt, who expanded his small Russian detachment into the "West Russian" army with "volunteers" from the Iron Division. Von der Goltz thus subverted the terms of the Riga armistice and ignored the summons of the Allies twice made to withdraw the Germans. Bermondt's force attacked Riga, but the Latvians, armed by the British and French, drove off the attack with the aid of British and French naval vessels. In November the Latvian army cleared the country of Bermondt's condottieri. The state of war with Germany caused by this affair ended with the conclusion of peace on July 15, 1920.[17]

The Poles joined the Latvians in common action against the Red forces that remained in Latgale. Together they freed the country of the last Bolsheviks by January 20, 1920. The peace treaty, signed at Riga on August 11, 1920, kept to the Estonian model. The treaty recognized Latvia's sovereignty irrevocably and determined Latvia's borders with Russia. The Allied Supreme Council by collective act finally accorded recognition to Latvia on the same day as Estonia, January 21, 1921.[18]

The National Council and the government of Kārlis Ulmanis, the leader of the Peasant Union, had already taken up the work of national reconstruction. A freely elected constituent assembly declared Latvia to be a sovereign and independent republic (May 29, 1920). The national and democratic revolution closed with the adoption of a liberal and democratic constitution making the cabinet responsible to a powerful unicameral parliament that elected the president.

3. THE LITHUANIAN REVOLUTION

The lands inhabited by the Lithuanian peoples were divided between the German and Russian sovereignties in 1914. The national movement developed primarily in Russian Lithuania, where the mass of the Lithuanian population was located. Politically, the national consciousness matured through resistance to the russification measures of the tsardom and to the polonizing tendencies of the polonized gentry and bourgeoisie.[19]

During the first year of the war the objective of the national movement

17. Bilmanis, *History of Latvia*, 324 ff.; Page, *Formation of the Baltic States*, 158 ff.
18. Graham, *Diplomatic Recognition of the Border States: Latvia*, 435–50 passim.
19. Constantine R. Jurgela, *History of the Lithuanian Nation* (New York, 1948), 469–502.

remained the unity and autonomy of ethnic Lithuania within the Russian empire. The vast movement of refugees gave the first impulse to wartime organizational activity supporting national interests. The Lithuanians formed a Lithuanian Relief Committee with political features, having its headquarters in Vilna, the ancient capital of Lithuania.

Lithuania was the only Baltic country under German occupation from September 1915 until the end of the war. Eventually, the occupation authorities consolidated the lands of Russian Lithuania into one unit, the Lithuanian Military District. Under this iron-fisted regime and the impact of catastrophic Russian defeat the national goal shifted from autonomy to independence. The political movement went underground and extended its activity abroad. The Lithuanian Relief Committee divided into two parts, one operating in Russia and the other under the German occupation from the Vilna center. In Switzerland the Lithuanian emigration held conferences of some import, sometimes attended by representatives of the Lithuanian Relief Committee. The Lithuanian Information Bureau of Lausanne acted with the force of a national council.[20]

The pace of the movement toward national independence quickened after the outbreak of the Russian revolution. Petitioned by the Lithuanians and pressed by the Reichstag majority, the German government permitted the Vilna leaders to organize a national conference. The assembly, convening at Vilna on September 18, 1917, declared that Lithuania should become an independent state with a democratic form of government and elected a Taryba, or national council.[21]

The Taryba quickly established itself among Lithuanians at home and in the west as the supreme organ of the nation and the independence movement. The Taryba directed its efforts to stabilizing Lithuania's relations with Germany on the basis of self-determination. Favorable to this endeavor were the positions of the German Social Democratic and Center parties. The Center under the lead of Erzberger, the friend and mentor of the Lithuanians, supported the early introduction of a parliamentary system in Lithuania. The occupation authorities, backed by the right, demanded that Lithuania enter into a union with the Reich. Confronted

20. Börje Colliander, *Die Beziehungen zwischen Litauen und Deutschland während der Okkupation 1915–1918* (Åbo, 1935), 22–31, 42–47; Jurgela, *History of the Lithuanian Nation*, 505; Georg von Rauch, *Staatliche Einheit und nationale Vielfalt* (Munich, 1953), 176–78.
21. Alfred Erich Senn, *The Emergence of Modern Lithuania* (New York, 1959), 25–26; Colliander, *Die Beziehungen zwischen Litauen und Deutschland*, 120–26.

with these contending forces, the Taryba proclaimed on December 11, 1917, "the restoration of an independent state" with the capital at Vilna. The Taryba appealed for the protection of the Reich and approved a close alliance with Germany to be effected through a military and a trade convention, as well as by means of a customs and currency union.[22]

Not acting on the declaration, the Germans postponed the recognition of Lithuania's independence. The Taryba then issued the proclamation of February 16, 1918, which abandoned the clauses relating to an alliance and conventions with the Reich. This avowal of independence became the birthright of the Lithuanian nation, and the date of February 16 the national day of free Lithuanians.[23]

The Reich government, attacked by Erzberger for vacillation and delay, was impelled to act. The kaiser's writ of March 23 recognized an independent state tied to Germany through the arrangements mentioned in the Lithuanian declaration of December 11. By the treaty of Brest-Litovsk Russia had already renounced sovereignty over the Lithuanian territory.[24]

Prince Max's government of defeated Germany recognized the unreserved independence of Lithuania on October 20, 1918. The Taryba adopted a provisional constitution by which this body, constituted as the State Council, would exercise supreme authority through a cabinet responsible to itself.

For more than a year Lithuania struggled in a time of troubles to make the national dream of a stable independent state a reality. The State Council had to cope with economic prostration, spreading Bolshevik influence, changing cabinets, and abject fiscal penury relieved only by a German loan and later by British financial aid. The gravest peril arose from Bolshevism and the Red Army. Acting in December 1918 on instructions of Bolsheviks sent from Moscow, the Communist party founded at Vilna the Provisional Workers' and Peasants' Government of Lithuania. The Red Army marched into Lithuania to support the Communist regime. The disintegrating occupation force of the Germans and the Lithuanian national government evacuated Vilna.[25]

22. Epstein, *Matthias Erzberger*, 237–38. The text of the declaration is in Colliander, *Die Beziehungen zwischen Litauen und Deutschland*, 150.

23. For the text of the declaration: Thomas G. Chase, *The Story of Lithuania* (New York, 1946), 265.

24. Senn, *Emergence of Modern Lithuania*, 32–33; Epstein, *Matthias Erzberger*, 237–38.

25. Senn, *Emergence of Modern Lithuania*, 49–100 passim.

The Lithuanian government, swept toward extinction in the maelstrom, implored Berlin to stop the withdrawal and the Allies to stay the Germans. The Lithuanians frantically tried to build up their own armed forces. The Germans established a defense perimeter around Kaunas and speeded up the arrival of their own volunteers. Through joint military action the Red Army was checked from taking Kaunas. The Red Army held on in Vilna and eastern Lithuania, and the Communist regime in the capital.

The winning of western support progressed slowly. A conflict with the Information Bureau at Lausanne proved to be a hindrance. The delegation to the Paris peace conference met unrelenting opposition to independence from the White Russians and from the Polish delegation and the Polish National Committee. The Lithuanian efforts nevertheless began to show results from the spring of 1919. The Allies lifted the Baltic blockade for traffic to Lithuania and Latvia and provided military aid. The separation of the Memel territory from East Prussia effected by the treaty of Versailles presumed the transfer of Memel to Lithuania.

The liberation of the country from the Bolshevik army and the Communist regime owed more to the aid of Poland—the unsolicited and unbestowed aid—than to that of any other country. The Poles had been waging their own campaign against the Red Army in Lithuania since January 1919. They pushed the Bolshevik forces steadily back and captured Vilna on April 19–21. The loss of the Communist center spelled the collapse of the Communist rule. The Lithuanians, who had been fighting the Bolsheviks in local cooperation with the Germans, had planned to take Vilna themselves.

The Polish capture of Vilna started a conflict with Poland that was conducted in the arena of diplomacy and political warfare as well as by intermittent armed action in 1919–20. The Lithuanians and Poles were divided by the Polish aim of restoring a union, or of forming at least a federative association, of the two countries and, when this aim could not be realized, by the issue of determining the Lithuanian-Polish boundary and the disposition of Vilna. Lithuania was saved from absorption by the Poles but at the sacrifice of Vilna and at the cost of embittered relations with Poland for years to come.[26]

The struggling Lithuanian state was also forced to take up arms for its

26. On the conflict with Poland, see Chase, *Story of Lithuania,* 274–82; Jurgela, *History of the Lithuanian Nation,* 517–24.

independence against Colonel Bermondt's army of White Russians and German "volunteers" from the Iron Division entering Lithuania from Latvia. The Germans completed the evacuation of their official troops in October 1919, which the Allies had ordered. The danger of the Germans establishing a position in the Baltic made the Allies and the Lithuanians partners in the removal of Bermondt's invaders. The Lithuanians routed them in November after two months of fighting. The last of Bermondt's Germans were evacuated under Allied supervision by December 1919.

The Lithuanians and Poles had continued to fight the Soviets in their separate zones of Lithuania during 1919. The Red Army was driven out of most of the Lithuanian territory. Lithuania's treaty of peace, concluded at Moscow on July 20, 1920, after the Estonian pattern, recognized the independence of Lithuania and ceded Vilna to Lithuania.

Diplomatic recognition was retarded because of German occupation at first and later owing to Polish ambitions supported by the French. Britain's more active interest in Lithuania, in fact in supplanting Germany's predominant influence there, was indicated by its grant of de facto recognition on September 23, 1919, and its moral support of Lithuania against the Poles and more tangible support against the Germans. France did not grant de facto recognition until May 11, 1920.

General recognition was assisted by the treaty of Moscow and by the work of the constituent assembly. This body, convening on May 15, 1920, formally proclaimed "that the independent Lithuanian state is reestablished as a democratic republic with ethnic frontiers." The constitution adopted on August 1, 1922, was comparable to Latvia's.[27]

The success of the national and democratic revolution of course depended to a great extent on the stamina and strenuous efforts of the Lithuanians themselves in war and state-building. Yet Lithuanian independence was saved repeatedly by the action of other states. Independence from Russia was gained through German occupation and with Germany's support. Lithuania was saved from probable Polish occupation by German volunteer soldiers; from Bolshevik control by German forces and the Poles; from the Germans by the Allies, mostly the British; from the Soviets by the Poles; and from the Poles by the Allies.

While the Allies conducted a crusade to save democracy—and insisted on maintaining the territorial integrity of Russia—Germany made possible

27. Senn, *Emergence of Modern Lithuania*, 216; Chase, *Story of Lithuania*, 268–69.

through its occupation the separation of the three Baltic nations from Russia and their assertion of independence eventually as democratic states. The opposition in turn to Germany's domination in the area cemented the national solidarity of each people east of the Baltic. That these Baltic countries survived the expansionist drive of the Bolshevik revolution was due in considerable part to the role of the White Russians and Allied intervention in compelling an exhausted Soviet Russia to make peace with the Baltic countries and recognize their independence.[28]

4. THE FINNISH REVOLUTION

The transfer of Finland to Russia in 1809 changed the Finnish position from being an integral part of Sweden to enjoying the special status of an autonomous grand duchy under the constitutional rule of the tsar-grand duke. The tsardom's policies of russification subverted Finland's special position and aroused Finnish nationalism to determined opposition. The conviction crystallized that the only way to escape absorption into the Russian empire was to sever completely the tie with the tsarist state.

Finland alone of the emergent eastern states waged the struggle for national independence from the immediate experience of having been a distinct political entity with its own constitution and institutional organization. In 1906 the Russian revolution had enabled Finland to update its constitution by replacing the ancient diet of four estates with a unicameral legislature elected on the universal franchise of both men and women. In separating itself from Russia, Finland was forced into a bloody and tragic conflict that was at once a civil war and a war of independence.

The final stage of russification, coming with the onset of the world war, threatened the complete integration of Finland into the Russian state. The Finnish patriots saw in Russia's defeat the hope of escape through successful armed rebellion. They prepared for the future by arrangements with Germany to train in the Reich a Jaeger battalion of young volunteers (eventually 2,000 men).[29]

The February revolution in Russia allowed immediate progress toward independence. The Russian Provisional Government's manifesto of

28. See C. Jay Smith, *Finland and the Russian Revolution, 1917–1922* (Athens, Ga., 1958), 213–15; Von Taube, "Die baltisch-deutsche Führungsschicht und die Loslösung Livlands und Estlands von Russland," 213–14.

29. L. A. Puntila, *The Political History of Finland, 1809–1966* (Helsinki, 1974), 91–93; John H. Wuorinen, *A History of Finland* (New York, 1965), 208–10.

March 20, 1917, abrogated all the imperial ordinances and decrees since 1890 that had gone far to destroy Finland's constitutional position of home rule. In addition, the Russian organization for the control of Finland broke down. The Provisional Government, however, refused to confirm an act of the Finnish parliament affirming its powers and dissolved the assembly. The bourgeois members of the parliament and cabinet acquiesced; the Social Democrats claimed that the dissolution procedure was illegal and resigned from the cabinet. The nonsocialists won a majority of seats in the election of October 1–2, 1917.[30]

After the Bolshevik coup in Petrograd the bourgeois majority of the new parliament resolved on November 15 to take over all the powers of the tsar-grand duke in Finland. The staunchest defender of the Finnish constitution before the war, P. E. Svinhufrud, formed a completely nonsocialist cabinet when the socialists rejected joining a coalition. The parliament approved the Svinhufrud cabinet's proposal for a new constitution establishing Finland as an independent republic. The parliament supplemented the statement with a public declaration of independence. The day of this action, December 6, became Finland's national day of independence. A cabinet delegation negotiated with the Russian Council of People's Commissars an agreement of December 31, 1917, recognizing Finland's independence. France, Germany, and the Scandinavian states quickly followed in according recognition.[31]

But the question of Finland's independence and national unity was not yet settled. The aggrieved socialists in a parliamentary minority refused to become a constitutional opposition. The revolutionary wing gained control of the Social Democratic party and the Federation of the Labor Unions of Finland. The socialist and labor leaders created a Revolutionary Central Council and staged a general strike for political aims from November 13–20.

The civil war about to begin reflected the impact of the Russian revolution and determined the nature of Finland's political system and its relations with Russia. The military forces on the two sides originated in the formation of local units of workers' guards and bourgeois civic guards

30. Puntila, *Political History of Finland,* 98–99; Wuorinen, *History of Finland,* 211–13; Eino Jutikkala and Kauko Pirenen, *A History of Finland,* rev. ed. (New York, 1974), 251–52; Smith, *Finland and the Russian Revolution,* 13, 18–19.

31. Puntila, *Political History of Finland,* 101; Wuorinen, *History of Finland,* 215–16; Justikkala and Pirenen, *History of Finland,* 253–54.

when conditions of anarchy prevailed. The local detachments of the workers' guard joined later in an independent, country-wide organization named the Red Guard, which was closely associated with the bolshevized Russian troops in Finland in forming the Red forces.[32] Carl Gustaf Mannerheim, a corps commander from the Russian army, took charge of the White civic guards or Protective Corps. Mannerheim contributed strategic skill and an unswerving power of decision. With the crucially needed aid of the Jaeger battalion returned from Germany, Finnish career officers from the Russian army, and volunteer Swedish officers, Mannerheim forged into being an army of standard military units and staff organization according to the German model. The initial scarcity of arms was relieved by those quickly captured from the Russians and by a large shipment obtained from Germany in February 1918. Mannerheim's army was assisted in combat by the Baltic Division of General von der Goltz and a separate German brigade as well as by a Swedish brigade of volunteers including also Danes and Norwegians.[33]

The radical trends of November—the increasingly violent campaign of the Social Democratic press, the general strike, and the effect of the Bolshevik revolution—were intensified by the growing food shortages and widespread unemployment. In the latter part of January 1918 the militant radicals captured control of the socialist party executive. The leftist socialist leadership and the Red Guard seized power in Helsinki on the night of January 27–28. This "minority of a minority" proclaimed a revolutionary government under the name of the Finnish People's Delegation.[34]

Members of the cabinet escaping from Helsinki joined Mannerheim at his headquarters in Vaasa to keep the legal government in operation. The Red bid for the rule of Finland left the cabinet no choice but war. Mannerheim's strategy was systematically designed on grand lines to neutralize

32. Henning Söderhjelm, The Red Insurrection in Finland in 1918 (London, 1919), 58–59; J. O. Hannula, La guerre d'indépendance de Finlande 1918 (Paris, 1938), 36, 51–52, 69–70; Smith, Finland and the Russian Revolution, 22, 47–48.

33. Puntila, Political History of Finland, 105–09 passim; Hannula, La guerre d'indépendance, 101; Carl Gustaf Emil Mannerheim, Memoirs (London, 1954), 133–37; Smith, Finland and the Russian Revolution, 48–50; Aurélien Sauvageot, Histoire de la Finlande, 2 vols. (Paris, 1968), 2: 318.

34. Wuorinen, History of Finland, 217–18; Söderhjelm, Red Insurrection in Finland, 40–47, 53–54, 57; Sauvageot, Histoire de la Finland, 2: 314–15; Justikkala and Pirenen, History of Finland, 256.

immediately the maximum number of Russian garrison troops and to cut off from the Red forces an escape route to Russia and support lines from the Soviets through the Karelian isthmus; and to deliver knockout blows against the western and eastern forces of the Reds, which were to be separated by a meeting of his own troops from the north and the German army advancing from the south. This strategic plan was executed to the letter. During April a quick succession of major actions took place to end the war with the fall of the rebel center at Viipuri (Vyborg). The Red government had already taken flight for sanctuary in Russia before its capture.[35]

The majority of the people and most of the civil servants supported the legal government. The Reds were constantly harassed by an underground resistance. Large segments of the population were increasingly alienated by the mass of badly administered or paper reforms and by the financial chaos due chiefly to the Red regime's lavish printing of paper money. The revolutionary tribunals typified the growing terror and violence of the dictatorial rule. The atrocities of the Red Guard against the civilian population and war prisoners inevitably bred vengeance. The legal government's forces executed possibly as many as 8,500, following summary courts martial, and 10,000 more died in prison camps while waiting for individual interrogation and handling by special courts. Altogether the toll from the war rose to more than 31,500, of whom 9,000 fell in battle.[36]

Foreign intervention widened the conflict from a civil war to a contest between Germany and Bolshevik Russia and in a larger sphere between Germany and the Allies. In the latter aspect the German interest was to counter from Finland the opening of an outflanking British front from the Murmansk base. Beyond training the Jaeger battalion and delivering the cargo of arms and munitions, Germany assisted the legal government of Finland by naval control of the country's Baltic coast, by the share in combat of 12,000 German soldiers, by the invasion of Russia during the Finnish war, and by diplomatic aid. The Germans wrote into the treaty of Brest-Litovsk an article requiring the Bolshevik government to evacuate Russian troops and the Russian Red Guard from Finland as well as Russian naval forces from Finnish ports.

35. On the military operations, see Hannula, *La guerre d'indépendance,* 106–202; Mannerheim, *Memoirs,* 141–45, 153–77; Von der Goltz, *Als politischer General im Osten,* 29, 51–52.

36. Söderhjelm, *Red Insurrection in Finland,* 110–19; Puntila, *Political History of Finland,* 109; Wuorinen, *History of Finland,* 223; Justikkala and Pirenen, *History of Finland,* 259.

Not only did the Russian garrisons in Finland take part in combat, but the Soviet authorities sent new detachments to Viipuri just before the rebellion began and during the war aided with staff officers and specialist troops. The Red Guards received from the Russian Bolsheviks necessary arms, ammunition, and training along with supplies of grain. Soviet Russia accorded diplomatic recognition to the People's Delegation, though by the Soviet name of the Socialist Workers' Republic of Finland.[37]

The fratricidal conflict deeply affected the Finnish nation. The blood drain had its counterpart in economic destruction. The war engendered a bitterness and spirit of vengeance in Finnish society. The Social Democrats were separated from the leftists who fled from Viipuri to Petrograd and founded the Communist party there in August 1918. The conservatives were driven further to the right, and a strong monarchical sentiment made its appearance. Finland was rent by cleavages between the victors and the defeated, between monarchists and republicans, and between those for and those against the pro-German orientation in policy.[38]

The consideration of the form of government involved a passionate struggle between the monarchists and republicans. The government's attempt to make the prince of Hesse the king of Finland was wrecked by the defeat of Germany and the German revolution. The issue of the form of government could not be resolved until a representative parliament was elected after a revived Social Democratic party, back again on the path of democratic reformism and the western tradition, was reintegrated into the nation's political life. With the Social Democrats restored to parliament, a new assembly on July 17, 1919, adopted a constitution creating a democratic republic based on ministerial responsibility and a presidency of substantial power.[39]

The German intervention and the pro-German orientation of Finnish policy interfered with the uninterrupted recognition of Finland's independence by the western powers. The collapse of Germany, however, assured the withdrawal of German troops in December 1918 and, on the demand of the Allies, the termination of the German military mission that controlled the Finnish defense organization. The elections of March 1919 produced a decisive majority that favored neutrality or was sympathetic toward the west. In view of this progress away from the German line, the

37. Smith, *Finland and the Russian Revolution*, 23–59 passim.
38. Puntila, *Political History of Finland*, 123.
39. Ibid., 119–20; Wuorinen, *History of Finland*, 235.

Council of Foreign Ministers on May 3 considered favorably the question of recognition. Britain and the United States agreed to recognize Finland as of that date, and France shortly followed.[40]

The normalization of relations with Soviet Russia was held up by the operations of the White Russians in the north and the attempt of the Finns to liberate East Karelia. Finally, by the treaty of Tartu, signed on October 14, 1920, Russia "recognized the independence and sovereignty of Finland within the frontiers of the Grand Duchy of Finland" and ceded the Petsamo corridor, which provided Finland an opening to the Arctic.

The winning of sovereign statehood came about not only through Finland's resolute struggle but also through the assistance of the Germans, the White Russians, and Allied intervention in Russia. Autocratic Germany had contributed, without so intending, to the creation of an independent Finnish democracy. The White Russians and the Allied intervention had assisted by helping to exhaust Soviet Russia so that it was ready to come to the peace table.[41]

40. Juhani Paasivirta, *The Victors in World War I and Finland* (Helsinki, 1965), 46–109.
41. See Smith, *Finland and the Russian Revolution*, 212.

Chapter Seventeen

THE WORLD RESHAPED

1. ECONOMIC AND SOCIAL CHANGE

OF all the convulsive transformations of the European system, the Great War and the peace settlement brought about the sharpest break with the past, economically and socially no less than politically. The prewar economic order of Europe was notable for its volume of capital accumulated from the production of the nineteenth-century industrial system, its free flow of international trade, its convertible currencies backed by gold, and its large overseas investments, making Europe the world's creditor. The mellow glory of that freely operating and productive system had vanished in the catastrophe of war. Instead, Europe had to cope with economic exhaustion and universal economic dislocation.

The degree of economic disruption varied from the greatest in Russia and the secondary states in the east to the least in Britain and the neutral states of the north. In the east the famine conditions of food and fuel imposed an elemental struggle for human survival. Mass hunger, malnutrition, and disease stalked the devastated and pillaged lands. In eastern Poland the people were reduced to a state of misery comparable to that inflicted on the population of central Europe by the Thirty Years' War. In Germany and Austria the urban consumers on inadequate diets were suffering apathy and diseases of nutritional deficiency.

Farming on the continent was set back by the losses of horses, cattle, and hogs. The livestock had been destroyed in wide areas of Poland, Serbia, Romania, and Russia; the German stock of pigs had diminished by 60 percent. Surviving livestock had deteriorated in quality. The soil was impoverished in central and eastern Europe and lowered in fertility elsewhere.

The industrial machine of Europe was in disrepair because of the heavy strain of wartime production and deferred maintenance and replacement. Stocks of raw materials were depleted, and shortages of fuel were crippling. The production of coal in Europe had fallen off by 30 percent since 1913. The industries of peace had atrophied.

Internal transport suffered a complete breakdown of the railway system in the east. Everywhere there were shortages of locomotives and rolling stock. Their condition was deteriorated, as was that of railway tracks. Overseas transport had to overcome the wartime losses to merchant shipping not offset by shipbuilding during the war.

The war disrupted the patterns of both intra-European trade and Europe's overseas trade. In the east, markets were lost through the effects of the Great War, continued wars in the creation of national states, the establishment of new boundaries, and the imposition of nationalist restrictions. The Russian market disappeared, and for about a year after the armistice Germany scarcely conducted a foreign trade. Everywhere the financial disorder within former belligerents and succession states inhibited external commerce. Germany and the Allied countries in Europe had been displaced in many overseas outlets during the war by the rising economic centers, the United States and Japan, and these two economic powers had developed new industries of their own to compete in the world market.

The war had played havoc with European finances. The national debt of each former belligerent had multiplied since 1913 (seven times in France and more than ten times in Britain). The national fiscal system and private economic activity were depressed by the enormous burden of external and domestic debt arising from the war loans, the costs of unemployment benefits and food relief, the costs of restoring devastated areas, and the loss of foreign assets belonging to the government or the country's private citizens exchanged for war imports or transferred from Germany by the treaty of Versailles. Most countries of the world had suspended the gold basis of their currency; raging inflation was bringing the old currencies to ruin in Russia, Austria, Hungary, and Germany.

In summary, the economic revival of Europe was retarded by the following conditions: the massive transfer of wealth to North America, converting the United States into a creditor country, through payments for war imports not offset by exports; the economic collapse of Germany, prolonged by the maintenance of the blockade after the armistice and the economic disabilities imposed by the treaty of Versailles; a shift in economic growth to the United States, Japan, and South America encouraged by the prodigious demands of Europe in wartime and the need for new sources of supply outside Europe for overseas lands; the widespread unemployment and labor disturbances incident to absorbing the rapidly demobilized soldiers into a peacetime economy; and economic separatism in Europe owing to the isolation of Russia, the autarchic tendencies engendered by the war, the number of rival economic sovereignties in eastern Europe engaging in restrictive practices to protect their new-born economies, and the beginning of postwar economic nationalism. It has been estimated that the war set back French economic growth by nearly ten years and that of Europe as a whole by eight years. The damage was so great that the European economy did not recover from stagnation and instability before the next world war struck.[1]

European society was also recast by the blasts of war. The belligerent populations were divided into distinct groups, each of which bore the marks of its separate experience and needed at the end of the war to be reintegrated into the national community. A chasm separated the soldiers at the front from the people at home. The French author Henri Barbusse wrote that there is no longer a single country of France; there are two, "the Front and the Rear."[2] The soldier returning on leave or convalescence frequently discovered that those he left at home could not imagine the realities of his front experience—trench squalor and despair, mechanized slaughter, combat comradeship. For his part he could only gag at the effusions of superpatriotism and mindless hate of the enemy that he heard at home, and in the case of some German soldiers at the betrayal attributed to the civilians. He seemed a stranger in his own land. This feeling often persisted when, on becoming a veteran, he attempted to fit himself into the civilian society again. The difficulty was evident among the demobilized German soldiers who joined the Free Corps.[3]

Besides these two larger components of the wartime population there were the lesser sections in the occupied areas, among the refugees, and in the camps for prisoners of war. The occupied areas were located mainly in France, Belgium, Russia, Serbia, Montenegro, Romania, Galicia, and

1. Arthur L. Bowley, *Some Economic Consequences of the Great War* (London, 1930), 90–99, 196–223 passim; Grebler and Winkler, *Cost of the War to Germany and Austria-Hungary,* 90–91; Pierre Renouvin, *War and Aftermath, 1914–1929* (New York, 1968), 123–25, 131; Clough, *Economic History of Europe in the Twentieth Century,* 9–11, 65–110 passim; *Cambridge Economic History of Europe,* 6, pt. 1: 19, 54–55; Fayle, *Seaborne Trade,* 3: 421–54; Wright, *France in Modern Times,* 401–02; Crouzet, *L'époque contemporaine,* 22; May, *Passing of the Hapsburg Empire,* 1: 329–35, 398–401; Thompson, *England in the Twentieth Century,* 50.
2. *Under Fire* (New York, 1917), 312–13, 339.
3. See Robert G. L. Waite, *Vanguard of Nazism; The Free Corps Movement in Postwar Germany* (Cambridge, Mass., 1952), 41 ff.

other Polish lands. The trail of refugees fleeing in masses before the sweep of armies or on the eve of far-flung battles marked the beginning of "the century of expellees and prisoners."[4] The mass flight of population was greatest in East Prussia and Galicia (1914), in Russia (1915), and in Romania (1916). The disordered waves of humanity, carting their possessions and driving their cattle with them, experienced difficulties everywhere in finding food and observing sanitary precautions sufficient to fend off diseases. In Russia their distress was indescribable before the zemstvos, town councils, and Red Cross arranged food and welfare stations along the routes and located the fugitives in refugee centers.

This was the first war in which prisoners numbered in the millions (8,400,000 altogether) and were detained for long periods of time.[5] While the great powers were obligated to treat prisoners in accordance with the Hague Convention, the treatment in general depended on the standards prevailing in the army of the captor power.[6] The captives of the Turks suffered the worst care. Russia provided no more than the minimum necessities in food and clothing, and the poor health care, along with the want of sanitary precautions, caused excessive sickness and mortality. The prison administration in Russia attempted to indoctrinate the Slavic captives in nationalist propaganda before the November revolution and all captives with Bolshevik propaganda after the revolution. The belligerents used prisoners of war in various modes of employment in grappling with their manpower problems.

The war altered the social structure and disrupted the normal patterns of social life. The soldier fatalities shifted the normal sex and age ratios of the population. The composition of society was unbalanced by the abnormally high number of single women, whether unmarried or widowed, and by the gaps in the ranks of the young men, depriving Europe of sorely needed resources of leadership for the future.[7]

The consequences of the war tended to level the classes in society. The aristocracy was decimated in the belligerents. In Russia both the aristocracy and bourgeoisie were liquidated as classes. In other countries the war

4. Heinrich Böll, "Hymn to a New Homeland," Saturday Review, May 3, 1975.
5. See the tables in Franz Scheidl, Die Kriegsgefangenschaft von den ältesten Zeiten bis zur Gegenwart (Berlin, 1943), 96–97.
6. See Daniel J. McCarthy, The Prisoners of War in Germany (New York, 1917), for treatment of Germany's prisoners.
7. France's war dead totaled 10 percent of the active male population and Britain's 9 percent of the men under 45 years of age.

accelerated the decline in social status, economic power, and political influence of the aristocracy. Where democratic constitutions were adopted, in Germany and the new states of eastern Europe, the nobles and gentry lost their special political privileges. Through land reforms in eastern Europe a great part of the land of this group was being transferred to the peasantry. The peasantry in areas not disturbed by the fighting had prospered during the war from the greatly increased demand and higher prices for their products. They added to their plots of land and paid off mortgages in depreciated currency. In eastern Europe agrarian elements exerted for the most part a dominant political influence in the interwar period.

In Britain the long-range progress of the landed aristocracy toward extinction was accelerated as this group merged with the plutocracy in the upper class, in which membership no longer required the ownership of land. The heavy taxes levied on landed estates to help defray the costs of war and the higher price of land after the war led to the sale or dismemberment of many estates. The aristocracy had become a declining element in Britain's political elite, the House of Commons, and even the Lords.[8]

The demarcation was receding between the bourgeoisie and the aristocracy on the upper side and between the bourgeoisie and the working classes on the lower side. Profits from war contracts and wartime construction largely escaping taxation propelled in central and western Europe a group of "new rich" to the upper bourgeoisie. The middle class was being recruited anew by the impressive growth in the salaried component of the population reflecting three phenomena of the maturing modern state—the rapidly expanding bureaucracy, the rise of the managerial class, and the broad entry of women into occupational life. At the same time that portion of the old middle class living on fixed or inadequately increased incomes had become the victims of vaulting inflation and higher taxes. Their descent in social status created unrest and instability as well as social antagonisms.[9]

The status of the working classes had risen. Industrial labor had generally gained the eight-hour day, and working conditions improved thanks

8. See W. L. Guttsman, *The British Political Elite* (London, 1963), 20, 109, 132–34, 356; Arthur Marwick, *The Deluge: British Society and the First World War* (Boston, 1965), 300–02; Charles F. G. Masterman, *England after the War* (New York, 1923), 27–47.
9. Masterman, *England after the War*, 49–83; Wright, *France in Modern Times*, 403.

largely to ameliorations associated with the entry of women into the factories. In the Allied countries of the west wages kept ahead of the rising living costs, and until the postwar recession the workers enjoyed more expectation of employment and material well-being than ever before. As the middle-class standards of comfortable living slipped downward, the living standards of the workers went upward. Labor, whose maximum output in the factories was essential for the waging of total war, moved toward dealing with management and government as an equal party.

The organization of the workers was strengthened through substantial expansion of trade-union membership and consolidation of separate unions. The workers' movement emerged as a powerful political force in Europe: the socialist parties came to dominate the Russian revolution, and the Bolsheviks established a workers' state; the Social Democrats in Germany supported by the trade unions captained the November revolution and took the lead in the formation of the Weimar republic; the British Labor party, after entering the government for the first time in the coalition cabinet formed by Lloyd George in 1916, founded a mass party of national scope by means of its constitution of January 1918 and an influx of new members. Labor showed in the elections of December 1918 that it was well on the way to displacing the Liberal party as the opposition to the Conservatives.

The war period witnessed conspicuous progress in the emancipation of women. The needs of modern war called women of all classes to work in munitions factories, transport, government offices, agriculture, and service organizations such as the British Women's Royal Naval Service (WRENS) and the Women's Auxiliary Army Corps (WAAC). Women retained many of their war jobs, and the beachheads thus established in the "man's world" were to be widened in the future. These women from the upper and middle classes were liberated from economic dependence on their families and confinements of the household; those of the working classes from the servitude of domestic work. The patriarchal dominance of European society was beginning to crack.

Political recognition was accorded women's wartime service to the state and their equal functional capacity by the extension of the franchise in the constitutions adopted by Germany and the new European states. Britain similarly granted the suffrage by the Representation of the People Act of February 6, 1918, to women who had attained thirty years of age, and in the following November qualified women to run for parliament.[10] The social behavior and dress of women altered concomitantly with these changes of status. Women and girls frequented the night clubs that had sprung up during the war, and single women dined in public restaurants without escorts. Women began to smoke in public, and their drinking increased. They took up the free use of cosmetics, the bobbing of hair, and the wearing of short skirts or slacks and uniforms at work. Their new social freedom encouraged freer sexual relations, with the consequences of increasing promiscuity and illegitimacy.[11]

Equalizing influences were thus breaking down rigid barriers between the classes and making for a mass society of more uniform and democratic character. While inflation and higher taxation operated in this direction, other factors were exerting a like effect. Under the system of rationing and state control of scarce commodities, everyone in the queues stood on an equal basis. Workers from all classes mingled together in the munitions factories. The prosecution of the war by any belligerent was an immense collective effort, and the collectivist drive toward greater community life received expression in an unceasing round of meetings and group activities concerned with refugees, charity, recruiting, articles for the soldiers, the sale of war bonds, and the singing of war songs.[12]

The diffusion of education and the advent of mass amusements contributed to the erasing of social differences. The war was an educational experience for the men who went to work in new industries, the peasants who came to the cities to work in new factories, the women and girls who left their homes for war work and war activities, and those who entered the armed services. The war was a stern schoolmaster in teaching the value of mass education in the competition of nations. Steps were taken consequently to found a thorough system of public education in the new eastern states and to remedy defects in the systems of western Europe. The British Educational Act of 1918, for example, established universal education for the young until fourteen years of age and further schooling thereafter for the unprovided.

10. Marwick, *Deluge*, 87–105, 278, 293; C. S. Peel (Mrs.), *How We Lived Then, 1914–1918* (London, 1929), 105–37, 171–72; Caroline E. Playne, *Britain Holds On, 1917, 1918* (London, 1933), 222; Michael MacDonagh, *In London during the War* (London, 1935), 323; Vivian Ogilvie, *Our Times* (London, 1953), 213.
11. Peel, *How We Lived Then*, 61, 66, 70; Marwick, *Deluge*, 105–13.
12. MacDonagh, *In London during the War*, 269; Peel, *How We Lived Then*, 72–73, 83–85, 116; Marwick, *Deluge*, 147–48.

Amusements were democratized in this period, above all by the movies. The movies became not only the poor man's theater but the theater of youth and in some measure of everybody else. In similar fashion radio (beginning commercially after its use during the war) was in time to spread until it entered most homes.

The changes in dress were also narrowing the gap between classes. In the blockaded lands the dearth of new fabrics reduced the classes generally to wearing old clothes. In the western countries upper-class women as a whole vested themselves in more practical and simple garments, while workers in the factories and government girls spent their higher pay freely to dress well. Among men, top hats and wing collars fell out of custom on the upper side at the time working men were wearing middle-class clothes outside their jobs.[13]

2. THE NEW INTERNATIONAL ORDER

The new international order was fashioned not simply by the peace settlement at the end of the war but by the peace settlement and the war. The settlement was a complex body of arrangements that defined and legalized the changes in the international state system generated by the war. The settlement comprised chiefly the treaties signed by the Allies with Germany at Versailles on June 28, 1919, with Austria at St. Germain on September 10, 1919, with Bulgaria at Neuilly on November 27, 1919, with Turkey at Sèvres on August 10, 1920, and again at Lausanne on July 24, 1923; the treaties between Soviet Russia and the four Baltic states and Poland recognizing their sovereignty and boundaries; the treaty of Rapallo concluded by Italy and Yugoslavia on November 12, 1920, yielding Fiume effectively to Italy; the expulsion of the Italians by the Albanians in August 1920; and the minority treaties and commitments of the states of eastern Europe with the Allies.

When the peace conference met, war and revolution had already effected the most radical metamorphosis of the European state system in modern times. The Russian and German empires had been overthrown; the territorial empires of the Dual Monarchy and the Ottoman state had been completely extinguished. There had risen a new Europe, consisting of twenty-seven established and emergent states. The Pentarchy of the five

13. Peel, *How We Lived Then,* 52, 67, 118; Ogilvie, *Our Times,* 77, 81–85; Playne, *Britain Holds On,* 240–41, 329.

great powers had vanished and with it the classical balance of power in Europe. America had entered European affairs under Wilson's leadership to play a military, political, and economic role of decisive importance and was exerting a primacy throughout the world.

The crisis of Europe continued, though the world war had ended. The chaotic conditions arising from economic debility and the national and revolutionary struggles exposed Europe to the spread of an expansive Bolshevism. The war had spawned not only revolution but also intense ideological warfare among Bolshevism, the nationalist, conservative right, and the liberal democratic principles of Wilsonism. The hard-line right desired to impose a tough peace that would make war pay and thereby pacify the left without surrendering all the privileges of the old order. They saw a liberal peace strengthening the drive for reform at home. The moderate center of Wilsonism, supported by liberals, bourgeois Radicals, labor, and moderate socialists, combated both the counterrevolutionary tendencies and old diplomacy of the right and Bolshevism on the extreme left. The conservative forces were strengthened by the upsurge of passions against Germany in the Entente countries when victory was attained and by the swing to the right in the American election of November 1918 and the Khaki election in Britain.[14]

The foremost tasks of the peace conference were to liquidate the war and to devise arrangements for the maintenance of peace and stability in the future. The delegations had to consider a means of equilibrium to replace the Pentarchy. Germany lay like a plastic mass before the conference. If that body was to realize its largest potential, it should deal constructively with the problem of Germany's future position in Europe and the problem of French security in relation to each other.[15] The ever-present ghost of Moscow challenged the conference to blaze a trail to a stable relation between the west and revolutionary Russia. The decisions reached at Paris would inescapably go far to fix the character and degree of America's continuing participation in European affairs. From the first the conference confronted the need for a European recovery program.

The awesome difficulties of achieving a peace were apparent from the many unsuccessful attempts since the outbreak of the war. On August 4,

14. Mayer, *Politics and Diplomacy of Peacemaking,* 18–30 passim.
15. See Harold I. Nelson, *Land and Power* (London, 1963), 198; Etienne Mantoux, *The Carthaginian Peace* (London, 1946), 21.

1914, Wilson tendered an offer of mediation to the warring powers.[16]
Both Bryan and Colonel House pursued efforts at mediation during the
fall of 1914.[17] House conducted a peace mission to Europe in 1915 and
another in 1916.[18] On the initiative of Bethmann Hollweg, the Central
Powers made an appeal for peace on December 12, 1916,[19] which was
followed by Wilson's peace note of December 18 to all the belligerents.[20]
This peace effort of Wilson was supported by Swiss and Scandinavian
notes and by parallel moves of the Vatican. The joint Allied note of
January 10, 1917, in reply to Wilson outlined victors' terms of peace and
affirmed the responsibility of the Central Powers for the war.[21] Wilson's
speech of January 22 on peace without victory promoted the prompt
conclusion of peace on the basis of negotiations between equal parties.

The peace moves of 1917–18 were mostly secret overtures conducted
by confidential agents. Those involving Austria included the initiative
undertaken through the mediation of Prince Sixte of Bourbon Parma,
brother of the Empress Zita of the Dual Empire, from January to May
1917,[22] French and British feelers extended in 1917 through intermediaries to the Austrian government, and the talks held at Geneva in December
between General Smuts and Count Albert Mensdorff, former Austrian
ambassador to Britain. Smuts discussed Allied terms for a separate peace;

16. Link, *Struggle for Neutrality,* 191–92.

17. On Bryan's action, see May, *World War and American Isolation,* 73–74; Baker, *Wood-row Wilson,* 5: 279–83.

18. On the genesis, conduct, and significance of House's peace venture of 1916—the more important of the two—see the references cited above, p. 251, n. 41.

19. Wolfgang Steglich, *Bündnissicherung oder Verständigungsfrieden* (Göttingen, 1958), 22–57, 67–140, 181. Steglich devotes most of this work to the preparation, issuance, and aftermath of the peace note of the Central Powers; it is the best study of the peace action. See also Birnbaum, *Peace Moves and U-Boat Warfare,* 192; American chargé (Grew) to secretary of state, November 22, 1916, and December 21, 1916, *Foreign Relations,* 1916, suppl., 69, 137. The text of the German note is available among other places in *Official German Documents,* 2: 1000–01.

20. See above, p. 251.

21. See above, p. 408. For the text of the Allied note: American ambassador in France (Sharp) to secretary of state, January 10, 1917, *Foreign Relations,* 1917, suppl. 1, 6–8.

22. The authoritative work on the subject is Wolfgang Steglich's *Die Friedenspolitik der Mittelmächte 1917–18,* vol. 1 (Wiesbaden, 1964), 15–58. A brief discussion of relevant literature and representative points of view regarding the peace bid is found in Robert A. Kann, *Die Sixtusaffäre und die geheimen Friedensverhandlungen Österreich-Ungarns im Ersten Welt-krieg* (Vienna, 1966). Kann reproduces Czernin's own notes on the affair and analyzes the weakness of this kind of secret diplomacy. Emperor Karl's letters involved in the Austrian move are given in *Ursachen und Folgen,* 2: 89–91. On the part of the Allies in the affair: Lloyd George, *War Memoirs,* 4: 1899–2035; Thomas Jones, *Lloyd George* (Cambridge, Mass., 1951), 127–28.

Mensdorff made clear that Austria would consider only a general peace.[23]

Germany's secret approaches in 1917 were made chiefly through Belgian confidants, the Spanish minister at Brussels, the Marquis de Villalobar, and the Danish king. Publicly, the Reichstag resolution of July 19 declared for a peace of understanding and lasting reconciliation between nations.[24] Pope Benedict XV addressed to the warring states peace notes dated August 1, proposing papal mediation to no avail.[25]

The rising sentiment among the Allies for peace was manifested in Lord Henry Lansdowne's public letter of November 29, 1917, calling for a negotiated peace and an Allied declaration of peace aims. Before this, the Soviet resolution of November 8 appealed "to all warring peoples and their governments [that they] begin immediately negotiations for a just and democratic peace."[26] Both the Soviet government and the Central Powers invited the Allies to take part in the peace parleys between them. On December 16 British Labor released its peace proposals. Lloyd George, induced by these pressures, gave his speech of January 5, 1918, on war aims.[27]

The public statements on peace terms attained the largest scope and highest moral force in Wilson's address of January 8, 1918, on the Fourteen Points.[28] These statements of Lloyd George and Wilson prompted Chancellor Hertling of Germany and the Austrian foreign minister Czer-

23. The intricacies of these soundings can be followed in Steglich, *Die Friedenspolitik der Mittelmächte*, 146–69 passim, 222–25, 248–63; Richard Fester, *Die politischen Kämpfe um den Frieden (1916–1918) und das Deutschtum* (Munich, 1938), 108–17, 135–41. The report of Smuts on the talks is published in full text in Lloyd George, *War Memoirs*, 5: 2461–2480; for Mensdorff's reports of December 19 and 20 to Czernin, see *Ursachen und Folgen*, 2: 91–97, and two courier telegrams of December 20, Fester, *Die politischen Kämpfe um den Frieden*, 177–78.

24. The text of the resolution is in *Ursachen und Folgen*, 2: 37–38. The British reception of the resolution is reported in Lloyd George, *War Memoirs*, 4: 2044–54, and Kent Forster, *The Failures of Peace* (Washington, 1941), 83. Its repercussions among the German nationalists, who regarded the resolution as a stab in the back, is recounted in Fester, *Die politischen Kämpfe um den Frieden*, 79–107.

25. On the papal peace moves as a whole, see Steglich, *Die Friedenspolitik der Mittelmächte*, 118–46, 169–206; Fridrich Engel-Jánosi, *Österreich und der Vatikan, 1846–1918*, 2 vols. (Graz, 1958–60), 2: 275–324; and the collection of documents in Wolfgang Steglich, ed., *Der Friedensappell Papst Benedikts XV. vom 1. August 1917 und die Mittelmächte* (Wiesbaden, 1970).

26. See above, p. 361.

27. See above, p. 410. Martin, *Peace without Victory*, 146–57.

28. On the genesis and historical role of the statement: Seymour, *American Diplomacy during the World War*, 279–84, 290–91; Seymour, *Intimate Papers*, 3: 316–43; Martin, *Peace without Victory*, 161–62.

nin to answer on January 24. Hertling's speech constituted a comprehensive formulation of Germany's position on peace and a further overture to the British, following Kühlmann's repeated efforts, toward getting negotiations started.[29]

Wilson replied to both pronouncements with his speech of February 11, enunciating the Four Principles for peace negotiations. This speech amplified the program of the Fourteen Points, and the process of its public development was completed with the address of July 4, 1918, on the Five Ends and that of September 27 on the Five Particulars of peace negotiations. The Fourteen Points and these speeches together formed the platform on which Wilson took up the leadership of the liberal forces throughout the west seeking a new order of world affairs and a reasonable peace.[30]

The peace flutters of the Central Powers continued into the early months of 1918. Kühlmann attempted further, apparently until April, to make contact with the west, and Czernin sent out feelers toward Wilson. Czernin's address of January 24 responded to Wilson's statement of the Fourteen Points with the purpose of starting an exchange that would enable the United States and Austria to mediate peace discussions between the two coalitions. Czernin continued his initiative through a message of February 17 for Wilson addressed to the president's Four Principles.[31] Talks were also under way in Switzerland between the Austrian businessman Julius Meinl at one time and the liberal professor of law Heinrich Lammasch at another and the American Protestant minister George David Herron, a one-time professor who was in contact with Wilson and American diplomatic representatives (November 1917–February 1918).[32]

The reasons are instructive for the failure of this many-sided search for peace. A line of secret communication through confidential intermediaries would frequently break down. Coordination was lacking between channels of approach and between parties involved for each coalition. Each side revealed an inability at times to agree on the procedure or substance affecting peace discussions. Each coalition endeavored to break up the opposing one by concluding a separate peace with one of its members.

29. See Steglich, *Die Friedenspolitik der Mittelmächte,* 365–72; Lloyd George, *War Memoirs,* 5: 2492–95; Hans W. Gatzke, *Germany's Drive to the West* (Baltimore, 1950), 256–57.

30. Seth P. Tillman, *Anglo-American Relations at the Peace Conference* (Princeton, 1961), 28–36.

31. The text of Czernin's message is in *Ursachen und Folgen,* 2: 97–99.

32. Heinrich Benedikt, *Die Friedensaktion der Meinlgruppe 1917–18* (Graz, 1962), 192–212, 230–45; Seymour, *Intimate Papers,* 3: 372–77.

Austria drew back when bids were pointed toward a separate peace. The Allies sniffed German approaches with suspicion in the fear that Germany was intent on splitting the Entente or playing the Allied powers off against one another.

The unbridgeable gulf appeared in a mutual unwillingness to accept a compromise satisfactory to the other side on territorial and political issues. The Germans held back from announcing any acceptable position on the crucial questions of Belgium and Alsace-Lorraine. The Allies insisted on the destruction of German militarism, whatever that meant. The Allies' note of December 30, 1916, in answer to the peace offer of the Central Powers was tantamount to a declaration of continued war until victory.

The statements of both coalitions contained provocative allegations about responsibility for the war, presaging a central difference at Versailles. Also suggestive of Versailles, the Allies would receive German terms only in written form instead of meeting for discussions of equal parties.

The Paris conference was thus called on to do what had not been possible during the war. The peacemakers, unlike those of Vienna in 1814-15, were not masters of Europe but subject to many influences that they could not escape or control. Overhanging the conference, constantly exerting its force, was the three-cornered ideological and political conflict. The Big Four were more occupied with the issue of Bolshevik Russia than with any other.[33]

Domestic politics intervened in the operation of the diplomatic process. The Republican victories in the election of 1918 turned Wilson into a lame duck whose crippled position was fully recognized by Europe's rightist exponents of a tough peace. The Khaki election of Britain made Lloyd George captive to a parliamentary coalition dominated by Bonar Law's conservative Unionists. Clemenceau and Orlando had to brace themselves against the high winds of an avenging nationalism demanding satisfaction.[34]

In contrast to the Vienna congress, public opinion was the most controlling force at Paris. The end of the war celebrated the universal participation of the masses in politics, and the diplomacy of democracy required respect for the opinion of this public. The opinion was dominated by the emotions of hate and revenge toward the former enemies and inflated

33. Mayer, *Politics and Diplomacy of Peacemaking*, 285.
34. The interaction of domestic politics and the work of the Paris conference is elaborated at length in Mayer's study of peacemaking.

expectations about the new world order to be created by the conference. Wartime propaganda had stirred up a frenzy of passions against the Germans, and now the peacemakers were its prisoners.[35] A large part of the French public demanded the Rhine boundary, and the British public and parliament clamored for excessive reparations.[36] If the experts could have been sealed off from these political pressures in drafting the treaty of Versailles, it would doubtless have been a more constructive instrument.[37] The pressure of time was felt both from the desire of the public in Allied countries to return to normal conditions and from the race with anarchy and Bolshevism for the survival of a democratic Europe.[38]

The framework for the settlement of concrete issues derived from the previous pronouncements on war aims, peace notes, and the secret treaties of wartime. Each coalition entered into secret treaties in order to strengthen it by adding new members, by insuring unity against defection through a separate peace, or by obtaining greater military and naval support from a member. The commitments so made consolidated the coalition but limited the freedom of action to negotiate a general peace.[39]

The secret agreements of most significance for the Paris conference were the treaty of London of April 26, 1915, with Italy, the Sykes-Picot agreement of May 1916, the commitments to the Arabs, and the agreements between the Allies and Japan of February 1917. The treaty of London violated the principles of nationality and self-determination as concerned the German element in the South Tyrol and many Yugoslavs in Dalmatia. The Sykes-Picot agreement would partition most of the dying Ottoman Empire into spheres of control under Allied states, a region of Arab states divided into French and British zones of economic exploita-

35. Geoffrey Barraclough, "Das Britische Reich und der Frieden," in *Ideologie und Macht-politik 1919*, ed. Hellmuth Rossler (Göttingen, 1966), 76–77; Dickmann, "Die Kriegs-schuldfrage auf der Friedensconferenz von Paris," 9; Schwabe, *Deutsche Revolution und Wilson-Frieden*, 576.

36. M. Baumont, "Clemenceau und der Friede von Versailles," in *Ideologie und Macht-politik*, 35; Tillman, *Anglo-American Relations at the Peace Conference*, 229, 259.

37. On this point Harold Nicholson, a participant at Paris, wrote: "Had the Treaty of Peace been drafted by the American experts it would have been one of the wisest as well as the most scientific and durable documents ever devised." See his *Peacemaking, 1919* (1933; London, 1945), 22.

38. John M. Thompson, *Russia, Bolshevism, and the Versailles Peace* (Princeton, 1966), 389–95.

39. This antithesis relating to the German peace offer of December 1916 is the theme of the germinal work by Steglich, *Bündnissicherung oder Verständigungsfrieden*.

tion, and a Palestine under international administration.[40] The British commitments to Arab independence were strengthened by the Anglo-French declaration of November 7, 1918, which pledged the formation of national governments and administrations in the Arab lands through self-determination.[41]

The agreements with Japan obligated Britain and France to support Japanese claims to the German rights in Shantung and to the German islands of the Pacific north of the equator. Japan had fortified its claims in Shantung by imposing on China the Twenty-One Demands of 1915, which also permitted Japan economic concessions and political domination elsewhere in China. Japan's exchange of notes with China on September 24, 1918, obtained police, administrative, and railway privileges in Shantung and railway concessions in Manchuria and Mongolia.[42]

The most binding engagement was the prearmistice agreement. This constituted a contract not only between Germany and the Entente victors but also among the Allied powers and the United States to negotiate a peace based on the Fourteen Points and related statements of Wilson.[43] These Wilsonian principles, representing for the most part the common program of the Anglo-American liberal heritage, held out the promise of Anglo-American cooperation in the framing of the peace. The antithesis of this program was embodied in the concepts of Carthaginian nationalism and "realist" diplomacy. The pivotal issue at Paris was the extent to which one would prevail against the other.

The delegations met in plenary conference at Paris on January 18, 1919, to agree on terms among themselves before dealing with the defeated Central Powers. The process proved so difficult and time-consuming that the preliminary conference turned into the final peace conference. The Allies imposed their agreed terms without permitting the negotiation at

40. Mansfield, *Ottoman Empire and Its Successors*, 44–45; Zeman, *Diplomatic History of the First World War*, 329–33; Smith, *Russian Struggle for Power*, 358–72; Grey, *Twenty-Five Years*, 2: 236–37.

41. A summary of the Allied engagements applying to the disposition of the remains of the Ottoman Empire is given in Conrad Oehlrich, "Die Friedensregelungen für die türkischen und arabischen Gebiete nach dem Ersten Weltkrieg," in *Ideologie und Machtpolitik*, 173–77.

42. Paul Birdsall, *Versailles Twenty Years After* (New York, 1941), 83–86.

43. Ibid., 10, 25; Tillman, *Anglo-American Relations at the Paris Peace Conference*, 52; Schwabe, *Deutsche Revolution und Wilson-Frieden*, 221–22; Peter Krüger, "Die Reparationen und das Scheitern einer deutschen Verständigungspolitik auf der pariser Friedenskonferenz im Jahre 1919," *Historische Zeitschrift* 221 (1975): 327.

the conference table of an agreement with the former enemy states or accepting more than a few slight changes suggested by them. The contents of the treaties evolved from the interaction of three approaches among the Allied delegations: a changed attitude toward war in the history of peace-making; the French concentration on security in terms of traditional power arrangements; and Anglo-American conceptions of a liberal society.

For the first time in history the general opinion of civilized mankind had moved from regarding war as an acceptable means of arbitrament between nations to viewing it with moral condemnation. Aggression and militarism had come under the same moral approach. From this standpoint the states-men at Paris asserted the sole responsibility of Germany and its allies for the war and in Article 231 of the treaty of Versailles required Germany to accept this responsibility. Although the assertion was of Germany's moral responsibility, there was at Paris a tendency, in spite of American jurists and especially with the French, to consider it a statement of criminal action and legal responsibility and to frame a punitive peace on this judgment rather than to base the peace on the prearmistice agreement. No part of the treaty aroused among the Germans such immoderate passion or enduring bitterness. Similarly proceeding in an *ex post facto* manner, the victor powers charged William II, and others to be indicated later, with war crimes, whether moral or legal, for judgment by special tribunals.[44]

The French pursuit of security and the Anglo-American desire for a European order based on self-determination and the avoidance of future Alsace-Lorraines collided in drafting the territorial terms. The dominant aim in the French government was to obtain security by breaking up the political and economic unity of Germany, as well as to increase wherever possible the size of Poland, Romania, and Czechoslovakia in building a balance with France against a reduced Germany, a barrier against German penetration in Russia, and a cordon against Russian Bolshevism.

The compromise worked out kept the Rhineland attached to Germany while demilitarizing it and placing the area under military occupation for fifteen years; transferred Alsace-Lorraine and the coal mines of the Saar

44. See especially Dickmann, "Die Kriegsschuldfrage auf der Friedenskonferenz." This is an enlightening inquiry into the genesis of the war-guilt charge and an impartial examina-tion of the subject from the standpoint of international law and its development. Also Winfried Baumgart, "Brest-Litovsk und Versailles," *Historische Zeitschrift* 210 (1970): 613–14; Hellmuth Rossler, "Deutschland und Versailles," in *Ideologie und Machtpolitik*, 222. And the immediate protest of the German delegation in its note of May 13, 1919, in Luchau, *German Delegation at the Peace Conference*, 241–42.

district to France; provided for determining the status of the Saar otherwise by plebiscite after it had been administered for fifteen years, or a
priorly reduced period, by a commission responsible to the League of
Nations; created a Free City of Danzig; and ceded to the restored Poland
the bulk of West Prussia and Posen along with border areas of Silesia and
a portion of Upper Silesia. A prohibition was laid on the union of Germany with German Austria. Altogether, Germany lost about 14–15 percent of its productive capacity.[45] Linked with the territorial compromise
in the west were treaties of guarantee between France and Britain and
France and the United States.[46]

Germany was required to carry out unilateral disarmament by giving up
its old navy and army for small military and naval establishments, to
surrender its colonies, and to submit to economic disabilities. The economic terms obliged Germany to renounce its merchant marine, German
property in Allied countries, and state and private assets in the ceded
territories. The economic warfare of the war period was continued
through maintenance of the blockade for seven months after the armistice
and through the denial of most-favored-nation treatment while obligating
Germany to grant it to the Allies. The reparations settlement seemed to
the Germans in being coupled with the charge of responsibility for the war
to demand the recovery of war costs beyond the reparation of damages
to civilians specified in the prearmistice agreement. The total sum demanded was so high that no accommodation could be reached with the
American stand for either a fixed sum or a fixed period of payment within
Germany's financial capacity. The final amount was left to be determined
in the future by a reparations commission of wide powers.

Despite the conflict over reparations the British and Americans cooperated notably in preparing the Covenant of the League of Nations, which
was incorporated into the peace treaties. The Covenant embodied the
common conceptions and purposes of the Americans and British.[47]

The treaties with Austria, Hungary, Bulgaria, and Turkey determined
the boundaries of those states and contained restraints and punitive measures corresponding to those of the treaty of Versailles. Austria was cut
down to a small state, separated from the Austrian Germans of the Sude-

45. Mantoux, *Carthaginian Peace*, 69–70.
46. Nelson, *Land and Power*, which offers a comprehensive treatment of the territorial
settlement with Germany.
47. Tillman, *Anglo-American Relations at the Paris Peace Conference*, 299–300, 404–05.

tenland and the South Tyrol, and prohibited from uniting with Germany. The truncated state of Hungary remained a boiling cauldron of wounded nationalism and passionate irredentism over the lost Hungarians in Transylvania. Bulgaria was punished and Greece rewarded, against the strong opposition of Wilson, by the cession of western Thrace to the latter.

The treaty of Sèvres carved up the remains of the Ottoman Empire. This instrument and an associated tripartite agreement among Britain, France, and Italy of the same date ceded eastern Thrace and certain Aegean islands to Greece. By Sèvres the Straits were neutralized under an international commission; in Asia Minor, Kurdistan was recognized as autonomous and Armenia as independent, while spheres of influence or control were assigned to Greece, Italy, and France. Sèvres recognized the independent state of the Hejaz, as well as the independence of Syria (or Syria-Lebanon), Mesopotamia (Iraq), and Palestine (or Palestine-Transjordan) subject to the establishment of mandates by the League. The arrangements in Africa sanctioned the British protectorates over Egypt and the Sudan and the French protectorates of Morocco and Tunis, while confirming the dominion of Italy over Libya and the Dodecanese islands. Britain, the mandatory for Palestine, assumed responsibility for the establishment of a Jewish National Home. The regime of capitulations was restored.[48]

The draconian dispositions in Asia Minor and Constantinople provoked a national uprising of the Turks, led by Mustapha Kemal. The intruding powers were driven out of Asia Minor, and the dictated peace rejected by force of arms. Kemal rewrote Sèvres in the treaty of Lausanne, which created a sovereign national state essentially in all the territory of Anatolia. The regime over the Straits and the regime of capitulations were abolished.[49]

Sèvres was a product of nineteenth-century imperialism, Lausanne a harbinger of the emancipation of the non-European world from unequal treatment. By overthrowing Sèvres, Kemal had won a historical victory over the European powers. Asians celebrated Turkey's triumph as far as China; it stimulated nationalist movements in Asia and universally the desire for independence from the colonial powers. The institution of

48. J. C. Hurewitz, ed., *Diplomacy in the Near and Middle East: A Documentary Record,* 2 vols. (Princeton, 1956), 2: 81–89; Oehlrich, "Die Friedensregelungen für die türkischen und arabischen Gebiete," 178.

49. Hurewitz, *Diplomacy in the Near and Middle East,* 119–27; Bernard Lewis, *The Emergence of Modern Turkey,* 2d ed. (London, 1968), 247–55.

mandates for the former German possessions in Africa and the Pacific and for the Arab lands of the Middle East formerly belonging to the Ottoman Empire was more than a fig leaf for the appropriation of these areas by the victor powers. The mandate system introduced the principle of stewardship under the supervision of the League and, casting an implicit condemnation of colonial status, held out the ideal of ultimate independence.[50]

Wilson tried to shield China against the imperialist designs of Japan, supported by the latter's secret agreements of the war period and actual physical possession of the Shantung peninsula. The best that Wilson could salvage from this critical controversy was a separate Japanese engagement affirming policy to be the restoration of the Shantung peninsula in full sovereignty to China while Japan retained economic privileges. The treaty of Versailles stipulated the surrender to Japan of German rights in Shantung. China in outrage refused to sign the treaty. There was, however, no practical alternative for Wilson to pursue, and in 1922 Japan lived up to its pledge with the restoration of Shantung.[51]

In dropping out of the war, revolutionary Russia dropped out of any European concert. The peace conference inevitably became deeply involved in the question of how to deal with the Bolshevik state. A number of unsuccessful attempts were made to solve the inscrutable problem: an undertaking to mediate between the warring groups in Russia on the island of Prinkipo; the mission of William C. Bullitt, a member of the American delegation, to Moscow to explore the possibilities of accommodation with the Soviet regime; the project hatched by Hoover to trade a relief program for termination of the civil war; the quixotic venture of obtaining Alexander Kolchak's paper assurances to introduce democratic government if the Whites won.[52]

When these initiatives failed, the treatment of the Russian problem drifted into a series of unplanned half-measures in resistance to the Soviet revolution: the continued blockade of Bolshevik Russia, a limited intervention of military forces, limited assistance to anti-Bolshevik groups,

50. See Barraclough's comments on Oehlrich's paper in *Ideologie und Machtpolitik,* 183–84; Penrose, *Revolution in International Relations,* 64; Smith, *Great Departure,* 131.
51. Birdsall, *Versailles Twenty Years After,* 83–115; Tillman, *Anglo-American Relations at the Peace Conference,* 33–43; Smith, *Great Departure,* 165–73.
52. George F. Kennan, *Russia and the West under Lenin and Stalin* (Boston, 1960), 125–46; Mayer, *Politics and Diplomacy of Peacemaking,* 417–87.

extension of military aid, relief, and economic assistance to the nationalities in the western borderlands seeking to establish independent states, and creation of a cordon sanitaire in the eastern zone. In the eyes of the Kremlin, the Paris conference had turned into an anti-Bolshevik concert. A legacy of suspicion and distrust settled down on Soviet relations with the west.

The condemnation of Wilson and Versailles had begun before the conference had finished. Thereafter the participants at Paris, John Maynard Keynes and Harold Nicolson, led the chorus of attack from disillusioned liberalism.[53] Nor was the Paris settlement acceptable to Germany, France, Italy, Poland, the United States, Japan (for not recognizing the equality of races), China, and Russia. The Paris decisions overturned the cabinets of Scheidemann in Germany, Clemenceau in France, and Orlando in Italy. Coalition peacemaking was even more difficult than coalition warfare.

The heart of the trouble was the revolution in Europe. As has been emphasized, the war was a mother revolution giving birth to a whole progeny of revolutions. The war had destroyed the old structure of Europe, and no consensus existed about its replacement. Four proposed solutions had competed for meeting the revolutionary situation: the concept of Mitteleuropa, Leninism, Wilsonism, and nationalist power politics. Mitteleuropa had fallen with the defeat of Germany. Revolutionary Russia was excluded from the Paris conference but not the specter of Bolshevism.

The forces of Wilsonism were never free to write a peace of their own making. They remained in contention with the forces of traditionalism, and a peace had to be hammered out with compromises between the two if there was to be any peace at all seemingly in time to save the world from utter ruin. It was a choice between a compromise peace and no peace at all, rather than between a Wilsonian and a traditionalist peace.

Even though the Paris treaties did not represent a purely Wilsonian peace, the settlement was impressed with Wilsonian features, or the features of Anglo-American liberal democracy. The reconstruction of Europe proceeded so far according to the principles of self-determination and nationality that the territorial order thus established continues today in fundamental structure. The founding of the League of Nations, regardless

53. In Keynes's *The Economic Consequences of the Peace* (London, 1919) and Nicolson's *Peacemaking, 1919.*

of its weaknesses, marked an epochal step in the supranational organization of the world. Plebiscites and minority treaties were attempts to protect the interests of lesser ethnic groups in Europe; the mandates system to assist the advance of non-European peoples toward independence.[54] In addition, the triumph of the democratic revolution that belonged to the total European settlement had been promoted by Wilson during the war and in the prearmistice agreement.[55] Without the Wilson program the shape of Europe in 1920 would have been different. Unlike the arrangements after the Second World War, this peace did not authorize mass expulsion of minorities from eastern European states or destroy German unity by partition.

The lesson of the interwar period is clear that the traditionalist plan of the French for peace was illusory and that the "higher realism" belonged to Wilsonian principles.[56] Germany, though defeated, still possessed the potential of a semisuperpower, which could not be eliminated or permanently put down by Versailles. Unless the Anglo-American powers were determined to join in compelling Germany's compliance by force, French supremacy on the continent linked with the eastern cordon was not sufficient to hold a resurgent Germany in check. Versailles, being provocative rather than draconian, had a part to play, but only a part, in preparing the ground for a nationalist resurgence in Germany.

A peace of the broadest vision would have avoided making Germany appear a pariah state in the eyes of the Germans and treated it even in defeat as an equal. The peace would have been framed to encourage the democratic forces in Weimar Germany. The settlement would have drawn in Germany's economic powerhouse, however battered it seemed at the moment, for the benefit of Europe's economic recovery. The victor powers, emphasizing a fresh start and concentrating on the good of Europe as a whole, could have asked Germany to join in a program of cooperation for the regeneration and growth of the European economy. This was not too far from the German counterproposals at Versailles.[57]

This solution might well have fostered the rise of an organized Euro-

54. See Ferdinand Czernin, *Versailles, 1919* (New York, 1964), 430.
55. Erwin Hölze, "Wilsons Friedensplan und seine Durchführung," in *Ideologie und Machtpolitik,* 16–17.
56. Link, *Higher Realism of Woodrow Wilson,* 137–39.
57. See Krüger, "Die Reparationen und das Scheitern einer deutschen Verständigungspolitik," 329–53, 372.

pean community and avoided the twenty years of economic stagnation Europe was condemned to undergo. Yet one has to face the realities whether domestic political currents and the frailties of the human perspective would have allowed so constructive a settlement without the experience of Europe's next generation. In the event it was Europe's fatal loss. The interwar period became a truce before a second cataclysm of war which in turn brought forth the need for Europe's consolidation if it was to exert its due weight in an age of superpowers.

3. THE WAR AND THE WESTERN MIND

The war made a profound and permanent impact on the western mind. Actors in the conflict, both individuals and governments, sensed a historical moment of singular importance. Memoirs, diaries, letters, poems, and novels of this perception have poured out from the participants in an unbroken stream. For the first time governments published official histories of land, sea, and air operations of war in many volumes. The Allies employed official artists on the Western Front to depict its scenes.

That the Indian summer of European civilization would vanish in the furnace of the war was borne home to men of the time. The Austrian liberal Redlich wrote in his diary on December 31, 1914, an obituary of the old Europe, commenting on the great force the war would exert on the psyche of the European peoples.[58] Hamilton, the Allied commander in the Gallipoli campaign, recorded in his personal chronicle that the "war will smash, pulverize, sweep into the dustbins of eternity the whole fabric of the old world."[59] Bethmann Hollweg's letter to Prince Max of January 17, 1918, characterized the war as "this most tremendous of all revolutions that has ever shaken the earth."[60]

The journey of the modern pilgrim through the war to the twentieth century proceeded from initial idealism and exaltation to a progressive disenchantment. At first the spirit of 1914—war enthusiasm, frenzied excitement, and patriotic fervor—welled up to the pitch of national intoxication. Germans spoke of the "exaltation of 1914," "Valhalla of national excitement," and "pathos of total identification" to describe the euphoric collectivism of war.[61] The pulpit everywhere became an altar of patrio-

58. *Das politische Tagebuch*, 1: 295.
59. *Gallipoli Diary*, 1: 125.
60. Zechlin, "Deutschland zwischen Kabinettskrieg und Wirtschaftskrieg," 356.
61. Schwabe, *Wissenschaft und Kriegsmoral*, 45.

tism; in Britain Westminster was converted into an oracle of propaganda. In Germany both the Protestant and Catholic churches, moved by "an ecstasy of nationalism," preached a war theology.[62]

The euphoria seized the streets, all classes, all professions and trades, all intellectual fields. Anatole France at seventy-eight was as eager to join the soldiers as was Isadora Duncan "all flame and fire."[63] The most powerful sources of this demoniac outburst of enthusiasm appeared to have been the feelings of national solidarity and belief in the agency of the war to regenerate a society considered by many critics to have grown corrupt and effete. As much as Romain Rolland deplored the catastrophe from his aerie in Switzerland above the passions of war, he could see in it "a scourge that chastizes the sins of Europe."[64]

There were intellectuals and men of the masses who rushed into the war for more personal reasons. Some sought adventure or flight from the empty routine of daily life—from the round of small responsibilities and "the prudence of private cares" (Rilke). Soldiers often went forth in quest of glory and the hero's deed or to answer the call of duty. Those who embraced the soldier's life like the Dying German Officer in Herbert Read's *The End of a War* and Julian Grenfell in his poem "Into Battle" "lived in the ecstasy of battle."[65] To a number the power to measure up to the grim test of combat conditions gave satisfaction. Others crusaded for the just cause.

Rupert Brooke, "the young Apollo, and golden-haired," found honor and nobleness returning to the earth. The poet glorified the war's sacrifice of youth as a way to personal redemption and purification:

> Now, God be thanked Who has matched us with His hour,
>   And caught our youth, and wakened us from sleeping,
> With hand made sure, clear eye, and sharpened power,
>   To turn, as swimmers into cleanness leaping,
> Glad from a world grown old and cold and weary . . .

In Anglo-Saxon countries, at least, Brooke caught the initial spirit of the wartime in a more representative way than any other war poet, and he was

---

62. Hammer, *Deutsche Kriegstheologie,* especially pp. 70, 74.
63. Roland M. Stromberg, "The Intellectuals and the Coming of War in 1914," *Journal of European Studies* 3 (1973): 111; Stengers, "July 1914," 106.
64. William Thomas Starr, *Romain Rolland and a World at War* (New York, 1956), 24.
65. Herbert Read, *The End of a War* (London, 1933), 12. Grenfell's poem is in Brian Gardner, *Up the Line to Death: The War Poets, 1914–1918,* rev. ed. (London, 1976), 34–35.

certainly more widely favored in the broad public as the poetic voice of
the war and its early idealism.[66]

Many others wrote "bardic verses" on these themes of the early period.
Rainer Maria Rilke was inspired in August 1914 to sing the god of war
in the Five Hymns. In mystic tones the poet told of "men in the grip of
something" and "the time speaking like a prophet." And again:

> And we?
> We melt together into one,
> Into a new creation to which he [the god of war]
>   gives life from death.
> Thus I exist no longer; my heart is beating
> With the beat of the heart of all . . .[67]

After the sacrificial holocausts at Verdun and the Somme the heroic
vision of war's glory gave way to the bitter disenchantment of the later
war years. The morning light of 1914 was followed by the night's despair
of 1916–17. The change of mentality was embodied in the literature and
art of the time. The nightmare of modern technological war evoked the
poetry of "the forlorn hope" and the passionate protest. Leading all the
other war poets of England in this "poetry of truth" were Siegfried
Sassoon, Wilfred Owen, and Isaac Rosenberg.

Sassoon on a convalescent leave experienced a personal crisis in which
he lost his faith in the war largely because of the humbug, the patriotic
lies, and the incomprehension of modern war that he encountered in
civilian life. From then on the officer made "war on the war" in poetry
of stabbing realism and powerful intensity. No poet surpassed Sassoon in
indicting the scourge of war with grisly and satiric pictures of the ravages
to which human beings were subjected on the Western Front.[68]

66 From Brooke's first War Sonnet, *The Poetical Works of Rupert Brooke*, ed. Geoffrey
Keynes, 2d ed. (London, 1970), 19. See Edmund Blunden, *War Poets, 1914–1918* (London,
1958), 17; John H. Johnston, *English Poetry of the First World War* (Princeton, 1964), 29;
Bernard Bergonzi, *Heroes' Twilight: A Study of the Literature of the Great War* (New York,
1966), 36–45.

67. The translation of this quotation is composite, following both Leishman and Wydenbruck with some modifications by this author. Rainer Maria Rilke, *Ausgewählte Werke*, ed.
Rilke-Archive, vol. 1, 3d ed. (Wiesbaden, 1948), 336, 338; *Rainer Maria Rilke: Poems 1906
to 1926*, trans. J. B. Leishman (Norfolk, Conn., 1957), 189; Nora Wydenbruck, *Rilke*
(London, 1949), 266.

68. Sassoon tells us of the personal crisis in the autobiographical novel *Memoirs of an
Infantry Officer*, 195, 256–98. His war poetry is in the *Collected Poems, 1908–1956* (London,
1961), 67–104. For critical appraisals: Bergonzi, *Heroes' Twilight*, 92–108; Johnston, *English*

Owen, the young poet-officer, dedicated himself to expressing "the truth untold." He came to realize that the church shared the mania of "the more hopeless war" at home. The poet then found "Christ in no man's land." His deep feelings of compassion moved him to write of "the greater love" among the foot soldiers whose sacrifice for one another he identified with Christ and the crucifixion: "Heart, you were never hot/ Nor large, nor full like hearts made great with shot." Indeed Owen defines the subject of his poems as "War, and the pity of War. The Poetry is in the Pity."[69]

In the poems "Greater Love" and "Strange Meeting" (between two dead and reconciled enemies), Owen reached his highest powers of poetic eloquence, rich sensuous imagery, original striking phrase, elegiac notes of haunting sadness, relating the concrete to the cosmic, and prophetic insight. He developed in maturity a style of his own, fully exploiting the technique of half-rhyme and fitting the form and poetic devices to the perception of his war experience. The poetry of passionate protest against the war achieved its most intense degree and greatest depth of meaning in the work of Owen. His poems are considered to have done more than the work of any other writer in the English language in changing the western view of war from the heroic attitude to a serious grasp of the realities of technological warfare. C. Day Lewis put this finest of the war poets together with T. S. Eliot and Gerard Manley Hopkins in being the poetic forebears of the Auden group of poets.[70]

Rosenberg, a private soldier and a *déraciné* of Jewish, urban, and working-class origins, brought to bear in his apprehension of the life at the front a cultural breadth and poetic development allowing a detachment not characteristic of the antiwar poetry. He avoided the aggressive, satirical realism of Sassoon and comprehended the war in more complex terms than Owen's pity. Like Owen, Rosenberg conveys the war's pathos and

Poetry of the First World War, 71–112; Arthur E. Lane, *An Adequate Response: The War Poetry of Wilfred Owen and Siegfried Sassoon* (Detroit, 1972), 87–120.

69. Wilfred Owen, *Collected Letters,* ed. Harold Owen and John Bell (London, 1962), 461, 562–71, 580. Wilfred Owen, *Collected Poems,* ed. with an Introduction by C. Day Lewis (Norfolk, Conn., 1964), 31, 39, 41.

70. For critical analysis of his poetry and assessment of Owen as a poet, see the outstanding study by D.S.R. Welland, *Wilfred Owen* (London, 1960), especially pp. 136–43; Lewis, Introduction to Owen's *Collected Poems,* 11–28; Bergonzi, *Heroes' Twilight,* 121–35; Johnston, *English Poetry of the First World War,* 155–209; Blunden, *War Poets,* 32–35; Lane, *Adequate Response,* 120–64.

tragedy for all mankind in a spirit of human tenderness. In his ultimate utterance, "Dead Man's Dump," the poet exhibits the transcendent power to communicate his vision by means of images and symbols. This work belongs with Owen's "Strange Meeting" to the two best poems in English to come out of the war.[71]

The changing attitude toward war manifested in poetry was paralleled in war fiction. Henri Barbusse's *Le Feu (Under Fire)*, published in France in 1916, was the most representative and influential novel of antiwar protest. This story, based on the author's ordeal at Verdun, turns into a fierce indictment of war and militarism. The book relates the grimmest details of the war's horrors with graphic realism and is widely inclusive of the themes subsequently common to the antiwar literature. Corresponding in the depiction of the madness of modern war were the German version of Verdun by Fritz von Unruh, *Der Opfergang (The Way of Sacrifice)* and the book by the Austro-Hungarian Andreas Latzko, *Menschen im Krieg (Men in War)*.[72]

Expressions in prose of the British attitude appeared in C. E. Montague's *Disenchantment* and letters of fallen soldiers. Montague, an older volunteer, produced a distinguished chronicle of the growing disillusionment of the front soldiers toward the war, its conduct, and the world emerging from the conflict.[73] Many of the published letters of the soldiers are in the vein of revulsion against the criminal folly of the war, its human degradation, the passion for killing, the lies of press and politicians, and the tremendous waste "of fine young bodies." The letters are noteworthy for avoiding generally expressions of hate or vengeance toward the enemy. They reveal the moral support deriving from the sense of brotherhood among the men in the fighting unit and from the hope of ending war through this war.[74]

Like the war poets and novelists, the British artists Paul Nash and C.R.W. Nevinson and some of the German Expressionists felt a compul-

71. For "Dead Man's Dump" and Rosenberg's other war poems: *The Collected Poems of Isaac Rosenberg*, ed. Gordon Bottomley and Denys Harding (London, 1949), 69–91. Critical assessments may be found in Johnston, *English Poetry of the First World War*, 211–49; Bergonzi, *Heroes' Twilight*, 109–21; Jean Liddiard, *Isaac Rosenberg* (London, 1975).

72. Fritz von Unruh, *Der Opfergang* (Frankfurt, 1919); Andreas Latzko, *Menschen im Krieg* (Zurich, 1918). See Eugene Lohre, *Armageddon: The World War in Literature* (New York, 1930), 7; William K. Pfeiler, *War and the German Mind* (New York, 1941), 91–96, 98–107.

73. C. E. Montague, *Disenchantment* (London, 1922).

74. Laurence Housman, *War Letters of Fallen Englishmen* (London, 1930).

sion to draw and paint the shocking reality of modern war. Though engaged as an official British artist, Nash was soon inspired with a sense of mission akin to Owen's in the will to paint the "bitter truth" of the "unspeakable, godless, hopeless" graveyard at the front.[75] Nevinson set out to make the war scenes give the impression that the soldiers were the mere creatures of the war machines or the forlorn victims of a vast mechanism.[76] Their works, particularly Nash's *We Are Making a New World, The Menin Road,* and *Year of Our Lord, 1917* and Nevinson's *The Mitrailleuse, La Patrie,* and *The Road from Arras to Bapaume,* picture in somber tones and stark forms the desolation wrought by technological warfare.

In Germany, the Berlin Secession, including such artists as Lovis Corinth, Emil Pottner, A. E. Herstein, Erich Büttner, and Hugo Krayn, published in 1915 a portfolio of four lithographs every two weeks under the title *Krieg und Kunst (War and Art).* The entire series of forty-eight lithographs pictured the barbarization incident to the war and its destructive consequences for European civilization.[77] During Oskar Kokoschka's long struggle to recuperate from nearly mortal wounds and from mental breakdown incurred in military service, he made two illegal antiwar lithographs and, before entering the army, painted the *Knight Errant* (1915). This famous portrait of himself as a prone knight in armor suspended above a storm-struck sea and a strange, unearthly landscape can be interpreted as a prophecy of his own fate on the battlefield, a vision of resignation before the forces of life and death confronting the artist, and a symbolic representation of man's destiny.[78] His army service caused the sensitive painter Ernst Ludwig Kirchner to suffer a complete physical and mental collapse. He gave vent to his bitter antimilitary reaction in the paintings *Soldiers in the Shower Room* (1915) and *Self-Portrait as Soldier* (1915).[79]

Under the decisive impact of the war experience, Otto Dix and George Grosz became social activists, and their work developed from Futurist semi-abstract stylized forms toward a more realistic art. Dix, wounded several times during his four years of combat service, could not exorcise

75. Paul Nash, *Outline* (London, 1949), 211.

76. C.R.W. Nevinson, *Pain and Prejudice* (London, 1937), 80, 87.

77. On the German Expressionists and the war, see Bernard Myers, *The German Expressionists* (New York, n. d.); Peter Selz, *German Expressionist Painting* (Berkeley, 1957).

78. J. P. Hodin, *Oskar Kokoschka: The Artist and His Time* (Greenwich, Conn., 1966); Edith Hoffmann, *Kokoschka: Life and Work* (London, 1947).

79. See the passages on Kirchner in Selz, *German Expressionist Painting.*

the grip of this nightmare until he recorded his impressions in the Futurist drawings of the war years, the great painting of the trench scene in *Schützengraben* (1922–23), the cycle of fifty war etchings (1923–24)—a pictorial parallel to the war novels of the time—and the monumental masterpiece, the triptych *Der Krieg* (1929–32). In the manner of Dürer, these works create an apocalyptic wasteland of indescribable horror documenting the naked truth of machine war with a pitiless detachment and a primordial power.[80]

Disgust with the military and German society, a violent hatred of war, and a nihilist despair followed Grosz's mental breakdown in military service. A therapy for his condition came through a political activism, antiwar and Spartacist in orientation, and in a savage, satirical art. In his scratchy drawings and macabre paintings of mechanical figures he portrays the madness of the war and the philistine features of German society. The distinction of a German Daumier or Hogarth that he won is borne out in the wartime works, *Pandemonium, August 1914* (1914), *Fit for Active Service* (1916–17), and *Germany, a Winter's Tale* (1917–19).[81]

Such artists belong with Sassoon, Owen, and Barbusse to those creative minds that brought an end to "the pride, pomp, and circumstances of glorious war." The altered attitude revealed in literature and art had its political counterpart in the changed view of war expressed at the Paris peace conference and in the treaty of Versailles.

Fiction concerning the Great War, much consisting of realistic anti-war novels, continued to have a wide public during the interwar period. Among others published, the following tales may be noted: Ford Madox Ford's trilogy *Parade's End,* R. H. Mottram's *The Spanish Farm Trilogy 1914–1918,* Jaroslav Hasek's *The Good Soldier Schweik,* Arnold Zweig's *The Case of Sergeant Grischa,* Erich Remarque's *All Quiet on the Western Front,* Ludwig Renn's (pseudonym for A. F. Vieth von Golssenau) *Krieg (War),* Paul Alverdes's *Die Pfeiferstube (The Whistler's Room),* H. M. Tomlinson's *All Our Yesterdays,* Frederic Manning's *Her Privates We,* and Jules Romains's *Verdun.* In spite of this array, a considerable part of which is of

80. Fritz Löffler, *Otto Dix: Leben und Werk,* 4th ed. (Dresden, 1977); Otto Conzelmann, ed., *Otto Dix* (Hannover, 1959); Otto Conzelmann, *Otto Dix: Handzeichnungen* (Hannover, 1968); Florian Karsch, ed., *Otto Dix: Das graphische Werk* (Hannover, 1970).

81. George Grosz, *A Little Yes and a Big No* (New York, 1946); Hans Hess, *George Grosz* (London, 1974); Herbert Bittner, ed., *George Grosz* (New York, 1960); John I. H. Bauer, *George Grosz* (New York, 1954); Beth Erwin Lewis, *George Grosz* (Madison, Wis., 1971).

literary craft as well as of some depth and imaginative insight, there is still to be written an epic tale of the Great War approaching the grand lines of Tolstoy's *War and Peace.* The war's effect on the creative powers of writers was mixed. The literary critic Edmund Gosse wrote that the war had forced writers in England out of their "lethargy of dilettantism."[82] The war dealt the final blows to the effeteness and pastoral placidity of Georgian poetry. D. H. Lawrence raised the battle cry of the new poetry in 1916: "The essence of poetry with us in this age of stark and unlovely actualities is a stark directness. . . ."[83] The war drove Sassoon and Owen in this general direction from their Georgian beginnings. Sassoon found his theme and voice in the war, and without it one may doubt that he would have won recognition as a poet. Under the molding influence of the war Owen was suddenly transformed into a mature poet of solid stature. Owen recognized this change in his poetic powers: "Tennyson, it seems, was always a great child. So should I have been, but for Beaumont Hamel."[84]

The trauma of the trenches seared so deeply the sensibilities of creative figures at the front that they could not take up autobiographical writing until a decade later. Then there appeared (1928–30) three extraordinary autobiographical works, in Edmund Blunden's *Undertones of War,* Robert Graves's *Good-Bye to All That,* and Siegfried Sassoon's *Memoirs of an Infantry Officer.*

The war had little or no effect on the craft and theme of some writers. In his cork-lined room Marcel Proust, protected alike from the noise of the Paris streets and from the alarms of war, forged ahead steadily without diversion in writing *Remembrance of Things Past.* After André Gide's initial preoccupation with news of the conflict and concern for the care of refugees, he stuck to a round of writing having no relation to the war.[85]

During the period of the war and revolution the influence of these events was exerted on the art of many European writers, and apparently the most, in a negative way. With the exception of the fourth of the Duino Elegies, written in the fall of 1915, the muse of Rilke was silent after the

82. *Correspondence of Gide and Gosse,* 138, n. 1.
83. Quoted in Lane, *Adequate Response,* 105–06.
84. Owen, *Collected Letters,* 482.
85. See Gide, *Journal.*

Five Hymns of 1914. The poet remained bewildered and anxious—in a state of "agonizing impotence"—during the rest of the war.[86] Romain Rolland was diverted from literary works to writing appeals in behalf of peace and to advancing the cause of a universal human unity.[87]

In Russia, world war, Bolshevik revolution, war communism, civil war, and the advent of a totalitarian regime did cataclysmic violence to the life of intellectuals and to literary creation. Trotsky pronounced a scornful epitaph on the passing of the old intellectual class. "The iron broom of history had swept them away together with other rubbish." An index to the destruction of literary life was furnished in the number of books published, dropping from 20,000 in 1913 to 3,260 in 1920.[88]

After the flood tide of revolution the struggle for physical survival was hard enough in these barebone times, but beyond that writers had to decide how to maintain their personal and artistic integrity when faced with a regime inimical to creative freedom. Some learned to live with the regime; some, led by the storyteller Ivan Bunin and joined eventually by the versatile craftsman Evgeny Zamyatin, went into exile; some, chiefly the laureate of the revolution Vladimir Mayakovsky and the peasant poet of the people Sergey Esenin, ultimately solved their conflicts by suicide; and some, such as the great poet Alexander Blok kept largely to their silence.

The poet and prose writer Osip Mandelstam protested against the totalitarian turn of the revolution in his fictive story "The Egyptian Stamp" and warned in an essay on humanism that the social engineering of the time must "build for man rather than with him." His revulsion against the Bolshevik state thus expressed led to his repression and ultimately to death in prison.[89] The suffering of the intellectuals exposed to the vagaries of revolutionary fortune are pictured in Boris Pasternak's *Doctor Zhivago*.

The transitional literature was not without certain noteworthy developments. Blok's masterpiece, "The Twelve," gained the rank of foremost

86. Wydenbruck, *Rilke*, 266–83; Leishman, Introduction to *Rilke: Poems*, 15–20.
87. Maurice Nadeau, "Romain Rolland," *Journal of Contemporary History* 2, no. 2 (1967): 212–14; Starr, *Romain Rolland and a World at War*, 6–170.
88. Marc Slonim, *Soviet Russian Literature* (New York, 1967), 3–5.
89. Clarence Brown, *Mandelstam* (Cambridge, England, 1973), 53–107; *The Prose of Osip Mandelstam*, trans. with a critical essay by Clarence Brown (Princeton, 1965), 167; *Complete Poetry of Osip Mandelstam*, trans. Burton Raffel and Alla Burago with an Introduction by Sydney Monas (Albany, 1973), 13, 23–24.

poem of the revolution.[90] While hating the war, Mayakovsky matured as a poet. With the revolution he led a revolt of the Futurists against literary tradition in the endeavor to create a virile poetry through innovations in verse form and through colloquial diction that would suit the revolutionary era. Sanctified by the regime as the official poet of the revolution, Mayakovsky captured its march and fire in verbal explosions, however much at times his verse turned propagandist.[91] Zamyatin showed his versatile originality in a whole series of short stories, novels, plays, and articles devoted to the defense of personal and creative freedom. His legacy, it has been said, is "a living image of his profoundly tragic epoch." Pasternak, who spoke for the "other Russia," came of age as a poet with publication of two collections of poems and the writing of a third, *My Sister, Life.* Pasternak notes in his autobiography, *Safe Conduct,* that he abandoned the Romantic style, believing it was unsuited to his poetry.[92]

The impact of the war period on the disposition of thought can be seen in numerous writings and their influence. Many intellectuals detected in the war the symptoms of the decline or ruin of European civilization; among those in whom the conviction of decay already existed it was strengthened. Ezra Pound's poem *Hugh Selwyn Mauberley* (1920) expressed this outlook: "There died a myriad,/ And of the best, among them,/ For an old bitch gone in the teeth,/ For a botched civilization."[93] George Bernard Shaw portrayed a sick society in *Heartbreak House.* D. H. Lawrence, obsessed by the savagery of the war, published a series of novels in the twenties beginning with *Women in Love* (written in 1916 but not published until 1920) in which the reiterated purport is the death of Europe and the foulness of urban civilization. His pilgrimage of doom took the road of revolt against the intellect; he rejected reason for the wisdom of the blood and the flesh.[94] T. S. Eliot was the premier poet of the war's aftermath in painting the

90. Of the numerous translations of "The Twelve," a recent one of special merit is in *Alexander Blok: Selected Poems,* trans. Jon Stallworthy and Peter France (London, 1974), 114–28. For an extensive gloss on "The Twelve," see Sergei Hackel, *The Poet and the Revolution* (Oxford, 1975), 49–190; for Blok's life and work, Sir Cecil Kisch, *Alexander Blok: Prophet of Revolution* (New York, 1960); for his place in Soviet literature, Vera Alexandrova, *A History of Soviet Literature* (Garden City, N. Y., 1964), 9–13.

91. Slonim, *Soviet Russian Literature,* 19–31.

92. Ibid., 11–18, 80–89, 218–30; Alexandrova, *History of Soviet Literature,* 80–111, 174–87; Boris Pasternak, *Safe Conduct* (New York, 1958), 128–30.

93. Quoted in Bergonzi, *Heroes' Twilight,* 140.

94. Horace Gregory, *D. H. Lawrence: Pilgrim of the Apocalypse* (New York, 1957), 44–100 passim.

bleakness of modern civilization. For a generation his poem *The Wasteland* (1923) became the symbol of the postwar world.

An *Untergangsgeist* was abroad in Europe. In Russia, Blok believed that the bourgeois civilization of the west was in decline. The war and the revolutionary gale in his vision would cleanse this world, which he called in "The Twelve" "a coarse-haired mongrel pup" and "a mangy beast."[95] In Germany, Oswald Spengler was writing *The Decline of the West* during the war, and when it appeared afterwards the popular success was phenomenal for so ponderous a work. Romain Rolland concluded that the war had completed the bankruptcy of European civilization. Henceforth the east would carry the torch, and to the east Europe must turn for help. André Malraux's imaginary letters between a Frenchman in China and a Chinese in France constituting *La tentation de l'Occident (The Temptation of the West)* also dwells on the sickness of Europe.[96]

The volcanic disturbance of the war wrought a determining effect on the intellectual climate of the twentieth century. Appalled by the impersonal and alien aspects of mechanized mass warfare, western man discovered that science and technology, whose progress, it had always been understood, was to advance human welfare, could get out of control and turn against mankind. Man's control of himself and the world about him came into question. The prophets of the irrational seemed to be confirmed. The final assault was made on the ruling concepts of the Enlightenment—the linear march of human progress, the perfectibility of man, and the sway of reason.

Western man of thought was shaken by the experience to the core of his being, with the legacy that he has felt less at home in the physical and social universe. There emerged from the war a climate variously described as of violence, restlessness, instability, confusion, uncertainty, skepticism, anxiety, and alienation. Central to this mentality was the changed attitude toward war. Since that time the possibility of obliterating war between technological societies has taken hold of the western mind with a deep apprehension about the future of civilization. This anxiety has surfaced in tales of imaginary warfare.[97]

95. Stallworthy and France, *Blok: Selected Poems*, 23, 124, 127; Hackel, *Poet and the Revolution*, 25, 48.

96. Starr, *Romain Rolland and a World at War*, 71, 76; Nadeau, "Romain Rolland," 214; Henri Peyre, *The Contemporary French Novel* (New York, 1955), 190–92.

97. I. F. Clarke, *Voices Prophesying War, 1763–1984* (London, 1966), 166–67.

A number of intellectuals felt the urge to escape these conditions. Charles Nordhoff and James Norman Hall fled to the south seas to write the Bounty trilogy. After completing *The Seven Pillars of Wisdom,* Lawrence of Arabia sought relief for his shattered spirit in a "brain-sleep" by joining the ranks of the Tank Corps and the RAF.[98] The Viennese philosopher Ludwig Wittgenstein withdrew from a sunny and outgoing disposition to the life of a recluse.[99] The people of the warring countries were exhausted from the tensions and overstimulation of the war experience and from being a "slave of the state." Many took flight into a jazz decade of hedonist extravaganza—a craze for jazz bands, dancing, movie-going, self-indulgence, and freedom from numerous moral and social restraints. In Italy, D'Annunzio and the Fascists, and in Germany, Hitler and the Nazis drugged themselves on a wild nationalism.

Yet there is a more positive side of the story. The prewar parochialism was lessened, and the horizons of ordinary people broadened by the wider reading of newspapers stimulated by the war, the introduction of broadcasting, the popularity of the theater, the contacts of soldiers with other lands for prolonged periods, and a start in the publication of inexpensive books and of popular books of informational character.

During the war the value of science and technology to the supreme national effort was forcefully demonstrated. Governments set up various agencies for science and research, and this marked the beginning of a broad expansion of the institutional foundations of science. Certain spectacular advances of peacetime value were made in Einstein's paper on the general theory of relativity (1916), the production of synthetic nitrogen, the discovery of vitamins C and D. These developments worked to popularize science and technology and to spur their advance. British society has been recognized as coming out of the war with "a new scientific orientation."[100]

The prevalent skepticism expressed itself in certain salutary ways. It scrutinized blind tradition in every field, played a part in the abandonment of woman's anachronistic status, and extended toward both state and press after the discovery of the falsities of war propaganda. The people were

98. Richard Meinerzhagen, *Middle East Diary, 1917–1956* (London, 1959), 39; Phillip Knightley and Colin Simpson, *The Secret Lives of Lawrence of Arabia* (New York, 1970), 251, 254.
99. Allan Janik and Stephen Toulmin, *Wittgenstein's Vienna* (New York, 1973), 177.
100. Marwick, *Deluge,* 229–36.

showing a well-deserved distrust of a state and ruling elites that could not avoid involving them in a catastrophic war and could only prolong the misery to the bitter end of the enemy's or the state's own collapse. Associated with the revolutions in Europe and social and political reforms, a spirit of emancipation and new beginnings animated a considerable part of the European society, notwithstanding the war's legacy of disruption and privation.

BIBLIOGRAPHICAL ESSAY

The volume of publications on the period of the First World War and its revolutions is massive and continues without end. No other period in modern history of this duration has called forth so many books and articles. Vladimir Dedijer found more than three thousand works on the assassinations at Sarajevo alone. The source material for this time is distinguished from that of preceding war periods in certain marked respects: (1) There is an immense wealth of memoirs, diaries, and letters because on the one hand the war was fought for the most part by nonprofessional mass armies whose literacy had noticeably increased over that of soldiers in previous combat, and on the other hand the nature of technological warfare penetrated deeply the sensibilities of many of these men. (2) For the first time the major belligerents compiled extensive official histories of their participation in war. (3) Critical reverses or discredited policies and regimes brought about extensive investigations by parliaments or cabinets. An example is: Germany, Nationalversammlung, 1919–1920, *Das Werk des Untersuchungsausschusses der Verfassungsgebenden Deutschen Nationalversammlung und des Deutschen Reichstages 1919–1930* (19 vols., Berlin, 1925–30), of which *Die Ursachen des deutschen Zusammenbruchs* comprises the fourth series (12 vols., Berlin, 1925–29). (4) Never before was there a monumental undertaking comparable to the series published by the Carnegie Endowment for International Peace and edited by James T. Shotwell, The Economic and Social History of the World War, in some two hundred volumes.

SCHOLARLY AIDS

Guides to pertinent libraries, museums, archives, bibliographies, and reference works have been compiled by that most productive of bibliographers, Max Gunzenhäuser, in *Die Bibliographien zur Geschichte des Ersten Weltkrieges* (Schriften der Bibliothek für Zeitgeschichte-Weltkriegsbücherei, Heft 3, Frankfurt, 1964) and by Gwyn Bayliss in *Bibliographic Guide to the Two World Wars* (London, 1977). The standard guide, Dahlmann-Waitz, *Quellenkunde der deutschen Geschichte* (10th ed., nos. 2 and 3, Stuttgart, 1965), is of use largely for items appearing before the sixties.

The following publications are helpful in keeping up with the current literature: The Historical Association (London), *Annual Bulletin of Historical Literature;* Centre de documentation sciences humaines (Paris), *Bibliographie annuelle d'histoire de France,* noting articles as well as books; the Imperial War Museum (London), *Monthly Accession List.*

The historical journal bearing entirely on the subject during the interwar period was the *Revue d'histoire de la guerre mondiale* (17 vols., Paris, 1923–39). Current journals of note in including articles, discussions of the literature, book reports or book notes concerning the period are the *Historische Zeitschrift* (since the Second World War), *Vierteljahrshefte für Zeitgeschichte, Geschichte in Wissenschaft und Unterricht,* and the *Journal of Contemporary History.*

Detailed maps are contained in the official histories. Convenient for reference are Arthur Banks, *A Military Atlas of the First World War* (New York, 1975); and Martin Gilbert, *First World War Atlas* (London, 1970).

Among annual surveys of contemporary events in the years 1914–1919, Friedrich Purlitz, ed., *Deutscher Geschichtskalender: Der europäische Krieg in aktenmässiger Darstellung* (10 vols., Leipzig, 1914–1919) is the best for the publication of documents. Schulthess's *Europäischer Geschichtskalender* (6 vols., Munich, 1917–23) is good for Germany's internal history. The *Annual Register* (6 vols., London, 1915–20) takes the form of a readable narrative rather than a calendar and incorporates few documents. The European press of the war years is surveyed in Britain's *Daily Foreign Press Review,* issued in 10 series by the War Office, General Staff.

THE OUTBREAK OF WAR

The European situation leading to war is covered in Oron J. Hale, *The Great Illusion, 1900–1914* (New York, 1971), in The Rise of Modern Europe series; and Dwight E. Lee, *Europe's Crucial Years: The Diplomatic Background of World War I, 1902–1914* (Hanover, N.H., 1974). Both have extensive bibliographical essays. The scholarly work of Karl Dietrich Erdmann, "Der Erste Weltkrieg," in *Die Zeit der Weltkriege (Gebhart Handbuch der deutschen Geschichte,* vol. 4, 9th ed., Stuttgart, 1976), includes considerable commentary on pertinent books.

Interwar study of the outbreak of war, oriented toward determining the responsibility of countries and individuals, reached its ultimate attainment in the classical work of microscopic detail published by the chief editor of the liberal daily *Corriere delle Sera,* Luigi Albertini, in *Le origini della guerra del 1914* (3 vols., Milan, 1942–43), appearing in English translation as *The Origins of the War of 1914* (London, 1952–57). This attributes primary responsibility for the war to Germany and its military leadership.

Since the Second World War the German historians, most of all Fritz Fischer and Gerhard Ritter, have taken the lead in studying the origins of the war. Beginning in 1959, Fischer came out with a series of articles and books, the chief of which was *Griff nach der Weltmacht: Die Kriegszielpolitik des kaiserlichen Deutschland 1914–1918* (Düsseldorf, 1961), appearing in English translation as *Germany's Aims in the First World War* (New York, 1967). Fischer's interrelated theses center in the claim that German policy before and during the war and extending to the Second World War exhibited a continuity of expansionist aims directed at gaining world power.

BIBLIOGRAPHICAL ESSAY

Fischer's interpretation of German policy provoked a vehement controversy in which the critics, headed by Ritter, rejected the claims of Germany's primary responsibility for the war, the continuity of war aims policy, and the generality of its support. That Bethmann Hollweg could not insure a purely political decision in the latter part of the July crisis and make his influence prevail in later peace efforts was due, Ritter stresses, particularly in his masterly study *Staatskunst und Kriegshandwerk* (4 vols., Munich, 1954–70), to the dominance of the military and militarism in Germany. The Fischer controversy can be pursued in an early collection of articles and essays in Ernst W. Graf Lynar, ed., *Deutsche Kriegsziele 1914–1918* (Frankfurt, 1964). The more comprehensive and best collection appeared in Wolfgang Schieder, ed., *Erster Weltkrieg: Ursachen, Entstehung und Kriegsziele* (Cologne, 1969). H. W. Koch, ed., *The Origins of the First World War* (New York, 1972), assembles some of the more influential articles in the argument, in English translation if not originally written in English. To these volumes may be added Jacques Droz, *Les causes de la première guerre mondiale* (Paris, 1973); and John A. Moses, *The Politics of Illusion: The Fischer Controversy in German Historiography* (London, 1975).

The extent to which the military factor, represented by militarism, military plans, and military commitments, must be taken into account is seen not only in the writings of Ritter but also in Paul M. Kennedy, *The War Plans of the Great Powers, 1880–1914* (London, 1979); John E. Tyler, *The British Army and the Continent, 1904–1914* (London, 1938); A.J.P. Taylor, *War by Time-Table* (London, 1969), attaching blame to the Schlieffen plan for the outbreak of hostilities.

The many works on the event precipitating the July crisis are largely superseded by the definitive study of Vladimir Dedijer, *The Road to Sarajevo* (New York, 1966), which extensively uses Bosnian and Serbian materials.

GENERAL HISTORIES

The single volume from the interwar period that has best stood the test of time is C.R.M. Cruttwell, *A History of the Great War* (Oxford, 1936). For a volume of ready reference, more recent in date, there is no better compact account of strictly military operations than Sir James E. Edmonds, *A Short History of World War I* (London, 1951). Similar in character, with a touch of the political, is Cyril Falls, *The Great War* (New York, 1959). Pierre Renouvin, *La crise européenne et la première guerre mondiale* (5th ed., Paris, 1969), is a lucid synthesis of the military and the diplomatic with political, economic, and intellectual affairs. Renouvin has also written a briefer account, *La première guerre mondiale* (4th ed., Paris, 1976). F. Gambiez and M. Suire, *Histoire de la première guerre mondiale* (2 vols., Paris, 1968), is characteristic of the broadening conception of the war among historians in that these military writers include chapters on the life of the soldiers, the life of civilians, the occupied areas, and social developments no less than on political institutions and political warfare.

Other recent syntheses are Hans Herzfeld, *Der Erste Weltkrieg* (Munich, 1968), and Gerhard Schulz, *Revolutionen und Friedensschlüsse 1917–1920* (Munich, 1967). These companion volumes are of accomplished scholarship, large perspective, and objective interpretation. Marc Ferro, *The Great War, 1914–1918* (London, 1973), is unconventional and stimulating.

THE MASS WAR

John Terraine, a distinguished military writer on the war in the west, critically examines its problems in a series of essays, *The Western Front, 1914–1918* (London, 1964). The manner of life that the technological war imposed on the frontline soldiers is best portrayed in Jacques Meyer, *La vie quotidienne des soldats pendant la Grande Guerre* (Paris, 1967); John Ellis, *Eye-Deep in Hell* (London, 1976), an unsurpassed description of the conditions, activities, and attitudes of the soldiers on the Western Front; and Dennis Winter, *Death's Men: Soldiers of the Great War* (London, 1978), an account that goes inside the infantrymen's war to convey the impact of the war experience.

Reflecting further the nature of the mass war is its perception by an individual participant in F. C. Hitchcock's plainly told *"Stand To": A Diary of the Trenches* (London, 1937). Collections of such simply narrated war experiences make up C. B. Purdom, ed., *Everyman at War* (New York, 1930); and Michael Mohnihan, ed., *People at War, 1914–1918* (Newton Abbot, England, 1973).

An attempt has recently been made to ascertain the collective response to some of the severest fighting by obtaining in each case the testimony of numerous participants. Thus Martin Middlebrook, *The First Day of the Somme* (London, 1971), draws on the experience of more than five hundred soldiers to evoke the battle in concrete detail. Proceeding in the same way, Martin Middlebrook, *The Kaiser's Battle 21 March 1918: The First Day of the German Spring Offensive* (London, 1978), concentrates on the participation of individual combat soldiers and fighting at the small-unit level.

Recent studies of most worth on bringing the war to a conclusion in 1918 are: H. Essame, *The Battle for Europe: 1918* (New York, 1972), the work of an Australian professional soldier with a broad, detached understanding of the art of war and of command; Barrie Pitt, *1918: The Last Act* (New York, 1963), a very readable account of worthy restraint and even judgment; John Terraine, *To Win a War: 1918, the Year of Victory* (London, 1978), concerned chiefly with British successes in the last hundred days of the war. The decisive battle of August 8 is the subject of Gregory Blaxland, *Amiens: 1918* (London, 1968); and Douglas Orgill, *Armoured Onslaught: 8th August 1918* (New York, 1972), excellent in narrative, technical grasp, select illustration, and diagrammatic representation.

THE MILITARY DIRECTION OF WAR

The major recent work on the supreme command is Corelli Barnett, *The Sword-bearers* (London, 1963). Robert Blake, *The Private Papers of Douglas Haig, 1914–1919* (London, 1952), is an invaluable selection from the thirty-eight volumes of unpublished papers of the British commander-in-chief, introduced with a splendid essay on the British army in the war. John Terraine, *Douglas Haig: The Educated Soldier* (London, 1963), commends itself as an expert and cogent study of the British supreme command though betraying a tendency to overjustify Haig. Sir William Robertson, in *Soldiers and Statesmen, 1914–1918* (2 vols., London, 1926), records his experience as chief of the general staff in memoirs that are illuminating on conflicts and leaders in the determination of British policy. An admiring biographer writes the story of this "master strategist" in Victor Bonham-Carter, *Soldier True* (London, 1963).

No satisfactory study exists of the successor of Robertson, yet Sir Henry Wilson possessed the most brilliant mind for military affairs of all the British leaders. Sir C. E. Callwell, *Field-Marshal Sir Henry Wilson: His Life and Letters* (2 vols., London, 1927), confines itself too narrowly to extracts from Wilson's highly personal and private diaries. Basil Collier, *Brasshat* (London, 1961), is rather undiscriminating in the attempt to do justice to the much-maligned Wilson.

The atmosphere at German general headquarters and the kaiser's connection with running the war are intimately conveyed in Georg Alexander von Müller, *Regierte der Kaiser? Kriegstagebücher, Aufzeichnungen und Briefe des Chef des Marine-Kabinetts 1914–1918*, ed. Walter Görlitz (Göttingen, 1959). The standard work on the general staff is Walter Görlitz, *Der deutsche Generalstab* (2d ed., Frankfurt, 1953). One sees the general staff in action during most of the first years of the war through Erich von Falkenhayn, *The German General Staff and Its Decisions, 1914–1916* (New York, 1920); and H. v. Zwehl, *Erich v. Falkenhayn* (Berlin, 1926), a solid, disinterested biography.

Much is to be learned about the Hindenburg-Ludendorff team in charge of the general staff from Paul von Hindenburg, *Out of My Life* (London, 1920); and Erich von Ludendorff, *Ludendorff's Own Story* (2 vols., New York, 1920), even though Ludendorff's memoirs are one-sided in attempting to exonerate the army command from blame for Germany's defeat. Studies of most value in probing Ludendorff's state of mind in 1918 are: Karl Tschuppik, *Ludendorff: The Tragedy of a Military Mind* (Boston, 1932); Wolfgang Foerster, *Der Feldherr Ludendorff im Unglück* (Wiesbaden, 1952); and Siegfried A. Kaehler, "Zur Beurteilung Ludendorffs im Sommer 1918" and "Die Waffenstillstandsforderung der O.H.L.," in *Studien zur deutschen Geschichte des 19. und 20. Jahrhunderts* (Göttingen, 1961), 241–80.

The French high command of the first years of the war is reflected in *Mémoires du maréchal Joffre* (2 vols., Paris, 1932). Pierre Varillon, *Joffre* (Paris, 1956), is the best recent work presenting a full picture of the life and achievement of the French leader. In scholarly investigation of Pétain's high command Guy Pedroncini, *Pétain général en chef, 1917–1918* (Paris, 1974), stands out as the premier work. The most interesting publication on Foch's role is his own *Mémoires pour servir à l'histoire de la guerre de 1914–1918* (2 vols., Paris, 1931). Substantial studies of Foch have come from British military writers: B. H. Liddell Hart, *Foch: The Man of Orleans* (London, 1931); Cyril Falls, *Marshal Foch* (London, 1939); and Sir James Handyside Marshall-Cornwall, *Foch as Military Commander* (New York, 1972).

Although in the nature of an apologia, Oskar Regele, *Feldmarschall Conrad* (Vienna, 1955), is the fundamental account of the Austrian commander-in-chief. Solomon Wank, "Some Reflections on Conrad von Hötzendorf and His Memoirs Based on Old and New Sources," *Austrian Yearbook* 1 (1965): 74–88, deflates the myth of Conrad's military prescience.

Norman Stone, *The Eastern Front, 1914–1917* (New York, 1975), supplies new information about the structure and operation of command in the Russian army. The following memoirs cast some light on the subject: A. A. Brusilov, *A Soldier's Note-Book, 1914–1918* (London, 1930); Basil Gourko, *War and Revolution in Russia, 1914–1917* (New York, 1919); Youri Danilov, *La Russie dans la guerre mondiale (1914–1917)* (Paris, 1927).

THE WAR AT SEA

Two multivolume sets are indispensable for a serious inquiry into the naval war: the British official history of Sir Julian S. Corbett and Sir Henry Newbolt, *Naval Operations* (5 vols., 1920–31; rev. eds. of vols. 1 and 3, 1938–40); and Arthur J. Marder, *From the Dreadnought to Scapa Flow* (5 vols., London, 1961–70), an achievement of exemplary scholarship and vibrant style, utilizing fresh materials and dwelling on matters of naval policy. An expert naval writer has also published a combat narrative in Geoffrey Bennett, *Naval Battles of the First World War* (London, 1968).

The memoirs and papers of the British wartime admirals are headed by John Rushmore Viscount Jellicoe, *The Grand Fleet, 1914–1916* (New York, 1919), particularly instructive regarding the battle of Jutland as well as the capabilities and problems of the British fleet in relation to the German. A. Temple Patterson, ed., *The Jellicoe Papers* (2 vols., Shortlands, England, 1966–68), is ably edited with informative summations and comment before each of its four sections. The same historian has contributed in *Jellicoe* (London, 1969) a needed biography, free of past controversies and supported with more recently available materials.

Apart from the German official histories of the naval war, comprising twenty-three volumes, the following books are of special interest in regard to the controversies over the use of the German navy: A. von Tirpitz, *My Memoirs* (2 vols., New

York, 1919); Reinhard Scheer, *Germany's High Sea Fleet in the World War* (London, 1920); Walther Hubatsch, *Die Ära Tirpitz: Studien zur deutschen Marinepolitik 1890–1918* (Göttingen, 1955); Bernd Stegemann, *Die deutsche Marinepolitik 1917–1919* (Berlin, 1970), noteworthy for its objectivity and interpretive insight.

THE WAR IN THE AIR

A bibliography of the literature has been compiled in Myron J. Smith, *World War I in the Air* (Metuchen, N.J., 1977). The ultimate authority on the wartime aviation of Britain is Walter Raleigh and H. A. Jones, *The War in the Air* (6 vols., Oxford, 1922–37). Nothing compares with this official history in scope, exhaustive inquiry, and accuracy of detail. Also of high technical merit is the work of a Secretary of the Royal Aeronautical Society in Harald Penrose, *British Aviation: The Pioneer Years, 1903–1914* (London, 1957), and his *British Aviation: The Great War and Armistice, 1915–1919* (London, 1969).

For a fine general account of aerial operations and developments, there is Aaron Norman, *The Great Air War* (New York, 1968). Alexander McKee, *The Friendless Sky* (London, 1962), deflates the legendry of air fighting and is negative toward strategic bombing. The multiplicity of planes is surveyed for Britain and France in J. M. Bruce, *War Planes of the First World War* (5 vols., London, 1965–72), and for Germany in Peter Laurence Gray and Owen Thetford, *German Aircraft of the First World War* (2d ed., London, 1970).

Strategic bombing and the defenses against air raids are investigated in Neville Jones, *The Origins of Strategic Bombing* (London, 1973); Raymond H. Fredette, *The First Battle of Britain, 1917–1918, and the Birth of the Royal Air Force* (London, 1966), stressing the legacy of the German raids for the theory—especially the doctrine of strategic bombing—and operations of the RAF; Douglas H. Robinson, *The Zeppelin in Combat* (3d ed., London, 1962), a superlative study, thoroughly researched and eminently fair and detached; Peter M. Grosz, *The German Giants* (2d ed., London, 1969), concerning the operations of long-distance bombers.

On the organizational side of the air war, there are these informative expositions: Great Britain, Royal Flying Corps, *Royal Flying Corps, 1915–1916* (London, 1969); Maurice Baring, *Flying Corps Headquarters, 1914–1918* (London, 1968); Christopher Cole, *Royal Air Force, 1918* (London, 1968).

THE MARITIME AND ECONOMIC WAR

For a single volume William Jameson, *The Most Formidable Thing* (London, 1965), is unequaled in tracing the development and uses of the submarine—a revolutionary weapon in the *Handelskrieg*—from the first rudimentary invention through the world war. The German official history in Arno Spindler, *Der Handelskrieg mit U-Booten* (5 vols., Berlin and Frankfurt, 1932–66), is the most thorough exposition of the submarine war on commerce from the side of the attack. The hot debate among the German authorities on the manner and extent of using the U-boats in the *Handelskrieg* is delineated in two works: Hermann Bauer, *Reichsleitung und U-Bootseinsatz 1914–1918* (Lippoldsberg, 1956), setting forth, in severe criticism of Bethmann Hollweg's stand, the views of the submarine establishment for an early all-out campaign against merchant shipping; and Stegemann, *Die deutsche Marinepolitik,* cited above, examining impartially the evidence to show the incorrect conclusions of the submarine command. The success of the various naval means of countering the U-boats is thoroughly analyzed in Robert M. Grant, *U-Boats Destroyed* (London, 1964).

The fight against the German submarine attack was also conducted through the control and adjusted use of merchant shipping and through the control of food supplies. The following studies are rewarding on these themes: James Arthur Salter, *Allied Shipping Control* (Oxford, 1921); C. Ernest Fayle, *Seaborne Trade* (3 vols., London, 1920–24), an official history of conspicuous excellence covering not only the dislocations of maritime trade but also more generally the economic disturbances arising from the wartime naval situation; Mancur Olson, *The Economics of the Wartime Shortages* (Durham, N.C., 1963), evaluating the British measures to adjust food supplies to meet the submarine peril.

A. C. Bell, *The Blockade of Germany, Austria-Hungary, Bulgaria, and Turkey* (London, 1961), is a detailed, technical account of the methods and machinery employed in this means of economic warfare as well as of the ensuing results. Marion C. Siney, *The Allied Blockade of Germany, 1914–1916* (Ann Arbor, 1957), is especially good for the maritime policies of the Allies and the operation of the blockade vis-à-vis the European neutrals.

A comprehensive and interpretive synthesis of the economic war is lacking. Gerd Hardach, *The First World War, 1914–1918* (Berkeley, 1977), with an extensive bibliography, is of some help in supplying this need despite its misleading title. Arthur L. Bowley, *Some Economic Consequences of the Great War* (London, 1930), is still one of the best books on the overall economic results of the conflict.

Among works on the pursuit and consequences of the economic war in individual belligerents, there are for Britain N. B. Dearle, *An Economic Chronicle of the War for Great Britain and Ireland, 1914–1919* (London, 1929); and Alan S. Milward, *The Economic Effect of Two World Wars on Britain* (London, 1970). In the case of France the reader may refer to Tom Kemp, *The French Economy, 1913–39* (London, 1972); Charles Ailleret, *L'organisation économique de la nation en temps de guerre* (Paris, 1935); and Arthur Fontaine, *French Industry during the War* (New Haven, 1926). The outstanding analysis of Germany's economic prosecution of the war is Gerald D. Feldmann, *Army, Industry, and Labor in Germany, 1914–1918* (Princeton, 1966).

Pertinent studies for Austria-Hungary are: Richard Riedl, *Die Industrie Öster-*

reichs während des Krieges (Vienna, 1932); and Gustav Gratz and Richard Schüller, *Der wirtschaftliche Zusammenbruch Österreich-Ungarns* (Vienna, 1930). Regarding the Italian economy, informative are Luigi Einaudi, *La condotta economica e gli effeti sociali della guerra Italiana* (Bari, 1933); and Giorgio Porisini, *Il capitalismo italiano nelle prima guerra mondiale* (Florence, 1975). Russia's economic role is surveyed in Boris E. Nolde, *Russia in the Economic War* (New Haven, 1928); and Rudolf Claus, *Die Kriegswirtschaft Russlands bis zur bolschewistischen Revolution* (Bonn, 1922). The economic involvement of Japan is treated in Ushiaburo Kobayashi, *The Basic Industries and Social History of Japan, 1914–1918* (New Haven, 1930); and Kakujiro Yamasaki and Gotaro Ogawa, *The Effect of the World War upon the Commerce and Industry of Japan* (New Haven, 1939).

POLITICAL WARFARE

Hans Thimme, *Weltkrieg ohne Waffen* (Berlin, 1932), affords the most searching examination of the contest of ideas in the war, plumbing the philosophical foundations of propaganda. James M. Read, *Atrocity Propaganda, 1914–1919* (New Haven, 1941), is a judicious and perceptive product of historical scholarship. Among the studies of Allied propaganda, George G. Bruntz, *Allied Propaganda and the Collapse of the German Empire* (Stanford, 1938), is extensively researched and well balanced in evaluation. H. C. Peterson, *Propaganda for War* (Norman, Okla., 1939), greatly overplays the influence of British propaganda in bringing the United States into the war. Sir Campbell Stuart, *Secrets of Crewe House* (London, 1920), tells the authoritative story of the destructive propaganda campaign against Austria-Hungary and of progress in inter-Allied cooperation in propaganda against the enemy. James D. Squires, *British Propaganda at Home and in the United States from 1914 to 1917* (Cambridge, Mass., 1935), is brief and first-rate. Cate Haste, *Keep the Home Fires Burning* (London, 1977), takes the most recent look at the sources, machinery, and lines of British propaganda.

Georg Huber, *Die französische Propaganda im Weltkrieg gegen Deutschland 1914 bis 1918* (Munich, 1928), analyzes French propaganda in a thorough and comprehensive survey. Using Italian archival sources, Luciano Tosi, *La propaganda italiana all'estero nella prima guerra mondiale* (Udine, 1977), traces the development of the foreign propaganda of Italy.

George Creel, *How We Advertised America* (New York, 1929), reflects an evangelical spirit of spreading the American gospel around the world. James R. Mock and Cedric Larson, *Words That Won the War, The Story of the Committee on Public Information, 1917–1918* (Princeton, 1939), covers some of the same ground as Creel's work but supplements it to a worthwhile extent from CPI files. Stephen Vaughn, *Holding Fast the Inner Lines* (Chapel Hill, N.C., 1980), recounts with detachment the origins and domestic activities of the CPI.

German propaganda in the United States was combined with a campaign of sabotage and subversion. George Sylvester Viereck, *Spreading Germs of Hate* (New York, 1930), gives an inside account of that propaganda. Henry Landau, *The Enemy Within* (New York, 1937), is a lawyer's version of German sabotage produced from the evidence assembled by American claimants suing Germany for damages after the war. Emanuel Voska and Will Irwin, *Spy and Counterspy* (New York, 1940), relates the efforts of the counterespionage organization formed by the Czech-American Voska from Czech, Slovak, and South Slav ethnics to combat German clandestine activities. The former British naval attaché Sir George Gaunt reveals in *The Yield of the Years* (London, 1940) the part played by the British intelligence service in the United States in detecting the activities of German agents.

In the intelligence field the thick collection of articles in Paul von Lettow, ed., *Die Weltkriegsspionage* (Munich, 1931), becomes a virtual handbook on espionage, taking up the subject from many angles. Max Ronge, *Kriegs- und Industrie-Spionage* (Zurich, 1930), provides an outstanding account, impressive in the extent and precision of information, of the intelligence system of Austria-Hungary. W. Nicolai, *The German Secret Service* (London, 1924), is useful in dealing with military intelligence primarily but also with propaganda, clandestine operations, and espionage in the conventional sense. Sir George Aston, *Secret Service* (London, 1930), strings together numerous stories of incidents drawn from the personal experience of a British career intelligence officer. Odoardo Marchetti, *Il servizio informazioni dell'esercito italiano nella grande guerra* (Rome, 1937), contributes an excellent study of the instrumentalities and activities of the intelligence service of the Italian army.

Yves Gyldén, *The Contribution of the Cryptographic Bureaus in the World War* (Washington, 1935), is brief but valuable in comparing the attainments of the warring powers in cryptographic services. Sir William James, *The Code Breakers of Room 40* (New York, 1956), is the best account of the widely ranging activities of the famous intelligence section in Admiralty under Admiral William Hall known as Room 40, which was engaged in its most important work in intercepting and decrypting secret wireless and cable traffic of the Germans.

Cartoons and posters reflected popular attitudes and emotions of the war period and served as vehicles of mass persuasion. Of greatest impact as a cartoonist was the Dutchman Louis Raemaekers, whose work may be followed in J. Murray Allison, ed., *Raemaekers' Cartoon History of the War* (3 vols., New York, 1918–19). Ferdinand Avenarius, *Das Bild als Narr* (Munich, 1918; reprint except for introduction, New York, 1972), noteworthy for having been published in Germany during the war, is a collection of pictures and cartoons, mostly Allied but also German, with limited commentary intended to reveal the practice of deception and the corruption of art in the fabrication of war propaganda.

Two recently published books on the war posters are especially good: Maurice Rickards, *Posters of the First World War* (New York, 1968), consisting of a broad selection illumined by a critical and comparative discussion of the poster art as it developed during the war; and Joseph Darracott, *The First World War in Posters* (New York, 1974), reproducing the better known posters from the Imperial War Museum, whose concise introduction treats the characteristics and sources of war posters as well as their historical importance.

THE STATE IN MODERN WAR

The British have published excellent studies of the political direction of the war and of the emergence of concrete institutional forms through which the wartime expansion of statism was expressed. Heading the list is the classic of Lord [Maurice] Hankey, *The Supreme Command* (2 vols., London, 1961), an incomparable handbook on running the war and a unique source on how Asquith and Lloyd George operated as war leaders. Hankey's *Government Control in War* (Cambridge, England, 1945) summarizes Britain's system of war direction, which laid the foundation for future governmental organization.

A study of note is John Ehrman, *Cabinet Government and War, 1890–1940* (Cambridge, England, 1958), which traces the genesis of institutions for the direction of Britain's part in the war and their relation to the British constitutional system. Samuel J. Hurwitz, *State Intervention in Great Britain* (New York, 1949), pertaining to the years 1914–1919, has won deserved recognition for its scholarly analysis. Meriting attention are: E.M.H. Lloyd, *Experiments in State Control: At the War Office and the Ministry of Food* (Oxford, 1924); and F.M.G. Willson, *The Organization of the British Central Government, 1914–1964* (2d ed., London, 1968).

Treating war government in other belligerents are: Pierre Renouvin, *The Forms of War Government* (New Haven, 1927); Stéphan Rials, *Administration et organisation* (Paris, 1977), maintaining that the "era of organization" began with the "explosion of statism" during the war; W. Dieckmann, *Die Behördenorganisation in der deutschen Kriegswirtschaft 1914–1918* (Hamburg, 1937); Joseph Redlich, *Austrian War Government* (New Haven, 1929); Paul P. Gronsky and Nicholas J. Astrov, *The War and the Russian Government* (New Haven, 1929); S. O. Zagorsky, *State Control of Industry in Russia during the War* (New Haven, 1928).

BRITAIN AT WAR

The political aspects of Britain's participation are taken up at length in Sir Llewellyn Woodward, *Great Britain and the War of 1914–1918* (London, 1967). Dealing with the politics and politicians of the time are Lord Beaverbrook, *Politicians and the War, 1914–1916* (New York, 1928), a rich source of telling summations; Lord Beaverbrook, *Men and Power, 1917–1918* (London, 1966); A.J.P. Taylor, *Politics in Wartime and Other Essays* (London, 1964), containing a good condensation of the subject; Cameron Hazelhurst, *Politicians at War, July 1914 to May 1915* (New York, 1971).

The *War Memoirs of David Lloyd George* (6 vols., London, 1933–36) constitute an indispensable source though prone to malice and mendacity, self-justification and denigration of past adversaries. Lloyd George wanted to run the war, and this is the vigorous tale of how he did it, or rather how he wanted the world to believe it. Although no definitive biography exists, among the more than fifty biographical works on Lloyd George three stand out: Thomas Jones, *Lloyd George* (Cambridge, Mass., 1951), discriminating in its estimate of the man; Kenneth O. Morgan, *Lloyd George* (London, 1974), admirable in impartial approach and final summation of character and achievement by the foremost current scholar of the subject; Peter Rowland, *David Lloyd George* (New York, 1976), open to Lloyd George's faults and fair in appraisal.

The role of the first wartime prime minister is reassessed by Stephen Koss, *Asquith* (London, 1976), in a biography that avoids hagiographical tendencies. The mass of publications on Britain's other principal war leader is vitiated in great part by the lack of critical inquiry. Randolph S. Churchill has done two volumes and Martin Gilbert three more to date in the monumental official biography, *Winston S. Churchill* (London, 1966–76), of which volumes 3 and 4 deal with the war years.

The story of political dissent is told in A.J.P. Taylor, *The Trouble Makers: Dissent over Foreign Policy, 1792–1939* (London, 1957); Marvin Swartz, *The Union of Democratic Control in British Politics during the First World War* (Oxford, 1971); Stephen Koss, *Nonconformity in Modern British Politics* (London, 1975); Gerda Richards Crosby, *Disarmament and Peace in British Politics, 1914–1919* (Cambridge, Mass., 1957).

For the chief developments in the party system, there are Trevor Wilson, *The Downfall of the Liberal Party* (London, 1966); Ross McKibbin, *The Evolution of the Labour Party, 1910–1924* (Oxford, 1974); Peter Stansky, ed., *The Left and the War: The British Labour Party and World War I* (London, 1969).

FRANCE AT WAR

La Grande Guerre (1914–1918) (Paris, 1957), volume 2 of the immense undertaking of Georges Bonnefous, *Histoire politique de la Troisième République,* covers the successive war ministries and the activities of parliament in regard to the problems of defense. A detailed and thorough treatment of French political life is also available in Jacques Chastenet, *Histoire de la Troisième République,* vol. 4 (Paris, 1958). Jacques Desmarest, *La Grande Guerre (L'évolution de la France contemporaine,* vol. 4, Paris, 1978), concerns political affairs, although a large part is devoted to the economic and social response to the war.

The personal chronicle of Raymond Poincaré, *Au service de la France* (11 vols., Paris, 1926–74), contains valuable entries on political events, even though the whole is clearly fashioned to defend his record as president. The biographical and political literature includes: Gordon Wright, *Raymond Poincaré and the French Presidency* (Stanford, 1942), a sound, scholarly study; Jacques Chastenet, *Raymond Poincaré* (Paris, 1948), a superior biography; Pierre Miquel, *Poincaré* (Paris, 1961); and Georges Wormser, *Le septennat de Poincaré* (Paris, 1977).

Grandeur and Misery of Victory (New York, 1930) presents Clemenceau's case against Foch about the treatment of Germany and replies to the critics of the Versailles treaty. Jean Jules Mordacq, *Le ministère Clemenceau* (4 vols., Paris, 1930–31), offers rewarding evidence about Clemenceau's methods of supreme direction of the war. Gaston Monnerville, *Clemenceau* (Paris, 1968), is authoritative and comprehensive; and David Robin Watson, *Georges Clemenceau* (London, 1974), an amply documented study of the minister's political career, is pro-Clemenceau in viewing strategy and the Germans.

Leftist political movements receive attention in Annie Kriegel and Jean-Jacques Becker, *1914: La guerre et le mouvement ouvrier* (Paris, 1964); Jacques Fauvet, *Histoire du parti communiste français*, vol. 1: *De la guerre à la guerre, 1917–1939* (Paris, 1964); Annie Kriegel, *Aux origines du communisme français, 1914–1920* (2 vols., Paris, 1964).

ITALY IN THE WAR

Pietro Pieri, *L'Italia nella prima guerra mondiale (1915–1918)* (Turin, 1971), with a review of the literature, and Emilio Faldella, *La grande guerra* (Milan, 1965), are the two best general studies of recent date dealing predominantly with military affairs but also taking up political problems. A fundamental synthesis of political affairs is Piero Melograni, *Storia politica della grande guerra, 1915–1918* (1960; Rome, 1977). Giorgio Rochat, *L'Italia nella prima guerra mondiale: Problemi di interpretatione e prospettive de ricerca* (Milan, 1976), is a perspicacious survey of the literature from the Marxist standpoint, rejecting the traditional interpretation consecrated in "the myth of the great patriotic war." Mario Isnenghi, *Il mito della grande guerra da Marinetti a Malaparte* (Bari, 1970), discusses the particulars of the mythic interpretation of the war.

Italian historians have concentrated on two themes: the passage from neutrality to intervention and the causes of, responsibility for, and the consequences of the disaster at Caporetto. Concerning the first, Brunello Vigezzi, *L'Italia di fronte alla prima guerra mondiale*, vol. 1: *L'Italia neutrale* (Milan, 1966), explores with authoritative thoroughness the foreign policy of the government and the attitudes of the political parties. Alberto Monticone, *La Germania e la neutralità italiana, 1914–1915* (Bologna, 1971), is an admirable study, larger in scope than the title might indicate, of Germany's efforts to win Italy to the Central Powers and the relation of these activities to the internal struggle.

Representative of recent writing on Caporetto are: Alberto Monticone, *La battaglia de Caporetto* (Rome, 1955), attributing the rout to military mistakes;

Emilio Faldello, *Caporetto, le vere cause di una tragedia* (Bologna, 1967), indicting the commander of the Italian Second Army; Mario Isenghi, *I vinti de Caporetto nella letteratura de guerra* (Padua, 1967), probing the meaning of the debacle through an analysis of the memoir literature.

The more direct interest taken recently in internal political forces is evident in the following studies: Leo Valiani, *Il partito socialista italiano nel periodo neutralità, 1914–1915* (Milan, 1963); Renato Mantelone, *Lettere al re, 1914–1918* (Rome, 1973), an investigation of political attitudes manifested in anonymous letters; Stefano Caretti, *La rivoluzione russa e il socialismo* (Pisa, 1974); Paolo Spriano, *Storia del partito communista italiano,* vol. 1 (Turin, 1967). The rise of the revolutionary right is reflected in Renzo De Felice, *Mussolini il rivoluzionario* (Turin, 1965).

THE NEUTRAL STATES OF EUROPE

The most comprehensive treatment of the Swiss case is Jacob Ruchti, *Geschichte der Schweiz während des Weltkrieges 1914–1919* (2 vols., Bern, 1928–30), which concerns political, economic, and cultural affairs. More specific in theme are Hans Rudolf Ehrbar, *Schweizerische Militärpolitik im Ersten Weltkrieg* (Bern, 1976); Heinz Ochsenbein, *Die verlorene Wirtschaftsfreiheit 1914–1918* (Bern, 1971), investigating the economic controls of the belligerents over Switzerland; Pierre Luciri, *Le prix de la neutralité* (Geneva, 1976).

The difficulties of the Netherlands as a neutral have been analyzed from all angles in M. J. van der Flier et al., *The Netherlands and the World War* (4 vols., New Haven, 1923–28). Eli F. Heckscher et al., *Sweden, Norway, Denmark and Iceland in the World War* (New Haven, 1930), is a collective volume compressed from separate studies on each of the four Scandinavian countries. The relations of Germany and Sweden are examined in W. M. Carlgren, *Neutralität oder Allianz* (Stockholm, 1962). Paul G. Vigness, *The Neutrality of Norway in the World War* (Stanford, 1932), competently analyzes Norway's problems and solutions in the crossfire of economic war between Britain and Germany. Olav Riste, *The Neutral Ally* (Oslo, 1965), emphasizes the political factors in the differences over neutral rights and the pro-Ally character of Norway's policy. José Subirá, *Los espagnoles en la guerre de 1914–1918* (Madrid, 1920), is noteworthy in view of the neglect over Spain's position as a neutral.

TURKEY AND THE MIDDLE EAST AT WAR

The latest authoritative works of general character include: Bernard Lewis, *The Emergence of Modern Turkey* (London, 1961); Howard M. Sachar, *The Emergence of the Middle East, 1914–1924* (New York, 1969); and Peter Mansfield, *The Ottoman Empire and Its Successors* (London, 1973).

Turkey's relations with the Central Powers are explored in Ulrich Trumpener, *Germany and the Ottoman Empire, 1914–1918* (Princeton, 1968), the primary work on the subject; Lothar Rathmann, *Stossrichtung Nah-Ost 1914–1918* (East Berlin, 1963), a Marxist study of German imperialism in the area; Frank G. Weber, *Eagles on the Crescent* (Ithaca, N.Y., 1970), dealing with the wartime diplomacy of both Germany and Austria toward Turkey.

The policies and activities of the western powers in the Middle East are treated from the Arab and western points of view, respectively, in Jukka Nevakivi, *Britain, France and the Middle East, 1914–1920* (London, 1969); and Ann Williams, *Britain and France in the Middle East and North Africa, 1914–1967* (London, 1968). Enlightening expositions of Britain's relation to the Middle East and the Arabs are Eli Kedourie, *England in the Middle East: The Destruction of the Ottoman Empire, 1914–1921* (2d ed., Hassocks, England, 1978); Elie Kedourie, *The McMahon-Husayn Correspondence and Its Interpretation, 1914–1939* (New York, 1976), relating the history of the original commitment made to the Arabs in revolt; Elizabeth Monroe, *Britain's Moment in the Middle East, 1914–1956* (Baltimore, 1963), a reliable examination of British policy. The latest study of the diplomatic process by which the Ottoman Empire was finally liquidated is Paul C. Helmreich, *From Paris to Sèvres: The Partition of the Ottoman Empire at the Peace Conference* (Columbus, Ohio, 1974).

The bulk of the literature on the Arab revolt has been written from the perspective of the relations of the great powers to the Middle East or of an episode in the Great War. This is true of the writings on the part T. E. Lawrence played in the liberation of the Arab lands. The magnification of Lawrence to the figure of heroic legend originated in such books as Lowell Thomas, *With Lawrence in Arabia* (New York, 1924); and Robert Graves, *Lawrence and the Arabs* (London, 1927). Lawrence's own contribution to the Arabian legend is told with rare literary artistry in *Revolt in the Desert* (London, 1927) and *The Seven Pillars of Wisdom* (London, 1935).

The legend was not assailed with destructive force until the landmark book of Richard Aldington, *Lawrence of Arabia* (London, 1955). Phillip Knightley and Colin Simpson, *The Secret Lives of Lawrence of Arabia* (New York, 1970), presents a more moderate biographical study, utilizing newly accessible materials chiefly from the British foreign office. In one of the most interesting biographies Jean Béraud-Villars, *Le colonel Lawrence: ou, La recherche de l'absolu* (Paris, 1955), approaches the subject as the rarest combination of warrior and artist.

An account that seeks to correct Lawrence's "flights of fancy" by stressing what the Arabs consider to be their own endeavors is Suleiman Mousa, *T. E. Lawrence* (London, 1966). Important along this line is George Antonius, *The Arab Awakening* (London, 1938), a pioneer effort to tell the story of the Arab national movement.

Significant in investigating the provision for a Jewish national homeland and the origins of the Palestinian question are: Leonard Stein, *The Balfour Declaration* (New York, 1961), the authoritative work in broad context; Isaiah Friedman, *The*

Question of Palestine, 1914–1918 (London, 1973), a thorough examination of British-Jewish-Arab relations, utilizing materials from the British cabinet and foreign office; A. L. Tabawe, *Anglo-Arab Relations and the Question of Palestine, 1914–1921* (London, 1977), a statement of the Arabs' case against British policy.

RUSSIA IN WAR AND REVOLUTION

There are valuable guides to aid the reader through the rain forest of literature on the Russian revolution. Robert D. Worth, "On the Historiography of the Russian Revolution," *Slavic Review* 26 (1967): 246–64, provides discerning evaluations. James H. Billington, "Six Views of the Russian Revolution," *World Politics* 18 (1965–66): 452–73, distinguishes types of writing on the revolution and, in discussing examples of each, gives a widely ranging and stimulating sketch of the literature. Current writing may best be followed through the articles and reviews of *Soviet Studies*.

The standard general account is still William H. Chamberlin, *The Russian Revolution, 1917–1921* (2 vols., New York, 1952), the most complete, objective, and factually accurate survey despite the fresh knowledge added since its writing. A notable achievement in scholarship is Edward Hallett Carr, *The Bolshevik Revolution, 1917–1921* (3 vols., London, 1950–53), which concentrates on the history of the Bolsheviks and the creation of the institutional order issuing from the revolution to the exclusion of revolutionary events and the civil war. Richard Pipes, ed., *Revolutionary Russia* (Cambridge, Mass., 1968), contains articles by Soviet experts in recognition of the fiftieth anniversary of the revolution.

A specialist reviews the tsarist empire on the road to collapse in Hugh Seton-Watson, *The Russian Empire, 1801–1917* (London, 1967). The role of the leading parliamentarian Paul Miliukov in the struggle with the regime is traced in the biography—a study long needed—by Thomas Riha, *A Russian European—Paul Miliukov in Russian Politics* (Notre Dame, 1969).

No satisfactory history of the February revolution has yet been written. Two recent ventures have attempted to correct the defects of the liberal interpretation of the revolution represented by Kerensky and Miliukov. Marc Ferro, *La révolution de 1917* (Paris, 1967), analyzes the conflicting claims of the main social groups in a loosely structured study finding the focus of the revolution in their aspirations. George Katkov, *Russia: The February Revolution* (New York, 1967), is a challenging revision from the monarchist standpoint.

Worthy of note are a number of fine monographs on the growing radicalism between the establishment of the Provisional Government and the Bolshevik seizure of power. John Shelton Curtiss, *The Russian Revolution of 1917* (Princeton, 1957), follows the successive changes in government and the associated political struggles during this stage. John L. H. Keep, *The Russian Revolution: A Study in Mass Mobilization* (New York, 1976), examines closely the role of the self-constituted mass organizations, above all the soviets of workers' and soldiers' deputies. Allan K. Wildman, *The End of the Imperial Army: The Old Army and the Soldiers' Revolt (March–April 1917)* (Princeton, 1980), studies similarly the politicized soldiery and the "reinstitutionalization of power" in the army through the soldiers' committees. Alexander Rabinowitch, *Prelude to Revolution: The Petrograd Bolsheviks and the July 1917 Uprising* (Bloomington, Ind., 1968), explains the failure of the uprising in terms of the contradictory policies pursued by the different Bolshevik groups. Rex A. Wade, *The Russian Search for Peace* (Stanford, 1969), demonstrates in detail how the moderates lost power through the failure to carry out an effective peace program.

Three volumes taken together permit a clearer insight into the Bolshevik advent to power: S. P. Melgunov, *The Bolshevik Seizure of Power,* ed. by Sergei P. and Boris S. Pushakarev (Santa Barbara, Cal., 1972); Alexander Rabinowitch, *The Bolsheviks Come to Power* (New York, 1976), an exemplary inquiry showing the developing correspondence between the aspirations of the workers and soldiers on the one hand and the proclaimed reform program of the Bolsheviks on the other; and Robert V. Daniels, *Red October: The Bolshevik Revolution of 1917* (New York, 1967).

The growth of the socialist movement and the rise of Bolshevism are investigated thoroughly in John L. H. Keep, *The Rise of Social Democracy in Russia* (Oxford, 1963); Richard Pipes, *Social Democracy and the St. Petersburg Labor Movement* (Cambridge, Mass., 1963); Leonard H. Haimson, *The Russian Marxists and the Origins of Bolshevism* (Cambridge, Mass., 1955); Harold Shukman, *Lenin and the Russian Revolution* (London, 1966). Searching study has been extended to other parties in Oliver H. Radkey, *The Agrarian Foes of Bolshevism* (New York, 1958), a model of research, dealing critically with the Social Revolutionary party; Oliver H. Radkey, *The Sickle under the Hammer* (New York, 1963), completing the story of the Social Revolutionaries; William G. Rosenberg, *Liberals in the Russian Revolution: The Constitutional Democratic Party, 1917–1921* (Princeton, 1974).

In the writing on the revolutionary leaders the most impressive separate volumes on Lenin's life and work are David Shub, *Lenin* (rev. ed., Baltimore, 1966); Adam B. Ulam, *Lenin and the Bolsheviks* (London, 1966); Louis Fischer, *The Life of Lenin* (New York, 1964). The latest edition of his complete writings is Vladimir Ilich Lenin, *Collected Works* (45 vols., Moscow, 1960–70). The classical biography of Leon Trotsky is Isaac Deutscher's trilogy, of which volume 1: *The Prophet Armed, 1879–1921* (1954; New York, 1975) pertains to this period. Deutscher's *Stalin* (2d ed., London, 1967) is generally recognized as not having the quality of the Trotsky trilogy. Adam B. Ulam, *Stalin* (New York, 1973), covers not only the man but the revolutionary movement in vibrant writing. Full-length studies of the lesser figures have been made in Israel Getzler, *Martov* (London, 1967); W. Lerner, *Karl Radek* (Stanford, 1970); and Stephen F. Cohen, *Bukharin and the Bolshevik Revolution* (New York, 1973).

The institutional foundations of the Soviet system are surveyed in volume 3 of Carr, *The Bolshevik Revolution,* cited above; Maurice Dobb, *Soviet Economic Developments since 1917* (6th ed., London, 1966); Merle Fainsod, *How Russia Is Ruled* (rev. ed., Cambridge, Mass., 1965); Oskar Anweiler, *Die Rätebewegung in Russland 1905–1921* (Leiden, 1958), a fundamental work on the development of the soviets from their spontaneous origin to their incorporation into the Soviet system. Leonard Schapiro, *The Origins of the Communist Autocracy* (London, 1955), recounts the rise and fall of the political opposition to the ruling leadership and the movement toward a monolithic state. The same writer's *The Communist Party of the Soviet Union* (2d ed., London, 1970) is the most reliable and best informed account.

GERMANY IN WAR AND REVOLUTION

The subject is treated with eminent craftsmanship and admirable historical balance in Ritter, *Staatskunst und Kriegshandwerk,* cited above. The most comprehensive single volume, showing the influence of Ritter, is Peter Kielmansegg, *Deutschland und der Erste Weltkrieg* (Frankfurt, 1968).

The best account of William II as war ruler is Michael Balfour, *The Kaiser and His Times* (London, 1964). The chancellor Bethmann Hollweg has recently been the central figure of the historian's political interest in wartime Germany. The picture of Bethmann revealed in the diary of his confidant, published as Kurt Riezler, *Tagebücher, Aufsätze, Dokumente,* ed. by Karl Dietrich Erdmann (Göttingen, 1972), accounts in part for this scholarly activity. The complexities of Bethmann's character give rise to many different interpretations of this political leader, which are reviewed in the biographical inquiry of Klaus Hildebrand, *Bethmann Hollweg—Der Kanzler ohne Eigenschaften?* (Düsseldorf, 1970).

Major studies of this statesman and his policies are: Wolfgang J. Mommsen, *Die Politik des Reichskanzlers von Bethmann Hollweg und das Problem der politischen Führung* (Cologne, 1967); Eberhard von Vietsch, *Bethmann Hollweg: Staatsmann zwischen Macht und Ethos* (Boppard, 1969); Konrad H. Jarausch, *The Enigmatic Chancellor* (New Haven, 1973); Willibald Gutsche, *Aufstieg und Fall eines kaiserlichen Reichskanzlers: Theobald von Bethmann Hollweg 1856–1921* (East Berlin, 1973), emphasizing the July crisis of 1914.

The most significant publication on Germany's representative institutions in wartime is Erich Matthias and Rudolf Morsey, eds., *Der Interfraktionelle Ausschuss 1917–18* (*Quellen zur Geschichte des Parlamentarismus und der politischen Parteien,* series 1, vol. 1, 2 pts., Düsseldorf, 1959). The subject is extensively researched in Udo Bermbach, *Vorformen parlamentarischer Kabinettsbildung in Deutschland: Der Interfraktionelle Ausschuss 1917–1918 und die Parlamentarisierung der Reichsregierung* (Cologne, 1967).

The most useful general account of party organization is Thomas Nipperdey, *Die Organisation der deutschen Parteien vor 1918* (Düsseldorf, 1961). Dieter Grosser,

Vom monarchischen Konstitutionalismus zur parlamentarischen Demokratie (The Hague, 1970), treats the role of the parties in the growing political force of the Reichstag during the last decade of the empire. Rudolf Morsey, *Die deutsche Zentrumspartei 1917–1923* (Düsseldorf, 1966), examines in detail the conduct and policies of this one of the two leading parties in the revolutionary period.

Of the other leading party Susanne Miller, *Burgfrieden und Klassenkampf: Die deutsche Sozialdemokratie im Ersten Weltkrieg* (Düsseldorf, 1974), offers a rounded and impartial treatment. Carl E. Schorske, *German Social Democracy, 1905–1917: The Development of the Great Schism* (Cambridge, Mass., 1955), has gained distinction for brilliance of analysis and interpretation. The Independent Socialist party has attracted these studies: Hartfrid Krause, *USPD: Zur Geschichte der Unabhängigen Sozialdemokratischen Partei Deutschlands* (Frankfurt, 1975); and David W. Morgan, *The Socialist Left and the German Revolution* (Ithaca, N.Y., 1975).

Reinhard Rürup, "Problems of the German Revolution, 1918–19," *Journal of Contemporary History*, 3, no. 4 (1968): 109–35, affords an introduction to trends and interpretations in the historiography of the revolution. These sources contribute substantially to our knowledge of the parliamentary revolution of October: Erich Matthias and Rudolf Morsey, eds., *Die Regierung des Prinzen Max von Baden* (*Quellen zur Geschichte des Parlamentarismus und der politischen Parteien*, series 1, vol. 2, Düsseldorf, 1962), stressing in the enlightening introduction the importance of the action taken by the political parties in the parliamentary revolution; Prinz Max of Baden, *Erinnerungen und Dokumente*, newly ed. by Golo Mann and Andreas Burckhardt (Stuttgart, 1968), which has a long, thoughtful, and interpretive introduction; Friedrich Payer, *Von Bethmann Hollweg bis Ebert* (Frankfurt, 1923).

Arthur Rosenberg, *The Birth of the German Republic* (1931; New York, 1962), is still one of the keenest analyses of the revolution, though it goes too far in interpreting the formation of Prince Max's government as a "revolution from above" to the neglect of the initiative taken by the majority parties of the Reichstag. The fullest work of recent origin is A. J. Ryder, *The German Revolution of 1918* (Cambridge, England, 1967), construed from the perspective of German socialism. F. L. Carsten, *Revolution in Central Europe, 1918–1919* (London, 1972), is a comparative study of the German and Austrian revolutions, focusing on the workers' and soldiers' councils.

The minutes of the revolutionary government that succeeded the monarchy are published in Susanne Miller, ed., *Die Regierung der Volksbeauftragten 1918–19 (Quellen zur Geschichte des Parlamentarismus und der politischen Parteien*, series 1, vol. 6, 2 pts., Düsseldorf, 1969), an invaluable collection with an illuminating introduction by Eric Matthias.

The mass movement expressed itself, above all, in the widespread formation of the characteristic revolutionary councils, chiefly workers' and soldiers' councils. The indispensable study of the conciliar movement, indeed essential for understanding the November revolution as a whole, is Eberhard Kolb, *Die Arbeiterräte in der deutschen Innenpolitik 1918–1919* (Düsseldorf, 1962). Superimposed on the workers' and soldiers' councils was a central organ in Berlin whose record of meetings is available in Eberhard Kolb and Reinhard Rürop, eds., *Der Zentralrat der deutschen sozialistischen Republik 19.12.1918–8.4.1919* (Leiden, 1968). The authoritative work on the trade unions in the revolution is Heinz Josef Varain, *Freie Gewerkschaften, Sozialdemokratie und Staat* (Düsseldorf, 1956).

For the chief German uprising outside Berlin, there is Alan Mitchell, *Revolution in Bavaria, 1918–1919* (Princeton, 1965), a lucid analysis presented with imagination and spirit. Also worthy of mention is Franz Schade, *Kurt Eisner und die bayerische Sozialdemokratie* (Hannover, 1961).

In manifesting a strong interest in the Spartacist movement, the East German historians have contributed, among other books, Walter Bartel, *Die Linken in der deutschen Sozialdemokratie gegen Militarismus und Krieg* (East Berlin, 1958); Heinz Wohlgemuth, *Die Entstehung der Kommunistischen Partei Deutschlands* (2d ed., East Berlin, 1978); Hans Wohlgemuth, *Karl Liebknecht* (2d ed., East Berlin, 1975), a full-length biographical study of the foremost leader of the Spartacist movement and uprising.

Expressive of the renewed interest in Rosa Luxemburg are Gilbert Badia, *Rosa Luxemburg* (Paris, 1975), the detailed inquiry of a specialist in the Spartacist field; and J. P. Nettl, *Rosa Luxemburg* (2 vols., London, 1966), in which a profound student of German socialist history portrays in glowing admiration, but without a rival, Luxemburg's political activity, thought, and personal life.

AUSTRIA-HUNGARY AT WAR

Robert A. Kann, *The Multinational Empire, 1848–1918* (2 vols., New York, 1950), supplies an acutely discerning and stimulating commentary on the fate of the empire confronted with nationality movements of growing force and the failure of political reform. The same historian's *The Habsburg Empire: A Study in Integration and Disintegration* (New York, 1957), is a cogent analysis of the conditions and core issues unresolved leading to the downfall of the monarchy. Varied essays dealing with specific aspects of political, military, and intellectual affairs are collected in Robert A. Kann, Béla K. Király, and Paula S. Fichtner, eds., *The Habsburg Empire in World War I* (Boulder, Colo., 1977).

The intimate journal, *Schicksalsjahre Österreichs 1908–1919: Das politische Tagebuch Josef Redlichs*, ed. by Fritz Fellner (2 vols., Graz, 1953–54), is a revealing source, recording by an insider the conversations, thoughts, anxieties, judgments, and moods of aristocratic and upper bourgeois circles. *Redlich's Emperor Francis Joseph of Austria* (New York, 1929) is still an unequaled biography of "the old emperor."

The last emperor and the collapse of the empire form the twin subjects of Reinhold Lorenz, *Kaiser Karl und der Untergang der Donaumonarchie* (Graz, 1959), an authoritative, very readable narrative of broad substantive dimensions. Arthur J. May, *The Passing of the Hapsburg Monarchy, 1914–1918* (2 vols., Philadelphia, 1966), becomes a long requiem on the empire's final agony, devoting unusual attention to intellectual developments. The bibliography is extensive and annotated. Leo Valiani, *La dissoluzione dell' Austria-Ungheria* (Milan, 1966), published in English translation as *The End of Austria-Hungary* (New York, 1973), emphasizes the role of Hungary in the collapse of the empire and Italian policy toward Austria-Hungary and its nationalities.

Richard Georg Plaschka and Karlheinz Mack, eds., *Der Auflösung des Habsburgerreiches* (Vienna, 1970), consists of papers for an international forum, a number of which deal with economic and social conditions and nationality questions. The *Austrian History Yearbook*, 3, pt. 3 (1967), contains a section of essays on the dissolution of the monarchy. Richard Georg Plaschka, Horst Haselsteiner, and Arnold Suppan, *Innere Front: Militärassistenz, Widerstand und Umsturz in der Donaumonarchie 1918* (2 vols., Vienna, 1974), examines in detail the internal resistance actions and repressive organization and measures to the final collapse of the internal front and the takeover of power in the national provinces. Hugo Hantsch, *Die Nationalitätenfrage im alten Österreich* (Vienna, 1953), provides an informative discussion of the baffling problem of nationalities, placing major responsibility on the Hungarians for the inability to reform.

EASTERN EUROPE IN REVOLUTION

Of most direct use among books concerned with the revolutionary developments in eastern Europe on an area basis is Z.A.B. Zeman, *The Break-Up of the Habsburg Empire, 1914–1919: A Study in National and Social Revolution* (London, 1961). Victor S. Mamatey, *The United States and East Central Europe, 1914–1918* (Princeton, 1957), achieves a high standard of scholarship in handling the subject across the board from the angle of Wilsonian diplomacy. The respected work of C. A. Macartney and A. W. Palmer, *Independent Eastern Europe* (New York, 1966), has initial chapters that summarize the achievement of independence.

Although actually the personal memoir of a socialist leader, Otto Bauer, *Die österreichische Revolution* (1923; Vienna, 1965), is a classical account of the revolution in Austria proper, extraordinary in interpretive power. Additionally, the most satisfactory study is Karl R. Stadler, *The Birth of the Austrian Republic, 1918–1921* (Leiden, 1966).

For the study of the Hungarian events as a whole, the acute analysis of the bourgeois socialist leader Oscar Jászi in *Revolution and Counter-Revolution in Hungary* (London, 1924) is still indispensable. A valuable recent work of this scope is Iván Völgyes, ed., *Hungary in Revolution, 1918–1919* (Lincoln, Nebr., 1971), a collection of essays by specialists in Hungarian history and political affairs. The Soviet stage of the revolution is the theme of a thoroughly professional inquiry, based on Hungarian and Soviet sources, in Rudolf L. Tökes, *Belá Kun and the Hungarian Soviet Republic* (New York, 1967). This work treats Hungary as a case study of major significance in explaining the failure of a "graduate of the October revolution" of Russia to transplant the Soviet system successfully. Andrew C. Janos and William B. Slottman, eds., *Revolution in Perspective* (Berkeley, 1971), consists of papers on the Hungarian Soviet Republic given at a conference held at the University of California.

The story of the Czech and Slovak revolution is told best by the two most prominent leaders of the liberation in Thomas G. Masaryk, *The Making of a State* (London, 1927), a great narrative of the crusade for independence in spite of minor inaccuracies; and Eduard Beneš, *Souvenirs de guerre et de révolution, 1914–1918* (2 vols., Paris, 1928), a complete translation of the Czech original, or *My War Memoirs* (London, 1928), a reduced version.

Recent studies most germane to the revolutionary movement among the Poles and the genesis of the Polish state include: Werner Conze, *Polnische Nation und deutsche Politik im Ersten Weltkrieg* (Cologne, 1958); Titus Komarnicki, *Rebirth of the Polish Republic* (London, 1957); Piotr S. Wandycz, *Soviet-Polish Relations, 1917–1921* (Cambridge, Mass., 1969); and Norman Davies, *White Eagle, Red Star* (London, 1972). The last is a major study, well documented and imaginatively written, of the military, political, and diplomatic events of the Polish-Soviet war in 1919–20.

Concerning the other eastern European lands, the single best study concerned with the Ukrainian movement is John S. Reshetar, *The Ukrainian Revolution, 1917–1920* (Princeton, 1952). The Balkan involvements in war and revolution are well summarized as a whole in the larger general history of Charles and Barbara Jelavich, *The Establishment of the Balkan National States, 1804–1920* (Seattle, 1977). The creation of the Yugoslav state is related in Emile Haumant, *La formation de la Yougoslavie* (Paris, 1930), and Pavle Ostović, *The Truth about Yugoslavia* (New York, 1952), with sympathy for the Yugoslav point of view as against the Serb. Alex N. Dragnich, *Serbia, Nikola Pašić, and Yugoslavia* (New Brunswick, N.J., 1974), is favorable to Serbia and the Serb premier Pašić.

The book most nearly treating on a regional basis the struggles in the Baltic lands for national independence and union is Stanley W. Page, *The Formation of the Baltic States* (Cambridge, Mass., 1959), although it does not deal with Finland. Jürgen von Hehn, Hans von Rimscha, and Hellmuth Weiss, eds., *Von den baltischen Provinzen zu den baltischen Staaten* (Marburg, 1971), is an informative collection of essays by specialists in Baltic history and affairs. The policies and activities of the great powers involved in the establishment of the Baltic states are analyzed in Albert N. Tarulis, *Soviet Policy toward the Baltic States, 1919–1940* (Notre Dame, 1959); Albert N. Tarulis, *American-Baltic Relations, 1919–1940* (Washington, 1965); Werner Basler, *Deutschlands Annexionspolitik in Polen und im Baltikum 1914–1918* (East Berlin, 1962).

Among studies of the movements in the separate Baltic lands, Andrew Ezergailis, *The 1917 Revolution in Latvia* (Boulder, Colo., 1974), examines the progress of Bolshevism in that country. Alfred Erich Senn, *The Emergence of Modern Lithuania* (New York, 1959), describes the founding of the Lithuanian republic in terms of its place in the power struggle in eastern Europe between Germany, Russia, Poland, and the Entente. The German part is investigated in Gerd Linde, *Die deutsche Politik in Litauen im Ersten Weltkrieg* (Wiesbaden, 1965). L. A. Puntila, *The Political History of Finland, 1809–1966* (Helsinki, 1974), achieves an impartial account, excellent in coverage and emphasis, of the Finnish revolution, civil war, and war for independence. The German link with the Finnish war is taken up in Dieter Aspelmeier, *Deutschland und Finnland während der beiden Weltkriege* (Hamburg, 1967). C. Jay Smith, *Finland and the Russian Revolution, 1917–1922* (Athens, Ga., 1958), explores the influence of Bolshevik Russia, while John H. Hodgson, *Communism in Finland* (Princeton, 1967), presents an interpretive inquiry.

THE DIPLOMACY OF WAR AND PEACE

The most extensive documentary material already published is found in the various series: Department of State, *Papers Relating to the Foreign Relations of the United States,* comprising the annual volumes for 1914–1918; the *Supplements, 1914–1918* (6 vols., 1928–33); *The Lansing Papers, 1914–1920* (2 vols., 1939–40); *1918: Russia* (3 vols., 1931–32); *Russia: 1919* (1937); and *The Paris Peace Conference, 1919* (13 vols., 1942–47), all of which appeared in Washington, D. C.

German documents are open for use in microfilmed copies, *Records of the German Foreign Ministry (1914–1918),* National Archives, Washington. André Scherer and Jacques Grunewald, eds., *L'Allemagne et les problèmes de la paix pendant la première guerre mondiale* (3 vols., Paris, 1962–66), selects from the German archives with scrupulously careful editing and annotating documents primarily concerned with Germany's war aims, peace efforts and attempts to subvert enemy countries.

On wartime diplomacy as a whole, Pierre Renouvin, *War and Aftermath, 1914–1929* (New York, 1968), contains a notable condensation showing the fruits of a lifetime's study of the subject. Z.A.B. Zeman, *A Diplomatic History of the First World War* (London, 1971), is well-furnished with pertinent information, organized in topical form. Based on the broadest research, Arno J. Mayer, *Political Origins of the New Diplomacy, 1917–1918* (New Haven, 1959), is an impressive exposition of the politics of war aims and the influence of liberalism. W. W. Gottlieb, *Studies in Secret Diplomacy during the First World War* (London, 1957), contributes to our knowledge chiefly of Turkish and Italian alignments.

The range of British policy at this time is treated in C. J. Lowe and M. L. Dockrill, *The Mirage of Power: British Foreign Policy, 1902–22* (3 vols., London, 1972); and V. H. Rothwell, *British War Aims and Peace Diplomacy, 1914–1918* (Oxford, 1971). Much briefer than the standard work of Albert Pingaud, *Histoire diplomatique de la France pendant la Grande Guerre* (3 vols., Paris, 1938–41), but excellent, is J. Neré, *The Foreign Policy of France from 1914 to 1945* (London, 1975). Studies in large part of Russian war aims and tsarist secret treaties comprise C. J. Smith, *The Russian Struggle for Power, 1914–1917* (New York, 1956); and Alexander Dallin et al., *Russian Diplomacy and Eastern Europe, 1914–1917* (New York, 1963).

Books of distinct interest or representative view concerned with the problem of American intervention are Ernest R. May, *The World War and American Isolation, 1914–1917* (Cambridge, Mass., 1959), a major work of superior scholarship; Edward H. Buehring, *Woodrow Wilson and the Balance of Power* (Bloomington, Ind., 1955); Daniel M. Smith, *The Great Departure: The United States and World War I, 1914–1920* (New York, 1965). Two important monographs of non-American historians are Karl E. Birnbaum, *Peace Moves and U-Boat Warfare* (Stockholm, 1958); and Klaus Schwabe, *Deutsche Revolution und Wilson-Frieden: Die amerikanische und deutsche Friedensstrategie zwischen Ideologie und Machtpolitik* (Düsseldorf, 1971).

Many writings relating to German foreign policy are involved in the Fischer controversy, mentioned above. The best introduction to German policy in the west is Hans W. Gatzke, *Germany's Drive to the West* (Baltimore, 1950), a pathfinding study of German war aims. In regard to eastern policy, Werner Hahlweg, *Der Diktatfrieden von Brest-Litovsk 1918 und die bolschewistische Weltrevolution* (Münster, 1960), constitutes the fundamental study. Winfried Baumgart, *Deutsche Ostpolitik 1918* (Vienna, 1966), looks into policy toward eastern Europe from Brest-Litovsk on.

No general survey of Austro-Hungarian policy has yet superseded Alfred Francis Pribram, *Austrian Foreign Policy, 1908–1918* (London, 1923). For Austrian policy in the east, there is Wolfdieter Bihl, *Österreich-Ungarn und die Friedensschlüsse von Brest-Litovsk* (Vienna, 1970). Gerald E. Silberstein, *The Troubled Alliance: German-Austrian Relations, 1914–1917* (Lexington, Ky., 1970), furnishes a substantial study of the difficulties bedeviling the two partners.

Concerning the numerous peace moves initiated during the war, Wolfgang Steglich has made the chief contribution in fundamental research in *Bündnissicherung oder Verständigungsfrieden* (Göttingen, 1958); and *Die Friedenspolitik der Mittelmächte 1917–18* (Wiesbaden, 1964). More restricted in scope is Leo Haupts, *Deutsche Friedenspolitik 1918–1919* (Düsseldorf, 1976). Robert A. Kann, *Die Sixtusaffäre und die geheimen Friedensverhandlungen Österreich-Ungarns im Ersten Weltkrieg* (Vienna, 1966), analyzes the deficiencies of the secret peace diplomacy on the basis of Austrian examples. The indispensable work on the pope's peace appeal of August 1, 1917, is Wolfgang Steglich, *Der Friedensappel Papst Benedikt XV. vom 1. August 1917 und die Mittelmächte* (Wiesbaden, 1970), a collection of documents along with an introductory exposition.

The thoroughly documented and well-balanced book of Harry R. Rudin, *Armistice, 1918* (New Haven, 1944), is still of essential use. Pierre Renouvin, *L'armistice de Rethonde* (Paris, 1968), treats related events more widely, uses materials available later, and contains useful documents in the annexes. R.-G. Nobécourt, *L'année du 11 novembre* (Paris, 1968), is a dramatic narrative of the end of the war and the conclusion of the armistice.

A helpful guide through the superabundant growth of literature on the peace conference and its settlement is Max Gunzenhäuser, *Die Pariser Friedenskonferenz 1919 und die Friedensverträge 1919–1920* (Frankfurt, 1970). A seasoned survey of the work of the peace conference and assessment of the peace treaties is Schulz, *Revolutions und Friedensschlüsse 1917–1920,* cited above. Pierre Renouvin, *Le traité de Versailles* (Paris, 1969), is an admirable résumé. Arno J. Mayer, *Politics and Diplomacy of Peacemaking* (New York, 1967), enlarges the purview of the history of the peace settlement by examining comprehensively on a comparative basis the impact of the internal politics of both victor and vanquished states and of the ideological struggle between the Bolshevik revolution, Wilsonian liberalism, and the forces of counterrevolution.

Of particular worth on the negotiating process are Lord Hankey, *The Supreme Control at the Paris Peace Conference, 1919* (London, 1963); and Howard Elcock, *Portrait of a Decision: The Council of Four and the Treaty of Versailles* (London, 1972).

The following works of merit deal with varied aspects of the conference. Seth P. Tillman, *Anglo-American Relations at the Paris Peace Conference of 1919* (Princeton, 1961), is an open-minded inquiry, fresh in approach and balanced in interpretation. Fritz Dickmann, *Die Kriegsschuldfrage auf der Friedenskonferenz von Paris* (Munich, 1964), studies impartially the genesis of the accusation of war guilt and war crimes from the standpoint of international law and its development. Harold I. Nelson, *Land and Power: British and American Policies on Germany's Frontiers, 1916–1919* (London, 1963), inquires into the goals and influences shaping policies, chiefly British, on territorial questions.

Basic for the relationship of Soviet Russia and the peace conference is John M. Thompson, *Russia, Bolshevism, and the Versailles Peace* (Princeton, 1966). Relevant are two books of distinct excellence: George F. Kennan, *Russia and the West under Stalin* (Boston, 1960); and Richard H. Ullman, *Britain and the Russian Civil War* (Princeton, 1968).

THE SOCIAL IMPACT OF THE WAR

The comparative survey of the effects of the war on daily civilian life, John Williams, *The Home Fronts: Britain, France and Germany, 1914–1918* (London, 1972), is weak on the German side. So far as British society is concerned, Arthur Marwick has made the most important recent studies in *The Deluge: British Society in the First World War* (Boston, 1965); and "The Impact of the First World War on British Society," *Journal of Contemporary History,* 3, no. 1 (1968): 51–63. The earlier books of Caroline E. Playne, *Society at War* (Boston, 1931) and *Britain Holds On: 1917, 1918,* assay the psychological temper of British society at war and its psychological consequences, but they tend to be pacifist briefs. Christopher Martin, *English Life in the First World War* (London, 1974), is a sketchy though imaginative reconstruction, supported by apt pictures.

Of direct interest in the case of French society is Gabriel Perreux, *La vie quotidienne des civils en France pendant la Grande Guerre* (Paris, 1966). Pierre Sorlin, *La société française,* volume 2: *1914–1968* (Paris, 1971), begins with social changes of the Great War.

There is no satisfactory volume dealing with the wartime social changes in Germany. While Albrecht Mendelssohn Bartholdy, *The War and German Society* (New Haven, 1937), observes attitudes induced by the war, it is largely concerned with political and economic developments. Jürgen Kochka, *Klassengesellschaft im Kriege: Deutsche Sozialgeschichte 1914–1918* (2d ed., Göttingen, 1978), is rich in information but restricts social history to the analytical framework of changes in relative class position and in orientation of various social groups. Otto Baumgarten et al., *Geistige und sittliche Wirkungen des Krieges in Deutschland* (Stuttgart, 1927), takes up moral conditions, churches, and youth.

The role of women in the war and the associated change in their position are discussed in Arthur Marwick, *Women at War, 1914–1918* (London, 1977); Mary Cadogan and Patricia Craig, *Women and Children First* (London, 1978); Ursula von Gerstorff, *Frauen im Kriegsdienst 1914–1945* (Stuttgart, 1969).

For the impact of the war on certain social classes and minorities, there are Jürgen Kochka, "The First World War and the 'Mittelstand': German Artisans and White Collar Workers," *Journal of Contemporary History,* 8, no. 1 (1973): 101–24; Arrigo Serpieri, *La guerra e le classi rurali italiane* (Bari, 1929); Frank Julian Warne, *The Workers at War* (1920; New York, 1976); George Lachman Mosse, *The Jews and the German War Experience, 1914–1918* (New York, 1977); Werner E. Mosse, *Deutsches Judentum in Krieg und Revolution 1916–1923* (Tübingen, 1971); Egmont Zechlin, *Die deutsche Politik und die Juden im Ersten Weltkrieg* (Göttingen, 1969); Emmet J. Scott, *Scott's Official History of the American Negro in the World War* (1919; New York, 1969).

The interest of German historians in the influence of the war on religious organizations is reflected in Gottfried Mehnert, *Evangelische Kirche und Politik 1917–1919* (Düsseldorf, 1959), dealing with political currents among Protestants; Wilhelm Pressel, *Die Kriegspredigt 1914–1918 in der evangelischen Kirche Deutschlands* (Göttingen, 1967); Heinrich Missala, *Gott mit uns: Die deutsche katholische Kriegspredigt 1914–1918* (Munich, 1968); Kurt Hammer, *Deutsche Kriegstheologie (1871–1918)* (Munich, 1971), showing how the Protestant and Catholic religions were overrun by nationalism, frenzied patriotism, and the war fever as the churches became propaganda instrumentalities for the conduct of war.

A corresponding interest in the Church of England has been manifested in Albert Marrin, *The Last Crusade: The Church of England in the First World War* (Durham, N.C., 1974), an impartial inquiry in a large social and historical perspective; and Alan B. Wilkinson, *The Church of England and the First World War* (London, 1978).

The war resisters are studied in H. C. Peterson and Gilbert C. Fite, *Opponents of War, 1917–1918* (Madison, 1957); John Rae, *Conscience and Politics: The British Government and the Conscientious Objector to Military Service, 1916–1919* (London, 1970).

THE WAR AND THE MODERN MIND

The invasion of the modern mind by the war is revealed in the outpouring of war books, both personal narratives and fiction, the war poetry, the war letters, and indeed every form of written expression as well as certain instances of pictorial art. Catherine W. Reilly, *English Poetry of the First World War* (London, 1978), provides a useful bibliographic guide to the war poetry of Britain.

The renewal of critical interest in the war literature has produced a number of noteworthy works of analysis and evaluation. The comparative study of the war literature from different countries is the approach taken in Holger Klein, ed., *The First World War in Fiction* (London, 1976), a collection of essays about stories concerned with all fronts; George A. Panichas, ed., *Promise of Greatness* (London, 1968), a collective work containing a long, reflective introduction on the significance of the war in literature and modern thought; Charles Dédéyan, *Une guerre dans le mal des hommes* (Paris, 1971); Sir Charles Bowra, *Poetry and the First World War* (Oxford, 1961), a masterly lecture.

A great part of the critical and interpretive scrutiny pertains to the war writings in the English language. One of the best of these studies is Bernard Bergonzi, *Heroes' Twilight* (New York, 1966). In a work of extraordinary conception Paul Fussell, *The Great War and Modern Memory* (New York, 1975), treats patterns and tendencies of war literature in the whole frame of literary tradition, leading to the thesis that the irony dominating our modern consciousness originated in the perception of the war by western man.

Excellent studies of poetry alone include Jon Silkin, *Out of Battle* (Oxford, 1972), an acute analysis, above all of the poetry of Wilfred Owen and Isaac Rosenberg; John H. Johnston, *English Poetry of the First World War* (Princeton, 1964), viewing the evolution of the war lyric through critiques of representative poets; J. M. Gregson, *Poetry of the First World War* (London, 1976), a slender volume of discriminating evaluations.

Most of the substantial studies of individual war poets have been done in the last two decades. The definitive biography of the most widely acclaimed war poet in his own time is Christopher Hassall, *Rupert Brooke* (London, 1964). The principal critical volume on Sassoon, and almost the only one, is Michael Thorpe, *Siegfried Sassoon: A Critical Study* (Leiden, 1966). The preeminent work on Owen is D.S.R. Welland, *Wilfred Owen: A Critical Study* (London, 1960), tracing his poetic development to mature achievement against the whole background of war poetry and the transition from nineteenth- to twentieth-century poetry. Note may be taken of these other books on Owen: Jon Stallworthy, *Wilfred Owen* (London, 1974); Arthur Orrmont, *Requiem for War: The Life of Wilfred Owen* (New York, 1972); Harold Owen, *Journey from Obscurity* (3 vols., London, 1963–65), being memoirs of the Owen family.

The growing recognition of Rosenberg's poetic attainment is suggested by the publication in 1975 of the three books: Jean Moorcroft Wilson, *Isaac Rosenberg: Poet and Painter* (London), a biography, written with the assistance of the Rosenberg family, focusing on the formative influences in his life; Joseph Cohen, *Journey to the Trenches: The Life of Isaac Rosenberg* (New York), distinctive in following the process of Rosenberg's recognition as a poet; Jean Liddiard, *Isaac Rosenberg* (London).

In the domain of prose, M. S. Grecius, *Prose Writers of World War I* (London, 1973), gives a brief overview, eminently fair and sensitive. Stanley Cooperman, *World War I and the American Novel* (Baltimore, 1967), concludes, in depicting the mental world of American soldiers and writers of war novels, that the American literature of a generation was in a sense created by the war.

The effect of the war on French literature is considered in general terms in Micheline Tison-Braun, *La crise de l'humanisme: Le conflit de la société dans la littérature française moderne,* volume 2: *1914–1939* (Paris, 1967); Germaine Brée and Margaret Guiton, *An Age of Fiction: The Novel from Gide to Camus* (New Brunswick, N.J., 1957); Maurice Rieuneau, *Guerre et révolution dans le roman française de 1919 à 1939* (Paris, 1974). Frank Field, *Three French Writers and the Great War* (Cambridge, England, 1975), studies the influence of the war on the development of the extremist ideologies of Henri Barbusse, Drieu la Rochelle, and Georges Bernanos.

The response to the war in German writings is taken up in Herbert Cysarz, *Zur geistesgeschicthe des Weltkrieges: Die dictherischen Wandlungen des deutschen Kriegsbilds 1910–1930* (Halle, 1931); William K. Pfeiler, *War and the German Mind* (New York, 1941), analyzing perceptively letters, diaries, and fiction but not war poetry; Michael Gollbach, *Die Wiederkehr des Weltkrieges in der Literatur* (Kronberg/Ts., 1978), which develops a typology of war novels and examines their social function and reception.

Certain books deal directly in a generic sense with the impact of the war on attitudes and consciousness. Eric J. Leeds, *No Man's Land: Combat and Identity in World War I* (Cambridge, England, 1979), is a psychological and anthropological study, rather abstract, of how the war shaped the mental character of an age. Robert Wohl, *The Generation of 1914* (Cambridge, Mass., 1979), portrays the European intellectuals of the war period as a generation "wandering between two worlds." Eckart Koester, *Literatur und Weltkriegsideologie* (Kronberg/Ts., 1977), is informative on reigning ideas and ideological currents in Germany during the war. Of general importance is I. F. Clarke, *Voices Prophesying War, 1763–1984* (London, 1966), which demonstrates how the First World War cut a deep chasm in western thought that resulted in an entirely changed view of war.

The transforming influence of the front experience on susceptible artists is not only manifested in their particular pictorial works but is also discussed in the autobiographical writings of Paul Nash, *Outline* (London, 1949); C.R.W. Nevinson, *Pain and Prejudice* (London, 1937); and George Grosz, *A Little Yes and a Big No* (New York, 1946).

Further light is cast on the impact of the Western Front on Nash's imaginative mind and on the nature and importance of his war art in Margot Eates, ed., *Paul Nash: Paintings, Drawings, and Illustrations* (London, 1948); Anthony Bertram, *Paul Nash: The Portrait of an Artist* (London, 1955), a detailed, dependable account of his life and achievement; and Margot Eates, *Paul Nash: The Master of the Image* (London, 1973), a critical assessment of Nash's development as an artist by an intimate and long-time student of the subject. C.R.W. Nevinson, *Modern War: Paintings* (London, 1917), provides a good collection of plates, introduced with an appreciation of Nevinson's war paintings by a friend and professional art critic, P. G. Konody.

Material on the changed attitudes of the German artists, conspicuously toward war and the military, may be found in the following books: Bernard Myers, *The German Expressionists* (New York, n. d.); Peter Selz, *German Expressionist Painting* (Berkeley, 1957); J. P. Hodin, *Oskar Kokoschka: The Artist and His Time* (Greenwich, Conn., 1966); Edith Hoffmann, *Kokoschka: Life and Work* (London, 1947); Fritz Löffler, *Otto Dix: Leben und Werk* (4th ed., Dresden, 1977); Otto Conzelmann, ed., *Otto Dix* (Hannover, 1959); Otto Conzelmann, *Otto Dix: Handzeichnungen* (Hannover, 1968); Florian Karsch, ed., *Otto Dix: Das graphische Werk* (Hannover, 1970); Hans Hess, *George Grosz* (London, 1974); Herbert Bittner, ed., *George Grosz* (New York, 1960); and John I. H. Bauer, *George Grosz* (New York, 1954).

INDEX

Illustrations are referred to by illustration number not by page number.

528 INDEX